An A–Z of Counselling Theory and Practice

An A–Z of Counselling Theory and Practice

Fourth edition

William Stewart
Freelance counsellor and trainer
Eastleigh, Hampshire, UK

First published in 1992 by:
Chapman & Hall
Second edition published in 1997 by Stanley Thornes (Publishers) Ltd
Third edition published in 2001 by Nelson Thornes Ltd

This edition published in 2005 by:
Nelson Thornes Ltd
Delta Place
27 Bath Road
CHELTENHAM
GL53 7TH
United Kingdom

05 06 07 08 09 / 10 9 8 7 6 5 4 3 2 1

A catalogue record for this book is available from the British Library

ISBN 0-7487-9592-8

Page make-up by Acorn Bookwork

Printed and bound in Spain by GraphyCems

Contents

RC
466
S74
2005

FOREWORD

The world of counselling, like many other disciplines and professions, is a dynamic one, and seems to change daily! There are new insights and under-standings, developing theories and models. The student of counselling has constantly to be looking for resources which will both assist and enhance their ability to understanding these new theoretical and skill developments, and to assimilate these into their personal and professional development.

For the past 25 years, I have been teaching counselling skills and theories to students who have been looking to enhance their professional expertise, and, in many instances, to use this in career development. The arena for this has been in the independent sector, Further and Higher Education settings, as a University External Examiner and as a Senior Examiner to a major Awarding Body. This has involved educational establishments in the UK and overseas. In the past I have been active in promoting the *A–Z of Counselling*, to students and practitioners, as a comprehensive resource book for such purposes, and I am particularly pleased to commend this Fourth Edition of this excellent publication, which includes new topics and an expansion of many previous ones. William Stewart brings a lifetime of professional knowledge and expertise to his writing, and the *A–Z of Counselling* clearly reflects this, as do many of his other publications. Whether as a student of counselling, or long time professional practitioner's viewpoint, this new edition of a very successful resource book provides a user-friendly compen-dium of insights and knowledge.

The *A–Z of Counselling* will open up the world of counselling to all of its readers, as it informs and educates. It will be an asset to the library of individual professional practitioners, and a resource tool for training departments and faculties.

Dr Phillip A. Rees
Easter, 2005

PREFACE TO THE FOURTH EDITION

It gives me great pleasure to be writing this preface for a fourth time. When I published the first edition in 1992, it was with some hesitation; how would such a book be received? From the start, it was obvious that it filled a niche. This has proved to be the case ever since.

In the 13 years since the publication of the first edition, I have been amazed and gratified by how well this book has been received. Students of counselling have found it particularly helpful, but I have been particularly pleased that many counsellors have told me how much they have benefited from dipping into it. One counsellor said that she always had it to hand when counselling, so that she could refer clients to specific parts that she considered might help them. For many colleges it is required or recommended reading.

In creating a fourth edition a decision has to be made as to what new material to include and what to leave out. I have carried out a major restructuring of the book, rationalising many of the subjects by bringing together related entries rather than scattering them throughout the book.

Many of the older, more fringe, entries have been removed, to be replaced with other entries more pertinent to present-day counselling. Wherever appropriate I have added examples of counselling skills to emphasise the 'practice' part of the book. There are several new entries.

This book draws its inspiration from over 30 years as a counsellor and many years as a teacher of counselling skills, and is an attempt to bring together in one volume many different ideas about counselling and many different approaches.

The number of topics covered is extensive, so it was a deliberate choice of what to include and what to leave out. It is my hope that there is enough detail to provide an insight into the subjects and that the index will act as referral points for people wishing to study specific subjects in more depth. So it is both a reference and a source book.

There is an increasing awareness and interest in counselling as a discipline and in applying the principles to other types of work. Students of counselling, in whatever area, need a handy reference book. This is what I have set out to write. From this book people will be able to dip into theory and practice and taste what is there. I also hope that what they read will help them to explore what particular approach to counselling may best suit them.

The style is deliberately brief and to the point. I felt that long discussion would act as a deterrent, particularly for people who have to fit counselling training around a full-time occupation.

I hope that you will find this new edition both helpful and instructive.

William Stewart
Eastleigh, March 2005

ABOUT THE AUTHOR

William Stewart spent 20 years in the Royal Army Medical Corps (RAMC) and gained experience in general and psychiatric nursing in the UK and abroad. He was commissioned in 1968 as a specialist officer in mental health and pioneered social work in the armed forces. Following his training as a psychiatric social worker he established a private counselling training practice.

On retiring from the RAMC in 1974 he worked as a Senior Nurse (Allocation) in the Southampton University Hospital's Combined School of Nursing until 1987.

Over 20 years ago he was one of the early pioneers of counselling within the health care professions. In 1987 he was invited to set up the Student and Staff Counselling service (part-time Student Counsellor/Lecturer) at St George's and Roehampton College of Health Studies, and St George's School of Radiography, London. In addition to providing a counselling service for students and college staff, he taught a variety of interpersonal skills within the college. He retired from that post in 1991.

Since 1992 he has been a distance learning tutor for the Institute of Counselling, Glasgow, and has written three texts for them.

In addition to *An A–Z of Counselling Theory and Practice*, William Stewart has written many other counselling and self-help books, and several devotional books, published privately for charity.

For several years he has been a supervisor of other counsellors.

William has been married to Margaret for 56 years.

LIST OF SUBJECTS

- Items annotated **N** are new
- Items annotated **E** are extended from the 3rd edition

'A' type personality **E**
Abreaction and catharsis **E**
Advice **E**
Analytical psychology
Anger and aggression
Anxiety **E**
Approval
Assertiveness
Attachment
Attending
Authoritarianism **E**

Behaviour therapy
Biblical basis for counselling **N**
Bibliotherapy **E**
Body-image
Bonding
Brainstorming **E**
Brief counselling
Burnout **E**

Challenging **E**
Child abuse **E**
Co-dependence **E**
Cognitive therapy
Communication
Communication modes of Virginia Satir
Competition versus cooperation
Complexes
Compliance
Concreteness
Conflict
Contract **E**
Core conditions
Counselling ethics
Counselling guidelines
Counselling process
Creativity
Crisis counselling **E**

A

'A' TYPE PERSONALITY (SEE ALSO: STRESS MANAGEMENT)

The type 'A' behaviour pattern was first described by two cardiologists, Meyere Friedman and Ray Rosenman (1974), who identified a strong link between stress and coronary heart disease (CHD).

Type 'A' behaviour is an ingrained pattern of behaviour observed in people who struggle to obtain something from their environment as quickly as possible. What they strive for is often not clear and may be in conflict with other things or persons.

Much of the work ethos of the presesnt day is geared towards the 'A' type personality, for whom competition and excessive hours present a constant challenge. Many young people already have their behaviour shaped into the type 'A' pattern as they feel that this is the one necessary to succeed in the business world.

Type 'A' behaviour characteristics

- Having difficulty sitting still and doing nothing
- Extreme competitiveness and hostility
- Striving for achievement
- Aggressiveness (sometimes very repressed)
- Haste
- Thinking of, or doing, two things at once
- Impatience and anger
- Restlessness
- Hyperalertness
- Explosiveness of speech and interrupting when others are speaking
- Tension in facial muscles
- Feelings of being under pressure of time
- Feelings of being under the challenge of responsibility
- Deep commitment to a vocation or profession. Other aspects of life may be neglected
- Playing every game to win, even when playing with children.

A study of 3411 men between the ages of 39 and 59 years showed that a high proportion of those who developed coronary heart disease were originally diagnosed as being type 'A' personality. The heart and circulatory systems seem particularly sensitive to type 'A' behaviours.

People who are high on type 'A' behaviours, although outwardly self-confident, have been shown to be prey to constant feelings of self-doubt. It would seem that this might be one of the reasons why such people push themselves to accomplish more in less time.

In contrast, type 'B' people do not exhibit these characteristics; they are able to relax without feeling guilty, they achieve what they have to, without feelings of being pushed and without agitation that they will not get it done; they are generally more patient and are not easily aroused to anger.

Although there are links between type 'A' behaviour and coronary heart disease, there is no agreement as to why this should be. The results of several studies suggest that impatience and ambition seem less damaging than being constantly angry. It is possible that it is not the competitive spirit but anger, hostile feelings and persistent annoyance that place the type 'A' person at risk. A further factor might be if the person is a smoker.

The two cardinal features of type 'A' behaviour are 'time urgency or time-impatience' and 'free-floating (all-pervasive and ever-present) hostility'.

Questions to assess the presence of time-impatience

- Do you eat quickly and leave the dinner table immediately after?
- Does your partner or any close friend tell you to slow down, become less tense or take it easy?
- Does it bother you a lot to queue at a cashier's counter or to be seated in a restaurant?
- Do you usually look at TV or read the paper while eating?
- Do you examine your mail or do other things while listening to someone on the telephone?
- Do you often think of other matters while listening to your partners or others?
- Do you believe that usually you are in a hurry to get things done?

Questions to assess pervasive and ever-present hostility

- Do you often find it difficult to fall asleep or difficult to stay asleep because you are upset about something a person has done?
- Do you believe that most people are not honest or are not willing to help others?
- Do you become irritated or swear at others when driving?
- Does your partner, when riding as a passenger with you, ever tell you to cool or calm down?
- Do you often have a feeling that your partner is competing against you or is too critical of your inadequacies?
- Do you grind your teeth or has your dentist ever told you that you have done so?
- Do the car-driving errors of other drivers, the indifference of shop assistants or the tardiness of mail delivery upset you significantly?

Vijai P. Sharma, PhD, www.mindpub.com/art207.htm

Modifying type 'A' behaviour

Learning how to modify one's type 'A' behaviour and hostility levels has been found to reduce the risk of heart disease. A counselling programme that concentrates on the following is the most promising, particularly in the reduction of hostility and urgency. This programme may be of benefit to people who have suffered coronary attacks:

- Education
- Relaxation training
- Cognitive therapy
- The use of imagery
- Behaviour modification
- Emotional support
- Don't limit your activities to work. Your family would probably appreciate your company, and time, more than seeing you completely wrapped up in your work or striving to bring home a fat income.
- Listen to other people's opinions and views without interrupting them, and value their differences.
- Praise other people, and praise yourself too – it's a great way of building self-esteem.
- Separate your work from other areas of your life.
- Trust other people and delegate. They might not do things as efficiently as you do, but give them a chance – you might be pleasantly surprised – and people appreciate being asked to help.
- Slow down – you move too fast. Give yourself a break before you break. Stop setting yourself such rigid deadlines.
- Nurture yourself. Stop making impossible demands on yourself. Take life as it comes, instead of trying to control everything and everyone. Learn the value of relaxing and having fun, instead of always doing and striving.
- Take up an activity or hobby that is non-competitive.
- Build some unstructured time into each day.
- Learn to share your feelings.

J. Sutton (1998) *Thriving on Stress: how to manage pressures and transform your life.*
How to Books (page 46), with permission from the author.

Questionnaires include
- The Jenkins Activity Survey
- The Framingham Type 'A' Scale
- The Cook-Medley Scale, derived from the Minnesota Multiphasic Personality Inventory, has been used to measure hostility, which may be the most risk-enhancing type 'A' attribute.

Recapitulation of type 'A'
- Persons having type 'A' patterns of behaviour are often so deeply committed to their vocation or profession that other aspects of their lives are relatively neglected.
- Not all aspects of this pattern of syndrome need to be present for a person to be classified as possessing it.
- Different situations evoke different reactions from different people.
- Type 'A' persons may exhibit multiple behaviour patterns – undertaking more than one job at any one time, resulting in poorly done work.
- Type 'A' persons may practise time restriction – trying to cram too much work into a given time – a race against the clock.

- Inappropriate competitiveness with hostility and aggression is a type 'A' behaviour. The competitive element pervades most activities. This is coupled with a persistent desire for recognition and advancement.
- Type 'A' persons may have an intense, sustained drive to achieve self-selected but usually poorly defined goals, coupled with extraordinary mental alertness.

Further reading

Friedman, M. (1969) *Pathogenesis of Coronary Artery Disease.* McGraw Hill, New York.
Friedman, M. and Rosenman, R. (1974) *Type A Behaviour and Your Heart.* Knopf, New York.
Manstead, A.S.R. and Hewstone, M. et al (1996) *The Blackwell Encyclopaedia of Social Psychology.* Blackwell Publishers, Oxford.
www.questia.com

ABREACTION AND CATHARSIS

Abreaction is emotional release or discharge after recalling a painful experience that has been repressed because it was not consciously tolerable. A therapeutic effect sometimes occurs through partial or repeated discharge of the painful affect.

Abreaction is sometimes seen as analogous to lancing the boil to allow the wound to heal.

Catharsis is the healthy release of ideas with the accompanying feelings. It also means the release of repressed material from the unconscious into the conscious.

Abreaction involves bringing repressed unconscious or preconscious material into conscious awareness. Abreaction does not eliminate the causes of conflict but it may open the way for further exploration of feelings and experiences.

Freud evolved the 'cathartic method' from hypnosis and in the early days of psychoanalysis abreaction was considered therapeutic in itself, whether or not the patient understood the significance of the repressed experience.

While there is no doubt that when a client experiences the release of hitherto forgotten experiences the relief is dramatic, abreaction is not the main purpose of counselling, mainly because it is a technique that involves working with the unconscious rather than with the conscious.

Abreaction is a difficult and painful process. The person is often re-experiencing the trauma as if it is occurring in the present. Pain is sometimes felt in the same part of the body that was hurt during the trauma, and they can experience sights, sounds, and smells that were present in the original traumatic situation. Many clinicians found that the pain that patients went through was severely disruptive to their daily life. A balance seemed to be needed between working on traumatic material from the past and helping the patient function in the present.

Leonard Holmes, PhD, *Abreaction: The Baby or the Bathwater*

However, there is the point of view that deliberate attempts to get the client to abreact could be harmful. Certainly abreaction would not be the aim in counselling, but 'If abreaction appears to be occurring spontaneously, then let's work to avoid re-traumatising while maximising the healing potential that seems to accompany abreaction.'

Dr Richard A. Chefetz, In response to 'Abreaction: baby or bathwater' by Dr Leonard
Holmes. In: *Dissociation*, X:4, 12/97.

Chefetz presents some excellent guidelines for therapists working with trauma survivors, for whom abreaction might be appropriate:

- Maintain a calm aura.
- Be capable of uncertainty.
- Track the affect in the patient and in the clinician.
- Make note of pressures towards enactment.
- Avoid re-victimisation and enactment of the traumatic transference.

The use of abreaction was linked to Freud's 'trauma theory' and early psychoanalytic experiments. Jung differed with Freud about the efficacy of using abreaction. Consideration of its inadequacy led to further definition of Jung's own method and clarification of the role that transference plays in treatment.

Used by itself (by suggestion or in the so-called cathartic method), Jung found abreaction to be insufficient, useless or harmful (just as Freud did later). He identified the aim of treatment as the 'integration of the dissociation' connected with trauma rather than its abreaction.

This re-experiencing, in his view, should reveal the bipolar aspect of the neurosis so that a person could once again relate to the positive or prospective content of the complex; hence, bringing affect under control. The manner in which this could be effected, he thought, was by way of relationship to the therapist, a relationship that reinforced the conscious personality of the patient sufficiently so that the autonomous complex became subject to the authority of the ego.

Abreaction is one form of enactment available in analysis. It is of central importance in some other therapies (e.g. primal therapy) (Samuels *et al.*).

The term 'catharsis' was used metaphorically by Aristotle to describe the effects of true tragedy on the spectator. Aristotle states that the purpose of tragedy is to arouse 'terror and pity' and thereby effect catharsis – purgation or purification of these emotions.

The term 'catharsis' was introduced into psychiatry by Freud and Joseph Breur, who used it to describe a method of treating hysterical patients under hypnosis. The patients relived, or at least remembered, the circumstances under which their symptoms originated. When the emotions accompanying those circumstances were expressed, the patient was thus relieved of the symptoms. People who block emotions may experience a great rush of feeling as the blockage is removed.

Abreaction, insight and working through are three main experiences in psychoanalysis. Catharsis is a prime treatment tool of such approaches as primal therapy, rebirthing, Z process attachment and many of the newer therapies, such as six category intervention (see entry, below).

Some of the ways to get something off your chest

- Relieving the emotions by talking about your problems and feelings with someone or a group
- Writing letters to others
- Keeping a diary
- Punching a punching bag
- Running
- Primal screams
- Drawing pictures.

Further reading

American Psychiatric Glossary. American Psychiatric Press, Inc. Washington, DC.
Samuels, A., Shorter, B. and Plant, F. (1986) *A Critical Dictionary of Jungian Analysis*. Routledge & Kegan Paul, London.
http://mentalhealth.about.com

ADVICE

The dictionary definition of advice is 'opinion, judgement (as it appears to me), probability, careful thought, consideration, deliberation, recommendation regarding a course of conduct, information or notice given or action to be taken'.

Advice is generally considered inappropriate in person-centred counselling and most humanistic and holistic approaches. It may be more appropriate and acceptable when working with the very young, with people who are disturbed or helpless, or in essentially practical issues.

While the dictionary defines counsel as advice, this one word is anathema to many counsellors. In its widest sense, and certainly as a lawyer would use it, it is not 'do this' but rather 'this is what is possible' – an opening up of alternatives and possibilities. In this sense the dictionary definition could be correctly applied to counselling. But, unfortunately, to the word 'advice' has been attached the undesirable meanings of 'this is what you should do' or 'what you ought to do'. In a way, 'this is what you should do' is direction and control, and not in legal terms advice. It is unfortunate that 'advice' and 'advising' have become unacceptable words in counselling.

One of the basic assumptions in any counselling is that the person is helped to work towards his own solution. This is why it is important to help him explore as many different avenues as possible; and it is in this area that the concept of advice appears to create conflict. It is how we present alternatives or point out the legal consequences of certain actions that must give some bias, but, provided that we leave with clients as much initiative as they are capable of exercising and give them every opportunity to discuss whatever they wish, then we do no violence to the principle of self-responsibility.

It is this self-responsibility which is implied in the above sentence about the person working towards his own solution. The more we severely limit the choices, then clients may well feel constrained. They may feel that there are no other alternatives open to them and attempt to follow what has been fairly strong (though veiled) direction. In other words, because exploration has been limited, the client has responded to 'closed advice', which implies direction, rather than to 'open advice', which implies freedom of choice.

Counsellors help clients look at what is possible, but do not tell clients what they should do. That would be the counsellor taking control rather than the client gaining control.

The counsellor who answers the question 'What would you advise me to do?' with 'What ideas have you had?' is helping clients to recognise that they have a part to play in seeking an answer. They help the client take responsibility for finding a solution that feels right for them.

Advice is often appropriate in crises; at times when a person's thoughts and feelings seem shocked by the event. At times like these the counsellor will exercise greater caution than when clients are fully responsive and responsible. Advice offered and accepted when in crisis, and then acted upon, could prove to be if not bad advice, not totally appropriate to meet the client's needs. When people are under stress they are vulnerable. For all those reasons, counsellors are wary about responding to a request for advice.

However, it is sometimes very difficult not to offer advice. If a client is stressed, for example, the counsellor may suggest relaxation techniques to help reduce stress levels. Even though the advice might be good, the choice should always remain with the client.

Gary Collins links advice with giving information, and that seems an important point to make. Information involves giving facts to people who need information. Try to avoid giving too much information at any one time, be clear and remember that when people are hurting they respond best to information that is relevant to their immediate needs or concerns. This kind of informing is a common and widely accepted part of counselling; advice giving is much more controversial.

Advice givers often lack enough knowledge of a situation to give competent advice, their advice giving encourages the client to be dependent and if the advice proves to be invalid it is the counsellor who later is made to feel responsible for giving bad direction.

Whenever you are asked for advice or are inclined to give advice, be sure that you are well informed about the situation.

- Do you have enough information and expertise to advise another competently?
- Ask yourself what might be the end result of this advice giving. Is it likely to make the counselee more dependent?
- Can you handle the feelings that might come if your advice is rejected or proven wrong?
- If you then do give advice, offer it in the form of a tentative suggestion, give the counselee time to react or talk through your advice, and follow up later to see the extent to which the advice was helpful.

Rowan Bayne *et al.* draw attention to the view that, 'not giving advice can be therapeutic in itself: it "says", in effect, "When you've explored what's troubling you, you'll see it more clearly and know what to do."' However, as Bayne *et al.* point out, 'Lazarus offers a radically different view: "I will often be fairly free with my advice," though he adds that he always phrases it ' "This is the way I see it."'

Directive therapies – behaviour therapy, cognitive therapy, crisis intervention and brief therapy – rely on advice-giving, although not in the lay understanding of the term – 'This is what I think you should do'. The advice so given is aimed at helping the person deal with the problem to achieve a goal.

It is useful to distinguish between advice on how the client's life should be lived and instruction about specific aspects of the therapeutic process.

Counsellors who offer a lot of advice run the risk of increasing the dependency of the client. Advice should always be 'this is what is possible', not 'this is what you should do'. The stronger the emotional content of the issue the less appropriate is advice.

There are occasions when counsellors put strength behind the advice; when they 'advocate' some course of action, e.g. seeking a medical opinion.

Further reading

Bayne, R., Horto, I., Merry, T. and Noyes, E. (1994) *The Counsellor's Handbook: a practical A-Z guide to professional and clinical practice.* Chapman & Hall. London.

Burnard, P. (1999) *Counselling Skills for Health Professionals*, 3rd edn. Stanley Thornes, Cheltenham.

Collins, G.R. (1988) *Christian Counselling: a comprehensive guide.* Word Publishing, Nashville, TN.

Stewart, W. (1983) *Counselling in Nursing: a problem-solving approach.* Harper & Row, London.

Sutton, J. and Stewart, W. (2002), *Learning to Counsel*, 2nd edn. How to Books, Oxford.

ANALYTICAL PSYCHOLOGY (C.G. JUNG, 1875–1961) (SEE ALSO: MYERS-BRIGGS TYPE INDICATOR, WOUNDED HEALER)

Carl Jung, a renowned Swiss psychologist and psychiatrist, was a contemporary of Freud. Jung had already formulated some of his major ideas before he came to know Freud, and he left the psychoanalytic movement in 1913. He used the term 'analytical psychology' to distinguish his method from psychoanalysis, even though it evolved from that source. Jung saw analytical psychology as a general concept embracing both psychoanalysis and the individual psychology of Alfred Adler. His work was influenced by religion, mysticism and parapsychology.

Psychological types

Jung's theory of psychological types has three dimensions:

- **Extroversion/introversion**: Extroversion typifies people whose interests and attention are directed outwards from themselves into the world of other people and objects, who feel easy in social situations and who feel free to carry out appropriate actions in the open. Introversion describes opposite tendencies. Introverts direct their attention inwards upon themselves into the realm of images and ideas, tend to withdraw from social situations and tend to be self-reliant. The mental or psychic energy responsible for producing both extroversion and introversion Jung called the libido. Everyone has tendencies to both extroversion and introversion, although one tendency will predominate.

- **Sensation/intuition**: Sensation and intuition are to do with how we perceive the world. The sensing part of us understands something by assembling the details, sees the individual trees of the wood and is more concerned with the here-and-now reality. The intuitive part of us sees the overall picture, rather than the detail – the whole forest rather than the individual trees – and prefers possibilities rather than reality.
- **Thinking/feeling**: This is how we process information and make judgements. The thinking part likes logic and things that are rational. Feeling involves making judgements through values and understanding relations.

Sensation ascertains that something exists. Thinking tells us what that something is. Feeling attaches values to it and intuition sees its possibilities.

Our individual psyche contains elements of all six types but most of us prefer some functions over the others, although this will depend on circumstances. Part of the process of individuation is to understand and integrate the functions that we least prefer.

Principal differences between Jung and Freud:

- Jung attached less importance to the role of sexuality in the neuroses.
- He believed that the analysis of patients' immediate conflicts was more important than the uncovering of the conflicts of childhood.
- He defined the unconscious as including both the individual's own unconscious and that which he inherited – the 'collective unconscious'.
- His interpretation of dreams was less rigid.
- He emphasised the use of the phenomenon of transference.
- He took a psychotherapeutic approach to the individual.

Analytical psychology does not possess a detailed personality theory. In analytical psychology, the psyche comprises several autonomous yet interdependent subsystems.

Ego

- The centre of consciousness
- The experiential being of the person
- The sum total of: thoughts, ideas, feelings, memories, sensory perceptions.

Personal unconscious

- Consists of everything that has been repressed during one's development
- Contains elements easily available to consciousness

- Contains complexes – emotionally toned ideas and behavioural impulses having an archetypal core.

Collective unconscious

- Jung's term to describe those aspects of the psyche that are common to humankind as a whole.
- It is part of everyone's unconscious and is distinct from the personal unconscious, which arises from the experience of the individual.
- Material in the collective unconscious has never existed in the conscious; it has not been repressed.
- Jung's evidence of the collective unconscious is found in myths, legends, folk tales, fairy tales and dreams.

The collective unconscious contains archetypes, which:

- express themselves as universal primitive images, accumulated down the ages and across cultures
- are inherited dispositions to perceive and experience typical or nearly universal situations or patterns of behaviour
- are transmitted in symbolic forms through myths, stories and dreams.

Persona

The persona (the Latin word for person – in classical Roman theatre it was a 'mask', worn by actors to express the role being played) is:

- The archetype of adaptation
- The mask or public face we put on to meet the world, which develops from the pressures of society
- The social archetype, something that involves compromises in order to live in a community
- The mediator between the unconscious and the conscious world.

People who identify too closely with their persona are not sufficiently self-aware and therefore run the risk of pathology.

Examples of persona:

- Gender identity
- A specific stage of development
- Social status
- Job or profession.

The anima (the feeling function) and animus (the thinking function)

In analytical psychology, the anima is the feminine principle latent in every male; the internalised female shadow image a man carries. The young man has a maternal anima, which relates to the heart rather than the head – the source of receptiveness and sensitivity.

To be fully integrated and make contact with his own unconscious (expressed in imaginative symbols) a man must recognise and accept the feminine qualities within him.

Anima is one of the archetypes of the collective unconscious, which derives, in part, from the man's relationships with his mother and other significant females and from his father's attitudes towards women. In addition, he is influenced by the deeper racial archetypal images of women.

The animus is the latent masculine principle that is present in every female. The anima is represented, in dreams, by a single figure; the animus by several or many figures. The animus can be negative and destructive but is very positive when integrated. To be fully integrated and make contact with her own unconscious (often expressed in concrete symbols) a woman must recognise and accept the masculine qualities within her.

Some anima/animus archetypes that may appear in a person's dreams or imagination are: good mother, harlot, spiritual guide, temptress, vampire, virgin, witch, hero/heroine, man of authority, scholar, dark or eclipsed sun, giants, satyrs and devils. Such archetypes are also represented in mythical figures: Aphrodite, Athena, Helen of Troy, the Virgin Mary, Beatrice in Dante's *Inferno*, Hermes, Apollo, Hercules and Romeo.

Analytical psychologists propose that a person's relationship with the opposite sex, and choice of mate, are influenced by the anima and animus, whose influence may be negative or positive. The internalised images of the anima and animus are influenced by cultural patterns and expectations of what someone of the opposite sex should be.

Part of the process of analytical therapy is helping clients recognise and integrate the repressed anima or animus.

Jung, in *Psychological Types* (page 468), says this of anima (although he speaks of anima, the same applies to the animus):

> *As to the character of the anima, my experience confirms the rule that it is, by and large, complementary to the character of the persona [the outward appearance of the person]. The anima usually contains all those common human qualities which the conscious attitude lacks. The tyrant tormented by bad dreams, gloomy forebodings, and inner fears is a typical figure. Outwardly ruthless, harsh, and unapproachable, he jumps inwardly at every shadow, is at the mercy of every mood, as though he were the feeblest and most impressionable of men. Thus his anima contains all those fallible human qualities his persona lacks. If the person is intellectual, the anima will quite certainly be sentimental.*

One of the tasks of therapy is to achieve balance. No man is so entirely masculine that he has nothing feminine in him. No woman is so entirely feminine that she has nothing masculine in her. People who ignore their anima or animus function only on half their psyche. Ignored, the anima or animus will rule without the person's knowledge. When people understand the true nature of their anima or animus, they can express their feelings more appropriately.

Yin and yang

The animus and anima are two complementary parts: similar to the yin (feminine principle) and yang (masculine principle) of Chinese philosophy.

Feminine principle, characteristics:

- Nature, creation and life
- Earthiness and concreteness
- Receptivity and yielding
- Dark and containing
- Collective and undifferentiated
- The unconscious.

Masculine principle, characteristics:

- Driving and energetic
- Creative and initiating
- Light and heat
- Penetrating
- Stimulating and dividing
- Separation and differentiation
- Restriction and discipline
- Arousing and phallic
- Aggression and enthusiasm
- Spirit and heaven.

The self

The self is an archetypal image of one's fullest potential and the unity of the personality as a whole. The self is our god within ourselves. The process by which we achieve the goal of realisation of self is individuation.

Individuation describes the lifetime process by which the person becomes who he was meant to become, whole, indivisible and distinct from other people. It means that each one of us comes to realise that we are truly individually unique, yet we are no more than a common man or woman.

Individuation does not mean an unhealthy, narcissistic preoccupation with one's own inner world; it does mean a looking inwards so that one may look outwards, to the world, with clearer eyes.

Individuation is not integration, which is social adaptation and ego-bound; it is bound to self, self-experience and self-realisation and emotional maturity and involves:

- Facing the dark side of one's personality, the shadow, progressing away from the constraints of the persona
- Understanding and separation from the controlling influences of the collective unconscious.

Individuation leads to more fulfilling relationships, not to isolation of self. It does not shut other people out, it gathers them in. Individuation is uniquely individual and cannot be forced on the client by the therapist.

The shadow

- The thing a person has no wish to be
- The negative, dark, primitive side of the self
- What is inferior, worthless, uncontrollable and unacceptable.

The shadow cast by the ego is what makes us fully human. If we did not know we had a shadow (in the physical sense) we would not be fully alive. So in the psychological sense: we need the awareness of the shadow side of us to bring balance to our inner world. The shadow is kept in check by the ego and the persona. The more we attempt to live in the persona, the more potent will be the shadow's strength. Analytical therapy aims to bring more of the shadow into the light.

The shadow involves the personal unconscious, instincts, the collective unconscious and archetypes.

The shadow is itself an archetype and as such it is impossible to eradicate.

The contents of the shadow are powerful and capable of overwhelming the most well-ordered ego.

Evidence of the shadow appears in:

- Projections, both negative and positive, which are powerful and potentially destructive and may be directed against individuals, groups or whole societies
- Dreams, as a 'shady' character, a 'tempter', in the same sex as the dreamer, but with characteristics that the dreamer would consciously not embrace.

Jungian counselling

In Jungian counselling, the client is helped to:

- Own, accept, come to terms with and integrate the shadow, as something personal and not attributable to other people
- Develop an awareness of the images and situations most likely to produce shadow projections
- Analyse the shadow and so break its compulsive hold.

It is helpful to reflect to the client that, as in the physical world we only become aware of our shadow when the sun shines, so it is in the psychological sense. The more we allow the sun of individuation to shine upon us, the more of the shadow will be revealed.

The four stages of Jungian counselling

- **Confession**: This is not meant in a 'religious' sense, but where the client tells his or her story.
- **Elucidation**: Where the therapist helps the client to understand the meaning of the story.
- **Education**: The therapist helps the client to move forwards, and this may include teaching her or him certain aspects of theory.

- **Transformation**: The end result of the previous three stages, although this is something ongoing rather than complete.

The goals of Jungian counselling

- To help the individual gain insight
- To journey towards individuation
- To facilitate greater integration of both conscious and unconscious components.

Jung, like Freud, believed that disturbance in the psyche often manifests itself in physical symptoms. He used dream analysis to understand the person's current problems as well as to uncover past conflicts. He also used interpretation and free association, as did Freud, but advocated a more active relationship between therapist and patient.

The Jungian counsellor may:

- Teach
- Suggest
- Cajole
- Give advice
- Reflect feelings
- Give support
- Interpret dreams.

Summary

In Jungian counselling, which deals extensively with dreams and fantasies, a dialogue is set up between the conscious mind and the contents of the unconscious. Clients are made aware of both the personal and collective (archetypal) meanings inherent in their symptoms and difficulties.

Under favourable conditions they may enter into the individuation process – a lengthy series of psychological transformations culminating in the integration of opposite tendencies and functions and the achievement of personal wholeness.

The Jungian counsellor does not work to a preset plan, and the therapeutic process hinges on creating an atmosphere of trust. The approach is more passive than active, and receptive rather than directive.

Heinrich Fierz, speaking of Jungian psychiatry, says, 'The task of psychotherapy, insofar as it is not exclusively concerned with consciousness, is to elucidate the unconscious circumstances that made the illness possible in the first place and sustain it in the present.' And, 'The psychotherapeutic process rests on the relationship between therapist and patient. It is a dialogue between two people, which forms the basis for a dialogue within society and an attempt to adapt to the environment.'

Speaking of the use of chair or couch, Ann Casement points out that in her experience client regression may be aided by using the couch; however, the chair is the more usual.

Casement sums up Jungian counselling thus: 'Above all, therapy is an inner journey and the goal of this quest is the individual's true identity, which may have been hidden for a whole lifetime under a "false self".' It is in fact in the patient's symptom or wound that his or her true identity lies hidden (see Wounded healer).

Further reading

A word on Jung: his writings are not easy to read. There are a number of books that simplify his work, but possibly the easiest introduction is in Samuels, A., Shorter, B. and Plant, F. (1986) *A Critical Dictionary of Jungian Analysis.* Routledge & Kegan Paul, London.

Casement, A. (1996) Psychodynamic therapy: the Jungian approach. In: *Handbook of Individual Therapy* (ed. W. Dryden). Sage Publications, London.

Fierz, H.K. (1991) *Jungian Psychiatry*, Daimon, Verlag, Switzerland.

Von Franz, K.L. (1974) *Shadow and Evil in Fairy Tales.* Spring Publications, Jung, Zurich.

Weiner, M.F. and Mohl, P.C. (1995) Theories of personality and psychopathology: other psychodynamic schools. In: *Comprehensive Textbook of Psychiatry*, 6th edn (eds H.J. Kaplan and B.J. Sadock). Williams & Wilkins, Baltimore, MD.

Wickes, F.G. (1988) *The Inner World of Man.* Sigo Press, Boston, MA.

http://encyclopedia.thefreedictionary.com/

ANGER AND AGGRESSION (SEE ALSO: COMPETITION VERSUS COOPERATION)

It is useful to consider anger and aggression together. When anger leads to aggression, it is said that we are acting out our anger.

Anger is an emotion, which arouses from displeasure at an undesired event, particularly for an event for which we believe someone is responsible. Some theorists believe anger to be a primitive response to something to which we are averse, such as frustration and pain.

Sources of anger

- **Blocked goal**: 'I want something, and someone or some event prevents my getting it.'
- **Breaking of personal expectations**: If we are not treated in the way we expect or when other people behave as we do not expect them to, anger is often the outcome.
- **As a defence**: When self-esteem is threatened, we may use anger to prevent our self-esteem being attacked. Anger may be a response to criticism.

The characteristics of anger

- Anger is a primary human emotion and needs to be experienced in order to be known.
- It has a distinct quality of its own, different from that of every other emotion; and no one could, by mere description, make it intelligible to someone who had never been angry.
- It is not derived from other emotions; it does not even presuppose experience of other emotions to give it being.

- Anger is not in itself malevolent: it is simply a protection or defence against harm or hurt and may be directed against things as well as against persons.
- It is a type of resentment and operates instinctively and, therefore, without due regard to consequences.
- As instinctive resentment, anger is neither to be praised nor to be blamed but is to be accepted as a part of the human constitution necessary to the welfare of the individual and therefore ultimately to the good of the community.
- People are often the cause of anger and often the anger is directed at objects that had no share in arousing it; for this reason it has to be brought under the control of reason.
- The three principal reasons for anger are injustice, hurt and frustration. We become angry with others for our hurts. We blame others for our own problems, yet often anger is not directed at the appropriate source.
- When anger is voluntarily nursed it tends to magnify the offence that caused it: vanity and offended dignity come in to intensify and transform the emotion; a rankling grudge naturally exaggerates the original cause.
- Anger readily associates itself with a desire to injure others or to inflict pain on them and so is easily changed into hatred, retaliation, revenge or, keener still, vindictiveness. Vindictiveness is exclusively aimed at people and in its nature is diametrically opposed to the sympathetic and humane sentiments, the tender emotions that bind people together; it is the very antithesis of love and, instead of attracting and cementing, alienates and repels. The feeling of 'an eye for an eye, and a tooth for a tooth' is often the feeling generated.
- When we harbour ill-will and feed our wrath, refusing to be pacified or to enter into mediation, waiting for the favourable opportunity, we are bordering on revenge. Revenge is in its very nature inequitable and relentless, blood-thirsty and cruel, satisfied with nothing less than 'the head of John the Baptist on a plate'. When revenge pursues its object spitefully with unremitting persistence and finds zest in every petty infliction of evil on the other person, it is vindictiveness.
- Anger is the first emotion we experience and often the last one we learn to manage effectively. For many people, a lifetime is spent in denying, suppressing, displacing or avoiding anger – this troublesome momentary insanity.

Recognising anger

- Anger is a feeling of extreme displeasure, hostility, indignation or exasperation towards someone or something. These feelings are associated with the fight response and accompanied by internal and external indicators. Such feelings are often accompanied by verbal or physical attack.
- Anger is often associated with mistrust and suspicion, destruction of some valued object and habitual overindulgence in alcohol.
- Very generally, anger is a fairly strong emotional reaction that accompanies a variety of situations such as being physically restrained, being interfered with, having one's possessions removed, being attacked or threatened, etc.
- Anger is often identified by a collection of physical reactions, including parti-

cular facial grimaces and body positions characteristic of action in the autonomic nervous system, particularly the sympathetic division. In many species anger produces overt (or implicit) attack. As with many emotions, anger is extremely difficult to define objectively.

- Angry people strive for superiority by strenuously applying all their powers. This may be a compensation for deep-seated inferiority. Any threat to their feeling of superiority will result in an angry response. Angry people generally find it difficult to tolerate equality.
- Inappropriate anger may be an indication of the feeling of lack of power, self-worth and recognition. An angry child is striving for recognition.
- A view of anger is that it is resentment, an experience that accompanies a demand or expectations that have not been made explicit. Anger seems to be a response to something outside of us, yet it is most often an intrapersonal event (within us): we make ourselves angry.
- Because anger is so unpleasant and we are so adept at turning it away from ourselves on to others, we usually attempt to locate the source of our anger outside ourselves with statements such as 'You make me angry', 'Your habits irritate me', 'You bother me'. We make ourselves angry and there is no one else who can honestly be blamed. Suffering the anger often seems to be the only alternative.
- Anger turned inwards is experienced as guilt; guilt produces feelings of depression, incompetence, helplessness and, ultimately, self-destruction.

Displaced anger

Anger may be directed at someone or something else that is convenient. We are angry at the traffic jam but we snap at an innocent spouse. The children consistently refuse to meet our expectations but we kick the dog. Such displacement of angry feeling serves to ventilate but not to resolve. The anger cycle still lacks closure. Expression of anger can lead to violence. Violence turned inwards produces depression. Displacement is ultimately ineffective and can damage innocent third parties. Repeated failure to close the anger cycle can produce a hostile, cynical, negative view of reality.

Dealing with your own anger

- Recognise it.
- Own it.
- Gauge your response – anger is never all-or-nothing.
- Diagnose the threat.
- Share the perceived threat.
- Letting go of the anger means: cancelling the feelings; cleaning the slate; you have forgiven.

Dealing with someone else's anger

- Define if you are the legitimate target.
- Acknowledge the other's feelings – don't sidestep them – and acknowledge your own feelings.

- Request feedback and give it.
- Remain relaxed.
- Recognise the difference between angry feelings and aggressive behaviour.
- Don't invade the other person's personal space.
- Encourage 'self-control' and suggest coping strategies: counting numbers, deep breathing, checking the number of joins in the wallpaper.
- Above all: listen. Strategies should never be at the expense of the client's feelings.
- Renegotiate the relationship.

Anger in counselling

Working with angry clients is very wearing, even when the counsellor is understanding, non-judgemental and empathic. While counsellors may recognise that the anger is not directed at them and that it arises from within the client, it is still demanding.

Helping clients to evaluate the level of their anger may be one way of introducing them to how to exercise control. A related point is to ascertain if the anger is justified or not.

There are different views about the benefit of encouraging clients to express their anger. Some writers hold the view that not to express it is repressing it and that it is cathartic to express it; others that expressing anger only consolidates it and makes the person even more angry. The client who is encouraged to recognise angry feelings and explore them within the safety of the counselling relationship is being helped to develop useful coping skills.

Questions you can ask yourself

- What is making me feel angry?
- Why am I feeling anger and not some other emotion?
- Am I jumping to conclusions about the situation or person who is making me feel angry?
- Is there something about this situation that threatens me and makes me feel afraid or inferior?
- Did my anger come because I had some unrealistic expectations?
- How might others, including the person who is angering me, view this situation?
- Is there another way to look at the situation?
- Are there things I can do to change the situation in order to reduce my anger?

Aggression is a variety of behaviour patterns in which (in human terms) a person shows a tendency to approach in attack rather than flee from something perceived as a threat. It is almost impossible to arrive at a concise definition of aggression. However, it could be said to be the deliberate and intentional infliction of harm upon another person who is motivated to avoid such treatment. Frustration, physical attack and verbal insult are most often what lead to aggression. Intense noise is also known to provoke aggression.

Aggression is viewed as:

- A motivated state
- A personality characteristic
- A response to frustration
- An inherent drive
- The need to fulfil a socially learned role.

In everyday terms, 'aggression' refers to acts of hostility and violence and meets with disfavour, yet there are contradictions. We speak approvingly of an athlete running an aggressive race or of the successful entrepreneur who conducts an aggressive sales campaign.

Competition, dominance, rivalry and victory all characterise aggression. Many murders or serious violent assaults appear to be instances of hostile aggression or explosive outbursts resulting from an argument or perceived threat. The majority of people who commit aggressive acts are more likely to commit them against people known to them, usually family members.

Direct aggression is the most likely outcome of anger, where we retaliate verbally or physically against a situation that arouses anger within us.

Passive aggression is a mechanism whereby the individual deals with conflict and stressors by expressing anger and aggression indirectly towards others. The person presents a facade of overt compliance, which masks the underlying feelings, often of resistance, resentment and hostility. The hostility is never entirely concealed. Hostile or destructive feelings and intentions may also be expressed through passive or submissive behaviour. Passive aggressive characters usually direct such behaviours toward others on whom they feel dependent or to whom they feel subordinate.

Manifestations of passive aggression include:

- Lack of interest
- Withdrawal
- Negativism
- Obstructionism
- Insufficiency
- Procrastination
- Sabotage
- Perfunctory behaviour
- Errors of omission
- Indifference
- Foot-dragging
- Lack of initiative
- Literalness in compliant behaviour that frustrates the outcome
- Dumb insolence.

The individual denies any hostile or negative intent, although there may be periodic angry outbursts.

Caregivers on the receiving end of such behaviour as wrist-cutting often feel they have been the victims of sadistic behaviour. Understanding the feelings, coupled with a matter-of-fact approach to the act, is often more productive than treating the behaviour as perverse. 'Time out' may be one way of breaking the pattern of the client who persists in self-defeating behaviour.

Redirected aggression is where we retaliate against some innocent person or object, for instance, kicking the cat.

In counselling, the clients to be wary of, when they express anger towards others, are:

- Those who lack perspective – they may misinterpret events
- Those who want to hurt specific people, in unspecified ways
- Those who have a history of episodic aggression
- Those unable to express anger towards another person on whom they are dependent.

Further reading

Bayne, R., Horto, I., Merry, T. and Noyes, E. (1994) *The Counsellor's Handbook: a practical A-Z guide to professional and clinical practice*. Chapman and Hall, London.

Collins, G.R. (1988) *Christian Counselling: a comprehensive guide*. Word Publishing, Nashville, TN.

Lion, J.R. (1995) Aggression. In: *Comprehensive Textbook of Psychiatry*, 6th edn (eds H.J. Kaplan and B.J. Sadock). Williams & Wilkins, Baltimore, MD.

Manstead, A.S.R. and Hewstone, M. et al. (1996) *The Blackwell Encyclopaedia of Social Psychology*. Blackwell Publishers, Oxford.

Pareek, U. (1983) Preventing and resolving conflict. In: *1983 Annual for Facilitators, Trainers, and Consultants.* University Associates, San Diego, CA.

Sutton, J. (1998) *Thriving on Stress: how to manage pressures and transform your life* (pages 108–115). How To Books, Oxford. Offers some thoroughly useful and practical guidelines on working with anger.

U'Ren, R.C. (1980) *The Practice of Psychotherapy*. Grune & Stratton, New York.

ANXIETY (SEE ALSO: BEHAVIOUR THERAPY, COGNITIVE THERAPY, POST-TRAUMATIC STRESS DISORDER, STRESS MANAGEMENT)

Anxiety is a distressing feeling of uneasiness, apprehension or dread. The fear may be rational, based on an actual event, such as when someone has palpitations and therefore fears a heart attack, or irrational, based on an anticipated event that may or may not take place, such as failing an exam that has not yet taken place. A certain amount of unrealistic and irrational anxiety is part of most people's experience; it seems to be an unavoidable part of human personality and usually takes the form of 'What if. . .'.

Existentialists describe anxiety as a fear of non-being, which may be fear of death but may also include a sense of meaninglessness and a powerful sense of guilt.

When anxiety is chronic and not traceable to any specific cause or when it interferes with normal activity, the sufferer is in need of expert help. Anxious people are in suspense, waiting for something, they know not what. A main source of anxiety is the fear of being separated from other persons who are felt to provide security.

Anxiety is a symptom in many mental disorders, including schizophrenia, obsessive-compulsive disorders, post-traumatic stress disorders and so on, but in phobias and other anxiety disorders proper, anxiety is the primary and frequently the only symptom.

The treadmill of anxiety

The analogy of the treadmill has been chosen to suggest that anxiety is both a prison and a punishment. By this is meant that the person who experiences severe anxiety is trapped within a process over which he seems to have no control, in the same way that a prisoner would be subjected to the treadmill. There the pace was set by a gaoler. If he felt particularly vindictive, a turn on the control lever increased the pace at which the prisoner was forced to run. There was no respite; no escape. Exhaustion was inevitable. This is the picture and the outcome of anxiety. It is a state from which the victim may not escape unless some influence can be brought to bear on the gaoler to slow the rate at which the mill turns and allow the prisoner to step out on to firm ground.

Mild anxiety is a common feeling, experienced by most people at some time in life. It is a feeling of uneasiness or apprehension. Most times, normal anxiety is based on reality. Some actual event is anticipated: an interview for a new job; having to tackle a difficult assignment; an examination; give a speech; admission to hospital. Not all events that produce feelings of anxiety are necessarily unpleasant. Getting married, or being presented with an award, are two events that could be termed 'pleasant', yet they may also produce feelings of anxiety. When the event has passed, feelings generally return quite quickly to normal, in much the same way as the heart rate, in a healthy individual, returns to normal after exercise. Normal anxiety, in small amounts, is biologically necessary for survival. Anxiety in doses too large for the individual to handle leads to panic: panic produces irrational behaviour. Panic is more likely to be caused by 'free-floating' anxiety: anxiety that cannot readily be attributed to any specific event or idea. It is there, constantly lurking in the background. When it attacks, the person is once again set a-running in the treadmill. At the 'normal' end of the anxiety scale, the person experiences butterflies in the stomach, restlessness and possibly some sleep disturbance. In more severe anxiety and panic, the physical accompaniments increase with the severity of the psychological disturbance. Anxiety, other than that which comes within the 'normal' range, which produces crippling emotional and physical symptoms, is pathological. People who suffer from such anxiety need expert help.

Levels of anxiety

Anxiety operates on three planes: emotional, cognitive and physiological. The more severe the anxiety, the more will these three planes become distorted. Very often it is what is happening within the body that brings the person to the notice of the physician. One of the characteristics of anxiety is that the more severe it is, the more it erodes every aspect of the person's life. The more this happens, the less able he is to function effectively. His total psychic energy is taken up with his anxious feelings. His thinking becomes unclear, and problem-solving ability is diminished. The inner struggle that he experiences, the constant feeling of pressure, coupled with the feeling of not coping, leads to exhaustion and defeat. The prisoner collapses on the floor of the treadmill, while the gaoler laughs.

Who is the gaoler?

It can be suggested that the gaoler is whatever, or whoever, it is that seeks to drive us on to exhaustion. This may be a punitive conscience, guilt, ambition, fear of failure or any of a multitude of fears. Less may be achieved by trying to fit the person into a theory than actually helping him identify what or who the gaoler is. It is possible that there are multiple gaolers, each of whom may be at war with the others; the resultant conflict increases the tension felt by the victim. Pathological anxiety is the likely outcome.

Various parts of our personality – in transpersonal psychology terms, 'sub-personalities' – may be the gaolers who will force the individual on to the tread-mill and keep up the pressure. They will resist all attempts by the Self to modify their punitive influence. They, the sub-personalities, have much to lose by surren-dering their power. The fear that drives the person on will be replaced by the peace and wholeness from central Self. That is what sub-personalities fear. They survive on power based on fear. When that fear is replaced by peace, they lose their sting. The person stops running and may then step out on to the firm ground of manageable, rather than pathological, anxiety.

Prevalence

Anxiety is widespread and common. Anxiety is found to rise with age, is greater in women than in men, is not significantly different between urban and rural populations and is more prevalent in the lower socio-economic groups. Another way of looking at it is that about 15 per cent of the patients on a GP's list will consult him, at least once a year, on conditions that are largely psychiatric in nature. The bulk of these patients (80 per cent) present with symptoms of anxiety or depression, of whom about half present with short-lived disorders, which are often stress-related and most of which resolve within four weeks. The other half have more chronic, recurring disorders that last for years.

These figures may not paint an accurate picture. They represent only those patients in whom anxiety is recognised. There are many others whose presenting clinical symptoms are treated but in whom the underlying anxiety remains undetected and untreated. Anxiety often accompanies depression and is present in many physical conditions. It is always difficult to assess if the anxiety the person experiences is caused by the condition or if the anxiety causes the condi-tion. It is sufficient to bear in mind that anxiety is likely to be present whenever the body, mind or emotions are put under stress.

Measurement of anxiety

Before moving on to discuss stress, it is worth looking briefly at the measurement of anxiety. Anxiety is accompanied by alteration in:

- Physiology (body)
- Cognition (mind)
- Mood (emotions).

The Hamilton Anxiety Rating Scale considers the following variables:

1. Anxious mood
2. Tension
3. Fears
4. Insomnia
5. Intellect
6. Depressed mood
7. Somatic general (muscular and sensory)
8. Cardiovascular system
9. Respiratory system
10. Gastro-intestinal system
11. Genito-urinary system
12. Autonomic system
13. Behaviour at interview.

While the administration of such a test was designed to assess anxiety neuroses, and would only be administered by people qualified to do so, a study of the variables and their sub-divisions provides excellent background material for a fuller understanding of the effects of anxiety.

Stress and life events

Life events studies demonstrate that breakdown is more likely in people who accumulate 200 Life Change Units over a period of six months. Since the studies by Holmes and Rahe in 1964, much attention has been focused on the relationship between events, stress and anxiety. Events that interfere with the life cycle, family relationships, social and work adjustment and the maintenance of psychological and physical integrity, are important contributory factors in psychiatric illness. It is not necessarily the event itself, but the symbolic meaning the event held for the person, that is significant. This is an important point to remember when counselling.

A moderate degree of anxiety is healthy and affords the person an opportunity to view the future realistically.

People can be helped to face reality by being given an opportunity to discuss their fears. It is also essential to look closely at the support systems available to the patient. It is possible that people may be able to endure more stress if they have another person with them, preferably one who has maintained a close relationship with the patient over some time.

The suspense of anxious people is characterised by:

- Watchful alertness
- Over-reaction to noise or other stimuli

- Helplessness in the face of danger, whether actual or imagined
- Mood that alternates between hope and despair.

Clients often have difficulty accurately describing the feelings of anxiety. Generally the fear is directed at some undefined threat to their physical or psychological wellbeing. They use such terms as 'tense', 'panicky', 'terrified', 'jittery' or 'wound up as tight as a clock spring'.

Bodily symptoms of anxiety may include:

- Tightness in the chest and throat
- Sinking feelings in the abdomen
- Dizziness or light feelings in the head
- Skin pallor
- Sweating or, less often, flushed
- Increase in pulse rate
- Undue increase in heart rate produced by mild exertion
- Muscle tension
- Loss of sexual interest
- Twitching of the limbs.

Cognitive symptoms of anxiety may include:

- Decreased concentration
- Acute alertness
- Confusion
- Fears of losing control or of going crazy
- Everything is a catastrophe.

Behavioural symptoms of anxiety may include:

- Withdrawal
- Irritability
- Hyperventilation
- Immobility.

Perceptual symptoms of anxiety may include:

- Depersonalisation (feelings of unreality or strangeness)
- Derealisation (a feeling of detachment from reality)
- Hyperaesthesia (abnormally high sensitivity of the skin to heat, cold and touch).

Anxiety frequently manifests itself as the result of opposing or conflicting wishes, desires, beliefs, life events or strain resulting from conflict between roles. An example of this would be in the newly married woman who experiences a conflict between being a wife and also maintaining a career, or the new husband who has a conflict between the roles of husband and member of the rugby team.

The more desperate the feeling of helplessness and indecision, and the more difficult the decision between two opposing forces, the more severe the anxiety will be. Defence mechanisms do not abolish anxiety. They try to bind or keep it from awareness.

Theories of anxiety

Learning theory proposes that anxiety is both a response to learned cues and a driver or motivator of behaviour. Most learning theorists maintain that anxiety is derived from reaction to pain. Anxiety can thus be reduced by removing or avoiding the source or sources of the situations that have produced pain. Avoidance may become firmly established and lead to constricted or bizarre behaviour such as phobias.

Psychoanalysis has three theories of anxiety:

- Repressed libido
- Repressed birth trauma
- A two-part theory – primary and signal:
  - Primary anxiety is perceived as a threat to the ego's equilibrium, which would result in the ego being dissolved. Primary anxiety would result from a failure of the defences.
  - Evidence of this is said to appear in nightmares.
  - Signal anxiety serves to warn the ego of a potential threat. The function of signal anxiety is to ensure that primary anxiety is never experienced.

Carl Jung did not deal comprehensively with the topic of anxiety and did not develop defence mechanisms to deal with it as Freud did. Jung's view of anxiety is:

- It does not always have a sexual foundation.
- It may serve a useful function by drawing attention to something that is undesirable.
- It may represent avoiding becoming consciously aware of suffering.

Cognitive behaviour theory postulates that anxiety is a response to perceived danger but that information has become distorted, leading to anxiety. In addition, sufferers perceive their resources as not adequate to cope with the perceived threat. One of the major threats is feeling a loss of control. Other significant threats are to self-esteem and excessive worry over how one is perceived by other people.

Some of the more florid mental disturbances, such as obsessive compulsion and panic attacks, which are characterised by a high degree of anxiety, are generally outside the scope of the average counsellor and should be referred for specialist psychiatric help.

However, it is appropriate here to draw attention to some of the more common anxiety conditions.

Panic attacks

The panic attack – a sudden, overpowering feeling of terror – is experienced by many people at some time in their lives. A panic attack typically lasts for several minutes and is one of the most distressing conditions that a person can experience. Many of the symptoms of acute anxiety are present in panic attacks. Symptoms of panic accompany certain medical conditions of thyroid, the inner ear, epilepsy, intoxication and substance withdrawal, and cardiac conditions, such as irregular heart rhythms or chest pains. People who suffer from post-traumatic stress disorder may experience panic when they are faced with situations (even on the television) that resemble the original traumatic event. It is vital to receive a thorough medical check-up and not take for granted that the symptoms are purely 'all in the mind'.

Phobias

A phobia is an extreme, irrational fear of a specific object or situation and the anxiety may vary in severity from unease to terror. A phobic disorder interferes with a person's ability to work, to socialise and go about a daily routine. A phobia that interferes with daily living can create extreme disability and the person needs medical treatment.

Phobias occur when fear produced by an original threatening situation is transferred to other similar situations, with the original fear often repressed or forgotten. All forms of phobias are disabling conditions and even mild forms can create problems of daily living. Phobias are associated with high incidence of distressing thoughts about suicide.

Fear of blood and injections may mean that the person avoids essential and urgent medical or dental care. Phobias generally respond to antidepressants and to behavioural forms of therapy. For example, cognitive restructuring therapy seeks to replace faulty thinking patterns with more constructive ones. The client says, 'I'm a complete failure'. The therapist then challenges this by getting the client to state in which areas of life he is successful. It is highly doubtful that someone is hopeless in everything.

Simple (specific) phobias

A simple phobia is of a specific object, animal or situation. Irrational fears of snakes, heights, enclosed places and darkness are examples. Receiving an injection or seeing blood may also assume phobic proportions.

Some common phobias are fear of:

- Mice or small animals (zoophobia)
- Spiders (arachnophobia)
- Height (acrophobia)
- Open spaces (agoraphobia)
- Enclosed spaces (claustrophobia).

In fact, almost anything can be the focus of a phobia. One medical textbook lists 33 specific situations. Phobias are quite resistant to change without treatment, although desensitisation therapy has proved effective. In desensitisation, the person is exposed, under relaxed conditions, to a series of stimuli that gradually come closer to the anxiety-provoking one, until the stimuli no longer produce anxiety. Some examples of phobias include:

- **Agoraphobia**: People with agoraphobia avoid open spaces, crowds and travelling. Agoraphobia, which literally means 'fear of the marketplace' and indicates fear of being away from the safety of home, commonly occurs with panic disorder. Where escape is impossible the feelings of anxiety are endured with marked distress.
- **Social phobia**: Social phobia is the irrational fear and avoidance of being in a situation in which a person's activities could be watched. Fear of public speaking or of eating in public are the most common complaints of socially phobic individuals. Social phobia sufferers are invariably loners and lonely, and often fail to develop intimate relationships. Social phobias are often associated with alcohol abuse. In children, the fear may take the form of tantrums, screaming, freezing, clinging or refusing to move away from a familiar person. Young children may be excessively timid, refuse to make contact with other children in play, are often seen on the fringes of a group and prefer to stay close to familiar adult figures.

The Diagnostic and Statistical Manual (DSM IV) identifies many more anxiety disorders, and is certainly worth studying.

Identifying useful approaches to helping clients control anxiety

Helping people cope with anxiety through counselling is likely to make use of support and encouragement and stress-management techniques of a behavioural nature. Within an empathic relationship the client can feel able to explore the reasons for the anxiety and learn to control it. And one of the most potent approaches, and often the easiest to learn, is deep relaxation. Learning to relax the body, then the mind, is often the first step in being able to control feelings of anxiety.

Behaviour therapy, which makes heavy demands on the person, is probably the most successful treatment, but that road is not an easy one for the client to tread.

Exposure is where the person is exposed to various carefully graded situations that build up confidence. When the person copes with the anxiety of one situation, the next one is tackled, until the most feared situation is tackled.

Homework and tasks are set. The behaviour therapist will constantly challenge what the client says, so bringing various parts of the client's statement or behaviour into focus. Generalisations are turned into specifics and excuses and rationalisations are disputed. At the same time, the counsellor offers a great deal of support as the client handles what seem terrifying situations and attempts to stop doing something. The support offered by the counsellor could be staying with the client while carrying out the feared task, giving practical advice like 'Take some deep breaths', 'Focus on becoming relaxed', 'Imagine yourself doing it'. The aim of support is to give clients the skills to use when they are on their own.

One important aspect of any counselling – and this applies with particular emphasis in teaching relaxation – is that the counsellor must be a believer. If you yourself are not relaxed, if you are tense and anxious, this will show and any attempt to help the client relax will be seen as technique and not of great value. The client might well say, 'Practise what you preach'.

Aspects of coping include:

- A positive and supportive network of family and friends all function to strengthen coping by providing validation of self-worth in the face of challenges that tend to lower a person's resistance.

Problems arising at work are less likely to be successfully coped with than those that arise within the family. This is attributed to the impersonality of the workplace and the lack of intimate support. If we can recognise the potential impersonality of our working environment, then take steps to make it less impersonal; to make it a place where feelings are recognised and acknowledged. Then stress can be dealt with effectively.

There is no one coping mechanism that would ensure a person being able to ward off the stressful consequences of strains. The most we can do, perhaps, is to help the person 'manage the strain', rather than 'change the strain'.

Successful coping appears to be linked to achieved status and to socio-economic status. Hardship is often linked to lower education achievement and low income. Such people are less likely to have the means to fend off the stresses resulting from the hardships.

Successful coping seems linked to:

- Lack of self-denigration
- Mastery
- Self-esteem.

Table 1: Coping strategies

1. Cognitive restructuring	finding something positive
2. Emotional expression	anger against others
3. Wish-fulfilling fantasy	pining, hoping
4. Self-blame	'all my fault'
5. Information-seeking	searching for information and advice
6. Threat minimisation	a refusal to dwell on thoughts about the illness and a conscious decision to put distressing thoughts aside

Cognitive strategies, including information-seeking, are related to positive affect, while emotional strategies, particularly those involving avoidance, blame and emotional ventilation, are related to negative affect, lowered self-esteem and poorer adjustment to illness. Deterioration of physical health may be the outcome of a vicious cycle of illness-based stress, ineffective coping and poor emotional adjustment.

The aim of counselling should be to help a person develop more effective coping strategies. This may be done by strengthening those strategies indicated in groups 1, 5 and 6 and diminishing the impact of items 2, 3 and 4. At the same time, however, it must always be remembered that being able to express one's negative feelings – about one's illness or one's self – is integral and essential to counselling. But there is a difference between the 'emotional expression' mentioned above and expressing one's feelings within a therapeutic relationship, where the essential aim is increased understanding and insight to assist in the process of readjustment.

Support and coping

The effect of primary group support is more important in readjustment than the severity of the disability or the length of time since the loss. Indeed, reliance on professional support, to the exclusion of primary group support, could be detrimental to recovery. The antidote to dependence lies in increasing the involvement of significant others and the support they are able to give.

Professionals engage in two types of support:

- **Resource compensation**: provision of resources; financial and physical; doing 'for'
- **Resource enhancement**: physiotherapy, vocational re-training, counselling; doing 'with'.

Many professionals engage in resource compensation rather than resource enhancement. The support of the primary groups rests on the relationship that exists between themselves and the client. On the other hand, no matter how supportive one's primary group, unless it is geared up to coping with trauma – and is adequately supported by professionals – help, appropriate to the need, may not be forthcoming.

It is necessary for the professionals to make certain that their expectations of the relatives' ability to cope are realistic. Most will need a great deal of support and guidance. If relatives do not cope, it will be so much more difficult for patients to make a satisfactory readjustment, and further deterioration of their condition may ensue.

A person who has someone to care for him is more able to resolve tension than one who does not. Simply knowing that someone is available is sufficient to increase one's strength. Clients who are not socially isolated, and are well supported, stay in treatment and follow recommended regimes. This applies particularly to people who have had to be hospitalised. Unless the support the client experiences while in hospital is maintained when he leaves, his motivation to continue the treatment on his own will suffer a decline. A valid assessment of the support available to him must be a high priority when deciding who can and who cannot be discharged.

Counsellors must be prepared not to demand more than these people can deliver, but to allow them time to approach the underlying conflict a little more closely. A counsellor's commitment to understanding the special language of emotional difficulties is under genuine trial at these times. Dealing with people who experience anxiety can be very stressful, but with a feeling for the difficulties these people experience, counsellors can work more effectively with them.

Taken from E. Kennedy (1977) *On Becoming a Counsellor.* Gill and Macmillan.

We must be constantly alert as to what other people's anxieties tell us about our own. Other people's vulnerabilities often find echoes somewhere in us. Other people's defences may make us equally defensive. On the other hand, we must be ever alert to our own reactions. If we find ourselves becoming uneasy and restive, we may be responding to the client's free-floating anxiety. If we feel under attack, it could be because we have become the focus of the client's paranoid feelings. Just as we should have a mentor relationship, so we should learn to listen to our own feelings when we work at close range with other people.

Summary

Anxiety can be considered as a normal experience, but in its pathological state the person usually requires psychiatric help. The treadmill analogy was used to describe anxiety, where the person experiencing it is often pushed to physical, intellectual and emotional exhaustion. The fact that most people would acknowledge that they have experienced some of the symptoms of normal anxiety provides a common base for an examination of a fairly universal phenomenon. For those people whose experience of anxiety has moved from the 'normal' end of the dimension towards the 'pathological', the theory was put forward that they are the victims of antagonistic sub-personalities who are at war with one another. Identifying these sub-personalities may be enough to drain them of the destructive power they hold over the person.

Imagery is one approach that can be used, not to control the anxiety, but to attempt to identify the gaoler of the treadmill. As with all counselling, it is essential that we use a broad repertoire of skills. A limited repertoire may prove to be too restricting on the client. One of the aims of counselling is self-awareness; this applies to both clients and those who counsel. Those of us who are counsellors need to know why we do it and why we prefer to use the particular approaches we do. If our counselling is to be truly effective, it is our duty to extend our awareness of ourselves as well as the approaches to counselling that other people have developed.

Further reading

Diagnostic and Statistical Manual of Mental Disorders (DSM IV) (1994) American Psychiatric Association, Washington, DC.

Holmes, T.H. and Rahe, R.H. (1967) The social readjustment rating scale. *Journal of Psychosomatic Research*, **11**, 213–218.

Papp, L.A. and Gorman, J.M. (1995) *Comprehensive Textbook of Psychiatry*, 6th edn (eds H.J. Kaplan and B.J. Sadock). Williams & Wilkins, Baltimore, MD.

Stewart, W. (1985) *Counselling in Rehabilitation*, Croom Helm, London.

Stewart, W. (2000) *Controlling Anxiety*, 2nd edn. How to Books, Oxford.

Sutton, J. (1998) *Thriving on Stress: how to manage pressures and transform your life.* How to Books, Oxford. This book has a comprehensive chapter on 'Learning the art of relaxation'.

Trower, P., Casey, A. and Dryden, W. (1988) *Cognitive-Behavioural Counselling in Action.* Sage Publications, London.

Weekes, C. (1995) *Self Help for Your Nerves: learn to relax and enjoy life again by overcoming fear and nervous tension.* Thorsons, London.

APPROVAL

Approval is a crucial element in the development of a child's self-worth and self-esteem. One definition of approval is 'to pronounce to be good, to commend'. Two other words linked with approval are acceptance and affirmation.

Approval, by parents or other significant figures in the life of the child (including siblings, particularly older ones, who exercise a profound influence on younger ones), is a form of control. People who as children have experienced little or no approval, in adult life often seem to go to extraordinary lengths to gain approval, almost as if the deficit can never be made up.

Approval is:

- Recognition that confirms our unique identity, and does not try to make us be someone we are not
- Acceptance of what we have to offer, without any preconceived ideas of what we should be or ought to be.

The results of approval are:

- Feelings of security
- Not being rejected because our abilities, opinions and what we think, feel or do, do not match up with other people's expectations of us
- Affirmation of our uniqueness and our existence
- Increased status and a sense of recognition
- A bond established between approver and approved
- Permission to take control of our lives, and responsibility for our actions.

The opposite of approval is rejection, and one of the principal ways we use rejection is by always passing judgement, always putting the other person in the wrong. Children are particularly prone to all that goes with judgement, and when this is reinforced with conditional love – 'I will love you if...' – then the child has little solid ground upon which to build a healthy self-esteem.

Approval, a form of social control, relates in some ways to Carl Rogers's 'unconditional positive regard', but only in the positive sense of approval. Some people will seem to go to extraordinary lengths to gain approval from significant others.

Conditional approval creates a relationship characterised by dependency and possessiveness. Unconditional approval empowers.

Any child reared in a relationship deprived of approval is likely to develop into an approval-hungry adult, for ever seeking and never finding approval; never able to trust other people's unconditional regard for them. This approval hunger may create difficulties in intimate relationships, where the person experiences a conflicting 'pull-push'. One part longs for intimacy, the other part rejects it because whatever the other person offers never satisfies and the one seeking approval pulls away.

A further characteristic of some approval-hungry people is their high drive to achieve, although seeking approval is not the only motivator for high achievement. One of the ways in which a child can get approval is by pleasing the significant person (or people). Achieving high grades at school is one way the child might gain this approval, yet this does not always work, for whatever the child does or achieves often leaves the significant person unimpressed. Indeed, what the child most wants and needs is not recognition for achievement but unconditional acceptance for just being who he is, without any strings attached.

Counselling approval-hungry clients means recognising their need. Within a relationship in which acceptance, empathy, genuineness, warmth and unconditional positive regard are lived out, the client can then feel accepted and achieve insight, then start to work towards change. The poem below, from an unknown source, encapsulates the discussion on approval.

If children live with criticism, they learn to condemn.
If children live with hostility, they learn to fight.
If children live with ridicule, they learn to be shy.
If children live with shame, they learn to be guilty.
If children live with tolerance, they learn to be patient.
If children live with encouragement, they learn confidence.
If children live with praise, they learn to appreciate.
If children live with fairness, they learn justice.
If children live with security, they learn faith.
If children live with approval, they learn to like themselves.
If children live with acceptance, they learn to find love in the world.

Further reading

Stewart, W. (1998) *Building Self-esteem: how to replace self-doubt with confidence and well-being*. How to Books, Oxford.

ASSERTIVENESS

Assertiveness is a clear, appropriate response to another person that is neither passive nor aggressive. It is communication in which self-respect and respect for the other person are demonstrated. Assertiveness is where one person's rights are not demanded at the expense of the rights of the other person.

Assertiveness is non-aggressive, non-defensive and non-manipulative, and it does not interfere with other people's freedom to take an assertive stance or make appropriate decisions. Although we may have to reach a compromise on a specific issue, this does not mean that we compromise our self-worth, neither should we nor the other person feel 'put down' or humiliated. If we or the other person feels this, manipulation or aggression and not assertion have been operating.

Many interpersonal difficulties and difficult behaviours arise because of people's inability to express positive or negative feelings clearly.

Assertiveness training helps people to:

- Gain and maintain respect for themselves and others
- Keep lines of communication open
- Achieve goals
- Recognise and develop inner resources.

Assertive rights

These are the basic rights we have as people, and assertion is the articulation of these rights. In maintaining 'rights' we must remember:

- One person's rights are never at the expense or another's. We must respect other people at all times.
- What a person does should always be based on her assessment of what she wants to do, and she should not be prevented from making such an appraisal. What she actually does is her own decision, and as such should not be judged by others.

Assertiveness training uses:

- Behavioural rehearsal
- Cognitive exercises
- Modelling
- Relaxation training
- Role play
- Simulation of feared situations
- Social skills training
- Structured exercises
- Systematic desensitisation.

Assertiveness training seeks to help people become aware of:

- **Aggressive behaviour**: Aggressive behaviour is a fight response. The goal is conflict.
- **Avoidance behaviour**: Avoidance behaviour is a flight response. The goal is to ignore conflict.
- **Assertive behaviour**: The goal is direct, honest, open and appropriate verbal and non-verbal behaviour.
- **Accommodating behaviour**: The goal is harmony at all costs.

Aggressive behaviour:

- We are competitive, motivated by results, power and control
- It can be offensive, because it violates the rights of other people
- Subtle, because it is often indirect
- Invasive of other people's psychological and/or physical space
- Other people are usually left feeling resentful.
- Aggressive people tend to get their own way by manipulating other people's feelings.
- Aggressive people spend a lot of time trying to repair hurt feelings.
- Aggression often shows when people stand up for their own rights.
- Aggressive people are often pushy and critical.

Avoidance behaviour

- We don't tackle intrusions on our rights, even when we feel they have been violated.
- We evade and avoid any honest confrontation by emotionally running away.
- We back down in the face of opposition.
- Other people easily invade our space.
- We may be more concerned with the image we present than being ourselves.

Assertive behaviour

- It means standing up for what we believe to be our personal rights.
- It means not attacking other people's rights.
- It means expressing our thoughts, feelings and beliefs in direct, honest and appropriate ways.
- It should nurture our esteem and the esteem of other people.
- It should lead to better respect and understanding in relationships.
- It should avoid the feeling of being constantly put down and frustrated.

Accommodating behaviour

- We often express our thoughts and feelings indirectly.
- What we say can be disregarded because it is indirect.
- We hope other people will be nice to us.
- We tend to shuffle problems around instead of dealing with them.
- We let problems build up, then – wow!
- Constant accommodating may mean that aggressive behaviour is just around the corner.

Obstacles to assertiveness

- Lack of awareness that we have the option of responding in an assertive manner
- Anxiety about expressing ourselves, even when we know what we want to say, in a way that expresses how we feel
- Negative self-talk inhibits self-assertion by what we tell ourselves.

- Verbal poverty: A difficulty in finding the right words at the right time leads to self-consciousness and hesitancy.
- Behavioural poverty: A non-assertive, non-verbal manner hinders all assertive expression.

Assertive speech

Many of us fail to be assertive because of the negative labels we carry or because we feel constrained by conforming to stereotypes.

An important technique in assertiveness training is getting people to make positive self-statements instead of negative ones. Participants are encouraged to create assertive hierarchies, starting with an encounter that would be relatively easy to handle and progressing to the most difficult, then to rehearse them in the group. One of the aims in assertive behaviour is to change from being indirect to being direct and from using generalisations to being specific.

Here are some examples:

- **Generalised**: You don't love me.
- **Specific**: When you come home from work, I would like you to kiss me.
- **Generalised**: You never think about anyone but yourself.
- **Specific**: If you know you're going to be late phone me. I worry about you.
- **Generalised**: You're a male chauvinist pig.
- **Specific**: I want you to listen to me while I'm stating my opinions, even if you don't agree.
- **Generalised**: All you ever do is work.
- **Specific**: I would like us to go to the beach next week.
- **Generalised**: You never talk to me any more.
- **Specific**: I'd like us to sit down together – with no TV, and talk for a few minutes each night.

Assertiveness is a dignified approach to human interaction that preserves the esteem of all parties while at the same time accomplishing a particular objective.

Further reading

Byrum, B. (1988) The nuts and bolts of assertive training. In: *1988 Annual: Developing Human Resources*. University Associates, San Diego, CA.

Cawood, D. (1988) *Assertiveness for Managers*. International Self-Counsel Press, Canada.

Davis, H., Eshelnan, E.R. and McKay, M. (1986) *The Relaxation and Stress Reduction Workbook*. New Harbinger Publications, Oakland, CA.

Dickson, A. (1982) *A Woman in Your Own Right*. Quartet Books, London.

Fensterheim, H. and Baer, J. (1980) *Don't Say 'Yes' When You Want To Say 'No'*. Futura, New York.

Kagan, C., Evans, J.S. and Kay, B. (1986) *A Manual of Interpersonal Skills*. Harper & Row, London.

Lindenfield, G. (1989) *Super Confidence: the woman's guide to getting what you want out of life*. Thorsons, Wellingborough.

Sharpe, R. (1989) *Assert Yourself*. Kogan Page, London.

Stubbs, D.R. (1986) *Assertiveness at work*. Pan Books, London.

Sutton, J. (1998) *Thriving on Stress: how to manage pressures and transform your life*. How to Books, Oxford.

ATTACHMENT (SEE ALSO: BONDING)

Attachment is a theory developed by John Bowlby at the Tavistock Clinic, London. Attachment describes the relationship between an infant and its mother or mother-substitute (caregiver). This early relationship is the foundation for all later relationships.

Attachment behaviour is evident from six months onwards when the infant discriminates sharply between the caregiver and other people. Early attachment influences adult behaviour, particularly during illness, in distress or when afraid. The primary attachment figure represents security. For attachment to be satisfactory, one principal caregiver needs to be identified.

Separation anxiety is anxiety at (the prospect of) being separated from someone believed to be necessary for one's survival. Separation anxiety may be objective, as in infancy or in adult invalids, or neurotic, when the presence of another person is used as a defence against some other form of anxiety. In both cases two factors are involved: dread of some unspecified danger, either from the outside or from mounting internal tension, and dread of losing the object believed capable of giving protection or offering relief.

Common manifestations are unrealistic worries about harmful things happening to the attachment figure (parent) while away, persistent fears of being lost, kidnapped or even killed if separated, social withdrawal and behaviour frequently showing protest, despair and detachment. When the caregiver returns, the child's behaviour may demonstrate avoidance, resistance and over-attachment. It is as if trust, broken by the separation, has to be re-established.

Homesickness is a lesser form of separation-anxiety disorder, although the feelings can be very powerful. It is thought that home-sickness and separation anxiety show in children who are unsure of their place within the family. The sickness and anxiety are a desire to return home to make certain that the family has not disintegrated.

The work of bonding and attachment has had significant practical implications for childbirth methods and how children's hospitals are run. The understanding of grief, bereavement, mourning, loss and loneliness have all been enhanced by attachment theory.

Reactive attachment disorder

In mental health, this is a condition that is found in infancy or early childhood. It begins before the child is five years old, characterised by markedly disturbed patterns of social relations.

In the inhibited type of reactive attachment disorder, failure to respond predominates and responses are wary, avoidant or highly ambivalent and contradictory.

In the disinhibited type, indiscriminate sociability is characteristic, such as excessive familiarity with relative strangers or lack of selectivity in choice of attachment figures.

The majority of children who develop this disorder (either type) are from a setting in which care has been grossly pathogenic. Either the caregivers have continually disregarded the child's basic physical and emotional needs or repeated changes of primary caregiver have prevented the formation of stable attachments.

In general, people who have experienced inadequate attachment are prone to experience difficulty establishing and maintaining intimate relationships as adults. Clients who have experienced 'insecure attachment' may present difficulties in counselling because their adult behaviour is a reflection of their attachment relationship. In other words, they are likely to display an anxious-avoidance or anxious-ambivalent relationship towards the counsellor.

Discussion of therapeutic techniques is outside the remit of this book; however, clients who do experience relationship difficulties of the types mentioned may respond to working with their inner child. Symbolically and through imagery, but also by using other body techniques and group work, they may find that they are able to reclaim their inner child, which feels trapped in deprivation. As in all deprivation work, the realistic aim is long rather than short term.

Further reading

Bowlby, J. (1969) *Attachment. Attachment and Loss*, vol. 1. Penguin, Harmondsworth.

Bowlby, J. (1973) *Separation. Attachment and Loss*, vol. 2. Penguin, Harmondsworth.

Bowlby, J. (1975) Attachment theory, separation anxiety and mourning. In: *American Handbook of Psychiatry*, vol. 6 (eds D.A. Hamburg and H. Hamburg). Basic Books, New York.

Bowlby, J. (1980) *Loss. Attachment and Loss*, vol. 3. Penguin, Harmondsworth.

Parkes, C.M. and Stevenson-Hinde, J. (eds) (1982) *The Place of Attachment in Human Behaviour*. Tavistock, London.

Zisook, S. (1995) Death, dying, and bereavement. In: *Comprehensive Textbook of Psychiatry*, 6th edn (eds H.J. Kaplan and B.J. Sadock). Williams & Wilkins, Baltimore, MD.

ATTENDING

Attending refers to the ways in which we physically and psychologically demonstrate our availability to other people. It means giving our full attention to what we are saying: the facts, the feelings and the accompanying body language.

Attending means concentrating and involves:

- Our body
  - The way we sit: distance, angle of chairs
  - A naturally open posture
  - Demonstrating involvement and interest, by moving forwards from time to time
  - Maintaining comfortable eye contact
  - Being aware of one's own facial expressions and body language
  - Being relaxed, without slouching

- Our mind
  - Thoughts uncluttered and focused
  - Open attitude
- Our feelings
  - To give full attention we must be secure, calm and confident. A disturbed spirit conflicts with attending. At some of the more dramatic moments of life, just having another person with us helps to prevent psychological collapse. Our face shows where our heart is.

When (though not necessarily during) counselling, we should ask ourselves:

- Was I effectively present and in emotional contact with this client?
- Did I give my whole attention or was part of it diverted?
- Did my non-verbal behaviour reinforce my internal attitudes?
- In what ways was I distracted from giving my full attention to this client?
- What can I do to handle these distractions?

AUTHORITARIANISM (SEE ALSO: PREJUDICE)

Authoritarianism, the favouring of blind submission to authority, is characteristic of certain individuals, of common belief systems shared by such individuals and, by extension, of elitist, anti-democratic governments based on such shared beliefs.

Totalitarianism is an extreme instance of authoritarianism, a political system designed to achieve complete control over people's inner and outer lives. This is, however, an extremely difficult if not impossible goal, which has rarely been achieved for very long. Even the most authoritarian societies such as Nazi Germany and the Soviet Union under Stalin failed to control most aspects of people's private lives or to stifle dissent and subversion. Since true democracy is quite rare, most governments are to some degree authoritarian and, therefore, problematic for those they govern.

Authoritarian personality

As an individual trait, authoritarianism was first systematically explored in research presented by Theodor Adorno and others in *The Authoritarian Personality* (1950). The study began as an investigation of anti-Semitism in the US, but led to the discovery of numerous correlations between anti-Semitism and other attitudes associated with stereotyped behaviour – although later work separated the attitudes towards authority from specific political views.

Adorno's hypothesis was that the origins of authoritarianism lay in childhood socialisation when the parents – and especially the father – adopted a very harsh disciplinary approach towards their children. All transgressions, however minor, were severely punished.

Drawing on psychoanalytic theory, Adorno and his colleagues argued that such an upbringing would lead children to repress their aggressive feelings towards their parents but that these feelings would later be displaced on to alternative and 'safer' targets. At the same time, children would develop an anxious and deferential attitude towards authority figures, since these symbolised the parents. Further, such people would be more susceptible than others to fascist or racist ideas, especially if these emanated from prestigious authority sources.

The 'F-scale' became widely used as a measure of prejudice. Consistent with the original hypothesis, high scores did reflect the respondents' childhood as a time of strict obedience to parental authority and they often manifested openly prejudiced views.

An example of authoritarianism in action was in an observation that, when solving mental puzzles, high authoritarians were less able or willing to change their problem-solving strategy once they had embarked on it. Low authoritarians solving the same puzzles were more adaptable. Prejudice was also reliably correlated with authoritarianism, a relationship that is still observable in more recent studies.

Characteristics of the authoritarian personality

- Aggression towards subordinates
- Closed-mindedness
- Contempt for weakness
- Curiosity about sexual behaviour
- Cynicism
- Dependence on conventional values
- Dominance
- Excessive concern with what is right or wrong
- Excessive conformity
- Insecurity
- Intolerance of ambiguity
- Lack of self-insight
- Need for strong external support systems
- Prejudice
- Respect (reverence) for power
- Ridged, stereotyped thought patterns
- Rigidity of thinking
- Sensitivity to interpersonal status
- Submissiveness to authority
- Superstition
- Tendency to use projection
- Uncritical submission to the authority of dominant groups.

Adorno's work on the authoritarian personality is best known for his ethnocentrism scale: a measure of the tendency to hold prejudiced attitudes towards all groups different from one's own.

High scores on this scale show a general tendency to see the world in terms of noble in-groups that must be supported and offensive out-groups that must be avoided, or rejected and attacked when they become threatening. In other words, people who are prejudiced against one group tend to be prejudiced against many groups with whom they do not agree, a hatred of Jews, for example, being associated with a hatred of Catholics.

Although controversial and the object of considerable criticism, Adorno's work is sociologically important because it seeks a connection between personality and how social systems are organised, in what it says about both how social conditions foster authoritarian personalities and how authoritarianism affects social life. The significance of more recent research findings is that it may be more appropriate to regard authoritarianism as a reaction to changes within society than as a consequence of a particular individual socialisation experience.

Some authoritarian statements:

- Obedience and respect for authority are the most important values children should learn.
- Young people sometimes get rebellious ideas, but as they grow up they ought to get over them and settle down.
- Business people and manufacturers are more important to society than artists and academics.
- When a person has a problem or worry, it is best for him not to think about it, but to keep busy with more cheerful things.

Authoritarianism and counselling

People with authoritarian personalities, because they see everything in 'either–or' terms and have great difficulty in tolerating ambiguity and uncertainty, do not cope well with disability. This inability to tolerate ambiguity could present a stumbling block in counselling if the person ever decides to risk this sort of relationship, for to engage in counselling would mean acknowledging that he is *not* the perfect person.

Counselling operates more in the realm of the possible, of what might be in the areas of feelings, rather than in what is factual and predetermined. It operates in the grey areas, rather than in black or white terms. Thus clients with authoritarian personalities are likely to experience difficulty in counselling, because any challenge to their preconceived ideas about themselves in relation to society could prove too threatening.

Open-mindedness

In contrast to authoritarianism is open-mindedness. Open-mindedness refers to how flexible and responsive one is to examine new evidence about one's belief systems. It is partially related to one's ability to receive, evaluate and act on information from the outside on its own merits. It also relates to how one is able to free oneself from internal pressures that would obscure, or interfere with incoming information.

The open mind is relatively unencumbered by irrelevant facts within the situation, which may arise from the person or from outside.

- **Examples of irrelevant internal pressures would be:** unrelated habits, beliefs and perceptual cues, irrational ego motives, power needs and the need for self-praise and the need to allay anxiety.
- **Examples of external pressures would be:** relying on reward or punishment from external authority, such as parents, peers and other authority figures, reference groups, social and institutional norms and cultural norms.

Open-minded people are more capable of discriminating between a message and its source and are less influenced by high status.

Indicators of closed Self

- Difficult to approach
- Insensitive to others' needs and goals
- Resists others' suggestions and ideas
- Expects too much of others
- Is highly competitive
- Is highly subjective
- Is resistant to change
- Unwilling to understand from someone else's point of view.

Indicators of closed Others

- Resentful of outside suggestions
- Refusal of offers of help
- Unwilling to cooperate
- Unwilling to adjust to the reality of the situation
- Resistant to changing their ways of working
- Insensitive to the effects they have on others
- Difficult to approach.

Further reading

Adorno, T.W., Frenkel-Brunswick, E., Levinson, D.J. and Stanford, R.N. (eds) (1950) *The Authoritarian Personality*. Harper, New York.

Manstead, A.S.R. and Hewstone, M. et. al. (1996) *The Blackwell Encyclopaedia of Social Psychology*. Blackwell Publishers, Oxford.

Rokeach, M., (1960) *The Open and Closed Mind*, Basic Books, New York.

Ruch, F.L. and Zimbardo, P.G. (1971) *Psychology of Life*, 8th edn. Scott, Foresman & Co., London.

Stubbins, J. (1977) Stress and disability. In: *Social and Psychosocial Aspects of Disability*, (ed. J. Stubbins). University Press, Baltimore, MD.

B

BEHAVIOUR THERAPY (SEE ALSO: COGNITIVE THERAPY AND RATIONAL EMOTIVE COUNSELLING)

This is the applied use of behavioural psychology to bring about changes in what people are doing and thinking, the central principle of which is that all behaviour is learned and maintained as a result of the person's interaction with the environment.

A useful definition is:

> *A mode of treatment that focuses on modifying observable and, at least in principle, quantifiable behaviour by means of systematic manipulation of the environment and variables thought to be functionally related to the behaviour. Some behaviour therapy techniques are operant conditioning, shaping, token economy, systematic desensitisation, aversion therapy, and flooding (implosion).*

> American Psychiatric Glossary, American Psychiatric Press, Inc. Washington, DC.

Rewarded behaviour will tend to increase in frequency, while behaviour not rewarded, or punished, will tend to decline. Behaviour therapy is a major form of therapy practised by clinical psychologists.

In the treatment of phobias, behaviour therapy seeks to modify and eliminate the maladaptive response that the person uses when confronted with a phobic object or situation. Although avoiding the feared situation, responding in this way reinforces the belief that whatever it is cannot be coped with in any other way and, unless challenged, will frequently persist.

Behaviour therapy interrupts this self-reinforcing pattern of avoidance behaviour by presenting the feared situation in a controlled manner so that it eventually ceases to produce anxiety.

The behavioural therapist is concerned with what can be observed – with what is said and done – not with experiences in the past that may have caused it nor with any postulated intrapsychic conflict – what must be inferred – unconscious motives and processes and symbolic meanings.

Although the focus is on changing behaviour, the relationship is important, not in itself, but to support the client through the difficult times of change and discomfort. In distinction from, for example, person-centred counselling, the behavioural counsellor is directive and active; but a relationship without warmth and empathy will be less likely to succeed than one where these are evident.

The roots of behaviour therapy

The behavioural approach has its roots in the 1950s and early 1960s as a radical reaction to the dominant psychoanalytic perspective. During the 1970s behaviour therapy emerged as a major force in psychology and made a significant impact on education, psychotherapy, psychiatry and social work. Behavioural techniques were developed and expanded, and they were also applied to fields such as business, industry and child rearing. This approach was now viewed as the treatment of choice for certain psychological problems.

Moving into the present, two of the most significant developments in the field are:

- The continued emergence of cognitive behaviour therapy as a major force
- The application of behavioural techniques to the prevention and treatment of medical disorders.

The main contributors are:

- Joseph Wolpe's work on experimental neuroses in cats and the clinical work that developed from that research; the most important technique is systematic desensitisation
- B.F. Skinner's contribution of operant conditioning
- Albert Bandura's social learning theory
- Albert Ellis created rational emotive behaviour therapy.
- Aaron Beck developed cognitive therapy.
- Donald Meichenbaum devised treatments such as stress inoculation and self-instructional training.
- Hans Eysenck's contribution to learning and trait theories of personality.

Systematic desensitisation

Desensitisation is the reduction or the extinction of sensitivity to something specific that causes a problem, e.g. allergies. The same behavioural principle is applied in the treatment of anxiety and phobic behaviours by counter-conditioning.

EMDR (eye movement desensitisation and reprocessing)

EMDR is a comparatively new therapeutic process developed by Francine Shapiro. EMDR integrates elements of many effective psychotherapies: psychodynamic, cognitive behavioural, interpersonal, experiential and body-centred therapies. EMDR is an information processing therapy and uses an eight-phase approach:

1. The first phase is a history-taking session during which the therapist assesses the client's readiness for EMDR and develops a treatment plan.
2. The therapist ensures that the client has adequate methods of handling emotional distress and good coping skills, and that the client is in a relatively stable state. New coping skills will be introduced if necessary.
3. **Assessment** is the next phase where the therapist:
   - Identifies a traumatic memory that results in anxiety
   - Identifies the emotion and physical sensations associated with the traumatic event
   - Evaluates the subjective unit of disturbance scale of images
   - Identifies negative thinking that is associated with the disturbing event
   - Finds an adaptive belief (or positive thinking) that would lessen the anxiety surrounding the traumatic event.
4. **Desensitisation:** The client:

- Visualises the traumatic image
- Verbalises the maladaptive belief (or negative thinking)
- Pays attention to the physical sensations.

- Exposure is limited, and the client may have direct exposure to the most disturbing element for less than one minute per session. Then other associations arise.
- During this process, the client is instructed to visually track the therapist's index finger as it is moved rapidly and rhythmically back and forth across the client's line of vision from 12 to 24 times. The client is instructed to:
  - Block out the negative experience momentarily and to breathe deeply to report what he is imagining, feeling, and thinking.
- Although eye movements are the most commonly used external stimulus, therapists often use auditory tones, tapping or other types of tactile stimulation. The kind of dual attention and the length of each set are customised to the need of the client. The client is instructed to just notice whatever happens. After this, the clinician instructs the client to let his mind go blank and to notice whatever thought, feeling, image, memory or sensation comes to mind.
5. **Installation**: Installing and increasing the strength of the positive thinking the client has identified as the replacement for the original negative cognition.
6. **Visualisation**: The client visualises the traumatic event and the positive thinking and scans his body mentally from top to bottom and identifies any bodily tension states. The body scan is completed when the client is able to visualise the target event and, at the same time, experience little bodily tension and be able to experience the positive cognition.
7. **Closure**: The therapist asks the client to keep a journal during the week to document any related material that may arise and reminds the client of the self-calming activities that were mastered in phase 2, such as relaxation, guided imagery, meditation, self-monitoring and breathing exercises.
8. **Re-evaluation**: Should be implemented at the beginning of each new session. This last phase of EMDR includes:
   - Reconceptualisation of the client's problems
   - Establishing new therapeutic goals
   - Engaging in further desensitisation
   - Continuing the work of cognitive restructuring
   - Continuing the self-monitoring process; and
   - Collaboratively evaluating the outcome of treatment.

The number of sessions depends upon the specific problem and client history. However, repeated controlled studies have shown that a single trauma can be processed within three sessions in 80–90 per cent of the participants. While every disturbing event need not be processed, the amount of therapy will depend upon the complexity of the history. In a controlled study, 80 per cent of multiple civilian trauma victims no longer had post-traumatic stress disorder after approximately six hours of treatment. A study of combat veterans reported that after 12 sessions 77 per cent no longer had PTSD.

The behaviour therapy technique

The client is exposed, under relaxed conditions, to a series of stimuli that increasingly approximate to the anxiety-provoking one, until the stimuli no longer produce anxiety.

The stages:

1. Relaxation training, which the client is urged to practise twice daily
2. The construction of a hierarchy of anxiety-provoking stimuli, ranked according to the level of anxiety they evoke from least to greatest
3. Presentation of scenes during relaxation, starting with the least anxiety-provoking and working in a step-by-step progression through the hierarchy.

Some people find it very difficult to relax, to carry out visualisation or to produce hierarchies that accurately reflect their problem.

Variations on the theme

Some therapists use a tape recorder for home desensitisation. Some work in groups, while others carry out the process in real situations.

The main features of behaviour therapy:

- It concentrates on behaviour rather than on the underlying causes of the behaviour.
- Behaviour is learned and may be unlearned.
- Behaviour is susceptible to change through psychological principles, especially learning methods.
- Clearly defined treatment goals are set.
- Classical personality theories are rejected.
- The therapist adapts methods to suit the client's needs.
- The focus is on the 'here and now'.
- There is a belief in obtaining research support for the methods used.

The stages of behaviour therapy

- A detailed analysis of the client's problems and behavioural factors.
- Specific treatment goals.
- Treatment plan using appropriate behavioural techniques.
- Implementation of the plan, including full discussion with the client.
- Evaluation.

Therapeutic techniques used

- **Exposure:** The aim is to extinguish the anxiety, and its associated behaviour, by systematic exposure to the feared situation. This may include modelling – observing someone carrying out the desired behaviour before attempting it.
- **Contingency management:** This means reinforcing positive behaviour but not reinforcing negative behaviour. Reward in the form of tokens is an example.

- **Cognitive behaviour therapy**: Concerned with thoughts and beliefs (see also Cognitive therapy).
- **Assertiveness and social skills training** (see also Assertiveness).
- **Self-control**: Behaviour therapy aims to teach people methods of self-control and self-help, to enable them to cope with situations they find difficult. For example, with exposure to the feared situation – rehearse the difficult situation and arrange for positive reinforcement when the task has been done.
- **Role play**: Clients may be asked either to replay an actual situation or to imagine one.
- **Guided imagery**: Clients symbolically create or recreate a problematic life situation.
- **Physiological recording**.
- **Self-monitoring**: For example, recording daily calorie intake.
- **Behavioural observation**: Assessment of problem behaviour is more accurate when based on actual observation.
- **Psychological tests and questionnaires**: Behaviour therapists will not generally use tests based on psychodynamic theories. They will use tests that yield the information necessary for a functional analysis or for the development of an intervention strategy.
- **Stress management**: Particularly the use of progressive relaxation.

The sequence of selecting and defining goals is described by Cormier and Cormier. This process demonstrates the essential nature of a collaborative relationship:

- The counsellor provides a rationale for goals, explaining the role of goals in therapy, the purpose of goals, and the client's participation in the goal-setting process.
- The client specifies the positive changes he or she wants from counselling. Focus is on what the client wants to do, rather than on what the client does not want to do.
- The client and counsellor determine whether the stated goals are changes 'owned' by the client.
- Together the client and the counsellor explore whether the goals are realistic.
- The cost–benefit effects of all identified goals are explored, with counsellor and client discussing the possible advantages and disadvantages of the goals.
- Client and counsellor then decide (1) to continue seeking the stated goals, (2) to reconsider the client's goals or (3) to seek a referral.
- Once goals have been agreed upon, a process of defining them begins. The counsellor and client discuss the behaviours associated with the goals, the circumstances required for change, the nature of sub-goals and a plan of action to work towards these goals (Corey, 2001).

Behaviour therapy does not ignore the importance of the therapeutic relationship. The client who is in a trusting, supportive relationship will generally work conscientiously through the therapy.

Behaviour therapy is tailor-made to suit individual clients' needs. Much of behaviour therapy is short-term – 25–50 sessions. Behaviour therapy is applicable over a full range of problems, for example:

- Anxiety disorders
- Cardiovascular disease
- Childhood disorders
- Depression
- Hypertension
- Interpersonal/marital problems
- Obesity
- Sexual disorders
- Speech difficulties
- Stress management
- Substance abuse
- Tension headaches.

While behaviour therapy is generally considered to be unsuitable in psychotic conditions, it is used in the treatment of people with chronic mental illnesses.

Self-management programmes and self-directed behaviour

Over the past two decades in particular, there has been a growing trend to help people manage their own problems, teaching them to manage their lives more effectively. However, the roots of this can be traced as far back as 1942 with Karen Horney's *Self-analysis*. At the time this approach was revolutionary, possibly equated with 'giving away secrets'.

Self-helpers are encouraged to control smoking, drinking and drugs; time-management skills; and dealing with obesity and overeating.

Five characteristics of an effective self-management programme are identified by Cormier and Cormier:

- A combination of self-management strategies is usually more useful than a single strategy.
- Self-management efforts need to be employed regularly over a sustained period or their effectiveness may be too limited to produce any significant change.
- Clients should set realistic goals and then evaluate the degree to which they are being met.
- The use of self-reinforcement is an important component of self-management programmes.
- Some degree of environmental support is necessary to maintain changes that result from a self-management programme.

Limitations and criticisms of behaviour therapy

In his book, *Theory and Practice of Counseling and Psychotherapy* Corey lists five major criticisms and then presents his rationale (it is worthwhile giving his rationale in full here) (pages 284–286).

1. Behaviour therapy may change behaviours, but it does not change feelings.

Some critics argue that feelings must change before behaviour can change. Behavioural practitioners generally contend that if clients can change their behaviour their feelings are also likely to change. They hold that empirical evidence has not shown that feelings must be changed first, and behavioural clinicians do in actual practice deal with feelings as an overall part of the treatment process.

I do not think behaviour therapy deals with emotional processes as fully or as adequately as do the experiential therapies. A general criticism of both the behavioural and the cognitive approaches is that clients are not encouraged to experience their emotions. In concentrating on how clients are behaving or thinking, counsellors play down the working through of emotional issues. Generally, I favour initially focusing on what clients are feeling and then working with the behavioural and cognitive dimensions.

2. Behaviour therapy ignores the important relational factors in therapy.

The charge is often made that the importance of the relationship between client and therapist is discounted in behaviour therapy. Although it appears to be true that behaviour therapists do not place primary weight on the relationship variable, this does not mean the approach is condemned to a mechanical and non-humanistic level of functioning. Behaviour therapists acknowledge that a good working relationship with their clients is a basic foundation necessary for the effective use of techniques.

Research has not shown the behavioural therapies to be any different from other therapeutic orientations in the relationship variables that emerge. Some therapists may be attracted to behaviour therapy because they can be directive, can play the role of expert, or can avoid the anxieties and ambiguities of establishing a more personal relationship. But this is not an intrinsic characteristic of the approach, and many behaviour therapists are more humanistic in practice than some therapists who profess to practise humanistic therapy.

3. Behaviour therapy does not provide insight.

If this assertion is indeed true, behaviour modification theorists would probably respond that insight isn't necessary. They do not focus on insight because of the absence of clear evidence that insight is critical to outcome. Behaviour is changed directly. If the goal of achieving insight is an eventual change of behaviour, then behaviour therapy, which has proven results, has the same effect. Moreover, a change in behaviour often leads to a change in understanding; it is a two-way street.

Nevertheless, many people want not just to change their behaviour but also to gain an understanding of why they behave the way they do. These answers are often buried deep in past learning and in historical events. Although it is possible for behaviour therapists to give explanations in this realm, in practice they usually do not.

4. Behaviour therapy treats symptoms rather than causes.

The psychoanalytic assumption is that early traumatic events are at the root of present dysfunction. Behaviour therapists may acknowledge that deviant responses have historical origins, but they contend that history is seldom important in the maintenance of current problems. Thus, behaviour therapy focuses on providing the client with opportunities to acquire the new learning needed for effectively coping with problem situations.

Related to this criticism is the notion that unless historical causes of present behaviour are therapeutically explored new symptoms will soon take the place of those that were 'cured'. Behaviourists rebut this assertion on both theoretical and empirical grounds. They do not accept the assumption that symptoms are manifestations of underlying intrapsychic conflicts. Instead, they contend that behaviour therapy directly changes the maintaining conditions, which are the causes of problem behaviours (symptoms). Furthermore, they assert that there is no empirical evidence that symptom substitution occurs after behaviour therapy has successfully eliminated unwanted behaviour.

5. Behaviour therapy involves control and manipulation by the therapist.

Some writers in behaviour therapy clearly acknowledge that therapists do have control, but they contend that this capacity to manipulate relevant variables is not necessarily undesirable or unethical. Kazdin (1994) believes no issues of control and manipulation are associated with behavioural strategies that are not also raised by other therapeutic approaches. He maintains that behaviour therapy does not embrace particular goals or argue for a particular lifestyle, nor does it have an agenda for changing society.

Surely, in all therapeutic approaches there is control by the therapist, who hopes to change behaviour in some way. This does not mean, however, that clients are helpless victims at the mercy of the whims and values of the therapist. Contemporary behaviour therapists employ techniques aimed at increased self-direction and self-control, which are skills clients actually learn in the therapy process.

Further reading

Agras, W.S. (1995) Behaviour therapy. In: *Comprehensive Textbook of Psychiatry*, 6th edn, (eds H.J. Kaplan and B.J. Sadock). Williams & Wilkins, Baltimore, MD.

Corey, G. (1991) *Manual for Theory and Practice of Counseling and Psychotherapy*. Wadsworth, Brooks/Cole, Pacific Grove, CA.

Corey, G. (2001) *Theory and Practice of Counseling and Psychotherapy*, 6th edn. Wadsworth, Brooks/Cole, Pacific Grove, CA.

Corey, G. (2001) *Case Approach to Counseling and Psychotherapy*, 5th edn. Wadsworth. Brooks/Cole, Pacific Grove, CA.

Cormier, W.H. and Cormier, L.S. (1991) Selecting helping strategies. In: Cormier and Cormier (eds), *Interviewing strategies for helpers: fundamental skills and cognitive behavioral interventions*, 3rd edn. Brooks/Cole, Pacific Grove, CA.

EMDR Institute, Inc. PO Box 750, Watsonville, CA 95077 USA. Tel: 831 761 1040. Fax: 831 761 1204. http://www.emdr.com. Email: inst@emdr.com

Goldstein, A. and Foa, E. (eds) (1980) *Handbook of Behavioural Interventions: a clinical guide*. John Wiley, New York.

Horney, K. (1942, reissued 1994) *Self-analysis*. W.W. Norton & Co., Inc., New York.

O'Sullivan, G. (1996) Behaviour therapy. In: *Handbook of Individual Therapy* (ed. W. Dryden). Sage Publications, London.

Kazdin, A.E. (1994) *Behaviour modification in applied settings* (5th edn). Brooks/Cole, Pacific Grove, CA.

Shephard, M. (1973, reprinted 1994) *Do-it-yourself Psychotherapy*. Optima Books, London.

Stewart, W. (1998) *Self-Counselling*. How to Books, Oxford.

Trower, P., Casey, A. and Dryden, W. (1988) *Cognitive Behavioural Counselling in Action*. Sage Publications, London.

BIBLICAL BASIS FOR COUNSELLING (SEE ALSO: PASTORAL COUNSELLING)

(I am indebted to my friend and colleague, Neil Morrison, for much of the input of this entry.)

The basic premise of this entry is that many of the qualities enshrined in counselling, particularly person-centred counselling, have their origins in Christian principles. This does not invalidate in any way beliefs held by other faiths. What is written here might make more sense if read alongside the entries: Core conditions and Relationship principles of counselling.

The principle of acceptance in Scripture

One of the strongest needs found in all of us, regardless of our circumstances, is the need to be accepted – loved for who we are rather than what we do for others. When we do not receive this acceptance, what can happen – and usually does – is that our emotions and ability to relate to others are stunted. Acceptance is one of the ways we know we have been justified and reconciled to God through the covenant of mercy, and the atonement of Christ.

Ephesians 1:6 reads '…wherein he hath made us accepted in the beloved'. Being accepted by God means that He delights in us; we are the objects of his love. Being accepted does not depend on what we do, but on our relationship with God. God is unchangeable, never put off by our lack of faith. God looks beneath the surface to the real, the unique, to the you and me who have been made acceptable through Christ. Because Christ is accepted, therefore those who are in him are accepted of God.

We know we are accepted of God because we are reconciled (Colossians 1:21, 22); made righteous (2 Corinthians 5:21); our sins are removed (Psalms 103:10–12); we are protected by angels (Psalm 34:7); nothing can take us out of his care (John 10:29).

Acceptance may prove difficult for some people whose value systems are rigid and inflexible; who see things in black and white terms, and who cannot work with shades of grey. What is important is not that we have to water down our cherished values, but to ever remember that our values are for us, and not for other people; we all have to arrive at our own value systems in our own way.

An example of this is how differently two people can interpret the same verse of Scripture or can have different beliefs about the Bible. One person might believe that the Holy Spirit is a power; someone else, that the Holy Spirit is a person, co-equal with God and Christ. Is the one person wrong and the other right? They hold different beliefs, but could we still accept the one who believes differently as a brother or sister in Christ? Could we accept Glen and his homosexual feelings without trying to 'put him right' by quoting Scripture?

Could we accept Joan and Bill who want to end their marriage and set up with different partners? Could we accept that Emily, riddled with cancer, now in a hospice, is saving up her medication so that she can end it all? Reflect on whether you can accept the above people as fellow human beings, while perhaps having to think through their way of thinking, beliefs, sexuality and a death wish.

An Old Testament theme is that 'Mercy overcomes Judgement'; and Jesus in the New Testament personifies this when he shouts from the cross, 'Father forgive them because they do not know what they do'.

Counselling will constantly challenge who we are; each and every client brings fresh opportunities for growth. If we reject a client who does not conform to what we think he should be, we stand in judgement on them. More, we stand in judgement of ourselves, for the very thing we reject in others, if we are honest, lurks in our own hearts. Helping a client explore a particular area of life that causes us pain, and from which we would rather run away, will open up new vistas, take us further along the road of self-awareness and bring us nearer to God.

When we reject a client, or something about the client, we stand in danger of rejecting someone who has been made in God's own image. If God accepts us while we were yet sinners (Romans 3:23) as we were, and as we are now, i.e. we are accepted in the beloved, then we can do nothing less than reach out empty hands and accept what clients offer – themselves.

Clients who are experiencing emotional upheaval have feelings of ambivalence; they feel the need to unburden themselves, yet they feel reluctant to do so. They feel a need to disclose, yet they feel hesitant that what they need to disclose will result in them being judged, criticised or even condemned. How the counsellor demonstrates acceptance of the merest detail will set the scene; if the client feels safe, he will continue, if not, essential disclosures will be bypassed and kept well hidden. The client will perceive when the counsellor's hands and heart are cluttered with motives, values and attitudes that get in the way of acceptance.

People who have plucked up courage to ask for counselling may also feel resentful that they have to approach us. They are likely to speak from behind defences, and only when they feel safe will they talk about the real issue or issues.

We fear what we do not know, and often what the client is hiding from the counsellor is also being hidden from him or her self. Within an atmosphere of acceptance, clients can begin to accept themselves. They can begin to accept that they are God's handiwork, and are precious to Him.

Thus acceptance is not just from counsellor to client; it is the client's self-acceptance. If the counsellor demonstrates acceptance of clients just as they are, clients are more likely to accept themselves. If the counsellor can accept the clients' feelings, positive or negative, clients have less need to deny these feelings. Acceptance by the counsellor sets the scene for change within the client. It is as if the client says, 'If the counsellor can accept me, then I must be OK'.

The counsellor is not happy that clients have feelings of doubt, are depressed, or anxious, or that they have suicidal thoughts and ideas, but is happy that they feel they have confidence enough in the counselling relationship to express and explore them.

The principle of non-judgementalism in Scripture

Judgemental is being convinced that we are right, and that someone else is wrong. Being non-judgemental is recognising that points of view are different, not necessarily wrong. To insist that one is right, and others are wrong, is patronising and arrogant. Passing judgement is against Scriptural teaching. Jesus tells us not to judge others, for if we do, we, ourselves, will be judged. The original meaning of Jesus' teaching against passing judgement on another person was of passing judgement as an accuser, judge and jury that results in a verdict of condemnation being passed, i.e. the person is acting as if he is accuser, judge and jury. The only righteous judge of humanity is God. When we pass judgement on people, we endeavour to elevate ourselves above them, to emphasise our superiority and, in doing so, in effect, depress them. Self-elevation is a desire to put one's self first, and arises from a sense of false pride. Although we may not voice it, our secret desire is to enhance our self-esteem at the expense of lowering someone else's.

If our Lord was speaking of not judging another's sins (behaviour) how much less are we able to judge human frailties? How can we tell someone else what to do, or not do? Often we pass judgement in order to bolster our own self-righteousness; it makes us feel good to do so. Passing judgement is more to do with bringing the other person into line with what we think, rather than for his benefit, although we may dress it up as such. When we pass judgement, we invariably do so by comparing the other person with ourselves. Judgement goes against the law of love. The minute we open the door to judgement, love flies out of the window. Judgement divides; love unites.

In his Commentary on the New Testament, the Revd W.B. Godbey translates judgement (Matthew 7:1) as criticism, and says this:

> *The critic's cap, manufactured in hell and dispensed by the devil, is not at all becoming a saint of the Lord. Luke says if you do not criticise others you cannot be criticised. Well, it has been said that curses, like chickens, will come home to roost. If you criticise no one, you will find no trouble by the criticism of others; if they undertake it, it will prove a failure, rebounding on their own heads. A critical spirit is incompatible with deep love, and if indulged will sap the foundation of a Christian experience, and retrogress sweet, perfect love back into sour godliness, which is Satan's counterfeit holiness. Lord, save us from a critical and condemnatory disposition!*

A story is told of a certain minister who, whenever he heard one person criticising another, would look meditatively into the far distance, and say, 'I'm so glad I'm perfect'.

The principle of listening in Scripture

Although there is no direct reference in Scripture to expressing feelings, the Psalmist David periodically shares his positive and negative feelings with God in some wonderful prose. We know that God hears what we say, and indeed, what is in our hearts, even before we speak it. God hears our distress. He hears our prayer for forgiveness, and accepts the penitent. If God is the giver of all good gifts, then just as He has a listening ear so may we. God does not need to have His ear trained to hear, but we do. God's hearing is perfect; ours is imperfect, because what we hear is filtered through screens that distort what is being said to us. God's hearing penetrates to the very core of what we say; He hears our weakest feeling and understands. God does not judge us by what we say to Him, for He understands however imperfectly we say it. Counselling seeks to encourage the client to say what is in the heart, depth communication, even though what is there may come out as indistinct and unclear, because sometimes words are inadequate to express how we feel.

The Scriptural principle of free will (see also Relationship principles of counselling)

(This relates to the principles of self-determination.)

The question of the free will of humans always arouses fierce debate, though this is not the place to expound that debate. Perhaps in some ways this intense debate emphasises people's free will to take up different theological positions to debate!

Charles Finney says this of free will:

> *By free will is intended the power of choosing, or refusing to choose, in every instance, in compliance with moral obligation. Free-will implies the power of originating and deciding our own choices, and of exercising our own sovereignty, in every instance of choice upon moral questions of deciding or choosing in conformity with duty or otherwise in all cases of moral obligation.*
>
> The Finney Sermon Collection, The Ages Digital Library.

And Adam Clarke says:

> *The free-will of man is a necessary constituent of his rational soul; without which he must be a mere machine, either the sport of blind chance, or the mere patient of an irresistible necessity; and consequently, not accountable for any acts which were predetermined, and to which he was irresistibly compelled.*
>
> Adam Clarke's Commentary on the Bible, The Ages Digital Library.

From these two biblical scholars we see that free-will gives us the power to make choices, and without free will we would not be human.

Arguments for free will are based on the supposition that we are fully respon-sible for personal actions; the belief in free will underlies the concepts of law, reward, punishment and incentive. Individual rights need to be respected because we must have an area of personal responsibility within which to make our choices about our lives or wherein to initiate our own actions. The need for this kind of respect assumes, again, that as human beings we have free will, that we can make basic choices about our lives, initiate basic conduct, which can turn out to be right or wrong. Free will extends to the issue of personal responsibility in such areas as how we conduct our everyday affairs; for the good and bad things that happen. If there were no free will then human beings would be less than God intended them to be. As we know from the Genesis story of Adam and Eve, free will also comes at a cost as it has the potential for the person to decide for good or evil.

In theology, the existence of free-will must be reconciled with the all-knowing God and His goodness (in allowing us to choose badly), and with divine grace, which allegedly is necessary for any virtuous act. Yet choice is not without its consequences, and often that choice is agonising. For some, having to wrestle with their free will might be worse than the alternative. This is where pastoral counselling comes in to help such people reflect, process and work through the various issues of exercising their free will, especially the potential consequences of their actions. In such counselling it is not a case of saying, 'You should not chose to do that'. It is more appropriate to say, 'Let's look at what might happen if you did do that'. In this way clients self-confront the potential consequences of taking such action. More is said about this important issue in the next section below.

The principle of the unique individual in Scripture

'But all the very hairs of your head are all numbered' (Matthew 10:3). This shows that even the minute details of life are considered. We know that one single hair is all that is enough to identify a person's DNA, and no two people's are identical. It is a similar case with fingerprints, and other parts of the body, such as the iris of the eye, and even speech patterns.

Although there are similarities between us all, there is also much that makes us unique. God does not turn us out like jellies from a mould. We all want to preserve that unique self, and resist attempts to wear down that precious part within us. Yet within that there is a paradox, found in Psalms 17:15 – 'I shall be satisfied when I awake with thy likeness'.

This implies that believers are being changed to become like Christ, and the paradox is that we shall not wish to be static and hold on to our uniqueness but be dynamic and develop more like Christ through God's revelation and grace. But just as we were created in the image and likeness of God, it is He who has created us as unique individuals. Yet it seems that although we cherish our uniqueness, God, in His wisdom, is drawing us ever onwards and upwards towards perfection, which can only be found in Him, and in Him our earthly individuality will develop and be enriched, becoming more like the nature of Christ. In theology this developmental and cleansing process of the believer is known as sanctification.

The Scriptural basis of empathy

In empathy – getting in touch with another's deepest feelings – we have the example of the suffering Christ who knows all our feelings, all our temptations and conflicts. Our empathy is never perfect, for we bring to any relationship so many of our imperfections. Yet even with all our limitations, we can still make deeply emotional contact and connection with people.

When a therapist truly hears clients and the meanings that are important to them at that moment, hearing not simply their words, but them, and when the therapist lets them know that their own private personal meanings have been heard, many things can happen. There may first of all be a grateful look, they may feel released, they may want to tell the therapist more about their world, they may surge forth in a new sense of freedom, or they may become more open to the process of change. The more deeply does the therapist hear their meanings, the more there may be that happens. Almost always, when people realise that they have been heard, their eyes moisten. It is as though they were saying, 'Thank God, somebody heard me. Someone knows what it is like to be me'.

J.C. Gunzburg (1997) Healing Through Meeting: Martin Buber's conversational approach to psychotherapy. Jessica Kingsley, London.

Thus, in spite of the limitations, the Holy Spirit knows no restrictions, and he it is who can speak to the heart of the person in deep need; he is the one who can neutralise our biases and prejudices, which might get in the way of effective hearing and responding. It is interesting that one of the titles of the Holy Spirit is 'Counsellor'. When a Christian is called to the ministry of counselling then years of training combined with the anointing of the Holy Spirit enhances the core qualities of the counsellor.

The Scriptural basis for unconditional positive regard

Two factors contribute to this one quality – benevolence and love. Although benevolence does not feature as a counsellor quality, it is closely linked with both unconditional positive regard and genuineness; genuineness is the precondition for empathy and unconditional positive regard.

Benevolence, which is based on love, puts the welfare of the other person before self, and it is free from ulterior motive. Thus benevolence and these two core conditions of counselling have the common root of love, unconditional love, of which the love of God is the model. Love has been discussed as being the basis for acceptance of other people just as they are; albeit it is a pale reflection of the unconditional agape (divine) love shown by God.

Unconditional positive regard is also linked to grace, which is the free and unmerited gift of God to humans. In the sense that grace is unmerited, it is also unconditional. It would be both arrogant and incorrect to suggest that counsellors are in the position of dispensing grace, and that certainly is not the intention. What we consider important is that something (and here we are calling it grace) within the counsellor makes contact with some need within the client.

In theology this personal need would include forgiveness. Forgiveness means cleansing, and renewing. An analogy would be that of cleansing a dirty vessel and filling it with clear, sparkling water. This is a useful symbol to use about counselling. While it is not the counsellor's task to 'cleanse' and 'fill', this is something like what happens, as the client 'gets rid of' and often experiences catharsis. We suggest that it is grace (or unconditional positive regard) that facilitates this process.

At first reading this might seem 'way out', but some of the synonyms of grace, such words as benevolence, love, and mercy, would support this view. God gives of His grace because it is His nature to do so. He does not debate whether He should. The counsellor, likewise, relates to clients with unconditional positive regard because he or she cannot help doing so. Counsellors do not 'give' it, any more than they give warmth; it is something they are which is drawn from them by the particular client. This quality cannot be acquired, like learning to swim; it can only be developed as we understand more about ourselves and others.

The Scriptural basis for genuineness

Although the word 'genuineness' does not occur in Darby's translation of the Authorised Version of the Bible, Darby translates 'sincerity' in 2 Corinthians 8:8 as genuineness, as do Weymouth and Young. When we regard genuineness as sincerity, we have a different perspective of it. To be sincere means to be free from pretence or deceit; the same in reality as in appearance; to be genuine, honest, frank.

Sincerity is one of the esteemed virtues of Confucianism. For Confucius, sincerity meant to be truthful and straightforward in speech, faithful to one's promises, conscientious in the discharge of one's duties to others. Added to this, Confucius held that sincerity is based on love of virtue, and that sincere people observe the rules of right conduct of heart as well as outward actions. No one could argue that these are not desirable qualities for counsellors, although putting them into practice might not always be easy.

John Calvin, in his *Institutes of the Christian Religion*, speaks of faith tried in the fire, in the same way as gold and silver are put to the test to prove their genuineness. Clients judge us by how genuine we are, how sincere, how consistent we are. They will assess our genuineness by how our words match with our actions. And, at a deeper level, they will be touched in their spirit by how utterly truthful we are.

While it is perfectly true that we cannot like every client, and we would not want them as friends, genuineness goes far beyond liking, for it, like unconditional regard, is based on love of and for people. Love, as in 1 Corinthians 13, is the essence of Christian character. Love, as in 1 Corinthians 13 can be thought of as 'other-centred', i.e. the opposite of self-centred. With this love the focus of attention is transferred from self to meeting the need of the other person. When we are asked to prove the genuineness of our love, through counselling, we can draw on the source of all love – God.

The quality of love

Love, as expressed in the Platonic concept of Eros (ideal beauty, immediate physical attraction, delight), was opposed in the Christian community by the biblical understanding of love, agape. Christians speak of Divine Love; love is the basis for Christian ethics. The Bible stresses that true love, while it is often tested by the sincerity that will not hesitate to rebuke (and it will accept rebuke), will also overlook faults.

Christianity received the main commandment of its ethic from the Old Testament: 'You shall love your neighbour as yourself' (Leviticus 19:18), but Jesus filled this commandment with a new, two-fold meaning. First, he closely connected the commandment 'love your neighbour' with the commandment to love God.

It is paradoxical that we find the greatest expression of God's love for humankind in the death of Jesus, echoing, perhaps, John 15:13, 'No one has greater love than this, to lay down one's life for one's friends'. But God's love was greater than that; Jesus gave his life for his enemies. Based on the connection of the Christian commandment of love with the understanding of Christ's person and work, the demand of love for the neighbour appears as a new commandment. Love for each other is supposed to characterise the disciples: 'By this all men will know that you are my disciples, if you have love for one another' (John 13:35).

This is an ethic that is based on an understanding and treatment of human beings as created in the image of God. Furthermore, the ethic does not deal with humanity in an abstract sense. Love, like many of the virtues, is useless if it remains locked within us, for the only way we shall ever know, and others will know if we have love, is if we express it.

From the beginning, the commandment (love one another), the practice of love of neighbour was characteristic of the young church. Christian congregations and, above all, small fellowships and sects have stood out throughout the centuries because of the fact that within their communities love of the neighbour was highly developed in the form of personal pastoral care, social welfare and help in all situations of life, crossing all social and religious barriers. Jesus uses the parable of the Good Samaritan to point to love in action – a non-Jew helping a Jew who was in need. Bringing the illustration nearer home are the many accounts of non-Jews risking their lives during the Nazi occupation to shelter Jews.

Summary

Christian counselling is primarily concerned with the individual's pilgrimage through the problems and crises of everyday life. It is concerned with the person's relationship with God and the breaking in of the Kingdom. Insofar as the mode is spiritual there is spiritual direction and awareness. And so far as it takes account of and uses psychological ways of attending to the client's inner world, it is counselling. At all times Christian counsellors, as with colleagues using other approaches, must be sensitive to the direction the client is facing. To push clients in the spiritual direction, when they are not ready, would be just as psychologically damaging as pushing them to perform some behavioural task of which they are mentally incapable.

Time is probably the major enemy to be overcome. That is why many counsellors may seek the problem-solving structure, with its solutions, relief of stress and reliance on techniques. Christian counselling, where the emphasis is on the client's story, can only be developed over time. Marital difficulties, vocational or situational stress such as illness or bereavement, are best understood and resolved within the total life story.

For example, the Psalmist David said he felt under stress, and his spiritual life was on the wane. On exploring his life story, we discover that he was a workaholic and always brought work home with him. This interfered with his home life and often with his attendance at church. Deeper exploration revealed that he was working to his father's script: make money. His father judged people by outward appearance, and the trappings of wealth and status. Slowly David began to take stock of his own values, and was able to achieve more balance between work, home and above all (for him) his spiritual life.

Whenever problem-solving techniques are used, they are best viewed as part of the resolution of the deep issues in the life of the soul. Christian counselling provides a structure for listening and responding to persons in a way that demonstrates deep caring. Christian counselling offers something more powerful than either theology or psychological counselling alone. The challenge for Christian counsellors is to hold together the skills and insights that come from clinical models, while at the same time working with the soul of the client whose spiritual life has been traumatised, from a pastoral perspective within a Christian context.

Further reading

Collins, G.R. (1988) *Christian Counselling: a comprehensive guide*. Word Publishing, Nashville, TN.

Thorne, B. (1998) *Person-centred counselling and Christian spirituality: the secular and the holy*. Whurr, London.

Thorne, B. (2000) *Person-centred counselling: therapeutic and spiritual dimensions*. Whurr, London.

BIBLIOTHERAPY

The Greek meaning is 'book-healing', the aim of which is to create a psychological interplay between the reader and the material, which may be literature or audio-visual.

The therapeutic relationship so formed may then be used to promote insight, personal awareness and growth, and psychological healing. It achieves this by overcoming moralisation, active involvement and fostering competence.

Bibliotherapy is often used as an adjunct to other forms of therapy. It may be conducted in a one-to-one relationship or in a group. It is used with client groups of all ages.

People can be helped through a story, play, music or songs to explore any major themes of life that are creating difficulties for them. They may create their own story.

Bibliotherapy can be helpful with people who have emotional or behavioural problems, where the objective is insight or behavioural change. The empathic or imaginative nature of the material would aim to produce catharsis. It may also be used with people who, apart from passing through a crisis, are not psychiatrically disturbed. The goal is self-actualisation and growth through using both imaginative and directive, factual material. The rationale is that people are encouraged to deal with their own threatening emotions and behaviours by displacing them on to the story. Identification takes place with the characters, which promotes change (Gunzburg and Stewart, 1994, pages 130–131).

The process

Reading can be very therapeutic. People find themselves entering the world described in the pages of a good book and becoming involved with the characters therein. They often close the cover having gained new insight and ideas.

That is the purpose behind the use of bibliotherapy: to assist people in overcoming the emotional turmoil related to a real-life problem by having them read literature on that topic. This story can then serve as a springboard for discussion and possible resolution of that dilemma.

- **Identification**: The person identifies with a book character and events in the story, either real or fictitious. Sometimes it is best to have a character of similar age who faces similar events. At other times, cartoon characters and stories are best.
- **Catharsis**: The person becomes emotionally involved in the story and is able to release pent-up emotions under safe conditions (often through discussion or art work).
- **Insight**: The person, after catharsis (possibly with help), becomes aware that her problems might also be addressed or solved. Possible solutions to the book character's and one's own personal problems are identified.

The power of the story

John Gunzburg says this of story telling:

Martin Buber believed in the potent healing effect of story on the aching soul. He understood story to be a medium within which various existential themes of life – belonging, yearning for companionship, loss of homeland, courage in adversity, the blossoming of love – could be woven and transmitted from one group to another and from one generation to the next. The telling of story could convey the struggle to understand the mystery of life, the dilemmas encountered and the myriad ways that such challenges could be met. Above all, story could convey both the uniqueness of individual experiencing and the connectedness of all living things.

We may use bibliotherapy to:

- Develop an individual's self-concept
- Increase an individual's understanding of human behaviour or motivations
- Foster an individual's honest self-appraisal
- Provide a way for a person to find interests outside of self
- Relieve emotional or mental pressure
- Show an individual that he is not the first or only person to encounter such a problem
- Show an individual that there is more than one solution to a problem
- Help a person discuss a problem more freely
- Help an individual plan a constructive course of action to solve a problem.

Further reading

Brown, E.F. (1975) *Bibliotherapy and its Widening Applications.* Scarecrow Press, Metuchen, NJ.

Cheripko. J. (2000) *Using Literature to Help Troubled Teenagers Cope with Health Issues.* Greenwood Press, Westport, CONN.

ERIC Clearinghouse on Reading and Communication Skills (1982) *Bibliotherapy. Fact Sheet.* Urbana, IL.

ERIC Clearinghouse on Reading and Communication Skills, Indiana University, 2805 E. 10th St, Suite 150, Bloomington, IN 47408-2698.

Gunzburg, J.C. (1997) *Healing Through Meeting: Martin Buber's approach to psychotherapy.* Jessica Kingsley, London.

Gunzburg, J.C. and Stewart, W. (1994) *The Grief Counselling Casebook.* Stanley Thornes, Cheltenham (now out of print but available on line at www.compassion-in-business.co.uk/fellowship/willstew.htm).

Howie, M. (1983) Bibliotherapy in social work. *British Journal of Social Work,* **13**: 287–319.

Jones, E.H. (2001) *Bibliotherapy with Bereaved Children: healing reading.* Jessica Kingsley, London.

Pardeck. J.T. (1992) *Bibliotherapy: a guide to using books in clinical practice.* Edwin Mellen Press Paperbacks, New York.

Pardeck. J.T. (1998) *Using Books in Clinical Social Work Practice: a guide to bibliotherapy.* Haworth Press, Inc., New York.

Smith, A.G. (1989) Will the Real Bibliotherapist Please Stand Up? *Journal of Youth Services in Libraries,* **2(3)**: 241–249.

BODY-IMAGE (SEE ALSO: FEMININITY/MASCULINITY)

Body-image is:

- The perception, conscious or unconscious, of one's own body
- The picture we have of our own body, which we form in our mind
- The way in which the body appears to ourselves
- Our mind's eye picture of ourselves.

Body-image is the root of identity, self-esteem and self-worth, the basis from which we function.

Somewhere a part of the brain is responsible for being able to bring to our conscious awareness the total representation of our body.

The development of body-image

- The awareness of body-image begins to develop at the toddler stage.
- Awareness is influenced by environment, by our attitudes, feelings, memories and experiences towards our bodies.
- We register our own thoughts and opinions about our body as well as the impressions we receive from other people of how they perceive us.
- Self-esteem is influenced by a positive or a negative regard for our bodies (or parts thereof).
- Socio-cultural environment influences body-image. People reared in one culture may experience devastating 'body-image shock' when they move into a

culture where different emphases are ascribed to various body areas. For example, in a society where strength and fitness are idealised, failing strength may produce unwelcome and unacceptable changes in our perception of ourselves because we no longer fit the ideal. These changes may be so resented that they produce emotional disturbances. That is when counselling may help.

Boundaries of body-image

- A clear awareness of our body-image separates us from other people or from our environment.
- The most obvious boundaries are height, size (slim/fat) and general appearance – how we appear to ourselves and how we think we appear to others. Part of this is the regard we have for our bodies.
- Clothes become a part of the body-image. The question could be asked: Do we use clothing to reinforce or deny certain body-image attitudes? If we wear clothes as a boundary to reinforce or deny something about ourselves, do we feel exposed and vulnerable when we remove our clothes?

Age-related changes in body-image

From babyhood to old age our body-image has to make various adjustments to what is happening in our bodies. At one end of the age scale we are developing quite rapidly in height, weight and strength; at the other end we again experience quite marked changes. In between these two age differences there is adolescence. Its accompanying sexual maturity brings dramatic changes; some of them are welcomed, others are so disturbing as to appear doubtful blessings. Adulthood brings with it different changes as new occupational and family responsibilities are taken on board.

Motherhood brings visible body changes to which women (and their partners) have to adapt. Pregnant women incorporate the foetus into their own body-image unless there are strong feelings against the pregnancy, in which case emotional disturbance or even psychosis is likely. Women who cannot conceive are likely to experience great body-image conflict.

In any pregnancy where the foetus was successfully incorporated into the mother's body-image, the woman has to make a dramatic adjustment if an abortion takes place. She has to adjust to the missing part of her. If the pregnancy was an unwanted one or if the foetus was not incorporated into the body-image, the woman still has an adjustment to make but in the first case, I would suggest, the adjustment is greater and may take longer.

Perhaps at no other time in her life is the woman subjected to such dramatic body-image changes as during the menopause. It is at this stage of her life when it seems that she is neither young nor is she yet old. Are the women who 'grow old gracefully' those who have successfully incorporated these changes into their body-image?

Men also experience body changes to which the body-image must adjust. Sexual difficulties, especially, create problems for many men, for most men's perception of masculinity centres around virility and potency. Thus, men who are infertile not only suffer emotionally; their whole concept of body is affected. Impotence and other sexual problems that interfere with a satisfactory sex life have a strong influence on body-image.

Although men do not have a menopause, in their middle years of life body changes do occur. The man who once prided himself on his strength and endurance now has to adjust to – if not exactly being a weakling – a body that does get tired much more quickly. Old age brings with it other changes – some welcome (like increased leisure and an increase in wisdom), others not so welcome. A man who has been the 'breadwinner' now has to adjust to being a 'pensioner' and all that means in reduced activity.

All the changes that have been mentioned – for both sexes – may seem to require nothing more or less than an emotional adjustment. But each change has very clear implications for body-image. No change can take place to or within our bodies without having some emotional impact. And, as was pointed out earlier, body-image is influenced by emotions of all kinds.

Other changes in body-image

Other changes considered normal occur during deep relaxation, when we often feel very heavy; that the body, or parts of it, becomes very large or very small. We may become aware of sensations within the body. We may hear strange sounds and see strange 'lights' and patterns. We may experience feelings almost of hallucination. We may have the sensation of floating in space and that we have become detached from our body.

All of these normal distortions may occur to any of us as we hover in the hypnagogic state between being awake and dropping into sleep. When in sleep, strange distortions may be experienced and many of these experiences are alarming and emotionally disturbing. The border between what is normal and what is pathological is a very narrow one and these feelings, experienced in dreams or near dreams, are what many mentally ill people – particularly psychotic patients – experience, only more so. The intensity and the frequency and the degree to which these experiences then start to influence a person's life are one of the characteristic differences between normal and pathological.

Pathological distortions of body-image

Distortion of body-image occurs in personality and psychiatric disorders and can be very frightening for the patient. One female schizophrenic patient, on looking in a mirror, said to a nurse, 'Where am I? I can't see myself.' The same patient said, 'Is it me talking or is it you?' Another schizophrenic patient felt that his body was 'spread over the world'. One central theme runs through many of the accounts of bizarre body-image fantasies: violation of the body boundaries – the boundaries are either obliterated or become so fluid and vague as to be worthless either as a defence against all perceived threats or as a reference point to be used in distinguishing self from the other world.

A physical example of distorted body-image is a person who has undergone an amputation of limb and still feels pain in the 'phantom' limb – the illusory feeling that the missing part of the body is still there. Although these phenomena are usually associated with limb amputations, the experience can occur when any part of the body is removed.

Distortion also occurs in eating disorders, where sufferers are convinced that they are fatter than they really are. Transsexuals who undergo surgery have to adjust to a new body-image. Acutely disturbed psychiatric patients sometimes say that they feel as if they had become diffused, like a sea mist before a wind.

When people have been the victims of crippling disease or accident or exposed to mutilating surgery, resulting in a change in the body, the body-image is forced to undergo a similar change if it is to be congruent with the 'new body'. This adjustment is often painful and emotionally disturbing.

Disturbance of body-image occurs in people who suffer from obesity. In psychiatric terms they may suffer from 'body-image disparagement', where the obese person believes that his body is grotesque and loathsome, and that others view it with hostility. The person's preoccupation with obesity swamps everything else and becomes the overruling personality factor. All other graces, talents and abilities take second place to the obesity. This disturbance is seen mostly in people whose obesity started in childhood and probably arises from the mocking and derision they received from both peers and older people.

Doubt about masculinity or femininity may make the person so ashamed of their body, either totally or parts of it, that they can only have sex in the dark or under the bedclothes.

So long as we feel certain that our body boundaries separate us from the world, we continue to feel significant and individual. If the client is able to feel a 'significant person' within the counselling relationship, this may help to maintain his feelings of self-esteem and self-worth and so prevent loss of body boundary.

Principal points to consider about body-image

- The regard the person has for his or her body – is it negative or positive?
- Does a specific part or parts cause concern?
- Generally satisfied or dissatisfied?
- What is the person's ideal?
- What body experiences make for pleasure or displeasure?
- What feelings are associated with size? The way we judge the size of our body or a part thereof is influenced by emotions and attitudes toward ourselves and our relationship to others.
- How aware is the person of his or her body? Some people have a high awareness while others have a minimal awareness. Most people focus more of their attention on specific sectors and less on others.
- Does the person have a clear idea of the demarcation between his or her body and the outside world, which includes other people?
- How accurately is the person able to judge body position? Spatial dimension is part of our ability to separate from our surroundings.
- Anxiety about the body – some people are very afraid of body damage while others seem unconcerned about such a possibility.

- Masculinity/femininity – does the person clearly affirm his or her gender and how does gender relate to body-image?

It is important to remind ourselves that, although some changes in body-image are pathological, what is considered pathological lies within the normal. Body changes – external and internal – are all likely to produce distortions in body-image. Some people need a great deal of emotional support in order to accommodate body changes within their body-image. Those who cannot may well wander over the border into the no-man's land of the pathological.

Further reading

Fisher, S. and Cleveland, S.E. (1985) *Body-image and Personality*. Van Nostrand, New York.
Stewart, W. (1985) *Counselling in Rehabilitation*. Croom Helm, New York.
Stewart, W. (1998) *Building Self-esteem: how to replace self-doubt with confidence and well-being*. How to Books, Oxford.

Bonding (see also: Attachment)

Bonding is the relationship that one individual maintains with either an inanimate object, e.g. a bird with its nest, or with animate objects, e.g. a child with its caregiver or an adult with a mate. Behaviour is directed exclusively towards the preferred object.

Bonding partners recognise each other as individuals. Bonding occurs rapidly between adults and their young. Bonded partners tend to defend each other.

Bonding is the formation of a close personal relationship (as between a mother and child), especially through frequent or constant association. The process of bonding between mother and baby starts long before the birth. If the baby in the womb responds to noise, then how much more is it likely to respond to feelings of already being loved or the reverse, of not being wanted, or of fear on the mother's part that she will not be a good mother?

For nine months, the environment within the womb is all-important to the developing baby; the mother's emotional and physical state plays a vital role in creating this environment. Sometimes events take over and the baby is catapulted prematurely into the world. Difficulty of delivery and premature birth add to the problems of the mother bonding with the new baby. Bonding is not just at birth; it is for life.

Babies born prematurely may induce feelings of great fear in the mother; when born with defects, the mother might not be able to accept the baby. Bonding is then fraught with difficulty. Early bonding difficulties are likely to lead to a decrease in the new mother's self-esteem. When this happens, the feelings are likely to be transmitted to the child.

Paternal bonding is said to be as important as maternal bonding and certainly, for the development of high self-esteem, the role of the father is necessary. The developing child needs to experience the feelings of being wanted and loved by both parents. When this love is deficient, the growing child is in danger of developing low self-esteem.

The effectiveness of the therapeutic relationship or alliance has characteristics of bonding. The relationship is influenced by:

- How the counsellor demonstrates the core conditions of empathy, genuineness, non-possessive warmth, unconditional positive regard
- The client's feelings towards the counsellor, which are influenced by: trust in the counsellor, feeling safe in the relationship, having faith in the counsellor
- The style of interaction of both client and counsellor – this is influenced by the 'fit' between the counsellor's approach and the ability of the client to work within it and how far the counsellor is able to adapt to the client's particular abilities and preferences
- The way transference and counter-transference are acknowledged and worked through. In very general (though not strictly in psychoanalytic) terms, transference and counter-transference refer to the tendencies we all have to perceive, feel and act towards other people in the present, based on previous experiences with significant others in our past lives.

Bonding between counsellor and client is generally strengthened when something within the relationship is challenged (by either person) and the potential conflict is dealt with constructively.

Further reading

Bowlby, J. (1969) *Attachment. Attachment and Loss*, vol. 1. Penguin, Harmondsworth.

Dryden, W. (1989) The therapeutic alliance. In: *Key Issues for Counselling in Action*. Sage Publications, London.

Volkmar, F. (1995) Reactive attachment disorder of infancy or early childhood. In: *Comprehensive Textbook of Psychiatry*, 6th edn (eds H.J. Kaplan and B.J. Sadock). Williams & Wilkins, Baltimore, MD.

BRAINSTORMING

This is an established technique for creative problem-solving, usually undertaken by a small group of between two and six members. One member of the group, or an outside adviser, acts as co-ordinator. The aim is to release the mind, increase the flow of creative ideas and assist decision-making. No discussion or evaluation is permitted until all ideas have been generated. This ensures that creativity is not blocked. One person may build upon the idea of someone else. All ideas are reviewed and graded for their usefulness.

Although brainstorming is especially successful for group problem-solving, because ideas generate other ideas, its principles can be modified for use by two people. Effective brainstorming hinges on all involved being willing to listen to one another and to develop ideas. It would seem that, for brainstorming to work, group members need to feel comfortable with and to have confidence in one another. Rivalry, competitiveness, the need to score, impress or put down will all get in the way of finding a solution, or solutions, to the problem. Lack of commitment to the outcome will interfere with creativity and generating ideas.

In counselling, brainstorming is a useful technique to use, particularly when helping clients set goals for themselves or in planning action. Brainstorming puts clients in the driving seat, as it were, for as they develop ideas they realise that they can exercise control. Encourage the client to come up with many different possibilities. One idea may well stimulate others. It doesn't matter how wild the idea seems. All have potential.

Brainstorming rules

- Collect as many ideas as possible from all participants with no criticisms or judgements made while ideas are being generated.
- All ideas are welcome no matter how silly or far out they seem. Be creative. The more ideas the better because at this point you don't know what might work.
- Absolutely no discussion takes place during the brainstorming activity. Talking about the ideas will take place after brainstorming is complete.
- Do not criticise or judge. Don't even groan, frown or laugh. All ideas are equally valid at this point.
- Do build on others' ideas.
- Do write all ideas on a flipchart or board so the whole group can easily see them.
- Set a time limit (e.g. 30 minutes) for the brainstorming.

Brainstorming sequence

1. One team member should review the topic of the brainstorm using 'Why', 'How' or 'What' questions.
2. Everyone should think about the question silently for a few moments. Each person might want to jot down his or her ideas on a sheet of paper.
3. Everyone suggests ideas by calling them out. Another way is to go around the room and have each person read an idea from his or her list until all ideas have been written on the board or flipchart.
4. One team member writes down all ideas on board or flipchart.

Making the final selection

- When all the ideas have been recorded, combine ideas as much as possible, but only when the original contributors agree.
- Number all of the ideas.
- Each member votes on the ideas by making a list of the numbers of the ideas he/she thinks are important or should be discussed further. This list should contain no more than one third of the total number of ideas.
- After counting the votes, cross out ideas with only one or two votes. Then vote again until only a few ideas remain (i.e. three or four). If there is no clear-cut winner, then vote again or discuss the remaining ideas and determine which idea best answers the original question.

Further reading

Fox, W.M. (1987) *Effective Group Problem Solving*. Jossey-Bass, San Francisco, CA.
Francis, D. (1987) *SO Activities for Unblocking Organisational Communication*. Gower, Aldershot.

www.mcli.dist.maricopa.edu/authoring/ studio/guidebook/brain.html
//www.jpb.com/creative/brainstorming

BRIEF COUNSELLING (SEE ALSO: GROUPS AND TAVISTOCK METHOD)

The term covers a range of planned, short-term therapies. Brief counselling does not mean superficial or merely relieving symptoms. In practice, the majority of psychotherapies are brief, whether or not that was the intention. By comparison with psychoanalysis, it is short, but that does not mean it is lacking in quality nor any less skilled or helpful. In fact, brief counselling requires great skill, for within a few sessions the counsellor has to make sufficient impact on the client so that the client feels able to continue his own work of healing. Many brief therapies are based on psychodynamic, behavioural, crisis or cognitive approaches, each with its own method of working. The results of brief therapy are said to be comparable with long-term therapy.

A brief psychotherapy is not simply one that is short. It is short because its goals are limited, as is its time, and number of sessions. Many brief therapies are associated with learning, crisis, cognitive, and systems approaches.

The origins of brief counselling

In the late 1950s, Michael Balint and colleagues at the Tavistock Clinic, London, met to explore how they could reduce the length of therapy yet still be effective. They researched techniques, indications, contraindications and effectiveness. Gradually, brief counselling was born, and the concept of 'focal conflict' or 'focal therapy'. This is where the central conflict is separated from the rest of the personality. Therapy then focuses on the dynamics of that conflict, not on all aspects of the client's unconscious life.

Characteristics of brief counselling

- Time limits, with an average of six to ten single sessions; this fits well with what is considered the norm for counselling, although in many instances the counselling relationship will continue far beyond the limit of the initial contract
- Limited goals, with the focus on specific areas
- Current problems are dealt with in the 'here and now'
- Direction – the counsellor is more active than in some other approaches
- Early assessment is needed to establish treatment rapidly; accurate assessment is essential to ascertain whether brief counselling, or something more long-term, is the most suitable option for a particular client.
- Flexibility of approach is emphasised, because of the time limit.
- Ventilation of feelings is considered essential.
- Therapeutic relationship and contract are stressed.
- Selection – brief counselling is more suitable with less disturbed clients and is not suitable for people who have chronic disturbances, which include drug or alcohol addictions, personality disorders and severe mental illnesses.

Brief counselling may benefit clients:

- Whose problem is acute, rather than chronic
- Whose previous adjustment was effective
- Whose ability to relate is adequate
- Whose motivation towards therapy is high
- Who are not severely disturbed and who function reasonably well
- Brief counselling has proved to be appropriate in stress management.

Similar to brief counselling is single-session counselling. Counselling may be planned where it is known by both counsellor and client to involve one session only, although it may be longer than the accepted 'therapeutic hour'. Counsellors who work in 'drop-in' centres are more likely to work in one session than with long-term counselling.

Suggested principles

- Identify one salient issue
- View the client's difficulties as a stepping stone to development
- Engage the client fully
- Keep interpretations to the minimum
- Understand with empathy
- Start the client on the road towards problem-solving
- Limit the number of issues to be explored
- Make provision for follow-up at the client's request.

'Therapeutic drop out' is a term used to describe the situation where the client terminates counselling, often after only one session. Studies show that a significant percentage of those who do drop out found what they were seeking and had no real desire to enter into ongoing therapy.

Three categories of clients who do poorly in brief therapy:

- Poorly motivated and hostile clients
- Clients who come with a history of poor relationships
- Clients who expect to be passive recipients of a medical procedure.

Further reading

Bayne, R., Horto, I., Merry, T. and Noyes, E. (1994) *The Counsellor's Handbook: a practical A-Z guide to professional and clinical practice*. Chapman & Hall, London.

Dryden, W. and Feltham, C. (1992) *Brief Counselling*. Open University Press, Buckingham.

Egan, G. (2002) *The Skilled Helper: a problem-management and opportunity-development approach to helping*, 7th edn. Brooks/Cole, Pacific Grove, CA.

Mohl, P.C. (1995) Brief psychotherapy. In: *Comprehensive Textbook of Psychiatry*, 6th edn (eds H.J. Kaplan and B.J. Sadock). Williams & Wilkins, Baltimore, MD.

BURNOUT (SEE ALSO: CORE CONDITIONS AND STRESS MANAGEMENT)

Burnout is a term used in two ways: to describe the injurious effects of the stress of counselling upon counsellors; and to describe the injurious effects of stress, particularly related to work.

Counsellor burnout

In counselling, burnout, resulting in physical or psychological withdrawal is characterised by:

- Chronic low levels of energy
- Defensive behaviour
- Distancing emotionally from people.

Counsellors often look forward to sessions where there is progress and dread sessions that don't go anywhere. Sessions that go badly have a debilitating effect on the counsellor, because prolonged client resistance depletes energy. Burnout may also be associated with the relationship in which there is a high level of empathy and with the high level of concentration that goes with giving full attention.

Counsellors who feel that they are starting to be impatient with clients or with members of the family, who are having difficulty sleeping, who feel that there are never, ever, enough hours in the day and that they simply could not face taking on another client, are probably heading for burnout.

If counsellors suggest that their clients take stock of their lives, can they do less with theirs? Finding satisfying ways to recharge the batteries is essential in order to prevent burnout.

Occupational burnout

In a more general sense, burnout is associated with stress, where people find increasingly that they feel unable to cope with the pressures at work, at home or within relationships. These factors are often compounded by feelings of failure, frustration, hopelessness and anger. These are all signs of running on under-charged batteries.

More specifically, when considering work, burnout is associated with:

- The high level of concentration that goes with giving full attention
- Situations where people have been exposed for prolonged periods to conflict in which there is little or no resolution
- Alienation from work – in this instance, burnout is more of a symptom than a cause.

The following are the main job factors linked to occupational burnout:

- **Variety of skills**: The fewer demands a job makes on our skills and talents, the more pressure we will feel.
- **Conflicting activities**: Where there is conflict between different activities, we will feel more pressure.
- **Influence over decisions**: The less opportunity there is to make independent decisions, and the less control we have over the outcomes, the more pressure we will feel.
- **Expertise**: Where there is not a good fit between our expertise and the required skills of the job, we will feel more pressure.

- **Workload**: The more we perceive our workload to be unduly heavy, the more pressure we will feel.
- **Boredom**: The more monotonous, uninteresting, dull and lacking in stimulation our work, the more pressure we will feel.
- **Identity**: If we are not able to clearly identify the role specifically as ours, we will feel more pressure.
- **Autonomy**: The less autonomy we are allowed, the more pressure we will feel.
- **Support**: If we do not feel supported in our work, we will feel more pressure.
- **Accountability**: When there is a disparity between accountability and the tasks we perform, we will feel more stress.
- **Significance**: The less significant our contribution, the more stress we will feel.
- **Upward communication**: The greater the gap between us and those in higher positions and the less our communication is listened to, the more stress we will feel.
- **Development**: The fewer opportunities our work provides for personal growth and development, to acquire work-related skills/knowledge, the more pressure we will feel.
- **Income**: The less we feel our income reflects our contribution, the more pressure we will feel.

Burnout and alienation from the job

The six main components of alienation can be traced in occupational burnout.

- **Meaninglessness**: When we expect that our future will not be good in our present position or profession
- **Cultural estrangement**: Where our personal goals are not in agreement with the goals of the organisation
- **Powerlessness**: Where we feel that our behaviour will have little or no effect on outcomes
- **Social isolation**: Where we feel excluded or rejected
- **Task estrangement**: Where we feel that the job we do no longer brings us satisfaction or enjoyment
- **Separation**: Where we feel dissociated from identifying with the work to which we claim membership by virtue of practice, qualification or employment.

Much of what applies to occupational burnout can be easily translated into counsellor burnout, particularly where the counsellor works in an agency or uses counselling skills in another job, such as nursing. There the 'counsellor' is part of a wider organisation and may experience some of the alienation discussed above.

Ways to prevent burnout

Although we may not always have control over stressful events, we do have control over how we interpret and react to them. We have to learn to attune ourselves to the signs of burnout. Corey (pages 39–40) gives some useful advice:

- Evaluate your goals, priorities, and expectations to see if they are realistic and if they are getting you what you want.
- Recognise that you can be an active agent in your life.
- Find other interests besides work, especially if your work is not meeting your most important needs.
- Think of ways to bring variety into your work.
- Take the initiative to start new projects that have personal meaning, and do not wait for the system to sanction this initiative.
- Learn to monitor the impact of stress on the job and at home.
- Attend to your health through adequate sleep, an exercise programme, proper diet, meditation and relaxation.
- Develop a few friendships that are characterised by a mutuality of giving and receiving.
- Learn how to ask for what you want, but don't expect always to get it.
- Learn how to work for self-confirmation and for self-rewards as opposed to looking externally for validation.
- Find meaning through play, travel or new experiences.
- Take the time to evaluate the meaningfulness of your projects to determine where you should continue to invest time and energy.
- Avoid assuming burdens that are properly the responsibility of others. If you worry more about your clients than they do about themselves, for example, it would be well for you to reconsider this investment.
- Take classes and workshops, attend conferences, and read to gain new perspectives on old issues.
- Rearrange your schedule to reduce stress.
- Learn your limits, and learn to set limits with others.
- Learn to accept yourself with your imperfections, including being able to forgive yourself when you make a mistake or do not live up to your ideals.
- Exchange jobs with a colleague for a short period, or ask a colleague to join forces in a common work project.
- Form a support group with colleagues to share feelings of frustration and to find better ways of approaching the reality of difficult job situations.
- Cultivate some hobbies that bring pleasure.
- Make time for your spiritual growth.
- Become more active in your professional organisation.
- Seek counselling as an avenue of personal development.

This is not an exhaustive list, but it does provide some direction for thinking about ways to prevent burnout.

Further reading

Cherniss, C. (1980) *Staff Burn Out: job stress in the human services*. Sage Publications, London.
Corey, G. (2001) *Theory and Practice of Counseling and Psychotherapy*, 6th edn. Wadsworth, Brooks/Cole, Pacific Grove.

Faber, B. and Heifetz, L.J. (1982) Process and dimensions of burn out in psychotherapists. *Professional Psychology*, **13**: 293–301.

Shearer, J.M. (1983) Surviving organizational burnout. In: *1983 Annual for Facilitators, Trainers and Consultants*. University Associates, San Diego, CA.

C

CHALLENGING (ALSO REFERRED TO AS CONFRONTATION)

Counselling is more than active and empathic listening. Part of effective counselling might also mean confronting the client with certain aspects of, for example, self-defeating behaviour or thoughts and feelings that are at odds with progress.

Using the basic active listening skills may take the client some way along the path of self-awareness, yet more may be needed to help the client gain a deeper understanding of the problem and its root cause. In this entry we provide insight into the skills the counsellor uses to facilitate understanding. These skills, unfortunately termed 'challenging' and 'confronting', invite clients to examine their behaviour and its consequences. In other words, by encouraging clients to come face-to-face with themselves, they develop the skill of self-challenge and the potential to change. However, it needs to be borne in mind that in the context of counselling, challenges and confrontations are always offered with the client's best interests at heart, as a gift, not an attack. The skills need to be used with great sensitivity, care and respect. They need to come out of a deep empathy with the client, and should not be used until trust has been well established.

Challenging and confronting

The aim of challenging is to provide accurate information and to offer our perspective. We challenge the strengths of the client rather than the weaknesses. We point out the strengths, assets and resources which the client may fail to fully use. Challenging and confronting helps clients develop new perspectives.

Confronting a client

Confronting clients with something they might prefer not to see, might not want to hear, or might not want to know, is not easy. It can be a painful learning process for the client, as well a risky business for the counsellor. It takes guts to challenge a client, and the counsellor may well be left wondering whether he has said the right thing. It can also be an exhausting experience for both.

In counselling, the aim of a challenge is to help the client face reality, as it is seen through the eyes of the counsellor. The force of the challenge depends on the type of counselling. In some instances it is offered as an observation, in others it is very strong and confronting.

There are times when it is wiser to ignore than to comment. There are times, however, when it could be valuable for the client to know how the counsellor feels about something.

The client may benefit from being confronted with the possible outcome of his behaviour or some contemplated course of action. Sometimes it is difficult to challenge without it being interpreted as a judgement.

Some specific points about challenging are:

- A challenge is not verbal fisticuffs!
- A challenge should be a tentative suggestion, not a declaration.
- A challenge is an observation, not an accusation.
- A challenge should be made only after careful deliberation.
- A challenge should never be used as a retaliation, nor as a put-down.
- A challenge is safest when the relationship is well established.

The main areas of challenge:

- Discrepancies
- Distortion of feelings
- Self-defeating thought patterns
- Self-defeating behaviours
- Games, tricks and smokescreens
- Manipulation
- Excuses:
  - Complacency
  - Rationalisation
  - Procrastination
  - Buck-passing
- Blind spots
  - Simple unawareness
  - Self-deception
  - Choosing to stay in the dark
  - Knowing but not caring
- Mindsets
  - Prejudices
  - Beliefs and assumptions
  - Passivity
  - Negative thought patterns.

A challenge should be preceded by careful consideration of:

- What is the purpose of the challenge?
- Can I handle the consequences?
- Does the challenge relate to the here and now?
- Whose needs are being met by the challenge?

Further reading

Ivey, A.E., Ivey, M.B. and Sinek-Downing, L. (1987) *Counselling and Psychotherapy: integrating skills, theory and practice*, 2nd edn. Prentice Hall, Englewood Cliffs, NJ.

Sutton, J. and Stewart, W. (2002) *Learning to Counsel: develop the skills you need to counsel others*, 2nd edn. How to Books, Oxford.

CHILD ABUSE (SEE ALSO: INCEST, RAPE COUNSELLING AND TRANSFERENCE)

The spectrum of child abuse is wide. It includes not only children who have suffered physical abuse with fractures and bruises (the 'battered child'), but also those who have experienced emotional abuse, sexual abuse, deliberate poisoning and the infliction of fictitious illness on them by their parents (Munchausen's syndrome by proxy).

Children under the age of two are most liable to suffer direct physical abuse at the hands of their parents, although it can happen to children of any age. Such abuse is more common in families who are living under stress and, in some instances, the parents themselves suffered cruelty as children.

Abused children are those of any age who have suffered repeated injuries, which may include physical, emotional and sexual abuse at the hands of a parent, parents or parent substitutes. Physical abuse often takes place as a response to minor infringements of behaviour. Child abuse also includes child neglect.

Child abuse or child maltreatment consists of different types of harmful act directed towards children. In physical abuse, children are slapped, hit, kicked or shoved or have objects thrown at them. Flesh wounds, broken bones or other injuries are common. Severe abuse may result in major injury, permanent physical or developmental impairment or even death.

Neglect, a form of child maltreatment, involves the failure to feed or care for a child's basic needs or to adequately supervise the child.

Emotional abuse involves humiliation, berating or other acts carried out over time that terrorise or frighten the child. Children are emotionally scarred when they are labelled as stupid or ugly or crazy or unwanted.

Sexual abuse consists of a wide range of sexual behaviour, including fondling, mutual masturbation, digital penetration, oral–genital contact and involvement of children in photography or filming for pornographic purposes and intercourse.

Sexual acts not involving intercourse between, for example, fathers and daughters constitute other criminal offences such as indecent assault or gross indecency with or towards a child. Sexual relationships with stepchildren count as unlawful sexual intercourse and indecent assault.

Father/son relationships come within the offences of buggery or indecent assault, not incest or unlawful sexual intercourse.

The majority of sexual assaults on children are by someone they know. The risk is higher when the child lives with a step-, foster or adoptive father. Child abusers come from every class, profession, race and religious background.

Sexual abuse is said to be symptomatic of a family in crisis and, unless it is dealt with, the victim will be continually abused and damaged. The wounds of a victim will bleed throughout life unless properly treated.

The child victim is never responsible for the abuse. The responsibility always lies with the perpetrator. The child needs constant reassurance of this.

Children who live in families where sexual abuse has occurred between family members have frequently been the subject of previous child abuse investigations. It is a myth that the spouse must have been aware of the sexual abuse taking place, although some are. The child victim is often blamed for what has taken place. The perpetrator rarely discriminates between the sexes or the ages of the victims.

Where the mother does know, secrecy, threats and silent acceptance hold the father, child and mother in a relationship to 'stabilise' the marriage and family and prevent break-up. There is an intense relationship between the father and child that is both powerful and dependent. The father is also dependent upon his wife. The coercive and threatening web of silence is spun.

The child is also dependent and could be said to have power. In fact, the child has little power, other than to expose and destroy the father and family unit. This is a heavy responsibility and is rarely used by the abused and very vulnerable child, because of the threat from the perpetrator and enormous fear of the unknown.

When sexual abuse occurs outside the family, there is more likelihood of the child confiding in the parents. But when the perpetrator is one of the family, disclosure is difficult. There is the public shame of failure for each person involved in their own role as father, mother and child, with resulting further loss of self-esteem by all.

Violent molestation and rape generally bring condemnation down on the heads of the perpetrators. Oro-genital molestation may leave no evidence except the child's story. This must be believed. Children rarely fabricate stories of detailed sexual activities unless they have witnessed them; and they have, indeed, been eyewitnesses to their own abuse.

Adult–child sex is wrong because the fundamental conditions of consent cannot prevail in the relationship between an adult and a child. Not only can the child not freely consent, the child also cannot give informed consent. A child is not likely to be aware of the social significance of sexuality, nor of the consequences. And in this, adult–child sex is morally wrong.

In the UK, a local authority can take abused children away from their parents by obtaining a care order from a family court under the Children Act 1989, amended as the Children and Adoption Act 2002.

Controversial methods of diagnosing sexual abuse have led to several high profile cases, which severely criticised the handling of such cases. The standard of proof required for criminal proceedings is greater than that required for a local authority to take children into care. This has led to highly publicised cases where children have been taken into care but no prosecution has eventually been brought. In some cases innocent parents have been pilloried, so the whole area of abuse is very difficult. There is also the related point of the abused child having to give evidence and all that that means. Although there is progress towards making the giving of evidence less of an ordeal, such facilities as video links are not yet universal.

Historical

The sexual abuse of children is as old as civilisation. Both the Bible and the Talmud encouraged sex between men and very young girls in marriage, concubinage and slavery. For generations we naively believed that the taboos against incest did actually operate and that, when incest did occur, it was as an isolated incident.

One of the first national laws designed to stop the mistreatment of children in their own homes was passed in 1884, when Britain's National Society for the Prevention of Cruelty to Children was organised. Earlier statutes had outlawed infant abandonment and failure to provide food, shelter, clothing and medical care for dependants. Child-labour laws regulated working conditions for underage factory workers and tried to improve the status of young apprentices, who lived almost as slaves while learning a skill from tradesmen.

Incidence

A particularly controversial aspect of the incidence problem is the number of individuals recalling memories of abuse. While repression of early traumatic memories is a concept that many psychotherapists accept, increasing concern is being raised over the alarming number of adult women in therapy who report repressed memories of abuse, particularly incest. At present, there is no way of determining whether such memories, in adults or in children, are valid or are the result of suggestive therapy or media probing.

Too often the crime goes unpunished because a child is afraid that exposing an abuser will only bring more pain. Abusive parents and caretakers may try to justify their actions as a way of punishing children for being 'bad' or of scaring them into being 'good'. A related point is the number of cases of children in care who have been abused. Much of this abuse occurred many years ago and only now have the victims had the courage to come forward.

Causes

No explanation of the cause of child abuse has emerged as conclusive but it is most likely to stem from a collection of factors, including poverty, substance abuse and societal violence. Like rape, child abuse may also have something to do with power and control over someone who is weaker and more vulnerable.

Childhood abuse is thought to lead to the person becoming an abuser in later life, although this theory does not take into consideration other moderating factors for the many people who were abused and have not become abusers. It must never be assumed that the one follows the other and to suggest this puts abused people under a fearful cloud when they themselves become parents.

Treatment

Child abuse is a multi-faceted problem best addressed through comprehensive, interdisciplinary interventions, including law enforcement and medical, mental health and social services. Most abused children require medical examination to detect the presence of injury or disease. Many abused children will suffer short- or long-term psychological or emotional trauma. Abusive adults require a range of mental health and social services to help them remedy the conditions associated with their behaviour.

Jan Sutton, in her book *Healing the Hurt Within*, draws attention to the fact that much self-harming behaviour is linked with experience of abuse as children. Thus the legacy of child abuse is a fearful one, which has brought many of its victims to the brink of despair.

Progress has been made in identifying not only effective therapeutic interventions for victims and perpetrators but also effective prevention strategies. One of the most promising of the latter is the provision of home-visitation services to new parents to promote positive parent–child interactions and ensure adequate support thereafter.

Recognising child abuse

The most important step in recognising child sexual abuse is to be aware of the possibility of such abuse. In other words you are not going to find sexual abuse if you don't believe it exists.

On the other hand, it is impossible to give hard and fast rules for identifying abuse. Each situation is different and children will find ways of coping with the abuse and their own way of trying to tell.

Children do not always know the words to explain clearly what is happening to them. They may try to tell, e.g. by saying, I don't like him', 'He's ugly', 'He acts funny'. These statements are often misunderstood or ignored.

Therefore, although in many cases the child's comment will relate to something harmless, it is worth asking a few gentle questions to find out why they are saying it.

Although there are few 'conclusive' signs it is helpful for anyone involved with children and young people to be aware of the types of behaviour often found in children who have been assaulted.

Signs of possible sexual abuse

- Repeated urinary infections/pain on urinating
- Sexually transmitted disease
- Stomach aches/cramps
- Inability to sit still (from sore bottom or genitals)
- Incontinence or bed-wetting
- Pregnancy
- Bruising, especially around genitals
- Chronic eating disorders/anorexia
- Depression
- Suicide attempts
- Self-mutilation
- Low self-esteem
- Self-neglect
- Nightmares/insomnia
- Panic attacks
- Compulsive washing/obsessive cleanliness

- Refusing to speak (elective mutism)
- Very sudden changes in behaviour
- Running away
- Truancy
- Fear of men or of one particular man
- Changes in school performance
- Regression to younger behaviour
- Falling asleep in school
- Uncharacteristic behaviour that is interpreted as sexual
- Inappropriate or detailed sexual knowledge in language or drawings.

Some of these sorts of behaviour are common to all distressed children and may not be a reaction to sexual abuse. To add to the difficulties, some abused children show none of these signs or symptoms and manage to conceal what is happening to them.

Again, the important thing to remember when dealing with any distressed child is that we keep our minds open to the possibility of sexual abuse. Remember, however difficult it is for children to tell openly about sexual abuse, it is through these and other signs that children are asking for permission to tell and for an end to the abuse. (Taken from a paper written by the Women's Support Project, 871 Springfield Road, Parkhead, Glasgow and used with permission.)

The term 'abusing parent' is applied to a parent guilty of child abuse but is also a label for a theoretical personality type possessing a particular set of characteristics, which postulates that it is highly likely that a person of this type will become an abusing parent. However, no clear-cut personality traits that typify abusing parents have been demonstrated other than the likelihood that they were themselves abused as children – but even that is not certain.

The abusers may spend a lot of time building the relationship before the abuse begins. This often results in the child trusting and becoming dependent on them. This is called grooming. The abuser may seem to be a safe and reassuring figure. He may also convince himself that he is doing no harm to children.

Keeping secrets

The child becomes more dependent on the abuser and in order to keep the abuse secret the abuser will use the child's natural fear, embarrassment or guilt about what is happening. A child who talks and shares feelings with parents and others is less likely to become dependent on a single abusing adult.

Surfing the internet safely: tips for young people

Chat rooms and messaging can be great fun, but remember, you never really know who you are talking to online. It could be someone trying to trick you, some kind of weirdo or someone really dangerous. Here are some tips to help you keep safe:

- Never use your real name in chat rooms – pick a special online nickname.
- Never ever tell anyone personal things about yourself or your family – like your address or telephone number, or the school or clubs you go to. That goes for sending them photos as well (that way if you don't want to hear from them again, you only have to log off). Remember, even if somebody tells you about themselves, never tell them things about you.
- If you arrange to meet up with someone you've only spoken to online, remember that they might not be who they said they were, so only meet people in public places and take along an adult – they should do this too, because they don't know who you really are either!
- Never respond to nasty or rude messages, and never send any either! If you feel suspicious or uncomfortable about the way a conversation is going, or if it's getting really personal, save a record of it and stop the conversation. That way you can show someone and ask what they think.
- Be careful with any email attachments or links that people send you; they might contain nasty images, or computer 'viruses' that could ruin your PC. So if you don't know who it's from, don't open it.
- Avoid sites that are meant for adults. You might be curious, but sometimes these sites can be difficult to get out of, they can cost more on the phone bill, and they can detect your email address and start sending you stuff you really don't want to get. If you see rude pictures where they shouldn't be, always let an adult know so they can get them removed.
- Agree some rules with your parents or carers about what you can and can't do on the Net. It'll save arguments later.
- Take a look at *Hands Off!* – the NSPCC magazine for teenagers on keeping safe from abuse. It's got some tips on safe surfing.
- Don't let the Net take over your life! Keep up your other interests and try and use the internet with friends and family, not just on your own.

Other sites with useful information on internet safety:

NCH (National Children's Homes)
Home Office Internet Safety
MSN web safety site, Websafe Crackerz
Internet Watch Foundation
Childnet
BBC Online
Parents' Information Network
IWF Hotline – for reporting illegal or harmful material
www.ivillage.co.uk
www.nch.org.uk

Further reading

Bradshaw, J. (1990) *Home Coming: reclaiming and championing your inner child.* Judy Piatkus, London.

Corby, B. (1993) *Child Abuse: towards a knowledge base*. Open University Press, Buckingham.

Diagnostic and Statistical Manual of Mental Disorders (DSM IV) (1994) American Psychiatric Association, Washington, DC.

Draucker, C.B. (1992) *Counselling Survivors of Childhood Sexual Abuse*. Sage Publications, London.

Saunders, P. and Myers, S. (1995) *What Do You Know About Child Abuse*. Gloucester Press, Gloucester.

Sutton J. (1999) *Healing the Hurt Within: how to relieve the suffering underlying self-destructive behaviour*. How to Books, Oxford.

CO-DEPENDENCE (SEE ALSO: COMMUNICATION MODES OF VIRGINIA SATIR)

Jan Sutton, speaking of self-destructive behaviour, says this of co-dependency:

Co-dependency may be an unfamiliar term. It is characterised by compulsive care-taking, a need to please or control others, and is often found in dysfunctional families, for example in adult children of alcoholics. Co-dependents frequently get enmeshed in other people's lives or problems, in an 'unconscious' attempt to avoid, deny or divert their own pain away from themselves. Another term for co-dependency is relationship addiction.

Sutton lists the following self-destructive behaviours:

- Unsafe sex
- Promiscuity
- Prostitution
- Staying in destructive relationships
- Co-dependency.

Co-dependent behaviour is often related to families where there is chemical addiction, but there are other situations in which co-dependence operates. Co-dependent behaviour is learned in dysfunctional families in which certain unwritten, and in many cases unspoken, rules prevail. The behaviour is reinforced within the culture. Many rules that produce people who are not wholly functional are linked to sex roles.

The main focus of the co-dependent person is other people, so much so that their own feelings and wishes do not feature at all. This ties in with Virginia Satir's 'Placater Mode'. The co-dependent person becomes so compliant and passive and eager to please the others that he really does forget to know what he wants/likes/prefers.

Typically, the co-dependent person came from a dysfunctional home in which their emotional needs were not met. Their parents were not able to provide the attention, warmth and responsiveness that children need in order to feel that their needs count. So, they grew up feeling that their needs did not matter, that their desires were unimportant, that they themselves were less important than anyone else.

Co-dependent people become addicted to emotional pain and to unhealthy relationships. They are drawn to people who are not available to them, or who reject them or abuse them. They often develop unhealthy relationships that eventually become unbearable. Because relationships hurt so much, co-dependents are more in touch with the dream of how the relationship could be, rather than how it is.

Examples of dysfunctional rules:

- 'Men should be...'
- 'Women should be...'
- 'Always do...'
- 'Never do...'

The rules stem from avoidance of interpersonal issues and the need to protect oneself from others. People from dysfunctional families learn to be 'people-pleasers'.

Examples of dysfunctional family rules:

- Never talk to others about your problems – 'Don't wash your dirty linen in public'.
- Never express feelings openly.
- Indirect communication is best.
- We have to be perfect – always; being ruled by 'shoulds' and 'oughts' creates fertile soil for shame, doubt, frustration and anger when we fail to attain perfection.
- Don't be selfish, ever – other people must always come first.
- Don't do as I do, do as I say.
- Play and fun are irresponsible.
- Whatever you do, don't rock the boat.

People who are the product of dysfunctional families tend to 'awfulise' events. Minor omissions are major transgressions. Dysfunctional behaviours become evident in people who do not know how to ask for help (asking for help implies an acceptance of vulnerability) or how to forgive themselves. Co-dependents may become dependent on other people, substances or behaviours.

Examples of dysfunctional coping:

- Compulsive, perfectionistic, approval-seeking or dependent behaviour
- May become 'doormat' co-dependents
- May suffer from physical exhaustion, depression and hopelessness
- May abuse or neglect their children
- May become suicidal
- May become self-destructive through overwork, chemical or any other form of dependency.

Development of co-dependence:

- The primary caregiver fails to allow the developing child to separate and establish his or her own boundaries.
- Male children are more likely to be encouraged to separate than female children.

- Masculinity is defined through separation from the primary caregiver while femininity is defined through attachment.
- Men, generally, are threatened by attachment, while women, generally, are threatened by separation.

The two most typical behaviours of co-dependence are compulsive care-taking and attempting to control others.

Characteristics of co-dependency:

- An exaggerated sense of responsibility for the actions of others
- A tendency to confuse love and pity, with the tendency to 'love' people they can pity and rescue
- A tendency to do more than their share, all of the time
- A tendency to become hurt when people don't recognise their efforts
- An unhealthy dependence on relationships. The co-dependent will do anything to hold on to a relationship to avoid the feeling of abandonment
- An extreme need for approval and recognition
- A sense of guilt when asserting themselves
- A compelling need to control others
- Lack of trust in self and/or others
- Fear of being abandoned or alone
- Difficulty identifying feelings
- Rigidity/difficulty adjusting to change
- Problems with intimacy/boundaries
- Chronic anger
- Lying/dishonesty
- Poor communications
- Difficulty making decisions.

Counselling can help co-dependent people:

- By helping them to build self-esteem through increased self-knowledge, identifying strong and weak points, and a full acceptance of themselves
- By working on accepting others as they are, without trying to change them to meet their own needs
- To lose interest in the struggles, drama and chaos of the past
- To become protective of themselves, their health and their wellbeing
- To come to realise that for a relationship to work, it must be between partners who share similar values, interests and goals, and who each have the capacity for intimacy
- To come to know that they are worthy of the best that life has to offer, and they know that with help, perhaps, they can find a way to achieve that.

Over-dependence versus self-reliance

Self-reliance is closely related to one's ability to cope with change and healthy life adjustment. People who are self-reliant, and are yet able to depend on others when appropriate, are better equipped to manage the challenges they meet than those who are not self-reliant.

According to Bowlby's theory of attachment, attachment behaviour is evident from six months onwards when the infant discriminates sharply between the caregiver and other people.

Early attachment influences adult behaviour, particularly during illness, distress or when afraid. The primary attachment figure represents security. For attachment to be satisfactory, one principal caregiver needs to be identified.

When our infant physical and emotional needs are not met, we experience separation anxiety, which involves feelings of isolation, loneliness and distress.

When separation anxiety is experienced frequently and intensely during childhood, it becomes a significant feature of the personality. It interferes with the person's normal development, and the formation of successful relationships. It can result in the feelings of anxiety, anger, depression, and a variety of health and emotional disorders.

An absence of self-reliance may be expressed either as over-dependence or counter-dependence. (See Loneliness for a discussion of counter-dependence.)

An over-dependent person – characteristics

- Needs to have other people around to feel secure
- Does not believe others will be there when they are needed
- Becomes very concerned over conflict at home or at work
- Has difficultly moving to a new location and new friends
- Is not comfortable working alone for long periods at a time
- Relies on frequent feedback to feel secure
- Invariably consults others before making decisions
- Often finds it difficult to leave home to go to work and vice versa.

Further reading

Beattie, M. (1987) Co-dependent No More: how to stop controlling others and start caring for yourself. Harper & Row, New York.

Beattie, M. (1989) Beyond Co-dependency and Getting Better at all Times. Harper & Row, New York.

Kramer, S. (1998–2004) Conquering Co-dependency from a Spiritual Point of View. Creations in Consciousness, Amsterdam.

Mellody, P., Miller, A.W. and Miller, J.K. (1989) Facing Co-dependence: what it is, where it comes from, how it sabotages our lives. Harper & Row, New York.

Pfeiffer, J.A. (1991) Co-dependence: learned dysfunctional behaviour. In: 1991 Annual: Developing Human Resources.University Associates, San Diego, CA.

Sutton, J. (1999) Healing the Hurt Within: how to relieve the suffering underlying self-destructive behaviour. How to Books, Oxford.

Simko, Patty Co-Dependency http://www.wholepersoninc.com

Co-dependency www.nmha.org

susan@susankramer.com

Cognitive therapy (see also: behaviour therapy and rational emotive therapy)

One way of defining the differences between approaches is to consider where their primary focus is – on feelings, thinking, behaviour or a combination of these.

Psychodynamic and person-centred approaches concentrate on feelings. Behaviourists believe that if the behaviour (including thinking) is adjusted, all other aspects will be put to rights. Cognitive theories (mainly concerned with thinking) put forward the view that all behaviour is primarily determined by what a person thinks. Eclectic or integrated counsellors may use any or all of these theories and approaches. What distinguishes one counselling approach from another is where the attention is focused, and the techniques and skills used.

Cognitive therapy was developed by Aaron Beck, who put forward the view that behaviour is primarily determined by what that person thinks. It is particularly relevant in treating depression, where thoughts of low self-worth and low self-esteem are a common feature. Cognitive therapy works on the premise that thoughts of low self-worth are incorrect and are due to faulty learning.

Such thoughts often centre on:

- 'I haven't achieved anything'.
- 'I have nothing to offer'.
- 'I deserve to be criticised'.

The aim of therapy is to get rid of faulty concepts that influence negative thinking. Karen Horney refers to the 'tyranny of the shoulds': should do this, should not do that. Cognitive therapists challenge all these assumptions, as well as all self-evaluations that constantly put the person down. Such evaluations are cumulative.

The person needs help to:

- Identify the internal rules of self-evaluations.
- See how self-evaluation influences feelings and behaviours.
- Decide how realistic the internal rules are.
- Discover the origin of the rule.
- See how the rule is maintained.
- Discover ways to get rid of redundant rules.
- Think through what it would mean to get rid of redundant rules.

Attributions are:

- Being told what we are, what we must do and how we must feel.
- Generally approving of obedience and disapproving of disobedience.

(See also Transactional analysis.)

The client is helped to explore:

- Personal responsibility

- Blame and self-blame
- Whether active or passive in meeting needs
- Attributions
- Alternatives
- Am I responsible for my behaviour?
- Am I in control or am I controlled?
- If I am controlled – by whom?

The challenge the client has to face is: to change or not to change? The person is helped to replace 'tunnel thinking' with 'lateral, flexible thinking'.

Common thinking difficulties:

- Memory lapse
- Concentration
- Incoherence
- Blocking
- Scatter
- Restrictive thinking, in 'either–or' terms.

Problem-solving involves being able to work with shades of grey. The counsellor needs to question behaviour based on unproven inferences such as: 'If I blush, people will think I am ...'.

Clients often need to learn decision-making and problem-solving skills as part of the process of thinking rehabilitation. Faulty self-evaluations, attributions and anticipations may lead to restricted perceptions and to restricted ability to solve problems.

Possible counselling interventions

- Giving appropriate information may clear up misinformation and facilitate movement
- Acceptance and empathic understanding
- Focused exploration
- Specificity – get away from generalisations: insist on 'I' instead of 'you' and 'my' instead of 'our'
- Challenge:
  - The discrepancies between thoughts, feelings and behaviours within and outside of counselling
  - The discrepancies between what is said and what is left unsaid
  - Attributions
  - False logic
  - Self-evaluations
  - Responsibility
  - Irrational beliefs
- Use disputation, a form of sustained challenging: 'Why...?' 'Yes, but why ...?' 'That's still not clear'

- Interpretation from the external frame of reference: 'It seems, from my point of view...'
- Teaching: the transactional analysis Parent/Adult/Child framework, for example, or problem-solving skills
- Information-giving: tasks; homework; questionnaires
- Direction:
  - Persuasion
  - Exhortation
  - Advice
  - Advocating
  - Encouragement
  - Reassurance
- Modelling:
  - The counselling relationship
  - Behaviour rehearsal
  - Group counselling
  - Observing tasks being carried out
- Role play:
  - Psychodrama
  - Dramatic enactment
  - Behaviour rehearsal
  - Imagery
- Encourage performance: anticipation about tasks is often more negative than results warrant
- Skills training
- Visual aids/homework.

Techniques to help clients with thinking

See also Rational emotive therapy.

1. **Explore and list negative thoughts**:
   - When do you think them?
   - Is there a pattern?
   - Do they occur all the time or only at specific times?
   - Are they concerned with specific people or events?
   - Do you always lose out? Come off worse?
2. Use imagination: Imagination is a powerful ally. Whenever a negative thought occurs, 'imagine the situation, then change the scene into something positive'.
3. Use 'thought stop': Every time a negative thought intrudes, say (aloud, if possible), 'STOP!' If thoughts are particularly troublesome, wear a loose elastic band on the wrist and, when the thought comes, snap the elastic.
4. **Substitute a positive thought to replace the invasive negative thought**: Substitution, coupled with imagination, is a powerful way to change from negative to positive thinking. Positive thinking can become as much a habit as negative thinking has been.

Further reading

Beck, A.T. and Rush, A.J. (1995) Cognitive therapy. In: *Comprehensive Textbook of Psychiatry*, 6th edn (eds H.J. Kaplan and B.J. Sadock). Williams & Wilkins, Baltimore, MD.

Horney, K. (1942) *Self-analysis*. W.W. Norton, New York.

Trower, P., Casey, A. and Dryden, W. (1988) *Cognitive Behavioural Counselling in Action*. Sage Publications, London.

COMMUNICATION (SEE ALSO: CREATIVITY, LISTENING AND RESPONDING, AND QUESTIONS)

Communication occurs when what takes place in one person's mind so influences the mind of another person that the resultant experiences of both are reasonably alike.

Communication is a sharing of:

- Attitudes
- Facts
- Feelings
- Information.

One (linear) model of communication has the following elements:

- Source – a person on the telephone
- Encoder – the mouthpiece
- Message – the words spoken
- Channel – electrical impulses
- Decoder – the earpiece at the other end
- Receiver – the mind of the listener.

Communication is influenced by:

1. **Entropy**, which is auditory or visual static that decreases the effectiveness of the communication
2. **Negative entropy**, which functions when the receiver, in spite of mixed or blurred messages, interprets enough of the message to make it intelligible
3. **Redundancy** is the repetition of parts of the message that ensures the message gets through. Redundancy works against entropy. Entropy distorts; negative entropy and redundancy clarify.
4. **Feedback** corrects the default between entropy, negative entropy and redundancy. Effective communication cannot take place without feedback. The term 'feedback' derives from cybernetic theory – a cybernetic example would be a room thermostat.

Methods of communicating:

- Words (10 per cent)
- Tones (40 per cent)
- Visual (50 per cent).

Styles of communicating:

- Telling
- Negotiating
- Persuading
- Listening
- Counselling.

There is more of self and less of the other person in 'telling'; more of the other person and less of self in 'counselling'.

Barriers to effective communication:

- Lack of trust
- Misinterpretation
- Stereotyped language
- Semantics – the words we use
- Emotional
- Intellectual
- Conceptual
- Cultural.

Effective communication hinges on:

- Creating a conducive atmosphere based on time and place, motivation and preparation
- Being clear about why we want to communicate, what the listener expects and how we can put the points over
- Active reception of information, which is influenced by the skills of:
  - Active listening
  - Attending
  - Paraphrasing
  - Reflecting
  - Open questions
  - Summarising
  - Focusing
  - Self-disclosure
  - Challenging.

Unclear reception of information may be influenced by:

- Lack of self-awareness
- Hidden agendas
- Preconceived ideas
- Arguing
- Interrupting
- Criticising
- Putting down
- Not being able to get into the internal frame of reference.

Feedback

Feedback is a term borrowed from rocket engineering by Kurt Lewin and gives one person the opportunity to be open to the perceptions of others.

Feedback is an essential mechanism in any interpersonal communication, particularly in group work. An example of social feedback is returning a smile.

Giving feedback is both a verbal and a non-verbal process where people let others know their perception of and feelings about the other people's behaviour. Soliciting feedback is asking for other people's perceptions of our behaviour.

The aim of giving and receiving feedback is to make someone more aware of:

- What he does
- How it is done
- The feelings
- The consequences.

Giving feedback requires:

- Courage
- Other-respect
- Self-awareness
- Self-respect
- Skill
- Understanding.

Feedback should focus on:

- Behaviour that can be changed
- Description
- Exploring alternatives
- Giving information
- Observation
- Sharing ideas.

Feedback should not focus on:

- Personal qualities
- Judgement
- Providing answers
- Giving advice
- Inferences
- Giving direction.

Guidelines for giving feedback

- Your intention must be to help.
- If the person has not asked for feedback, check whether he is open to it.
- Deal only with observable behaviour.
- Deal only with modifiable behaviour.

- Describe specifics, not generalities.
- Describe behaviours.
- Do not judge the person.
- Do not make assumptions or interpret.
- Let the person know the impact the behaviour has on you.
- Check that the message has been received and understood.
- Suggest, rather than prescribe means for improvement.
- Should be directed towards meeting the need of the other person, not designed to punish.
- Encourage the person to check out your feedback with other people.
- Feedback, if well timed and accurate, enhances the relationship.

Guidelines for receiving feedback

- When you ask for feedback, be specific in describing the behaviour about which you want feedback.
- Try not to act defensively.
- Try not to rationalise the behaviour.
- Summarise your understanding.
- Share your thoughts and feelings.
- Accept the responsibility for the behaviour.
- Try to see things through the other's eyes.
- Explore the feedback; don't use it as an excuse to attack.
- Don't brush it off with misplaced humour or sarcasm.
- Don't put yourself down, assuming that everyone else is correct.
- Plan how you could use the feedback.
- If it is hard to take, remember, you did ask!

Examples of feedback

- Direct expression of feelings: 'I like you'
- Descriptive feedback: 'Your fists are clenched'
- Non-evaluative feedback: 'You are angry and that's OK'
- Specific feedback: 'When you shouted, I felt anxious'
- Freedom of choice to change: 'When you called me "son" I felt put down and small'
- Immediate feedback: 'I'm feeling angry at what I consider to be a sexist remark'
- Group-shared feedback: 'Does this group see me as being supportive?'

To be effective communicators, counsellors should:

- Be clear what they want the other person to understand
- Consider their attitudes and the attitudes of the client
- Have an accurate assessment of their own communication style
- Be able to assess the communication style of the client
- Try to get on the client's thinking and feeling wavelength

- Strive for clarity of expression
- Make certain the message is understood before continuing
- Try to get into the client's frame of reference
- State ideas in simplest possible terms
- Define then develop
- Explain then clarify
- Present one idea at a time
- Take one step at a time
- Make use of appropriate repetition to ensure understanding
- Compare and contrast ideas
- Use analogies and metaphors
- Use appropriate emphasis to underline ideas
- Use language which appeals to all five senses
- Use body language, congruent with the verbal message
- Give, encourage and acknowledge verbal and non-verbal feedback
- Be sensitive to go at the client's pace
- Be aware of when they are in danger of losing the client.

We should consider how much feedback to give and then evaluate how clear and how accurate the feedback was. Effective communication leaves people feeling OK and is therefore a basis for change.

Defensive and supportive communication

Communication, in addition to the foregoing, also depends on climate. Climates may be supportive or defensive.

Supportive climates promote understanding and problem-solving and are characterised by:

- Empathy (see Core conditions)
- Spontaneity and openness
- Agreement, cooperation and teamwork.

Defensive climates are motivated by control, recognised by persuasion, coercion and convincing. The desire to control results in:

- **Evaluations**: Characterised by criticism and judgement
- **Strategies**: With the focus on winning
- **Superiority**: The person who feels superior views the other as unintelligent and inferior
- **Certainty**: Correctness with no room for negotiation.

Barriers to supportive climates

These are cultural, time/energy, risk, emotional.

- **Culture**: In some cultures competition, not cooperation, listening and understanding is emphasised.
- **Time/energy**: Creating a supportive climate takes time, energy and commitment.

- **Risk**: Every time we view the world through someone else's eyes, from another person's frame of reference, we run the risk of having to change something within ourselves.
- **Emotions**: Hostile, angry feelings get in the way of offering support.

Facilitating supportive communication

This depends on three things:

- **Being genuinely open**: False openness will create alarm. Some people are very good at putting on a show of being open but something about their motives is not genuine.
- **Active listening, which is grasping the facts and meaning of the message**: Clarifying and checking.
- **Feedback, which is sharing perspectives**: Moving from 'me versus you' to 'you and me together' and thinking of the goal(s), then seeking solutions to reach it (them).

Direct and indirect communication

Indirect communication is pseudo-communication, carried out with the purpose of manipulating, control, avoiding risks and self-protection.

Characteristics of indirect communication

- **Non-communication**: Attempting to get support which is not genuine: 'I think I speak for the whole group'.
- **Non-genuine questions**: These are generally indirect communication and seek to direct the person toward a certain response:
  - Limiting questions: 'Don't you think that...?', 'Isn't it a fact that...?'
  - Punishing questions, where the motive is to expose the other person without appearing to do so and so put the person on the spot
  - Hypothetical questions, which are often motivated by criticism and typically begin with 'If', 'What if', 'How about': 'If you were making that report, wouldn't you say it differently?'
  - Demand or command questions, where the motivation is to impress urgency or importance:
  - 'Have you done anything about...?'
  - Screened questions, where the motivation is to get the other person to make a decision that fits with the speaker's hidden wish. This type of question puts great pressure on the person being questioned, not being sure what answer is required: 'Would you like to go to ...?'
  - Leading questions, where the motive is to manoeuvre the other person into a vulnerable position. Leading questions are often used by lawyers in court to confuse the witness:
  - 'Is it fair to say that you ...?' 'Would you agree that...?'
  - Questions that don't need an answer, where the motive is to forestall a response because the questioner fears it may not be a favourable one. The

attempt is to secure a guaranteed agreement. No response is required: 'You don't mind if I come for the weekend?'

– 'Now I've got you' questions, where the motive is to dig a trap for the other person to fall into: 'Weren't you the one who …?'

- **Clichés**: Here the motive is to appear to be communicating, without sharing anything significant. The frequent use of tired, worn-out phrases reduces the effectiveness of communication.

The effects of indirect communication

- **Guesswork**: Without direct, open communication, people cannot get to know each other. What we do not know, we will make guesses about. Inaccurate guessing means making assumptions and often we get the wrong answers.
- **Inferences**: When communication is not direct, we are forced to infer the other person's motives. Pseudo-questions and clichés hide motives.
- **Playing games**: Indirect communication encourages game-playing, leading to deception and dishonesty.
- **Defensiveness**: This is one of the surest effects of indirect communication (see also Defence mechanisms).

Direct communication is characterised by:

- Being two-way, in which ideas, opinions, values, beliefs and feelings flow freely
- Active listening (see also Listening and responding)
- Giving and receiving feedback
- Not being stressful
- Being clear and relatively free from ambiguity and mixed messages.

We can foster direct communication by:

- **Making direct statements**: When we make statements, based on what we have heard, rather than ask questions, we are more likely to be communicating directly
- **Actively listening**
- **Owning** that what we say and feel belong to us and not to someone else
- **Locating the context**: This means that in order to make a genuine response we have to understand the context in which the statement is made; we must not make assumptions
- **Sharing**: All true communication is a sharing process. For communication to be effective, we must be prepared to take risks and work towards a mutual understanding through genuine sharing of a common meaning.

Further reading

Combs, G.W. (1981) Defensive and supportive communication. In: *1981 Annual Handbook for Group Facilitators*. University Associates, San Diego, CA.

Gibb, J.R. (1961) Defensive communication. *Journal of Communication*, **11**: 141–148.

Hanson, P.C. (1975) Giving feedback: an interpersonal skill. In: *1975 Annual Handbook for Group Facilitators*. University Associates, San Diego, CA.

Jones, J.E. (1972) Communication modes: an experiential lecture. In: *1972 Annual Handbook for Group Facilitators*. University Associates, San Diego, CA.

Rogers, C.R. (1970) *Encounter Groups*. Harper & Row, New York.

COMMUNICATION MODES OF VIRGINIA SATIR (SEE ALSO: FAMILY THERAPY)

Virginia Satir – a family therapist – identifies four universal patterns of responses we use to get around the threat of rejection. We feel and react to the threat but, because we do not want to reveal 'weakness', we attempt to conceal our feelings. A fifth mode – the Leveller – is positive and genuine.

The five communication modes

Placaters

Placaters are frightened that people will get angry, go away and never return. However, they don't dare admit this.

Typical Placater speech:

> *Oh, you know me – I don't care, really I don't.*
> *Whatever anybody else wants to do is fine with me.*
> *Whatever you say, darling; I don't mind, really.*
> *Oh, nothing bothers me! Do whatever you like.*
> *What do I want to do? Oh, well! What would you like to do?*

Two Placaters conversing cannot make decisions, however minor.

Blamers

Blamers feel that nobody cares about them; there is no respect or affection for them; that people are indifferent to their needs and feelings. Blamers react to this with verbal behaviour intended to demonstrate who is in charge, the boss and the one with power.

Typical Blamer speech:

> *You never consider my feelings.*
> *Nobody around here ever pays any attention to me.*
> *Do you always have to put yourself first?*
> *Why don't you ever think about what I might want?*
> *I've had all I'm going to take.*
> *Why do you always insist on having your own way, no matter how much it hurts other people?*

When two Blamers talk, the conversation is not a dead-end, as it is with two Placaters. It is a rapid road to a screaming match, nasty in every way.

Computers

Computers are terrified that someone will find out that they have feelings. Computers work hard to give the impression that they have none. Star Trek's Mr

Spock – except for the troublesome human side of him that makes him so interesting – is a classic computer type.

Typical Computer speech:

There is undoubtedly a simple solution to the problem.
It's obvious that no real difficulty exists here.
No rational person would be alarmed by this minor event.
Clearly the advantages of this activity have been exaggerated.
Preferences of the kind you describe are rather common in this area.

Two Computers talking is like listening to people from another planet!

Distracters

Distracters are tricky people to keep up with, as they shift rapidly between the other modes, yet never stay long in any one of them. The underlying feeling is of panic: 'I don't know what on earth to say, but I've got to say something and the quicker the better!'

The surface behaviour is a chaotic mix.

Levellers

Levellers are the most contradictory type of all – either the easiest or the most difficult to handle.

Levellers do what the term implies – level with you. There's no one simpler to deal with than the Leveller – just level back. What Levellers say is what Levellers feel. The Leveller verbal message is congruent with the body language. The aim is single, straight messages.

Levelling relationships:

- Free and honest
- Few threats to self-esteem
- Potential for healing and for building bridges
- Genuine
- More likely to criticise and evaluate the behaviour not the person. Developing levelling attitudes will give us a good opportunity to stand on our own feet. It may not be easy; it may not be painless; but it might make the difference as to whether we grow or not.

The benefits of levelling:

- Levelling is a way of responding to real people in real-life situations.
- Levelling permits us to agree because we really do, not because we think we should.
- Levelling allows us to disagree when we really do.
- Levelling allows us to use our brain freely but not to score off others.
- Levelling allows us to change course, not to get someone off the hook but because we want to and there is a genuine need to do so.

Fake Levellers are more dangerous than all the other categories combined and very hard to spot. One way to spot the fake is to listen to your gut reaction. You may not unmask this person straight away, but after a time you will start to feel very uncomfortable without being able to identify the reason. When this happens, start to do a check on things that don't add up – inconsistencies, discrepancies, ambiguities.

You don't have to stay in one mode, even though the Leveller has the most to offer. To be able to switch modes has distinct advantages. When you are uncertain which mode to move into, become a Computer, who:

- Is never angry or emotional or hurried or upset
- Never uses 'I', 'me', 'my', 'mine', 'myself'
- Always talks in abstractions and generalities
- Says, 'One could...' or 'Any reasonable person would...'
- Says, 'It is ... that...' [It is obvious that there is no cause for alarm]
- Always looks calm and relaxed
- Maintains one physical position throughout the conversation
- Never commits himself to anything
- Deliberately creates emotional distance.

The computer mode at work

Meg was a graduate student nurse, in the last year of training, having counselling because she felt uncertain about her choice of career, coupled with panic attacks. This is part of her account.

We weren't very close, any of us and this was something I very much regretted. I knew I was harbouring a lot of resentment against my mother. She is a very dominant, self-centred and possessive woman, towards us all, but particularly towards me, for some reason. On talking things through with William I realised that Mother made very heavy demands on me. She would use words like, 'If you really loved me...' or 'Other daughters don't treat their mothers like you do'. I felt stifled by her. So strong were my feelings that I was often troubled by bad dreams in which, for example, I would be going upstairs with a knife in my hand to kill Mother. In fact, I was afraid that some day I might actually do this. The thought terrified me. I didn't know how to deal with Mother. William talked through with me a way of responding called the 'Computer'. I tried this and found I could handle my feelings better. I think Mother is jealous of me, though I can't think why she should be.

The aim was to help Meg cope with her mother's Blamer mode; the Blamer is the person who makes statements like, 'Why don't you ever think what I might want?' This seemed to be Meg's mother's mode, which usually put Meg into the Placater mode – anything for peace, even at the expense of feelings. One way to cope with the Blamer is to adopt the Computer mode. A Computer has no feelings, does not react from an emotional base. Everything directed at the Computer is filtered through the impersonal screen that deflects the other person's feelings. Computers work very hard at not saying 'I', for that would be too personal. The Computer response is aimed at taking the heat off. It helps the target person by putting the question back at the sender. Meg was able to achieve some success and a little success paves the way for other successes.

Further reading

Satir, V. (1972) *Peoplemaking*. Science and Behaviour Books, Palo Alto, CA.
AVANTA The Virginia Satir Network,, 2104 SW 152nd Street #2, Burien WA 98166 USA.
   Tel: 206 241 7566. Fax: 206 241 7527. Email: office@avanta.net.

COMPETITION VERSUS COOPERATION

Cooperation is a coordinated effort to reach mutual goals; competition is the struggle that occurs when we try to maximise our own rewards at the expense of others. Competition and cooperation can be regarded as opposite ends of a continuum of human interaction. At the one end are what could be considered positive outcomes – actions that result in gains for all. At the other end are negative outcomes, which result in one person or group gaining at the expense of other people or groups. Generally we will choose either one or the other, depending on the situation and what we stand to gain from either orientation.

Many societies are intensely competitive and this is obvious throughout all sections from a very early age. This statement will be easily confirmed by studying a group of children playing at school – how they will strive for mastery over other children.

It could be argued that competition is a natural tendency, and it could quite well be, but it could equally be argued that it is a natural instinct to kill. We are encouraged in one activity and positively discouraged in the other. It is also possible that competition is a relatively harmless channelling of this primitive drive. At the same time as competition is encouraged at school, in sports, at work and in many other areas of life, attempts are made to foster cooperation. Undue competition at work may be quite a significant factor in producing intolerable levels of stress in certain individuals.

Competition has more excitement, more immediate thrill to it than cooperation; for example, the thrill of the downhill ski competition is immediately appealing because of the high level of adrenalin produced.

Whatever the outcome, physiological or psychological, the question that must be asked is: Can highly competitive people move easily into an essentially cooperative role?

The language of business, politics and education is dotted with win–lose terms. One 'wins' promotion or 'beats' the competition. Students strive to 'top the class' or 'outsmart the teacher'. Although we do recognise cooperative effort and collaboration, it seems that we tend to emphasise 'healthy' competition. Competition means an event or contest in which people compete. Generally we compete against other people who represent the opposition.

Examples of competitive behaviour:

- Interrupting when others are talking
- Getting one's own ideas across
- Not acknowledging other people's contribution or ideas
- Forming partnerships and power blocks to get one's own way.

Examples of cooperative behaviour:

- A football team, even though the focus is competition
- An orchestra; every person playing their part to produce a whole.

We so easily drop into competing when the situation would benefit from co-operation. Win–lose contests can also develop in an organisation. People strive for dominant positions. Battles rage between departments. People sabotage new ideas in order to prove that they won't work. Although there are instances where win–lose is positive, it is often destructive. Win–lose is a poison to relationships. Win–lose is a stressor that interferes with working effectiveness. Win–lose 'victories' often turn into lose–lose for both parties.

Summary of win–lose/win–win:

- Win–lose is characterised by each person seeking his own advantage, usually to the detriment of the other person – the 'win at all costs' approach.
- Lose–win is where one person decides in advance to yield to pressure. In the lose–win approach, one party seeks the acceptance of the other party. This is the 'peace-at-any-price' approach – appeasement.
- Win–win is characterised by each person seeking an agreement that provides joint gain. This is the 'everybody's-a-winner' approach.
- In a mixed approach, each person strives to be realistic. Both persons realise that usually one wins more than the other.

Applied to counselling

Counsellors must learn to cooperate with their clients; if we do not learn to do this, the client's needs will not be fully met. The spirit of competition, harmless on the playing field, may spell disaster in relationships where, instead of fighting to gain possession of a ball or to score a goal, each person is constantly trying to dominate the other, to gain possession of an emotional ball.

Counsellors have to cooperate with clients and not compete with them. The counsellor who enters into a spirit of competition with the client is sure to end up in conflict with him. It is possible that the seeds of competition lie deeply buried in some emotion or experience that is reawakened by contact with a particular client.

On the other hand, if the counsellor is someone who always wants to win, always wants to score, always wants to get on top, then cooperating with the client may prove difficult. A client who is prepared to cooperate may very well be swamped by a competitive counsellor and be persuaded to make choices that have mental rather than emotional assent.

A highly competitive client may try very hard to engage the counsellor in a competition rather than in exploring the problem. If the counsellor does not 'play the game', conflict may be generated within the client. This could very well be the spark to kindle the desire to change.

Further reading

Hersey, P., Blanchard, K.H. and Natemeyer, W.E. (1979) *Situational Leadership, Perception, and the Impact of Power*. Leadership Studies, Escondido, CA.

Wiley, G.E. (1973) Win/lose situations. In: *Annual Handbook for Group Facilitators*. University Associates, San Diego, CA.

COMPLEXES

A complex is a group of associated ideas that are emotionally charged and have been partially or wholly repressed. These are usually outside awareness and evoke emotional forces that influence a person's behaviour.

Complexes are archetypal in character, have their origins in early relationships with parents and significant others, and have a 'magnetic' quality that attracts associated ideas and memories to them.

A complex may arise from the personal unconscious, from the collective unconscious or from both. Complexes always contain the characteristics of a conflict – shock, upheaval, mental agony, inner strife.

Complexes are the 'sore spots', the 'skeletons in the cupboard' that come unbidden to terrorise us and always contain memories, wishes, fears, duties, needs or insights that somehow we can never really grapple with.

They constantly interfere with our conscious life in disturbing and usually harmful ways. The presence of complexes acts as an obstacle to new possibilities of achievement of growth. They act as filters through which life is perceived.

Castration complex

In psychoanalytic theory, castration is the unconscious fear of losing the male genital organs or the feeling (in the female) that they have already been lost. Boys fear punishment by castration from their fathers because of their (unconscious) wish for a sexual relationship with their mothers, leading to castration anxiety.

Girls, so the theory goes, feel that the punishment has already been carried out; that is why they do not have a penis; they therefore have a residual penis envy. Female analysts, however, have pointed out that many males can be as envious of the reproductive power of females as females are of the male's penis.

The concept of castration complex is controversial, especially outside psychoanalysis. Not all psychoanalysts of Freud's era, or since, totally agreed with Freud. The question must also be asked: Who is the castrator? Does the threat arise from without or within?

In the 19th century the threat of castration was often used as a deterrent against masturbation. Freud linked the castration complex with the incest taboo, for which it serves as a major prohibition.

People who constantly undermine the self-confidence of others are said to be castrating. It can apply to females who, because of penis envy, are constantly disparaging men and are aggressively competitive towards them.

The term also applies to men who undermine their sons. An extension of the word is where men make a habit of putting women down and do their best to make them feel incompetent and second-rate.

If this and other complexes remain unresolved and persist into adult life, they can produce disturbances in the person's love relationships and ability to work productively. There is also the suggestion that castration anxiety is part of some sexual perversions.

In these days, the idea of the castration complex may seem outmoded but, although the modern term is castration anxiety, castration complex is still very much a part of psychological language and part of the wider myth.

Electra complex

In mythology, Electra was the daughter of the Greek leader Agamemnon and his wife Clytemnestra. Electra saved the life of her brother, Orestes, by sending him away when their father was murdered. Later, when he returned, she helped him avenge their father's death by slaying their mother and her lover, by whom Agamemnon had been killed.

Freud adopted the term as the female equivalent of the Oedipus complex, although it is rarely used in modern psychoanalysis. It is where a female child has an erotic attraction to her father, accompanied by hostility toward her mother.

Oedipus complex

This is a psychoanalytic concept derived from the Greek myth in which Oedipus, unknowingly, falls in love with his mother and kills the rival for his love, his father.

The oedipal triangle – father, mother and child – applies equally to male and female children during the 'phallic' stage of development, about three–five years. It is during this stage of development, in psychoanalytic theory, that the loving desire for the parent of the opposite sex reaches a climax. Feelings of intense rivalry are generated towards the parent of the same sex, who is the real love partner.

The rivalry resurfaces during adolescence, to be finally resolved when the young person chooses a love partner who is not the parent.

The 'Electra complex' is the female equivalent, although the resolution of the conflict is different for male and female children. The male child perceives the threat of castration by his father, so he gives up his incestuous desires toward his mother. The conflict for the female child culminates in her recognition that she has no penis – castration has already taken place. The resolution of the oedipal conflict leads to the formation of the superego and the internalisation of the prohibitions and taboos of society.

Repressed oedipal wishes provide fertile ground for irrational guilt in later life. If relationships between child and parents are loving and basically non-traumatic, and if parental attitudes are neither excessively prohibitive nor excessively sexually stimulating, the oedipal stage is passed through without difficulty. Children subjected to trauma are likely candidates for 'infantile neurosis'; an important forerunner of similar reactions in adult life.

Melanie Klein believed that Freud interpreted the myth too literally. For her, the complex started during the first year of life and unresolved oedipal conflict did not necessarily set the scene for all future neuroses.

It is possible that the Oedipus complex is never totally resolved or overwhelmed, as Freud suggested, but that it persists in varying degrees throughout life.

Freud also applied the myth to the whole of society and in all cultures. Every social and psychological phenomenon Freud related to the Oedipus complex. However much the concept may be open to criticism, the central place of the triangle of mother, father and child is an important concept in any school of psychotherapy.

Inferiority complex

This is a term used in individual (Adlerian) psychology to describe exaggerated feelings of inadequacy or insecurity resulting in defensive and neurotic behaviour. Inferiority complexes are usually abnormal.

As a result of its initial helplessness, an infant feels inferior and strives to overcome this feeling of incompleteness by developing to a higher level. The feeling of inferiority and compensating for that feeling becomes the prime motivator in moving the person from one level of development to another. Adler refers to this as the 'great upward drive' towards perfection.

Constant incapability, discouragement from others, faulty self-evaluation of one's own worth, abetted by being put down and ridiculed, all sow the seeds of inferiority.

People who view themselves against others on a vertical plane (a typical hierarchy) are bound to put themselves either higher or lower (better or worse) than someone else.

People who view relationships on a horizontal plane are more likely to adopt a view of equality, each recognising his/her own unique attributes and contributions.

Superiority complex

In literal terms this means the conviction that one is better than or superior to others. Adler used the term to describe the mechanism of striving for recognition and superiority as a compensation for the feelings of inferiority, inadequacy and insecurity.

Inferiority is acted upon through the processes of socialisation and education. The superiority complex helps to rid the developing child of feelings of inferiority.

The striving for power and dominance may become so exaggerated and intensified that it then must be called pathological. When this happens, the ordinary relationships of life will never be satisfactory.

The pathological drive to achieve power is characterised by:

- Effort
- Haste and impatience

- Violent impulsiveness
- Lack of consideration for others
- Dominance from an early age
- Defensiveness
- Feeling of being against the world and the world being against one
- Achievements that do not benefit anyone but oneself
- Trampling on others to get to the top
- Lack of importance attached to human relationships
- Pride, vanity and the desire to conquer
- Constantly putting other people down in order to elevate oneself
- A marked distance between oneself and other people
- Joy in life is rarely experienced.

Further reading

Adler, A. (1956) *The Individual Psychology of Alfred Adler* (eds H.L. Ansbacher and R.R. Ansbacher). Basic Books, New York.

Hamilton, V. (1982) *Narcissus and Oedipus.* Routledge & Kegan Paul, London.

Jung, C.G. (1958) *The Collected Works – Psychological Types*, vol. 6. Routledge & Kegan Paul, London.

Klein, M. (1932) *The Psychoanalysis of Children.* L. and V. Woolf, Institute of Psychoanalysis.

Weiner, M.F. and Mohl, P.C. (1995) Theories of personality and psychopathology: other psychodynamic schools. In: *Comprehensive Textbook of Psychiatry*, 6th edn (eds H.J. Kaplan and B.J. Sadock). Williams & Wilkins, Baltimore, MD.

COMPLIANCE

Compliance is a response to social influence in which the person towards whom the influence is directed publicly conforms to the wishes of the influencing source but does not change his private beliefs or attitudes. This is termed 'public compliance' and may or may not lead to private attitude change.

When a source obtains compliance by setting an example, it is called conformity; when a source obtains compliance by wielding authority, it is called obedience; e.g. the child eats tapioca pudding but continues to dislike it. In compliance the person does not need to believe in what he is doing.

Forced 'compliance' (also called induced compliance), on the other hand, is when a person is induced to make a public declaration which is contrary to his previously held attitudes.

The term 'compliance' has a different meaning in health care, where it refers to a patient's adherence to a treatment programme prescribed by a doctor. Faulty compliance can represent a serious problem to the patient's wellbeing and mental health.

Karen Horney (1885–1952), the German-born American psychoanalyst, departed from some of the basic principles of Sigmund Freud, suggesting that environmental and social conditions, rather than biological drives, determine much of individual personality and are the chief causes of neuroses and personality disorders. Horney developed a theory of neurosis that included the 'compliant character'.

According to Horney, neurosis is a disturbance in the relationship between self and others. Feelings of helplessness and despair drive us into making decisions that are not fulfilling and leave us feeling dissatisfied. Such feelings (formed early in childhood into defensive patterns) are self-perpetuating strategies against anxiety. Three strategies are available to the child in its search for safety:

- **Compliant, self-effacing**: Moving towards others, seeking affection approval – this 'moving towards' only emphasises helplessness
- **Aggressive, expansive**: Moving against others and in so doing accepting a hostile environment
- **Detached, resigned**: Moving away from others and in so doing accepting the difficulty of relating to people at an intimate level.

Behaviour, then, is influenced by whichever one of these strategies is found to bring the greatest rewards. Only one strategy is used, so the child does not explore the feelings and impulses of the other two. A deep sense of instability is thus created, which leads to ever greater restriction and repression of genuine feelings. Feelings are mistrusted and projected on to the outside world, where they develop into neurotic trends.

The compliant, self-effacing, moving-towards type seeks constant approval, is highly dependent, is ultra-sensitive to others' needs, constantly subordinates himself; is poor on assertiveness, values goodness, sympathy and ultra-unselfishness and tends to panic at the first hint of rejection.

Clients who tend towards being compliant are likely to agree with whatever the counsellor suggests, however tentatively it is put. They are also likely to be very clinging and not open to being challenged, for this would be interpreted as rejection. These two behaviours alone make progress difficult and the counsellor may be left with the feeling of treading very carefully on eggshells.

Further reading

Horney, K. (1937) *The Neurotic Personality of Our Time*. W.W. Norton, New York.

CONCRETENESS

To get clients to be concrete or specific may, at times, be quite difficult, yet it is essential if they are to come to terms fully with whatever is causing them concern. The counsellor picks up on generalisations, omissions and distortions.

The opposite of being concrete, direct and specific is making generalised, indirect and vague statements. So often, in general conversation, as well as in counselling, we confuse the issue by not being concrete, specific and direct.

A generalisation does not discriminate but lumps all parts together. A generality, common in everyday speech, is 'you'. Clients who say, 'You never know when people approve of what you're doing', when encouraged to rephrase it to, 'I never know when people approve of what I'm doing', will usually be able to perceive their statement in a different light. The client needs to be able to identify thoughts, feelings, behaviour and experiences in specific ways.

Personalising a statement in this way makes it pertinent and real. In one sense it is 'owning the problem'. Being specific opens the way for a realistic acknowledgement of feelings. Owning and not merely reporting such feelings opens the door to exploring them. While this may be uncomfortable for the client, it is vital.

Sometimes thoughts, feelings and behaviours are expressed before the counselling relationship has been established firmly enough to explore them. That is why, in Egan's model, concreteness is a second-stage skill. If such thoughts, feelings and behaviours are central to the client's problem the client will return to them at some stage.

Concreteness requires clients to be prepared to examine themselves closely and not to hide behind the facade of generality. Clients may fiercely resist attempts to encourage them to be specific, particularly about feelings. They may have to be led gently into what, for many, is a new experience.

Counsellors can collude with clients by allowing them to talk about feelings second-hand, as if they belonged to other people and not to them. 'I wonder if this is how you feel?' or 'It sounds as if that is something like your situation' may be enough to bring the interview back into focus from second-hand reporting to 'This is what is happening to me, now'.

Counsellors who themselves speak in generalities would find it difficult to challenge a client about not being concrete.

Further reading

Egan, G. (2002) *The Skilled Helper: A problem-management and opportunity-development approach to helping.* 7th ed., Brooks/Cole, Pacific Grove, CA.
Sutton, J. and Stewart, W. (2002) *Learning to Counsel.* How to Books, Oxford.

CONFLICT

Conflict is a psychological state of indecision, where the person is faced simultaneously with two opposing forces of equal strength that cannot be solved together.

Types of conflict

- Choice between positives both of which are desirable: approach–approach. Chance factors determine the outcome, e.g. the choice between two attractive careers.
- Choice between negatives, where both are undesirable: avoidance–avoidance. For example, a man may dislike his job intensely but fears the threat of unemployment if he resigns.
- Choice between negative and positive: approach–avoidance. This creates great indecision, helplessness and anxiety, e.g. in a child, dependent on her mother, who also fears her because she is rejecting and punitive.

Conflicts are often unconscious, in the sense that the person cannot clearly identify the source of the distress. Many strong impulses, such as fear and hostility, are not approved of by society, so children soon learn not to acknowledge them, even to themselves. When such impulses are in conflict, we are anxious without knowing why.

Related concepts are cognitive dissonance and Kurt Lewin's field theory.

Conflicts may be avoided or resolved by:

- Active listening
- Appropriate disclosure.

Poorly handled, conflicts can result in negative behaviours such as:

- Aggression
- Defiance
- Forming alliances
- Gossiping
- Physical and psychological withdrawal
- Retaliation.

Conflict resolution is strongly influenced by feelings of self-worth. People with low self-worth expect to be treated badly; they expect the worst, invite it and generally get it.

People who do not feel confident generally feel small and, therefore, view others as threateningly larger.

Thinking about resolving conflict:

- Identify the rules that encourage conflict.
- How much autonomy do people have and give?
- How much do we control each other?
- Identify 'musts', 'oughts' and 'shoulds'.
- Examine attributions (see Transactional analysis).
- Who blames whom and for what?
- What are the risks and gains of resolution?
- Are there any possible compromises?
- What roles sustain the conflict?
- What 'games' do people play? (see Transactional analysis).

Helping people change:

- Teach assertiveness.
- Use video feedback.
- Teach empathic listening.
- Develop open communication.
- Concentrate on changeable behaviour.
- Work at a time free from distractions.
- Teach how to give specific and non-evaluative feedback.
- Encourage the giving of written contracts.
- Explore agreed areas.
- Be an example of an effective, caring communicator.

Conflict: a problem-solving model

Let each person:

- Describe the situation as they see it.
- Describe what they feel about the conflict and what personal meaning it has for them.
- Describe a desired situation.
- Identify changes necessary to achieve the desired situation.
- Outline a problem-solving agenda or plan of action.

Further reading

Deutsch, M. (1973) *The Resolution of Conflict*. Yale University Press, New Haven, CT.

Lewin, K. (1969) Quasi-stationary social equilibria and the problem of permanent change. In: Bennis, W.G., Benner, K.D. and Chin, R. (eds) *The Planning of Change*. Holt, Rinehart and Winston, New York.

Main, A.P. and Roark, A.E. (1975) A consensus method to reduce conflict. *Personnel and Guidance Journal*, 53: 754–759.

CONTRACT

A contract is a formal, explicit agreement between counsellor and client. A contract helps to ensure the professional nature of the relationship and may include:

- Venue
- Frequency of sessions
- Boundaries of confidentiality
- Broad requirements of the treatment
- Duties and responsibilities of each party
- Goals of therapy
- Means by which the goals may be achieved
- The provision and completion of 'homework'
- The setting of boundaries and expectations
- The terms of the therapeutic relationship
- Time limits – of sessions and of counselling
- Provision for renegotiation of contract
- Fees, if appropriate
- How therapy will be evaluated
- Process of referral, if and when necessary
- Supervision.

The contract may be written, signed by both therapist and client or each person in a group.

In family therapy, the children need to be included in the terms of the contract – how, and at what age, needs to be considered. In group therapy, part of the contract would include a full and frank discussion on 'ground rules'.

The British Association for Counselling and Psychotherapy Code of Ethics and Practice for Counsellors says this about contracts:

Counsellors are responsible for reaching agreement with their clients about the terms on which counselling is being offered, including availability, the degree of confidentiality offered, arrangements for the payment of any fees, cancelled appointments and other significant matters. The communication of essential terms and any negotiations should be concluded by having reached a clear agreement before the client incurs any commitment or liability of any kind.

Further reading

Sager, C.J. (1976) *Marriage Contracts and Couple Therapy.* Brunner/Mazel, New York.

Sutton, J. and Stewart, W. (2002) *Learning to Counsel: develop the skills you need to counsel others*, 2nd edn. How to Books, Oxford.

CORE CONDITIONS (SEE ALSO: BIBLICAL BASIS FOR COUNSELLING)

The core conditions are the relationship qualities embraced in most humanistic therapies and considered to be crucial in person-centred counselling.

The core conditions are:

- Empathy
- Genuineness or congruence
- Warmth
- Unconditional positive regard.

Empathy

Mearns and Thorne say this of empathy:

One of the central dimensions of the therapeutic relationship is empathy. Brief definitions seldom capture the full meaning of processes, but as a prelude to the more complete description offered in this chapter, the following might suffice: Empathy is a continuing process whereby the counsellor lays aside her own way of experiencing and perceiving reality, preferring to sense and respond to the experiences and perceptions of her client. This sensing may be intense and enduring with the counsellor actually experiencing her client's thoughts and feelings as powerfully as if they had originated in herself.

Empathy is thus the ability of one person to step into the inner world of another person and to step out of it again, without becoming that other person. An example is the singer or actor who genuinely feels the part he is performing.

It means trying to understand the thoughts, feelings, behaviours and personal meanings from the other's internal frame of reference.

For empathy to mean anything, we have to respond in such a way that the other person feels that understanding has been reached or is being striven for. Unless our understanding is communicated it is of no therapeutic value.

Empathy is to feel 'with'. Sympathy is to feel 'like'. Pity is to feel 'for'.

Empathy is not a state that one reaches, nor a qualification that one is awarded. It is a transient thing. We can move into it and lose it again very quickly. Literally, it means 'getting alongside'.

Empathy is the central core condition of the person-centred approach, although therapists from a wide range of approaches rank empathy as being one of the highest qualities a therapist can demonstrate.

Levels of empathy are related to the degree to which the client is able to explore and reach self-understanding. It can be taught within an empathic climate.

Primary empathy works more with surface or stated facts and feelings; advanced empathy works more with implied facts and feelings.

The difference between empathy and identification is that in identification the 'as if' quality is absent. We have become the other person.

Some client statements about counsellor empathy:

- 'Helps me to learn a lot about myself'
- 'Understands how I see things'
- 'Understands me'
- 'Can read me like a book'
- 'Is able to put my feelings into words'
- 'Knows what it's like to feel ill'.

In their book (page 42), Mearns and Thorne give a useful empathy scale.

Genuineness or congruence

Genuineness is the degree to which we are freely and deeply ourselves and are able to relate to people in a sincere and undefensive manner. Also referred to as authenticity, congruence or truth, genuineness is the precondition for empathy and unconditional positive regard.

Mearns and Thorne define congruence as: 'the state or being of the counsellor when her outward responses to her client consistently match the inner feelings and sensations which she has in relation to the client' (page 74).

Effective therapy depends wholly on the degree to which the therapist is integrated and genuine. In person-centred counselling, skill and technique play a much less important role than relating to the client authentically. Genuineness encourages client self-disclosure.

Appropriate therapist disclosure enhances genuineness. The genuine therapist does not feel under any compulsion to disclose, either about events, situations or feeling aroused within the counselling relationship.

An essential element in genuineness is that it is not a role adopted specially for the counselling relationship. If it were, then it would be false. This means that in all our relationships we strive to be genuine.

Some client statements about counsellor genuineness:

- 'What she says never conflicts with what she feels'
- 'He is himself in our relationship'

- 'I don't think she hides anything from herself that she feels with me'
- 'Doesn't avoid anything that is important for our relationship'
- 'I feel I can trust her to be honest with me'
- 'Is secure in our relationship'
- 'Doesn't try to mislead me about her own thoughts or feelings'
- 'Is impatient with me at times'
- 'Is sometimes upset by what I say'
- 'Sometimes looks as worried as I feel'
- 'Treats me with obvious concern'.

J.R. Gibb gives the following guidelines on being role-free:

- **Do not over-emphasise the helping role**: Genuine helpers do not take refuge in the role of counsellor.
- **Be spontaneous**: Be tactful and respectful, but do not let caution stop you being natural.
- **Avoid defensiveness**: Try to examine negative criticism honestly.
- **Be open**: Use deeper levels of self-disclosure when and if it is appropriate. Be open with no hidden agendas: 'What you see is what you get.'

Non-possessive warmth:

- Is genuine
- Springs from an attitude of friendliness towards others – a relationship in which friendliness is absent will not flourish
- Makes us feel comfortable
- Is liberating
- Is non-demanding
- Melts the coldness and hardness within people's hearts.

Possessive warmth, on the other hand:

- Is false
- Makes us feel uncomfortable and wary
- Is more for the needs of the giver than for the receiver
- Is smothering and cloying
- Robs us of energy.

Warmth is conveyed by:

- **Body language**: Posture, proximity, personal space, facial expressions, eye contact
- **Words and the way we speak**: Tone of voice, delivery, rate of speech and the use of non-words – all these are 'paralinguistics'.

All the indicators of warmth – the non-verbal parts of speech and body language – must be in agreement with the words used; any discrepancy between the words and how we deliver them will cause confusion in the other person.

Warmth, like a hot water bottle, must be used with great care. Someone who is very cold, distant, cynical and mistrustful could feel threatened by someone else's depth of warmth. A useful analogy would be to think how an iceberg would react in the presence of the sun.

Some client statements about counsellor warmth:

- 'Always responds to me with warmth and interest'
- 'Her feelings towards me do not depend on how I feel towards her'
- 'I can express whatever feelings I want and she remains the same towards me'
- 'I can be very critical of her or very appreciative without it changing her feelings towards me'.

Ways of communicating warmth

Mearns and Thorne give the following ten guidelines for communicating warmth:

1. Going to the door to meet the client
2. Shaking hands with the client
3. Using the client's first name
4. Smiling
5. Using a 'warm' tone of voice
6. Holding eye contact
7. Genuinely laughing as the client recounts a funny incident
8. Agreeing to extend the session where that is possible and appropriate
9. Using words to show warmth, showing genuine interest in the client, physically moving towards the client, touching the client's arm, touching the client's shoulder, holding hands, hugging the client.

Unconditional positive regard (UPR)

This is a non-possessive caring and acceptance of the client, irrespective of how offensive the client's behaviour might be. The counsellor who offers unconditional positive regard helps to create a climate that encourages trust within the counselling relationship. It is where we communicate a deep and genuine caring, filtered through our own feelings, thoughts and behaviours.

Mearns and Thorne define it thus:

Unconditional positive regard is the label given to the fundamental attitude of the person-centred counsellor towards her client. The counsellor who holds this attitude deeply values the humanity of her client and is not deflected in that valuing by any particular client behaviours. The attitude manifests itself in the counsellor's consistent acceptance of and enduring warmth towards her client.

Conditional regard, on the other hand, implies enforced control and compliance with behaviour dictated by someone else.

Some client statements about counsellor unconditional positive regard:

- 'She always seems very concerned about me'
- 'Always appreciates me'
- 'Thinks I'm a worthwhile person'
- 'Still likes me even if I criticise her'
- 'I feel safe with her'
- 'I feel free to be myself'
- 'Makes it OK to talk about anything'
- 'Seems to trust my feelings about myself'
- 'Would never knowingly hurt me'.

When the core conditions are present and appropriately expressed, a climate is created in which a positive therapeutic outcome is likely. When clients are in a relationship in which the core conditions are demonstrated, they will learn to relate to themselves with respect and dignity.

Criticism of the core conditions centres more on their efficiency than their necessity. Some theorists argue that, while the core conditions must be present, by themselves they are insufficient. Other interventions are necessary.

There is a body of opinion that neither a 'relationship' nor a 'skills' approach is sufficient. Both are needed. This would depend on the nature of the problem and the personality of both client and counsellor. Counsellors generally choose an approach or method that suits their personality.

Further reading

Barrett-Leonard, G.T. (1981) The empathy cycle: refinement of a nuclear concept. *Journal of Counselling Psychology*, **28**: 91–100.

Gibb, J.R. (1968) The counsellor as a role-free person. In: Parker, C.A. (ed.) *Counseling theories and counselor education*. Houghton Mifflin, Boston.

Mearns, D. and Thorne, B. (1988) *Person-centred Counselling in Action*. Sage Publications, London.

Rogers, C.R. (1961) *On Becoming a Person: a therapist's view of psychotherapy*. Constable, London.

Rogers, C.R. (1967) *The Therapeutic Relationship and its Impact*. Greenwood Press, Westport, CT.

Rogers, C.R. (1975) Empathic: an unappreciated way of being. *Counselling Psychologist*, **3**: 2–10.

Rogers, C.R. and Truax, C.B. (1967) The therapeutic conditions antecedent to change: a theoretical view. In: *The Therapeutic Relationship and its Impact* (ed. C.R. Rogers). University of Wisconsin Press, Madison, WI.

Thorne, B. (1987) Beyond the core conditions. In: *Key Cases in Psychotherapy* (ed. W. Dryden). Croom Helm, London.

COUNSELLING ETHICS

Counselling and psychotherapy have incurred criticism because of the lack of a common frame of reference for practitioners. The British Association for Counselling and Psychotherapy issues guidelines to its members.

The following has been constructed by the author along the lines of the International Code of Medical Ethics, although this does not imply approval by any counselling body.

The therapeutic relationship

Counsellors should:

- Make clear and explicit contracts with their clients
- Ensure that the counselling relationship does not exploit clients
- Use all their skill to discourage clients from becoming dependent on the counsellor and on the relationship
- Use all their skill to encourage personal autonomy of their clients
- Ensure that they do not collude with clients against other people
- Ensure that they do not sexually exploit their clients
- Handle transference and counter-transference skilfully and to the benefit of both themselves and their clients
- Ensure that they do not enforce or impose value or attitude change on their clients
- Ensure the physical and psychological safety of their clients
- Ensure that they do not intrude, coerce or use persuasion
- Ensure that their need for regular supervision is discussed with clients
- Make explicit to clients the nature and extent of confidentiality of records, whether handwritten or computerised, to third parties, such as the courts, other agencies or case conferences.

Competence of counsellors

Counsellors should:

- Recognise and work within limits of their competency
- Recognise their own needs
- Regularly update their knowledge, experience and technical skill
- Ensure that they seek regular supervision
- Know when to refer clients and to whom.

Responsibilities

Counsellors should:

- Exercise responsibility towards their clients by maintaining their effectiveness and ability
- Exercise responsibility to themselves to stay fresh and to protect their private and social life
- Exercise responsibility to the counselling relationship by monitoring their performance
- Exercise responsibility to their clients through personal and professional development
- Exercise responsibility to their colleagues and other professionals
- Exercise responsibility to the wider community, so as not to reduce confidence in counselling
- Exercise responsibility to know and work within the law of the land

- Exercise responsibility to be aware of the requirements of the law regarding client confidentiality.

Other issues

Counsellors should:

- Ensure the accuracy of their advertisements and announcements
- Ensure that research material and writings preserve client anonymity
- Ensure that ethical conflicts are resolved through discussion.

Ethical decisions

Speaking of ethical decisions, Gerald Corey says:

> *As a practitioner you will ultimately have to apply the ethical codes of your profession to the many practical problems you face. You will not be able to rely on ready-made answers or prescriptions given by professional organisations, which typically provide only broad guidelines for responsible practice. Part of the process of making ethical decisions involves learning about the resources from which you can draw when you are struggling with an ethical question. Although you are ultimately responsible for making ethical decisions, you do not have to do so in a vacuum. You should also be aware of the consequences of practising in ways that are not sanctioned by organisations of which you are a member or the state in which you are licensed to practise. Professional maturity implies that you are open to questioning and that you are willing to discuss your quandaries with colleagues. Because ethical codes do not make decisions for you, demonstrate a willingness to struggle, to raise questions, to discuss ethical concerns with others, and to continually clarify your values and examine your motivations. To the degree that it is possible, include the client at all phases of the ethical decision-making process.*

These are wise words. He goes on to outline some steps in ethical decision-making:

- **Identify the problem or dilemma:** Gather information that will shed light on the nature of the problem. This will help you decide whether the problem is mainly ethical, legal, professional, clinical or moral.
- **Identify the potential issues:** Evaluate the rights, responsibilities and welfare of all those who are involved in the situation.
- **Look at the relevant ethics codes for general guidance on the matter:** Consider whether your own values and ethics are consistent with or in conflict with the relevant guidelines.
- **Know the applicable laws and regulations:** It is essential to determine whether any laws or regulations have a bearing on the ethical dilemma.
- **Seek consultation from more than one source to obtain various perspectives on the dilemma:** Obtain consultation with professionals who are knowledgeable about the issues involved in the situation under question.

- **Brainstorm various possible courses of action:** Continue discussing options with other professionals. Include the client in this process of considering options for action.
- **Enumerate the consequences of various decisions,** and reflect on the implications of each course of action for your client. Again, include the client in this process.
- **Decide on what appears to be the best possible course of action:** Once the course of action has been implemented, follow up to evaluate the outcomes and to determine if further action is necessary.

Further reading

Code of Ethics and Practice for Counsellors (AGM/9/90) British Association for Counselling and Psychotherapy, 1 Regent Place, Rugby, Warwickshire, CV21 2PJ.

Corey, G. et al. (1979) Professional and ethical issues. In *Counseling and Psychotherapy*. Brooks/Cole, Pacific Grove, CA.

Corey, G. (2001) *Theory and Practice of Counseling and Psychotherapy*, 6th edn. Wadsworth, Brooks/Cole, Pacific Grove, CA.

COUNSELLING GUIDELINES

These guidelines are offered from my own work as a teacher. When given to a group, they generate lively discussion.

1. Skill and art

Counselling is a balance between skill and art. Some people may be very skilled in the theory but lack the art; some may have a natural flair and would be more effective if they acquired some of the theory. Learning any job demands hard work and patience; counselling is no different.

2. Generate alternatives

Get agreement that there is a problem; that something is unacceptable. Then explore alternatives that are acceptable to the other person. People who are free to choose, however difficult the decision, are more likely to be committed to change.

3. Don't argue

We all tend to increase our resistance to match the force of an argument raised against us. Don't get into a 'win–lose' interaction.

4. Be prepared to listen

Being prepared to listen to people and help them explore what's bothering them does not mean we have to agree with them. Give people time and space to think, feel and talk.

5. Focus on behaviour

When we direct attention to specific behaviour that people are able to change, they will feel more in control and less under attack.

6. Give feedback

Concentrate less on what has gone wrong and more on what can be changed, and how and what the benefits of that change might be. Negative feedback should be given in small doses. Small changes achieved over a long period of time have more chance of success.

7. People have feelings

Try to see the world through their eyes; from their frame of reference.

8. Be careful of advice

Advice that opens alternatives is helpful. If the other person has a weakness in a specific, clearly measurable aspect of the job, coaching may be necessary and direct advice may be appropriate. If, however, the problem lies in a clash of attitudes, values or interpersonal difficulties, direct advice in the form of 'If I were you...' is inappropriate. More will be achieved if the person's feelings are understood.

9. Ask skilled questions

Since the purpose is to help the person solve a problem, past facts are far less important than present feelings and attitudes. Remember! Strong, negative feelings act as stoppers to thinking or expressing positive feelings and interfere with full functioning.

10. Watch for signals

Become aware of verbal and non-verbal cues that signal the person's willingness to start looking at the possibility of change. Once a person assumes responsibility for overcoming his own shortcomings, our task is almost complete.

11. Impartiality

Counselling aims at objectivity. Total objectivity is seldom, if ever, achieved. Partiality interferes with objectivity – so be careful about being pulled over to the side of the client against someone else. It is easy to become partial, especially when our own feelings about the other person are involved. For instance, the client is complaining about person 'A' and you don't like 'A' very much. Unless you are very careful your dislike of 'A' may affect your judgement of the situation.

12. Authority and power

You have a certain authority and power by virtue of your role. Do not use that authority to persuade the client to make a decision he would rather not make.

13. Other people

Do not allow the focus of the interview to be drawn away from the client by discussing other people unless their behaviour has a direct bearing on the situation. It is far better to concentrate on the way the client's behaviour has been affected as a result of interaction with the person in question.

14. Personal experiences

Be careful what you say about yourself. You may be tempted to use an experience from your own life to illustrate a point. This may be interpreted as 'I can see she copes, but does she see that I can't?'

Sometimes a personal experience can be used effectively. For instance, the client may be trying desperately to get a specific point over but cannot bring himself to spell it out. If you think that you have got his message, a short personal experience will let him see that you do know what he is talking about. But remember: he is the one on whom the attention should be focused so don't let it remain on you longer than is necessary (see Self-disclosure).

15. Interpretations

Psychological interpretations are more appropriate to in-depth psychotherapy and psychoanalysis, which deal with personality change, and must be left to those qualified to make them.

16. Credibility

The perceived ability of the counsellor to possess the knowledge and skill required by the client together with the willingness to use them on behalf of the client.

The essential elements of credibility:

- Effective communication
- Empathy and warmth
- Expertness – qualifications and experience
- Reliability
- Reputation
- Trustworthiness.

COUNSELLING PROCESS (SEE ALSO: RELATIONSHIP PRINCIPLES)

The main aspects are:

- Getting on the client's wavelength and staying there
- Active listening and appropriate responding
- Remaining impartial and suspending judgement
- Using the skills of:
  - Attending
  - Paraphrasing the content
  - Reflecting feelings
  - Open questions
  - Summarising
  - Focusing

- – Challenging
- – Self-disclosure
- – Immediacy
- – Concreteness
- Waiting for a reply
- The constructive use of silences
- Keeping pace with the client
- Reading between the lines
- Demonstrating the principles of the counselling relationship:
  - – Individualisation
  - – Feelings
  - – Involvement
  - – Self-determination
  - – Confidentiality
  - – Acceptance
  - – Non-judgement
- Expressing understanding of the client's feelings
- Being able to enter the client's frame of reference
- Demonstrating empathy
- Expressing support
- Keeping the interview moving forwards
- Keeping objective when planning action
- Dealing with transference and counter-transference
- Saying goodbye constructively.

CREATIVITY (SEE ALSO: IMAGERY AND PSYCHOSYNTHESIS)

Most people are born with the ability to be creative, yet not everyone makes use of that potential. Conformity thwarts expression of creativity in the developing child. The spark of creativity will be extinguished if it is not given expression. Increasing personal effectiveness requires creativity, plus unlearning non-productive and self-defeating behaviours. Helping clients tap into their creative potential, particularly through the use of imagination and intuition, may help to restore an essential part they may have lost.

Creative people are generally:

- Open to experience
- Flexible in thinking
- Able to deal with conflicting information
- Not unduly swayed by criticism or praise.

Creativity develops within a psychologically safe environment in which there is acceptance, a non-judgemental attitude and freedom to think and feel.

Barriers to developing creativity

Barriers are mental fogs that prevent us from perceiving a problem correctly or conceiving possible solutions.

- **Perceptual – how we see things**: These barriers are recognised by:
  - Failure to use all the senses in observing
  - Failure to investigate the obvious
  - Inability to define terms
  - Difficulty in seeing abstract relationships
  - Failure to distinguish between cause and effect
  - Failure to use the unconscious, such as not using visualisation or fantasy
  - Inability to use the conscious mind, such as inability to organise data.
- **Cultural – how we ought to do things**: These barriers are recognised by:
  - A need to conform
  - An overemphasis on competition or on cooperation
  - A drive to be practical and economical at all costs
  - Belief that fantasy is time-wasting
  - Too much faith in reason and logic
  - A deep-seated need to find the proper setting and to give oneself every advantage
  - A work-orientated need to keep trying and to be always prepared and ready.
- **Emotional – how we feel about things**: These barriers are recognised by:
  - Fear of making mistakes
  - Fear and distrust of others
  - Grabbing the first idea that presents itself
  - Personal feelings of insecurity, such as low self-esteem
  - Feelings of anxiety, fear of criticism, fear of failure or lack of curiosity
  - Need for security, such as lack of risk-taking or of not trying new things.

Further reading

Cameron, J. (1995) *The Artist's Way*, Pan Books, London.
Hambrook, C. (2000) *Healing through Creativity, Speaking our Minds: an anthology.* Open University Press, Milton Keynes.
Martin, L.P. (1990) Inventory of barriers to creative thought and innovative action. In: *1990 Annual: Developing Human Resources.* University Associates, San Diego, CA.
Stewart, W. (1996) *Imagery and Symbolism in Counselling.* Jessica Kingsley, London.
Stewart, W. (1998) *Dictionary of Images and Symbols in Counselling.* Jessica Kingsley, London.
Stewart, W. (1998) *Self-counselling: how to develop the skills and the insights to positively manage your life.* How to Books, Oxford.

CRISIS COUNSELLING (SEE ALSO: POST-TRAUMATIC STRESS DISORDER)

A crisis is a limited period of acute psychological and emotional disorganisation brought about by a challenging or hazardous event.

Crisis counselling is a brief form of social and/or psychological treatment offered to people who are experiencing a personal crisis, whose usual methods of coping have proved ineffective. Their thinking, emotions and behaviours are all affected, and not coping adds one more factor to the stress they are experiencing.

Types of crisis intervention:

- Appropriate social and material assistance
- Emotional 'first aid' – supportive therapy, containment of the crisis and care, particularly during the early days following the event
- Crises, such as bereavement, have a similar meaning and effect upon individuals, regardless of their personalities, and can usually be approached in the same way
- A dynamic approach that helps the client understand current reactions to previous crises.

The goals of crisis intervention

Collins identifies the goals of crisis intervention as:

- To help the person cope effectively with the crisis situation and return to his usual level of functioning
- To decrease the anxiety, apprehension and other insecurities that may persist during the crisis and after it passes
- To teach crisis-management techniques so the person is better prepared to anticipate and deal with future crises.

Examples of crises:

- Addictions
- Birth of a disabled child
- Death of a relative or friend
- Disaster
- Divorce
- Family break-up
- Gender identity crisis
- Hearing bad news about self or a close relative
- Long-term illness
- Loss of part of the body
- Mental illness
- Rape or sexual assault
- Redundancy or retirement
- Sexual abuse
- Suicide or threatened suicide
- Terminal illness
- Wife/partner battering
- Witnessing a horrific event.

The objective of all crisis intervention is the restoration of psychological balance to at least what it was prior to the crisis. The aim is not insight or exploration of feelings or of working towards change but of coping with the immediate difficulty.

Dealing with crises usually means, initially, that a more direct approach is often appropriate, because the person's inner resources have been paralysed.

When someone needs to take control, the authoritarian person often turns up trumps. They are not afraid of action and are often excellent in emergencies.

Another plus for an authoritarian approach is when we recognise that the person is immobilised by some trauma, e.g. at a road accident or some other traumatic experience. Very often people in deep shock need others to take temporary control.

After the acute stage has passed, therapy should be directed towards:

- Helping the person to talk about the crisis
- Helping the client to think clearly
- Helping the client to focus on his wants and resources
- Catharsis and ventilation of feelings and to understand what it means from the client's frame of reference
- Nurturing self-esteem and positive self-image
- Developing problem-solving behaviour and coping skills
- Helping the client to formulate a plan to get what he wants
- Encouraging the client to act positively and realistically.

Crisis counselling means just that; it does not mean that the person takes on a commitment to long-term counselling. In fact, when a person is in crisis, the counsellor might be well advised to discourage the client from undertaking long-term counselling. People who are in crisis are already vulnerable and may take decisions that are not founded on reality. Just as post-traumatic stress disorder counselling is not mixed up with debriefing, so crisis counselling should not be mixed up with long-term counselling. A related point is possibly to help the person find support from friends and relatives, for this is part of what is normal.

One of the basic principles of counselling is that the client is helped to help himself. Thus in crisis, the object is to do no more for the client than will aid the client to do whatever is necessary for get himself back to normal.

Further reading

Collins, G.R. (1988) *Christian Counselling: a comprehensive guide.* Word Publishing, Nashville, TN.

Everstine, D.S. and Everstine, L. (1983) *People in Crisis.* Brunner/Mazel, New York.

Kennedy, E. (1981) *Crisis Counselling: the essential guide for non-professional counsellors.* Gill and Macmillan Ltd, Dublin.

Langsley, D.G. (1981) Crisis intervention: an update. In: *Current Psychiatric Therapies*, vol. 20 (ed. J.H. Masserman). Grune & Stratton, New York.

homepage.ntlworld.com/nick.heap/Careercounsbro.htm

D

DEFENCE MECHANISMS

Defence mechanisms (also called mental mechanisms) are unconscious mental processes that enable us to reach compromise solutions to problems that we are unable to resolve in any other way. These internal drives or feelings, which threaten to lower our self-esteem or to provoke anxiety, are concealed from our conscious mind. Thus they function to help us cope.

In Freudian theory, these unconscious drives are in conflict with one another and are the cause of mental disorders. Defence mechanisms are developed unconsciously to ward off internal and external dangers, and to protect the individual from being annihilated. Their purpose is thus to protect the ego and maintain the status quo by diverting anxiety away from consciousness. The functioning of the adult should be controlled by the perceptive and intelligent ego, and action by the ego ideally should satisfy the demands of id, superego and reality.

Defences are not necessarily pathological, even although the ego may not function adequately. They become pathological when they fail to ward off anxiety and when more defences have to be used to control the ego. Neurotic symptoms are then formed that interfere with pursuing a satisfactory way of living. Psychosis is where there is a complete breakdown of the defence system.

Although defence mechanisms derive from psychoanalytic theory, they have become widely used in psychology, even although some of the basic tenets may not apply other than in psychoanalysis. There is lack of agreement as to the number of defence mechanisms but there is agreement on the following characteristics:

- They manage instincts, drives and affect.
- They are unconscious.
- They are singular and distinct.
- They are dynamic and reversible.
- They can be adaptive (working for the individual) or pathological.

Defences do not remove the cause of the anxiety; they change the way we perceive, or think about, a situation. All defence mechanisms hide the truth and are therefore self-deceptive. We all use defence mechanisms at some time or other. They help us over rough patches until we are more able to deal with the stressful situation. They become pathological when a particular way of coping becomes so ingrained that we are oblivious to any other way of responding.

The defence mechanisms

- **Acting out:** Acting out is where the individual expresses an unconscious wish or impulse through action to avoid being conscious of the accompanying feeling.

- **Altruism**: Through this defence mechanism (similar to reaction formation) the individual experiences inner satisfaction from unselfish service to others.
- **Anticipation**: Where conflict and stressors are dealt with by living in the future and experiencing the full gamut of feelings associated with an event that has not yet taken place.
- **Asceticism**: Where any pleasure resulting from experiences is eliminated.
- **Avoidance**: Thinking and acting in ways that evade dealing with reality. From a counselling perspective, working with such clients might prove difficult, partly because they will generally not voluntarily seek counselling and partly because, if they do, they may be so hungry for approval and eager to please that they are ultra-sensitive to any sense of challenge, fearing rejection. Refusal on the part of the counsellor to extend the relationship into friendship might be interpreted as rejection.
- **Blocking**: A temporary or fleeting restraint of thinking, feelings or action that resembles repression but differs in that tension results from the inhibition. Blocking may manifest itself at any time during counselling. It may become apparent in the way the client refuses to consider what is being said or argues against it without consideration.
- **Compensation**: The tendency to cover up a weakness or defect by exaggerating a more desirable characteristic.
- **Controlling**: Attempting to manage or regulate events or objects in the environment to minimise anxiety and to resolve inner conflicts.
- **Conversion**: In psychoanalytic terms, conversion is where repressed material, ideas, wishes and feelings are converted into physical manifestations, such as hysterical paralysis of a limb. The physical symptom symbolises the original conflict.
- **Denial**: A mechanism employed to avoid becoming consciously aware of some painful thought, feeling or experience or event or part of self.
- **Devaluation**: Where the individual deals with emotional conflict and stressors (internal or external) by attributing exaggerated or excessively negative qualities to self or to others.
- **Displacement**: The shifting of affect (feeling) from one mental image to another (normally less threatening) to which it does not belong, in order to avoid anxiety.
- **Dissociation**: A temporary but extreme change in a person's character or personal identity in order to avoid emotional distress. It is the separating off of thoughts, feelings and fantasies from conscious awareness.
- **Distortion**: Where external reality is grossly restructured to preserve the person's inner world. Its function in dreams is to make acceptable the content that otherwise would be unacceptable.
- **Externalisation**: Tending to perceive in the external world and internal objects elements of one's own personality, including thoughts, feelings and behaviour.
- **Fantasy**: People who are most likely to make use of this as a defence are those

who are lonely and frightened; eccentric people and those labelled schizoid; aloof and unsociable people; and those who fear intimacy.

- **Humour**: Using comedy to overtly express feelings and thoughts without personal discomfort or discomfort in other people.
- **Hypochondriasis**: Excessive preoccupation with bodily symptoms (especially pain) and often accompanied by fears of serious physical illness, such as cancer or heart disease.
- **Idealisation**: Where the person, as a defence against guilt, attributes exaggerated positive qualities to self or others in order to deal with emotional conflicts and internal or external stressors.
- **Identification**: The process by which we model aspects of ourselves upon other people. We behave, or imagine ourselves behaving, as if we were the person with whom we have a strong emotional tie and take on the attitudes, patterns of behaviour and emotions of that person.
- **Inhibition**: Consciously limiting or renouncing some ego functions, alone or in combination, to evade anxiety arising out of conflict with impulses arising from within or from the environment or from other people.
- **Intellectualisation**: Where the ego deals with threats by using the mind rather than dealing with feelings. The person excessively analyses problems in remote, intellectual terms, while emotions and feelings are ignored or discounted. The process is closely allied to rationalisation.
- **Introjection**: Where aspects of the outside world are internalised into the ego as fantasies or mental representations. Introjection is similar to internalisation and identification and the opposite of projection.
- **Isolation**: Where anxiety-provoking feelings and impulses, and the associated feeling and impulse, are pushed out of consciousness.
- **Passive-aggressive behaviour**: Expressing aggression towards others indirectly through passivity, masochism and turning against self. Manifestations of passive-aggressive behaviour include failures, procrastination and illness that affects others more than oneself.
- **Projection**: In psychoanalysis, projection is the process by which one's own traits, emotions, dispositions, ideas, wishes and failings are attributed to others, who are then perceived as an external threat.
- **Projective identification**: Similar to projection, where the individual copes with stressors and conflicts by attributing unacceptable parts of self – feelings, thoughts and impulses – and putting them on to another. Unlike projection, the person remains aware of the feelings, but considers them justified. It serves to protect the ego against the anxieties of being persecuted by others and being separated from them.
- **Rationalisation**: In psychoanalytic terms it means giving an intellectual, rational explanation in an attempt to conceal or justify attitudes, beliefs or behaviour that might otherwise be unacceptable.
- **Reaction formation**: In psychoanalytic terms, this is a mechanism that is used to defend the ego against the anxiety of expressing a repressed wish, whereby we believe as though the opposite were true. It is where one's anxieties about

unacceptable impulses are kept at bay by developing behaviour patterns that are directly opposed, as a means of controlling the impulses.

- **Regression**: A return to an earlier (fixated) level of functioning, with the feelings and behaviours attached to it. Regression is prompted by an unconscious desire to avoid anxiety, tensions and conflicts evoked at the present level of development.
- **Repression**: In all depth psychology it is where an idea or feeling is banished or not allowed to enter consciousness. It is the cornerstone concept of psychoanalytic theory.
- **Sexualisation**: Endowing an object or a function with sexual significance that is not appropriate, in order to ward off anxieties associated with prohibited impulses.
- **Somatisation**: Where psychic disturbances are converted into physical symptoms that preoccupy the individual. The physical symptoms are not in keeping with any actual physical disturbance. Somatisation is a way of dealing with emotional conflicts or internal or external stressors.
- **Splitting**: A psychoanalytic term to describe a division within the psyche, where the self or others are reviewed as all good or all bad, with failure to integrate the positive and negative qualities of self and others. Splitting is commonly seen in clients with behavioural and anti-social problems.
- **Sublimation**: In psychoanalysis, sublimation is the channelling of what would be instinctual gratification into new, learned behaviour; something that is more conforming to social values and behaviours.
- **Suppression**: In psychoanalytic terms, the conscious banishment of disturbing ideas, feelings or memories from the conscious to the preconscious, where they are more easily accessed.

Further reading

American Psychiatric Glossary. American Psychiatric Press, Inc., Washington, DC.
Gabbard, G.O. (1995) Theories of personality and psychopathology: psychoanalysis. In: *Comprehensive Textbook of Psychiatry*, 6th edn (eds H.J. Kaplan and B.J. Sadock). Williams & Wilkins, Baltimore, MD.
Heller, T. et al. (1996) *Mental Health Matters: a reader*. Open University Press, Milton Keynes.
[A browse through the Amazon Books website shows many books related to psychiatric nursing and psychiatry, all of which will have detailed descriptions of defence mechanisms.]

DEFINITION OF COUNSELLING

There are many definitions of what counselling is. Simply, it is a working relationship in which clients are helped to explore what is happening in their lives, and through the relationship to work towards living life with greater well-being, which empowers them to take control of the direction of their life.

The British Association for Counselling's (BAC, now The British Association for Counselling and Psychotherapy (BACP)) old definition was:

People become engaged in counselling when a person, occupying regularly or temporarily the role of counsellor, offers or agrees to offer time, attention and respect to another person temporarily in the role of client. The task of counselling is to give the client an opportunity to explore, discover and clarify ways of living more resourcefully and towards greater well-being.

The newer (1989) BACP definition reads:

Counselling is the skilled and principled use of relationship to facilitate self-knowledge, emotional acceptance and growth and the optimal development of personal resources. The overall aim is to provide an opportunity to work towards living more satisfyingly and resourcefully. Counselling relationships will vary according to need but may be concerned with developmental issues, addressing and resolving specific problems, making decisions, coping with crisis, developing personal insights and knowledge, working through feelings of inner conflict or improving relationships with others. The counsellor's role is to facilitate the client's work in ways that respect the client's values, personal resources and capacity for self-determination.

Points about the two definitions

Not every person who uses counselling skills is designated 'counsellor'. We can distinguish two broad groups of people who use counselling skills: people who are called 'counsellors', who engage in counselling as a distinct occupation; and 'others' who use counselling skills as part of their other skills. They would be 'temporarily in the role'.

Most people enter into counselling of their own volition and it is something agreed between client and counsellor. Sometimes, particularly where counselling is part of another job, the need for counselling may be perceived and suggested. In any case, counselling should not be entered into without agreement from both parties. The relationship should be made explicit and the roles clearly defined.

People who engage in counselling make a contract where one of the boundaries is time – number and length of sessions. Giving total, undivided attention means being able to free oneself from external and internal distractions.

One of the aspects of respect is that we recognise and accept the uniqueness of each and every person, while at the same time taking account of shared similarities. Many people who have difficulties – in whatever area of life, be it work or at a personal level – suffer from damaged self-esteem. The counselling relationship encourages people to repair their damaged self-esteem, for it is here that, free from judgement and criticism, they are able to start to respect themselves. It is almost as if the damaged self-esteem devalues all they are and all they do. Respect should be total – for the person and for what transpires during counselling.

- People are not clients for life. The counselling relationship is only one of many and takes place for one hour out of the 168 hours in the week.
- Counselling helps clients to make order out of confusion, choice from conflict and sense out of nonsense. Counselling helps clients to discover resources not hitherto recognised and to put those resources to work on their behalf.

- Counselling makes use of relationship skills (see Relationship principles) for the benefit of the client.
- Counselling harnesses the client's own resources.
- Counselling makes a difference in the client's overall wellbeing, in that the client is more able to take control of the direction of his life.
- Whatever the focus in counselling, it must always be on the client's needs and the action taken must always be the client's decision.

Further reading

British Association for Counselling and Psychotherapy (1989) *Definition of Counselling*, British Association for Counselling and Psychotherapy, 1 Regent Place, Rugby, Warwickshire, CV21 2PJ, UK.

Woolfe, R. (1989) *Counselling Skills: a training manual*. Scottish Health Education Group, Edinburgh.

DEPRESSION (SEE ALSO: PSYCHIC PAIN)

In this entry I have deliberately taken a broad approach to this distressing condition because it needs to be tackled on as wide a front as possible. Our knowledge of depression is great; but like the bottomless pit into which depressives invariably tumble, our understanding of this condition can never be fully satisfied. This entry attempts to plumb, still further, the depths of the ocean of depression.

The 'limbo' of depression

In the entry on anxiety I use the analogy of anxiety being a treadmill, where the person is constantly driven to exhausting activity. In many ways depression is the opposite: people are caught in a trap that cuts them off from their environment, so preventing them reacting appropriately to it and with the people in it. This feeling of being cut off – of not being able to make emotional contact – leads me to the analogy of the limbo of depression.

Limbo, according to theological belief, is a region on the border of Hell. It is the abode of those who died before the birth of Christ; they died without salvation. It is also the place of unbaptised infants and of mentally subnormal people. The souls in limbo are there through no fault of their own. Some theologians maintain that the infants in limbo are affected by some degree of sadness because of felt deprivation. Without becoming caught up in the vagaries of philosophical and religious discussion, it would be useful to consider the similarity between limbo and the state of depression.

In psychology, depression is a mood or emotional state that is marked by sadness, inactivity and a reduced ability to enjoy life.

A person who is depressed usually experiences one or more of the following symptoms, although this will depend on the basic personality and the severity of the depression:

- Feelings of sadness, hopelessness or pessimism
- Guilt and worthlessness

- Lowered self-esteem and heightened self-depreciation
- A decrease or loss of ability to enjoy daily life
- Reduced energy and vitality
- A lowering of thought or action
- Paranoid ideas and deep suspicion
- Disturbed sense of time
- Suicidal thoughts, preoccupations and tendencies. Depression is a major contributory factor to suicide. The future seems grey, then black. Sufferers see no future and only exist from day to day, with no joy or pleasure. They wish never to have been born and that they could fall asleep and not wake up. Existence seems so bleak that the only remedy is to end it all.
- Anxiety and obsession
- Loss of appetite; and disturbed sleep or insomnia
- Physical symptoms, such as loss of weight
- Loss of sexual function.
- Retardation and agitation (retardation refers to a general slowing down of bodily functions; agitation comprises severe anxiety together with over-activity of the limbs).
- Pain is a common manifestation of depression, and may show as backache, rheumatic pains or facial neuralgia, against which normal pain-killers are ineffective.

Sadness

This entry will consider sadness within depression, because there is no sadness as profound as that experienced by a person caught in the grip of depression. Grief and the sadness of depression are close relatives; indeed it could be said that depression has many elements of unresolved grief. One of the differences is that in grief the sadness has a focus – the loss of someone treasured. In the sadness of depression there is no such identifiable focus. A parallel can be drawn between specific anxiety and free-floating anxiety, where no known cause can be identified.

Sadness is unhappiness brought down a degree. Most people know the feeling of unhappiness. Many know the feelings of sadness. Not everyone understands the deep, lasting, incapacitating sadness of a person depressed to the point of feeling like a dried-out husk and where tears – therapeutic in normal sorrow – dry up in the eyes before they can be shed.

Depending upon the particular theoretical approach, the sadness of depression is considered to have its genesis in:

- The loss of some valued person, possession or status
- The way we attribute meaning to our ideas, feelings, ideals and circumstances – the sense of lack or loss of positive emotions, such as love, self-respect and feelings of satisfaction
- A sense of deprivation, pessimism and self-criticism.

While sadness is a normal and healthy response to any misfortune and is common, sorrow that does not lessen with the passage of time is pathological. People who experience normal sadness are usually able to talk about it, to know why they are sad and still feel hope that the sadness will lift. Depression sets in when normal exchanges are absent or greatly diminished. The words that would express how a depressed person feels are blocked in the well by the dried-up tears. Sadness is also referred to as 'psychic pain' – pain that is not physical but mental (see entry on Psychic pain).

If sadness is psychic pain, is the psyche able to tolerate only so much pain? Is it possible that excess psychic pain is transformed into other feelings – anxiety, anger, rage and psychosomatic manifestations? Sadness, particularly when it follows a definite event such as a death, is reparative, but renewal may take a long time. Are people who pass from normal sadness to depression those in whom the reparative work of sorrowing has not taken place? Is it that they have not been able to do 'sorrowing work'? Such people are psychologically ill-equipped (because life experience has not prepared them) to solve their sorrow or their sadness.

People consistently use figurative language to describe the feelings of depression such as: the heart is heavy, dark, constricted, sunk; they may feel they have a stone in their heart; a dark cloud hangs over their head; if they pray, they may feel that the heavens are as brass.

Loss of joy and lack of pleasure feature as much as actual feelings of sadness and there is an increasing inability for depressed people to enjoy themselves. This affects relationships with their families; hobbies become boring; art and music, which they previously enjoyed, lose their appeal; the world of nature and sound is dull and insipid. The fact that life is dull and cheerless causes them concern. They know the joy has gone but they cannot find out where or how to recapture it. The fact that they find no pleasure in things or people has the effect of cutting them off emotionally from activities and people who would normally stimulate them.

That such a feeling of joylessness causes problems should come as no surprise. When any mood separates husband from wife, parent from children, work colleague from mates, neighbour from neighbour, and when all these relationships are affected all at once, the emotional world shrinks so much that even they themselves are reduced to nothing.

One of the characteristics of depression is that it is contagious. We may well find ourselves 'picking up' the sadness and reacting to it by ourselves becoming sad and losing some of our own joy. The effect that depressed people have on others is an important factor in their increasing isolation. On the one hand, depressed people desperately need human contact, yet there is very little that they can offer to establish or maintain affectional relationships. Indeed, depressed people's ability to love and be loved is impaired. A measure of this – which reinforces the feeling of isolation – is a decrease of libido. The decrease may range from 'little desire' to total inability and impotence. For couples who have hitherto enjoyed satisfactory and fulfilling sex, loss of desire or inability may put their relationship under great strain.

Another part of an 'affectional relationship' is communication. Yet the profound feeling of isolation usually makes communication burdensome. One of the difficulties expressed by depressed people is that the conversations of others jar; their normal laughter seems totally out of place; their attempts to 'keep things going' become sources of irritation. The wavebands of communication have become distorted by depressed feelings. Communication – of any meaning – virtually ceases.

Depression and grief

Depression differs from simple grief, which is an appropriate emotional response to the loss of loved persons or objects. Where there are clear grounds for a person's unhappiness, depression is considered to be present if the depressed mood is disproportionately long or severe in relation to the precipitating event. Severity can range from feeling low to crippling and incapacitating.

Abnormal depression can be an accompaniment of a physical illness or to any emotional illness or disturbance. It frequently accompanies anxiety and may occur following the birth of a baby, as postnatal (postpartum) depression.

Bipolar disorder (formerly manic depression – some sufferers still prefer this term to the more modern one) is when a person experiences alternating states of depression and mania (extreme elation of mood). Many people never experience full-blown manic phases but there is a swing of mood. The term 'unipolar' describes single phase depression, with repeated attacks, rather than the swings of mood of the bipolar type.

The whole subject of depression is fraught with difficulties of terminology. The DSM-IV (page 317) describes several variants under the heading 'Mood disorders' and the ICD-10 (page 112) describes similar mood states under the heading 'Mood (affective) disorders'. Mania and severe depression are at the opposite ends of the affective spectrum.

Where depression accompanies suicidal thoughts, the person is best treated in hospital.

Depression is probably the most common psychiatric complaint and has been described by physicians from as early as the time of Hippocrates, who called it melancholia. The course of the disorder is extremely variable from person to person; it may be fleeting or permanent, mild or severe, acute or chronic.

Depression is more common in women than in men. The rates of incidence of the disorder increase with age in men, while the peak for women is between the ages of 35 and 45.

Depression can have many causes. When there is substantial reason for suspecting a definite cause, it is called reactive depression. Frequently, no direct 'cause' can be demonstrated. The loss of one's parents or other childhood traumas and privations can increase a person's vulnerability to depression later in life. Stressful life events in general are potent precipitating contributors to depression, although why some people develop a severe mood depression is still not certain. Depression often occurs in members of the same family, although it is not clear if the illness is genetic or if it results from being exposed to someone with the illness.

Guilt and worthlessness

In a severe case of depression, the person becomes preoccupied with feelings of guilt and worthlessness: 'I am worthless'; 'The world is meaningless'; 'The future is hopeless'. There may be a discrepancy between what they think, 'I will get well', and how they feel, 'I feel blue'. This distinction between thinking and feeling is crystallised in the following maxim: 'It's not what I think I am, but what I think, that I am'.

In the most severe cases of depression, these feelings of guilt and worthlessness assume full-blown delusional proportions. In such cases the belief cannot be reversed by evidence to the contrary, despite being out of keeping with the person's social, educational and cultural background. Minor misdemeanours and omissions are blown up into mountainous breaches of morals. Delusional responses may include the firm conviction that the individual is the worst possible sinner; he has committed 'the unforgivable sin'; it is his fault that the world is in the state it is, and so on. It seems that when depressed, our normal feelings of doubt become so exaggerated as to 'take over' and crowd out rational thought and feeling.

Self-esteem

Self-esteem is defined as the degree to which one feels valued, worthwhile or competent'. Very low self-esteem equates to feeling worthless.

- Lowered self-esteem is accompanied by feelings of unhappiness, anger, sense of threat, fatigue, withdrawal, tension, disorganisation, feelings of constraint, conflict and inhibition.
- High self-esteem is accompanied by feelings of integration, freedom, positive emotion and availability of energy.

The first list equates very directly to the list of symptoms of depression and one cannot but speculate as to the place of self-esteem in the onset and course of depression.

Positive self-esteem relates to parental warmth, acceptance, respect and clearly defined limit-setting. A person with high self-esteem carries, in effect, a loving parent within him. The person who does not carry a loving parent within him becomes one of life's vulnerable personalities, prone to become caught in the quicksands of depression. Esteem for others is as necessary as esteem for one's self. So long as we have a reasonable degree of self-esteem and esteem for others, we have little grounds for feeling helpless or hopeless; hopelessness is a significant factor in the genesis of clinical depression.

Anxiety with depression

Some practitioners believe that depressive and anxiety states are inseparable. Anxious, depressed patients are tense, jumpy, irritable and apprehensive, worry about trivial matters and agonise over decisions.

Anxiety is the emotional reaction to the expectation of danger or damage.

When the event has taken place – e.g. death of a loved one or loss of job – and the damage has already been done, sadness results. But in many people the anxiety has become trapped in the feelings of sadness, thus preventing the completion of 'sorrowing work'.

Sleep disturbances

Disturbances of sleep often accompany depression. In severe cases the content and quality of sleep is altered. The alterations may assume the form of dark and foreboding dreams and nightmares. Some people are tortured by early morning waking, after which they try miserably to get back to sleep. Sleep deprivation is a stressful experience. Sleep is nature's way of ensuring rest and restoration. Any disturbance will produce anxious feelings. In sleep, many bodily functions are suspended but during sleeplessness these functions, which should be resting, remain activated. This, plus the anxiety that inevitably accompanies disturbed sleep, leads to increased irritability and tiredness, but that tiredness does not induce sleep. So, depressed people not only have their depressed mood to contend with, they are caught in a cycle of depressed mood, sleep deprivation, tiredness, anxiety and less sleep, leading to increased depression.

During periods of lying awake, the individual has ample opportunity to ruminate upon many of the dark facets of his emotions. Lying awake for several hours, after getting into bed, or lying waiting for the dawn to set the world astir, are not the best times to fill one's mind with light, positive thoughts. If the person is to climb out of his depression, he needs help to break the vicious cycle. Improved sleep, and with it improved wellbeing, may be the first step.

Limbo revisited

The picture of the depressed person that has been painted here may appear sombre and perhaps depressing. This is precisely the effect depression has. Very often counsellors discern on the radar screens of their own feelings the shapes of the depressions that others cannot consciously describe. It is with radar-like intuition that we try to pierce the limbo-gloom that surrounds the depressed person. One of the points about limbo is that it is a prison: a prison from which the only escape rests in eternity. Nothing the condemned soul can do, no prayers, no oblations – neither by himself nor by others still in this world – may effect an escape. The soul is powerless to escape from the darkness. In limbo there is no light. Milton in *Paradise Lost* contrasts Hell (and with it, limbo) with Heaven. The one is dark and punishing. The other is perfect. People who are trapped in depression do feel cut off from the light. The word pictures they paint are of being in dark prison cells; of being in a dark hole; of being enclosed by thick soundproof glass; in solitary confinement. And as the days pass, the torture grows worse.

Negative thinking characterises those who suffer from depression. None of us is entirely free from negative thoughts about ourselves and others, and how we shall respond to them, but when most of our thinking and reacting is negative, we will spend increasingly more time (and emotional energy) in the dark halls of limbo, far removed from the light. Cognitive theorists believe that depression and other mood disorders are caused by irrational thinking. The person interprets events, his own self-worth and the expected outcome of events, in a negative fashion. Other theorists believe that depression is 'learned helplessness'. The person becomes a victim of circumstance, and as such he cannot be held responsible for what happens. He learns, therefore, to exploit his weakness and complaints, in order to force others to give him his way. But this drives him still deeper into the darkness, and isolates him further from others. Every manipulation that results in increased isolation reinforces the negative view he holds of himself.

Life events, health and depression

Psychic stress has been classified as: situational; social; family; psychosexual; or physical. 'Health' is a significant contributory factor in depression. When thinking of disability and health, mobility and the lack of social relationships seem to be factors leading to depression.

There is a close connection between disability, lowered self-esteem and independence. This state creates a fertile soil for the development of depression. Depression is common at the outset of a disabling condition and may recur periodically thereafter. Patients who face life-threatening surgery often are depressed. These feelings can be regarded as a grief reaction of severe loss. However, the majority of patients are not able to make clear to the doctor their depressed feelings and anxieties. They are grieving for the loss of health but also for loss of self-esteem which is linked to:

- Loss of autonomy
- Reduced earning power
- Having to give up certain activities
- Sexual restriction
- Invalidism
- Premature old age.

The emotional tension and stress following accidental trauma or major surgery will be high when what has happened produces dramatic changes in body image. Depression, secondary to loss and combined with grief, may develop or be aggravated and may lead to further impairment of general physical health.

Pain and depression

Pain is frequently present in illness, and is invariably a prominent feature of surgery and trauma. Pain is linked with depression, and when depression and anxiety are relieved, persistent pain is reduced to the extent that pain-relieving medication can also be reduced. Emotional support plus the marshalling of family and social resources, is often more effective than administering anti-depressant drugs. Pain sometimes develops after loss – of loved ones, status, occupation and when depression follows after a period of pain, the mood change is likely to be secondary to the pain; but where pain and depression occur almost together, it is more likely that the pain is a symptom of depressive illness. The pain that depressed people experience may include atypical facial pain or 'neuralgias', vague 'rheumaticky' joint pains and headache. In some instances the preoccupation with the pain becomes hypochondriacal. Pain is one more stress, which, when added to the stress of illness or disability, makes the person vulnerable to depression.

Vulnerable personalities

The characteristics of personalities vulnerable to develop depression are:

- Breakdown under stress
- Lack of energy
- Insecurity
- Introversion and sensitivity
- Tendency to worry
- Lack of social adroitness
- Unassertiveness
- Dependency
- Obsessionality
- Negative thinking.

When illness or accident come as additional burdens, a person already vulnerable may collapse under the weight.

There can be little doubt but that 'the family' is one significant and dominant force in the creation of a vulnerable personality. Disturbed children are more likely to occur in families where there is a depressed parent. Where it is the mother who is depressed there is conflict between her own feelings of deprivation and need for support versus her need to cope with heavy maternal role demands. The conflict experienced by such mothers creates an atmosphere in which the 'learned helplessness' theory gains credence. Children reared in an atmosphere dominated by depression, where affectional relationships are neither established nor maintained, where the depressed parent constantly dwells in the underworld of negative thought and feeling are, themselves, likely to respond similarly. They have learned what emotional capital may be gained from being the helpless victims of circumstance.

Loss and depression

The link between actual loss and symbolic loss has long been recognised, particularly in psychoanalytical theory, which includes death and separation from key inter-personal figures, but also includes loss of limbs and other bodily parts and loss of self-esteem.

Illness exerts a profound influence on most people, for it represents a symbolic loss of health, and heralds a decline and eventual death. People tend to think more of death when they are ill than when they are fit. When trauma is considered, particularly where part of the body is actually removed, the resultant depression may be invested with a symbolic significance far beyond reality. The impact of loss due to illness or disability is affected by:

- The function of the part
- The symbolic value
- Any alteration of appearance
- Visibility of the change
- The feasibility of rehabilitation
- The degree of restoration possible
- Altered lifestyle
- Whether or not it is permanent.

Health care workers need constantly to remind themselves that the patients for whom they care, whatever the nature of their illness, may experience feelings of loss, which, if not dealt with, can lead to depression. The psyche will respond with feelings of loss whenever any part of the body, which it inhabits, is attacked by disease or trauma. That is why any illness or accident, however minor, may act as a precipitator to depression.

Treatment

There are three main treatments for depression. The two most important are psychotherapy and drug therapy. Psychotherapy aims to resolve any underlying psychic conflicts that may be causing the depressed state while also giving emotional support to the patient. Cognitive behavioural therapy is proving a useful intervention.

Antidepressant drugs, by contrast, directly affect the chemistry of the brain and presumably achieve their therapeutic effects by correcting the chemical imbalance that is causing the depression.

In cases of severe depression in which therapeutic results are needed quickly, electroconvulsive therapy (ECT) is a third treatment that has proved helpful. In this procedure, a convulsion is produced by passing an electric current through the person's brain. In many cases, the best therapeutic results are obtained by using a combination of psychotherapy with drug therapy or electric shock treatment.

The one theme that repeats itself is the isolation felt by depressed people, cut off as they are from emotional contact. In a sense, depressed people pre-empt and pre-experience their own death – the final isolation. The relationship between counsellor and client is crucial in maintaining contact and thereby reducing the risk of isolation. Human contact has a calming effect on the cardiovascular system of a person under stress. Thus it is quite feasible that our very presence achieves as much, or more, than our words of counsel, however profound.

What we do when we counsel is to offer ourselves in a relationship that makes no demands for itself. When we reach out to make emotional contact with depressed people we break through the invisible barrier that keeps them isolated. This emotional contact builds a bridge. Across this bridge they may walk away from their isolation.

Counselling: an intervention

The role of confidant – spouse or someone else – is significant. If it is important to share intimacies within a caring relationship, then the lack of such a relationship could be conducive to developing depression. Counselling offers the sort of support that avoids smothering feelings.

Theories and therapies dealing with depression are legion, but when all else fails, when theories fall flat, and when techniques fail to satisfy, all we have left are our relationship skills. It is surely upon these, and through these, that theories become fact and techniques become reality. Rapport, immediate and intense, must be established immediately. Depressed people often feel themselves to be 'losers'. It is important that we help them to feel 'winners'. A small task accomplished is infinitely more beneficial than an unrealistic task that is doomed to failure. The change in self-esteem that comes with even small successes is essential if the person is to step out of his depression. Maintaining self-esteem is vital if the ill or disabled person is to stop himself sliding into depression.

This may sound easy. But, as with all counselling, working with those who are depressed is not always easy or successful. Some people construct their lives and relationships on a purely negative foundation and are very resistant to change. It seems that they need to be 'poorly'. In a curious way it makes them feel 'good'. This is the construct of the 'martyr'. Such people resist giving up their suffering. What they gain from being 'ill' is more than they would gain from being well. Thus, counselling – of even the most intense sort – may not always work. Moving out of limbo – with its implication of being there through no fault of our own – would mean that we could no longer regard ourselves as helpless victims of circumstances imposed upon us by others.

Measurement of depression

The most widely used measurements of depression are:

1. Completed by an observer:
   - Hamilton's Rating Scale for Depression (HRSD). This scale contains 17 items.
   - World Health Organisation (WHO) Schedule for Standardised Assessment of Depressive Disorders. This scale contains 57 items.
2. Completed by the person:
   - Zung's depressive scale, which comprises 20 sentences.
   - Beck's Depressive Inventory (BDI 46), which consists of 21 categories of symptoms and attitudes.

Further reading

Akiskal, H. (1995) Mood disorders. In: *Comprehensive Textbook of Psychiatry*, 6th edn (eds H.J. Kaplan and B.J. Sadock). Williams & Wilkins, Baltimore, MD.
Gilbert, P. (1992) *Counselling for Depression*. Sage Publications, London.

Hirschfield, R.M.A. (1995) Mood disorders: psychosocial treatments. In: *Comprehensive Textbook of Psychiatry*, 6th edn (eds H.J. Kaplan and B.J. Sadock). Williams & Wilkins, Baltimore, MD.

Rowe, D. (2002) *Beyond Fear*, 2nd edn. HarperCollins, London.

Rowe, D. (2003) *Depression: the way out of your prison*, 3rd edn. Brunner-Routledge, London.

Stewart, W. (1985) *Counselling in Rehabilitation*. Croom Helm, London.

Worden, J.W. (1983) *Grief Counselling and Grief Therapy: a handbook for the mental health practitioner*. Routledge, London.

DILEMMA (SEE ALSO: DOUBLE BIND)

In popular use, a dilemma is a choice between two (or, loosely, several) alternatives that are or appear to be equally unfavourable; a position of doubt or perplexity, a 'fix'. The alternatives are commonly spoken of as the 'horns' of the dilemma.

An example of a dilemma would be: 'If I don't go on holiday with my in-laws, my wife will make my life a misery; if I do on holiday, my in-laws will make my life a misery. So I am stuck with being miserable, whichever way I jump – a double bind.'

The dying patient who asks his doctor to give him a lethal dose of pain-killing drugs places the doctor on the horns of an ethical and moral dilemma.

Social dilemmas exist; for example, there is a need for transport yet the increasing number of vehicles on the roads produces health hazards.

Another example of a moral dilemma would be if my son, whom I knew to be addicted to drugs, came home covered in blood. I hear on the radio that a shop has been robbed and the owner seriously wounded by a man answering the description of my son. If I obey my conscience I will report my son; if I don't, I don't know that I could live with my guilt.

Resolution of a moral dilemma means the overriding of one of the obligations by the strength of the other. Once overridden, it is no longer obligatory. However, it also appears that what influences us in making the choice is the sense of duty, although deciding which course of action evokes the stronger sense of duty is not always easy.

Choosing means making a decision and for some people making decisions is very painful and tortuous. And whatever decision is made, we have to live with the consequences. In deciding to 'shop' my son, I have to live with the consequences of him, and possibly my other children, rejecting me for being an uncaring father and not putting family interests first. If my family's opinion means more to me than law and order and justice, then I might decide to turn a blind eye and then I would have to live with the consequences of not being a citizen of integrity.

The choice of action might be influenced by the fact that I don't have a very high regard for my son anyway, and that the shopkeeper is a friend. Here I have conformed to what I believe is the 'highest intrinsic good'.

People often feel caught on the horns of a dilemma, feeling that whichever way they move they will lose out or the solution is too difficult. For example, the child whose father is sexually abusing her feels she cannot tell anyone, for if she does, she knows he will be taken away and the family will be split up. The mother of the child who knows about the abuse, yet fears she would not be able to handle the scandal, is also trapped.

Not all moral dilemmas are as dramatic as have been quoted, yet so often clients do feel hopelessly stuck; being able to sort the 'problem' into two opposing forces – 'On the one hand it seems that ... and on the other it seems that ...' – is often the first step towards helping sort out the two forces. When the client can give some value to the opposing obligations, he is well on the way towards resolving the moral dilemma.

DOUBLE BIND (SEE ALSO: DILEMMA)

Double bind is Gregory Bateson and Donald Jackson's description of the contradiction experienced by people who receive contradictory messages from someone more powerful. It means that the person is placed in a situation in which there is no winning, no matter what is said or done.

The term evolved from the study of the nature of schizophrenic communication. Now it is applied to a wide range of interpersonal communications. Only repeated exposure within a survival relationship produces severe pathology.

It is likely to arise in a family where one or both parents, who cannot express affection, respond coldly to the advances of the child. When the child withdraws, confused, they respond in simulated love, coupled with accusations such as, 'You don't love your mother; after all she's done for you!' Or, the one refusing an embrace and then saying, 'Why don't you love me?' The result is 'I'm damned if I do and damned if I don't.'

As relationships are mutual, both parties become 'victims' of the double bind. It is experienced by people suffering from schizophrenia who, whatever they do, will be labelled either 'mad' or 'bad'.

The essential elements

In their original 1956 paper, Bateson et al. defined the necessary ingredients for a double-bind situation:

- Two or more persons
- Repeated experience
- A primary negative injunction
- A secondary injunction conflicting with the first at a more abstract level, and like the first enforced by punishments or signals which threaten survival
- A tertiary negative injunction prohibiting the victim from escaping from the field.

Finally, the complete set of ingredients is no longer necessary when the victim has learned to perceive his universe in double-bind patterns (pages 253–254).

Paradoxes and double binds abound in life; what is pathological is staying trapped and entangled in futile attempts to unravel them from within. The aim of counselling is to help the person identify the double binds and 'mixed messages', and then to re-learn effective patterns of communication.

Double-bind is similar to Catch-22.

Catch-22

Catch-22 is a conflict – a psychological state of indecision – where the person is faced simultaneously with two opposing forces of equal strength that cannot be solved together.

Writers experience a Catch-22 in 'Sorry, we cannot be your agent until you are a published author'; 'Sorry, we only accept new work through agents'.

The term 'Catch-22' entered the English language as the title of a black-humour novel by Joseph Heller, published 1961. (Joseph Heller died in December 1999 at the age of 76.)

The plot of the novel centres on the anti-hero Captain John Yossarian, stationed at an airstrip on a Mediterranean island in the Second World War, and portrays his desperate attempts to stay alive. The 'catch' in *Catch-22* involves a mysterious Air Force regulation, which asserts that a man is considered insane if he willingly continues to fly dangerous combat missions; but, if he makes the necessary formal request to be relieved of such missions, the very act of making the request proves that he is sane and therefore ineligible to be relieved.

Clients often present in this state of conflict, where they feel trapped, stuck, unable to move. Although the exact meaning of Catch-22 may have become lost to many people, the general feeling is there, so it is a useful analogy. (For a more detailed discussion of Conflict, refer to entry). Generally movement is possible only after counsellor and client have clearly identified the various parts of the two sides of the catch. Only then will the client feel energised to be able to make a decision and move in one direction.

Further reading

Bateson, G., Jackson, D.D., Haley, J. and Weakland, J.H. (1956) Towards a theory of schizophrenia. *Behavioral Science*, **1**: 251–264.

Bateson, G., Jackson, D.D., Haley, J. and Weakland, J.H. (1962) A note on the double bind. *Family Process*, **2**: 154–161.

Berger, M.M. (1981) *Beyond the Double Bind: communication and family systems*. Brunner/Mazel, New York.

Kiley, F. and McDonald, W. (eds) (1973) *A Catch-22 Casebook*. Thomas Y. Crowell, New York.

McGlashan T.H. and Hoffman R.E. (1995) Schizophrenia: psychodynamic to neurodynamic theories. In: *Comprehensive Textbook of Psychiatry*, 6th edn (eds H.J. Kaplan and B.J. Sadock). Williams & Wilkins, Baltimore, MD.

Sluzki, C.E. and Ransom, D.C. (eds) (1976) *Double Bind: The foundation of the communication approach to the family*. Grune & Stratton, New York.

www.ncyclopedia.yahoo.com

DREAM THERAPY

Dreaming is generally defined as imaginary, sensory, motor and thought processes occurring during sleep. Neither sleep nor dreaming, however, can be precisely defined. What is called dreaming depends on how it is measured and in which of the four basic stages of sleep it occurs. Dreaming takes place in varying degrees in all stages of sleep. Dreams are not necessarily visual imagery; congenitally blind people dream in auditory and sensory-motor modes. One difference between waking and dreaming consciousness is that the latter tends to be an internal hallucinatory-like experience disconnected from the external world.

An Australian Aboriginal expression says 'He who has no dreaming is lost'. The Dreaming refers to the creative period when mythic spirits were believed to have shaped the land, bringing into being various species and establishing human life. These beings were thought to live on eternally in spirit form and to have left tangible evidence of their presence in the shape of certain prominent land forms considered sacred.

Dreams are hallucinatory experiences that occur during sleep. People have had experiences where complex problems have been solved in dreams. So dreams can aid creativity.

Views on the nature of dreams

Freud referred to dreams as 'the royal road to the unconscious'. He believed that dreams reflect waking experience. He developed a highly systematised approach to interpret and use dreams in therapy. Thinking during sleep is primitive and dips into repressed material. Dreaming is a mechanism for maintaining sleep and fulfilling wishes.

Wish fulfilment (Freud)

In dreams, wishes and desires are disguised to keep us from waking and being confronted by repressed material too difficult to handle. This is all the more important if a frank expression of those wishes would be in conflict with our moral or social values and standards.

The original wish or desire corresponds directly to the dream's latent content. The meaning of any dream lies in the latent content.

The transformation of 'latent' into 'manifest' content is done by 'dream-work', which is initiated by the 'dream-censor'.

The latent material has been suppressed because of its sexual, aggressive or otherwise frightening nature.

We employ mechanisms of symbolic imagery to deal with the repressed material:

- **Condensation**: In which we combine certain elements within the dream into a single image.
- **Displacement**: In which we shift an impulse from one object to another.

- **Secondary elaboration**: The process of imposing structure to increase the coherence and logic of the dream.

Therapy aims to retrace the dream-work and understand it by interpretation. The analyst does not interpret by referring to a dream guide in the manner of the ancients, but by understanding the general principles of transformation on which we all create our own highly personalised dream language.

Analytical interpretations

Jung's theories are different from those of Freud. For Jung, dreams are forward-looking, creative, instructive and, to some extent, prophetic.

Jung believed that dreams draw on the collective unconscious. Archetypes are the common symbols, which enshrine universal, even mystical perceptions and images. Dreams serve to enlarge our insight into our own resources, and contain hints on how to solve our own problems.

Research into dreaming and cognitive functioning shows the following:

- People with right brain orientation, divergence and creativity find it easy to recall their dreams.
- People with left brain orientation, verbal, analytical, recall dreams less easily.
- Problem-solving and creative dreams occur because one's habitual thought patterns are relaxed in sleep.
- Dreams may be attempts to clear pathways and resolve cognitive conflicts due to blockages and dissonances within the system.
- Research suggests that sleep may be dreamless or dream sleep. Dreams are likely to occur in all extended periods of sleep and their function seems to be to process sensory inputs throughout periods of wakefulness.
- The value of dream interpretation depends very much on the content, the relationship between the dreamer and the other person, and the dream can only be considered as a part of (for example) the client's overall work.
- Although scientists, for years, have investigated dreams, we do not know for certain why people dream or what dreams do. What is known is that dreams are connected to the REM (rapid eye movement) stage of sleep. While there may be various explanations of how we dream, there is still no direct test to prove one theory as being superior to another. What is important for counsellors is that if a client is worried by a dream, then it has some importance to the client, and while interpretation might be inappropriate, the dream should be listened to with as much attention as any other communication.

The Gestalt approach

- The Gestalt approach does not interpret and analyse dreams. Instead, the intent is to bring dreams back to life and relive them as though they were happening now.
- The dream is acted out in the present, and the dreamer becomes a part of his dream.

- The suggested format for working with dreams includes making a list of all the details of the dream, remembering each person, event and mood in it, and then becoming each of these parts by transforming oneself, acting as fully as possible and inventing dialogue.
- Each part of the dream is assumed to be a projection of the self, and the client creates scripts for encounters between the various characters or parts.
- All of the different parts of a dream are expressions of the client's own contradictory and inconsistent sides, and, by engaging in a dialogue between these opposing sides, the client gradually becomes more aware of the range of his own feelings.

Using dreams to develop your creative self

Analysis of dreams provides valuable information about your unconscious inner conflicts. Dreams more often arise from the hidden self, and nearly always have a message. The task to find that meaning is not made easier by the fact that dreams are couched in symbolic terms. Yet they direct your attention to what you are in most danger of not seeing, or neglecting.

Make your dreams work for you

Dreams can work for you. Most of us will have had the experience of going to sleep with a problem on our mind and when we wake next day the answer 'comes'. Some dreams are transparent; others come like encrypted messages on the Internet, for which we need a decoder. Free association can help to decode the hidden message.

An understanding of symbols and symbolic language will help your understanding of your dreams. There are various books on the use of symbols listed below.

Further reading

Corey, G. (2001) *Theory and Practice of Counseling and Psychotherapy*, 6th edn.Wadsworth, Brooks/Cole, Pacific Grove, CA.

Freud, S. (1900) *The Interpretation of Dreams*, Standard Edition (vol.4). Hogarth Press, London. Reprinted by Penguin 1991.

Jung, C.G. (1934) The practical use of dream analysis. In: *The Practice of Psychotherapy* (vol. 16). The Collected Works of C.G. Jung. Routledge & Kegan Paul, London.

Jung, C.G. (1936) Individual dream symbolism in relation to alchemy. In: *Psychology and Alchemy* (vol. 12). The Collected Works of C.G. Jung. Routledge & Kegan Paul, London.

Jung, C.G. (1964) *Man and His Symbols*. Doubleday & Company, Garden City.

Powell, R. (2000) *Interpretations and Insights into the Power of Dreams*. Anness Publishing, London.

Shohet, R. (1985) *Dream Sharing*, Turnstone Press, Wellingborough.

Ullman, M. (1983) *Working with Dreams*. Hutchinson, London.

Wickes, F.G. (1988) *The Inner World of Childhood: a study in analytical psychology*. Sigo Press, Boston.

Zdenek, M. (1983) *The Right-Brain Experience*. Corgi, London.

Stages of dying – Kubler-Ross

The science of the study of death is called thanatology, a term invented by Russian biologist Elie Metchnikoff. The field includes not only the biological changes associated with death but also the social, psychological, emotional, legal and ethical factors that may be involved.

In 1969 the Swiss-born psychiatrist Elisabeth Kubler-Ross conceptualised five stages in facing one's terminal illness: denial, anger, bargaining, depression and acceptance. Although most thanatologists accept the Kubler-Ross stages, they also recognise that these stages occur neither with predictable regularly nor in any set order.

Further, the five Kubler-Ross stages are simply general reactions to many situations involving loss, not necessarily dying. Seldom does a dying person follow a regular, clearly identifiable series of responses. With some, acceptance may come first, then denial; others may cross over constantly from acceptance to denial. Some may never go through denial.

Thanatology also examines attitudes towards death, the meanings and behaviours of bereavement and grief, and the moral and ethical questions of euthanasia, organ transplants and life support.

Kubler-Ross found that many dying patients are comforted if someone sits and listens to their openly expressed fears and thoughts. Patients may be assisted in reaching acceptance by the hospital staff's and family's openly talking about death when the patient so desires.

Fear not death; remember those who have gone before and those who will follow after. (William Stewart)

Tasks of dying – Worden

Opposition to the 'stages' model, because it is linear in nature, has led to a model that sees grief more as a cycle, or even a series of cycles. The bereaved move in their emotions in a sort of never-closing circle, oscillating from one painful emotion to another and perhaps experiencing more than one of the so-called stages simultaneously. What is more, the circle or cycle may not end, the bereaved may learn new coping skills, but will not therefore cease to grieve.

William Worden devised a model, which suggests that the bereaved work through a series of tasks. The idea of tasks seems very appropriate, as anyone who has suffered grief, or seen the suffering of another, can testify that it is hard work. Worden's tasks are:

- To **accept** the reality of the loss. Until this task is completed the bereaved cannot move on.
- To **experience** the pain of the loss. Many people try to escape this but Worden considers that it is necessary and that the pain may be physical as well as emotional.

- To **adjust** to an environment which no longer contains the dead person. Many difficult, practical, tasks may be involved here, as well as emotional work.
- To **withdraw** emotional energy from the deceased and reinvest it in new relationships.

Manifestations of normal grief

Worden identifies:

1. Feelings
   - Anger
   - Anxiety
   - Emancipation
   - Fatigue
   - Guilt and self-reproach
   - Helplessness
   - Loneliness
   - Numbness
   - Relief
   - Sadness
   - Shock
   - Yearning.
2. Physical sensations
   - A sense of depersonalisation
   - Breathless, feeling short of breath
   - Hollowness of the stomach
   - Lack of energy
   - Oversensitivity to noise
   - Tightness of the chest and throat
   - Weakness of the muscles
   - Dry mouth.
3. Cognitions
   - Confusion
   - Disbelief
   - Hallucinations
   - Preoccupation
   - Sense of presence.
4. Behaviours
   - Absent-minded behaviour
   - Appetite disturbances
   - Avoiding reminders of the deceased
   - Crying
   - Dreams of the deceased
   - Restless over-activity
   - Searching and calling out
   - Sighing

- Sleep disturbances
- Social withdrawal
- Treasuring objects that belonged to the deceased
- Visiting places or carrying objects.

There is much more that could be said about the stress of grief and bereavement, but enough has probably been said to draw attention to one of life's major stressors.

It is appropriate to close this entry with a quote from Gibran – *The Prophet*.

For what is it to die but to stand naked in the wind
and to melt into the sun?
And what is it to cease breathing
but to free the breath from its restless tides,
that it may rise and expand and seek God unencumbered?

Further reading

Gibran, K. (1923, reprinted 1984) *The Prophet*. Heinemann, London.

Grief and Bereavement, Counselling Skills (1991–1994) Institute of Counselling, 6 Dixon Street, Glasgow, G1 4AX.

Kubler-Ross, E. (1970) *On Death and Dying*. Tavistock, London.

Poss, S. (1981) *Towards Death with Dignity*, National Institute Social Services Library No. 41. George Allen & Unwin, London.

Worden, J.W. (1983) *Grief Counselling and Grief Therapy: a handbook for the mental health practitioner*. Routledge, London.

Zisook, S. (1985) Death, dying and bereavement. In: *Comprehensive Textbook of Psychiatry*, 6th edn (eds H.J. Kaplan and B.J. Sadock). Williams & Wilkins, Baltimore, MD.

E

EATING DISORDERS

Three eating disorders will be considered here:

- Anorexia nervosa
- Bulimia
- Compulsive over-eating.

Anorexia nervosa

Anorexia nervosa, named about a hundred years ago and existing in many countries of the world, is refusal to eat or an abnormality in eating pattern, not a loss of appetite. It occurs most commonly among adolescents but is also observed in older people.

Anorexia nervosa is commonly referred to as a 'female' problem but, although there are more females than males who suffer from it, it is not an exclusively female condition. Statistics from the Eating Disorders Association (EDA) show that around 5 to 10 per cent of sufferers from this condition are males. The greater emphasis on anorexia as a female illness is possibly due to the fact that the number of men with eating disorders is not known to doctors, self-help groups and other agencies. A second reason could be ignorance or disbelief among some professionals that anorexia could be a male problem. The fact that men do suffer from what traditionally has been considered to be a female problem might indicate that the psychology of men and women is closer than we generally accept (Eating Disorder Association (EDA)). Men who are anorexic seem more achievement-orientated and show more sexual anxiety, being athletic and placing a high value on being physically fit.

The onset of anorexia is usually between the ages of 15 and 25. The starvation regime may be pursued relentlessly, resulting in a range of health complications – involving all systems of the body – and often death. It is estimated that fatalities from anorexia run at around 13 to 20 per cent per annum (EDA).

Osteoporosis – thin bones – is a major problem. One of the first complications of anorexia nervosa is a loss of fertility.

The EDA says, 'The illnesses [anorexia nervosa and bulimia nervosa] generally develop between the ages of 15 and 25 years, although they can occur at any age, even as young as 7 or 8 years. Bulimia is rare before the age of 13. Eating disorders can persist throughout life and people may fluctuate between anorexia and bulimia.'

Physical symptoms

- Malnutrition, resulting in extreme body weight loss and emaciation

- Drastic fasting, which may be interspersed with eating sprees, usually at night, after which vomiting is induced
- Cessation of menstruation and, in males, a drop in the levels of testosterone.

Emotional symptoms

- Ranging from a neurotic preoccupation with reducing weight to full-blown schizophrenic delusions, with an overwhelming fear of getting fat
- There is often a history of relationship difficulties and fear of meeting strangers
- Irritability and depression
- Extreme weight loss over prolonged periods results in impaired reasoning and logic.

Possible causes

- **Biological**: There is no known proven cause. A disorder of the hypothalamus in the brain is a theory. A function of the hypothalamus is the control of metabolism and intestinal activity.
- **Psychological**: The major psychological factor appears to be an inability to face womanhood, with all its changes and responsibilities. Not being able to face responsibilities may be a factor in males who suffer from anorexia. However, there is sufficient anecdotal evidence to suggest a disparity between the outward appearance and the inner body-image that the person never seems able to resolve. Stress and how it is perceived and dealt with is an important trigger for anorexia.

Characteristics of the anorexic's immediate family

- Dysfunctional communication: closed, indirect, veiled, defensive
- Parental over-protectiveness
- The anorexic person is over-concerned for and feels responsible for the well-being of the others
- Intense relationships with excessive togetherness and sharing
- Rigidity with resistance to change
- Anorexics often feel that if they get well their parents' marriage will fail.
- There is often a family history of eating or weight problems.
- Anorexics are discouraged from developing personal autonomy and their own unique identity.
- Recent research shows that anorexia is more common where family members have also suffered from it. Identical twins are more likely to have anorexia than non-identical twins.

Characteristics of the person
Anorexics have a self-esteem characterised by:

- A pathological need for approval

- Stern disapproval of themselves
- A compulsion to strive for perfection
- Considering themselves unworthy
- Fixed, almost delusional, beliefs about being unattractive
- Overestimation of their body width
- Starving themselves to achieve a still smaller body-image
- Appearing unconcerned at their undernourished state
- Self-imposed social isolation, involving eating and drinking.

Sexual relationships

- Extreme weight loss leads to reduced sexual interest and activity.
- Anorexics fear taking on the sexual roles observed in their parents.
- They feel that they cannot love another when they do not like themselves.
- The slightly masculine look that many adopt warns males off.
- The break-up of a relationship may be the result of curing anorexia.
- Pregnancy is unlikely because of the extreme and prolonged weight loss.

Achievement

- Academic success is highly valued by anorexics and their families.
- An extreme fear of failure pushes them on to constantly seek approval.
- Anything less than a 100 per cent pass is a failure; praise for achievement is almost impossible to accept.
- Their weight is the only thing over which they feel they have control.
- They must control the intake of food and every function of the body, mind and emotions.

Dieting and exercise

- Obsessive rigidity and unbalanced diets characterise the anorexic's goal of ever lower weight and slimmer figure.
- So much has calorie-counting taken over that they no longer control the diet; it controls them.
- Many engage in a killing schedule of exercises and sport.
- There is a close parallel between anorexics and long-distance runners. Both are likely to be from fairly affluent backgrounds, introverted, with depressive tendencies and high achievers, with an obsessive interest in keeping up physical appearances.

Physical treatment

Hospital admission may be necessary to restore correct dietary intake and a balanced blood chemistry. Cooperation is vital, so undue pressure must be avoided. Weight gain alone is not necessarily a cure.

Emotional treatment

- Anorexia can be totally reversed, without lasting effects.

- Anorexics must want to be cured; and this means putting on weight.
- Treatment started within one year of the onset of anorexia has a far greater chance of quick recovery.

Treatment may be:

- Personal counselling concentrating on: adolescent conflict, interpersonal problems and personal experiences of stress and failure
- Behaviour modification
- Trance therapy and hypnotherapy
- Group therapy
- Family counselling – one particular approach includes taking meals with the family to identify the mealtime dynamics
- Self-help groups, such as Anorexic Aid, offer help in much the same way as Alcoholics Anonymous.

Recovery

Recovery rests with:

- Acceptance that there is a problem
- A sincere desire to get better
- A willingness to accept change of lifestyle and circumstances
- Exploration, understanding of the underlying issues and feelings
- Setting and striving to achieve realistic targets of attitudes to food and weight.

Early warning signs

- Becoming isolated in their room
- Missing meals or making excuses of having eaten
- Eating alone in room
- Slimming and diet magazines
- Scales in the bathroom
- Reluctance to eat in public
- Small amounts of food eaten
- Bread, potatoes and carbohydrates avoided
- Bulky, loose sweaters that disguise shape
- Food thrown away
- Ultra health-conscious
- Failure to put on weight
- Preoccupation with calorie-counting
- Excessive amounts of exercise
- Poor sleep, restlessness, hyperactivity
- Cessation of menstruation.

Prevention

- Establish effective communication.
- Don't insist on increased intake.

- Encourage outside help.
- Don't pressure for weight gain.
- Encourage self-action and responsibility.
- Parents may need counselling themselves.
- Remove pressure to succeed.
- Encourage independence.

What happens afterwards?

- Anorexics may lapse when under pressure.
- Anorexia is like alcoholism in that the person must always be on guard; joining a group of ex-anorexics may provide the support necessary to cope with living.
- Forming relationships with the opposite sex is a huge hurdle for many ex-anorexics.

Bulimia nervosa (binge-eating)

Russell (quoted in Garfinkel) first used the term in 1979 to describe a group of patients who feared putting on weight yet had a compulsive urge to eat. It is most common in societies where slimness is considered desirable and attractive.

Important points about the condition

- The excessive eating, which causes distress, is not within the person's control.
- People who have also experienced anorexia are more prone to develop bulimia. This is thought to be when the iron-like control over not eating suddenly cracks and results in a binge. Guilt takes over, resulting in self-induced vomiting. The starvation and binge cycle starts all over again.
- Bulimia never comes of its own accord but follows a period of self-imposed starvation. The body revolts against this deprivation and the food gorged is what the body most needs, especially carbohydrates.
- Binge-eating is accompanied by self-induced vomiting or the abuse of purgatives, or both. Self-induced vomiting ensures a secret method of maintaining weight at a level that keeps other people satisfied.
- Bulimia may start just as the anorexic is reaching optimum body weight.
- Pressure may push the recovering anorexic into bulimia.
- Not all bulimics have been anorexic but they are just as fearful of putting on weight. They seem not to have the same iron control to do without food for such long periods.
- Bulimics are thrown into panic when they feel that their body has taken control away from them.
- Bulimics fear that if they start eating they will eat everything in sight.
- The mind of the bulimic is constantly full of thoughts about food. They dream about it. This is similar to the experiences of prisoners of war in concentration camps, whose daydreams were often about food.

- Binge eating is usually done in secret and the buying of the food is so arranged that no one could be suspicious.
- The person may resort to strenuous exercise and the use of stimulants or diuretics.
- Bulimics often feel depressed, brought on by feelings of having lost control and self-disgust. Sustained use of stimulants often brings depression in its wake. Deterioration of relationships is also a factor in this depression.
- Constant vomiting is harmful because the body is deprived not only of food but of gastrointestinal juices essential for health. Juices that have their function in the stomach have a harmful effect on the upper parts of the alimentary tract. Continual loss of fluid often leads to dehydration.
- People who cannot make themselves vomit often resort to repeated purging, also damaging to health.
- Bulimia is but one indication of lack of control; many also overspend and get into financial difficulty. So overpowering is the desire for food that some will steal to get it. Relationships are also entered into in the same overboard way. Few succeed in a long-term, lasting sexual relationship.
- Most bulimics, male and female, have low self-esteem and desperately seek approval.
- There is some evidence to support the theory that female bulimics identify with their fathers and males with their mothers.
- The basic conflict is between their need to be admired and desired by a member of the opposite sex, on the one hand, and a fear that they are not good enough and will be rejected, on the other.
- Unlike anorexics, bulimics normally continue to menstruate. Some conceive and a few give birth. Many, however, are against the idea of becoming pregnant.
- Because bulimics normally weigh more than anorexics, their eating habits may escape notice for years. Their preoccupation with weight and size equates to that of anorexics.
- Bulimics generally feel afraid when they feel the desire to binge coming on, when they have successfully controlled it for a while.
- A recent study in Switzerland showed that women who binge and purge are more likely to have attempted suicide in the past, regardless of whether they have been diagnosed with anorexia nervosa, bulimia or another eating disorder.

Treatment

A normal eating pattern must be established. This is not easy, for the patterns of eating and vomiting are firmly established.

As bulimics are intent on keeping their weight down, cooperation is problematic, but essential if their programme is to work.

Hospital treatment, where skilled help is available, is desirable if the pattern of binge eating and vomiting is to be interrupted. Hospital admission is essential if there are physical complications or if there is depression.

Repeated information-giving about the effects of binge eating and persistent vomiting is a necessary part of treatment, supported by an equally forcible plugging of the physical and emotional advantages of a balanced eating programme.

Eating small amounts slowly in the company of others encourages a normal eating pattern. Water intake is restricted; too much water gives a sensation of fullness. No eating is allowed between meals.

Some effort is made to gradually increase the weight beyond what the client thinks is desirable.

Those not in hospital are trusted to keep a daily journal of all food they eat as well as times they want to, or actually do, vomit.

Supervision is likely to continue for months or even years.

Compulsive over-eating

The characteristics of compulsive over-eating are:

- Uncontrollable eating with consequent weight gain
- Food is used as a way to cope with stress, emotional conflicts and daily problems
- Food is used to block out feelings and emotions
- Feel out of control
- Aware that their eating patterns are abnormal
- Usually recognise that they have a problem.

Onset of compulsive over-eating

- Usually starts in early childhood
- Have never learned to deal with stressful situations other than by eating as way of coping
- Victims of abuse may eat to gain weight as a protection, to keep others at a distance, and make them less attractive.
- Unlike anorexia and bulimia, there is a high proportion of male overeaters.
- Binges occur after a determined attempt to diet and lose weight.
- Feelings of powerlessness, guilt and shame accompany failure to gain control.
- Like anorexia and bulimia, compulsive overeating is a serious problem and can result in death.
- With the proper treatment, which should include therapy, medical and nutritional counselling, it can be overcome.

Signs and symptoms

- Binge eating
- Fear of not being able to stop eating voluntarily
- Depression
- Self-deprecating thoughts following binges
- Withdrawing from activities because of embarrassment about weight

- Going on many different diets
- Eating little in public, while maintaining a high weight
- Believing they will be a better person when thin
- Feelings about self based on weight
- Social and professional failures attributed to weight
- Feeling tormented by eating habits
- Weight is focus of life.

Physical/medical complications

- Weight gain
- Hypertension or fatigue
- Heart ailments
- Mobility problems
- Diabetes
- Arthritis
- Sciatica
- Varicose veins
- Hiatus hernia
- Embolism
- Sleep deprivation
- Toxaemia during pregnancy
- High blood pressure
- Shortness of breath
- High cholesterol levels
- Cardiac arrest and death.

Trends among men

Men seem more aware of their image than previously and, with the adverts for chiselled, muscular male models, eating disorders could become worse among men. Added to this is the guilt and shame of succumbing to what has been known as a 'woman's disease'.

According to researchers, men can also suffer from bulimia, binge eating and, to a lesser extent, anorexia.

Athletes whose weight is crucial to their performance – jockeys, wrestlers, distance runners and gymnasts – are reported to have a higher incidence of eating disorders.

The root causes can be similar for men and women: genetics, low self-esteem, trauma and cultural influences.

Trends among children

It is reported that:

- Many 10 year olds are afraid of being fat
- Many 7 year olds are dieting
- Young girls would rather be dead than fat

- In the US, the number of children with eating disorders and related issues continues to increase.

Further reading

Boskind-Lodahl, M. (1981) Cinderella's stepsisters: a feminist perspective on anorexia nervosa and bulimia. In: *Women and Mental Health* (eds E. Howell and M. Bayes). Basic Books, New York.

Eating Disorders Association Newsletter, July 1997. First Floor, Wensum House, 103 Prince of Wales Road, Norwich, NR1 1DW.

Garfinkel, P.E. (1995) Eating disorders. In: *Comprehensive Textbook of Psychiatry*, 6th edn (eds H.J. Kaplan and B.J. Sadock). Williams & Wilkins, Baltimore, MD.

MacLeod, S. (1981) *The Art of Starvation: anorexia observed*. Virago, London.

Melville, J. (1983) *The ABC of Eating: coping with anorexia, bulimia and compulsive eating*. Sheldon Press, London.

Siegel, M., Brisman, J. and Weinshel, M, (1988) *Surviving an Eating Disorder: perspectives and strategies for family and friends*. Harper & Row, New York.

Sutton, J. (1999) *Healing the Hurt Within*. How to Books, Oxford.

Vaughan, E. (1979) Counselling anorexia. *Marriage Guidance Journal*, September.

Vredevelt, P. and Whitman J. (1985) *Walking a Thin Line*. Mullnomah Press, Oregon.

www.hypnosis-hypnotherapy.co.uk

www.justbewell.com

www.MySelfHelp.com

ECLECTIC COUNSELLING

The word 'eclectic' means deriving ideas, tastes, style etc. from various sources – generally, not following any one system but selecting and using whatever is considered best in all systems. There is a growing trend towards integration and eclecticism.

Some practitioners regard eclecticism as being healthy; others think that a more formal and structured approach is more appropriate. Eclecticism is usually put at one pole of a dimension that runs from the eclectic to the formal.

Those who favour eclecticism feel that such an approach suits their personality and that they can offer variety, rather than expecting the client to fit some theoretical model that suits the counsellor.

While many counsellors work to one model of counselling, probably an equal number are eclectic counsellors, using a variety of approaches. They are most likely to have one core framework but borrow from other models and apply them to suit their particular needs.

Purists might not approve of this varied use of theories or models but eclectic counsellors would possibly counter this with, 'If it will help, use it'. Eclectics would also believe that, instead of trying to fit the client into one framework or model, the counsellors should be adaptable and find what works for you, rather than the other way round. Every person is unique and has needs and goals specific to his own life stage, particular problem(s) or degree of self-awareness.

Thus a counsellor using an eclectic or integrated approach may use a psychodynamic approach to bring unconscious drives and/or defences into conscious awareness. Behavioural therapy may be appropriate if a particular behaviour pattern is inhibiting, e.g. if the client has a specific sexual difficulty. Cognitive therapy could help if the messages from the client's earlier life are leading to self-defeating or self-destructive thought patterns or behaviours. Most counsellors using an eclectic approach work with the person-centred core principles.

Norcross and Tomcho point to the difference between eclectic and syncretic counselling, which is an attempt to unify or reconcile differing schools of thought. Syncretic counsellors 'fly by the seat of their pants'. They operate in a muddle.

Eclectic counselling is systematic, based on the counsellor being trained and skilled in several therapeutic systems and using them appropriately. Eclectic counselling is backed by research and experience.

The authors quoted above end their article by saying (speaking to would-be therapists seeking therapy for themselves) that competence, clinical experience, professional reputation, warmth and caring rank much higher than theoretical orientation.

Sue Wheeler highlights a difference between eclectic and integrated. The one fits with the general view of being eclectic; the integrated approach is a hybrid, made up of different theories, models and approaches. This corresponds with what Norcross and Tomcho call syncretic.

Wheeler points out that for a counsellor to be fully trained in at least two models, the counsellor would have to be in training (part-time) for at least five to six years. She also says that offering 'modules' is not a satisfactory substitute for eclectic training, mainly because there is no true integration of the theory and practice.

Further, 'if there is no core theoretical model that is studied in depth, students have no secure frame of reference in which to conceptualize their clients' concerns or on which to rely when the going gets tough'. Whatever the core model, that does not preclude the counsellor from exploring other models.

At a practical level, and this is perhaps where the counsellor might experience great conflict, is the therapeutic relationship. For example, in person-centred counselling, the counsellor works with being warm, accepting, genuine and real; in psychodynamic counselling the counsellor interprets unconscious motivation from a theoretical base, not from what something means to the client, as in person-centred counselling. In transpersonal counselling, working with the body through touch and movement may be totally acceptable.

Corey lists eight motives in the growth of eclecticism:

1. A proliferation of therapies
2. The inadequacy of a single theory that is relevant to all clients and all problems
3. External socio-economic realities, such as restrictions for insurance reimbursement and the prospect of national health insurance
4. The growing popularity of short-term, prescriptive and problem-focused therapies
5. Opportunities to observe and experiment with various therapies

6. A paucity of differential effectiveness among therapies
7. Recognition that therapeutic commonalities play a major role in determining therapy outcome
8. Development of professional societies aimed at the integration of psychotherapies.

Future trends in integration

- Multicultural issues
- Spiritual/religious issues
- Common goals
- Implications for assessment and treatment
- The role of the counsellor.

The basic approaches

- Analytical psychology (Jungian)
- Behaviour therapy
- Cognitive behaviour therapy
- Existential therapy
- Family systems therapy
- Feminist therapy
- Gestalt therapy
- Individual (Adlerian) therapy
- Person-centred therapy
- Psychoanalytic therapy
- Reality therapy.

Corey sums up this important development thus (the text has been anglicised):

Therapists cannot simply pick bits and pieces from theories in a random and fragmented manner. In forming an integrated perspective, it is important to ask: Which theories provide a basis for understanding the cognitive dimensions? What about the feeling aspects? And how about the behavioural dimension?

Developing an integrated theoretical perspective requires much reading, thinking, and actual counselling experience. Unless you have an accurate, in-depth knowledge of these theories, you cannot formulate a true synthesis. Simply put, you cannot integrate what you do not know.

Besides considering your own personality, think about what concepts and techniques work best with a range of clients. It requires knowledge, skill, art and experience to be able to determine what techniques are suitable for particular problems. It is also an art to know when and how to use a particular therapeutic intervention.

Further reading

Corey, G. (2001) *Theory and Practice of Counseling and Psychotherapy*, 6th edn. Wadsworth, Brooks/Cole, Pacific Grove, CA.

Norcross, J.C. and Newman, C.F. (1992). Psychotherapy integration: setting the context. In: *Handbook of Psychotherapy Integration* (eds J.C. Norcross and M.R. Goldfried). Basic Books, New York.

Norcross, J.C. and Tomcho, T.J. (1993) Beyond specific orientations. In: *Questions and Answers on Counselling in Action* (ed. W. Dryden). Sage Publications, London.

Wheeler, S. (1993) Reservations about eclectic and integrative approaches to counselling. In: *Questions and Answers on Counselling in Action* (ed. W. Dryden). Sage Publications, London.

EMOTIONAL FREEDOM TECHNIQUES (EFT)

EFT is becoming known to many amazed users as a modern miracle. It can dramatically relieve emotional disturbances along with many physical symptoms. It often works in minutes, its results are usually long lasting and side effects are almost always positive.

With remarkable consistency, EFT relieves symptoms by an unusual (but scientific) routine of tapping with the fingertips on a short series of points on the body that correspond to acupuncture points on the energy meridians. Where there is an imbalance, there is a corresponding blockage in the flow of energy through the meridian system.

EFT was developed early in the 1990s by Gary Craig, whose academic training includes a Stanford engineering degree.

EFT encompasses a longer term approach to relationship counselling, structured in nine steps that may take as many as 26 sessions. The change process in EFT involves identifying the cycle of pursuit/withdrawal in the couple being counselled, cycle de-escalation, engagement of the withdrawer and softening of blame on the part of the other person.

It is apparent, however, that EFT is most effective with clients who are not suffering deep hurts or major trauma, and with clients who are capable of self-reflection and are comfortable with emotional presence.

EFT involves the use of individualised tapping routines. EFT differs in that it employs only one comprehensive tapping routine, which is used for all emotional and physical problems. Because of this, it is easy enough to be mastered by most people.

www.emofree.com
www.businessballs.com/eftemotionalfreedomtechniques.htm
RodBenson@bigpond.com

EFT – benefits of

- Remove negative emotions
- Reduce food cravings
- Reduce or eliminate pain
- Implement positive goals.

Further reading

www.garycraig.com for CDs on EFT.
Rowe, Dr J.E. *Keep tapping.* www.emofree.com/articles/theoreti.htm

EUTHANASIA

Euthanasia describes an easy and painless death or the means for producing one. It is advocated by many for those suffering from intractable pain that accompanies the terminal stages of many incurable diseases.

Passive euthanasia is when one simply ceases to supply support measures specifically needed to keep an individual alive. Active euthanasia is when specific means are taken to terminate life.

Because there is no specific provision for euthanasia in most legal systems, it is accounted either suicide (if performed by the patient himself) or murder (if performed by another).

The opinion that euthanasia is morally permissible goes back to Socrates, Plato and the Stoics. It is rejected in traditional Christian belief, chiefly because it is thought to come within the prohibition of murder in the Sixth Commandment.

The organised movement for legalisation commenced in England in 1935, when C. Killick Millard founded the Voluntary Euthanasia Legalisation Society (later called the Voluntary Euthanasia Society). The society's bill was defeated in the House of Lords in 1936, and so also was a motion on the same subject in the House of Lords in 1950. In the United States, the Euthanasia Society of America was founded in 1938.

Counsellors may become drawn into moral, ethical and legal conflict if clients they are counselling are actively seeking to end their lives.

The Voluntary Euthanasia Society:

- Promotes greater patient choice at the end of life
- Campaigns for people with terminal illnesses to be allowed to ask for medical help to die at a time of their choosing, within proper legal safeguards
- Wants to make back-street suicides and 'mercy killings' a thing of the past
- Is the leading supplier of living wills in the UK. A living will is a legally binding document that sets out how you wish to be treated, should you no longer be able to communicate your wishes to your medical team.

What is a living will?

Whereas an ordinary 'last will and testament' deals with your wishes on the disposal of your money and property, a 'living will' deals with your wishes on what medical treatment you are to receive or not receive, should there come a time in the future when you are, through specified illnesses, no longer capable of making such decisions or of communicating them to your medical attendants or family.

One final aspect of making a 'living will' is that should you be in a coma through illness or accident – be on a life support machine for example – you have taken the responsibility away from any member of the family concerning what treatment you are to receive or not receive in the given circumstances – even to when to switch the machine off.

People's views on euthanasia

Research by the Imperial Medical School of Medicine, London (published in the *British Medical Journal*, 16 August 2000, carried out on patients aged between 66 and 97 years at two hospitals) found that once the idea of making a 'living will' had been explained to them:

- 92 per cent said they wanted to register in advance that they would not wish their lives to be prolonged by doctors if they became too ill to communicate themselves.
- 90 per cent stated they would not want their lives prolonged if they developed a terminal illness and would refuse surgery, artificial feeding, ventilation and resuscitation.
- Almost as many were against having intravenous fluids or antibiotics.
- Many disabilities were unacceptable to the patients, such as being bedridden, doubly incontinent or unable to speak.
- Many patients would prefer 'comfort only' care and nursing to active treatment – even if it meant they might die.
- The most feared condition was advanced Alzheimer's, whilst the least feared was having to use a wheelchair.
- Around 75 per cent expressed interest in writing a 'living will' (advanced directive), one of the main reasons being to relieve the burden on the family of taking such treatment decisions, or conversely they suffer loss of dignity and quality of life by having it medically prolonged.
- When researchers made it clear that they were talking about the difference between active care and letting nature take its course, the majority wanted comfort-care only.

The British Medical Association, the Patients Association, the Royal College Of Nursing and the government all support the concept of 'living wills'.

> *Planned legislation to allow people to register 'advance decisions' on future treatment they wish to refuse should they lose their mental faculties, was published yesterday [18 June 2004]. But Lord Filkin, minister in charge of the mental capacity bill – recently renamed from the politically incorrect 'mental incapacity bill' – said a series of discussions with prominent members of the Catholic church, including the archbishop of Cardiff, the Most Rev Peter Smith, had led to a tightening of the proposed restrictions on living wills.*
>
> *He said: 'Earlier drafts of the bill have been quite wrongly linked with the idea of legalising euthanasia. This bill expressly provides that it does not affect the law on murder, manslaughter or assisted suicide.'*
>
> Bob Sherwood, Legal Correspondent, *Mirror* (19 June 2004)

The anti-euthanasia lobby

Euthanasia is a highly contentious subject worldwide. The *New Zealand Herald* (19 June 2004) said: 'Nearly 700 doctors have admitted hastening the deaths of terminally ill patients despite legal constraints, a study in the *New Zealand Medical Journal* revealed today.'

The anti-lobbyists argue that the promotion of living wills and advance directives create a climate for the acceptance of euthanasia. A grey area is where there is dispute between the medical staff and the patient or the patient's relatives, as in 1993 when the Law Lords ruled that Tony Bland, in a so-called 'persistent vegetative state', could be made to die of dehydration. They also maintain that living wills enable doctors to end the lives of patients, whilst protecting the doctor from civil or criminal liability.

ALERT www.donoharm.org.uk

Arguments against euthanasia

- Euthanasia is forbidden by God.
- Euthanasia could not be regulated safely.
- Human beings should never be killed.
- The slippery slope argument.
- Accepting euthanasia weakens society's respect for human life.
- Suffering may have real value.
- Euthanasia gives doctors too much power.
- Euthanasia will make people scared of doctors.
- Euthanasia may not be in the best interests of the patient.
- Good pain control makes euthanasia unnecessary.
- Proper end of life care makes euthanasia unnecessary.
- Euthanasia sends the wrong message about disability.
- Euthanasia may infringe other people's rights.

Arguments in support of euthanasia

- Euthanasia can be merciful.
- Human beings have the right to die how and when they want to.
- The libertarian argument.
- Euthanasia may be necessary for the fair distribution of medical resources.
- Allowing euthanasia can be universalised as a moral rule.
- Euthanasia will always occur – so it's better to allow it and regulate it properly.
- Death is not always an evil to be avoided.

www.bbc.co.uk

The religious point of view

I sincerely believe that those who come after us will wonder why on earth we kept a human being alive against his [sic] will, when all the dignity, beauty and meaning of life had vanished; when any gain to anyone was clearly impossible and when we should have been punished by the state if we had kept an animal in similar conditions.

Dr Leslie Weatherhead (the late leader of the Methodist church in the UK)

Some Christians who disagree with euthanasia but support the idea of dying with dignity have been involved with the setting up of the hospice movement. Many hospices have a Christian foundation.

All Christians also believe in life after death and so would not consider death as the end of life but as a stage on the road. This idea could be applied to both sides of the argument.

Websites

The Voluntary Euthanasia Society: www.ves.org.uk
The Church of England's views on: www.cofe.anglican.org/view/index.html
www.portfolio.mvm.ed.ac.uk

Further reading

Emanuel, E.J. (1994) Euthanasia: Historical, Ethical and Empiric Perspectives. *Arch Intern Med*, 154: 1890–1901.

Emanuel, E.J., Emanuel, L.L. (1998) The promise of a good death. *The Lancet*, 351 ii: 21–29.

Gillon, R. (1994) Medical ethics: four principles plus attention to scope. *British Medical Journal*, 309: 184 (16 July).

Institute of Medical Ethics Working Party on the Ethics of Prolonging Life and Assisting Death (1990) Assisted death. *The Lancet*, 336: 610–613.

Keown, J. (ed.) (1995) *Euthanasia Examined: ethical, legal and clinical perspectives*. Cambridge University Press, Cambridge.

Zisook, S. (1985) Death, dying and bereavement. In: *Comprehensive Textbook of Psychiatry*, 6th edn (eds H.J. Kaplan and B.J. Sadock). Williams & Wilkins, Baltimore, MD.

EVALUATION

Individual counselling sessions

By evaluating or analysing counselling sessions, counsellors will continue to make progress. Evaluation encourages the growth of both client and counsellor.

If counsellor and client are active partners in the evaluation process, they can learn from each other.

Ongoing evaluation gives both partners an opportunity to explore their feelings about what is happening and also to appraise, constructively, what should be done next.

What happened within the counsellor?
Was the counsellor:

- Fully attentive
- Listening actively
- Asking too many questions
- Leading the client
- Open or closed
- Afraid to challenge
- Insensitively challenging

- Able to empathise
- Relaxed or tense
- Friendly or aloof
- Anxious or at ease
- Quiet or talkative
- Interested or bored?

What happened within the client?
Was the client:

- Fully present
- Responding to the counsellor
- Showing evidence of blocking
- Open with feelings
- Prepared to explore
- Waiting for answers
- An active partner?

What happened between counsellor and client?
Was there:

- Participation
- Involvement or over-involvement
- Argument
- Persuasion
- Feeling versus intellect
- Reassurance versus exploration
- Tolerance
- Achievement of insight?

Was the following behaviour exhibited: if so, by whom?

- Tension release
- Support
- Caring
- Aggression
- Hostility
- Manipulation
- Rejection?

Body language and its significance
Was there:

- Physical contact
- Proximity and position
- Gestures
- Facial expressions
- Eye contact?

Atmosphere:
Was the atmosphere:

- Formal/informal
- Competitive/cooperative
- Hostile
- Supportive
- Inhibited/permissive
- Harmonious/destructive?

On termination of counselling

A terminal evaluation gives both client and counsellor a feeling of completeness. It gives the counsellor an opportunity to look at some of those things that did not go according to plan, as well as those that did.

A well-carried-out evaluation not only looks backwards, it also looks forwards. A final evaluation provides the client with something positive to carry into the future.

Termination should be well planned and worked through. Abrupt termination can be very traumatic to both client and counsellor. It should be approached with as much sensitivity and caring as any stage in the counselling.

When counselling has taken place over a long period, the original reason(s) may have faded into insignificance. Counselling is like taking a journey: we know from where we have come and roughly the route taken, but looking back, the starting point has become obscured, partly through distance but also through time.

Unlike a journey, it is necessary for both counsellor and client to look back in order to firmly establish the final position.

Looking back to where and why the journey began may prove difficult; feelings, as well as memories, fade with time. Looking back is not always comfortable. It may reveal obstacles not previously recognised.

Evaluation should identify:

- The different problems and how these were tackled
- The goals and how they have been achieved
- Areas of growth and insights.

The relationship between counsellor and client is not an end in itself. Evaluation helps to establish just how the client has been able to transfer the learning into relationships outside of counselling.

Evaluation helps the client to realise and acknowledge personal gains. The counsellor, in return, receives something from every counselling relationship.

Success in counselling is not easily measured, however:

- Clients who have succeeded in climbing a few hills are more likely to want to tackle mountains and, emotionally, are better equipped to do so.
- Counsellors who have helped create an atmosphere of trust and respect, and have helped a client travel a little way along the road of self-discovery, are entitled to share the success the client feels.

The feeling of failure in counselling is difficult to handle. Blame should not be attributed to either counsellor or client. Both (if that is possible, but if not, the counsellor alone) should examine what did happen rather than what did not happen.

If counselling goes full term, it is unlikely to be a failure. The feeling of failure and consequent blame is more likely when the client terminates prematurely.

If counsellors have created a conducive climate and clients are unable to travel their own road towards self-discovery, then the responsibility for not travelling that road must rest with them. We can only take those people along the road of self-discovery who are willing to travel with us. We can only travel at their pace. Unless two (or a group) are in agreement, the journey towards self-discovery will be fraught with impossibilities.

Some possible indicators of impending termination

- Abandonment
- Acting out
- Apathy
- Decrease in intensity
- Denial
- Expressions of anger
- Feelings of separation and loss
- Futility
- Impotence
- Inadequacy
- Intellectualising
- Joking
- Lateness
- Missed appointments
- Mourning
- Regression
- Withdrawal.

Further reading

Cormier, W.H. and Cormier, L.S. (1979) *Interviewing Strategies for Helpers: a guide to assessment, treatment and evaluation.* Brooks/Cole, Pacific Grove, CA.

Ivey, A. (1983) *Intentional Interviewing and Counselling.* Brooks/Cole, Pacific Grove, CA.

Sutton, J. and Stewart, W. (2002) *Learning to Counsel: develop the skills you need to counsel others,* 2nd edn. How to Books, Oxford.

Ward, D.E. (1989) Termination of individual counselling: concepts and strategies. In: *Key Issues for Counselling in Action* (ed. W. Dryden). Sage Publications, London.

EXISTENTIAL THERAPY (SEE ALSO: LOGOTHERAPY)

Existential therapy is a psychodynamic approach within psychotherapy influenced by existentialism, rather than a distinct school of therapy. The existential therapy movement was not founded by one person or by a singular group of people. It grew out of the need to help people resolve such issues as isolation, alienation and meaninglessness.

The key figures of the existentialist movement are:

- Viktor Frankl, who developed logotherapy, which means therapy through meaning
- Rollo May, who was instrumental in bringing existentialism from Europe to the US. According to May, it takes courage to 'be', and how we choose influences the type of person we become
- James Bugental, who views therapy as a journey undertaken by the therapist and the client, where the focus is the client's inner world. This relationship demands of counsellors a willingness to be in contact with their own inner world
- Irvin Yalom, whose approach focuses on:
  - death
  - freedom
  - existential isolation
  - meaningless.

Enshrined in this approach is a belief in the individual's capacity to become healthy and fully functional; to rise above self through self-consciousness and self-reflection. This is achieved as the client concentrates on what is happening in the present; accepting that what happens in life is partly his personal responsibility and influenced by decisions.

Existentially oriented psychotherapists concern themselves with how the client experiences life rather than with diagnosis and cause. Psychoanalysis, conversely, concentrates on cause and effect, and on trying to reduce complicated patterns to individual parts.

Important principles

- The immediate moment of experience
- Conscious, personal identity
- Unity of the person
- The search for the meaning of life
- Pathology arises from the need to defend against alienation from self and others and the anxiety generated by the threat of the immediate experience.
- Alienation from self leads to rigid, restrictive behaviour, a clinging to the past and a desire to impose a false order on the present and future.
- Existential therapists engage in a dialogue within an authentic and equal relationship, in which the therapist is totally present.

The aims of existential therapy are to help clients:

- To take responsibility for their own being in the world
- To become independent and self-governing
- To move beyond self into full fellowship with others

- To exercise conscious intention
- To make ethical choices
- To accept high ideals
- To engage in loving relationships
- To confront normal anxiety, an unavoidable part of being human
- To confront and reduce anxiety that is related to fear – anxiety is more basic than fear
- To live without neurotic anxiety but to be able to tolerate normal, existential anxiety.

The cost of change may mean having to deal with anxiety and inner crises. The person's only authentic response to the contribution of the family and other social institutions may be to choose madness.

Existentialism is similar to humanistic therapies, although it may be more confronting. It is the opposite of the more technical, behavioural and strategy-dominated therapies. It is an attempt to grapple with the meaninglessness and extinction that threaten present-day societies.

Basic concepts

The 'I am' experience

- The 'I am' experience is known as an 'ontological' experience, which translated from the Greek means 'the science of being'.
- It is the realisation of one's being and the choice one has of saying, 'I am the one living, experiencing. I choose my own being'.
- Being is not tied to status or what one does, occupation or the life one leads.
- When everything else is stripped away, one can still say 'I am'.
- The experience of being also points to the experience of non-being or nothingness.
- Examples of non-being would be the threat of death, destruction, severe and crippling anxiety or sickness.
- The threat of non-being is ever present, e.g. in a remark by someone that puts us down.

Normal and neurotic anxiety

In existential terms anxiety arises from our personal need to survive, to preserve and to assert our being; it is the threat to our existence or to values we identify with our existence. The characteristics of normal existential anxiety are:

- It is proportionate to the situation.
- It does not require to be repressed.
- It can be used constructively, e.g. to discover the underlying dilemma that created the anxiety.

The characteristics of neurotic anxiety are:

- It is not appropriate to the situation.

- It is repressed.
- It is destructive and paralysing, not constructive and stimulating.

Guilt feelings

- Neurotic guilt feelings usually arise out of fantasised transgressions.
- Normal guilt feelings make us sensitive to social and ethical aspects of behaviour
- Existential guilt feelings arise from locking up our potentialities.

The world

- The world includes all past events and influences that condition our existence.
- The way one relates to these events and influences is what holds meaning.
- There are three forms of world:
  - **The 'world around'** (environment): the world of objects, the natural world, biological drives
  - **'Own world'** (relationship to self): self-awareness, self-relatedness, grasping the meaning of something in the world
  - **'With-world'** (fellow humans): interpersonal relationships and love. To truly love, one must have become truly individual and sufficient unto oneself. The 'with-world' is empty of vitality if 'own world' is lacking.

The significance of time

Time is considered to be the heart of existence.

- Experiences such as anxiety, depression and joy are usually related to time.
- People who cannot relate to time, who cannot hope for the future, who view each day as an island with no past and no future, are seriously disturbed.
- The ability to relate to time is one of the characteristics of being human.
- Time fixes us in the here and now, and prevents us from being lost in space.
- Some experiences, such as the development of life, cannot be measured by time.
- Experiencing in the 'now' breaks through time.
- Insight is not time-controlled; it comes complete.
- When one's past does not come alive, it is probably because one's future has no attraction.
- Being able to change something, however small, in the present, gives hope to work towards a future.

The capacity to transcend the immediate:

- Existing means a continual going beyond the past and present to reach out to the future.
- Transcendence means being able to think in terms of 'the possible'.
- People who are unable to think in terms of the possible feel threatened by the lack of specific boundaries – it is as if they already perceive themselves as 'lost in space'.

- People who are unable to think of what is possible experience a world that has shrunk around them, with consequent loss of freedom.
- The existential model of personality postulates that the basic conflict is between the individual and the 'givens' (or 'ultimate concerns') of existence.

Death

A core conflict exists between one's awareness of death and the concurrent wish to continue living. It is an emotional disturbance that is often the result of inadequate death transcendence, which then leads to terror of death.

Freedom

In existential terms, freedom is bound to dread. Inherent in freedom is self-responsibility, for life design and its consequences. Responsibility for one's situation is bound to the principle of 'willing', which consists of wishing and then deciding.

Many people cannot wish, because they cannot feel. When we fully experience a wish, we are then faced with a decision. Some people experience 'decisional panic' and try to pass the decision-making on to others.

Isolation

- Interpersonal isolation is the separation of oneself from others, which results from either a deficiency in social skill or a pathological fear of intimacy.
- Intrapersonal isolation is where we have dissociated parts of ourselves – experiences, desires, feelings – out of awareness.
- Existential isolation is a fundamental isolation from people and from the world. People who suffer from depression may also experience existential depression, where they can no longer find meaning in their activity and can find no sense of purpose.

There is always a gap that cannot be bridged. The personal dilemma is that, no matter how intimate the relationship, there is always a part that we will never be able to share. This has been referred to as 'the fundamental loneliness'. The most poignant example of the fundamental loneliness is the experience of death.

The fear of death and of isolation keeps many people from entering relations – of any depth and intimacy. Some people doubt their own existence so much that they only feel they exist in the presence of another. Many undergo a fusion with others, so that 'I' becomes 'we', resulting in the safety of conformity. Compulsive sexuality is a common antidote to the terrifying prospect of isolation. The sexually compulsive person relates only to part of the other, not to the whole.

Meaninglessness

This often revolves around questions such as:

- What possible meaning can life have?
- Why do we live?

- How shall we live?
- Is my self-created meaning of life strong enough to bear my life?

In the same way as we need to organise random events into something we can understand, so we deal with the existential situation. Were we not able to find some meaning, we would be desperately unsettled. From a sense of the meaning of life, we generate values that provide a master-plan for life conduct. Values not only tell us why we live, but how to live.

The dilemma of existential meaninglessness, then, is: How do I find meaning in a universe that has no meaning?

Defence mechanisms
To an existentialist therapist, anxiety results from confrontation with death, freedom, isolation and meaninglessness. Two defence mechanisms ensue:

1. **Specialness**
   - This involves a deep, powerful belief that one cannot be destroyed, is totally invulnerable and will never die.
   - The person believes that the laws of biology do not apply.
   - These beliefs (of delusional quality) give rise to narcissism, search for glory, search for power or suspicious behaviour.
   - Such people often seek therapy when their defence of specialness no longer holds up and they are hit by anxiety.
2. **An ultimate rescuer**
   - This is the belief in an omnipotent protector who will always snatch us from the deepest hell.
   - These beliefs (of delusional quality) give rise to passivity, dependency and servile behaviour.
   - Such people often dedicate themselves to living for the 'dominant other', which is fertile ground for depression.

Existential therapy is not a system of psychotherapy, it is a frame of reference, a pattern for understanding a client's suffering in a distinctive manner.

Further reading
Binswanger, L. (1967) *Being-in-the-World*. Harper & Row, New York.
Corey, G. (2001) *Theory and Practice of Counseling and Psychotherapy*, 6th edn. Wadsworth, Brooks/Cole, Pacific Grove, CA.
Deurzen-Smith, E. van (1988) *Existential Counselling in Practice*. Sage Publications, London.
Frankl, V. (1973) *Psychotherapy and Existentialism*. Penguin, Harmondsworth.
Macquarrie, J. (1972) *Existentialism*. Penguin, Harmondsworth.
May, R., and Yalom, I. (1995) Existential psychotherapy. In: *Current Psychotherapies*, 5th edn (eds R.J. Corsinie and D. Wedding). F.E. Peacock, Itsaca, IL.
Yalom, I.D. (1981) *Existential Psychotherapy*. Basic Books, New York.

F

FAMILY THERAPY

Family therapy brings all the members of one family into a therapy group, on the assumption that families operate as an interacting system and that one member's problems are only symptomatic of problems in the system. Thus the focus of therapy is on the whole family (the system) as the client. A family is more than the sum of its members.

The family as a focus for treatment usually comprises the members who live under the same roof, sometimes supplemented by relatives who live elsewhere or by other people who share the family home. Family therapy may be appropriate when the person referred for treatment has symptoms clearly related to such disturbances in family function as marital discord, distorted family roles and parent–child conflict or when the family as a unit asks for help. It is not appropriate when the patient has a severe disorder needing specific treatment in its own right.

The approach may be psychoanalytical, systems or behavioural. The psychodynamic approaches will concentrate on interpreting behaviour and increasing insight. The systems therapist concentrates on the present and on changing how the family functions, by helping the family look at its rules and assumptions. The behaviourist will help the family look at what reinforces certain behaviours that the family regard as undesirable.

The aim of family therapy is fourfold:

- Understanding the dynamics of the specific family
- Mobilising the psychological resources of the family
- Working to so change relationships between family members that dysfunctional behavioural symptoms disappear
- Developing problem-solving and coping skills.

The family as a system

A system has in common:

- Interconnected and interdependent parts
- Every part is consistently related to the other over a period of time. Systems may be closed (house heating) or open (the family).

Properties of an open system

Wholeness

- Wholeness is the sum of the parts plus the interaction.
- One part cannot be understood unless its relationship to the other parts is also understood.

- Wholeness is a Gestalten – the interdependence between parts.
- The family consists of the members and the relationships between them.

Relationship

- Relationship concerns the 'what' rather than the 'why' of what is happening.
- The shift is from what is happening within the members to what is happening between them.

Equifinality (self-perpetuation)

- When interventions are made in the 'here and now', changes are produced in the family open system.
- Concentrating on the here and now and not becoming involved in blaming the past is valid, because a system has no memory.

The building blocks of the family system are a series of interlocking triangles, the function of which is to reduce or increase the emotional intensity within the family.

The man in a partnership that is shaky who becomes a workaholic could be seen as creating a triangle to reduce tension.

The prime therapeutic task is to analyse the various triangles in a family and make interventions to change the system.

The family systems school of thought considers triangles over three generations. The structuralist school of thought is more concerned with triangles within the nuclear family.

Feedback, the mechanism by which the system is constantly being adjusted and equilibrium restored, is an important concept and function in systems theory. Positive feedback forces change on the system by not allowing it to return to its former state.

Main schools

1. Object relations family therapy

Here the identified 'patient' is often seen as the one who carries the split-off, and therefore unacceptable, impulses of the other family members; the 'sick' one; the one on whom the family focuses their dysfunctional behaviour.

2. Family systems therapy

This works with eight concepts:

- Triangles
- Differentiation of self; which measures the amount of fusion between members
- The emotional system of the family
- Family projection process; how a family selects the identified patient
- Emotional cut-off; the extent to which one member relates to the others
- Transmission; the mechanism by which pathology is passed through generations

- Sibling position – determines one's existential view of the world
- Societal regression; patterns that occur in the family are also found in society.

Families are taught not to react but to respond. Reacting means acting only on the basis of feeling and ignoring the needs of other people. Responding is making a rational, not a purely emotional, choice and taking into account the needs of others. Family members learn to be both 'self' and a member of the system.

3. Structural family therapy
This views pathology as either 'enmeshed' or 'disengaged'. In an enmeshed structure, the therapist works on loosening the boundaries. In a disengaged structure, the therapist works towards establishing or strengthening the boundaries.

4. Strategic intervention family therapy
This views therapy as a power struggle between client and therapist. In family therapy, the identified 'patient' is the controller who makes the others feel helpless. The role of the therapist is to restructure the system by re-establishing family boundaries and changing the balance of power. Family therapy seeks to answer three questions:

- What is a family? A family has physical and emotional needs, and the basic emotional needs are intimacy, self-expression and meaning.
- What is a 'dysfunctional family'? Such a family has an inability to meet basic emotional needs. In family systems therapy, all members are an essential part of the therapeutic process. The functional family will work to solve conflicts, while the dysfunctional family will not.
- Why must a family change? In order to be functional, families must become 'we' as well as retaining their individual 'I'. Feedback, possible with adults, is entirely different with children and is not immediate. The birth of subsequent siblings changes the system. Entry to school admits others into the system, so forcing further change. Children with school phobia may be responding to the family's inability to widen the boundaries. Adolescence, with its need for greater freedom, is a potential for dysfunction, as parents experience loss of meaning. The 'empty nest syndrome' is often experienced by parents when children leave home. Dramatic change may allow marital differences to surface.

Three family dimensions

Marital subsystem

- Two people become a couple.
- 'Fusion' or 'enmeshment' is where one or both members of the couple are unable to separate from their family of origin – the boundaries of the new relationship are thus blurred.
- The ability to close a door and shut out others (symbolically) is important in the development of a functional family system.

- In functional families, it is spouse first and others next.
- Children-oriented marriages are invariably dysfunctional, because the children are needed to give meaning to the marriage.
- A firm alliance between parents prevents a child from forming an alliance with one or other of the parents.

A point about triangles: when a couple add a child and become a family, a triangle is formed. In a stable, functional family, the child is at the apex, supported by the firm base of the parents. However, in a child-centred family, the triangle is reversed and the child supports the parents, for all attention is directed at the child. This can only lead to dysfunction, as this configuration prevents integration, where the child feels supported. Children will exploit the family relationship and strive to drive a wedge between the parents, and create alliances. Unless the parents stand united, such alliances will lead to dysfunction.

Sibling subsystem

- The alliance between parents forces children into forming their own subsystems with brothers and sisters or others of their own generation.
- The sibling subsystem has its own boundaries.

Questions to ask:

- Are parents clearly separated from children?
- Is the difference between children clear?
- Are older children treated differently from younger ones?
- What are the levels of responsibility?
- What are the levels of respect for their uniqueness, privacy, common courtesies and freedom?
- What is the influence of the neighbourhood culture? The school culture? Peer group pressure?

Homeostasis

This is the balance between marital and sibling subsystems. If disrupted limits cannot be corrected, homeostasis is upset and the system will eventually disintegrate. Homeostasis is threatened, for example, when a family moves to a new neighbourhood or culture. 'Destructive behaviour' may be an attempt to restore homeostasis.

Tony Gough identifies five obstacles to growth:

1. Mistaken assumptions about the relationship
2. Taking each other for granted
3. Dishonesty
4. Self-denial. To always put the other person first denies one's own right for recognition
5. The absence of quality time together.

Goals of family therapy

A primary goal in family therapy is to produce visible change in behaviour, even though family members may not be totally aware of what is happening. Insight, helpful for the therapist, is not considered important for the family; getting them to be aware of the interactions is.

The history of the family is important for object relations and family systems therapists, but less important for structural and strategic intervention therapists, for whom the present is what is relevant. Family therapists are less concerned than are traditional therapists with arriving at a correct diagnosis.

Feelings, which are thought to arise from behaviours, are not given first place; possibly because of the emphasis on the 'system'.

Learning and teaching form an essential part of the therapies of schools 1 and 2 (object relations therapy and family systems therapy), but less so in 3 and 4 (structural family therapy and strategic intervention family therapy).

Transference and working through it do not form an explicit part of family therapy; the concentration is on the family interaction, not on the relationship between individual and therapist.

The therapist is viewed as a model, a change agent or teacher, who helps the family develop problem-solving skills.

Therapists are active; they are not 'blank screens'.

Techniques in family therapy

- **Re-enactment**: Instead of 'talking about', the family are encouraged to 'talk' and interact; sometimes called 'psychodrama in situ'
- **Homework**: To build bridges between the sessions and interaction in the home
- **Family sculpting** (see Psychodrama)
- **Genogram**: This is a multigenerational diagram that graphically illustrates family relationships
- **Behaviour modification** (see Behaviour therapy)
- **Multiple family therapy**: Some of the advantages of involving several families at the same time are that it:
  - Points up similarities and differences in interactions
  - Permits the family members to act in a co-counselling role
  - Loosens the authority of the therapist
  - Helps to hasten the formation of the therapeutic alliance.

A phenomenon of family dynamics has been referred to above: the 'sick role' – a label attached to a person that affords that person certain privileges and obligations as 'the sick one'. The sick role may perform a function for the person but it also does so for the rest of the family: the sick one becomes the focus of attention and, often, the scapegoat (see Scapegoating) for all that goes wrong within the family.

The family may show great unity, as distinct from a 'delinquent' family, which is often fragmented. However, the person filling the sick role feels a weight of responsibility for keeping the family together and when the sick person is removed the family often disintegrates. This places the person in a double bind – the sick person may want to get well, yet if he or she recovers, blame for family break-up is likely to follow.

Family therapy does produce change, although it is not clear how that is accomplished or why one approach works with one family and not with another.

Counselling couples

When counselling couples, it is essential to be aware of the dynamics of what is happening between the couple. This is what makes couples counselling different from other counselling, and more akin to working in a group.

Mutuality: a sign of a healthy marriage

When counselling a couple, the counsellor should be aware of the degree of mutuality that exists. Mutuality is interpersonal communication in a non-value, non-judgemental style that results in a bonding taking place. As the couple respond to each other and to the questions asked by the counsellor, mutuality is either present or absent. If the counsellor says something and the couple agree and 'hook up' because of their non-judgemental stance then mutuality is again noticeable and experienced.

When a couple can disagree and respect each other's point of view without trying to force their own point of view on to the other, then mutuality is experienced, if both partners are being honest.

Little or no mutuality may be due to:

- Lack of time alone together
- Lack of respect for each other
- Not being honest with each other
- Complete breakdown of relationship.

Divorce

If death is the final parting, divorce is the spectre that haunts the living, with rattling chains of what once was and might have been. The marriage knot is easily tied, and with the passing of time the knot bites deep. The untying of it is not achieved without leaving deep scars.

In the Life Change Chart, divorce scores the second highest. Divorce is death of a marriage. People who suffer the breakdown of their marriage experience similar feelings to those experienced when a death occurs, namely:

- Shock
- Denial
- Anger
- Grief
- Loneliness
- Acceptance
- Resolution.

These emotional adversities for the divorcee have one major difference: the partner is still around! A death is final, and nothing can alter it. But, for the one whose close and intimate relationship has fractured, the loss experienced is one of confusion, feeling abandoned, and loss of self-worth and dignity.

Many people do not realise the depth of pain couples go through during, and after, a divorce. Some dash straight into another intimate relationship, and expect the new partner to carry them, with all their hurt and pain. Difficulties may be compounded by the fact that the new partner may also have come from a failed relationship. So this new relationship is already fraught with stress.

When a woman initiates the break, she is very likely to feel a deep sense of failure and guilt, particularly where children are involved, and more so if the husband is given custody of the children.

The lifestyle of divorcees undergoes dramatic changes, as both assume new responsibilities and duties as single people or single parents. Each assumes a new identity as a 'divorcee'.

Regrets over divorce

The loss of 'what used to be' home, family and security is often compounded by feelings of responsibility and guilt for what has happened. There is a constant looking over one's shoulder, to the past, and a refusal, or inability, to risk looking at what the future may hold.

Recovery from divorce

Generally, much anger and bitterness has to be overcome before any resolution is possible. In fact, the road to recovery may be very slow indeed, and painful, and may never be resolved satisfactorily.

The death of a divorced partner can reawaken feelings concerning the former marriage, and subsequent divorce. These feelings may be suppressed because the person thinks that such feelings are irrational.

In addition, the ex-partner is likely to experience all sorts of mixed feelings, not just associated with the deceased, but about other losses. It is a peculiar fact about loss, that very often the most innocuous event may trigger off old feelings that have lain dormant for years.

Advice to divorced people

- Do not withdraw from life.
- Do not deny the way you feel.
- Do not back away from relationships.
- Do not put yourself down for feeling vulnerable.
- Do not be surprised at sudden physical problems.
- Do not dwell on the unfairness of it all.
- Do not base relationships entirely on trying to please.
- Do not rush into remarriage if you are single or a one-parent family.
- Do not make visits to children a series of spectaculars.
- Do not indulge in guilt about sometimes being away from children.

Dealing with stress in a relationship

Stress can come from many sources, but if the relationship is to succeed the couple must find a way of handling the stress without it wrecking the relationship. There is no easy way, and no iron-clad blueprint, either for avoiding stress or coping with it. We all must find our own strategies. However, if we recognise some of the ways in which stress can develop, we are part-way to dealing with it.

When there is stress at home and at work, that is when the emotional knees start to buckle.

Long-lasting and intimate relationships are prone to experience stress. To take marriage as an example, when the excitement and thrill of being in love is replaced by loving and life settles into a well-established routine, that is the time when stress develops. When children are added to the equation, there is added stress.

Children bring their own tensions, and unless the parents are firmly rooted in each other children can drive a wedge between them. When children are reared in a shaky parental relationship they sense the tensions and experience their own stresses.

Some couples come into marriage with the idea that they can change the partner in some way. Attitudes and beliefs are notoriously difficult to change, so are habits. Change will happen gradually and naturally, but it can never be forced or demanded. People who love want to please each other, but there has to be a balance between pleasing because you want to and pleasing because you feel manipulated into doing so. A relationship with that as the motive will result in disharmony. People who love each other do grow to be like each other.

Further reading

Gough, T. (1991) *Couples Growing*. Darton, Longman & Todd, London.

Gurman, A.S. and Kniskern, D. (1981) *Handbook of Family Therapy*. Brunner/Mazel, New York.

Hoffman, L. (1981) *Foundations of Family Therapy*. Basic Books, New York.

Keinglass, P. (1995) Family therapy. In: *Comprehensive Textbook of Psychiatry*, 6th edn (eds H.J. Kaplan and B.J. Sadock). Williams & Wilkins, Baltimore, MD.

Stewart, W. (2001) *Making the Most of your Relationships*. How to Books, Oxford.

FEMININITY/MASCULINITY (SEE ALSO: ANALYTICAL PSYCHOLOGY, FEMINIST THERAPY, MYERS-BRIGGS TYPE INDICATOR, SELF)

Femininity/masculinity generally refers to gender, those personal characteristics that are believed to differentiate one sex from another. Gender is more than the manifest biological differences between the sexes.

Family patterns and wider cultural behaviours exert a powerful influence on the development and acceptance of what is 'feminine' or 'masculine'. It can be said (in Freudian terms) that men adopt the masculine role and women accept the feminine role and only do so when they have renounced the penis. This view has been strongly criticised by female psychoanalysts.

Gender difficulties occur when people feel pressured into denying attributes that they feel are vital to their identity and other people feel are inappropriate.

Feminist issues

The feminist issue has to be addressed in counselling, for there is a whole ideology – assumptions, ways of thinking, attitudes, values and beliefs – that needs to be examined.

The word 'different' is important in counselling. The words 'superior' and 'inferior' carry connotations of competition, win–lose, hierarchy, strong–weak, capable–incapable.

Alfred Adler (see Individual psychology) speaks of the difference between 'horizontal' and 'vertical' relationships. A hierarchy is a vertical relationship that does not respect differences but places people in superior/inferior positions. Many of the differences will disappear and true equality (not uniformity) will be established when we relate to men and women in horizontal, not vertical relationships.

In order for men to truly accept women and women to accept men as equals they must accept the male or female within themselves, which is so often our shadow side. An acceptance of our shadow brings a wholeness and richness hitherto seen only through darkened glass.

Much of the difference between men and women is learned rather than genetic. There is tremendous variation within the two groups. Many women behave more aggressively than some men. Many men are involved at a higher level of caring than some women. Many men never resort to physical violence; some women are violently aggressive.

We can make a conscious choice to incorporate traits or values associated with either men or women if they are appropriate for us. Rigid sex roles restrict behaviour. Sex-typed feminine women attend to babies and people in need but do not exhibit appropriate independent and assertive behaviours. Sex-typed masculine men are the opposite of this.

When we integrate characteristics of both sexes, we incorporate independent-assertive behaviours and responsible-helping behaviours. Integration helps us to be more spontaneous. We are able to respond appropriately to situations calling for both assertiveness and caring.

Counselling, of whomsoever, is about wholeness and integration. Counsellors who ignore the fact that for centuries women have been put down and made second-class citizens (and in some respects, still are) will never be able to make effective contact with female clients, which is essential if integration and wholeness is to take place.

Likewise, we need to recognise when the feminine side of male clients is being repressed and help them work towards liberation, integration and wholeness so that they, too, can become wholly alive. Women and men have to believe that they are both equal and different from the other sex, and that their unique differences are valuable to each other.

However much women tell other women this, the greatest change will come when men start valuing women for themselves. It is not what men say but what they do that will convince women that their uniqueness is respected for what it is.

Cross-gender counselling

Many cultures in the world are still very male-dominated; this is reflected in the way women relate to men and is demonstrated in the way power is shared.

Men have assumed, and women for centuries have colluded with them, that their role is to provide and the role of women is to do. Male counsellors (the archetypal 'doctors') may (unconsciously) reinforce this power difference.

The female client who is compliant and submissive and does not argue openly may well be caught in this power trap. The reverse may be true. A male client with a female counsellor may feel uncomfortable with what he (consciously or unconsciously) perceives as a reversal of roles, and attempt to dominate the session.

Cross-gender counselling may also create difficulties where the subject is a delicate one. Just as some female patients prefer male doctors and some prefer female doctors, so it is with counselling. However, there are many issues where same-sex counselling is more appealing than dealing with someone of the opposite sex.

Some women may prefer to talk with a female counsellor about, for example, the problems associated with pre-menstrual syndrome, rape or abortion. Likewise, some men would probably find it easier to talk with another man about sexual impotence.

Another area of potential difficulty in cross-gender counselling is sexual attraction and, in some instances, sexual harassment. While there are many jokes about clients 'falling in love' with therapists (of either gender) the reality of it is far from humorous. The possibility should always be hovering in the wings of the counselling room. Apart from any overt involvement, these transference feelings (see Transference and counter-transference) may cause the relationship to flounder unless they are recognised and dealt with.

A potential difficulty lies in expressing an opinion. Between two people of the same sex an opinion can be expressed and both parties will generally be able to discuss and argue it through. When the same statement is made by a person of one gender to someone of the other, the statement is filtered through gender values. What is said by a man to a woman may be interpreted as a pronouncement rather than a suggestion or a possibility. What was acceptable in one situation could be perceived as patronising or domineering in another.

Counsellors, of whichever gender and of whatever professional persuasion, will never fully understand femininity or masculinity unless they are willing to enter the other's frame of reference. Only as we risk leaving our own frame of reference will any of us be able to understand anyone else's personal meanings. The more one person can work with and understand someone's personal meanings, the more that person will understand himself and will achieve new insights into himself.

Entering the client's frame of reference in cross-gender counselling will mean confronting our own hidden anima or animus. When we accept the challenge of integrating our shadow, our personality will be more complete and our counselling will be richer.

The concept of androgyny refers specifically to the blending of the behaviours and personality characteristics that have traditionally been thought of as masculine and feminine.

The androgynous individual is someone who is both independent and tender, both aggressive and gentle, both assertive and yielding, both masculine and feminine, appropriate to the situation.

Further reading

Bem, S.L. (1977) *BEM Sex-Role Inventory (BSRI). The 1977 Annual Handbook for Group Facilitators.* University Associates, San Diego, CA.

Brown, L. and Liss-Levinson, N. (1981) Feminist therapy. In: *Handbook of Innovative Psychotherapies* (ed. R. Corsini). John Wiley, New York.

Chaplin, J. (1988) *Feminist Counselling in Action.* Sage Publications, London.

Chaplin, J. (1989) Counselling and gender. In: *Handbook of Counselling in Britain* (eds W. Dryden, D. Charles-Edwards and R. Woolfe). Tavistock/Routledge, London.

Dickson, A. (1982) *A Woman in Your Own Right.* Quartet Books, London.

Orbach, S. and Eichenbaum, L. (1985) *Understanding Women.* Pelican, London.

FEMINIST THERAPY

Gerald Corey devotes a whole section of his book to a therapy that '. . . puts gender and power at the core of the therapeutic process' (page 343). It is a fact that the majority of therapies were conceived by white males from Western cultures. Corey goes on to say:

A central concept in feminist therapy is the psychological oppression of women and the constraints imposed by the socio-political status to which women have been relegated. The socialization of women inevitably affects their identity development, self-concept, goals and aspirations, and emotional well-being.

Some people might argue with the premise that women are still oppressed; however, it is important to recognise that this is how many women feel, hence the rise of feminist therapy. Feminist therapists believe that we cannot separate psychotherapy from the culture in which the client and therapist live.

Historical development

Thus feminist therapy has developed to meet the needs of women, and has its roots in the feminist movement of the 1960s, when there was a sharp rise in self-help, rather than using traditional psychotherapy. Gradually groups were formed with the express aim of empowering women. Therapy was viewed as a partnership between equals, where the emphasis is not on pathology but on understanding the cultural forces that damage and constrain women. More recently the trend is to establish feminist psychoanalysis, feminist family therapy and feminist career counselling.

Four main orientations can be identified:

- Liberal feminists, whose focus is helping women overcome the constraints and limitations of their socialisation
- Cultural feminists, whose focus is on the way society devalues the strengths of women
- Radical feminists, whose main focus is to redress the oppression of patriarchal societies
- Socialist feminists, whose main focus is on multiple oppressions, which include considerations of class, race and other forms of discrimination.

Key concepts

1. View of human nature

- Feminist therapists challenge the assumption that because of the difference in gender men and women are predestined to pursue different directions in life, and that these differences apply across races, cultures and nations.
- They challenge the view that heterosexuality is the norm and desirable, thus devaluing same-sex relationships.
- They challenge the view that present personality patterns and behaviour are fixed from an early stage of development.
- Feminist therapies are gender-free, flexible, interactionist and deal with the whole lifespan.

2. Feminist perspective on personality development

- From birth we are programmed by society into certain roles, and these expectations influence our personality.
- Broadly, girls learn from their mothers to be nurturers, and boys from their fathers to be power-seeking. Some people would argue with this premise, for although feminists profess to be against stereotyping, this view does carry certain stereotyping of both mothers and fathers.
- From society girls and boys learn different things about their gender identity, and this can cause confusion and conflict when personality traits do not match expectations. Thus gender can organise our lives.

3. Characteristics associated with traditional roles

- Women, more than men, are expected to exhibit the qualities of warmth, expressiveness and nurturing. They are expected to be kind, thoughtful and caring. Many women have difficulty asking for these very qualities from others and do not allow themselves to receive nurturing.
- Women should not display an independent spirit. If women are assertive, they might well be viewed as being hostile and aggressive. If they display indepen-

dence, men may accuse them of trying to 'prove themselves' by taking on masculine roles.

- Rather than being rational and logical, women are traditionally viewed as being emotional and intuitive.
- Traditionally, traits such as passivity and submissiveness, a home orientation, being prone to tears and excitability in minor crises, indecisiveness, religiosity and tactfulness are expected of the female role. If women deviate from these behaviour patterns, they run the risk of being labelled 'unfeminine'.
- Women are viewed as being 'naturally' interested in relationships more than in accomplishments. Rather than competing or striving to get ahead, women are expected to maintain relationships.

Feminist therapists teach their clients that uncritical acceptance of traditional roles can greatly restrict their range of freedom to define the kind of person they want to be. Today many women and men are resisting being so narrowly defined. Women and men in therapy learn that, if they choose to, they can experience mutual behavioural characteristics such as being both dependent and independent, giving to others and being open to receiving, thinking and feeling, and being tender and using touch.

Principles of feminist psychology

1. **The personal is political**: What this means is that the aim is social transformation; to change the status quo and to improve the status and well-being of all women.
2. **The counselling relationship**: This is a partnership of equals, where the therapist is alert to hear evidence of oppression. The person in the client role is seen as having the capacity and the will to change. The therapist is not seen as an expert, but rather as one who has more information.
3. **Women's experiences are honoured**: In this respect, the feminist therapy is akin to the person-centred therapy. These experiences may include such themes as rape, sexual assault, sexual harassment, childhood sexual abuse, eating disorders and domestic violence.
4. **Definitions of distress and 'mental illness' are reformulated**: Feminist therapy rejects the 'disease model' of mental illness; rather, it strives to understand the external forces as well as the internal forces that create imbalance, with a focus on distress as the client communicating something about unjust systems. Pain is regarded as evidence of resistance and the skill and will to survive, and of being alive.
5. **Feminist therapists use an integrated analysis of oppression**: Feminist therapists recognise that both women and men are affected by being raised in cultures where sexes are treated differently, and are expected to behave differently. It is worth considering this statement alongside what Alfred Adler said about the masculine protest. Feminist therapists are committed in the struggle against oppression based upon discrimination.

Some comparisons between counselling approaches

- Although feminist therapy fits broadly with humanistic therapies, it aims to empower clients to live according to their own values, and to develop an internal locus of control in determining what is right for them.
- Feminist therapists offer all the core conditions associated with person-centred therapy. However, unlike person-centred therapy, the therapist is more active in working with the client to set goals for change.
- With some modification, psychoanalytic therapy, Gestalt therapy and cognitive behaviour therapy all have a contribution to make to feminist therapy. For example, cognitive behaviour therapy would teach the client assertiveness and behavioural rehearsal techniques, and have the client do homework assignments, as well as focusing on the client's thinking about gender issues and women's roles.
- Feminists, like existentialists, view therapy as a shared journey, in which change occurs for both client and therapist.

Themes clients might explore

- Exploring anxiety and defences
- Understanding power and control issues
- Examining external forces that influence behaviour
- Identifying messages received in growing up
- Learning to accept appropriate responsibility
- Critically examining social dictates and expectations
- Exploring one's values
- Reflecting on the meaning of life.

Corey, quoting Walden, says:

- When counsellors make decisions about a client *for* the client rather than *with* the client, they rob the client of power in the therapeutic relationship. Collaboration with the client in all aspects of therapy leads to a genuine partnership and empowerment of the client.
- Bringing the client into ongoing dialogue regarding decisions about the therapy demonstrates a true respect for the client's views. This dialogue increases the chances that the client's therapy will be guided by self-determined goals, drawing on the client's successes and strengths.
- Including the client in the therapeutic process increases the chances that the interventions will be more culturally appropriate. Through the exchange of views, client empowerment and solutions consistent with the client's cultural values are possible.

This is an important point with which to close this entry, for this sums up not only feminist therapy, but also the views of many other therapies and therapists, certainly those that fall under the broad umbrella of humanist therapies.

Further reading

Corey, G. (2001) *Theory and Practice of Counseling and Psychotherapy*, 6th edn. Wadsworth, Brooks/Cole, Pacific Grove, CA. On pages 364–365 you can read the case study of feminist therapy applied to the case of Stan.

Enns, C.Z. (1987) Gestalt therapy and feminist therapy: a proposed integration. *Journal of Counseling and Development*, 66: 93–95.

Enns, C.Z. (1997) *Feminist Theories and Feminist Psychotherapies: origins, themes, and variations*. Haworth Press, New York.

Walden, S.L. (1997) Inclusion of the client perspective in ethical practice. In: *Boundary Issues in Counseling: multiple roles and responsibilities* (eds B. Herlihy and G. Corey). American Counseling Association, Alexandria, VA, pages 40–47.

FOCUSING

Focusing is:

- A body-centred therapy technique
- A counselling skill.

Gendlin's body-centred therapy

- Focusing helps the client get to grips with a complex problem, with its feelings, by examining the problem in stages.
- Specific instructions concentrate attention on what is happening in the body.

Examples of focusing in body therapy

1. How does the body feel inside?
2. What feelings are being experienced?
3. Allow a problem to emerge and gain a sense of it as a whole.
4. Pay attention to the most powerful feeling.
5. Allow the feeling to change.
6. Put an image to the feeling.
7. Watch the image change.
8. Relax and reflect on the changes.

Focusing tries to address the client's problems directly rather than just talking about them. It is also used in existential and humanistic therapies.

Focusing in counselling

- Focusing helps the client get to grips with a complex situation by teasing out details and exploring specific parts in depth.
- Focusing helps the client look beyond the problem to possible solutions or alternatives.
- Focusing helps both client and counsellor not to get lost.
- Focusing involves a certain degree of direction and control by the counsellor, which has to be carefully used.

Principles of focusing
- If there is a crisis, first help the client to manage the crisis.
- Focus on issues that the client sees as important.
- Begin with a problem that seems to be causing the client pain.
- Focus on an issue that the client is willing to work on, even if it does not seem important to you.
- Begin with some manageable part of the problem.
- Begin with a problem that can be managed relatively easily.
- When possible, move from less severe to more severe problems.
- Focus on a problem where the benefits will outweigh the costs.
- Make the initial experience of counselling rewarding as an incentive to continue.
- Work for something with quick success.
- Work from the simple to the complex.

Underlying focusing is the client's need to feel some reward and some hope. Focusing implies a certain degree of direction and guidance of the exploration and not everything can be worked out at once.

Focusing uses specific questions to tease out detail and to explore particular topics in depth. There needs to be a focus in the helping process, around which the resources of the client can be mobilised. Focusing helps client and counsellor to find out where to start or, having started, in which direction to continue.

Some useful focusing guidelines
- Does the problem use a lot of energy?
- Is the problem of high, moderate or low significance?
- What priority would the client give to this problem?
- Could it be managed if it was broken down?
- If it is resolved, would it influence other issues?
- Small issues resolved give a boost.
- Is it within the client's direct control?
- In cost terms, how important is it? In other words, would the client be spending 80 per cent of time to get 20 per cent result?
- Is the client open to explore this issue?
- Does it need more time than is available now?

Three responses help the client to focus:

The contrast response
'Contrast' describes a marked awareness of the differences between two conditions or events that results from bringing them together.

Example: 'If you think about (for example) staying in your present job or moving to another job, what would it be like then?'

The choice-point response
'Choice-point' describes any set of circumstances in which a choice among several alternatives is required.

Example: 'From what you've said, it looks as if these are the major issues (itemising them); which of these would you feel most comfortable working with first?'

The figure-ground response

'Figure-ground' describes how a person perceives the relationship between the object of the attention or focus (the figure) and the rest of what is around the perceptual field (the ground). The figure generally has form or structure and appears to be in front of the ground. The figure is given shape or form and the background is left unshaped and lacking in form.

Thus, figure-ground focusing helps to give one part of the problem shape and form and so helps the client to more readily grasp hold of something and work with it.

Example: 'These are the various points of the problem; it seems to me that the most worthwhile to address first could be the need for you to get a job. How do you feel about that?'

When working on any of the above techniques, the choice is best put last, otherwise it becomes lost. There should be no further exploration after you have invited the client to consider a particular response. The specific response should be the last thing the client hears, and so responds to.

In *The Skilled Helper* (pages 238–239), Egan sets out a useful aid to focusing.

Focus and Leverage: The Lazarus Technique
The technique highlights how important language is in helping and how important it is to ask questions that help clients point themselves in the right direction.
Step 1: ask the client to use just one word to describe the problem.
Step 2: ask the client to put the word in a phrase.
Step 3: put the phrase into a simple sentence that describes the problem.
Step 4: ask the client to move from a simple sentence to a more detailed description.
This is a simple technique to bring a session into focus, and can be used at any stage or step of the helping process. For instance, clients can be asked to use one word to describe what they want.
Leverage questions for Step I-C that you can help clients ask themselves:
What problem or opportunity should I really be working on?
Which issue, if faced, would make a substantial difference in my life?
Which problem or opportunity has the greatest payoff value?
Which issue do I have both the will and the courage to work on?
Which problem, if managed, will take care of other problems?
Which opportunity, if developed, will help me deal with critical problems?
What is the best place for me to start?
If I need to start slowly, where should I start?
If I need a boost or a quick win, which problem or opportunity should I work on?

Helping the client focus is one way of moving the interview forward, and helps to prevent stagnation.

Further reading

Egan, G. (2002) *The Skilled Helper: a problem-management and opportunity-development approach to helping*, 7th edn. Brooks/Cole, Pacific Grove, CA.
Gendlin, E. (1981) *Focusing*. Bantam, New York.

FRAMES OF REFERENCE (SEE ALSO: PERSON-CENTRED COUNSELLING)

This is a two-part concept that is emphasised in person-centred counselling, and relates closely to empathy.

If people with whom we relate are to feel that we receive them loud and clear, we need the ability to 'get inside their skins', 'walk in their shoes' and 'see the world through their eyes'. The skill of really listening to and understanding another person is based on our choosing to get into their internal rather than remain in our external frame of reference.

At the heart of listening is a basic distinction between:

- 'You' and 'me'
- 'My view of me' and 'your view of me'
- 'Your view of you' and 'my view of you'.

'My view of me' and 'your view of you' are both inside or internal viewpoints, where-as 'your view of me' and 'my view of you' are both outside or external viewpoints.

To the extent that I understand 'your view of you' I am inside your internal frame of reference. If I then respond in a way that illustrates an accurate under-standing of your viewpoint, I am responding as if inside your frame of reference. If, however, I choose not to understand 'your view of you', or lack the skills to do so, I remain within my external frame of reference in regard to your world. When I respond from the external frame of reference, my responses reflect more where I am or think you should be than where you actually are.

(Taken from R. Nelson-Jones (1986) *Human Relationship Skills*. Holt, Rinehart & Winston, New York.)

Examples of external frame of reference responses

- I'm interested in what's going right for you, not what's going wrong.
- You should always respect your parents.
- My advice to you is to drop him.
- You have troubles. Let me tell you mine.

Examples of internal frame of reference responses

- Though you don't like to show it, you've been feeling very depressed recently and even contemplated suicide.
- You are thrilled that you've just got this promotion and can't believe your good fortune.

- You are pretty scared at the thought of being unemployed.
- You have mixed feelings about the wedding ceremony and will be glad when it is out of the way.

Examples of internal frame of reference (the inner world of the client)

- Behaviours
- Cultural influences
- Experiences
- Feelings
- Meanings
- Memories
- Perceptions
- Sensations
- Thoughts
- Values and beliefs.

External frame of reference (the inner world of the counsellor)

The contents of the counsellor's frame are similar to those of the client's frame and therein lies a danger. When the experiences of one person are similar to those of someone else, it is tempting to 'know' how the other person feels. This knowing cannot come from our experience. It can only resonate within us as we listen to what it means to the other person.

The external frame of reference is when we perceive only from our own subjective frame of reference and when there is no accurate, empathic understanding of the subjective world of the other person.

Evaluating another person through the values of our external frame of reference will ensure lack of understanding.

When we view another person within the internal frame of reference, that person's behaviour makes more sense.

The principal limitation is that we can then deal only with what is within the consciousness of the other person. That which is unconscious lies outside the frame of reference.

For person A to understand the frame of reference of person B, person A needs to:

- Build a bridge of empathy, in order to enter the other person's world
- Help the other person to communicate
- Understand the personal meanings of B
- Communicate that understanding to B.

The bridge of empathy is built upon the foundations of self-awareness. Lack of self-awareness acts as an obstruction to being able to enter someone else's frame of reference. The more we feel able to express ourselves freely to another person, without feeling on trial, the more the contents of our frame of reference will be communicated. Indeed, it is impossible to understand what something means to another person unless you are able to engage that person's frame of reference.

Communicating with another person's frame of reference depends on:

- Careful listening to the other person's total communication – words, non-verbal messages, voice-related cues
- Trying to identify the feelings that are being expressed and the experiences and behaviours that give rise to those feelings
- Trying to communicate an understanding of what the person seems to be feeling and of the sources of those feelings
- Responding by showing understanding, not by evaluating what has been said.

Example of engaging a client's frame of reference

- Jane says, 'My mother died and I feel devastated.'
- Person A says, 'That sounds really awful.'
- Person B says, 'It sounds as if your whole world has collapsed.'

Further reading

Rogers, C.R. (1961) *On Becoming a Person: a therapist's view of psychotherapy*. Constable, London.

FREE ASSOCIATION (SEE ALSO: SELF-COUNSELLING)

Free association is the psychoanalytic technique whereby the patient reports spontaneous thoughts, ideas or words. The 'golden rule' in psychoanalysis is that the patient reports everything that comes to mind, without any attempt to control or censor it; the unconscious mind is thus tapped. The analyst refrains from any prompt that might influence the patient's selection of material.

The rationale for free association is that all lines of thought tend to lead to what is significant; that the patient's unconscious will lead the associations towards what is significant; resistance will influence this process but that resistance is minimised by relaxation and concentration.

Free association is similar to Jung's word association test, where the person responds to a stimulus word with the first word that comes to mind. Conclusions are drawn about the associated words. Jung, building upon the work of Bleuler, Galton and Wundt, perfected the technique for tapping the personal complexes.

Where Freud and Jung differed is that Freud continued to use free association, while Jung developed his work with the archetypes to overcome complexes.

Identifying difficulties in free association

It is possible that free association is not for everyone. Some people take to it like the proverbial duck to water; others shy away from anything approaching introspection. Free association is not a miracle-worker, neither is it a panacea. But if it is persevered with, and undertaken with as much dedication as learning any other skill, the majority of people will find it answers many of their questions, and certainly shows the inner workings of the mind.

The following types of people might experience difficulty working with free association, but that does not mean that they should not try:

- People who steer clear of anything to do with self-development
- People who have difficulty with intimate relationships
- People who cannot make judgements for themselves; who are afraid to speak lest what they say does not meet with approval
- People who are so caught up in the trap of their conflicts that their whole life is over-controlled by negative thinking
- People who would be so ashamed by what free association reveals that they would feel safer if they never started.

Further reading

Samuels, A. (1985) *Jung and the Post-Jungians.* Routledge & Kegan Paul, London.

Stewart, W. (1998) *Self-counselling: how to develop the skills to positively manage your life.* How to Books, Oxford.

Zdenek, M. (1983) *The Right-Brain Experience*. Corgi, London.

G

Gestalt counselling

Gestalt is a German word that, when translated loosely, means 'pattern' or 'form'. When the pattern or Gestalt, is incomplete we talk of 'unfinished business'.

The chief tenet of Gestalt psychology is that analysis of parts, however thorough, cannot provide an understanding of the whole. An analogy is the human body, each part of which has its distinct function, yet all are integrated to make up the body. Parts are not understood when analysed in isolation. Mental processes and behaviours come complete. An example is that we hear a melody as a whole and not merely as a collection of individual notes.

Gestalt psychology sprang out of dissatisfaction over the inability of both psychoanalysis and behaviourism to deal with the whole person. Gestalt therapy, developed by Fritz Perls (1893–1970) and his wife Laura (1905–1990), aims to help the person to be self-supportive and self-responsible, through awareness of what is going on within the self at any given moment, the 'here-and-now'. Gestalt therapy is heavily influenced by existentialism, psychodrama and body therapies.

The theory is based on the principle that mental processes and behaviour cannot be analysed into elementary units. They come complete.

Gestalt therapy is usually performed in groups, though many of the techniques are applicable in individual work. The aim of therapy is to get clients to move from environmental support to self-support through their increased ability to use the world actively for their own development instead of manipulating the environment by playing neurotic roles.

Key aims of Gestalt therapy

Perls rejected the belief that human beings are determined and controlled by external and/or internal factors. This belief is reflected in two of his basic ideas:

- That human beings are responsible for themselves and their lives and living
- That the important question about human experience and behaviour is not why but how. The more we strive to be what we are not, the more entrenched we become in not being who we are not.

Implicit in these ideas is the belief that human beings are free and can change. He rejected the dualities of mind and body, body and soul, thinking and feeling, thinking and action, and feeling and action. The rejection of dualities is inherent in the concept of holism. Human beings are unified organisms and always function as a whole.

Principles of Gestalt therapy theory

1. **Holism.** The whole is greater than the sum of its parts. Thus the client must be viewed as a whole person, all dimensions of human functioning. The emphasis is on integrating every part.
2. **Field theory.** The client must be viewed in the context of his environment. Thus therapy would concentrate on what is happening at the boundary between the person and the environment.
3. **The figure-formation process.** This distinguishes between background and the figure. (See the figure-ground response in Focusing.) Identifying what is figure and what is ground is important to help the client make sense out of chaos.

The principle of homeostasis

Homeostasis is a state of equilibrium produced by a balance of functions within an organism. The basic tendency of every organism is to strive for balance. The organism is faced with external and internal factors that disturb this balance. Restoration of balance is self-regulating. The need is satisfied. The process starts again. Incomplete gestalts are called 'unfinished business'.

The emphasis of Gestalt counselling is on:

- Change through activity
- The central meaning of present experience
- The importance of fantasy and creative experimentation, particularly using the right, creative hemisphere, though not ignoring the contribution of the left, structured hemisphere
- The significance of language.

Here-and-now awareness

The Gestalt therapy slogan is 'I and thou, here-and-now'. Only the 'now' exists. Problems solved in the present solve problems of the past. The client is not allowed to talk 'about' problems in the past tense or in terms of memories. The client is asked to experience them now in his breathing, gestures, feelings, emotions and voice. The manner of expression, not the content or the words, is what is important.

The basic sentence the client is required to repeat is 'Now I am aware ...' Variations are:

- 'What are you aware of now?'
- 'Where are you now?'
- 'What are you seeing? Feeling?'
- 'What are you doing with your hand? Foot?'
- 'Are you aware of what you are doing with your ...?'
- 'What do you expect?'
- 'What do you want?'

Draw attention to the client's behaviour, feelings and experiences, do not interpret them and discover how he is preventing awareness of unfinished business, of holes or missing or rejected parts of his personality. Awareness, or formation of Gestalt, cannot be forced.

The therapist makes the client responsible by getting him to use 'I' not 'it' when referring to parts of his body and activities. Any statement or behaviour that does not represent self is challenged.

Unfinished business

Unfinished business means that figures that emerged from the background are not completed, so the person is left with unfinished business; the Gestalten is not completed, and like a complex in psychoanalysis will draw energy to itself, something like a black hole in the universe.

Unfinished business makes itself known through preoccupations, compulsive behaviour, wariness of others and self-defeating behaviour, and may be experienced as some physical symptoms, or difficulty in establishing or maintaining satisfactory relationships.

Clients may complain of feeling stuck, or having reached an impasse. When clients fully experience the feeling of being stuck, they are then able to get in contact with their frustrations and are then able to do something to change.

Peeling the onion

Perls likens the unfolding of the personality as peeling five layers of an onion:

- **The phoney**: Reacting to others in stereotyped and non-genuine ways and playing games instead of being real.
- **The phobic**: This is where we strive to avoid emotional pain by keeping parts of ourselves out of sight.
- **The impasse**: This is where our maturation is stuck and we do not feel alive.
- **The implosive**: This is where we fully experience our deadness; where we expose our defences.
- **The explosive**: This is where we let go of phoney roles and pretences. Energy is released and we become alive and authentic.

Contact and resistances to contact

Contact is necessary for change and growth to take place. Effective contact is through the senses, and interacting with nature and with other people, yet all the while retaining our individuality.

The resistances or the defences we erect to prevent contact are:

- **Introjection**: This is the tendency to passively incorporate other people's beliefs and standards and make them our own. This binds up energy.
- **Projection**: This is the opposite of introjection, where we disown certain aspects of ourselves, and put them onto the environment, with the effect that the distinction is blurred between ourselves and the environment.
- **Retroflection**: This means turning back to ourselves what we would like to do to someone else. Equally it is doing to ourselves what we wish someone would do to us.

- **Deflection**: This is the process of distraction so that it is difficult to maintain a sense of contact, by such defences as humour, abstractness, generalisations and questions.
- **Confluence**: This means a blurring between the self and the environment. Some people blend so with the environment that they lose all sense of self, and confluence characterises people who have a pathological need to be accepted and liked.

The counsellor draws attention to:

- What the client says
- How it is said
- The client's behaviour
- Non-verbal communication
- Breathing pattern
- Tensions within the session.

Clients are encouraged to act out various roles in life that they, and others, have played or are currently playing and to take responsibility for their own conflicts.

Gestalt counsellors believe:

- That human beings are responsible for themselves, for their lives and for living; therefore counsellors do not foster dependency
- That the important question about human experience and behaviour is not 'why' but 'how'
- That each person functions as a whole, not as separate parts
- In the philosophy of holism
- In the principles of homeostasis – a state of equilibrium produced by a balance of functions within an organism
- That the past exists only within a faulty memory. The future exists only in present expectations and anticipations. The past affects the individual and persists as unfinished business.

Counselling goals

- To re-establish contact and normal interaction; restore ego function and restore the whole
- To foster:
  - maturation and growth
  - independence
  - self-support
  - awareness
- To help the client:
  - deal with unfinished business
  - learn to live in the 'here and now'.

The counselling process

Clients are asked, and sometimes actively encouraged, to experience as much of themselves as possible – gestures, breathing, voice and so on. In so doing they become aware of the relationship between feelings and behaviours, and are thus able to:

- Integrate their dissociated parts
- Establish an adequate balance and appropriate boundaries between self and the environment.

Unfinished business must be concentrated on and re-experienced, not just talked about, in order to be resolved in the here and now. Unfinished business is something that acts as a block or interruption to the flow of energy, the task of which is to form a Gestalt. When there is completion we can move on because we are able to build only on what is completed. As each piece of unfinished business is resolved, a Gestalt is completed and the way is thus prepared for the client to move on to the next unfinished business. When a prior need was left unsatisfied, that particular Gestalt could not be completed. Part of the counselling task is to help the client to close off and complete what was previously unfinished – similar to closing the chapter of a book.

Clients are constantly required to repeat and complete the basic sentence, 'Now I am aware . . .' and its variations:

- 'What are you aware of now?'
- 'Where are you now?'
- 'What are you seeing? . . . Feeling?'
- 'What is your hand, foot, doing?'
- 'What do you want?'
- 'What do you expect?'

Therapists make clients take responsibility by getting them to use 'I' not 'it' when referring to their body. Any statement or behaviour that does not represent self is challenged.

Integration means:

- Owning disowned parts of oneself
- Being responsible for one's own life goals
- Expressing everything that is felt in the body
- Expressing the vague feelings associated with shame and embarrassment at expressing certain thoughts and feelings. Shame and embarrassment are the prime tools of the defence mechanism of repression. Endurance embarrassment brings repressed material to the surface.

Techniques of Gestalt therapy

- **The 'chair':** Clients move forwards and backwards from one chair to another and engage in dialogue between parts of themselves, between other people or between dream objects.
- **Skilful frustration:** In this the therapist:
  - repeatedly frustrates clients' avoidance of uncomfortable situations, until they show willingness to try and cope

- helps clients to identify the characteristics they project on to others that are most missing in themselves
- helps clients express and understand resentment, in the belief that the expression of resentment is one of the most important ways of helping people make life a little easier; Gestalt theory proposes that behind every resentment there is a demand, and that expressing the demand is essential for real change
- **Monotherapy**, where the client creates and acts every part of the production
- **Fantasy**: Through the use of symbols – fantasy can be verbalised, written or acted
- **Shuttle**: Directing the client's attention back and forth from one activity or experience to another
- **Topdog-underdog**:
  - topdog represents the 'shoulds' that the person has introjected; topdog is righteous, perfectionist, authoritarian, bullying and punishing
  - underdog is primitive, evasive, 'yes, but', excusing, passively sabotaging the demands of topdog
  - the client enters into a dialogue and alternately takes the part of topdog and underdog.

Disowned parts of the personality are integrated into the whole to complete that person's Gestalt. When a need is satisfied, the situation is changed and the need fades into the background. If a need is not fulfilled – if a Gestalt is not completed – it may produce a conflict that is distracting and draining of psychic energy.

Critics of Gestalt therapy say that it may help clients get in touch with their needs but does not necessarily teach them the skills or wisdom to deal with those needs.

Confusion

All clients demonstrate confusion, by way of hesitation between contact and withdrawal. Because confusion is unpleasant, the client will attempt to get rid of it by avoidance, blanking out, verbalism and fantasy. The client is encouraged to become aware of, to tolerate and to stay with this confusion. When it is not avoided or interrupted and allowed to develop, it will be transformed into a feeling that can be experienced and can lead to appropriate action.

Example of 'blankness' – client cannot see anything but black curtain. In fantasy, the client can throw open the curtain and discover what lies behind.

Dreams

According to Perls, the dream is the royal road to integration. The Gestalt therapist attempts to have the client relive the dream in the present and to act it out. The interpretation is left to the client. The more we refrain from telling the client what he is like or what he feels like, the more we encourage him to discover himself. Dreams are existential messages. We find all we need in the dream, if all parts of it are understood. Dreams reveal missing personality parts.

Homework

The client is encouraged to review the session by imagining himself back in it. He is encouraged to re-experience blocks and say what could not be said in therapy.

Integration

All techniques operate towards integration. What the client does is, step by step, to re-own the disowned parts of the personality and, eventually, to be responsible for his own growth. In addition to expressing thoughts and feelings, the client is expected to express everything that is felt in his body, including major physical symptoms but also unobtrusive sensations, including the shame and embarrassment felt at expressing thoughts and feelings. Shame and embarrassment are the prime tools of repressions.

Endurance of embarrassment brings the repressed material to the surface.

The awareness of, and the ability to endure, unwanted emotions are the precondition for a successful cure. It is this process, and not the process of remembering, that is the royal road to health.

Further reading

Clarkson, P. (1989) *Gestalt Counselling in Action*. Sage Publications, London.

Corey, G. (2001) *Theory and Practice of Counseling and Psychotherapy*, 6th edn. Wadsworth, Brooks/Cole, Pacific Grove, CA. See pages 217–219 for a case study of applied Gestalt therapy.

Patterson, C.H. (1980) *Theories of Counselling and Psychotherapy*. Harper & Row, New York.

Perls, F.S. (1969) *Gestalt Therapy Verbatim* (Stevens, J.O. ed.). Bantam, New York.

Van de Riet, V., Korb, K. and Gorrell. J.J. (1980) *Gestalt Therapy*. Pergamon, Oxford.

GOALS AND GOAL-SETTING

Many people become counselling clients because they feel stuck in situations from which they can see no way out. Counselling can help them to develop a sense of direction, which often accompanies hope.

One important part of problem-solving that can sometimes be difficult is goal-setting – working out a satisfactory solution. Goal-setting is a highly cognitive approach, which many people have difficulty working with. Goal-setting must take into account the affective and behavioural factors as well as the creative potential of the client.

Eight important tasks can be identified in the process of problem-solving and goal-setting.

1. Assessment – **helps clients identify**:
   - What they feel is OK about their life
   - What they feel is not OK about their life

- The resources they have to draw on
- Assessment continues throughout the counselling relationship.

2. **Identifying the initial problem:** Help the client to focus on the initial problem by using Rudyard Kipling's 'six honest serving men and true': What? Why? How? Where? When? Who?

3. **Develop new ways of looking at the problem:** Looking beyond the now, to what could be.

4. **Goal-setting:** A goal is what a person would like to attain so that the problem can be managed more easily and constructively. Clients may need help to distinguish clearly between a wish and a goal.

5. **Opening up possibilities:** There are often several ways in which a problem may be tackled using resources the client may not have recognised.

6. **Making an informed choice:** Achieving the best fit between resources, personality and abilities in order to achieve the desired outcome.

7. **Implementing the choice**

8. **Evaluation.**

Direction

In order to move from Point A (now) to Point B (the desired outcome) counsellor and client need to explore:

- Feelings
- Thoughts
- Behaviours

in order to develop a new perspective and work through hindrances.

Table 2: *Tom and problem solving*

Point A:	Tom is dissatisfied with work.
Point B:	Tom to look for satisfying job.
Perspective	There is no reason why Tom should stay in an unsatisfying job.
Hindrances	Tom's self-defeating beliefs and attitudes
	Tom's misplaced loyalty
	Tom prefers the comfort zone.

Problem-solving counselling is successful only if it results in problem-handling action. Listening, as part of problem-solving, is effective only if it helps clients to become more intentional and leads to realistic goal-setting.

Characteristics of intentional people:

- Are in charge of their own lives
- Do not waste time and energy blaming other people or circumstances for their problems
- Refuse to capitulate to unfavourable odds

- Have a sense of direction in their lives, characterised by:
  - having a purpose
  - feeling they are going somewhere
  - engaging in self-enhancing activities
  - focusing on outcomes and accomplishments
  - not mistaking aimless actions for accomplishments
  - setting goals and objectives
  - having a defined lifestyle
  - not indulging in wishful thinking
- Are versatile – thinking about and creating options
- Become involved in the world of other people – social settings
- Evaluate their goals against the needs and wants of others
- Are ready to work for win-win rather than win-lose situations.

Advantages of goal-setting

- Focuses attention and action
- Mobilises energy and effort
- Increases persistence
- Is strategy oriented.

The goal-setting model of Gerard Egan

Dr Gerard Egan is professor of psychology and organisational studies at Loyola University in Chicago. He has written many books, including *The Skilled Helper*. He currently writes and teaches in the area of counselling, counsellor education and management and organisation development.

Stage 1 – The present scenario

The aim of stage one is to help clients:

- Understand themselves
- Understand the problem
- Set goals
- Take action.

The client's goal is self-exploration: the counsellor's goal is responding.
  The counsellor helps clients to:
- Tell their story
- Focus
- Develop insight and new perspectives.

Stage 2 – Creating new scenarios and setting goals

The aim of stage two is to help clients:

- Examine their problem
- Think how it could be handled differently
- Develop their powers of imagination.

The client's goal is self-understanding: the counsellor's goal is to integrate understanding.

The counsellor helps clients to:

- Create new scenarios
- Evaluate possible scenarios
- Develop choice and commitment to change.

Stage 3 – Helping clients act

The client's goal is action: the counsellor's goal is to facilitate action.

The counsellor helps clients to:

- Identify and assess action strategies
- Formulate plans
- Implement plans.

Some useful questions for clients to ask:

- What would this situation look like if I managed it better?
- What changes would there be in my lifestyle?
- What would I do differently with the people in my life?
- What behaviours would I get rid of?
- What new behaviours would there be?
- What would exist that doesn't exist now?
- What would be happening that isn't happening now?
- What would I have that I don't have now?
- What decisions would I have made?
- What would I have accomplished?

Working for commitment

1. Ownership of the plan is essential for it to work.
2. A plan that has appeal encourages commitment.
3. A detailed plan has a logic to it.
4. An effective plan has an emotional content.
5. Flexibility increases the chance of commitment.
6. Clients need to see that the plan is within their capabilities, and that they have the personal and external resources.
7. Client commitment is often influenced by counsellor enthusiasm.
8. Getting started by using problem-solving skills.

Action plans

There is more to helping than talking and planning. If clients are to live more effectively they must act. When they fail to act, they fail to cope with problems in living or to exploit unused opportunities. Attaining goals cannot be left to chance.

Three steps in action are:

- Discovering strategies for action
- Choosing strategies and devising an action plan
- Implementing plans and achieving goals.

A goal is an end; a strategy is a means for achieving a goal. Many people fail to achieve goals because they do not explore alternatives. Brainstorming ways of achieving a goal increases the probability that one of them, or a combination of several, will suit the resources of a particular client.

Planning helps to initiate, and give direction to, action. Clients and the counsellors will know that the goal has been reached only when the clients feel sufficiently free from the forces that have been restraining them to take constructive action. The aim is to help the client discover, then harness, inner resources that have been locked in. Increased self-awareness and insight are often the keys that will release these resources.

The stages of the action plan:

1. Thinking it through – inadequate thinking through may spell disaster
2. Carrying it out.

Goals should be:

- Stated as accomplishments or outcomes rather than means or strategies
- Clear and specific
- Measurable or verifiable
- Realistic
- Genuine
- In keeping with the client's overall strategy and values
- Set in a realistic timeframe.

Force field analysis

Force field analysis (FFA) is a decision-making technique, developed from Lewin's field theory, designed to help people understand the various internal and external forces that influence the way they make decisions. For most of the time these forces are in relative balance; but when something disturbs the balance, decisions are more difficult to make.

When the forces are identified, counsellor and client work on strategies to help the client reach the desired goal.

Stages:

- What is the goal to be achieved?
- Identify the restraining forces.
- Identify facilitating forces.
- Work out how either the strength of some of the restraining forces can be reduced or how the strength of some of the facilitating forces can be increased.
- Use imagery to picture moving towards the desired goal and achieving it.

Forces may be external or internal. There follow some examples of internal forces:

- Type of personality
- Age
- Health
- Previous experiences
- Motivation
- Attitudes
- Beliefs.

Some examples of external forces:

- Family and friends
- Locality
- Job and career
- Finance
- Mobility
- Commitments
- Hobbies.

The underlying principle is that, by strengthening the facilitating forces and diminishing the restraining forces, a decision will be easier to make because energy, trapped by the restraining forces, has been released.

The hindering forces are the obstacles that are, or seem to be, restraining us from implementing our plan of action. Once the hindering forces have been identified, ways of coping with them are explored. We must ensure that we do not dwell on these forces and become demoralised.

Our resources are the positive, facilitating forces. These forces can be persons, places or things. Any factor that facilitates or assists us to attain our goal is to be utilised. This part of the process of searching for facilitating forces actually pushes us to look at our positive attributes.

The plan of action is born out of using the facilitating forces to reach the defined goal. The plan needs to be simple and easily understood.

Coping with complex problems

Complex problems may need the creation of sub-goals, steps towards a larger goal. Each sub-goal has the same requirements as a goal. Workable plans may flounder on the rocks of:

- Too much detail
- Not taking into account the difficulties some people experience with a cognitive exercise if it does not take feeling, intuition and initiative into account.

There is more to helping than talking and planning. If clients are to live more effectively they must act. When they refuse to act, they fail to cope with problems in living or do not exploit opportunities. The attainment of goals cannot be left to chance.

Only when the client speaks of the problem in the past tense has the goal been reached. Many programmes may have to be devised before the final outcome is reached. Clients cannot know whether or not they are making progress if they do not know from where they started or the milestones they should have reached.

Goals should be set neither too low nor too high. Goals set inappropriately high can cause the client to feel inadequate, while goals set too low do not generate enthusiasm:

- Goals must be tailored to the uniqueness of the individual client
- Goals that are to be accomplished 'some time or other' are rarely achieved.

Further reading

Egan, G. (1988) *Change-Agent Skills B: managing innovation and change*. University Associates, San Diego, CA.
Egan, G. (2002) *The Skilled Helper: a problem-management and opportunity-development approach to helping*, 7th edn. Brooks/Cole, Pacific Grove, CA.
Sutton, J. and Stewart, W. (2002) *Learning to Counsel: develop the skills you need to counsel others*, 2nd edn. How to Books, Oxford.

GRIEF AND BEREAVEMENT COUNSELLING (SEE ALSO: DYING – STAGES AND TASKS OF)

It is helpful to distinguish grief from bereavement. Grief, according to the dictionary, is 'mental pain, distress, or sorrow: deep or violent sorrow caused by loss or trouble; keen or bitter regret or remorse'. Bereavement is where one is deprived, robbed, stripped of, dispossessed of, life, hope. Bereavement is the process that includes grief and mourning, over the loss of a significant person or object. Ideally, counselling is commenced before the loss.

Thus, grief is consequent upon something, some event or happening. It is the normal response to loss and its absence is indicative of psychopathology.

Grief is a normal reaction of intense sorrow, following:

- The loss of an emotionally significant person
- The loss of a material object or objects
- The loss of a part of the self
- The end of a stage of the life cycle
- An event such as divorce or separation
- The loss of a limb or a faculty, e.g. blindness or deafness
- The scarring of one's body, possibly through drastic surgery such as mastectomy.

The psychoanalytic view is that grief allows ties with the lost object to be broken through the withdrawal of libido. Freud identified a period of between one and two years as the normal period for accomplishing 'grief work', with improvement after about six months.

John Bowlby's view is that grief is an attempt to re-establish ties rather than withdrawing them. Grief can also be viewed as the working out of conflicting impulses. Grief is the price we pay for loving; we would not know grief if there were no attachment to what we have lost.

Some definitions

- **Bereavement.** Loss through death
- **Bereavement reactions.** Psychological, physiological or behavioural response to bereavement
- **Bereavement process.** The term that covers bereavement reactions over time
- **Grief.** The feelings and associated behaviours, such as crying, that accompany bereavement
- **Mourning.** The social expressions of grief – funerals and rituals.

Murray Parkes identifies the following types of grief:

1. Typical
2. Chronic
3. Inhibited
4. Delayed
5. Anticipatory grief.

1. Typical grief

- Numbness
- Attacks of yearning and anxiety alternating with longer periods of depression and despair
- Preoccupied with thoughts of the dead one
- Insomnia
- Anorexia
- Irritability
- Social withdrawal.

All of these soon begin to decline in intensity.

2. Chronic grief

All the symptoms of normal grief but they are all pronounced. The general impression is one of deep and pressing sorrow.

3. Inhibited grief

The person shows little reaction to the death, but every unresolved grief is given expression in some form. It is most common in children under 5 years of age. Bowlby says that some forms of depression in adult life may be attributable to losses in early childhood. People over the age of 65 experience a process of 'disengagement' – a mutual severing of the ties between them and others in society.

4. Delayed grief

This is where a typical or chronic reaction occurs after a period of delay, during which the full expression of grief is inhibited. The grief may only be called to mind when some later loss is experienced. Crying, a normal reaction in grief, often absent in inhibited grief, has been linked with feelings of guilt.

One approach in counselling is to help the person explore and express her feelings about all the losses she has experienced throughout her life.

Life expectancy has increased and, with it, has the age of 'disengagement' also increased?

5. Anticipatory grief

This is where grief is expressed in advance of a loss that is perceived as inevitable. By definition, anticipatory grief ends with the occurrence of the anticipated loss, regardless of what reactions follow. Anticipated grief may increase in intensity as the expected loss becomes more imminent. Reactions differ with different person-alities and the nature of the anticipated loss. Anticipated grief may occur in professional care-givers and may thus influence the quality of the care given.

The normality of grief

Grief is considered normal following any bereavement. Indeed, not to experience grief could be considered inappropriate and even pathological. However, it has to be pointed out that feeling grief and showing it openly are two different things. Freud considered that grief work was complete when the person was able to invest energy elsewhere other than in what had caused the grief reaction.

John Bowlby's work on attachment and loss draws attention to grief as an expression of separation anxiety and the intense desire to recapture the lost relationship (see separation anxiety, in Attachment). The following stages of separation from an attached object (not necessarily a person) related to bereave-ment can be identified:

- Protest, a great deal of crying
- Searching behaviour, characterised by restlessness and inability to tolerate any attempt to hinder the search – anything, everything must be done to keep the memory of the person alive
- Despair and detachment, as the searching and hope of re-establishing the relationship diminishes, despair sets in
- Reorganisation and acceptance that the 'lost' person is not going to return. Now the person has an opportunity to redefine the relationship with the deceased and move forwards alone. At the same time, it is important to forge realistic ties to the deceased. Accepting the loss is likely to generate anguish; establishing realistic ties is likely to bring comfort.

The intensity of grief

1. Acute grief

Acute grief has several sub-stages:

- Shock, where the focus is on the past, is characterised by alarm and denial
- Realisation, where the focus is on the present, is characterised by:

- intermittent denial
- searching behaviour
- preoccupation and identification with the lost object
- idealisation
- regression
- crying
- bodily symptoms
- depression/helplessness
- guilt, anger, shame
- Integration, where the focus is on the future, is characterised by acceptance and a return to physical, social and psychological well-being.

2. Morbid or pathological grief
This may be:

- Inhibited, where reactions are absent or distorted
- Chronic, where severe reactions are prolonged
- Delayed, where severe reactions occur later.

Pathological grief is more likely to occur following:

- Experience of loss or separation in childhood
- Lack of effective support
- Sudden or violent death
- Where the bereaved one is not able to separate from the deceased
- The loss of a child.

Influences on grief reactions
Grief reaction is influenced by:

- Coping strategies
- Relationship support
- How a person normally functions
- Psychological strength
- Self-esteem
- Previous life experiences
- The significance of the loss
- State of health.

Phases of grief
The work of Kubler-Ross on death and dying gives insights into similar phases of grieving, principally:

- **Initial shock, disbelief and denial, where numbness prevails.** The period of mourning, with the meeting of friends at the funeral, is often accompanied by severe separation pangs and searching behaviour.
- **Immediate period of acute discomfort and social withdrawal, where acute**

anguish prevails. Acute anguish may last weeks or months, gradually moving into well-being and the ability to get on with life.

• **Resolution and reorganisation.** Grieving has been accomplished, although the person may be surprised by how small things can again trigger tears.

The Kubler-Ross Model of Stages and Worden's Model of Tasks are not discrete phases, but overlapping and fluid.

Grief versus depression

In both states the person may show sadness, may cry and express tension in retardation or agitation. The grief-stricken person, however, will show shifts of mood from sadness to a more normal state within a reasonably short time and will increasingly find enjoyment in life's experiences as the loss becomes more remote. The complaints and lamentations of the depressed person may come to irritate and annoy the listener, almost as if they were actually designed for that purpose.

In normal grief, the response is accepted as appropriate and normal by both the grieving person and those around. In depression, the response readily conveys the notion that something is not right about what is going on. People who have experienced previous depressions are more likely to experience depression, rather than normal grief, at the time of a major loss. A depressed person much more frequently presents the threat of suicide than does the grieving person.

In normal grief the individual does not usually show the marked lowering of self-esteem and the sense of worthlessness that may be of delusional proportions in melancholic depression, which may also give rise to suicide attempts.

During grief the person is in a vulnerable physical state, so much so that perhaps it should be viewed as an illness in its own right. Bereaved relatives have a much higher mortality rate during the first year of the bereavement, the greater risk being for widowed people. The risk of a close relative dying during the first year of bereavement is significantly greater when the death causing the bereavement occurred somewhere other than at home.

The psychological origins of grief

The universality of grief reactions seems to rest on what has been called 'bonding'; the attachment that provides protection and the basic sustenance necessary for emotional existence. The premature severance of the attachment to the mother elicits a response from the child that bears a striking similarity to the protest, despair and final detachment found in adult grief reactions.

How the separation and lessening of the attachment to the mother are integrated by the child is assumed to predetermine the later capacity for coping with loss, deprivation and frustration. This experience is assumed to establish the model for the way in which later losses will be handled: with basic optimism or despair; with passive resignation or angry unwillingness to 'let go'; with a felt sense of competence or of incompetence when a detachment occurs.

It is, then, the capacity of the human, or animal, to form an affiliation with another that carries with it the potential for grief when that affiliation is broken.

It is not only the course and quality of the initial and major separation from the mother that influences the adult's response to loss. The person brings to any major crisis a backlog of experience that leaves that person relatively prepared or unprepared, competent or incompetent, for integrating a present loss.

The psychodynamics of grief

The magnitude and nature of the loss bears some direct relationship to the kind of reaction. Death of a loved one normally elicits a more profound reaction than separation from living persons. Suicide or death by violence presents special problems to the bereaved, because of the difficulty in accepting and integrating the reality of what has happened. Guilt and hostility often accompany such deaths. Death of an old person is often easier to accept than the death of a child.

The loss of a husband greatly alters the social role of the widow and may encompass the loss of: a companion, sexual partner, breadwinner, chauffeur and handyman. Who can replace all these roles?

Most of the symptoms of grief can be understood as attempts to search for and to regain the lost object, efforts that serve a successful purpose in most separations, by reuniting the person with the object of attachment – crying or anger bring the mother to the child. The very facial expression characteristic of adult grief has been considered the result of the inhibition of the tendency to scream like an abandoned child. When the grief behaviour does not elicit its usual response, the person's sense of frustration and anger is further intensified.

Anger in grief, whether as a reaction to grief, and thus designed to alleviate it, or whether an essential component of it, cannot be ignored.

Identification can be used to adjust normally to a loss – e.g. unconsciously adopting mannerisms or characteristics that were those of the dead person. In some instances this means developing physical symptoms similar to those accompanying the fatal illness of the dead person. Fond memories, recollections and preserving possessions are all links with the dead one. With the passage of time the person becomes free to seek some other replacement. Such a mature adjustment to loss is possible only when a sense of self-identity, or firm ego-boundaries, has been established before the loss.

Ambivalent feelings towards the person before death may give rise to depression, self-accusations and feelings of worthlessness that reflect the previously unacceptable aspects of the relationship. That is, the ambivalence originally directed against the dead person is now directed against the self, because the object and the self are not distinguished. The self-accusations of a depressed person can thus be the unconscious accusations the person would like to direct at the dead person. The person's cry for attention, love and service may contain an element of unconscious desire to punish, which leads to further guilt and depression.

Mourning

Mourning is the period of time that follows a bereavement, which allows the expression of grief through accepted rituals. Mourning follows bereavement, is accompanied by grief and may or may not be followed by attachment to a new object.

Mourning is distinguished from grief in that it involves physiological and psychological processes. Mourning is more to do with the customs and traditions of a particular culture or society.

Grief and mourning do not necessarily occur at the same time but, for some, a period of ritualised mourning aids the grieving process. The mourning for a spouse is the loss most frequently ritualised in most societies. Mourning rituals are frequently linked with religious observance and practice.

Mourning and burial customs

Mourning customs are influenced by beliefs about life and death that are passed down through the generations. Religion is concerned with questions of mortality and immortality. All the major religions have a belief system that influences the way the rituals of burial and subsequent mourning are carried out.

Central to the Christian belief is the hope of resurrection. At the same time, there must be an acknowledgement of the reality of the grief of parting. The funeral will usually take place at a church or chapel, followed by a short committal at the graveside or the crematorium. The choice of flowers, procession and headstone is for the family, in contrast with several generations ago when the ritual was more predictable. Mourning clothes are also a matter of choice. Normally there is some sort of social gathering as farewell. The role of the funeral director has become more prominent in recent years.

The basic belief of the Hindu religion is that the cremated body returns to its elements of fire, water, air and earth and is thus reunited with God. The eldest son lights the funeral pyre, while mantras and sacred texts are recited by the priest. Then follows a period of ritual where gifts of food are left for the soul of the departed. When this period is over, the bones of the deceased may be buried. Hindus believe in reincarnation (transmigration), which is the rebirth of the soul in one or more successive existences, which may be human, animal or, in some instances, vegetable.

The basis of Judaism is the first five books of the Old Testament (the Torah). Death and mourning are highly ritualised. The funeral must take place within three days of death, but not on the Sabbath or on a festival day. The body is dressed in a simple white garment and is never left unattended. Burial is the norm but some non-orthodox Jews living in countries other than Israel will permit cremation. A seven-day period of formal mourning (Shivah) is observed after the death of a close relative. Prayers are said, candles are lit, family and friends will visit and bring gifts of food. Though normal life will be resumed after Shivah, certain social activities are not resumed until 30 days have passed.

The followers of Islam believe that the one God was revealed through the prophet Muhammad. When a Muslim dies, the body is turned to face Mecca. Death for the Muslim is but a parting for a short space of time, so prolonged grief is not encouraged. The body is washed, wrapped in clean white sheets and buried shortly after death. Prayers are said before the burial.

Sikhs believe in one God and the equality of humankind. They also believe in reincarnation. The body is dressed in white by the family, prayers are said, then cremation takes place. Prayers and the reading of sacred scriptures continue for a further 10 days. The death of an elderly person is not a time of sadness and is usually followed by feasting and rejoicing.

Buddha is seen not so much as a god, rather as a model for life. For the Buddhist, belief is demonstrated by good behaviour. Buddhists believe that the qualities of the deceased are reincarnated to become the 'germ of consciousness' in the womb of a mother. A monk leads the cremation service.

People of other world religions, living in an alien society, may observe compromised rituals instead of orthodox observances.

Rituals help the grieving person to make some sense of the experience; within a socially accepted framework, they allow for a sharing of the experience and for eventual reintegration. All of this may not be so easily achieved where traditions have been eroded, as in many Western societies.

Mourning is an essential part of grief and whatever the religious belief (or none at all) understanding what mourning means to that person is of utmost importance in grief counselling. Of equal importance is the fact that, for some people, where the ritual has been interrupted or has not been observed, it may not be emotionally possible to close the grief chapter, e.g. where the eldest son of a Hindu has not been able to light the funeral pyre or where the body has never been found, as in loss at sea or some other tragedy.

Management of grief

People should not be deprived of an opportunity to experience grief, which can ultimately be a rewarding and maturing process. Grief cannot be permanently postponed, for it will reach expression in some way. Ventilation of feelings is to be encouraged. The more sustained the inhibition of feelings, the more intense are they likely to be when finally expressed.

Counselling that places emphasis on living through and talking about the loss may prevent depressive reactions or pathological mourning. Counselling emphasises the present and recent past, and the aim should be to help the person deal with the loss, rather than aim at personality or character change. Within an atmosphere of trust and support, the grieving person can be encouraged to ventilate and explore negative as well as positive feelings towards the dead person. In order to work through grief, the person may need to confront the over-idealised image he retains. But as with all challenges in counselling, this skill should only be used when the relationship is firmly established.

Counselling guidelines following a death

- Support is necessary to help deal with the many practical issues surrounding the death.
- Work with feelings and encourage catharsis, but do not push the person too far, too fast, too soon.

- Helpers need to be able to accept the bereaved person's feelings, whatever they are.
- Feelings, however negative, are valid.
- Support by repeated telling of the story, with the associated feelings.
- Encourage the acceptance of the finality of the loss.
- Facilitate disengagement and establish separateness from the deceased.
- Help the bereaved person to gain a positive but realistic memory of the deceased through repeated discussion.
- Help the deceased to accept the changes in role, social situation and self-image in becoming a widow/widower, fatherless, childless, no longer pregnant, disabled.
- Encourage the bereaved person to think about new relationships, activities, self-help groups.

Depression is a common feature of many bereaved people, particularly after the death of the lifetime partner, often occurring after about a month. In severe cases, psychiatric illness may be precipitated by bereavement.

Some helpful counselling aids

- **Journals and diaries**: Writing down what is happening, including feelings and thoughts, can be very therapeutic. Some people feel able to burn the writings at some stage, thus signifying a letting go.
- **Pictures**: These need not be 'artistic'. What is important is what the person includes, as well as what is left out. The picture can then be used as a talking point, not as something to be 'interpreted'. This method is superb when dealing with children. Children's drawings may take the form of fantasy, with monsters and other frightening figures.
- **Photographs**: Family 'snaps' provide a focus for communication. The person in a photograph always has a certain substance. The viewer often has to contain the 'then' within the reality and pain of the 'now'.
- **Scrapbooks**: As with photographs, collecting material to paste into a scrapbook may be painful. The therapeutic benefit of having put together a memorial in this way, as something to look back on, is of inestimable value.
- **A family tree**: A family tree is a visual record of one's heritage and should include those dead as well as those still alive. It is an ideal medium for the grieving person to talk about the interaction between various people on the tree. A related technique is family sculpting, where shapes can be used to represent members of the family.
- **Bibliotherapy** (see Bibliotherapy entry)
- **Relaxation therapy**.

Some things to avoid in grief counselling

Being afraid to confront the client's pain often makes people resort to euphemisms, like 'I'm sorry you have lost your husband', or 'I hear he has passed over/gone to his great sleep/passed away/departed this life' or simply 'I hear he has gone'. We use euphemisms to protect the other person and ourselves from reality.

There is a difference between 'You have lost your wife' and 'You are suffering loss'. The one is an avoidance; the other highlights the feelings of loss. For the process of healing is accepting that the loved one is dead, not lost. Certainly the person feels great loss, but that is a different meaning. When we speak of 'the loss of a person' we confuse the issue, particularly when we then try to help the person explore feelings of loss. It is true that many people who are bereaved seek for their loved one as if that person was lost. We can add to that confusion by not helping them acknowledge the finality of death. No one can come out of the experience of loss and be the same as before.

Another pointer is the difference between 'You are grieving' and 'You are going through the grieving process'. The first phrase is more immediate and accepts the uniqueness of the client. Drawing attention to a 'process' makes it sound detached and predictable. And, as we know from all the literature, while models are useful, they are only guidelines and bereaved people dip in and out of the various stages or phases rather than progress neatly from one to the other. Helping adults to confront the reality of death is often a difficult enough task – helping children may be doubly difficult, yet surprisingly simple. Children often have a clearer grasp of reality than adults give them credit for. We all hate being told untruths and children are very quick to detect what is not true. 'Dad's gone away and he won't be coming back' is cruel and deceptive. Adults often say they only said what they did to protect the child. While this might be true, the whole truth is that they needed to protect themselves.

One of the counselling tasks in bereavement, where children are involved, is to help the survivor to realise that any disturbance within the child is likely to be an expression of the survivor's inability to accept the loss and know how to deal with it.

Nothing can protect the child from the fact and it is proved to be healthier that the child knows the truth, although not every detail, rather than fobbing the child off with lies or evasions. For example, I grew up with the clear knowledge that at the age of 10 months a brother of mine had died in a fire in Australia before I was born. This was no secret to be hidden away but neither did my parents dwell on the horrors of the event. It was enough that I knew that John was a part of my family tree, even though his life had been cut off.

Who helps most after a death?

Outcomes are favourable if soon after bereavement the bereaved person experiences positive interactions with others.

The table that follows (taken from A.J. Davis (1984) *Listening and Responding*, The C.V. Mosby Company) is based on the experiences of 119 widowed persons between the ages of 28 and 70 years whose spouses either had died in an acute general hospital or were pronounced dead on arrival at the hospital. These widowed persons were interviewed after 13 to 16 months of bereavement and were asked which people inside and outside the hospital gave them help (little, some or great) before and after the death of their spouse.

Nurses were praised for being solicitous, showing concern, and helping explain tests and equipment when this was not done by the physician. It was also appreciated when nurses extended visiting hours or helped give the spouse confidence about caring for the client at home. Physical comfort meant a great deal, though it was not frequently offered. The major complaint was a coldness of attitude and unconcern.

Table 3: *Support groups who were identified as being of great help*

SUPPORT GROUP	Percentage of respondents who said support group was of great help	
	WIDOWERS	WIDOWS
Social workers (most respondents had no contact)	5%	5%
Physicians	47%	40%
Nurses	56%	55%
Chaplains	44%	71%
Neighbours	56%	68%
Local clergy	56%	62%
Funeral directors	76%	76%
Family	80%	80%

It would appear that bereaved people find that relatives and funeral directors give more support than professionals such as doctors, nurses and social workers.

Particularly helpful are groups that bring bereaved people together to share expression of loss and to offer companionship, social contacts and emotional support. It should be more generally recognised and accepted that even in deepest grief it is not unusual for a person to experience transient feelings of relief for a death that occurred at the particular time it did; feelings of anger over seemingly having been abandoned by the dead person; thoughts of the gains and rewards possibly accruing from the death; and many other 'unacceptable' feelings that seem inappropriate to the depth of feeling about the magnitude of the loss.

Bereaved persons have rights that should be respected. When these rights are respected, the goal of making grief easier to bear will become more of a reality.

The bereaved have a right to professional and lay bereavement support, including assistance regarding insurance, medical bills and legal concerns.

If we are to give the kind of help to a bereaved person that we should all like to give, it is essential we see things from his point of view and respect his feelings – unrealistic though we may regard some of them to be. For only if a bereaved person feels we can at least understand and sympathise with him in the task he sets for himself is there much likelihood that he will be able to express the feelings that are bursting within him – his yearning for the return of the lost figure, his hope against hope that miraculously all may yet be well, his rage at being deserted, his angry, unfair reproaches against 'those incompetent doctors', 'those unhelpful nurses', and against his own guilty self; if only he had done so and so, or not done so and so, disaster might perhaps have been averted.

Bowlby

For what is it to die but to stand naked in the wind
and to melt into the sun?
And what is it to cease breathing
but to free the breath from its restless tides,
that it may rise and expand and seek God unencumbered?

Gibran, *The Prophet*

Further reading (see also references under Dying – stages of)

Ainsworth-Smith, I. and Speck, P. (1982) *Letting Go: caring for the dying and bereaved*. SPCK, London.

Backer, B. et al. (1982) *Death and Dying*. John Wiley, New York.

Bowlby, J. (1979) *The Making and Breaking of Affectional Bonds*. Tavistock Publications Ltd, London.

Carr, A.C. (1985) Grief, mourning, and bereavement. In: H.I. Kaplan and B.J. Sadock (eds) *Comprehensive Textbook of Psychiatry/IV*. Williams & Wilkins, Baltimore.

Cook, B. and Phillips, S.G. (1988) *Loss and Bereavement*. Lisa Sainsbury Foundation, London.

Cruse – Bereavement Care (Spring 1993) *Supporting Bereaved Children and their Families: a training manual*. Cruse, Richmond, Surrey.

Gibran, K. (1923, reprinted 1984) *The Prophet*. Heinemann, London.

Glick, I. et al. (1974) *The First Year of Bereavement*. John Wiley, New York.

Gunzburg, J.C. and Stewart, W. (1994) *The Grief Counselling Casebook*. Chapman & Hall, London.

Kubler-Ross, E. (1970) *On Death and Dying*. Tavistock, London.

Lewis, C.S. (1961) *A Grief Observed*. Faber & Faber, London.

Machin, L. (1990) *Looking at Loss: bereavement counselling pack*. Longman, Harlow.

Parkes, C.M. (1972) *Bereavement: studies of grief in adult life*. Tavistock, London.

Poss, S. (1981) *Towards Death with Dignity*, National Institute Social Services Library No. 41. Allen & Unwin, London.

Schoenberg, B. (ed.) (1980) *Bereavement Counselling*. Greenwood Press, London.

Worden, J.W. (1983) *Grief Counselling and Grief Therapy: a handbook for the mental health practitioner*. Routledge, London.

Ziscook, S. (1995) Death, dying and bereavement. In: *Comprehensive Textbook of Psychiatry*, 6th edn (eds H.J. Kaplan and B.J. Sadock). Williams & Wilkins, Baltimore, MD.

GROUPS (SEE ALSO: TAVISTOCK METHOD)

A group is a social system involving regular interaction among members and a common group identity. This means that groups have a sense of togetherness, that enables members to identify themselves as belonging to a distinct entity and usually distinguished from other groups.

Some social systems have intense involvement and strong group identity, such as families, a neighbourhood association or a close-knit 'circle' of friends (all of which can be thought of as a group). Groups also vary in how often and how extensively members interact, how long the group survives and the reasons that people join and participate.

The group is an important sociological concept because groups play such a complex and important part in social life. Group membership, for example, is an important part of an individual's social identity. The group is a key agent of social control over individuals, for it is in groups that social pressures towards conformity can be most directly applied, especially when those who deviate are at risk of being alienated from other members.

Groups are also important because it is in groups that many of the most important social activities take place, e.g. the socialisation and care of children in families, the production of goods, religious worship, formal education, social movements, scientific research, politics and the making of war. Attention to how groups work is thus essential for a full understanding of social life.

The study of groups is an important topic, because most of us work in groups of one kind or another. Some groups we choose to be in, although there are some, such as work groups, in which we have little choice. The very nature of being present with a number of people has the potential for producing stress. Therefore, learning what makes groups tick is an important factor in reducing stress levels.

Types of group

- **Simple groups**: The dyad, or two-person group, and the triad, or three-person group
- **Formal groups**: Where each person has a specific role allocated
- **Informal groups**: A group of people who join together
- **Primary groups** (also called small groups): Usually bound by ties of affection and personal loyalty; involve many different aspects of people's lives and endure over long periods of time; involve a great deal of face-to-face interaction where the focus is on people's feelings and welfare more than accomplishing specific tasks or goals. The family is an example of a primary group.
- **Secondary groups**: Organised around secondary relationships and usually task-oriented. The services one receives from the bank are an example of secondary relationship.

Group dynamics

Group dynamics refers to the psychological and social forces arising from the interaction of people in such groups as families, committees and athletic teams and in work, educational, therapeutic, religious, racial and ethnic groups. The study of group dynamics is concerned with such processes as power and shifts of power, leadership, how the group is formed and how the group interacts with other groups, how cohesive the group is and how decisions are made within it.

As group size increases, a smaller proportion of the group's members take part in group discussion and decision making, interaction becomes more impersonal, satisfaction declines, group cohesiveness is reduced and the group tends to become divided into factions. Most groups, especially those that include seven or more people, begin to develop role specialists, such as task leaders, who try to get people to do the work of the group, and the best-liked group members, who generally are not the task leaders.

Group-think

Group-think, a concept developed by Irving Janis, is a process through which the desire for consensus in groups can lead to poor decisions. Rather than object to poor decisions and risk losing a sense of group solidarity, members may remain silent and thereby lend their support. The presence of a directive leader strengthens the desire to be with everyone else. Defective decision-making is characterised by:

- Limited discussion of only a few alternatives
- Failure to re-evaluate previous solutions
- Failure to seek the advice of experts
- Options presented are strongly biased.
- Objectives are not scrupulously examined.
- Little or no account is taken of the views of other groups.
- No contingency plans are developed.

Group-think can be minimised by every person:

- Identifying the problem
- Writing down the solutions
- Privately ranking each solution.

The group then selects the highest ranking solution as the group decision.

Group psychotherapy

Group psychotherapy or group therapy is a form of psychotherapy carried out with groups of patients, of both sexes, who come together regularly with therapist as group leader. They are encouraged to talk freely about themselves, their problems and their feelings towards each other and the therapist.

There are many kinds of group psychotherapy; some are based on psychoanalysis, while others involve or are derived from psychodrama. A group usually consists of six to eight patients who meet for treatment once or twice a week. A closed group keeps its membership for the duration of the treatment (about two years) whereas membership of an open group changes when patients leave or are discharged and new patients join the group.

While the majority of counselling is carried out on a one-to-one basis, counsellors may become involved in group counselling. They may also be involved in teaching. In both situations, knowledge of how groups work is an advantage. It must not be assumed that knowledge of groups applies only to groups that we join willingly; knowledge of group interaction can be of enormous benefit wherever people gather. Being aware of what is happening is one sure way of relieving stress. The more intimate the group, the more possible it is for stress to develop.

Among the strategies for survival are fight or flight responses. We can observe both of these reactions to situations that are perceived as threats. Part of the skill of handling groups is to intervene in such a way that people don't feel put down. The aim is for the interaction to help people feel OK.

We all may experience stress when we meet in a new group or when a new leader takes over, as in a work group. A knowledge of group dynamics would help us realise that even though 'The king is dead, long live the king', the old leader still has to be mourned and we may demonstrate our suspicion of the new leader, even though we are too polite to say it verbally.

The role of the group facilitator is important – not that the facilitator is infallible but the role carries with it certain responsibilities and duties that reflect the facilitator's training, competence and experience. Of equal importance are the personal qualities of the facilitator; one may have a great deal of experience, yet, if there is no integrity, the group will flounder and be unproductive.

It is important to identify the different roles we adopt within groups: roles that focus on the task, that build the group or that work against the group. How these roles are played and held in balance determines how productive the group is.

Groups are born, live, work and then die. The death of a group has echoes of all death; something that is not easy to come to terms with or accept.

Two other types of groups

1. Human potential movement
The human potential movement began as an endeavour to examine interpersonal skills and group dynamics through educational means; today it emphasises personal psychological growth for normal persons through increased self-awareness and the attainment of their full potential. The movement consists of loosely organised centres where people visit for periods of a few days to a few weeks.

Fritz Perls, the founder of Gestalt therapy, strongly influenced the growth of the human potential movement. Most growth centres have modelled themselves after the Esalen programme, which incorporated many philosophical and meditative aspects of Eastern religions.

2. Encounter, sensitivity and training groups (T-groups)
These groups are not traditional therapy groups, and they attempt to screen out people with known psychiatric problems and illnesses. Typically, the group leaders are not trained in traditional group therapy; they concentrate mostly on the present and use such approaches as sensory awareness techniques, physical contact, role playing and marathon sessions.

They advocate leader transparency; the leaders participate fully as members of the group and tend to ignore issues of transference, intrapsychic conflict and resistance. Instead, they explore issues of leadership, competition, intimacy and sub-grouping, which may revolve around concerns dealing with race, minority status and gender differences.

Encounter, sensitivity and training groups had their heyday in the 1960s and 1970s. Today they have largely passed from the scene, but their principles have been incorporated into many retreats and workshops conducted by secular and religious organisations.

Concluding a group

Basic issues
Grief, integration of the experience, and transfer of learning.

Basic questions

- 'Do we have to say goodbye?'
- 'What have I learned?'
- 'What will I do with this learning?'
- 'How can I add to what I've learned?'

Behavioural indicators
Non-verbal behaviours include leaving early, clinging, turning inwards and reverting to habitual behaviours.

Verbal behaviours

- Joking, excessive talking and laughing.
- Indication of self-affirmation: 'I learned. . .'
- Avoiding goodbyes or experiencing regrets: 'This isn't really the end. We'll see each other.'
- Indication of disowning responsibility: 'If only it were like this everywhere.'
- Offering feedback: 'You really changed.'

The facilitator must model and encourage ways to integrate the group experience and to apply learning to everyday activities.

Suggested activities in closure

- Members select partners and establish contracts with each other regarding what they will do outside the group.
- Have a group discussion on how they intend applying the learning.
- Engage in a goodbye fantasy.
- Lead a farewell toast or express wishes for members.
- Engage in a total-group activity with each member making personal contact with every other member.
- Have members give direct feedback by stating how the group experience has changed them, by presenting make-believe gifts or awards, or by giving compliments.

Further reading
Institute of Counselling, Crisis Module, Lessons 8 and 9. Institute of Counselling, 6 Dixon Street, Glasgow, G1 4AX.

Janis, I.L. (1982) *Victims of Group-think*. Houghton-Mifflin, Boston.

Manstead, A.S.R. and Hewstone M. et al. (1996) *The Blackwell Encyclopaedia of Social Psychology*. Blackwell Publishers, Oxford.

Rowan, R. (1988) *Group Processes: dynamics within and between groups*. Blackwell, Oxford.

Wong, N. (1995) Group psychotherapy, combined individual and group psychotherapy, and psychodrama. In: *Comprehensive Textbook of Psychiatry*, 6th edn (eds H.J. Kaplan and B.J. Sadock). Williams & Wilkins, Baltimore, MD.

GUILT AND SHAME

Guilt

The distinction between these two emotions is blurred. Both are characterised by self-reproach. Guilt is focused on specific blameworthy actions that one has performed, or one feels responsible for, whereas shame is focused on the inadequacy of the entire self. Thus, the negative evaluation of shame is more global and painful than that of guilt.

The feelings associated with shame may be helplessness, a fear of others' disapproval, and a desire to hide from interpersonal situations. These feelings may motivate the shamed person to externalise blame to others and become angry. On the other hand, guilt may motivate one to make restitution, encouraging empathy and a change in behaviour.

Objectively, guilt is a fact or state attributed to a person who violates the will of and/or some moral or penal code. Subjectively, guilt is awareness of having violated personal norms or the norms of family, religion or society. The offence may be real or imaginary. Normally the reason for the guilt is known only to the person concerned.

The feeling of guilt may or may not be proportionate to the nature of the offence. Guilt is often experienced as an alienation from the relationship with God, others or self. The act that causes shame is often inconsequential, but the self feels attacked.

- 'False guilt' is usually associated with sexuality, self-assertion, self-love and putting oneself first. A distinction needs to be made between having desires to do 'wrong' and acting upon such desires.
- Pathological guilt is present when a person not only feels the guilt but also considers himself to be a bad person deserving of punishment. This is linked with self-blame and might, in the case of a person suffering from depression, lead to self-harm.

Guilt about having wrong desires often wreaks havoc with the psyche, producing severe neuroses and sometimes psychoses. Guilt and shame are both concerned with internalised standards of conduct. Guilt is more abstract and judgemental than shame.

It is possible to say one feels guilty without experiencing it; one cannot be ashamed without feeling it. Shame is more tied to threat of exposure than is guilt. Shame is the more fundamental of the two feelings.

Psychoanalytic theory regards guilt as internalisation of prohibitions and is not so much concerned with the fact of guilt as with the sense of guilt. Psychoanalysis distinguishes 'normal' guilt (remorse), which would respond to 'confession', from 'pathological' guilt for which therapy would be more appropriate. Behaviourists regard guilt as a conditioned response to past actions that have involved punishment.

One view of guilt is that it is anger turned inwards. A total absence of guilt is one of the features of 'character disorder'. Dealing with guilt is difficult. Working at it indirectly by tackling the underlying feelings that support the guilt may be more productive.

Carl Jung makes a distinction between 'collective guilt' and 'personal guilt'; a sense of guilt may arise from either. Collective guilt may be compared to fate or to a curse or to a form of pollution. An example of collective guilt would be where a nation feels guilty about the crimes of a previous generation, such as the Holocaust.

A sense of guilt may be necessary to avoid the projection on to other people of those parts of the personality called the Shadow, the dark side of us, which, was it known, would invoke moral condemnation. The sense of guilt inspires reflection on what is evil – which is as important as reflection on what is good.

Guilt differs from anxiety in the following ways:

- Anxiety is experienced in relation to a feared future occurrence, while guilt is experienced in relation to an act already committed.
- The capacity to experience guilt is related to the capacity to internalise objects whereas the capacity to experience anxiety is not.

While animals and infants seem to feel anxious, so far as we know only humans with some awareness of time and of others feel guilt. Neurotic guilt and anxiety may, however, be indistinguishable owing to the fact that the neurotic sense of guilt is associated with dread of punishment and retribution.

All defences used to reduce anxiety can also be used to reduce the sense of guilt but one defence – reparation, the making good of damage imagined to have already been done – is used specifically to reduce the sense of guilt.

Some expressions of guilt

- 'I feel I've let someone down so badly, I deserve to be punished'
- 'I've done something wrong against someone'
- 'I've not done anything wrong, but I feel I've left something undone I should have done'
- 'I feel caught between what's realistic and the selfish desires of other people'
- 'I've made a mistake and can't live with it'
- 'I can't forgive myself and I'm being punished'
- 'I can't help people making me feel guilty'
- 'I need to get a balance between guilt and what I've done or feel I've done'
- 'I feel guilty because other people make demands on me that I can't meet and I feel I should'
- 'My burden of guilt robs me of any self-esteem and makes me feel so unworthy'.

Counselling points to remember about guilt

- Guilt may be anger turned inwards. Work, therefore, with the anger.
- Guilt often has delusional qualities, in that it cannot be shaken by reason or logic. Sometimes there is the feeling of being excommunicated, even though the person may not be 'religious'.
- Guilt is a common symptom of depression.
- No one can make us feel guilty (or feel anything else) if we do not want to. When we say 'That person makes me feel...', we pass on to that person the responsibility for how we feel. We have chosen to take on board something someone else wants to off-load on to us.
- In all work with guilt, there is an urgent need to help the person balance conscience with responsibility.

Authentic awareness of guilt seems to be a necessary aspect of healthy human beings. Religious guilt is a warning system that we are at odds with God or with the structures, values and truths to which we subscribe, although this would depend on whether the person had a religious belief.

Shame

Shame is a complex, painful feeling resulting from a strong sense of guilt, unworthiness or disgrace. We feel shame when we are faced with something that draws attention to a discrepancy between what we are and what, ideally, we would like to be. The act that causes shame is often inconsequential, but the self feels attacked.

Shame is an emotion of self-abasement experienced when we are conscious of acting contrary to, or below, the standards of which we approve and by which we know (or feel) others judge us. This sense of self-abasement is stronger than in the related states with which it is often confused – modesty, bashfulness, shyness and coyness, which are marked rather by hesitation, caution and inhibition. They arise through consciousness of being under the gaze of others whose attitude is that of curiosity or superiority or searching criticism. But shame involves a sense of unworthiness and demerit. Like its kindred states it may arise in connection with matters of sex, but it is also found in a great variety of situations not concerned with sex. The sense of shame consists in the consciousness of failure and exposure before other persons in connection with a point of honour or of strong self-esteem.

Blushing is often an expression of shame and is frequently accompanied by other signs, such as drooping of the body, lowering of the head and averted gaze. We tend to hide or want to hide, to escape notice and, in extreme cases, to inflict injury upon ourselves as a kind of self-imposed punishment for some imagined wrong committed. Shame may also arise from a conflict between impulses or resulting from comparison with someone with whom we consider ourselves to be inferior in some way. We then act in a way that draws attention to the powers and attributes in which we consider ourselves deficient. So the self-fulfilling prophecy is completed.

We are more likely to feel shame when we feel in competition with someone, e.g. when there is one rival who can excel us, as in athletics. On the other hand, if we have no athletic prowess or ambition we will not be depressed by the fact that everyone can surpass us. When we have great expectations of success, our self-esteem might result in shame when lack of success reinforces our inadequacies, particularly if those expectations were unrealistic and boosted by unrealistic claims.

Social psychology emphasises the fact that one's social group furnishes the determining influences in forming one's standards of taste and conduct. Infringement of social conventions, or mores, is likely to be accompanied by shame. Some sociologists speak of 'shame cultures', e.g. the traditional Japanese culture, and 'guilt cultures', e.g. Judaeo-Christian cultures.

In psychology shame has received less attention than guilt, anxiety and depression. Freud interpreted shame as fear of ridicule. Guilt occurs when we fail to meet a standard imposed from outside; shame, when we fail to meet self-imposed standards or when we are aware of being tactless or of behaving in bad taste.

We feel shame when we are faced with something that draws attention to discrepancy between what we are and what, ideally, we would like to be. The act that causes shame is often inconsequential, but the self feels attacked. This highlights what could be a difficult area for the client, for if the client is to be true to himself, then certain things need to be explored, yet it is possible that it is these very things that bring a sense of shame. The fact that I feel I should be generous and forgiving expresses what I would like to be, what I feel I 'should' be, yet the reality is that I am vindictive and unforgiving; hence there is a discrepancy between the two parts of self.

As a client I might find it relatively easy to disclose that I am not always kind, and not feel ashamed, yet the knowledge that I secretly harbour murderous thoughts and feelings towards someone might create so much shame in me that I cannot disclose that. The deeper the feelings of shame, the more the client will feel resistant to disclose them; yet the more trust the client has in the counsellor, the more able the client will feel able to disclose and then explore. Movement and growth depend so much on the strength of the counselling relationship but also on the client's willingness to move towards healing.

Challenging the feelings of guilt or shame is one way of working with these feelings; on the other hand, working with the underlying anger, in the case of guilt, or the feelings of self-devaluation, in the case of shame, could be productive. A second approach, with guilt, is to help the client clarify whether it is justified or false. But in either case, the feelings are just as real and not easily dealt with.

Forgiveness

Guilt is often linked to not being able to forgive, either someone else or one's self. In Christian thought, forgiveness is one of the constituent parts of justification. In pardoning sin, God absolves the sinner from the condemnation of holy law because of the work of Christ, i.e. he removes the guilt of sin or the sinner's actual liability to eternal wrath on account of it.

Justification is a legal term opposed to condemnation. As regards its nature, it is the legal act of God by which he pardons all the sins of those who believe in Christ and accounts, accepts and treats them as righteous in the eyes of the law, i.e. as conformant with all its demands.

In addition to the pardon of sin, justification declares that all the claims of the law are satisfied in respect of the justified. Justification is the act of a judge and not of a sovereign. The law is not relaxed or set aside but is declared to be fulfilled in the strictest sense; and so the person justified is declared to be entitled to all the advantages and rewards arising from perfect obedience to the law (Rom. 5:1–10).

In counselling, the client may be looking for absolution for some wrongdoing – real or imagined. Part of forgiveness is being able to accept forgiveness from God and from other people. Just as relevant are clients being able to forgive themselves – to act as their own God, to mete out absolution and justification, particularly where the forgiveness is not related to some religious omission or commission.

The desire (and note that this is a conscious act of will) to hold on to bitterness and resentment against someone who has injured us lies deep in the human heart. Unforgiveness, however, has serious spiritual and psychological consequences.

The longer a person holds on to bitterness and resentment, the harder it is for him to forgive. Listing the hurts and offences that need to be forgiven is useful and brings things into the open and stops them coming up at another time.

The next step is to get the person to view these hurts and offences from the other person's point of view. A useful technique is to get people to post each point on a board, then to get them to read each one out aloud as if it were a notice, or for the counsellor to read it out. Looking at it dispassionately in this way may bring the degree of objectivity necessary – for the client to stand back from the problem.

When working with self-forgiveness, help the client to find a part of self that can act as a forgiving, all-loving God, who will offer absolution. In the entry on Psychosynthesis there is a section on subpersonalities; a study of this, and of using imagery, may well show a way in which the client can create a subpersonality who can act as internal priest.

Finally, show the client that forgiveness is an act of the will. If we wait until we feel like forgiving, we may never do it.

The Bishop of Singapore spent the years of the Second World War in a Japanese concentration camp, where he suffered deprivation and cruelty at the hands of the Japanese soldiers. His life hung on a slender thread as his health was severely threatened by starvation and physical punishment.

At the end of the war he was repatriated to England. Two years later he was invited back to Singapore to conduct a confirmation ceremony. When he approached the last person to be confirmed, the bishop recognised him as one of the most cruel guards in the concentration camp, now confessing his new-found faith in Jesus Christ. As the bishop laid hands on the head of the Japanese confirmant, he knew in his heart that God, through Jesus Christ, had forgiven them both.

Further reading

Coleman, V. (1982) *Guilt: why it happens and how to overcome it*. Sheldon Press, London.

Lewis, H. (1971) *Shame and Guilt in Neurosis*. International Universities Press, New York.

Manstead, A.S.R. and Hewstone, M. et al. (1996) *The Blackwell Encyclopaedia of Social Psychology*. Blackwell Publishers, Oxford.

H

HIERARCHY OF HUMAN NEEDS (ABRAHAM MASLOW, 1908–70)

Abraham Maslow, an American psychologist who became an influential figure in humanistic psychology and humanistic psychotherapy, is probably best known for his hierarchy of human needs, related to motivation and problem-solving and his work on self-actualisation and peak experiences. Maslow was active in the development of the human potential movement and the founding of the Esalen Institute in California.

His self-actualisation theory of psychology proposed that the primary goal of psychotherapy should be the integration of the self and that integration is achieved as needs are experienced and met. Our behaviour motivations, priorities and actions are determined by these needs. Motivated behaviour thus results from tension when a need presents itself, whether the tension is pleasant or unpleasant. The goal of behaviour is the reduction of tension.

Maslow identified five levels of human needs. In order to progress upwards, the person must have experienced secure footing on the first rung in order to proceed to the next. Inability to fulfil a lower-order need may create locked-in, immature behaviour patterns.

The theory is that it is only as each need is satisfied that we are motivated to reach for the next higher level; thus, people who lack food or shelter or who do not feel themselves to be in a safe environment are unable to concentrate on higher needs such as self-actualisation. Our drive for self-actualisation may conflict with our rights and duties and responsibilities to other people who are involved. Maslow did not say that all needs of a certain level must be fulfilled before progress upwards was possible. It is a question of how much energy is being used up at a lower level.

While people might be high on self-actualisation today, tomorrow something could happen that would change that and thrust them back into satisfying their basic needs. For example, if I lost my job, then, however much I might want to continue the upwards climb towards reaching my potential, my prime concern would probably be trying to find another job, trying to meet the security needs. If I were flying over the desert and the plane crashed, my immediate need would be very basic – food and water, not self-actualisation.

Another way of looking at Maslow's model is that, rather than moving on from stage to stage, as in climbing a ladder, all five needs are being met simultaneously, to some degree.

The hierarchy

The term 'self-actualisation' is used by most humanistic therapies to describe the dominating, motivating life force that drives the individual towards ever-devel-

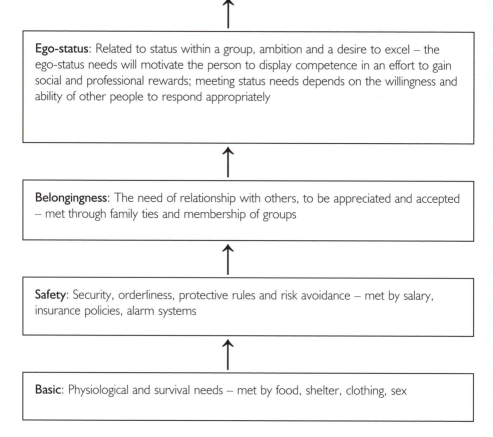

Self-actualisation: The capacity of human beings to grow and develop towards emotional and psychological maturity and self-fulfilment. This level of personal growth may be met through the challenge of creativity or demanding greater achievement. Self-actualising behaviours include risk-taking, seeking autonomy and freedom to act

Ego-status: Related to status within a group, ambition and a desire to excel – the ego-status needs will motivate the person to display competence in an effort to gain social and professional rewards; meeting status needs depends on the willingness and ability of other people to respond appropriately

Belongingness: The need of relationship with others, to be appreciated and accepted – met through family ties and membership of groups

Safety: Security, orderliness, protective rules and risk avoidance – met by salary, insurance policies, alarm systems

Basic: Physiological and survival needs – met by food, shelter, clothing, sex

Figure I: Hierarchy of human needs

oping, ever-perfecting his capacities to the highest heights and deepest depths. Therapies that emphasise minimal direction or person-centred philosophy also embrace the principle of self-actualisation.

Self-actualisation is the road; to be self-actualised is the goal, striven for but never absolutely attained. Self-actualisation involves the successful mastery of conflicts, which always involve anxiety. It is closely linked with 'peak experiences', although not synonymous with them. Our drive for self-actualisation may conflict with our rights and duties and responsibilities to other people who are involved.

The characteristics of self-actualisation

- Psychological growth and maturation
- The awakening and manifestation of latent potentialities
- Ethical, aesthetic and spiritual experiences and activities.

For Maslow self-actualisation is:

- A liberating of the person from factors that stunt personal growth
- Freeing of the person from the neurotic problems of life – infantile, fantasy or otherwise 'unreal'
- Something that enables the person to face, endure and grapple with the real problems of life; a moving from unreal towards real issues.

Self-actualisation is not:

- A state of no conflict
- A state of once-and-for-ever full unity
- An absence of problems.

Further reading

Maslow, A.H. (1970) *Motivation and Personality*. Harper & Row, New York.
Stewart, W. (1998) *Self-counselling: how to develop the skills to positively manage your life.* How to Books, Oxford.

HONESTY AND OPENNESS

Honesty or the quality of being honest is a virtue that belongs to the ethic of justice. In common speech it usually means being honourable or having integrity. Honesty involves regard for the rights of other people, whatever those rights are. Breaches of the law of justice often involve dishonesty, untruthfulness or covetousness and are judged to be bad because they inflict harm on others.

In Christian theology, we are urged not to distinguish the welfare of other people from our own well-being, so one cannot be dishonest without harming one's self. Honesty, then, is not just about obeying the laws of the land; honesty is a moral code of practice.

Honesty means that there are no contradictions or discrepancies in thoughts, words or actions. To be honest to one's real self and task earns trust and inspires faith in others. Honesty is never to misuse that which is given in trust. Inner honesty needs to be examined to provide wisdom and support, and ensure strength and stability, giving confidence to be grounded in one's self-esteem.

An honest person is one who aspires to follow the highest codes of conduct, one who is loyal to the benevolent and universal principles of life and whose decisions are based clearly on what is right and wrong. Such an individual maintains standards that provide guidance and courage to understand and respect the subtle connections of the world in relation to his life. An honest person does not take for granted his own resources such as mind, body, wealth, time, talents or knowledge.

When applied to counselling, honesty, although similar to openness, should not be confused with it. Counsellors talk of 'genuineness' and 'congruence', and openness is about those, but it is more. Some people enjoy relationships where they talk about their feelings, their secrets and their innermost thoughts. They enjoy having one person or at most a few people in whom they confide. Other people avoid being open. They prefer to keep things impersonal and have acquaintances rather than close friends.

Some people are very high on openness, as if they can't get close enough to people. As a consequence they tend to treat everyone in a close, personal way. They have a strong desire to be liked and for intimacy. They fear rejection and being unloved by all. They may be possessive and they may punish people who do not respond with intimacy.

On the other hand, some people are very low on openness, as if they don't want to get emotionally involved with people at any level. As a consequence, they tend to avoid close personal ties. They have a fear of being 'discovered', which results in superficial relationships. They fear not being loved and being rejected and they feel unloveable. Distrust of others often shows in antagonism. By keeping everyone at a distance they avoid having to show affection to one person.

Between these two extremes there are many gradations and the ideal is to achieve a balance between the two extremes. But at all times, openness has to be appropriate. Behaviour appropriate in the bedroom is inappropriate in the high street. What is appropriate between close friends is inappropriate between strangers. Counsellors who have no problem with being open with clients always have to remember that they are who they are and the clients have travelled to counselling by a very different life journey. They may have to be led very gently into honesty and openness.

HUMANISTIC PSYCHOLOGY

The roots of humanistic psychology are in humanism, a philosophy that attaches importance to humankind and human values. It derives much of its impact from the 'growth movement' of the 1960s.

It is often described as the 'third force' in modern psychology. It is seen as a reaction against the strict formalism of psychoanalysis and behaviourism, which has been described as the 'first force'.

The 'second force' is linked to the depth psychologies of Alfred Adler, Erik Erikson, Erich Fromm, Karen Horney, Carl Jung, Melanie Klein, Otto Rank, Harry Stack Sullivan and others, making way for the 'third force' of Carl Rogers's person-centred approach, which emerged during the late 1950s, Roberto Assagioli's psychosynthesis, Abraham Maslow's theory of self-actualisation, Albert Ellis's rational emotive therapy, Eric Berne's transactional analysis, Jacob Moreno's psychodrama, Rollo May's existential psychoanalysis, Fritz Perls's Gestalt therapy.

From their work, sensitivity-training sessions or T groups developed, in which facilitators lead group activities and observe interactions between members as they actually occur. Such groups are designed to help people develop sensitivity, awareness of self and others, interpersonal skills and personal effectiveness, and are said to reduce authoritarianism, prejudice and the need for structure and control.

Within the broad framework of working in a partnership, in which the client becomes a conscious partner with the therapist in determining the course of treatment, many different approaches have developed.

Humanistic psychology emphasises that psychotherapy is restricted to working with mentally ill people, but is equally relevant to many healthy people who are interested in exploring the further reaches of their potential and their place in the wider world.

Humanistic psychology is guided by a conviction that the interaction of the body, mind and spirit, and the capacity to become more aware, free, responsible, life-affirming and trustworthy, are the guiding values in life. Individual freedom has to be matched by recognising our responsibilities to one another, to society and culture, and to the future.

What humanistic psychologists share:

- An understanding of life as a process, change is inevitable
- An appreciation of the spiritual and intuitive
- A commitment to ecological integrity
- A recognition of the profound problems affecting our world and a responsibility to hope and constructive change
- A belief that an individual's behaviour is primarily determined by his perception of the world around him
- A belief that individuals are not solely the product of their environment
- A belief that individuals are internally directed and motivated to fulfil their human potential.

Humanistic views of human behaviour

- A person is more than just a sum of his parts. A person should be viewed holistically.
- A person does not live alone. People are social by nature and their interpersonal interactions are a part of their development.
- A person is aware. People have an awareness of their existence and themselves. How a person reacts to a situation is in part influenced by previous events. Future responses will be influenced by past and present experiences.
- A person has free will. People are aware of themselves; therefore, they make conscious choices. Animals, unlike humans, are driven by instincts and do not reach a conscious level of choice.
- A person is consciously deliberate. A person seeks certain things for himself such as value or meaning in his life. How a person seeks meaning or value for himself results in a personal identity. This personal identity is what distinguishes one person from another.

Three key components relate to reaching the highest level of self-understanding and development:

1. Self-actualisation
2. Self-fulfilment
3. Self-realisation.

The focus of humanistic counsellors is on:

- Working with clients to achieve their goal of a healthy personality
- Helping clients to become aware of and communicate their feelings
- Focusing on what the client's life is like from the client's own frame of reference
- Affirming the client's freedom of choice and emphasising the striving for the highest potential for each individual
- Helping clients to develop and recognise inner resources, identify choices and formulate goals.

Although fundamentally eclectic, there are common themes in humanistic psychology:

- Personal growth, human potential, responsibility and self-direction
- Lifelong education
- Full emotional functioning
- The need to learn, or to relearn, what play and joy are about
- Recognition of a person's spirituality, with an acknowledgement of the human capacity for altered states of consciousness.

Humanistic psychology is a way of dealing with problems related to the following beliefs:

- Intense personal experiences radically alter attitudes to self and others. Unity of the human and natural worlds is achieved through 'peak experiences'. Peak experiences describe life events that are ecstatic, overwhelmingly intense, positively valued by those who experience them and have long-term effects. The experience can be neither earned nor manufactured, nor even worked up. Maslow used art, music, dance and sex in the search for the paths to peak experiences. For Maslow such an experience is where the person feels in harmony with all things, is clear, spontaneous, independent and alert and often with little awareness of time or space.
- Existential experiences lead to being completely independent and totally responsible for one's thoughts and actions.

Criticisms of humanistic psychology

- Its concepts are too vague.
- Subjective ideas such as authentic and real experiences are difficult to objectify.
- An experience that is real for one individual may not be real for another person.

- Conclusions drawn from subjective experiences are almost impossible to verify, making humanistic psychology unreliable.
- It is not a true science because it involves too much common sense and not enough objectivity.

Strengths of humanistic psychology

- It emphasises individual choice and responsibility.
- It satisfies most people's idea of what being human means because it values personal ideals and self-fulfilment.
- It provides researchers with a flexible framework for observing human behaviour because it considers a person in the context of his environment and in conjunction with his personal perceptions and feelings.

Humanistic psychology has a strong influence on education, as summarised below. The basic objectives of humanistic education are to encourage students to:

- Be self-directed and independent
- Take responsibility for their learning
- Be creative and interested in the arts
- Be curious about the world around them.

The five basic principles of humanistic education can be summarised as follows:

1. Students' learning should be self-directed.
2. Schools should produce students who want and know how to learn.
3. The only form of meaningful evaluation is self-evaluation.
4. Feelings, as well as knowledge, are important in the learning process.
5. Students learn best in a non-threatening environment.

Association for Humanistic Psychology
1516 Oak St, #320A
Alameda, CA 94501–2947
Phone: 510/769–6495
ahpoffice@aol.com

Association for Humanistic Psychology in Britain
BM Box 3582
London, WC1N 3XX
Phone: 0845 707 8506
www.ahpb.org.uk

Further reading

Assagioli, R. (1980) *Psychosynthesis.* Turnstone Books, Wellingborough.
Ferrucci, P. (1982) *What We May Be.* Turnstone Press, Wellingborough.
Journal of Humanistic Psychology, SAGE Publications.
Maslow, A.H. (1969) *Motivation and Personality.* Harper & Row, New York.
Maslow, A.H. (1971) *The Farther Reaches of Human Nature.* Penguin, Harmondsworth.
Ornstein, R.E. (1975) *The Psychology of Consciousness.* Pelican, Harmondsworth.
Rowan, J. (1983) *The Reality Game.* Routledge & Kegan Paul, London.

HUMOUR

Humour is defined simply as a type of stimulation that tends to elicit the laughter reflex. The coordinated contraction of 15 facial muscles, accompanied by altered breathing, combines to produce a conventional pattern we call smiling or laughter.

The only biological function of laughter is to provide relief from tension. It is the only form of communication in which a complex stimulus produces a predicable, physiological response. Humour, then, can be applied to a stimulus, a response or a disposition.

Humour is also regarded as a form of play involving symbols, images and ideas. Through laughter and smiling, it serves a variety of social functions:

- Assisting interaction
- Revealing attitudes
- Engendering fellow feeling
- Aiding understanding
- Raising esteem
- Confirming the standing of relationships.

Humour is different from wit, which involves distraction from the feelings associated with the issue. The emotion discharged in laughter often, though not always, contains an element of aggression. Malice may be combined with affection in friendly teasing and the aggressive component in civilised humour may no longer be conscious. There is often a relationship between laughter and ugliness, deformity and cruelty, delight in suffering and contempt for the unfamiliar.

Humour as a defence mechanism:

- Is an antidote to sympathy
- Is a protection from the shortcomings of others
- Is a defence against showing true feelings
- Allows the individual to focus on something in a way that makes bearable what, in reality, is too terrible to be borne.

Humour in counselling requires a distinction between that which is used to attack and humour as a shared response. Appropriate humour may aid therapy, it lowers anxiety, reduces distance, focuses attention on the material being discussed, assists in building the relationship and promotes catharsis.

Freud regarded jokes and parapraxis as revelations of the unconscious. The *Oxford English Dictionary* defines parapraxis as 'the faulty performance of an intended act; in psychoanalysis, a minor error said to reveal a subconscious motive'. Parapraxis is a general term that includes momentary amnesias, slips of the tongue and pen, errors in action and forgetting. In psychoanalytic thought, parapraxis is caused by the intrusion of unconscious processes on the conscious, causing the 'mistake', the 'Freudian slip' that somehow betrays the truth.

Examples of parapraxes:

- 'I'm glad you're better' was the intention, which turned into 'I'm sad you're better'.
- 'My husband can eat what he wants' was the intention, which turned into 'My husband can eat what I want'.
- Man entering a restaurant with a woman: 'Do you have a table?' was the intention, which turned into 'Do you have a bedroom?'.
- King Henry VIII greeting Anne Boleyn: 'Good morning, beloved' was the intention, which turned into 'Good morning, beheaded'.

Humour is as essential to healthy interaction, to healthy people and to any productive relationship, as oil is to smooth-running machinery.

Humour is a tool, which helps to:

- Prevent the build-up of stress
- Improve communication
- Enhance motivation and morale
- Build relationships
- Encourage creative problem-solving
- Smooth the way for change
- Make learning fun
- Decrease problems with discipline
- Focus listening and attention
- Decrease the pressure to be perfect
- Increase retention, by freeing attention through laughter
- Increase the comfort level
- Build interest and energy through laughter
- Contribute to achievement and productivity
- Enhance self-confidence
- Build empathy
- Hear feedback and new information
- Develop a new perspective on problems.

Sharing humour with your client, when based on caring and empathy:

- Builds confidence
- Involves your client in the fun
- Amuses and encourages your client to laugh
- Is supportive
- Brings you both closer
- Encourages positive exchange
- Demonstrates that counselling is not always deadly serious.

Further reading

Cade, B.W. (1982) Humour and creativity. *Journal of Family Therapy*, 4: 35–42.

McGhee, P.E. (1976) *Humour: its origins and development*. W.H. Freeman, San Francisco, CA.

McGhee, P.E. and Goldstein, J.H. (1983) *Handbook of Humour Research*. Springer-Verlag, New York.

HYPNOTHERAPY

Hypnosis is a special psychological state with certain physiological attributes, resembling sleep only superficially and marked by a functioning of the individual at a level of awareness other than the ordinary conscious state. Hypnotised people appear to heed only the communications of the hypnotist, and respond in an uncritical, automatic fashion, ignoring all aspects of the environment other than those pointed out to them by the hypnotist. They see, feel, smell and otherwise perceive in accordance with the hypnotist's suggestions. Even the subject's memory and awareness of self may be altered by suggestion.

The history of hypnosis is as ancient as that of sorcery, magic and medicine, to whose methods it belonged. Its scientific history began in the latter part of the 18th century with Franz Anton Mesmer, a Viennese physician who used it in the treatment of patients. Because of his mistaken belief that it was an occult force, which he termed 'animal magnetism', that flowed through the hypnotist into the subject, he was soon discredited; but hypnotism – or mesmerism, as it was named after him – continued to interest medical practitioners. A number of clinicians made use of it without adequate recognition of its nature until the middle of the 19th century, when the English physician James Braid studied its phenomena and coined the terms 'hypnotism' and 'hypnosis'.

Freud adopted and then rejected hypnotism in the treatment of neurotic patients, but despite his rejection, it continues to flourish.

The techniques used to induce hypnosis share common features:

- The most important consideration is that the person to be hypnotised (the subject) be willing and cooperative and that he trust in the hypnotist.
- The subject is invited to relax in comfort and to fix his gaze on some object.
- The hypnotist continues to suggest, usually in a low, quiet voice, that the subject's relaxation will increase and that his eyes will grow tired.
- Soon the subject's eyes do show signs of fatigue, and the hypnotist suggests that they will close.
- The subject allows his eyes to close and then begins to show signs of profound relaxation, such as limpness and deep breathing.
- He has entered the state of hypnotic trance.

A person's responsiveness to being hypnotised is greatest when he believes that he can be hypnotised, that the hypnotist is competent and trustworthy, and that the undertaking is safe, appropriate and congruent with his wishes. Therefore induction is generally preceded by the establishment of suitable rapport between subject and hypnotist.

One fascinating manifestation that can be elicited from a subject who has been in a hypnotic trance is that of post-hypnotic suggestion and behaviour. By this is meant the subject's execution, at some later time, of instructions and suggestions that were given to him while he was in a trance. With adequate amnesia induced during the trance state, the individual will not be aware of the source of his impulse to perform the instructed act.

Posthypnotic suggestion, however, is not a particularly powerful means for controlling behaviour when compared to a person's conscious willingness to perform actions. Many subjects seem unable to recall what happened while they were in deep hypnosis. This post-hypnotic amnesia, as it is called, can either result spontaneously from deep hypnosis or it can result from suggestion by the hypnotist during the trance state. The amnesia may include all the events of the trance state or only selected items, or it may be manifested in connection with matters unrelated to the trance. Post-hypnotic amnesia may be successfully removed by appropriate hypnotic suggestions.

Uses of hypnotherapy

Hypnotherapy is a general term for any psychotherapy that makes use of hypnosis. It is a directive therapy, since hypnosis produces a passivity during which the client accepts direction from another person.

Hypnosis has been found most useful in:

- Preparing people for anaesthesia
- Enhancing the drug response and reducing the required dosage
- In childbirth it is particularly helpful, because it is effective in alleviating the mother's discomfort while avoiding drug-induced impairment of the child's physiological function
- In the management of otherwise intractable pain, including that of terminal cancer
- In reducing the widespread fear of dental procedures; the very people whom dentists find most difficult to treat frequently respond best to hypnotic suggestion
- In the area of psychosomatic medicine, hypnosis has been used in a variety of ways. Patients have been trained to relax and to carry out, in the absence of the hypnotist, exercises that have had salutary effects on some forms of high blood pressure, headaches and functional disorders.
- In psychotherapy, hypnosis has been used in a variety of ways. For example, the technique of revivifying traumatic events in order to produce an emotional catharsis continues to be a useful treatment in relieving neuroses with traumatic onset, such as those that develop in combat, among individuals with relatively stable prior adjustments.

Though the induction of hypnosis requires little training and no particular skill, when used in the context of medical treatment, it should never be employed by individuals who do not have the competence and skill to treat such problems without the use of hypnosis.

Hypnosis has been repeatedly condemned by various medical associations when it is used purely for purposes of public entertainment, owing to the danger of persons suffering adverse post-hypnotic reactions to the procedure. Indeed, in this regard, several nations have banned or limited commercial or other public displays of hypnosis on such grounds.

Cautions

1. Many experts caution that the revelations under hypnosis are best corroborated using other means.
2. Therapists must be absolutely certain that any suggestions do not ride counter to the client's beliefs and values.
3. Therapists must be certain that any altered thinking suggestions are morally and ethically correct.
4. Hypnosis with seriously emotionally disturbed clients may release too many feelings too quickly, and leave the client and the therapist floundering.

www.hypnos.co.uk
www.gpotter.com/clinical.htm

Further reading

Orne, M.T., Dinges, D.F. and Bloom, P.B. (1995) Hypnosis. In: *Comprehensive Textbook of Psychiatry*, 6th edn (eds H.J. Kaplan and B.J. Sadock). Williams & Wilkins, Baltimore, MD.

I

IMAGERY (SEE ALSO: CREATIVITY AND PSYCHOSYNTHESIS)

At a primitive level imagination is thinking in pictures, and it is possibly this faculty that many of us have lost, because we use words. Imagination is free and unlimited, not bound by established rules of grammar. It works with what might be, rather than what actually is or what might have been.

Memory and imagination

- Memory and imagination are two different functions, and are often at odds with each other. We use imagination to construct or prepare for a new experience, something which we have not yet realised.
- Imagination faces the future.
- Memory faces the past.
- Imagination produces something that is essentially new, spontaneous and original.
- Memory reproduces what was and is imitative.

A child reads a book – that is memory. Imagination takes the child into the pages of the book and makes the characters live. The characters become real people. Too heavy a reliance on memory can stifle imagination; too much dependence on imagination can interfere with accurate recall of factual material. As with all other aspects of personality, imagination and reality must be in balance.

Exploring imagination and reality

Reality and imagination are opposites. Imagination uses images, but also works with ideas and perceptions. Reality is concerned with what is correct, predictable, logical and true. Imagination works with myths, legends and fantasy and understands them, because imagination looks beyond, to the truth or truths.

In the story of Creation in Genesis, realists will argue about the date, the feasibility and the details. Imagination will see the possibilities, the symbols, the metaphors, the underlying message and grasp them – those are the truths, hidden from the realist's mind.

Does it matter that the Creation story cannot be proven? Does it matter that the fairy story of Snow White and the Seven Dwarfs is improbable? Imagination has wings and will take you wherever you want to go, and if you trust your psyche it will take you where you need to go, on your personal journey of discovery.

This article draws together imagination, guided fantasy, directed daydream and guided affective imagery (GAI).

- **Imagery**: The inner representation of objects and events created at will by the conscious mind

- **Fantasy**: Imaginary activities that are produced spontaneously (as in daydreams) or as a requested response to stimuli such as inkblots or ambiguous pictures
- **Imagination**: Expresses repressed parts of personality.

Imagery has an obvious and a hidden meaning:

- The obvious is conscious and concrete
- The hidden is unconscious and implied and takes the form of symbols. Understanding the fantasy means working with the symbols.

Guided imagery (also referred to as 'symboldrama')

This is a form of creative imagination facilitated by the therapist, who prompts, encourages, develops and brings the fantasy experience to a close. The material may then be analysed in terms of its meaning and symbolism – similar to dream analysis. Symbols, which may conceal or reveal, always derive from archetypes. Symbols have four meanings:

- Literal
- Allegorical
- Moral
- Mystical.

Kinds of symbols

- Nature
- Animal
- Human
- Man-made
- Religious
- Mythological
- Abstract
- Individual/spontaneous.

Guided imagery is used in one form or another in many different therapies. May also be used in groups, either for individuals or for the whole group-fundamental truth of therapeutic imagery is that the psyche always strives to represent itself in fantasy using images.

Two examples of symbolic meaning

Finding words to convey an image or a feeling is not always easy, for images do not have a literal meaning. That is why a study of symbols aids conveying meaning. A symbol encapsulates much more than the obvious or the external.

The cross

The simple cross can be just an ornament to be worn, but at a deeper level there are many different symbolic meanings. A cross stands for both the actual crucifixion and the concept of the Christian church. In contrast, it is often used in decorations awarded for military distinction for bravery.

The rose

Probably no other flower has received so much attention or been interpreted as much as the rose. In the language of flowers over 40 different sentiments can be expressed by choosing different colours and varieties of roses, for instance the golden rose for perfection, the blue rose for the unattainable, the seven-petalled rose for the days of the week, the planets and the seven degrees of enlightenment, while the eight-petalled rose symbolises regeneration.

Thus in your meditation if you have an awareness of a cross, or of a rose, or any other image, it needs to be explored to establish its unique meaning for you. Engaging in free association is one way of delving into the meaning the symbol has for you.

(The cross and the rose are extracts from W. Stewart (1998) *Dictionary of Images and Symbols in Counselling*. Jessica Kingsley, London.)

Principles of guided imagery therapy

- **The principle of symbol confrontation**: The client is encouraged to be courageous and to confront images (usually a part of self) that cause anxiety. Successful confrontation causes transformation and removal of anxiety.
- **The principle of feeding**: Where confrontation is inappropriate or unacceptable – the challenge may be too great – the therapist may suggest that the client feeds the frightening figure, to make it lazy and sleepy.
- **The principle of transformation**: While transformation may take place in confrontation, sometimes the transformation has to be more clearly directed if it doesn't occur spontaneously. Changing the feared object into something more acceptable is not just a way of coping; the new object often reveals significant psychological growth.
- **The principle of reconciliation**: This is where the client makes friends with a hostile symbolic figure, by addressing it, touching it, making friends with it.
- **The principle of the magic fluid**: The brook or stream represents the flow of psychic energy and the potential for emotional development. Bathing in the stream or drinking from it may prove therapeutic. Bathing in the sea can be very revealing, from what is felt and from what one discovers in the depths.
- **The principle of exhausting and killing**: Should only be used by experienced therapists, because it is very often an attack against the client's self.

Table 4: *Principal motifs in guided imagery*

Meadow	Brook
Mountain	House
Edge of woods	Animals
Rosebush	Lion/dragon
Significant person	Cave

Swamp	Volcano
Book	Sword
Container	Witch/sorceress/wizard/magician
Sleeping Beauty	Wise person – guide

Principal groups of symbols

- **Introversion or interiorisation**: The external life must be counterbalanced by an adequate inner life. The task is to discover our centre.
- **Deepening – descent**: The exploration of the unconscious. To become aware of and incorporate one's Shadow, the lower parts of one's personality.
- **Elevation – ascent**: The mountain-top, sky or heaven. The levels of the inner worlds are:
1. Emotions and feelings
2. Mind/intellect – concrete, analytical, philosophical reason
3. Imagination
4. Will
5. Transcendence.
- **Broadening – expansion**: Consciousness can be enlarged or broadened to include increasingly larger zones of impressions and contents. This happens spherically, in all directions, not just in one direction.
- **Awakening**: The natural conscious state is that of being asleep. In this dreamlike state we see everything and everyone through a thick veil of colouring and distortions, which derives from our emotional reactions, the effect of past psychic traumas and from external influences. To awaken from this state requires courage.
- **Light – illumination**: Illumination is the means by which we move from consciousness to intuitive awareness.
- **Fire**: The function of fire is essentially one of purification.
- **Development and evolution**: The principal symbols are:
  - The seed
  - Flower (lotus, rose).
- **Strengthening – intensification**: The reinforcement of all our latent, underdeveloped energies and functions. This may include transpersonal or peak experiences.
- **Love**: Human love is an attempt to come out of oneself and to enter communion with another.
- **The way, path, pilgrimage**: The 'mystic way', e.g. Bunyan's *Pilgrim's Progress*, Dante's *Divine Comedy*, passing through Hell, Purgatory and Paradise.
- **Transformation**: Transformation, or transmutation, is the theme of psychospiritual alchemy, which Jung explores in relation to dreams and symbols. Transformation occurs through the combined actions of elevation and descent.
- **Rebirth – regeneration**: Transformation paves the way for regeneration, which, in its most profound meaning, constitutes a 'new birth'.
- **Liberation**: Elimination of encumbrances, a process of liberation from our

complexes, from our illusions and from identification with the various roles we play in life, from the masks we assume and from our idols. Freedom from fear is a goal to be won and safeguarded every single day.

What imagery does is to cut through the control of the mind, which so often blocks tapping into the feelings. This does not mean that the client is out of control; that would be too frightening to contemplate and would certainly not be therapeutic. At all times clients are totally aware of what is happening and where their imagination is taking them, although the reason why and the outcome are obscured. Using imagery is a rewarding experience for both counsellor and client, for it takes them both beyond the realms of normal dialogue into the client's inner world in ways that normal dialogue cannot.

Further reading

Gallegos, S.E. and Rennick, T. (1984) *Inner Journeys.* Turnstone Press, Wellingborough.
Leuner. H. (1984) *Guided Affective Imagery: mental imagery in short-term psychotherapy.* Thieme-Stratton, New York.
Ornstein, R.E. (1975) *The Psychology of Consciousness.* Pelican, Harmondsworth.
Stewart, W. (1996) *Imagery and Symbolism in Counselling.* Jessica Kingsley, London.
Stewart, W. (1998) *A Dictionary of Images and Symbols in Counselling.* Jessica Kingsley, London.
Zdenek, M. (1983) *The Right-Brain Experience.* Corgi, London.

IMMEDIACY (HERE-AND-NOW)

Immediacy is also referred to as 'here-and-now', or 'you-me' talk, or 'mutual talk'. It is where the counsellor helps the client to look at the interaction within the relationship, as it is happening. There is often a natural tendency to talk about feelings in the past (the 'then-and-there'), rather than in the 'now'. People who rarely talk in the present often dilute the interaction by the use of 'you' instead of 'I'. They may be helped to feel the immediacy of the statement when 'I' is used. As with challenging, immediacy is more appropriate when the counselling relationship is firmly established.

As concreteness contrasts with generality, so 'here-and-now' immediacy contrasts with 'then-and-there'. The principal difference is that, in the one, clients are encouraged to own their feelings and not to generalise; in the other, they are encouraged to own their feelings as they exist at that moment.

Immediacy involves:

- Being open with the client about how you feel about something within the relationship
- Disclosing a hunch about the client's behaviour towards you, by drawing attention to discrepancies, distortions, avoidances, games
- Inviting the client to explore what is happening, with a view to developing a more productive working relationship.

Types of immediacy

Egan identifies the following:

- **Overall relationship immediacy:** This refers to your ability to discuss with a client where you stand in your overall relationship with him or her and vice versa. The focus is not on a particular incident but on the way the relationship itself has developed and how it is helping or standing in the way of progress.
- **Event-focused immediacy:** Here-and-now immediacy refers to what is happening between the two of you in the given transaction. It is not the entire relationship that is being considered but rather the specific interaction or incident.
- **Self-involving statements:** Such statements can be either positive or negative in tone. Clients tend to appreciate positive self-involving statements. Negative self-involving statements are much more directly challenging in tone.

Situations calling for immediacy

- **Lack of direction:** When the session, or the relationship seems stuck
- **Tension:** 'We seem to be getting on each other's nerves. It might be helpful to stop a moment and see if we can clear the air'
- **Trust:** 'I see your hesitancy to talk, and I'm not sure whether it's related to me or not. You're talking about pretty sensitive issues. It might still be hard for you to trust me'
- **Diversity:** When something like age, culture, interpersonal styles and personality types is getting in the way
- **Dependency:** 'You don't seem willing to explore an issue until I give you permission to do so or urge you to do so. And I seem to have let myself slip into the role of permission giver and urger'
- **Counter-dependency:** 'It seems that we're letting this session turn into a kind of struggle between you and me. And, if I'm not mistaken, both of us would like to win'
- **Attraction:** 'I think we've liked each other from the start. Now I'm wondering whether that might be getting in the way of the work we're doing here.' Care is needed in this situation. Talking about attraction can increase it. Someone once described romantic moments as 'when we are alone together and the topic is only us'.

Immediacy is a difficult skill, because we need to be aware of what is happening in the relationship without becoming preoccupied with it.

It is demanding because it calls on strength of character, as well as social intelligence and social courage to bring up relationship issues.

Immediacy can help both counsellor and client move beyond a variety of relationship obstacles.

It is also a learning opportunity for clients. If we use immediacy well, clients can see its value and learn how to apply it to their own sticky relationships.

Further reading

Egan, G. (2002) *The Skilled Helper: a problem-management and opportunity-development approach to helping*, 7th edn. Brooks/Cole, Pacific Grove, CA.

Sutton, J. and Stewart, W. (2002) *Learning to Counsel*. How to Books, Oxford.

INCEST (SEE ALSO: CHILD ABUSE, RAPE COUNSELLING)

Incest is defined as:

Any overtly sexual contact between people who are either closely related or perceive themselves to be ... if that special trust that exists between a child and parent figure or sibling is violated by a sexual act, that act becomes incestuous.

S. Forward and C. Buck (1981) *Betrayal of Innocence*. Pelican Books, London.

Incest is universally condemned and usually greeted with horror. (Punishment for incest may be very severe.) It has been countenanced in exceptional circumstances, usually associated with the marriage of royal children.

Initiation ceremonies at puberty reinforce the idea that the mother and sister are forbidden to the young male as sexual partners.

Sigmund Freud and the French sociologist Emile Durkheim both contributed to understanding the incest taboo. Freud sees the Oedipus complex – son–mother love – as a fundamental psychological conflict.

Jung interpreted incest fantasies as symbolic of wanting close emotional contact, although acknowledging the sexual feelings to be real.

To act upon the sexual urges and not acknowledge the taboo leads to abuse. To acknowledge the taboo and deny the sexual urges leads to repression, with all its consequent pathology.

Adult–child incest strikes at the very core of civilisation. It disturbs both the social order and the developing child. Although sibling incest does exist, unless it happens by force, it does not generally constitute abuse in the same sense as does adult–child incest.

Within the category of sexual abuse, the most prevalent examples are incestuous.

Child abuse may take the form of:

- Fondling a child
- 'Talking dirty'
- Pornography
- Masturbating a child
- Forcing a child to masturbate an adult
- Oral, anal or vaginal intercourse.

Social, cultural, physiological and psychological factors all contribute to the breakdown of the incest taboo. There is a higher incidence of incest among families where remarriage has occurred. Incest, because it usually involves a stronger male, is a variation of child abuse and rape. Children are cajoled or intimidated into incestuous relationships. Bribes and threats are used to keep children silent. Children are further damaged and confused because they are told by the abusing relative that there is nothing wrong with the incestuous behaviour.

Father–daughter incest is reported to be more common than either sibling or mother–son incest. Families at risk of father–daughter incest include those with violent fathers, as well as those with mothers who have been disabled because of depression, alcoholism, psychosis, frequent involuntary childbearing or chronic illness.

Incestuous daughters tend to develop character disorders such as promiscuity, antisocial behaviour, frigidity, homosexuality, learning difficulties and depression.

There is role confusion: is the father paternal or sexual? The incestuous father, fearful of exposure, is jealously possessive of the victim and this has an adverse influence on her relationships with siblings, other children and other adults.

In father–son incest, the taboos against incestuous behaviour and against homosexuality are both violated. The son is frequently the eldest child and, if he has sisters, they are likely to be sexually abused by the father as well.

Authoritarian fathers with poor impulse control who were abused as children, abuse alcohol, view children as property and are sexually attracted to children place their children at risk of incest abuse unless mitigating factors intervene.

Mitigating factors

Mitigating factors are conditions that serve to decrease the likelihood of incest:

- Adherence to proscription ('I want to, I could, but I shouldn't')
- Social support groups often help to reinforce society's norms
- Close family ties outside the nuclear family
- Official intervention and/or the threat of it
- Sex education is potentially the single most effective mitigating factor
- Media reporting.

Rape and other sexual attacks by strangers, however traumatic, are usually single events, but incest may continue for years with intercourse taking place daily or several times a week. Survivors sacrifice a part of their childhood to exploitation, pain, fear and secrecy.

Some of the consequences for child victims:

- Pregnancy
- Physical injury
- Secrecy
- Helplessness
- Entrapment and accommodation
- Disclosure brings shame
- Retraction of accusation.

Many women presenting severe psychological or behavioural difficulties admit a history of incest. Many prostitutes claim that their first sexual experience was with their fathers.

Incest survivors persistently describe how they tried to cut themselves mentally from the act, freeze up or pretend it wasn't happening. This can spread into other areas of life beside sex, causing feelings of social isolation, inability to communicate or to get close to other people. Self-disgust is compounded by intense shame and guilt, particularly when the act is exposed, with publicity and family break-up. There is no escape from the 'Catch-22' – the emotional burden of silence; the trauma of disclosure.

Myths of incest

The victims

- It preserves the family.
- It didn't happen.
- They must have asked for it.
- Children are very sexy, encourage and invite sex with adults.
- Incest is an accepted part of some sub-cultures; they enjoy it.
- Incest is a caring relationship.
- They are that sort of children anyway.

The mothers

- She colluded. What could be her 'Catch-22'?
- The marriage is faulty – her fault.
- She is the 'silent partner'.
- She must be an inadequate or flawed personality.

The perpetrators
Which view do you subscribe to?

- Most incest aggressors are criminals and need to be locked up.
- The offender can be helped and should be kept close to his family.
- He is a deviant – 'There's got to be something wrong or ill about a father who does that sort of thing to his child'.
- He is a product of his family history – the sins of the father. Is incest carried around in the genes like a genetic illness?
- A normal man has to have sex – 'The poor fellow must have been driven to it'.
- Incest is a sign of a dysfunctional family.

Further reading
Carter-Lourensz, J.H. and Johnson-Powell, G. (1995) Physical abuse, sexual abuse, and neglect of child. In: *Comprehensive Textbook of Psychiatry*, 6th edn (eds H.J. Kaplan and B.J. Sadock). Williams & Wilkins, Baltimore, MD.
Nin, A. (1993) *From a Journal of Love: the unexpurgated diary of Anais Nin*. Peter Owen, London.

INDIVIDUAL PSYCHOLOGY (ALFRED ADLER, 1870–1937)

Alfred Adler was one of the neo-Freudians and the first to break with Freud. He resigned as president of the Vienna Psychoanalytic Society in 1911 and formed a society that later became the Society for Individual Psychology.

Adler established many child guidance centres in schools in Vienna and is credited with being the pioneer psychiatrist of group counselling. He disagreed with Freud over the libido theory, the sexual origin of neurosis and the importance of infantile wishes.

Individual psychology is a broad, socially-orientated, humanistic and holistic personality theory of psychology and psychotherapy. Adler's system is invested with a great deal of common sense, for it makes sense to the average reader.

According to this theory, people are guided by values and goals of which they may be aware, not driven by unconscious instincts. Adler believed that the main motives of human thought and behaviour lie in the individual's striving for superiority and power, partly in compensation for feelings of inferiority. The individual moves from a sense of inferiority to a sense of mastery.

Every individual is unique and our personality structure, including our unique goal and ways of striving for it, is our style of life, a product of our own creativity. The individual cannot be considered apart from society, for all human problems – relationships, occupation and love – are social. Adler coined the term 'inferiority complex'.

The neurotically disposed person is characterised by increased inferiority feelings, underdeveloped social interest and an exaggerated, uncooperative goal of superiority. These characteristics express themselves as anxiety and aggression.

Individual psychology emphasises:

- Social relationships, rather than biological factors
- Self, rather than the id and the superego
- Striving for self-actualisation, rather than the sex instinct
- The present, rather than early experiences
- Equality and cooperation between the sexes

The person moves away from situations that make him feel inferior and towards goals of success and superiority.

Basic assumptions

1. All behaviour has social meaning

- Social interest creates an attitude towards one's own place within society and one's relationship to others. The tasks of living are to love and to be loved: to experience friendship; to work; to develop a satisfactory self-concept; and to search for meaning. Thus the person has to be viewed within his social environment.
- People choose their own goals.
- A person with high self-esteem and high social interest will move towards others in an encouraging manner.
- A person suffering from self-doubts or inadequacies or who has few concerns for the rights and needs of others will move away from others in swamping dependency or in an independent manner that cuts other people off.

2. The human personality is a unity

'Unity' means synthesising our physical, emotional, intellectual and spiritual aspects. Adler used the term 'style of life', a key term that describes variously:

- Self
- Personality
- A personal problem-solving method
- An attitude towards life
- A line of movement
- A pattern
- A technique.

The unique life style is developed from an early age and is as characteristic as a theme in a piece of music.

3. Behaviour is subjectively determined

Personal reality is determined through subjective experience, perceiving and learning. Every person develops a 'private logic'.

4. All behaviour is goal-directed

By seeking to discover the payoff or purpose of behaviour, therapists can more readily understand dysfunctional behaviour. Goals are not always conscious.

5. Motivation explains striving for significance

Each of us moves from a feeling of relative inferiority to a feeling of superiority. This striving for success and superiority is the upward drive towards perfection.

Neurosis and psychosis force people to impose their (often unfounded) achievements on to others in order to boost a weakened self-esteem. This weakened self-esteem frequently leads to overcompensation, which takes the form of deprecating others, a tendency that is at the root of sadism, hatred, quarrelsomeness and intolerance.

6. Behaviour

Behaviour changes throughout life, to meet current demands and long-term goals.

7. People are not pushed by causes

We are determined neither by our heredity nor by our environment.

8. Self-realisation is other-directed

Self-realisation, if it does not help to make the world a better place, is sterile.

9. Every person has the freedom of choice

Some choose to remain neurotic; others choose to strive towards the goal of wholeness.

10. The concept of mental health

Mental health is the sum total of the individual's:

- Social interest
- Contribution to society
- Degree of self-respect and self-confidence
- Degree of belongingness as social equals in the family, groups and the wider society.

Adler's 'masculine protest' describes the drive for superiority or completeness arising out of a felt inferiority or incompleteness, femininity being regarded as incomplete and inferior.

The myth of masculine superiority

Society has been so structured that in the division of labour, males assume dominance and superiority over women. In Adlerian psychology, the differences between males and females are very slight, so assumed dominance by males creates tension between the sexes.

From a very early age, boys and girls are conditioned into an acceptance of dominance or submission. Adler insists that this masculine superiority is a myth that creates many psychological problems.

The thought of such superiority scares male children and imposes on them an obligation they can never expect to fulfil. At the same time it compels female children to rebel against enforced inferiority.

Individual psychology emphasises horizontal relationships between the sexes, a position of difference but of equality, rather than vertical relationships, in which, for ever, we compare ourselves favourably or unfavourably with someone else who happens to be of a different sex. The idea is also applied to relationships in general. A hierarchy is an example of vertical relationships.

The concept of organ inferiority (see also Complexes)

Adler uses the term to describe the perceived or actual congenital defects in organs of the body or their functions. For example, children compare themselves in stature with adults and adult abilities, and this sense of inferiority is reinforced by adults, who draw attention to the failings of the child as compared with adult standards. The move towards mastery and high self-esteem is often blocked by such organ deficits as poor eyesight, speech difficulties, physical disability or poor health.

Adler referred to children who suffered from organ inferiorities as 'stepchildren of nature'. They are engaged at an early age in a bitter struggle for existence where social feelings become strangled. A consequence of this is that there is morbid preoccupation with self and in trying to make an impression on others. This may lead to intense approval-seeking.

Adler also believed that a child's educational potential may be shattered by exaggerated, intensified and unresolved feelings of inferiority, and a goal that demands security and peace fuelled by a striving to express dominance over others. Such children, Adler says, are easily recognised. They are 'problem children' who interpret every experience as a defeat and consider themselves always to be neglected and discriminated against, both by nature and by people.

Adults who demand more of the child than the child can do reinforce the child's helplessness and pave the way for the realisation that there are but two things over which the child has power: the pleasure and displeasure of adults.

Adler also believed that organ inferiority resulted in compensation, a striving to overcome the weakness.

Birth-order theory

Another factor contributing to personality development is birth order. Adler, along with Jung and others, disputed the importance of sexual motives. Adler assigned a prominent place to family dynamics in personality development. Children's position in their family – their birth order – was seen as determining significant character traits.

Oldest child: reported characteristics

- Parents' undivided attention
- Afraid of losing parents' favour, conforms to standards
- Often becomes quite responsible
- May feel 'dethroned' initially by other arrivals and may refuse to share
- When a male firstborn child is only slightly older than a female, permanent dethronement can occur because of the girl's accelerated rate of growth and development
- Frequently ambitious and anxious to achieve
- Often serves as pacesetter for the other children in their families
- Dislikes change and may develop conservative viewpoints
- Likely to be authority-oriented
- Tends to relate better to adults than to peers
- Tends towards being conservative.

Middle child: reported characteristics

- May feel an intruder between the oldest child and the parents
- Often becomes proficient in areas in which the oldest child is not
- Often more sociable than oldest children
- Often sensitive to injustices, unfairness and feelings of being slighted or abused, or of having no place in a group
- Tend to favour change and become interested in social change
- May feel dethroned by the competition from any new arrival.

Youngest child: reported characteristics

- The youngest child is never dethroned
- Adept at inducing others to do things for him

- Often 'spoiled', usually the most powerful person in the family
- Often not taken seriously.

Single child: reported characteristics

- Similarity to the youngest child
- May become very demanding
- Often expects a 'special place' in life without having earned it
- May try to reach his parents' adult level of competence
- May remain helpless and irresponsible as long as possible
- Usually establishes better relationships with people much older or much younger than with peers
- Often experiences difficulty with sharing and often becomes a loner.

Adopted child: reported characteristics

- Reaps the benefits of having been planned and wanted by the parents and of the adoption agency's investigation of the home environment prior to placement
- When adopted by parents who are unable to bear their own children, the adopted child may be overprotected or pampered
- A child adopted into a family where there are already children may be in an 'in' or 'out' situation with the siblings.

Theories are given for guidance, not to be interpreted as infallible or predicable. In some instances the above structure does not apply; for others it may apply in part. However, birth order is one more factor to consider in counselling.

Life tasks

The basic challenges of life are:

- Love
- Living in society
- Working
- Sex
- Spiritual growth
- Self-identity.

Lifestyle mistakes

- Tendency to over-generalise
- False or impossible goals of security
- Misperceptions
- Minimisation or denial of one's worth
- Faulty values.

Adlerian counselling goals

- To establish and maintain a therapeutic relationship in which there is equality, trust and acceptance and which does not reflect differences but sameness

- To uncover the uniqueness of the client
- To give insight
- To encourage redirection and reorientation.

The stages of Adlerian counselling

1. The therapeutic relationship

This encompasses the qualities of unconditional positive regard, genuineness, empathy, non-possessive warmth, self-disclosure and concreteness.

2. Psychological investigation

This is in four parts:

- The subjective situation – what is happening within the client
- The objective situation – what is happening in the client's external world
- Getting the answer to 'the fundamental question' – 'What would be different if all these problems or concerns were solved?' – gives clues as to possible payoffs or reasons why the person persists in a specific behaviour
- Lifestyle investigation – may involve psychometric testing, an examination of the family atmosphere and an exploration of the client's early recollections.

3. Interpretation

Interpretation is not counsellor-centred, it is a mutual sharing of basic attitudes about life, self and others, where the emphasis is on goals and purposes, not on causes.

An interpretation identifies:

- Problems and feelings of deficiency
- Directions taken to overcome the perceived deficiencies
- The relationship between direction and other significant areas in the client's life
- Specific life-task difficulties
- Strategies used to avoid resolution
- Feelings of superiority about avoidances
- Contribution of past influences.

Adler disapproved of the 'red pen' approach, where only weaknesses are examined. We can build only on strengths, not on weaknesses.

4. Reorientation

Counsellor and client work together to consider what changes could be made in the client's life style. Two basic techniques are:

- **'Stroking'**, which is synonymous with encouragement and caring
- **'Spitting in the soup'**, which is a discouraging response, based on the idea that a bowl of soup would no longer be appetising if spat in. When clients have insight into faulty thinking and self-defeating behaviours they become contaminated and no longer appealing.

Confronting illogical, faulty thinking is also an important part in their therapy. Illogical thinking may be:

- **Causal inference** – false logic
- **Blowup** – exaggeration
- **All-or-nothing** – thinking in extremes
- **Responsibility projection** – failing to own
- **Perfectionism** – idealistic demands on self
- **Value-tainted** – 'shoulds', 'oughts', 'bad'
- **Self-depreciation** – punitive statements.

Faulty thinking may be corrected by:

- Factual description
- Generating alternative explanations
- Designing positive course of action.

Adlerian general counselling skills

- Active listening
- Reflection of feelings
- Empathic understanding
- Challenging
- Interpretation
- Encouragement.

Adlerian specific therapeutic techniques

Paradoxical intention (Adler originally called this 'prescribing the symptom')
The client is encouraged to emphasise the symptoms or develop them even more. When people discover that they cannot intentionally do what they feared would happen, they are often able to laugh at the situation.

Viktor Frankl, the originator of logotherapy (see below), said that such an intervention 'takes the wind out of the sails of fear'.

Acting 'as if'
To 'If only I could...', the counsellor replies 'Pretend – act as if you could do it that way'. Acting 'as if' is like wearing a different suit. Feeling different is important.

Catching oneself
When clients become aware of engaging in behaviour they want to change, they are encouraged to say, 'There I go again'.

Creating movement
The element of surprise may encourage the client to change behaviour. Agreeing with the faulty logic and 'going over the top', provided it is not an attack, nor sarcastic, may jolt the client into action.

Goal-setting and commitment

Homework, assignments and change cards related to some change in behaviour. An example of a 'change card' might be:

- 'This week I will...' (something specific)
- 'I know I could sabotage my task by...'
- 'I will evaluate my achievement on...'

Adler's social relations, interpersonal behaviour, ego development, self-direction and group work have influenced many other approaches to therapy.

Child-guidance

Whenever a child lies you will always find a severe parent. A lie would have no sense unless the truth was felt to be dangerous.

Attributed to Alfred Adler, *New York Times* (1949)

Child-guidance clinics – staffed by psychiatrists, psychologists and social workers specialising in child development – work on parent–child relationship problems through individual and group counselling; the guidance clinics also give help to parents with emotionally disturbed children.

The traditionally accepted working relationship is that the psychiatrist works directly with the child while the social worker works with the parent(s). The premise is that, while it would be inaccurate and mistaken to imply that the parents are to blame for the child's behaviour, it is certainly true to say that when there is a problem child the whole family is disturbed. If the child is to change, then the whole family also needs to change; hence the focus of the social worker.

Areas of application

- Education
- Parent education
- Marriage counselling
- Family counselling
- Group work.

Comment

People who have studied cognitive behavioural therapy will be struck with certain similarities to the work of Adler. The two models complement each other.

Further reading

Corey, G. (2001) *Theory and Practice of Counseling and Psychotherapy*, 6th edn. Wadsworth, Brooks/Cole, Pacific Grove, CA. Corey includes a case study of working with Adlerian therapy (pages 128–130).

Eckstein, D. (1981) An Adlerian primer. In: *1981 Annual Handbook for Group Facilitators*. University Associates, San Diego, CA.

Kern, A. et al. (1978) *A Case of Adlerian Counselling*. Alfred Adler Institute, Chicago, IL.

Mosak , H. and Dreikurs, R. (1973) Adlerian psychotherapy. In: *Current Psychotherapies* (ed. R. Corsini). F.E. Peacock, Itasca, IL.

INFERTILITY COUNSELLING

Since the birth, in 1978, of the first baby to be born using in-vitro fertilisation (IVF), there has been a constant debate about IVF and other methods of giving would-be parents hope of having a family. The government set up a Committee of Inquiry in Human Fertilisation and Embryology, chaired by Mary Warnock. Their report was published in 1984.

The discussions surrounding this report strongly supported the view that adequate counselling provision should be made available for people considering the use of the new reproductive techniques.

The Human Fertilisation and Embryology Act (referred to as the Act) was passed in 1990. This Act requires that those undergoing investigation and treatment, as well as those donating gametes, be 'given a suitable opportunity to receive proper counselling'.

Added to this requirement was that such counselling must take into account the needs of the child born as an outcome of regulated infertility treatment. With this, the needs of any other child who may be affected by the birth must also be considered.

The Human Fertilisation and Embryology Authority (HFEA) is a non-departmental government body that regulates and inspects all UK clinics providing IVF, donor insemination, or the storage of eggs, sperm or embryos. The HFEA also licenses and monitors all human embryo research being conducted in the UK.

The term 'proper counselling' is interpreted as:

- Giving of relevant information
- Providing an opportunity to discuss and explore the personal implications associated with this information
- Providing an opportunity to come to an informed and considered decision concerning the choice to be made from among the options that may be available.

The Code of Practice of the Human Fertilisation and Embryology Authority and the King's Fund Report, Counselling for Regulated Infertility Treatments (1991), identify four types of counselling:

- Information counselling
- Implications counselling
- Support counselling
- Therapeutic counselling.

The Act made it obligatory for centres engaged in regulated infertility treatment to employ at least one trained infertility counsellor, with the availability of other counsellors. There is a shortage of trained infertility counsellors.

Many couples are able to produce children with no difficulty. Many couples, however, do have difficulty. Those who do not may not always understand the depth of feeling when a couple keep trying for a baby and do not succeed.

Couples who enter a fertility treatment programme are starting out a very difficult path, often beset by disappointment. The drain on their emotional, physical and financial resources is often such that they feel under great stress.

The stress they feel may be added to by their not receiving adequate emotional support in the form of counselling.

Fertility is the ability to achieve a spontaneous conception. Infertility is the absence of the ability to produce offspring. Half the fertile population take about five months of unprotected sex before conception takes place. Most couples who have unprotected sex will conceive within one year. If conception does not take place within 18 months, there may be a problem.

Causes of infertility

About 20 per cent of marriages are barren.

- Known causes   70–80 per cent
- Unknown causes   20–30 per cent
- Male infertility   20–30 per cent
- Female infertility: hormonal and tubal   40–50 per cent
- Female infertility: uterine, cervical and others   5–10 per cent.

Attachment and bonding before birth

The two theories of attachment and bonding are mainly applied after birth. It is suggested that the process starts long before birth. At the moment conception takes place, many women say they feel different, although as yet there are no physical indications of pregnancy. When we talk of attachment and bonding, we should be thinking of the very early days in the womb.

One could even say that attachment and bonding start with the expressed desire to conceive. If this is so, then couples who try unsuccessfully, perhaps for many years, to start a family, are experiencing a succession of breaking of attachment as every try fails to result in a pregnancy.

With every failure in conception, so the loss becomes greater as the possibility of parenthood is wrenched from them. At some stage, when the couple face the reality that normal parenthood is not for them, they will have to face the truth of the loss.

A couple who have been trying for a family may well have been receiving ongoing counselling. That counselling will take on a different dimension when the harsh reality dawns that parenthood is not to be realised.

The work of Elisabeth Kubler-Ross on death and dying gives insights into how to help the couple who stand at the crossroads between trying for a child and moving into a child-free future.

Unresolved grief and infertility

Couples who feel they must contain their grief about infertility, because society does not understand the depth of their feelings, are in danger of driving the grief deeper. Suppressed grief will find an outlet somehow, somewhere, some time.

Many couples fear that if they do express their feelings, they might 'crack up' completely.

Unresolved grief is an illness with recognisable symptoms: loss of sleep, loss of appetite, headaches and general exhaustion are a few. Confronting the pain of grief requires courage, which some couples find difficulty in harnessing. Delaying it may sound a reasonable option, but all that does is to bottle up the pain. Unresolved grief may be reawakened by another loss, which may be totally unrelated.

Communicating with people suffering from loss

Some people never talk to people suffering from loss because of a fear of saying the 'wrong' thing. There is not a 'right' thing to say. Warmth, caring and genuineness are of more value than any stereotyped response that says nothing. Non-verbal language, such as eye contact, appropriate touch, facial expression and tone of voice, says more than words to someone suffering from the pain of grief. Many people cannot become involved with someone else's pain because of their own present or unresolved pain.

Counselling for loss

The aim of counselling is to help the couple identify their feelings about infertility and the deep drive within them to have children. Exploring these issues is one way of helping them face their own reality. They may find it helpful to belong to a local support group or one of the national organisations, such as CHILD, the National Association for the Childless (NAC), or PROGRESS.

The four tasks (see worden's tasks in death and dying, pp. 144–6)

1. To accept the reality of the loss

When a couple enter a fertility programme, they have already experienced loss – the loss of hope of a natural pregnancy. When the end of the fertility programme road is reached, and has failed, a second, and more final, hope-shattering loss is experienced, which increases with every failed attempt.

2. To experience the pain and grief

Anything that allows the couple to avoid or to suppress the pain will, inevitably, prolong the mourning period. Avoidance or suppression of grief may show itself, sooner or later, in some form of depression, often associated with not 'letting go'. Task two is to do with healing and transformation. The negation of this task is not to feel. When we experience the pain, and work through to greater awareness and wholeness, we are ready to move on to the next task.

3. To adjust to a childless life

This may involve taking on new roles, and discovering new avenues and outlets of fulfilment.

4. To redirect energy

The energy that has been used up struggling through a fertility programme is now available to be redirected. When a loved one dies, the person left is then able to start to form other relationships. This is not the same with a couple who are infertile; there is no new baby for them. Some people feel that they lost the ability to love when their loved one died. The successful completion of task four is trusting oneself to fully love again.

How feelings of loss may be expressed

Grief, loss and attachment are linked. If there was no attachment, there would be no feelings of loss. Animals experience loss when the links that attach them are broken. The greylag goose that loses its mate will become restless, uttering its distinct long-distance call, night and day. So far will it extend its search that it may lose itself. That is grief; the price we pay for loving. Feelings of loss may be expressed through five channels:

- **Physical:** These may manifest themselves in any part of the body and are synonymous with stress reaction. Any physical symptom following on a loss may be linked to it.
- **Mental:** Disbelief, confusion, preoccupation, changes in perception and a need to repeatedly talk about what has happened, in an attempt to make sense of what has happened.
- **Behaviour:** Disturbance in sleep, appetite, memory, dreams, socialising. Searching, calling out, sighing, restless activity, crying.
- **Emotional:** Numbness, guilt, self-reproach, sadness, anger, anxiety, loneliness, fatigue, shock, yearning.
- **Spiritual:** Arguments with God and with life, with the whole question of 'Who am I?'. Troughs of doubt about existence and meaning. For many people, making peace again with God is a prelude to healing.

Counselling guidelines

- Support to help deal with the practical issues surrounding the loss
- Working with feelings and encouraging catharsis, but not to push the couple too far, too fast, too soon
- Helpers need to be able to accept the couple's feelings, whatever they are.
- Feelings, however negative, are valid.
- Repeated telling of the story with the feelings
- Encourage the acceptance of the finality of the loss.
- Facilitate disengagement and establish separateness from the object of loss.
- Help the couple to accept the changes in role, social situation and self-image in becoming childless or no longer pregnant.
- Encourage the person to think about new activities and self-help groups.

Principles of loss counselling

- Help the couple to face the loss. The loss is real and devastating, but it is not one's own death. A helpful technique is to get the couple to affirm, 'I am experiencing pain, but I am not that pain'.

- Help the couple to identify and express their feelings, both negative and positive. Rage must be given a voice and an expression if the couple are to move forwards.
- Assist the couple to live with each other, without their cherished dream.
- Facilitate emotional withdrawal from the dream of being parents. A useful and powerful technique is to get the couple to write letters: one to each other and one to the fantasy baby. Get both of them to write a joint letter to the fantasy baby. All letters are read aloud as if to the baby. This technique dips into other unresolved loss, so counsellors who use it should be prepared to deal with expression of deep pain.
- Work and other responsibilities may not leave the couple with enough time and space to grieve, unless something definite is arranged. They need to discover how and with whom they want to express their grief.
- To know that their behaviour is normal is reassuring at a time when irrational and sometimes bizarre thoughts are bewildering and frightening.
- Grief is likely to resurface from time to time, and when least expected. The death of a pet, for example, may trigger off some unresolved parts of grief associated with loss of their dream. Continued support should, therefore, be available.
- Counselling people for loss requires us to understand their coping strategies and the influence that personality has on those strategies.
- We develop strategies by association with other people, either from what they do or what they say.
- How one has coped with previous loss has a strong bearing on how one coped in the present.
- The greatest gift a counsellor can give sorrowing couples is to share their burden and their loss, and to help them discover that even in the darkest moments, slowly but surely, healing is taking place.

Remaining child-free: the final choice

While some couples keep trying for a child, others try for adoption. There is a third choice – to remain child-free.

The term 'child-free' has a different meaning from 'childless', which implies an unwilling surrender to circumstances. The decision to remain child-free indicates a maturity that can contemplate a future without children. This is looking forwards, not backwards. Couples who choose this option are in the position of being available to many children, of all ages and in many situations. The couple may, for example, sponsor a child in another country. The decision to do this may not meet with general approval or understanding.

Please help me!

If self-awareness is important for counsellor development, support is vital. The more intense and prolonged the counselling, the more risk there is of burn-out. Receiving others' pain calls on reserves that need constantly to be topped up by the strength from loving, caring relationships.

Types of counselling for infertility

1. Information counselling

The Act makes it obligatory for centres to give clients 'such relevant information as is proper'. Information should be distinguished from the requirement to offer counselling, which the client(s) need not accept. Verbal information may not be taken in and understood, and, therefore, ought to be backed by written material, which should be fully discussed with the clients.

The King's Fund Report draws together eight principal areas where verbal information should be backed by suitably worded leaflets and provided in languages other than English and regularly updated:

- Providing advice about infertility
- Infertility treatments
- Semen donation
- Egg donation
- Information for younger children
- Information for older children
- How to tell your child about gamete donation
- Approaching the HF&E Authority for information.

The 'person responsible' has a duty to ensure that clients have received adequate information about their treatment options, and that they have consented in a free and informed way to a particular treatment, and that consent may be subsequently varied or withdrawn.

2. Implications counselling

The aim of implications counselling is to enable the person concerned to understand the implications of the proposed course of action; for herself, himself, for her or his family, and for any children born as a result.

Implications counselling deals with the meaning of the information and involves the consequences and outcomes of the options available.

Implications counselling covers the following areas:

- Social responsibilities to ensure the best possible outcome for all concerned
- To explore, understand and resolve painful feelings, which may be linked to the infertility of one of the partners and the possibility that treatment might not be successful
- To explore the feelings about the use and possible disposal of any embryos derived from their gametes
- To return to implications counselling as and when necessary, at various stages of the treatment, or as circumstances change
- The advantages and disadvantages of openness about the procedure envisaged, and how they might be explained to relatives and friends
- To be available at a later stage to enable people who make an enquiry about their genetic origins

- Potential recipient of donor gametes or embryos need to be able to explore the social and psychological implications for relationships now and in the future
- Couples also need to explore their feelings about not being the genetic parents of a child born from donor gametes or embryos.

Counselling for recipients of donated gametes should be separated from counselling about the implications of treatment, and donated gamete treatment should not proceed until counselling has taken place, or has been offered.

Potential donors of gametes and embryos should be offered counselling to consider the implications of:

- Their reasons for wanting to become donors
- Their attitudes to any resulting children, and the understanding that they will have no future responsibility for such children
- The possibility of their own childlessness
- Their perception of the needs of any children born as a result of their donation
- Their attitudes to the prospective legal parents of their genetic offspring
- Their attitudes to allowing embryos that have been produced from their gametes to be used for research.

Counselling once given to a donor or to a client should be available in the future should a client request it.

3. Support counselling

The aim of support counselling is to give emotional support at times of particular stress, for example, for people who are not suitable for treatment, where there is failure to achieve a pregnancy, or where a pregnancy is not viable, or where there is multiple pregnancy. Support could be through a group. Centres should ensure that, as part of professional development, all staff are trained to offer appropriate emotional support to clients who are suffering distress.

4. Therapeutic counselling

Therapeutic counselling focuses on healing, which may be the gradual adjustment of expectations, and the eventual acceptance of whatever is reality for this particular couple. Not every couple will require therapeutic, on-going, in-depth counselling. Part of the skill is being able to assess which clients need this type of counselling.

People for whom therapeutic counselling may be indicated by the treatment centre are those suffering from:

- Acute emotional distress
- Disruption of social functioning.

People for whom therapeutic counselling may be indicated by another agency, not the treatment centre, are those suffering from:

- Marital disharmony
- Psychosexual difficulties
- Neurotic or psychotic disorders, not caused by, but which may have been exacerbated by, the experience of, and treatment for, infertility.

Counselling may be needed following the birth, as many people experience emotional difficulties, reawakened by various life events, for example, the developing child and independence; the child's request for information about donor identity. Such counselling is probably best referred to other agencies.

A record should be kept of all counselling offered (not the details) and whether or not the offer is accepted.

The content of counselling sessions must be held in strictest confidence. As with all matters of confidentiality, the counsellor may have to exercise professional judgement whether to keep certain information secret or ask the client's permission to disclose it to other members of the team.

Centres must ensure that information provided in confidence is kept confidential and only disclosed in the circumstances permitted by law.

The financial costs of counselling should be regarded as part of the overall treatment budget.

Monitoring of counselling services is a function of the Authority.

ICSI – what is it?

Intracytoplasmic sperm injection is a comparatively new procedure, particularly suited to male infertility. ICSI involves injection of single sperm into single eggs in order to achieve fertilisation. First, the woman must be stimulated with medication and have an egg retrieval procedure so that several eggs can be obtained in order to attempt in-vitro fertilisation. The eggs are injected using specially designed microscopes, needles and micromanipulation equipment.

Male factor infertility can include any of the following problems: low sperm counts, poor motility or movement of the sperm, poor sperm quality or sperm that lack the ability to penetrate an egg.

While at a clinic in Belgium, Dr Gianpiero D. Palermo, currently assistant professor of embryology, the Center for Reproductive Medicine and Infertility, The New York Hospital–Cornell Medical Center, pioneered the ICSI process.

When a single sperm was injected directly into the egg, it virtually eliminated the problems and limitations found with previous treatments. Palermo and others studying ICSI found that not only did it address the issues of poor sperm motility and low count, but it was also successful with sperm that were considered less than ideal for an IVF process.

www.inciid.org/icsi.html

Egg sharing

Egg sharing involves a woman having infertility treatment donating some of her eggs in return for a reduction in the costs of her treatment. Egg sharing can mean patients pay half the cost of their treatment or even receive free treatment. There is a need for egg sharing because of the shortage of donated eggs – some women have had to wait three to five years to receive donated eggs.

The HFEA decided to allow egg sharing in 2000. A Chairs letter went out to advise clinics of the new guidelines and these were incorporated in the 5th Edition of the Code of Practice in 2001.

Current situation

Clinics wishing to use egg sharing must submit papers to the HFEA licence committee including: protocols, consent forms, patient leaflets etc. The licence committee then decides if the clinic has all the appropriate standards and criteria for patients before granting permission for them to practise egg sharing. Clinics are inspected annually and part of that inspection will include the egg sharing scheme. Most large hospitals have local ethics committees which discuss the issues and decide whether egg sharing is appropriate for that hospital.

Sperm donor anonymity

Some fear donors may be deterred by a law change that threatens donor anonymity.

Children conceived with donor sperm may be able to trace their biological fathers, if a change in the law proposed by Baroness Warnock comes about. This is a reversal of the decision the Baroness made in 1984, which enshrined the principle of anonymity for donors.

At the moment, when children reach the age of 18, they can find out information such as the height, hair colour and race of their father.

Surrogacy

Surrogacy is where one woman carries a baby for an infertile couple. There are two types of surrogacy – straight or host.

- **Traditional (straight) surrogacy:** The surrogate uses her own egg fertilised with the intended father's sperm. This is done by artificial insemination using a syringe, which the surrogate may do herself, or there are an increasing number of infertility clinics willing to help with traditional surrogacy.
- **Gestational (host IVF) surrogacy:** The surrogate carries the intended parents' genetic child conceived through IVF, for which specialist doctors are needed. For this treatment the infertile woman must still have working ovaries.

www.surrogacy.org.uk

Opinion on the morality of surrogacy is divided. Surrogacy is legally accepted in the UK as a treatment option for selected groups of patients. However, surrogacy is still not allowed in many countries.

Surrogacy for social reasons, such as the inconvenience of carrying a child, fear of pregnancy or interrupting a career, is not acceptable.

Women who agree to become surrogates may do so for compassionate reasons to help a sister, daughter or friend. Some women may agree to become surrogates for financial remuneration. However, commercial surrogacy is not allowed in the UK.

www.ivf-infertility.co.uk

Human Fertilisation Embryology Authority
21 Bloomsbury Street
London
WC1B 3HF
Tel: 020 7291 8200
Fax: 020 7291 8201
E-mail: admin@hfea.gov.uk
The HFEA is open from 9 a.m. to 5 p.m. Monday to Friday.

News from the HFEA
The HFEA has announced strict new guidelines to protect the safety of frozen sperm, eggs and embryos stored at fertility clinics throughout the UK. The guidelines have been produced following an HFEA review into a small number of incidents where inadequate temperature levels in storage vessels led to the irretrievable loss of patients' stored material.

The Human Fertilisation and Embryology Authority welcomes the government's decision to remove anonymity for those donating sperm, eggs and embryos in the future.

Following a review, the HFEA has decided to write to all licensed clinics telling them not to practise egg giving. The review was in response to a number of enquiries and expressions of concern from patients and clinics.

A new technique might bring hope to thousands of couples to become parents. Pioneered in Germany and developed at The Churchill Clinic, London, it helps men who have a zero sperm count, caused by blockage of the vas deferens either at birth or by a vasectomy. A biopsy is taken from the testes and then frozen. Mature sperm is then extracted from the biopsy then used to fertilise the woman's egg. The resultant embryos are then placed in the womb. The new operation can also be used to preserve sperm from men who have to undergo chemotherapy or radiotherapy for cancer treatment.

Further reading
Jennings S.E. (ed.) *Infertility Counselling*. Blackwell Science, Inc., Oxford.
Kubler-Ross, E. (1970) *On Death and Dying*. Tavistock, London.
Snowden, R. and Spiby, J. (1991) Counselling for Regulated Infertility Treatments: The Report of the King's Fund Centre Counselling Committee, London.
Issue – The National Fertility Association. National charity providing information, support, counselling and literature on infertility and reproductive health. Message board feature. www.issue.co.uk
Opening the Record: the Provision of Counselling to People applying for Information from the HFEA Register available online at BICA (British Infertility Counselling Association), www.bica.net

INTERNALISATION

Internalisation is a term that describes the process whereby one incorporates beliefs, values, attitudes, practices, standards, norms and morals into one inner world as one's own. As children develop, they become able to give themselves the instructions that were previously given by significant others. Full internalisation is achieved when the behaviour takes place not in response to reward or fear of punishment but because it is perceived to be correct or appropriate.

When children learn to value hard work or financial success or a belief in God, they tend to acquire a sense of vested interest in such ideas and feelings as these become their own. Internalisation maintains social systems through voluntary means rather than requiring them to be monitored and corrected by external authorities. In contrast, coercion is a far less effective means of social control.

The goal of parents, educators and, indeed, counsellors, is not compliance but internalisation. Internalisation is generally obtained by an influential source who has credibility, whose message is persuasive and believable.

In psychoanalytic theory, the superego is the last of three agencies (with the id and ego) of the human personality to develop. The superego is the ethical component of the personality and provides the moral standards by which the ego operates. The superego's criticisms, prohibitions and inhibitions form a person's conscience, and its positive aspirations and ideals represent one's idealised self-image or 'ego ideal'.

The superego is assumed to develop through the process of internalisation of the standards and values of the parents, a process greatly aided by a tendency to identify with the parents. The superego continues to develop into young adulthood as a person encounters other admired role models and copes with the rules and regulations of the larger society. Within traditional approaches to social psychology and the study of personality, an important issue is the degree to which a person attributes his behaviour to such internalised motives. Identification is a major link between the psychoanalytic and social learning theories of development and it is a powerful influence in the socialisation process.

Identification, by which we model aspects of ourselves upon other people, is an essential part of internalisation. Most of our important beliefs and attitudes are probably initially based on identification. Whenever we start to identify with, for example, a new reference group, we start 'trying on' the new set of beliefs and attitudes. From the moment we engage in this process our belief system is in a state of flux; the more so if the new beliefs contrast sharply with previously held ones. The test of whether identification has led to internalisation is whether induced beliefs, values and attitudes stay the test of time.

Counselling is neither persuasion not compliance, yet in a sense it is a process of internalisation. Clients are challenged to face up to the fact that something in their lives has to change if they are to move forwards. While it is not the aim that the client internalises the counsellor's beliefs, values and attitudes, as someone to be admired, there is the sense that the counsellor holds up to the client alternative beliefs, values and attitudes, as together they engage in the process of reframing. Neither is it that the client looks upon the counsellor as the 'ideal'; the counsellor holds up the mirror so that the client can identify with his own ideal self. When the client has done this, internalisation takes place and the client can then begin to separate from the counsellor.

Further reading

Meissner, W.W. (1981) *Internalization in Psychoanalysis*. International Universities Press, New York.

INTIMACY (SEE ALSO: LONELINESS)

Intimacy is like a harp. The music it produces comes from all its strings. Intimacy means discovering the particular harmony and melody that is enjoyed by the people involved. Sometimes the melodies will vary. Sometimes a minor key will be more appreciated than a major one.

Source unknown

Intimacy has been used to describe the process of revealing one's inner self to others; to refer to relatively intense non-verbal engagement; or to describe the stage of life in which the primary developmental task is to establish an emotionally close, trusting and sexual relationship with another person. It is also used as a synonym for closeness, sexuality or marriage. In a more general sense, intimacy is the state of being closely familiar with another person, not necessarily of the opposite sex and not necessarily sexual. Intimacy with at least one other person is generally regarded as an essential ingredient of a healthy and satisfying life. It is thought that intimate relationships are an essential component of human well-being and that their absence causes distress.

Self-disclosure seems to be essential in the development of an intimate relationship; however, too little or too much disclosure, in comparison to personal standards and situational norms, tends to hamper the development of a relationship. We also convey feelings related to intimacy by body language, such as distance, through facial expressions, eye contact and non-vocal cues.

Erik Erikson, in his lifespan model of development, proposes that young adults must resolve the crisis of intimacy versus isolation. Intimacy achieved in a primary relationship has several characteristics: mutual trust and openness; coordination of work, procreation and recreation; mutually satisfying sexuality; feelings of love; mutual support and understanding; and trust, openness, shared experiences.

The absence of an intimate relationship, the inability to share emotions, trust others or make a commitment to a stable, lasting relationship, is often a significant cause of mental and/or physical distress and an indication of an intimacy disorder. The capacity for intimacy fosters self-worth and a feeling of belonging. Many people, of either sex, have difficulty talking about intimate matters.

Intimacy applied to counselling

Erikson defined the major task of the young adult as resolving the ambivalence between intimacy and isolation. The ability to be intimate has its origins in the early parent–child relationship and the successful resolution of any parent–child power struggles (in psychoanalytic terms, the Oedipus complex).

The loneliness of Erikson's theory is that the adolescent feels isolated from the love once experienced from the parents; the intimacy of the young child is no longer felt to be appropriate for the new stage of life. Whatever sexual experiences the adolescent has had do not fill the void and no longer boost his self-esteem. Mere repetition of the sexual act no longer satisfies. There is a deep hunger for intimacy, which can only be found in a relationship of commitment. The young adult who fails to develop the capacity for intimate relationships runs the risk of living in isolation and self-absorption in later life.

By implication, people who have been deprived of parental love and a family to act as a role model – children brought up in care, for example – are likely to have difficulty in establishing and maintaining intimate relationships.

The counselling relationship is one of depth and intimacy, unlike any other relationship. For, within the security of this unique relationship, clients have the freedom to express their feelings knowing that the relationship exists primarily for them. The counsellor makes no demands for self, and the clients can be exactly themselves. This freedom to be themselves within a warm and trusting and at times challenging relationship can be scary for some clients.

The person who finds intimacy difficult may be so terrified of allowing the counsellor into his inner world that dialogue is stilted and sterile. In just talking about feelings, the client is forced to come out from behind the safety barrier that he has erected to protect the vulnerable self. If the inability to be intimate has its origins in the parent–child relationship, then it would seem obvious that, in counselling, the remedy lies in the client experiencing intimacy, albeit not from a parent, but delivered with as much love and caring as if the counsellor were a parent. As the client begins to experience intimacy, so he is able to redraw the boundaries and gradually begin to feel safe with intimacy.

The role of confidant – spouse or someone else – is significant in depression and in working through the sadness of loneliness and isolation and lack of intimacy. If it is important to share intimacies within a caring relationship, then the lack of such a relationship could be conducive to developing depression. Everything must be done to foster an atmosphere in which intimate feelings may be shared. There is no doubt that having an opportunity to talk with someone, to express one's feelings, is a safeguard not only against loneliness and isolation but also against weaving, out of one's defensive mechanisms, a blanket to suffocate feelings. Counselling offers the sort of support that avoids smothering feelings.

In human intimacy there is a secret boundary; neither the experience of being in love nor passion can cross it, though lips be joined together in awful silence, and the heart break asunder with love.

Anna Akhmatova, Russian poet (1889–1966) *In Human Intimacy* (1915), translated by Dimitri Obolensky

Further reading

Hinde, R.A. (1979) *Towards Understanding Relationships.* Academic Press, New York.
McAdams, D.P. (1989) *Intimacy: the need to be close.* Doubleday, New York.

J

Jealousy and envy

Jealousy is a close relative of envy. They have much in common, although they are distinct emotions. They are selfish and malevolent, they are both concerned with persons, and both imply hatred of, and a desire to harm, their object. But there is a deeper malevolence in jealousy than in envy, and jealousy is the stronger and more demanding passion.

Envy

In general, envy is classified as a special form of anxiety, based on an overpowering desire to possess what someone else has.

Kleinian theory relates envy to the conflict between love and hate. The developing infant may experience hate towards the good objects. This love–hate relationship may be seen in adult life where something is hated because of its goodness.

Schizophrenic states have been attributed to prolonged and early envy, with continued confusion between love and hate.

For Adler, envy is present wherever there is a striving for power and domination. The person who is consumed by envy has a low self-evaluation and is constantly dissatisfied with life.

Envious people act as if they wanted to have everything. The universality of the feeling of envy causes a universal dislike of it.

People who envy someone else's achievements tend to blame others for their own lack of success.

Envious people tend to be aggressive, obstructive and officious, with no great love for relationships and with little understanding of human nature.

Envy may go so far as to lead a person to feel pleasure in someone else's suffering and pain. Working to raise self-esteem may help to reduce envy.

Jealousy

Jealousy differs from envy in that it involves three parties: the subject, an object whom the subject loves and a third party who arouses anxiety in the subject about the continuing security of the second party's affections. Envy involves only two parties: the subject and an object whose good fortune or possessions the subject covets. Jealousy is related to possessiveness of the other, envy to comparison of the self with the other. Jealousy is a complex emotion implying the existence of the sentiment of love.

Jealousy is grounded on some estimate of what is due to self rather than a consciousness of inferiority, as in envy. Secondly, there is irritation and displeasure to the jealous person arising from the circumstance that there is a rival to contend (individuals or group). When I am jealous of a person it is because he has gained possession of the regard of another whose attachment I claim. This means that I hate the usurping person, but also that I am annoyed with the other who has allowed the rival to intrude. When I feel jealous of an individual's popularity with one person or a group of people, my meaning is that I hate this person for taking away a popularity that I myself claim or aspire to, which I feel is rightly mine. I also resent the person or group that has allowed itself to come under this person's influence.

It is characteristic of jealousy that it distorts the nature of the person who harbours it. It deprives the person of the power to see things as they really are, rendering the person's judgements unjust. It makes the person suspicious, leading him to catch at straws and make much of trifles, and driving us on to acts of cruelty.

Jealousy or something like it seems to be present to some degree in animals, as well as in humans. An example is the response of one's favourite dog when petting another dog or a neighbour's cat. It will sometimes slink away and hide and appear to be sulking or will keep pushing itself forwards to be patted, with sidelong glances at the cat. Some very young children behave in a similar way when their mother pays attention to another child. In both cases the jealous creature is apt to exhibit anger towards the intruder.

Jealousy is a complex reaction involving emotions, thoughts and behaviours:

- Common emotions include pain, anger, rage, sadness, envy, fear, grief and humiliation.
- Thoughts include resentment, blame, comparison with the rival, worry about image and self-pity.
- Behaviours include feeling faint, trembling and sweating, constant questioning and seeking reassurance, aggressive actions and even violence leading to crimes of passion.

The paradox of jealousy

Jealousy can protect love. It can encourage couples to appreciate each other and make a conscious effort to make sure the other person feels valued. In small, manageable doses, jealousy can be a positive force in a relationship. But when it's intense or irrational, the story is very different.

Jealousy can damage love. When one partner is constantly suspicious, this can create the feeling of walking on eggshells. This can lead the jealous partner to swing between self-blame and justification.

The psychoanalytic view

In psychoanalytic terms, jealousy typically forms part of the Oedipus complex. Pathological jealousy, i.e. persistent, unfounded, delusional jealousy, appears to have some fundamental connection with paranoia. According to Freud, jealousy and paranoia are defences against latent homosexuality, but the contemporary psychoanalytic view is to regard the paranoia as the primary member of the triad of jealousy, paranoia and homosexuality.

Pathological jealousy

Marked jealousy is a symptom (usually termed pathological or morbid jealousy) of many psychiatric disorders, including schizophrenia, epilepsy, mood disorders, drug abuse and alcoholism. When jealousy occurs in delusional disorder or as part of another condition it can be a potentially dangerous feature and has been associated with violence in both suicide and murder.

One form of jealousy expresses itself in self-destruction, another expresses itself in energetic obstinacy. Spoiling the sport of others, senseless opposition, the restriction of another's freedom and that person's consequent domination are some of the protean shapes of this character trait.

Jealousy can also be put to the purpose of degrading and reproaching people in order to rob them of their freedom of will, to set them in a rut or to chain them down. Jealousy is an especially well-marked form of the striving for power.

Delusional jealousy, also called 'Othello syndrome', afflicts men, often with no prior psychiatric history, and is the false belief that one's sexual partner is unfaithful.

Alfred Adler's view

On a wider front, jealousy is a character trait, interesting because of its frequency. Jealousy is found in children who want to be superior to one another. Adler says that jealousy is the sister of ambition and that the trait, which may last a lifetime, arises from the feeling of being neglected and a sense of being discriminated against.

Jealousy occurs almost universally among children with the advent of a younger brother or sister who demands more attention from his or her parents and gives an older child occasion to feel like a dethroned monarch. Those children become especially jealous, who basked in the warm sunshine of their parents' love prior to the advent of the younger child. Jealousy may be recognised in mistrust and the preparation of ambushes for others, in the critical measurement of others and in the constant fear of being neglected. Just which of these manifestations comes to the fore is dependent entirely upon the previous preparation for social life. Jealousy is an especially well-marked form of the striving for power.

Jealousy also invariably involves the spirit of competition and a client who has strong jealous feelings (although not necessarily directed at the counsellor) may also harbour feelings of suspicion, and these may well be directed at the counsellor. Such a client may also experience great difficulty in the intimacy of the counselling relationship.

Further reading

Adler, A. (1932) *Understanding Human Nature*. George Allen & Unwin Ltd, London.
Paula Hill. www.bbc.co.uk/science

Relate
Herbert Gray College
Little Church Street
Coventry
CV21 3AP
Relate centre. You can get details from their site at www.relate.org.uk or freephone 08454 561310 or at 01788 573241

K

Born in Vienna, Klein lived most of her life in England and is linked with the Objects Relations School. Her interest in psychoanalysis arose from her time as a patient of Sandor Ferenczi, although she never trained in psychiatry. Her therapeutic techniques for children had great impact on present methods of child care and rearing.

Encouraged by Ferenczi (1873–1933) and Karl Abraham (1877–1925), she developed her own system of child analysis and it is her contribution to child psychiatry for which she is mostly remembered, showing that how children play with toys reveals earlier infantile fantasies and anxieties. She used free play with toys to gain insight into the fantasies, anxieties and defences associated with the early years of life. In *The Psychoanalysis of Children* (1932), she showed how these anxieties affected a child's developing ego, superego and sexuality to bring about emotional disorders. Through her methods she attempted to relieve children of disabling guilt by having them direct towards the therapist the aggressive and Oedipal feelings they could not express to their parents.

Klein's personality theory agrees with Freud's about the life and death instincts, and that inborn aggression is an extension of the death instinct. Oral sadism is where the death instinct is directed outwards, giving rise to fantasies of the bad, devouring breast. These unconscious fantasies, from birth onwards, become the origins of love and hate.

Other powerful, negative emotions include:

- Envy, which is derived from the fantasy of the wilfully withholding breast and finds expression in greed, penis envy, envy of the creativity of others and guilt over one's own creativity
- Jealousy, which develops from the Oedipus triangle. A third person is hated because that person takes the love and libidinal energy from the desired object. In Oedipal terms, the son directs hate at the father for stealing the mother's love, love that is rightfully his.

The 'good breast' is responsible for all positive, gratifying feelings associated with the life instinct, feelings that reinforce trust and balance the life and death instincts.

Gratitude, the predominant emotion, allows the expression of trust and decreases greed. It is the origin of authentic generosity.

The term 'part object' refers to parts of the person that are perceived by the infant and related to as the 'whole'.

Some major Kleinian concepts

Anxiety
Anxiety, the ego's expression of the death instinct, becomes fear of persecutory objects, which in turn leads to fear of internalised persecutors. The major fears are oral – the fear of being devoured; anal – the fear of being controlled and poisoned; and Oedipal – the fear of castration.

Introjection and projection
Both contribute to the growth of the ego through trust and to ego defence through paranoid feelings. Which one is dominant depends on whether what is introjected or projected is perceived as good or bad.

Splitting
Splitting characterises the very young. It is the active separation into good or bad of experiences, perceptions and emotions linked to objects. Splitting interferes with the accurate perception of reality and nurtures denial. The opposite of splitting is synthesis. This takes place when the infant is able to distinguish part from whole objects.

Internalisation
Internalisation of the good object is a prerequisite for the development of a healthy ego firmly rooted in reality. A predominance of aggressive feelings works against a healthy ego. An ego that is based on unhealthy internalisation leads to excessive idealisation and excessive splitting.

Paranoid-schizoid position
The paranoid-schizoid position, which occurs during the first six months of life, is characterised by:

- Splitting
- Idealisation
- Denial
- Projective identification
- Part object relationships
- Persecutory fears about self-preservation.

Depressive position
The depressive position, adopted during the second six months of life, is characterised by idealisation of the good object, to avoid destroying the object. Depressive idealisation creates an over-dependence on others in later stages of development.

Superego
Klein believed that the superego starts to develop within the second six months

of life. A return to the paranoid-schizoid position may occur when excessive pressure from the superego prevents working through the depressive position.

Split-off, and projected, bad objects are later introjected and form the basis of the superego. Sadism, once projected, is then re-introjected, resulting in guilt.

The internalisation of mainly bad objects is normally outweighed by internalisation of good objects, although there is always some contamination by the objects. A perfectionist superego imposes the harsh demands of infantile virtues. A balanced superego responds realistically to demands for improvement on the one hand and sublimation on the other.

The Oedipus complex

In Kleinian theory, the early stages of the complex develop from the first year of life. The desire in both sexes for the good breast becomes a desire for the father's penis. Likewise, the bad breast is displaced on to the bad penis. When a boy perceives his father's penis to be bad, it makes a healthy father–son relationship difficult.

When the Oedipal relationship is not resolved, the boy is likely to develop sexual inhibitions and a fear of women. Castration fears arise from an oral-sadistic desire to destroy the penis.

For a girl, the good breast prepares the way for expecting a good penis. Intense oral aggression prepares the way for rejecting a positive Oedipal relationship with the mother. An Oedipus complex in a girl develops when the mother is perceived as possessing the father's penis. Penis envy arises from oral sadism, not from an envy of the male genitals. Envy of the opposite sex occurs in both sexes.

Working through (see also main entry)

Working-through of the depressive position consists of:

- **Reparation** (the origin of sublimation) is the mechanism of trying to repair damage done to a good object by expressing love and gratitude, and by so doing, preserve it.
- **Reality testing** increases as splitting decreases; love from the mother accelerates reality testing.
- **Ambivalence** is the infant's awareness and acceptance of both love and hate towards the same object, with the eventual triumph of love over hate.
- **Mourning** in adult life reactivates the depressive position and guilt of infancy. In the latter, however, the mother is present to help the infant to work through towards wholeness.

Fixation at the paranoid-schizoid position

This may result in either a paranoid or a schizoid personality.

- The paranoid personality combines:
  - Denial of reality
  - Excessive projective identification
  - Pathological splitting
  - Confusional states

- Development of paranoia (fear of external persecutors)
- Hypochondriasis
- The schizoid personality combines:
  - Shallow emotions
  - Limited capacity to tolerate guilt feelings
  - Tendency to experience objects as hostile
  - Withdrawal from object relations
  - Artificiality and superficiality in social adaptation.

Fixation at the depressive position

This may result in pathological mourning or the development of manic defences.

Pathological mourning may lead to the development of a sadistic superego, which evokes extreme guilt and feelings that the whole world is empty of love. Pathological mourning is characterised by:

- Cruelty
- Demands for perfection
- Hatred of anything instinctual
- Despair
- Self-reproach
- Suicide, which may be an attempt to protect the good object by destroying the bad self
- Hypochondriacal delusions
- Fantasies of world destruction.

Manic defences include:

- Omnipotence, based on identification with an idealised good object, accompanied by
- Denial of reality
- Identification with the sadistic superego
- Introjection – object hunger that can never be satisfied
- An exalted state of power
- Manic idealisation; the merging of one's exalted self with idealised objects.

Kleinian therapy

Klein believed that analysis of children could protect them from serious guilt-producing impulses. She favoured:

- Direct, immediate interpretations of the child's unconscious motivations
- The analysis of the child's feelings, displaced from the parents and transferred to the analyst
- The analyst, from the very commencement, interpreting the unconscious paranoid-schizoid and depressive fantasies within the transference.

In interpreting play as the symbolic expression of conflicts and anxieties, the analyst does not offer the child reassurance but works exclusively with the transference, in language the child can understand.

Counselling from a Kleinian perspective, as with almost every other approach, is based on the development of the relationship between counsellor and client. Within this relationship clients are encouraged to face whatever it is that is causing their immediate anxiety and to achieve a healthy balance between feelings of love and hate. The hoped-for outcome of counselling is that clients:

- Will achieve insight into the causes of their anxiety
- Will be able to establish and maintain more satisfactory relationships because they feel released from their fixations and repressions
- Will experience freedom to live their lives with increased well-being
- Will enjoy more ego strength to cope with the stresses of life
- Will feel that they want to survive rather than feel they are always losers.

Professor Cary Cooper identifies five criteria in selecting clients for counselling:

- Their problems can be clearly defined in psychodynamic terms.
- They are motivated enough to change.
- They have insight into their previous behaviour.
- They have enough internal strength to cope with the counselling process.
- There is evidence that they are able to accept and sustain a long-standing therapeutic relationship and a relationship with significant others in their immediate surroundings.

The Kleinian style is formal, with the client being offered a chair or a couch. The number of sessions is five or six a week for analysis, but in counselling this would not be the norm. Free association and interpretation are used within a relaxed and facilitative atmosphere.

Whatever the client's needs, however caring and compassionate the counsellor, the counsellor must never become a surrogate parent. However close counsellor and client become, the counsellor must remain detached and separate; this helps the client face reality. The boundary between counsellor and client must remain firmly established. Client and counsellor are two separate and distinct people.

Further reading

Cooper, C. (1996) Psychodynamic therapy: the Kleinian approach. In: *Handbook of Individual Therapy* (ed. W. Dryden). Sage Publications, London.
Klein, M. (1932) *The Psycholanalysis of Children*. L. and V. Woolf, Institute of Psychoanalysis.
Solomon, I. (1995) *A Primer of Kleinian Therapy*. Jason Aronson, Lanham, MD.
A useful website for a complete list of books by Melanie Klein: psychematters.com/bibliographies/klein.htm

L

LABELLING

In its broad sense, to label is to describe, classify, categorise and designate objects, and labelling helps us make sense and order of the world around. It is also used to describe the process by which people are designated by some behaviour that society has called 'deviant'.

Labelling is a two-way process: the person so labelled has one set of responses; the person labelling has another set. Clusters of behaviours are attached to specific labels or stereotypes; the role and its behaviours have to be learned and internalised. People so labelled then tend to behave in a way that reinforces the negative feeling attached to the labels.

People and society may derive gains from the labels and roles people are given and have accepted, e.g. 'the sick one'. Society may feel freed from a burden. Removing the label may itself be therapeutic but new behaviours also have to be learned, as well as changing attitudes of others. The stigmatising and dehumanising effect of labelling was one of the processes that the anti-psychiatry movement brought to notice, leading to a more humane and personalised approach to psychiatry.

At a different level, clients may carry around invisible labels put upon them by other people, often at an age when they are too young to refuse to accept them. Some examples of labels are: 'You're stupid'; 'You'll never do anything with your life'; 'You're too delicate'; 'You need looking after'. Such labels seriously affect the person's self-esteem. Getting the client to identify the labels is the first step towards change. When the label has been identified, getting the client to substitute a positive label is often a major step in building self-esteem.

Labelling and anti-psychiatry

One of the things that Thomas Szasz and R.D. Laing and the anti-psychiatry school loudly condemned was diagnosing someone as mentally ill. The *Oxford English Dictionary* defines diagnosis as 'determination of the nature of a diseased condition; identification of a disease by careful investigation of its symptoms and history; also, the opinion (formally stated) resulting from such investigation'. A medical definition is 'the process of determining, through examination and analysis, the nature of a patient's illness'. Both of these definitions are straightforward and logical, so why should diagnosis create problems?

Stage 1 – diagnosis

Diagnosis is the first stage in the process of what has become known as 'labelling'. A person is diagnosed, but then a curious thing happens: the person becomes the illness. John is not referred to as 'John, who is suffering schizophrenia' (or depression, or any other illness) but 'John, who is a schizophrenic'. John's character has thus changed – he has been labelled. The same thing applies to all sorts of conditions – 'He is a geriatric'; 'She is a Down's syndrome'; 'He is an amputee'. The list is endless.

It is so easy to drop into the trap of referring to 'the mentally ill' or 'the mentally handicapped' or 'the disabled'. Labelling dehumanises the person and in so doing emphasises difference, implying that those who are so labelled are deviant – not normal – in some way. It was precisely this dehumanising that sparked off the anti-psychiatry movement.

A related aspect is that, once a diagnosis is made, the person becomes a 'patient' and enters into a different sort of relationship; the patient assumes a new identity, a labelled identity. Once the diagnosis has been made, the person (now called 'the patient') becomes one of a vast number of people – past and present – who all carry the same label.

Stage 2 – treatment and prognosis

The next stage after diagnosis and labelling is treatment and prognosis. Doctors (in almost all branches of medicine) are expected to have certain god-like qualities mixed with the divination when it comes to declaring a prognosis – the duration and direction of a particular illness or condition. That is something society has come to expect, and this in turn puts the psychiatrist into a strait-jacket, for the psychiatrist can only work on assumptions and experience, and in order to do this he may resort to treating all patients with a certain diagnosis in very much the same way. Again, this is what the anti-psychiatrists call 'dehumanising the individual' – lumping all such people together without regard for their individuality. Medication is prescribed according to what works for the majority – again, without account being taken of the real person.

The anti-psychiatry lobby tried very hard to remove the label of mental illness from people and to introduce a more humane regime. To some extent they have succeeded, and counselling, where the individual is respected, is one way of redressing the balance. Perhaps the growth of counselling skills for people working with people with mental illness will – over the next few decades – prove to be another quiet revolution, as they somehow strive to perform a delicate balancing act between dehumanising and humanising regimes.

Further reading

Horowitz, A.V. (1982) *The Social Control of Mental Illness*. Academic Press, New York.

Laing, R.D. (1967) *The Divided Self*. Penguin, Harmondsworth.

Scheff, T.J. (1996) Labelling mental illness. In: *Mental Health Matters* (eds T. Heller et al.). Open University Press, Milton Keynes.

Szasz, T. (1962) *The Myth of Mental Illness*. Secker & Warburg, London.

Szasz, T. (1973) *Ideology and Sanity*. Calder & Boyars, New York.

Wing, J.-K. (1978) *Reasoning About Madness*. Oxford University Press, Oxford.

LEFT/RIGHT BRAIN

The left and right hemispheres of the brain specialise in different activities.

Left brain

The left, logical, systematic brain:

- Controls movements on the right side of the body
- Is more concerned with 'active doing'.

Left brain cognitive style is predominantly concerned with:

- Analysis and deduction
- Convergent thinking
- Facts, data, figures
- The end product
- Structure
- Logical, sequential, linear thought
- The mathematics mode
- Order
- Processing
- Rationality
- Reducing problems to workable segments
- Science and technology
- Step-by-step precision
- Using a highly sequential approach
- Verbal, literal, concrete language
- Working to well-defined plans.

Left brain language patterns

- 'Why don't we look at the facts?'
- 'These data show us that. . .'
- 'We must work to specific objectives'
- 'Here is what I think – A, B, C'
- 'You haven't explained yourself'
- 'Where's the logic in that?'
- 'This is what you do – 1, 2, 3'
- 'I'll have to work it out carefully'.

Left brain non-verbal patterns

- Creates endless lists
- Puts everything down in strict time order
- Spends much time on detail
- Must get one point clear before moving on.

Some typical left brain occupations

- Accountant
- Administrator

- Computer programmer
- Engineer
- Personnel specialist
- Production manager
- Purchasing agent
- Systems analyst.

Right brain

The right, intuitive brain:

- Controls movements on the left side of the body
- Is more concerned with the whole, not parts.

Right brain cognitive style is predominantly concerned with:

- Abstract topics
- Artistic expression
- Body image
- Concentrating on ideas and feelings
- Constructive tasks
- Crafts
- Creativity
- Divergent, global thinking
- Emotions
- Focusing on the process, not the outcome
- Using experience
- Non-verbal knowledge through images
- Perception
- Prayer, meditation, mysticism
- Problem-solving
- Perceiving
- Remembering faces
- Spontaneity
- What is visual
- Working with symbols and fantasy, dreams
- Working with metaphors and imagery
- Working with opposites
- Working with the unknown.

Right brain language patterns

- 'My gut feeling is...'
- 'I sense that...'
- 'Can't we look at the whole picture?'
- 'Let's look at things on global terms'
- 'The solution is really quite simple'
- 'Common sense tells me...'
- 'I know the answer, but I'm not sure how'.

Right brain non-verbal patterns

- Uses a lot of visual aids
- Becomes agitated over data
- Often appears to be disorganised
- 'Thinks' with the eyes
- Displays the problem graphically.

Some typical right brain occupations

- Advertising agent
- Counsellor/therapist
- Graphic artist
- Marketing manager.

In Jungian typology

Left-handed (right brain) activities are also associated with the feminine principle. The left brain is more associated with extroversion, sensing, thinking and judgement. The right brain is more associated with introversion, intuition, feeling and perception. For left-handed people the specialisation is not so consistent. Even in right-handed people it is not an 'either/or'.

Damage to the left hemisphere often interferes with language ability. Damage to the right hemisphere is likely to cause disturbance to spatial awareness of one's own body. Damage to the left brain may prove disastrous to an author, scientist or mathematician but may not prove so damaging to a musician, craftsman or artist. The hemispheres have a partnership function. A poet using deep feelings, imagery and metaphor draws on the right brain, and then the left for the words to express what the right side creates. The hemispheres may also be antagonistic: when, for example, the left hemisphere becomes too aggressive, trying to solve everything with logic and analysis, intuition and feelings are subdued.

Some clients experience difficulty moving between left and right hemisphere activities, but this does not mean that they should not be encouraged to do so. A person who is more left- than right-brain orientated, might choose to work with intuition or imagery, thus tapping into parts that normal activity leaves untouched. A person who is more right- than left-brain orientated might choose to work with a cognitive approach, thus developing sharper thinking ability.

Further reading

Buzan, T. (1983) *Use Both Sides of Your Brain*. E.P. Dutton, New York.
Edwards, B. (1982) *Drawing on the Right Side of the Brain*. Collins, London.
Ornstein, R.E. (1975) *The Psychology of Consciousness*. Pelican, Harmondsworth.
Wonder, J. and Donvan, P. (1984) *Whole-Brain Thinking*. William Morrow, New York.
Zdenek, M. (1983) *The Right-Brain Experience*. Corgi, London.

LIFESPAN PSYCHOLOGY

Erik Homburger Erikson (1902–1994) was a German–American psychoanalyst who had a major influence on the behavioural and social sciences.

In his classic study, *Childhood and Society* (1950; 2nd edn 1963), Erikson introduced his theories on identity, identity crisis (which term he popularised) and psychosexual development. Erikson proposed that people grow through experiencing a series of crises. They must achieve trust, autonomy, initiative, competence, their own identity, generativity (or productivity), integrity and acceptance.

Lifespan psychology is the study of people throughout life. Erikson, building on the work of earlier theorists, is the name most associated with lifespan psychology. Erikson's view of personality development has widely influenced the views of educators.

Psychological development does not necessarily parallel physical maturity. Physical maturation is predictable within reasonable time limits, within specific societies and cultures. The eight stages represent points along a continuum of development and each stage is accompanied by physical, cognitive, instinctual and sexual changes. How these changes are resolved results either in regression or in growth and the development of specific virtues, defined by Erikson as inherent strengths. With every stage the individual acquires a specific 'virtue' or quality but only if that stage has been worked through and all the conflicts resolved.

Table 5: *Erikson's stages ('nuclear crises') of the psychosocial development model*

Stage of development	Approximate age	Virtue
Basic trust versus mistrust	Infancy: birth to about 18 months	Hope

If the caretaker provides for the infant's needs, hope develops. Severe disturbance of this early relationship that does not result in the development of a sense of trust or the virtue of hope is likely to lead to severe emotional disturbance in later life.

Autonomy versus shame and doubt	Toddler: about 18 months to about 3 years	Will

Parental control that is too strict or rigid, or control exercised too early, may interfere with the child's developing need for autonomy. Lack of appropriate control exposes the child to dangers from his or her own desires. Judicious control helps the child to develop a healthy balance between loving goodwill and hateful self-insistence; between cooperation and wilfulness; and between appropriate self-expression on the one hand and compulsive self-expression on the other. Too rigid a control can result in compliance. Problems with control in early life may manifest later as being suspicious of other people. According to Erikson, the obsessive–compulsive personality is rooted in the earlier conflicting tendencies to hold on or let go.

Initiative versus guilt	Pre-school: about 3 years to about 5 years	Purpose

A stage characterised by inquisitiveness, competitiveness and physical aggression, jealousy and rivalry. The stage in which the Oedipus complex is manifested. The development of conscience, as 'forbidden' impulses, thoughts and desires are repressed. The virtue of purpose grows as the child develops ambition. Inability to resolve the conflict between initiative and guilt, says Erikson, is the foundation for the personality of the person who creates stress by driving himself or herself too hard.

Industry versus inferiority	School age: about 5 years to about 13 years	Competence

This is the stage where the young person discovers the value and rewards of the 'work principle' through diligence and persistence. In order to move through this stage, conflict from previous stages has to be resolved. Interference with the development of this stage can lead to despair of ever achieving anything, coupled with feelings of inferiority and inadequacy. The ability to work with and get on with people has its beginnings in this stage of development.

Identity versus role confusion	Adolescence and young adulthood: about 13 years to about 21 years	Fidelity

The burning issue is identity – who am I? Young people in this stage are more concerned with appearing right in the eyes of others than with knowing how and who they feel they are. This is the stage of cliques, of alliances, coupled with an intolerance of individual differences. The young person complies with the group, rather than with his own self-identity. The group gives identity. This is the stage of falling in love and a developing concept of faithfulness. Failure to form a clear sense of identity can lead to gender-identity confusion and delinquency.

Intimacy versus isolation	Young adulthood: about 21 years to about 40 years	Love

The main issue of a balanced identity is that the person develops an ability to both love and work. Love is to be interpreted as the ability to be intimate and not to be limited to genital love. People who do not have a clear identity might find difficulty in establishing and maintaining intimate relationships, because intimacy demands mutual giving and receiving. Both loving and work have to be held in balance; obsession with either can be destructive and indicate unresolved conflicts over identity.

Productivity versus stagnation	Middle adulthood: about 40 years to about 60 years	Care

Erikson refers to 'generativity', the concern for the next generation. It implies the passing on of knowledge and skills, having concern for all the generations as well as for social institutions. The person has usually achieved a satisfying role in life. Failure to develop generativity may lead to excesses at work or in personal life, including infidelity; mid-life crises or premature physical or psychological old age may occur.

Ego integrity versus despair	Later adulthood: about 60 years to death	Wisdom

Integrity, according to Erikson, is acceptance; acceptance of self, of the significant people in one's life. One of the crucial elements of this stage is the realisation (and that is acceptance) that the significant people (parents, for example) were as they were and that no amount of wishful thinking will change that; that is, accepting responsibility for one's own life story. Integrity helps a person face the reality of death. On the other hand, failure to attain integrity leads to a deep contempt for the whole, coupled with resentment, bitterness and regret that there is not enough time left to start again.

Lifespan psychology in counselling

Lifespan psychology has produced major contributions in the fields of:

- Relationships between generations
- Cognitive development
- Age and the social system
- Social policy
- Occupational choice.

One of the implications of the above model for counsellors is that development is lifelong. Secondly, to view a client from a psychosocial development perspective adds another dimension to one's understanding of the client's frame of reference. It is highly doubtful that every last conflict of one stage could ever be resolved in order to make sense of the next stage, but what Erikson's model does imply is that serious disturbance in one stage of development might give the counsellor a focus to work on and enable him to grow.

Further reading

Newton, P.M. and Newton, D.S. (1995) Erik H. Erikson. In: *Comprehensive Textbook of Psychiatry*, 6th edn (eds H.J. Kaplan and B.J. Sadock). Williams & Wilkins, Baltimore, MD.

LISTENING AND RESPONDING

The ultimate proof of active listening is effective responding.

Sensitive, active listening is an important way to bring about personality changes in attitudes and the way we behave towards ourselves and others. When we listen, people tend to become:

- More emotionally mature
- More open to experiences
- Less defensive
- More democratic
- Less authoritarian.

When we are listened to, we listen to ourselves with more care and are able to express thoughts and feelings more clearly.

Self-esteem is enhanced through active listening, because the threat of having one's ideas and feelings criticised is greatly reduced. Because we do not have to defend, we are able to see ourselves for what we truly are, and are then in a better position to change.

Listening, and responding to what we hear, is influenced by our own frame of reference. Therapeutic listening is also influenced by one's theoretical model.

Poor listening habits identified

- Not paying attention
- Pretend-listening
- Listening but not hearing the meaning
- Rehearsing what to say
- Interrupting the speaker in mid-sentence
- Hearing what is expected
- Feeling defensive, expecting an attack
- Listening for something to disagree with.

What to avoid

- Trying to get people to see themselves as we see them or would like to see

them: This is control and direction and is more for our needs than for theirs. The less we need to evaluate, influence, control and direct, the more we enable ourselves to listen with understanding.

- **Responding to a demand for decisions, action, judgement and evaluation or agreeing with someone against someone else**: We are in danger of losing our objectivity. The surface question is usually the vehicle with a deeper need as its passenger.

- **Shouldering responsibility for other people**: We remove from them the right to be active participants in the problem-solving process. Active involvement releases energy; it does not drain it from the other person. Active participation is a process of thinking with people instead of thinking for or about them.

- **Passing judgements – critical or favourable**: Judgement is generally patronising.

- **Using platitudes and clichés**: These demonstrate either lack of interest or verbal poverty.

- **Giving verbal reassurances**: This is insulting, for they demean the problem.

What to do

- Get into the person's frame of reference. Listen for total meaning, which is content and feelings. Both require hearing and responding to. In some instances the content is far less important than the feeling for which the words are but vehicles. We must try to remain sensitive to the total meaning the message has to the speaker:
  - What is he trying to tell me?
  - What does this mean to this person?
  - How does this person see this situation?

- Note all cues. Not all communication is verbal. Truly sensitive listening notes:
  - Body posture
  - Breathing changes
  - Eye movements
  - Facial expression
  - Hand movements
  - Hesitancies
  - Inflection
  - Mumbled words
  - Stressed words.

What we communicate by listening

We communicate interest in the importance of the speaker, respect for the speaker's thoughts (not necessarily agreement) and non-evaluation, and we validate the person's worth.

Listening demonstrates; it does not tell. Listening catches on. Just as anger is normally met with anger, so listening encourages others to listen. Listening is a constructive behaviour and the person who consistently listens with understanding is the person who is most likely to be listened to.

Responding as a part of listening

Passive listening, without responding, is deadening and is demeaning. We should never assume that we have really understood until we can communicate that understanding to the full satisfaction of the other person. Effective listening hinges on constant clarification to establish true understanding.

What effective listeners do

- Put the talker at ease
- Limit their own talking
- Are attentive
- Remove distractions
- Get inside the talker's frame of reference
- Are patient and don't interrupt
- Watch for feeling words
- Are aware of their own biases
- Listen to the paralinguistics
- Are aware of body language.

Listening with the 'third ear'

The phrase 'listening with the third ear' was coined by Theodor Reik to point up the quality of psychotherapy where active listening goes beyond the five senses. The 'third ear' hears what is said between sentences and without words, what is expressed soundlessly, what the speaker feels and thinks.

Principles for third ear listening

- Have a reason or purpose for listening
- Suspend judgement
- Resist distractions
- Wait before responding
- Repeat verbatim
- Rephrase the message accurately
- Identify important themes
- Reflect content and search for meaning
- Be ready to respond.

We convey non-acceptance by:

- **Advising, giving solutions:** 'Why don't you …?'
- **Evaluating, blaming:** 'You are definitely wrong'
- **Interpreting, analysing:** 'What you need is…'
- **Lecturing, informing:** 'Here are the facts…'
- **Name-calling, shaming:** 'You are stupid'
- **Ordering, directing:** 'You have to…'
- **Praising, agreeing:** 'You are definitely right'

- **Preaching, moralising**: 'You ought to. . .'
- **Questioning, probing**: 'Why did you . . .?'
- **Sympathising, supporting**: 'You'll be OK'
- **Warning, threatening**: 'You had better not. . .'
- **Withdrawing, avoiding**: 'Let's forget it'.

More than any other communication skill, responding with understanding helps to create a climate of support and trust between two people or among the members of a group. There are three basic ways of responding:

- **Evaluating**: Our first instinct. Whenever we evaluate others, we *decide* whether they are right or wrong. The process of evaluating and judging doesn't pull people closer together; it sets them further apart.
- **Hollow listening**: Listening without responding. Listening is hollow if it consists merely of listening and nothing more.
- **Responding with understanding**: The most effective, yet the least used response in interpersonal communication. Responding with understanding means:
    - careful listening to the other person's total communication – words, non-verbal messages, voice-related cues
    - trying to identify the feelings the person is expressing and the experiences and behaviours that give rise to these feelings
    - trying to communicate to this person an understanding of what he or she seems to be feeling and of the sources of these feelings
    - responding not by evaluating what he or she has to say, but by showing your understanding of the other person's world from his or her frame of reference.

    (The above is an extract from G. Egan (1977) *You and Me*. Brooks/Cole, Pacific Grove, CA.)

Further reading

Reik, T. (1972) *Listening With the Third Ear*. Pyramid Publications, New York.
Wismer, J.N. (1978) Communication effectiveness: active listening and sending feeling messages. In: *1978 Annual Handbook for Group Facilitators*. University Associates, San Diego, CA.

LISTENING (BELIEFS ABOUT)

These 22 points about listening are adapted from Nelson-Jones, R. (1986) *Human Relationship Skills,* Holt Rinehart & Winston, London, and used with permission. I have altered and developed this questionnaire to include the results of several years' work with it. People are asked to score each question as True or False.

1. Most people are brought up to be good listeners.
   False. Many people answer this as True, possibly because as children we were very often told to 'listen' or 'pay attention'. And very often if the child does

not, there is some punishment. But this is not the listening we mean in counselling.

2. Listening to others means also listening to ourselves.

True. 'Listening to myself' often causes confusion. Many confuse listening to the words and how they are expressed with the inner listening to attitudes and one's own judgements.

3. It is always up to other people to communicate precisely what they want to say.

False. This often results in heated discussion in training groups. In normal conversation, yes, each one of us does have an obligation to say clearly what we want to. But do we always? In counselling, however, many clients do not have the facility of clear speaking. Part of counselling skill is to help the person to clarify constantly.

4. We sometimes listen because we are afraid of revealing something about ourselves.

True. This is getting at the fact that, here, 'listening' has moved from being active and has become passive, and that if we respond we may reveal something we would rather keep safe.

5. Talking is more important than listening.

False. Only a few people believe that talking is more important than listening in counselling.

6. What people reveal about themselves is likely to influence what others tell them.

True. Some people find this difficult. They confuse 'reveal' with verbal disclosure. After discussion they usually agree that we reveal many things about ourselves, indirectly, through speech and non-verbal behaviour. This question is also to do with openness in communication.

7. To be a good listener, one has to feel emotional about issues.

False. When we are impassioned about something, there is a danger of getting so 'hot' over it that we cease to listen.

8. When we repeatedly do not listen to and understand someone, we could be accused of a form of psychological violence.

True. The phrase 'psychological violence' generally pulls people up with a jolt. Some modify their views, others react strongly against it; others reserve judgement. Most people agree, whatever the word used, that repeated non-listening is psychologically damaging.

9. We are more likely to hear messages that agree with the views we hold of ourselves than messages that challenge our views.

True. Some people argue quite strongly against this, putting forward the view that they often look for views that are contrary to their own. In counselling, we need constantly to be aware that this is a possibility.

10. We listen well when we have something to say on a subject.

False. This is similar to question 7. However, the difference is that it focuses on the fact that so often we cease to listen effectively because we have something to say. When we start formulating a reply, we have stopped listening.

11. Our thoughts may interfere with how we listen.
    True. Very few people have difficulty with this question.
12. Listening is a natural ability for most people.
    False. As with question 1, many people believe they have a natural ability, until they explore exactly what listening (in the counselling sense) means.
13. We may resist listening to people when we blame them.
    True. Most people accept this statement, for blame is passing judgement and it is also related to point 7.
14. Being a good listener does not require self-discipline.
    False. Many people get this wrong because they miss the word 'not'. This is a useful demonstration that even in reading sometimes we 'skip', so, in listening, we may not hear everything the other person says.
15. People will feel able to talk with us if they feel safe and accepted.
    True. Most people would agree with this.
16. Keeping confidences is important in developing trust.
    True. This generally does not present any difficulty.
17. Fatigue never affects the quality of listening.
    False. Most people do not agree with this statement. As with 14, some miss the 'never'. Some people just have difficulty with double negatives.
18. Effective listening entails making a series of correct choices in receiving what is being said.
    True. Many people score this as False, possibly because they think that they should remain completely open to what the client is saying and not make judgements. This is true, of course, and I normally get them to consider the possibility that it is only in retrospect that we can determine if the choices were the 'correct' ones or not. The question would probably cause less difficulty if 'accurate' were substituted for 'correct'.
19. Observing body language and voice quality plays no part in effective listening.
    False. Few people get it wrong, though some dispute the degree to which it plays a part.
20. When we are angry we are not very good listeners.
    True. As with 7 and 10, listening is affected by emotions.
21. Our listening is not affected by our previous experiences.
    False. This is another question where the 'not' is often missed. When this little word is pointed out, it makes all the difference.
22. We sometimes send mixed messages that are difficult for the other person to understand.
    True. Few people argue with this, although some want to know more about 'mixed messages'.

LOGOTHERAPY

Viktor Frankl (1905–1992) was a Viennese neurologist and psychologist, and founder of the school of logotherapy or existential analysis. He was imprisoned in German concentration camps between 1942 and 1945. He saw the meaning of his life as helping others to see a meaning in their lives.

Frankl's method of psychotherapy, sometimes referred to as the 'third Viennese school' (Freud and Adler being the first two) focuses on the meaning of human existence as well as one's search for such a meaning to help people change their lives, and recover from crisis and trauma.

Definition

Logotherapy means 'therapy through meaning'. It's an active-directive therapy aimed at helping people specifically with meaning crises, which manifest themselves either in a feeling of aimlessness or indirectly through addiction, alcoholism or depression.

Logotherapy also employs techniques useful for phobias, anxiety, obsessive-compulsive disorders and medical ministry. Other applications include working with juvenile delinquents, career counselling and helping all of us find more meaning in life.

The foundations of logotherapy

1. **Logotherapy is existentialist** because it emphasises the freedom of the will and the accompanying responsibility. It asserts the importance of the meaning of life. Freud said humans have a 'will to pleasure' and Adler the 'will to power'. Frankl says we have a 'will to meaning'. In spite of physical and psychological restraints, we are free to stand against whatever circumstances confront us. We all have the potential to rise above even the most adverse conditions. Each of us has to find our own unique meaning of life.
   - If the will is frustrated, spiritual neuroses result. Frankl argued that the spiritual dimension of man should be added to the physical and psychological dimensions. To find and to fulfil meaning and purpose is fact, and we are all required to find and respond to this fact. To discover meaning, in itself, produces a sense of fulfilment.
   - Ultimate meaning does exist and is unique to each person and each situation.
   - Every moment we live has a meaning and can never be repeated.
   - Meaning cannot be invented but must be discovered.
2. **Logotherapy is stoic**, because no matter what the situation or condition, our *attitude* can always help us. In other words, it is not the situation that moves us but how we interpret the situation. Many people facing death have found a meaning in it.
3. **Frankl's own experiences.** His three years in Auschwitz and Dachau concentration camps contributed towards the development of his approach to psychotherapy.

Looking for intentions

Logotherapy investigates the questions for whom or for what I am doing something. It is important to find out what is being expressed. When we say something it is not accidental, it has a purpose and it is the relationship with the person to whom we are expressing something that is the carrier of the message.

Finding the person

Frankl showed that the core person is not affected by illness, ailment, crisis, fate or success. The person is integrating the very specific and unique human qualities into all situations and conditions in life.

The therapeutic process

Therapy involves helping clients face the fact that while some circumstances may be changed, others may never be. Finding and responding to the meaning of life will then require an acceptance of whatever is involved in accepting change and also accepting what cannot be changed.

Every client should be approached 'holistically'; mentally, physically, emotionally, socially and spiritually. To gain fulfilment means to go beyond self-actualisation, to become 'other-directed' and accountable.

Existential frustration refers to the individual's sense of meaninglessness. Existential vacuum refers to the emptiness that results from existential frustration. People can be helped to move out of their existential vacuum by finding meaning through love, work, suffering and death.

While logotherapy, as an intervention, has characteristics of both psychoanalysis and spiritual counselling, it is neither. Therapy concentrates on examining the person in terms of responsibility. It does not deal directly with symptoms but with the person's attitude towards them. Logotherapy does not encourage homeostasis, it encourages tension, struggle and striving for some goal that is worthy of the person.

Techniques of logotherapy

1. Paradoxical intention

A paradox is an apparently self-contradictory statement; the underlying meaning is revealed only by careful scrutiny. The therapist encourages clients (with appropriate humour, something Frankl strongly emphasises) to do exactly and deliberately what they believe they do involuntarily, and over which they believe they have no control.

The technique is used primarily to overcome obsessions. An example would be where a client is terrified to leave the house in case she faints. The therapist might say (with relevant humour) 'Go on, faint. Faint twice. In fact, why not have a heart attack into the bargain.' When the client realises that her intention does not produce the feared symptom, she begins to appreciate the uselessness of her behaviour. By reversing the habitual avoidance of the feared event or object the anxiety cycle is broken.

2. Dereflection

The therapist diverts patients away from their problems towards something else meaningful in the world. Used specifically for sexual dysfunction, deflection is indicated because (for example) the more you think about potency during sex, the less likely you are to achieve it. It's no use just telling clients to stop thinking about something – what is needed is to substitute something positive (for example, with an insomniac – don't just tell them to stop trying to sleep, tell them to count sheep).

More generally, logotherapy can be seen as deflecting the patient away from their presenting problem towards searching for meaning. The client is dereflected from their disturbance to something other than themselves.

3. Orientation towards meaning

A. **Meaning through creative values**: The therapist's role is to bring into conscious awareness the whole spectrum of meaning and values. A major source of meaning is through the value of all that we create, achieve and accomplish.

B. **Meaning through experiential values**: Find what is meaningful to the client and ask if, having had this experience, what life would be without it.

C. **Meaning through attitudinal values**: People always have the freedom to find meaning through meaningful attitudes even in apparently meaningless situations.

Assessing logotherapy

Table 6: *Assessing logotherapy*

Strengths	Weaknesses
Inspired by Viktor Frankl's life	Too authoritarian
Relatively simple to understand, potentially life-changing and enhancing	Too religious and not sufficiently scientific or rigorous
Addresses dimension of life not addressed by other therapies	Too dependent on Frankl and his intuitions
Optimistic and constructive	Too narrow

Developments in logotherapy

James Crumbaugh has devised six lists that are used throughout analysis.

1. Lifelong aims, ambitions, goals and interests going back as far as the client can remember, including those he no longer considers important
2. The strong points of personality, physical and environmental circumstances, 'good luck'
3. The weak points of personality, failures, 'bad luck'
4. Specific problems that cause the client's conflicts
5. Future hopes
6. Future plans.

Further reading

Crumbaugh, J. (1973) *Everything to Gain.* Institute of Logotherapy Press, Berkeley, CA.

Frankl, V.E. (1955) *The Doctor and the Soul: from psychotherapy to logotherapy.* Knopf, New York.

Frankl, V.E. (1962) Basic Concepts of Logotherapy. Paper read before the Annual Meeting of the American Ontoanalytic Association in Chicago on 7 May 1961. Reprinted from *Journal of Existential Psychiatry*, No. 8 Spring 1962 and available from The Institute of Psychosynthesis, London.

Frankl, V.E. (1967) *Psychotherapy and Existentialism.* Simon & Schuster, New York.

Frankl, V.E. (1969) *The Will to Meaning: foundations and applications of logotherapy.* New American Library, New York.

Frankl, V.E. (1978) *The Unheard Cry for Meaning.* Simon & Schuster, New York.

LeBon, T. (2001) *Wise Therapy: philosophy for counsellors.* Sage Publications Ltd, London.

Wong, P. and Fry, P. (1998) *The Human Quest for Meaning: a handbook of psychological research and clinical applications.* Lawrence Erlbaum Associates, Mahwah, NJ.

www.geocities.com

http://members.aol.com/timlebon

LONELINESS (SEE ALSO: INTIMACY, EXISTENTIAL THERAPY)

Loneliness is an unpleasant experience that occurs when a person's network of social relationships is deficient in some important way. Loneliness exists when there is a discrepancy between the needs of a person and the social contacts available to meet those needs. Loneliness is something felt by the person and relates to the degree of emotional contact one person has with others. So being with a crowd of people does not mean that one stops feeling lonely.

Emotional loneliness stems from the lack or absence of a close attachment. This form of loneliness results in intense and unpleasant feelings of anxiety and apprehension. Social loneliness stems from the absence of adequate or effective social networks. The feelings associated with this type of loneliness – boredom and exclusion – are not so intense as emotional loneliness.

It would appear that it is not the number of relationships that ward off loneliness but the depth of the relationships we do have – in other words, intimacy. It also seems that loneliness is linked to low self-esteem, anxiety, depression, shyness, self-consciousness and the lack of social skills that help in forming new relationships.

Loneliness is characterised by:

- Apathy
- Distress
- Emptiness 'as vast as a frozen wilderness'
- Feeling of drifting, without rudder or line
- Futility
- Helplessness
- Lack of concentration
- Lack of motivation

- Over-sensitivity
- Restlessness
- Suspicion
- Withdrawal
- A worn-out feeling.

Loneliness is often precipitated by:

- Age
- Disability
- Extreme introversion
- Infirmity
- Isolation through environment
- Isolation through loss of partner
- Low self-esteem
- Over-dependence
- Poor social skills
- Rigidity of personality
- Self-deprecating trait
- Shyness
- Being a single parent.

Loneliness may be coped with through denial. Social contact may be devalued and refuge sought in work, hobbies or addiction.

The link between loneliness and depression is an important consideration. Feeling lonely may result from knowing that one has fewer friends than other people. People who attribute being lonely to some personality deficit are likely to experience depression and pessimism. When relationships end, other than by mutual consent, the person ending the relationship is reported to experience less loneliness than the other person. The one who was 'dumped' is very likely to feel a victim.

People who have a schizoid personality disorder have great difficulty with intimate relationships and are characteristically loners. They are often to be found in occupations where they can work in isolation. People with a paranoid personality, likewise, often experience difficulty with intimate relationships. People with social phobia are invariably loners, and lonely, and as such often fail to develop intimate relationships. People with a histrionic personality often consider relationships to be more intimate than they actually are.

The aim of counselling is to help the client live with the deep loneliness that lies at the heart of existence. Counselling should not propel the client into establishing relationships that may simply be perpetuating the denial.

The stress of loneliness

Loneliness is a personal, subjective experience of discomfort, distress and pain resulting from the lack of intimate relationships. We are likely to feel lonely where there is an unacceptable gap between our expectation and the reality of how we interact with people.

Loneliness is associated with many psychological, physical and social conditions. Many people feel ashamed to admit to being lonely.

Four forces contribute to loneliness:

1. **Independence**: Independence is highly valued in the British culture. The myth is that if we can grow up not needing anyone else, then we have made it.

   The person who believes in this myth is more likely to strive to be autonomous *all of the time*. Autonomy, when carried to extremes, separates us from the group, who pick up the cue, 'I don't need you'.

   Leaders are more likely to be able to work in a solitary fashion than are managers without feeling stressed. The work of the leader is not so dependent upon interaction with others.

2. **The hierarchy**: (see: Individual Psychology for a discussion on vertical versus horizontal relationships)

   This applies more to the work place, but as the majority of people do work, it has an application. A hierarchy is vertical in nature; this forces those who are higher up into increasing isolation from those on lower levels. The discrimination that creates this separation is based on authority and responsibility.

   Hierarchical relationships mean that those above have a self-enhancing bias; while those lower down have a self-diminishing bias. The implied message is that those at the top are 'better' or more perfect. The social distance feeds the problem of emotional isolation.

3. **Counter-dependence**: (see also Co-dependency)

   Children who grow up in the security of knowing that the 'attached figures' are there and will supply their basic needs tend to become self-reliant adults who can accept responsibility for their own well-being. At the same time, they maintain a support network of people who will be willing to help in times of need.

   Children who grow up without that security tend to suffer from separation anxiety. As adults, such people may then employ dysfunctional strategies for achieving a sense of felt security in times of danger or threat. One of these dysfunctional behaviours is overdependence – a desperate clinging to others.

   A second strategy, more damaging to health, is counter-dependency. The main effect is an attempt to achieve total self-sufficiency. This results in the lack of close, personal or professional, relationships, on which to draw in times of need. In times of stress, counter-dependent people become isolated and withdrawn, although this is the time when they most need the support of others.

   A counter-dependent person:
   - Makes very strong efforts to work alone and in a solitary way
   - Finds it difficult to delegate at work
   - Makes little effort to spend time regularly with people
   - Believes that close relationships will backfire
   - Thinks he is the only one who can do a job right

- Avoids depending on people because of a fear of being crowded
- Is frequently suspicious of people's motives
- Feels uncomfortable asking for help and admitting a need.

4. **Defensiveness:**

Defensiveness always establishes barriers between people, creating distance in relationships, and may result in a wide range of communication dysfunction.

Active defensiveness results in aggressive, controlling, dictatorial form of interpersonal interaction. The manager who uses an active defence likes to hold the upper hand.

Passive defensiveness relies on being submissive, withdrawn, non-aggressive and non-assertive. Apologies, inappropriate to the situation, and self-deprecation, are clearly forms of passive defensiveness.

The person who is non-defensive chooses how to relate, and is not simply reacting to the behaviour of the other person.

Impacts of counter-dependency on health

Psychological

Emotional isolation can lead to depression and burnout. The depressed person may experience decreased ability to make decisions, judgements and in other cognitive processes.

Social

Isolation leads to the loss of key information and expectations, which normally come through the social network. Serious social deficit may result in errors and miscalculations of planning risks or problem-solving failures. Social deficit affects relationships and morale. There may be a strong link between counter-dependency and social deficit.

Physiological

Less serious than premature death, emotional isolation can lead to psychosomatic illness. Emotional isolation can produce symptoms in all the vulnerable bodily systems. Physiological or medical breakdown often occurs in the weakest link of the body.

Anxiety/insomnia

The higher the level of self-imposed autonomy and the more counter-dependency, the higher is the risk of anxiety and insomnia. It seems that the anxiety associated with counter-dependency reawakens the separation anxiety of childhood.

The difference between self-reliance and counter-dependency lies in the well-developed support network of the one and the lack of it in the other.

Work groups

An interesting development over the last two decades is the development of work groups and the emphasis on work teams, as well as personal growth groups. This could be interpreted as an attempt to redress the balance, and move away from the idea that independence is more valuable that interdependence. Perhaps this century will witness a revolution, as work groups are recognised as a viable way to overcome loneliness and isolation.

Although not directly connected, loneliness can lead to feelings of alienation and separation. For example, managers and executives at the top of a hierarchy, the 'pedestal syndrome', are in a precarious position. The risk of being toppled from power is ever-present. The 'loneliness of the bridge' eats away at them. But the stress of loneliness is not confined to those at the top; many situations at work isolate people from contact with others. Without contact many of us shrivel, like plants in the hot sun deprived of moisture.

Further reading

Bowlby, J. (1979) *The Making and Breaking of Affectional Bonds.* Tavistock, London.

Hobson, R.F. (1974) Loneliness. *Journal of Analytical Psychology,* **19**: 71–89.

Peplau, L.A. and Perlman, D. (1982) *Loneliness.* John Wiley, New York.

Quick, J.C., Nelson, D.L. and Quick, J.D. (1990) *Stress and Challenge at the Top: the paradox of the successful executive.* John Wiley, Chichester.

Quick, J.C., Nelson, D.L., Joplin, J.R. and Quick, J.D. (1992) *Emotional Isolation and Loneliness: executive problems.* The 1992 Annual: Developing Human Resources. University Associates, San Diego, CA.

M

Manipulation

Identifying why counselling is not exercising undue influence

Some people believe that successful counsellors are those who are able to suggest solutions to clients' problems in such a way that the clients feel they are their own. This is commonly called 'manipulation', behaviour from which most counsellors would recoil. However, situations are seldom clear cut. There is a fine line between legitimate influence and manipulation. Manipulation always carries with it some benefit to the manipulator. Influence is generally unconscious. In any case, suggesting solutions is not part of effective counselling. There is a difference between exploring alternatives and suggesting solutions and manipulation. Manipulation will always leave you feeling uncomfortable, used and angry.

Identifying why counselling is not manipulation

Counselling definitely *is not* manipulation, which is 'unfair influence'; something underhand, a plot, duplicity.

When one person persuades you to do or attempt something (even though it may be against your better judgement or wishes), it is usually done in such a way that you realise what is happening. The person who manipulates you to do what he wants does so subversively, not in the open, and (this is the essential difference) usually for some personal gain and not in your best interests.

The dividing line between manipulation and seeking ways and means to resolve a problem may not always be easily seen, but the deciding factor must be who benefits. Is it you, or is it the other person?

An example of manipulation, taken from a training session, illustrates the point. Joe was passing through a difficult time with his girlfriend. The trainee counsellor, in the belief that it would be best for Joe to end the relationship, introduced a whole gamut of moral issues, which made Joe feel so guilty that he said he would sever the relationship. This would have been inappropriate and would have left both Joe and the girl feeling resentful. That is manipulation.

Some students of counselling think, initially, that the counsellor manoeuvres clients so adroitly that they agree with what the counsellor proposes as if they themselves had thought of it. This can be done and it is a very subtle means of ensuring that the client takes the direction that the counsellor feels is right. This can be done by loading the exploration in favour of the direction you have chosen, by limiting the exploration to one avenue or by putting forward all the difficulties against any other choice.

Sometimes people who counsel will manipulate the client's feelings to satisfy their own emotional needs. It is probably true to say that we all counsel to get something out of it, but the majority of us have enough awareness of our own emotional needs not to let them overshadow our counselling. When referring to 'the counsellor', I mean anyone doing counselling; I would not want to imply that counsellors who have undergone training would be guilty of this sort of manipulation but neither would I want to suggest that those who have not received such a training would be any more guilty. Manipulation of any kind is caused by underlying, and often well-hidden, motives.

Counsellors must also be watchful that their own emotional needs do not intrude to the extent that they could be accused of manipulation. It is not always easy to detect when we have moved from exploration to manipulation but, as I have already said, a great deal depends on motives. If you are not clear when you are manipulating, the clients will be, although they may not use that word. They may not realise at the time what is happening but, when the session has ended and they have time to reflect, their feelings are likely to be something like: 'The cunning *****' (with a suitable expletive), 'so that's what he was after. I won't trust him again!'

The other side of the coin is graphically portrayed by Gary Collins. He draws attention to how the counsellor, in the desire to please, can be manipulated. He quotes one case where counselling became more frequent, and the counsellor ended up running errands, making phone calls, giving small loans and even doing shopping for the client who 'constantly expressed gratitude and mournfully kept asking for more'.

Collins goes on to say that manipulated counsellors cease to be helpful. Instead, the counsellor must learn to '. . . challenge these tactics, refuse to be moved by them, and teach more satisfying ways of relating to others'. We can halt this process by asking: 'Am I being manipulated? Am I going beyond my responsibilities as a counsellor? What does this client really want?' Finally, this is where adequate supervision is a must.

David Mearns and Brian Thorne make a different point about manipulation. They say that being prepared to be manipulated is an indication of a healthy relationship. 'Such a belief [in the basic trust in human nature] does not mean that the counsellor is gullible and blind to human perversity, but it does imply that she is prepared to trust those who are manifestly untrustworthy so that they may gradually discover their own untrustworthiness.' This extract might well confuse readers who are not grounded in the person-centred approach, however, the authors go on to say, 'The willingness to submit to manipulation if need be is but one sign of the counsellor's determination to stay with her client through thick and thin.'

Further reading

Collins, G.R. (1988) *Christian Counselling: a comprehensive guide.* Word Publishing, Nashville, TN.

Mearns, D. and Thorne, B. (1988) *Person-centred Counselling in Action.* Sage Publications, London.

Stewart, W. (1999) *Going for Counselling.* How to Books, Oxford.

MEDIATION AND NEGOTIATION

Mediation

Mediation is a legal/therapeutic process whereby a counsellor mediates between a husband and wife at the point when they have begun or are considering beginning the legal process to end their marriage.

Mediation requires close liaison with solicitors and extensive knowledge of divorce law and court procedures, as well as therapeutic skills appropriate to working with couples in conflict.

The aim of mediation is to help the parties to negotiate with each other over matters that are in dispute. These may include the divorce itself (where one party's decision to end the marriage is opposed by the other), the settlement of finances and property and the custody of children.

The aim is to make the divorce as amicable as possible so that both parties can walk away with dignity and without recrimination. Mediation starts the grieving process and allows the couple to express their feelings openly and appropriately. Effective mediation prepares the way for counselling.

A couple engage the assistance of one or two impartial mediators who have no authority to make any decision for them, but who have certain skills to help them to resolve their issues by negotiated agreement.

Mediation does not aim to save the marriage, but to help parties deal by agreement rather than through the courts with the consequences of its breakdown.

It should be noted that mediation is in essence an assisted form of negotiation, leaving responsibility for decision making in the hands of the parties.

Mediation helps resolve issues arising from the breakdown of a relationship, such as:

- Whether to divorce and on what grounds
- With whom the children will live
- How to manage shared care of the children
- Contact with the children
- What will happen to the family home
- Division of capital
- Financial support for family members.

Negotiation

While negotiation is similar to mediation, it is sufficiently different to warrant a section of its own.

Negotiation is the most mature of the approach-style modes. Negotiation is possible only when both parties are interested in peace. Negotiation involves continuous interaction and dialogue in order to find a solution with maximum advantages to both.

By using the Nine-Step Negotiation Model, mutual interests are met and the most satisfactory solution is determined.

Step 1 – Unfreezing

Conflict may become 'frozen' into stereotyped responses. Before movement can take place, those patterns and expectations have to be 'unfrozen'. This can be done by each person describing exactly how they see the situation.

Step 2 – Openness

People may be 'closed' with each other and need to develop the ability to express different points of view without fear of repercussions. Openness is usually most difficult when the conflict involves critical issues, and when the atmosphere is emotionally charged.

Step 3 – Empathy

When we see only our own points of view, we gain little understanding of others. When we share their main concerns, apprehensions or goals, we start to see things from their frame of reference. Such sharing may help us and them to gain new insight about the common difficulty.

Step 4 – Themes

People involved in conflict may be helped to search for common goals or other areas of overlap by listing their expectations, apprehensions, perceptions and goals.

Step 5 – Choices

Once aware of others' perspectives, alternatives for solving some of the issues can be generated. If both parties participate in generating alternatives, they are likely to feel mutually responsible for finding an acceptable solution.

Step 6 – Responding

After alternatives have been generated, both parties should study and respond to them. Every effort should be made to see issues in a positive, problem-solving way. Outright rejection of alternatives should be avoided, but all should be discussed to seek clarification and for sharing concerns.

Step 7 – Solution

A number of alternatives may be explored in depth to find what is considered the most likely.

Step 8 – Movement

Sometimes the conflict may be so emotionally deadlocked that people cannot move towards a solution by themselves. In such cases, a third party, who is both objective and experienced with this type of problem, may be brought in to arbitrate.

Step 9 – Commitment

After solutions are generated, the people concerned can debate and consider these solutions and make their commitments to some of them. Openness among group members will help for genuine commitment. All doubts must be resolved or must be put aside at this point.

UK College of Family Mediators
Alexander House
Telephone Avenue
Bristol
BS1 4BS
Tel: 0117 904 7223
Fax: 0117 904 3331
E-mail: ukcfm@btclick.com

These are useful websites:
www.familymediation.org.uk
www.concilia.org.uk
www.familymediationscotland.org.uk
www.solicitorsupontyne.co.uk

Further reading

Howard, J. and Shepherd, G. (1987) *Conciliation, Children and Divorce: a family systems approach.* Batsford, London.

MOMENTUM, MAINTAINING

During the early stages of counselling, as counsellor and client are getting to know each other, as clients spend time telling their story, there may not be any pressing need for you to find ways to keep the interview on the move. Later, however, when the tale has been told and the problem has been identified, or partially so, and as counselling enters the exploratory stage, it may happen that the process slows up or comes to a halt. There are a number of possible reasons for this. Sometimes you may get the impression of 'having been here before' – a sense of repetition. A moment's reflection may be enough to reveal that the wheel has come full circle. This is the time either to move on or to terminate the session. Perhaps the client has had enough, or perhaps you have.

To move the interview on, it may be sufficient to say something like, 'We seem to have come full circle. Maybe I missed something important before.' If this approach is not used, you may refer to something that emerged earlier in the session or you may ask at which point the person would like to restart. This may provide an opportunity to explore why the session has come back to the beginning.

The point may have been dealt with inadequately at a previous time, and it has now reappeared. But it is also possible that only by going back can the person speak about something that caused difficulty before. It could also mean that you are trying to direct the person into an avenue that the client felt could have been explored before, but was not.

Comments such as 'And then?', 'What happened?', 'What was the outcome?', 'Tell me about ...', 'What were your feelings at the time?' are all aimed at moving the interview forwards – gently, not pushing it. But there is usually a natural time for a session to end. If momentum slows down, that may be the appropriate time to stop, by summarising what has taken place.

On the other hand, momentum may slow down because the client is thinking deeply about some comment you have made or something that has been triggered off as part of a chain reaction. The client may be hesitating to mention something, not certain of its relevance, its importance or possibly its controversial nature. You may have become preoccupied, allowing your attention to waver. When this happens, the client will feel uneasy; conversation most likely will falter. A simple, 'Sorry, I've lost track' will be enough to get you both back on track.

MULTICULTURAL ISSUES

Cross-cultural counselling is similar in many ways to cross-gender counselling. Counselling has its roots in white cultures and it is possible that this way of relating is not readily accepted by people from different cultures. However well versed and aware we are, our counselling could benefit from a study of three important factors.

Firstly, we could learn from our clients how the history of their own culture influences them now. We also need to have explored our own cultural influences and recognised how our attitudes, beliefs, prejudices, stereotypes and judgements influence our interactions.

Secondly, we must be prepared to take on board what our clients say of their experiences of discrimination, exploitation, stereotyping and those indefinable but palpable phenomena, 'awkwardness' and 'joking', and how these affect them. Discrimination applies not only to people of different colour; many other groups of people are also subjected to as much prejudice and discrimination as people of African and Asian origin.

Thirdly, however self-aware we are, it is only as we become involved in cross-cultural counselling that we will truly be able to explore our own values and attitudes towards people from different cultures.

For centuries white nations conquered, then dominated, other races and considered them ignorant and of lower intelligence. These beliefs still lurk in our cultural unconscious. For an example of how insidious the process of cultural superiority is, one only has to look at picture books, adverts and comics, to pick out how discrimination is still being thrust at the reader or viewer. Cross-cultural counselling, then, may be as fraught with difficulty as cross-gender counselling.

The major influences that make for cross-cultural difficulties in counselling are language, education, religion, gender, values, beliefs and attitudes.

Language

Language unites people on the one hand and separates them on the other in a more powerful way than even skin colour does. Language conveys thoughts. Thinking is any cognitive or mental manipulation of ideas, images, symbols, words, propositions, memories, concepts, precepts, beliefs or intentions. Concepts are structured in hierarchies; with increasing complexity the more the original idea is broken down into properties. Conceptual thought often creates difficulty in cross-cultural counselling.

People with English as their second language often have to translate what they have heard into their own language and then retranslate into English before replying. They understand the meanings of broad concepts but not every property in the hierarchy. This difficulty is similar to two people listening to a piece of music. The one may hear only the melody; the other hears all the notes of both melody and harmony.

The way people from other cultures respond in counselling is moderated by the length of time they have spent in the new culture. Skin colour or, indeed, accent (although accent is more open to moderation) is not a reliable guide to how a person will respond. Many people with different skin colours are in fact second-, third- or fourth-generation residents of the UK. In every respect they would respond as anyone else.

Education

Methods of education vary from culture to culture. People who have come through an education system where discussion is the norm are generally more able to deal with sophisticated concepts, while a person (of no matter what culture) who has learned mainly by rote usually experiences difficulty handling them. So it is necessary for the counsellor to be sensitively alert to the cues given out that something has not been understood.

'Talk and chalk' and rote learning are the methods of an authoritarian, obedience-dominated, system of education. An outcome of the authoritarian approach is that experiential learning is difficult. People who have been educated under a heavily authoritarian system expect to be told what to do and what to learn. Many such people cannot see the relevance of experiential work; they have little by which to measure their learning. When they can leave a session with pages of notes or dictation, they feel satisfied that the session has been productive.

This has implications in counselling. Apart from the restriction of conceptual thinking, a relationship of equality, in which the client works towards finding solutions, is to many an alien concept, unproductive and time-wasting. At the same time, the fundamentals of accepted counselling practice conflict with the client's value system.

Religion

Religion has a profound bearing on the values and beliefs of both client and counsellor, on the style of education they have received and on their relationships with the opposite sex. Many people have been saddled with a double authority: an authoritarian style of teaching within a religious system of education. This atmosphere of traditionalism supports the belief that women are inferior to men. Males and females from such a culture develop a deep and unhealthy fear of authority, which shows itself in compliance and submission. It also perpetuates the male–female dominance and submission system.

The male counsellor may then be related to with the same awe and reverence as the priest, as possessing the same god-like function and qualities. Clients from such a background would find a relationship of equality difficult to accept. As most religions are male-centred, clients with a religious-based culture may find it difficult to accept the credibility of female counsellors.

On the one hand, the client (of whichever gender) may not be able to enter into a relationship of active equality and will expect the counsellor to be directive and prescriptive. On the other hand, the female counsellor could be rejected because a woman in a position of perceived authority creates too much ambiguity in the client's belief system.

Aids to cross-cultural counselling

- We should always aim for clarity of expression in the language we use.
- We should be aware of our use of jargon and unfamiliar figures of speech.
- Constant checking for understanding, essential in any counselling, is crucial in cross-cultural counselling; to be aware that the client is agreeing with something when it is not fully understood demonstrates empathy.
- If possible, allotting extra time may be an advantage, in order to facilitate exploration.
- We should be alert to how our personal experiences can colour our judgement; we should also be careful to separate our experiences from other people's prejudices and from myths and legends.
- We should be aware that such moral concepts as truth, honesty, loyalty, politeness and respect may not mean the same in the client's culture as they do in ours.
- In some cultures, showing feelings to a comparative stranger is taboo.
- The client's verbal and non-verbal language should not be filtered through the screen of our own standards. What we might consider 'rude' may be perfectly acceptable in the client's culture. The more we are able to suspend judgement, the more we shall be able to stay on the client's wavelength.

Finally, it has to said that not all people within the white, western culture accept counselling, preferring to work things through for themselves. People from other cultures might find great difficulty in speaking to a stranger about their innermost feelings, preferring to talk with some wise person of their own culture. However, this entry intends to pave the way by highlighting some important areas of potential difficulty when counselling someone from a different culture.

Egan gives some guidelines for integrating diversity and multiculturalism into counselling:

- Place the needs of the client above all other considerations.
- Identify and focus on whatever frame of reference, self-definition or belief system is central to any given client, with consideration for, but not limited to, issues of diversity.
- Select counselling interventions on the basis of the client's agenda. Do not impose a social or political agenda on the counselling relationship.
- Make sure that your own values do not adversely affect a client's best interests.
- Avoid cultural stereotyping. Do not over-generalise. Recognise that within-group differences are often more extensive than between-group differences.
- Do not define diversity narrowly. This client's concern about being unattractive deserves the helper's engagement just as much as that client's concern about racial intolerance.
- Provide opportunities for practitioners to be trained in the working knowledge and skills associated with diversity-sensitive counselling.
- Subject the assumptions, models and techniques of diversity-sensitive counselling to the same scrutiny as other aspects of the counselling profession.
- Create an environment that supports professional tolerance.

Further reading

Dummett, A. (1980) Nationality and citizenship. In: *Conference Report of Further Education in Ethnic Minorities*. National Association for Teachers in Higher Education, London.

Egan, G. (2002) *The Skilled Helper: a problem-management and opportunity-development approach to helping*, 7th edn. Brooks/Cole, Pacific Grove, CA.

Jones, E.E. (1985) Psychotherapy and counselling with black clients. In: *Handbook of Cross-cultural Counselling and Therapy* (ed. P. Pederon). Praeger, London.

Katz, J.H. (1978) *White Awareness: handbook for anti-racism training*. University of Oklahoma Press, Norman, OK.

Lago, C. and Thompson, J. (1989) Counselling and race. In: *Handbook of Counselling in Britain* (eds W. Dryden, D. Charles-Edwards and R. Woolfe). Tavistock/Routledge, London.

Sue, D.W. (1981) *Counselling the Culturally Different*. John Wiley, New York.

MYERS-BRIGGS TYPE INDICATOR

The Myers-Briggs Type Indicator (MBTI) is a widely used psychometric test, based on the work of Carl Jung and developed by Isabel Myers and her mother Katherine Briggs. It measures eight personality preferences along four dimensions:

Extroversion (E) →Introversion (I)
Sensing (S) →Intuition (N)
Thinking (T) →Feeling (F)
Judgement (J) →Perception (P)

Generalisations

- People who have similar strengths in the dimensions will seem to 'click', to arrive at decisions more quickly and to be on the same wavelength. Their decisions, however, may suffer because of their similar blind spots.

- People with dissimilar strengths in the dimensions will not be on the same wavelength and may have difficulty accepting the views, opinions and actions of the other person. Decisions arrived at through their interaction will, however, generally be more sound and therefore more acceptable.
- The parts of our dimensions we don't use much – the 'Shadow' side – we are more sensitive about and are more prone to react negatively when they are criticised. As a result, conflict may occur when we must work with our Shadow sides or when our deficiencies are pointed out by others.
- We are generally attracted to people who display similar preferences. On the other hand, we are often drawn to others because of the strengths we observe in them – the flip side of our own preferences.
- Our values, beliefs, decisions and actions are all influenced by the four stronger dimensions of our typology.
- Although our preferences are fixed, we can work with our Shadow sides and strengthen them in order to overcome problems that result from the weaknesses.

A person's type is made up of the four dominant functions. Helping a client to understand his personality preferences is just one more way in which the client will gain insight into how to mange his life with less stress.

Preferences and communication

- Es may feel under pressure in a group to do all the talking both for themselves and for Is. Is may feel ignored by Es, who are often more willing to enter a conversation and keep it going.
- Ss may feel irritated by Ns, who jump to conclusions (sometimes correctly) without working through obvious stages. Ns may feel irritated by the caution of Ss, who, to them, often take a long time to arrive at conclusions.

Table 7: *Personality types*

Extroversion/introversion	
Extroversion/introversion describes the way we relate to the world around us.	
Extroversion People who are more extroverted than introverted (Es):	Introversion People who are more introverted than extroverted (Is):
Are generally sociable and outgoing Relate to people and things around them Endeavour to make their decisions in agreement with the demands and expectations of others Are interested in variety and in working with people May become impatient with long, slow tasks Do not mind being interrupted by people	Prefer making decisions independently of other people Tend to be quiet, diligent at working alone Tend to be socially reserved Dislike being interrupted while working Are liable to forget names and faces

Sensing/intuition
Sensing/intuition describes the way we perceive the world.

Sensing People who are more sensing than intuitive (Ss):	Intuition People who have more intuition than sensing (Ns):
Prefer what is concrete, real, factual, structured, tangible, here-and-now Tend to mistrust their intuition Think in careful, detail-by detail accuracy Remember real facts Make few errors of fact May possibly miss a grasp of the overall	Prefer possibilities, theories, patterns, the overall, inventions and the new Become bored with the nitty-gritty details, the concrete and actual Feel that facts must relate to concepts Think and discuss in spontaneous leaps of intuition May leave out or neglect details Find that problem-solving comes easily May show a tendency to make errors of fact.

Thinking/feeling
Thinking/feeling describes the way we make judgements.

Thinking People with more thinking than feeling (head types, Ts):	Feeling People with more feeling than thinking (heart types, Fs):
Make judgements about life, people, occurrences and things based on logic, analysis and hard evidence Avoid irrationality and decisions based on feelings and values Are interested in logic, analysis, and verifiable conclusions Are less comfortable with empathy, values and personal warmth May step on others' feelings and needs without realising it Often neglect to take into consideration the values of others	Make judgements about life, people, occurrences and things based on empathy, warmth and personal values Are more interested in people and feelings than in impersonal logic, analysis and things Feel that conciliation and harmony are more important than in being on top or achieving impersonal goals Get along with people in general

Judgement/perception
Judgement/perception describes the way we make decisions.

Judgement People with more judgement than perception (Js):	Perception People who have more perception than judgement (Ps):
Are decisive, firm, and sure Like setting goals and sticking to them Want to make decisions and get on to the next project Will leave an unfinished project behind and go on to new tasks and not look back, if that's what has to be done Give priority to work over play Are good at meeting deadlines Tend to be judgemental of themselves and other people	Always want to know more before making decisions and judgements Are open, flexible, adaptive, non-judgemental Are able to appreciate all sides of an issue Always welcome new perspectives and new information about issues Are difficult to pin down Hate working to deadlines Are often so indecisive and non-committal that they frustrate themselves and other people Are often involved in many tasks Give priority to play rather than work

- Ts may feel irritated by Fs, who do not approach a problem logically and want to talk about how they feel. Fs may feel irritated by Ts, who want to analyse everything with cold logic before making a judgement.
- Js may feel irritated by Ps, who never seem to be able to make a decision, always want to put things off and always want to put play first. Ps may feel irritated by Js, who insist on having everything planned, won't let things just happen and insist upon work first.

Temperament and marriage

Although this section discusses marriage, the principles apply to all intimate relationships.

To deal with all 16 types would be beyond the scope of this book. Instead, the four basic temperaments of Kiersey as applied to marriage will be summarised below: SP, SJ, NT, NF.

Many factors influence our choice of partner: social, economic, educational, physiological, racial and cultural. Where there is choice, temperament is a powerful attraction.

The Shadow

Carl Jung put forward the view that we search for a mate who represents our shadow, in order to complement, or bring completion.

The Shadow is:

- The things we have no wish to be
- The negative, dark, primitive side of the self
- What is inferior, worthless, uncontrollable and unacceptable
- All the parts of us that are unacceptable either to us or to our idea of what other people will think if they knew about them
- At the same time the Shadow is what makes us fully human, because without it we are not complete.
- In typology, the Shadow is made up of our undeveloped preferences.
- If person A's E, S, F and J are all low this would make up his Shadow.
- If person B's I, N, T and P are all low this would make up her Shadow.
- Part of the work they have to engage in is starting to feel comfortable with their underdeveloped preferences.

Pairing

When two come together as a couple, a process of merging begins and, over time, they come to be more like each other. Sometimes, however, one, or both, is not content for time to work the change. They bring out the heavy guns to try to force change on the other.

It would seem that by far the greatest source of broken relationships is because partners seem hell-bent on forcing change. The partner is treated as an inanimate chunk of marble to be sculpted to the partner's wish.

A marriage, based on the hidden agenda of 'You're not what I want, so I will change you' has already within it the seeds of destruction. When we are forced into someone else's preconceived blueprint, we end up betraying ourselves or rebelling.

Differences in type between people may give rise to friction, although this can often be diminished or eliminated when the origins are understood. Opposites have much to offer each other, provided we accept each other's differences as being valid and worth while.

Extroversion/introversion (E/I) differences

- The major differences appear to be sociability versus privacy.
- When the work of the I is socially demanding, time and space is needed at home to recharge the emotional batteries – some silence and a chance to think quietly is essential.
- On the other hand, E requires an opportunity to talk, especially if that has been denied during the day.
- The E partner is more likely to reach decisions by talking them out and getting feedback.
- The I partner is more likely to work things out then give a conclusion. When this happens the E partner feels excluded from mutual sharing – something of great importance to the E.

The sensing perceptive (SP) partner

- As with most other activities, sex for the SP is there to be enjoyed – to the full – now, not later. They respond to tactile, auditory and visual sexual stimuli.
- A relationship that develops with great speed may soon become a burden on the SP independent spirit. So, just as quickly, the relationship may end, and the burden be shed.
- The SP often operates on a short fuse, then it's back to normal. Confrontation, however, is difficult; the preferred course of action is to retreat into silence. When under pressure they can become very tactless or even cruel. This may also lead them to be insensitive to any harm they may have done.
- They are not good at arranging priorities and they are so caught up living in the present, that they may overlook their obligations.
- The SP delights in giving and receiving gifts, often extravagant ones. Gifts may be at the expense of necessities; something which may irritate the partner.
- The SP has little respect for saving for the future. Living for today is central to the SP temperament. Money, sex, friends, are all there to be enjoyed – now. They are often into the latest and the best.
- The SP finds an outlet for creativity in arts and crafts. Clutter does not seem to bother them. They are drawn to strong colours. Plants are likely to adorn every windowsill.
- SP parents expect, and get, obedience from children, though it is balanced with autonomy and freedom. They are not given to sentimentality.

The sensing judging (SJ) partner

- The idea of enjoying or needing sex does not sit easily with the SJ. Sex is a service offered for security and comfort. Many injunctions surround sex not being 'the thing'.
- Purpose is important to the SJ. Children are there for the purpose of extending the family line. Family history is kept alive with stories and anecdotes.
- Affection is expressed in standard, almost stereotyped, ritualised ways. Gifts are intended to be treasured. Flowers fade and wilt so will seldom be given.
- Possessions are significant, but they are valued for their usefulness and long-lasting qualities. They should be functional and without show.
- The SJ is careful with money; budgeting, planning well for the future, investment in insurance, bonds and savings accounts. Sacrifice now for benefit later.
- Home may assume a focus to the exclusion of all else. Spouse and children may become the reason for existing; life without them is unthinkable.
- Children are expected to toe the standard line. The SJ has a strong sense of right and wrong, and they tend to see things in black and white terms.
- The SJ is the typical 'pillar of society'; involved in church, civic or community activities. Small talk is time-wasting and frivolous. Punctuality is a virtue.
- Life with an SJ is predictable and safe. They like to take the same weeks of the year and the same place for holidays, going with the same like-minded friends.

The intuitive thinking (NT) partner

- The NT may appear cold, serious and unemotional. The intellect is likely to get in the way of sexual enjoyment. Public display of affection does not appeal.
- The NT wastes few words, and rarely states the obvious. This can lead to problems with the partner to be told, 'I would have thought it was perfectly obvious I love you'.
- If a relationship fails, the NT is just as likely to shrug it off as 'one of those things'. Once committed, however, the NT seldom looks back.
- The NT does not tolerate emotional conflict such as quarrels; debate and logical argument, yes, but acrimony is destructive. They will walk away from emotionalism.
- Spontaneity and play are difficult. Pleasure is in discussing abstract issues, playing around with words and their meanings. They are often offended by practical jokes.
- The pursuit of wealth rarely interests NT people. Possessions are accumulated, not as symbols of status, simply to be enjoyed. They like to feel comfortable. The home of the NT is likely to be bulging with books, as representing knowledge. The partner may feel that the thirst for knowledge is at the expense of family priorities.

- The NT often needs to be reminded of birthdays and anniversaries. Family responsibilities are taken seriously. Parenthood is a pleasure, although they often give the impression of not being emotionally involved.

The intuitive feeling (NF) partner

- NF people are skilled in the art of romantic relationships. They respond with tenderness, sympathy and frequent passionate expressions of love. The partner of an NF will always feel that this is perfect love.
- Before marriage, both male and female NFs are often totally blind to any flaws in the loved one. Later, the male NF can lose interest in the partner and continue his quest for perfect love. The female NF sees only perfection, rarely the flaws. For her, the main delight is to bring sexual pleasure to her mate. To fall in love once is a lifetime fulfilment.
- They rarely forget birthdays and anniversaries; however, they can be deeply wounded when people don't remember their milestones.
- The NF is naturally empathic, which can be both a strength and a weakness. Someone who has felt encouraged to become dependent may then feel rejected by the NF when suddenly told, virtually, 'Stand on your own feet'. This is not being unkind or callous; it is the only way the NF can handle such overwhelming dependency.
- NF people can become so overloaded with their own concerns that they find it difficult to cope with conflict or pain of those close to them.
- NF people often fail to organise priorities. The demands of other people may take precedence over family needs. NF people are always seeking new relationships, which may be at the expense of those already established.
- No other type has the same capacity for empathic understanding, and a relationship with an NF holds the promise of warmth, appreciation and support.

How personality preferences might influence counselling

- People who are too extroverted often get on people's nerves; someone who is too introverted often has difficulty making contact with people at all.
- People who are high on sensing can get so caught up in counting the trees that they miss the beauty of the wood; people who are too intuitive often seem 'away with the fairies'.
- People who are too high on thinking often intellectualise everything; people who are too high on feeling often swamp others by their warmth.
- People who are too high on judgement often become judge, jury and executioner; people who are too high on perception often give the impression of being grown-up children.

These are generalisations, however, about how client and counsellor interact, and an understanding of what is going on could be significantly enhanced by knowing why you, the counsellor, prefers certain ways of working above others.

Counselling is almost always linked to change. What follows demonstrates how each of the eight preferences may help or hinder change in counselling.

Extroverted/introverted types

The E part will tend to accept change with enthusiasm, mainly because change brings with it the possibility of new relationships. If anything, the E may rush into change with open arms before counting the cost. The E part of us likes to talk, to hold the floor, but might have trouble listening.

The I part proceeds with caution. Change for the introvert brings more questions than answers, and that is unsettling. The I part likes to take things in, digest them, then – and only then – speak, and the response is given with caution. The E part would be less comfortable with silence than the I part, which might prompt you to say anything just to keep things moving. The E part tends not to like reflection, which is one of the strengths of the I.

Sensing/intuitive types

The S part tends to resist change, because it disturbs the status quo. When the S part cannot find the next logical piece in the plan, there is anxiety. S needs to know what is, to have hands on. The S is cautious, rarely jumps to conclusions and often needs careful explanation and to work through logical stages.

The N part enjoys possibilities and revels in the unknown and new beginnings. N is creative. Change energises. Because the N sees things with the intuition, it often jumps ahead to make what might seem illogical conclusions but which are often correct. The S prefers to work with the obvious; the N is comfortable working with the imagination.

Thinking/feeling types

T asks if it is 'true or false'. Analysis requires time, so if change is hurried, before the logic is fully accepted, it will produce stress and will be rejected. Thus if something is not logical it is likely that the client will feel irritated. The thinking part would prefer to debate than to discuss feelings and will generally want to make judgements based on logic and reason.

F asks if it is 'agreeable or disagreeable'. Change would be acceptable provided there was sufficient attention paid to the 'human' aspect and ample time for discussion. The F tends to become irritated if asked to be too logical and reasoning. Feelings are what make the world go round, not cold logic.

Judgement/perception types

The J part excels in plans, decisions and conclusions. If change is protracted by people who can't make up their minds, stress is likely to occur. The J part will plan an event well in advance and expect other people to comply. The J part puts work first and is often judgemental of people.

The P part puts off making decisions. Open-mindedness is a P strength. Putting perceptive people under pressure, such as deadlines, will create stress. The J part would be comfortable working towards set goals, whereas the P part would find it difficult to look that far ahead, as they prefer to live in the moment.

Although the eight preferences have been presented as if they were separate entities, each is modified by all the other preferences. However, having an idea of basic preferences is one way of making sense of what is happening in counselling. When counsellors are aware of their own and their client's personality preferences, even though they may not work specifically with the Myers-Briggs Type Indicator, they will certainly add another dimension to the counselling interaction.

Further reading

Bayne, R. (1990) A new direction for the Myers-Briggs Type Indicator. *Personnel Management,* March.

Kiersey, D. (1998) *Please Understand Me II.* Prometheus Nemesis, Del Mar, CA.

Myers, I. (1980) *Gifts Differing,* Consulting Psychologists Press, Palo Alto, CA.

Myers, I. (1980) *Introduction to Type.* Consulting Psychologists Press, Palo Alto, CA.

Myers, I. and McCaulley, M.H. (1985) *Manual: a guide to the development and use of the Myers-Briggs Type Indicator.* Consulting Psychologists Press, Palo Alto, CA.

Stewart, W. and Martin, A. (1999) *Going for Counselling: how to work with your counsellor to develop awareness and essential life skills.* How to Books, Oxford.

N

Narcissism

In Greek mythology, Narcissus was the son of the river god Cephissus and the nymph Leiriope. Narcissus was beautiful and his mother was told that he would have a long life provided he never looked upon his own features. He fell in love with his own reflection in the waters of a spring and pined away and died. The narcissus flower sprang up where he died. The myth possibly arose from the Greek superstition that it was unlucky to see one's own reflection.

Freud used the myth to describe a morbid condition in which sexual energy, which naturally focuses firstly on self and then upon the parent and then on others, remains focused on self. The person can rarely achieve satisfactory sexual relationships because of mistrust of other people.

A narcissistic personality disorder (NPD) is characterised by:

- A grandiose sense of self-importance (e.g. exaggerates achievements and talents, expects to be recognised as superior without commensurate achievements)
- A need for attention and admiration that is exhibitionistic in character
- A preoccupation with fantasies of success, wealth, power, esteem or ideal love
- Inappropriate emotional reactions to the criticisms of others
- The narcissistic adult person is cut off from others, self-absorbed, vain and somewhat superior in manner
- Belief that he is 'special' and unique and can only be understood by, or should associate with, other special or high-status people (or institutions)
- Requirement for excessive admiration
- A sense of entitlement, i.e. unreasonable expectations of especially favourable treatment or automatic compliance with his expectations
- Being interpersonally exploitative, i.e. takes advantage of others to achieve his own ends
- Lack of empathy: is unwilling to recognise or identify with the feelings and needs of others
- Being often envious of others or believing that others are envious of him
- Showing arrogant, haughty behaviours or attitudes.

It is suggested that narcissism develops when a child's fears, failures and vulnerabilities are responded to with disdain, criticism or neglect. However, no hard and fast evidence exists as to why some people develop a narcissistic personality.

Cognitive effects

Beck and Freeman list typical beliefs associated with narcissistic personality disorder:

- I am a very special person
- Since I am so superior, I am entitled to special treatment and privileges
- I don't have to be bound by the rules that apply to other people
- It is very important to get recognition, praise and admiration
- If others don't respect my status, they should be punished
- Other people should satisfy my needs
- Other people should recognise how special I am
- It's intolerable if I'm not accorded my due respect or don't get what I'm entitled to
- Other people don't deserve the admiration or riches that they get
- People have no right to criticise me
- No one's needs should interfere with my own
- Since I am so talented, people should go out of their way to promote my career
- Only people as brilliant as I am understand me
- I have every reason to expect grand things.

People with NPD won't (or can't) change their behaviour even when it causes problems at work or when other people complain about the way they act, or when their behaviour causes a lot of emotional distress to others. They seldom if ever admit to being distressed by their own behaviour – they always blame other people for any problems. NPD interferes with people's functioning in their occupations and in their relationships.

Levels of impairment

1. **Mild impairment,** which may result in occasional minor problems, but the person is generally doing pretty well.
2. **Moderate impairment,** which may result in:
   - Missing days from work, household duties or school
   - Significant performance problems as a wage-earner, homemaker or student
   - Frequently avoiding or alienating friends
   - Significant risk of harming self or others (frequent suicidal preoccupation; often neglecting family, or frequently abusing others or committing criminal acts).
3. **Severe impairment,** which may result in:
   - Staying in bed all day
   - Totally alienating all friends and family
   - Severe risk of harming self or others (failing to maintain personal hygiene; persistent danger of suicide, abuse or crime).

Counselling a person who is strongly narcissistic is a long-term process involving a relationship in which the client's self-involvement is slowly changed to involvement with others, confronting the client's defences of devaluation and idealisation to avoid acknowledging weaknesses and interpreting what some consider are the basic issues of anger and envy. Other therapists allow an idealising transference to develop, constantly reflecting what is taking place, until disillusionment sets in and then the work is to establish a positive transference and a more satisfying relationship. Group therapy is often useful alongside individual therapy.

Further reading

Beck, A.T and Freeman A, (1990) *Cognitive Therapy of Personality Disorders.* Guilford, New York.
Diagnostic and Statistical Manual of Mental Disorders (DSM-IV) (1994) American Psychiatric Association, Washington DC.
Jacoby, M. (1981) Reflections on H. Kohut's concept of narcissism. *Journal of Analytical Psychology,* 26(1): 19–32.
www.mentalhealth.com
www.halcyon.com
groups.msn.com/NARCISSISTICPERSONALITYDISORDER – this website has some useful case studies.

NEURO-LINGUISTIC PROGRAMMING (NLP)

NLP is a model developed by Bandler and Grinder. It describes how the brain works with language, and how language relates to other brain functions, and how this knowledge may enable people to achieve more satisfaction in their behaviour.

NLP builds on the work, and uses some of the techniques, of other communications theorists. Techniques specific to NLP are:

- **Anchoring:** Similar to the behavioural technique of conditioning
- **Eye movements:** A very precise technique, using the clients' eye movements to gain access to their inner states.

Eye movements indicate whether we are:

- Making pictures
- Listening to internal tapes
- Concentrating on feelings.

Following a person's eye movements gives lots of information about that person's mental processes at the moment, but not the content. When reference is made to 'right', 'left', 'down', it means the other person's, not yours.

Visual:	eyes up and right,
	eyes up and left,
	eyes straight ahead and
	out of focus.
Auditory:	eyes level right,
	eyes level left,
	eyes down left.
Kinaesthetic:	eyes down right.

Information that comes through the kinaesthetic channel is genuine and not usually open to being disguised. Each of the three 'representational systems' finds some words easier to understand than others.

Visual people work with pictures and may be recognised by:

- Conversation which contains many visual words: 'I see what you mean'; 'I get the picture'
- They have a tendency to breathe high up in the chest.
- Their voice tempo is faster than the auditory or kinaesthetic modes.
- They have a tendency to tighten the neck and shoulder muscles in order to make the pictures more clear; this is likely to lead to neck tension.
- They are more able to recount colours and shapes, and they may be deeply affected by room colour.
- They seldom get lost, and are able to remember directions.

Some typical visual words:

- Clear
- Graphic
- Perspective
- Picture
- Short-sighted
- Spectacle.

Auditory people work with sounds and may be recognised by:

- Conversations that contain a predominance of auditory words: 'That rings a bell'; 'I hear you'.
- They have a tendency to breathe in the middle of the chest.
- They trust sounds.
- They do not generally trust feelings.
- They often use internal dialogue, and in consequence may have difficulty making decisions, because thoughts go round and round.

Some typical auditory words:

- Alarm
- Harmonise
- Hear
- Ring
- Static
- Tune.

Kinaesthetic people work with feelings and may be recognised by:

- Conversations that contain a predominance of feeling words: 'I get a feel for the problem'; 'Can you remove the stumbling block?'; 'Help me untangle this knot'
- They have a tendency to breathe low down.
- Their voices are deeper than the other two modes.

- They like to have space to check out their feelings.
- They like or hate, feel warm or cold about lots of issues.

Some typical kinaesthetic words:

- Flat
- Impact
- Impress
- Move
- Tangle
- Touch.

Most people favour one mode. Sometimes we use two, not often do we use all three. Sensory awareness is enhanced by opening all doors.

People who are 'thinkers' tend to filter out the communication, thus making detection of eye movement difficult. An open-ended question such as, 'Tell me about your best experience with this', may evoke a sequence of eye movements, and words to go with them, and give insight into the obscured mode.

Matching language systems

It has been suggested that using the same primary language system as someone else could help to build rapport.

It also seems that people will learn best when we present something to them in their primary representational systems.

Visuals:

- Remember graphs, illustrations and seeing new things.

Auditories:

- Remember sounds and will be stimulated by changes in vocal tone, pitch and pacing.

Kinaesthetics:

- Learn best from 'hands on' experience and will remember how they 'felt'. Thus, more impact may be gained from showing things to visuals; providing interesting sounds for auditories; and working alongside kinaesthetics.
- If a person is kinaesthetic or visual, and the presentation is verbal, the content may not be easily translated, and the person may not 'get it'.
- Of course, we must first be aware of our own primary and secondary language systems. Then, by paying attention to the predicates used by others, we can determine the systems valued by those others.

Examples:

The following example illustrates *mismatched* language systems, with a kinaesthetic teacher and a visual student.

Student: *I just can't see myself doing any better in this test.*
Teacher: Well, how do you feel about not being able to do better?
Student: *I just don't have a clear picture of what you want from me.*
Teacher: How do you feel about not being able to handle things we are doing?
Student: *I don't see what you're trying to do. It's really hazy to me.*

It is apparent that the teacher is not paying attention to the language system used by the student, who 'sees' the teacher as a person who just does not portray things clearly.

On the other hand, the teacher may 'feel' frustrated in his attempts to 'reach' this student. Neither of them profits from this type of interaction.

The following example illustrates *matched* language systems, where both are visuals.

Student: *I just can't see myself doing any better in this training session.*
Teacher: It did appear to me that you looked confused when I was giving out the work assignment.

Further reading

Bandler, R. and Grinder, J. (1976) *Structure of Magic* (vols 1 and 2). Science and Behaviour Books, Palo Alto, CA.

Bandler, R. and Grinder, J. (1979) *Frogs into Princes*. Real People Press, Moab, Utah.

Bandler, R. and Grinder, J. (1982) *Reframing*. Real People Press, Moab, Utah.

Grinder, J. et al. (1973) *Guide to Transformational Grammar*. Holt, Rinehart & Winston, New York.

Laborde, G.Z. (1987) *Influencing with Integrity*. Syntony Publishing, Palo Alto, CA.

O

OBSERVING COUNSELLING

Sometimes it is possible to observe a counsellor at work. More often, observing is associated with counselling training, where students observe each other. Observing means listening to:

- What is said
  How it is said
  What is not said

and watching the unconscious communication of body language.
  Some guidelines:

- Did the counsellor seem certain/uncertain in the counselling role?
- How was the client put at ease?
- What evidence was there of rapport?
- What evidence was there of empathy?
- What evidence was there of acceptance of the client by the counsellor?
- What evidence was there of genuine concern?
- Did the counsellor concentrate on facts at the expense of feelings?
- How would you rate the counsellor's listening with the 'third ear' and responding skills?
- Was there any evidence of argument?
- How did you feel as the observer?
- How would you describe the pace of the interview?
- The particular comments by the counsellor that seemed most helpful were...
- What evidence was there of the counsellor 'reading between the lines'?
- What body language was there?
  - Eye contact
  - Personal spacing and distance
  - Gestures
  - Body posture
  - Facial expressions
  - Tone of voice
  - Timing of speech
  - Evidence of being relaxed/tense.

The above questions are a useful self-appraisal.

OWNING THE PROBLEM (SEE ALSO: COMMUNICATION MODES OF VIRGINIA SATIR)

Owning the problem 'as mine' is a vital stage to be reached before effective counselling can really get going, just as alcoholics must reach this stage before they can start to climb out of the pit into which they have dropped.

Owning that the problem is mine is only part of what could be a difficulty in counselling: owning feelings may be equally important. Owning feelings depends on being able to recognise and identify them, and an essential part of counselling might simply be helping the client to do just that. Not owning the problem could lead to blaming someone or something else.

Blame

The *Oxford English Dictionary* gives the following definitions of 'blame':

1. The action of censuring; expression of disapprobation; imputation of demerit on account of a fault or blemish; reproof; censure; reprehension
2. Responsibility for anything wrong, culpability
3. To find fault with; to censure (an action, a person for his action): the opposite of 'to praise'.

Thus blame is making a judgement of responsibility against someone. We can innocently blame people for how we feel – 'He makes me feel ...'. This is blaming the other person. Such a reaction would be better put: 'I feel ... at what you have done'. 'I was startled when you jumped out on me', not 'You made me jump'. This is placing responsibility outside of one's self. It is passive and turns the person into a victim.

The rationale is that nobody can make us feel anything. The fact that we do feel something has to be acknowledged but we also have to acknowledge the feeling as ours. Saying 'You made me ...' is, in a way, blaming the other person and is guaranteed to rouse a 'fight' response.

> *Neither he, she, nor they ever make me feel this way. Rather, it's the thoughts I choose that do the trick. That makes me feel sick.*
>
> Dr Gerald Kushel

Blame is anger directed outwards at someone else. But blame may also be self-blame, whereby the person internalises the feelings of responsibility. Self-blame is detected in such sentences as, 'I should have known better', 'Idiot!', 'I never get things right'. Such discounting language has a detrimental effect on self-esteem.

Blame is linked with guilt (see: Guilt and shame) and guilt may be anger turned inwards. Many people spend much of their life accepting blame for what goes wrong and feeling guilty over what is clearly not their fault. This is closely allied to the martyr attitude (see below), where the person is weighed down by constantly feeling hard done by. Self-blame is also to do with making oneself socially acceptable. Very often such feelings border on the delusional and are not amenable to logic or reason.

Feelings of self-blame rarely respond to direct confrontation. Changing the word to 'responsibility' may be more effective.

The person who, when driving a car, kills a child who runs out in front of it would quite naturally feel guilt, blame and responsibility. Such feelings and thoughts as, 'If only I'd been driving more carefully' or 'more slowly', 'If only I'd been more observant' would be perfectly normal. They are all the sorts of self-questions that take place during grief.

The person who kills innocently is just as likely to be caught up in grief as the parents of the dead child. If such thoughts persist beyond what is normal for grieving and if, say, 10 years later, the person is still blaming himself for the death, here is a case of chronic self-blame bordering on delusion.

Many people are caught up in chronic self-blame when they are the innocent victims of, for example, crimes committed by parents, the relatives of someone who has committed suicide or the survivors of some horrific accident.

> *It is extremely common in Western cultures for clients to view their struggles in a 'linear' or 'blaming' context. The philosophy underlying this context is that there is one underlying reason to a problem for which there is one sole cure. The problem is being created by something or someone and if only the specific cause can be uncovered, a solution will become readily apparent. Clients often regard counsellors as the experts who will discover the cause of their pain and provide the cure. One of our initial tasks, then, as counsellors is to indicate that we are facilitators rather than experts. Our job is to divert our clients' energies from searching for an underlying treatable cause towards trying to view the context of the problem from a different angle.*
>
> Gunzburg and Stewart, 1994

Martin Shephard (1973) says:

> *Blame is totally illogical. It is a game we can well do without. If something doesn't work out the way you or I would like it to, disappointment is natural enough. Blaming yourself, however, only adds further unhappiness. You are already disappointed. Why add further aggravation in the form of self-blame? And if you blame* me – or some third party – *for your disappointment, that will only get our hackles up ... Blame of other people usually occurs when they fail to live up to* your *expectations. But why should they? Would you be willing to live up to theirs?*

Blame applied to counselling

Even though clients may blame, attributing blame gets them nowhere. So changing the word to something like 'responsibility' may have the effect of changing something in their minds. Otherwise, if they keep on attributing blame, it may be necessary to change tack and work with the underlying anger.

Counselling is not about establishing innocence or guilt or of attributing blame, punishment or judgement. One of the tasks might be to help clients accept responsibility for their own actions and their consequences. All the time the client engages in 'passing the buck' movement forward will be stopped. Owning the problem is a crucial step in the client's progress towards healing. Helping clients take responsibility for their thoughts, feelings and behaviours means that they stop blaming. Attributing motives, claiming that 'the devil made me do it', is a sneaky, dishonest attempt to be irresponsible.

But as counselling is a two-way street, it is sometimes easy for counsellors to 'blame' clients when counselling does not go well. When counsellors own their thoughts and feelings, both counsellors and clients know where they are and can respond more authentically. We are all entitled to have thoughts and feelings.

Being aware of them and the differences between them is one way to improve communication. However, blaming someone is one way of avoiding self-examination. 'If I pass the buck, then I don't have to bear the consequences.'

The martyr attitude

The martyr attitude is based on the belief that sorrows and troubles are evil machinations heaped upon the defenceless heads of suffering saints. Martyrs will invariably use the concepts of religious duty and spiritual living as flights from reality.

Behaviourally, martyrs shoulder other people's burdens and then complain to make sure that everyone around commiserates with them. The burdens of others weigh them down and they experience little joy or peace.

Martyrs are subservient and humble and create an impression of everlasting goodness, sweetness and light. Were the Inquisition to return, they would be the first to be burned at the stake. They often need to enjoy poor health; in a curious way it makes them feel 'good'. Martyrs accept all the blame that others heap upon them, for that is their perceived role in life.

Counselling, even of the most intense sort, is difficult. What martyrs gain from being ill is more than they would gain from being well. So, identifying the gains and losses is a positive step along the road.

Counselling is not a one-way process; it involves the client and the counsellor. Just as the client has to own his feelings, so does the counsellor need to acknowledge her part in the interaction and this would invariably involve owning one's feelings, which are generated within the relationship. It might not be appropriate to disclose all feelings to the client, although this would depend on the approach one is using, but certainly in debriefing or recording, or in supervision, one's feelings, unless owned, will interfere with the counselling relationship.

Further reading

Gunzburg, J.C. and Stewart, W. (1994) *The Grief Counselling Casebook*. Stanley Thornes, Cheltenham (pages 57–58) (now out of print but available on line at www.compassion-in-business.co.uk/fellowship/willstew.htm).

Rowe, D. (1971) Poor prognosis in a case of depression as predicted by the repertory grid. *British Journal of Psychiatry*, **118**: 297–300.

Shephard, M. (1973, reprinted 1994) *Do-it-yourself Psychotherapy*. Optima, London.

P

Parables and Metaphors (see also: bibliotherapy)

Parables

Parables, fables and allegories are forms of imaginative literature or the spoken word, so constructed that the reader or listener is encouraged to look for meanings hidden beneath the literal surface of the fiction.

A poet may describe the ascent of a hill in such a way that each physical step corresponds to a new stage in the soul's progress towards a higher level of existence.

An allegory is usually a long narrative full of symbols conveying a moral message. Well-known allegories include *The Pilgrim's Progress, The Divine Comedy, Animal Farm, Gulliver's Travels* and *The Picture of Dorian Gray*.

Fables and parables are short, simple forms of allegory, usually about animals or inanimate objects, who behave as though they are human. Fables tend towards detailed, sharply observed realism, sometimes satirical, and use impossible events to teach their lesson. The 200 or so fables of Aesop (6th century BC) are probably the best-known collection, although other writers have achieved acclaim: John Gay and Edward Moore (England) and La Fontaine (France) are three examples.

Parables also tell a simple story with a moral message, this time about humans, and depend heavily on analogy. The story of the Good Samaritan in the New Testament is an example. Only the elite can decipher the inner core of truth of the parable. Christ's disciples had 'ears to hear'.

Parables possess a certain mystery that makes them useful for teaching spiritual values. The counsellor can use stories (fictional or true, taken from literature or the Bible or from clinical experience) to draw analogies with some aspect of the client's life, to show how another client successfully solved a similar problem. Such a technique must be used with care, lest it put undue pressure on the client. The essential ingredient is the symbolic connection between the story told and the client's problem.

Metaphors

A metaphor is a figure of speech, an indirect method of communication, by which two distinctly separate elements are brought together in comparison to form a new meaning and where an abstract concept is expressed by means of analogy.

Metaphors abound in everyday conversation: the arms of a chair; the legs of a table; a sparkling personality; rivers of blood. The ability to use metaphors is a right brain activity.

The therapist needs to be able to decode the client's metaphors and so assist the development of insight. In the same way, the client needs help to understand the metaphors used by the therapist.

The difference between a symbol and a metaphor is that the symbol *represents* something else, while a metaphor *is* something else. Interpretation of metaphors is central to psychoanalysis. It is possible to work within the metaphor, rather than tackle it directly. The use of a metaphor is useful when working with resistance, because it is indirect.

Metaphors, along with myths, parable and symbols are used in the process of transformation, of metamorphosis, for example:

- Seed/ovum – womb state
- Larva – separation, ego development
- Chrysalis – intermediate stage of growth
- Imago – fully unfolded being that is able to move in other dimensions.

Ten classical metaphors

1. From dream-sleep to awakening
2. From illusion to realisation
3. From darkness to enlightenment
4. From imprisonment to liberation
5. From fragmentation to wholeness
6. From separation to oneness
7. From being on a journey to arriving at the destination
8. From being in exile to coming home
9. From seed to flowering tree
10. From death to rebirth.

Further reading

Black, M. (1962) *Models and Metaphors*. Cornell University Press, Ithaca, NY.

Cade, B.W. (1982) Some uses of metaphor. *Australian Journal of Family Therapy*, 3: 135–140.

Felner, C. (1976) The use of teaching stories in conjoint family therapy. *Family Process*, 15: 427–433.

Gordon, D. (1978) *Therapeutic Metaphors*. Meta Publications, CA.

Gunzburg, J.C. (1997) *Healing through Meeting: Martin Buber's approach to psychotherapy*. Jessica Kingsley, London.

Metzner, R. (1980) Ten classical metaphors of self-transformation. *The Journal of Transpersonal Psychology*, **12(1)**: 47–62.

Te Selle, S. (1975) *Speaking in Parables: a study in metaphor and theology*. SCM Press, London.

http://www.edgeoftheforest.com/metaphors.htm

PARAPHRASING AND REFLECTING

Paraphrasing the facts

A paraphrase is a brief response, in the hearer's own words, that captures the main points of the content of what the other person has said. It may condense or expand what has been said.

In general conversation, many assumptions are made about what has been said. Counselling is not an 'ordinary' conversation. Effective paraphrasing is part of effective listening, which ensures understanding.

Words carry feelings, so not only is it necessary to understand the client's words, we must also try to understand why particular words are used in preference to others. If clients have been expressing their thoughts with difficulty, then is a good time to paraphrase. Letting clients hear the meaning as understood by someone else may help them to clarify more precisely what they do mean. Paraphrasing may echo feeling words without responding to them.

Our response need not be a repetition of the details. Rather, we paraphrase the client's content by summarising and using our own words. Paraphrasing is not parroting. A paraphrased response will capture the main points communicated by the client in a brief statement, thus ensuring that the client clearly understands our summary.

A useful format for responding to content is:

- 'You're saying . . .' or
- 'In other words . . .' or
- 'It sounds as if . . .'

Such formulated responses can sound stilted unless freshness is retained.

Reflecting the feelings

Reflecting concentrates on the feelings within a statement. Paraphrasing and reflecting are invariably linked and it may be artificial to try to separate them. Reflecting feelings accurately depends on empathic understanding.

Pity = feeling for
Sympathy = feeling like
Empathy = feeling with.

Neither pity nor sympathy is constructive. Reflecting involves listening and understanding, then communicating that understanding. If understanding remains locked up within us, we contribute little to the helping process.

Being able to reflect feelings involves viewing the world from the clients' frame of reference – what their thoughts, feelings and behaviours mean to them.

Effective responding shows that we accept people. It does not act as a 'stopper' on their flow of talk and their emotions. They do not feel inadequate, inferior or defensive talking to us, or as though they are being talked down to.

To respond effectively:

- Observe facial and bodily movements.
- Listen to words and their meanings.
- Tune into your own emotional reactions to what the client is communicating.
- Sense the meaning of the communication.
- Take into account the degree of client self-awareness.
- Respond appropriately.

- Use expressive, not stereotyped language.
- Use vocal and bodily language that are in agreement with each other.
- Check the accuracy of your understanding.

Paraphrasing mirrors the content of a statement; reflecting mirrors the feelings of a statement. It is a clarification of the emotional content. Accurate paraphrasing and reflecting communicate empathy. Accurate mirroring of feelings will demonstrate deeper empathy.

Further reading

Sutton, J. and Stewart, W. (1997) *Learning to Counsel: how to develop the skills to work effectively with others.* How to Books, Oxford.

PASTORAL COUNSELLING

Charles V. Gerkin's hermeneutical model of pastoral counselling is introduced here because in many ways it provides a balance to some of the other models included in this book. What Gerkin has to say also develops some of the psychological concepts and principles discussed elsewhere in the book. He also introduces some new ones.

Although Gerkin writes from a Christian perspective, what he says is applicable to other religions. Although this article has a pastoral counselling emphasis and some counsellors and clients might not subscribe to Christian theology, the principles go far beyond doctrine and dogma. A study of Gerkin's model provides valuable insights across many different counselling approaches.

Gerkin, a professor of pastoral psychology at Emory University in the US, draws upon the work of another visionary, Anton Boisen. Boisen believed that a person's struggle must be interpreted in much the same way as a historic Bible text. Although pastoral counsellors make use of a number of secular theories, their work must essentially be founded in Christian faith.

Traditionally there has been a conflict of ideology between theological ministry and the psychodynamic theory of the person. Gerkin attempts to resolve this conflict by introducing a hermeneutical alternative.

Hermeneutics is the critical interpretation and the science of the Bible, used by both Jews and Christians to discover the truths and values of the Old and New Testaments.

Gerkin proposes that hermeneutical pastoral counselling can bring together the two language worlds of theology and psychology. Pastoral counselling needs to incorporate the insights coming from secular psychotherapy, although not to be so absorbed into the general stream of psychotherapy that it loses its own identity.

Pastoral counsellors: who are they?

Pastoral counsellors listen to and interpret other people's stories and help them make sense of what seems senseless. Clients, through counselling, are helped to change the plot and counterplot of their life story. The pastoral counsellor and client are likely to use different language systems, symbols and images to interpret the meaning of experiences. The counsellor must strive to understand the client's frame of reference and the personal meanings. Failure to do so will result in the client going away empty-handed.

The more the counsellor understands the language of the client and helps the client to understand his own language, the more the distance between their worlds will be reduced. Gerkin sees people in crisis as being caught between despair on the one hand and an interpretation of hope and expectation on the other. Much of the problem of the crisis experience is seen as a loss of the sense of continuity, with accompanying difficulty in moving into the open-ended future of hope and faith.

Anton Boisen's vision

Boisen is generally considered the spiritual ancestor of the development of the pastoral counselling movement. His term 'living human document' was coined to highlight how essential it is that theory *about* people should be supported by direct experience *of* people. For Boisen, the soul's cure is fundamentally to do with the raw stuff of religious experience.

Boisen viewed the person in distress as a troubled soul whose inner world had become so disorganised that the world had lost its foundations. If we interpret and understand the language and gestures of the troubled soul, we will gain understanding of the specific inner world of this particular client.

The troubled person's own reporting of his inner world of experience is to be respected and heard, as having authenticity and integrity of its own, no matter how peculiar its language. What the person needs is an interpreter and a guide. One event must be interpreted in the light of all other experiences in the life story.

Boisen's philosophy was that the pastoral counselling tenets of faith and salvation, sin and redemption, have been replaced by the psychological language of neurotic symptoms, identity conflicts and compensatory behaviour; useful, but sterilised of religious meaning.

The client cannot be read as a living document unless the counsellor is willing to be read by the client. In person-centred counselling, this is the process of empathy, rapport and acceptance.

Horizon of understanding (empathy)

Experiences, prejudices, previous understandings, personal meanings and biases all limit our horizon of understanding. Listening to someone's inner world of meaning involves extending our horizon of understanding to admit something of the other person's world. Change takes place in the transitional space between the two horizons of understanding. The integrated language worlds used in Gerkin's model may be imagined as bridges between what is known – the past – on the one hand and the unknown – the yet-to-be – on the other.

Psychological theory and pastoral counselling

Pastoral counselling is concerned with communicating the inner meaning of the Gospel to persons at their point of need. Pastoral counsellors search for clues to understand the nature and purpose of God in His relationship with people. Theological and biblical images, themes and symbols need to be part and parcel of the pastoral counsellor's self-understanding and self-expression. Pastoral counselling ministry – seen as the communication of the inner meaning of the Gospel – flows first out of that level of inner meaning that has been informed and influenced by the images of faith. Pastoral counsellors draw from biblical and theological tradition a broad range of images, symbols and narrative themes. These provide a language with which to broaden the horizon of understanding and move towards self-identity.

What pastoral counselling is not, according to Gerkin's model, is indiscriminate quoting of Bible verses to clients. That is not active listening, whereas what Gerkin is proposing is listening of the highest order.

Self-identity and pastoral counselling

Self-identify involves taking into self the contents of the world; to refuse to do so is to become an empty self. Yet to be too open to do so brings with it the risk of chaos. The Spiritual Presence is both a fundamental answer and a safeguard. Where the Spiritual Presence is effective, life is turned towards the ultimate direction of the Kingdom.

People who come for pastoral counselling are usually aware of the suffering that comes from being stuck in their history, although that awareness may be hazy. Counselling aims to liberate clients' inner resources so they can handle the suffering more positively and help to restore their identity.

For the pastoral counsellor, change involves the work of the Spirit. The Spirit is seen as an energy or power, whose subject is God or Christ. The counsellor cannot force change. Change is achieved through the mediating influence of the Spirit. The counselling relationship is undertaken in the hope, and with the expectation, that in the search for new directions the client will be accompanied by the Spirit.

Identity and pastoral counselling

Identity is the self's effort to maintain some level of consistent attitude in the face of forces that would cause fragmentation. It is both an individual uniqueness and something conferred upon the individual by the significant figures in the person's life.

Identity is received, in part, from the person's historic circumstances in which human life takes place and in part from the individual's participation in the coming kingdom of God. The ego, self and soul are analogous to the Trinity: Father, Son and Holy Spirit – functionally distinct but coexistent and indivisible.

Working with the life of the soul model

It is helpful to present the model as a triangle; then, together, client and counsellor identify the various factors. Having done that, they work out the tensions between them.

The task of the self is to hold in tension the three force/meaning dimensions, which come from three general directions in the life space of the individual.

- Self/ego
- Social context
- The interpretations of faith and culture.

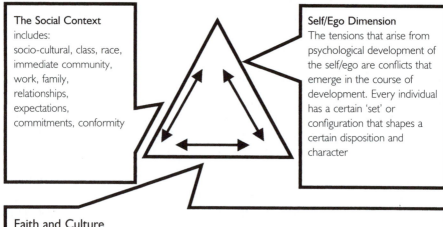

The Social Context
includes:
socio-cultural, class, race,
immediate community,
work, family,
relationships,
expectations,
commitments, conformity

Self/Ego Dimension
The tensions that arise from psychological development of the self/ego are conflicts that emerge in the course of development. Every individual has a certain 'set' or configuration that shapes a certain disposition and character

Faith and Culture
Faith and culture give rise to myths and symbols by which a tradition or way of life is shaped over time in a given location. Faith and culture provide languages by which behaviours and relationships are given meanings and the way an individual perceives self and the world. Faith and culture tell us what relationships should be, and why; what thoughts and behaviour should be assigned guilty, accusatory meaning and what should receive commendation

Figure 2:   Three force/meaning dimensions

The constant interaction between all three dimensions makes up the flow of life in which the soul is either nurtured or kept in bondage. Our relationship to God is part and parcel of the self in all our relationships, including our struggle to hold the tension between forces and meanings.

Gerkin identifies three approaches to counselling:

- A 'force approach', where the counsellor sifts truth from falsehood; searching for hidden memories, forgotten facts and unconscious forces

- A 'meaning approach', where the facts are considered to be secondary to the client's interpretation of the meaning attached to the facts – this relies on acceptance and affirmation, without questioning the truth or falsity of the statement, an approach closely allied to Carl Rogers's unconditional positive regard
- Gerkin's 'integrated approach' holds in either hand the languages of force and meaning, two parts of a whole that are in constant tension – to truly understand a human situation we must understand both force and meaning: what happened, what is happening, the interpretation of those events.

The self as a story

The story creates a pathway between the known and the unknown, although it is often narrated as a muddle and portrayed in highly symbolic language. The self is a book of many chapters. When chapters remain open, we cannot fully move forward. Part of counselling is to enable the client to examine chapters that are still open, work through the contents and close the chapter.

Elements of a narrative

Atmosphere
Pastoral counsellors attune themselves to hear the hidden positive and negative forces that influence the way a story is portrayed.

Plot
The deep story of the soul has a plot with a beginning, a principal story line, minor lines and an anticipated ending. People who cannot construct their story line are in danger of losing their sense of self.

Characterisation
Character is how the person describes him or herself and how significant others in the life story are described. We use both imagination and behaviour to characterise someone.

Tone
Tone has three interlinked facets:

- We select or choose material to tell.
- Language is used in a certain way.
- Certain attitude are used to tell the story.

The way counsellors listen reinforces how and what they interpret. Vital lines may be missed because we are blinkered. We need to ask, 'Why is this particular part of the story being told? What is being left out and why?'
Examples of language the client may use:

- Blame and accusation: 'It's all my parents' fault'
- Helplessness and weaknesses: 'What can I do, I'm a failure'

- Determination against odds: 'I won't let this thing beat me'
- Emotional or intellectual: 'I feel...' or 'I think...'.

The changing tones in the reporting of a life story are often a reliable indicator of changes in the life of the soul.

Stage 1: Evoking the story
The story may be painful and difficult to tell. What is told may not be the story, but merely a connecting line. Many sidelines may be told before the central story emerges. The pastoral counsellor must constantly be alert to the line that will lead to the person's central line. Most stories indicate some sense of an obstruction, damming the flow. When the line of life is blocked, that is the time to seek the client's interpretation.

How we listen and interpret is influenced by the ego conflicts and object relationships of our own pre-understandings. These must be as soft wax, to allow our horizon of understanding to come somewhere near the client's inner world. In the gap between these two worlds, the Christian counsellor can work with an understanding enhanced by the Holy Spirit. Or, in humanistic terms, the counsellor can work with an understanding enhanced by the psyche.

Stage 2: Exploring the story
Psychoanalytic therapies regard the development of insight as a central principle. Gerkin's theory emphasises not only insight but also the need for integration and wholeness, the development of an authentic selfhood to replace the fragmented and dissociated self-image.

The soul needs to integrate and hold in balance the tensions coming from the three dimensions of self/ego, social situations and belief; not to do so will result in fragmentation.

The fragmented soul is unable to achieve integration. The narrative account of the life of the self must achieve a certain unity and cohesion, so that the various sub-themes and issues in the life of the soul hold together. Integration and wholeness are not static goals but an open-ended process of movement and change.

Stage 3: Changing the story
Changing the story involves working with two concepts: the horizons of understanding and the living human document. Five ways of using language help to understand this process.

- **Myth** *establishes* the client's story: The counsellor risks immersion in the client's world in order to change the myth from within.
- **Apologue (moral fable)** *defends* the client's story: Pastoral counselling defends the self-story and explores relationships, attitudes, feelings, behaviours, evaluations of self and others within it.
- **Action** *investigates* the story, by asking questions and posing hypotheses about what is going on or will go on: Action language can be intrusive if it does not

understand the language of images, symbolism and feeling-laden words; when we understand those, we begin to understand the client's story.

- **Satire** *attacks* the story by mocking it and encouraging us to laugh at ourselves: If there is a place for satire in pastoral counselling it must be handled with every bit as much care as a physician administers a highly powerful but potentially dangerous medicine.
- **Parable** *transforms* the client's story: The well-told parable is an ordinary story with a familiar ring. As the story progresses, it takes a new and unexpected turn and stretches the imagination of the hearer. A well-told parable involves the person as participant, not just a passive hearer.

Levels of counsellor suffering

Counsellors who are involved in this gradual transformation process of another require a level of personal involvement and interpersonal engagement that taps the deepest suffering of the soul at a number of different but related levels.

- **Level 1: Anxiety.** No counsellor has foreknowledge of a client's journey.
- **Level 2: Vulnerability.** Certain themes of the client's life story may awaken within the counsellor unfinished business that requires reworking.
- **Level 3: Balance.** As client and counsellor move in the transitional space between their worlds, a balance between objectivity and subjectivity is essential. This is the space where the Spirit works and transformation begins to take place. It is there where one's own vulnerabilities become open to challenge and change, in the light of the Spirit's work with the client.
- **Level 4: Transference.** This is the unconscious process whereby the counsellor becomes the focus of the client's unresolved feelings towards significant others.

The hermeneutical circle of understanding

Understanding is like a circular feedback system, taking in, interpreting data and then adding it to what already exists to produce new data. The circular flow moves from the present counselling relationship to the history of significant relationships, then back again. This leads to an ever-enlarging arena. A danger is that both counsellor and client may be so taken up exploring one line of the story that all other lines remain unnoticed.

The ending phase of counselling

Gerkin identifies four issues related to ending counselling:

- How to help people make the transition from an intense, therapeutic relationship back into everyday life without that relationship. The return to the community, for many, may not be an easy journey. Where, for them, is the understanding, totally accepting, non-judgemental person to whom they have said farewell?
- The degree of control the counsellor exercises as to the outcomes of counselling. Where the person already has allegiance to a community of faith, the aim of counselling will be to strengthen that commitment.

- How the pastoral counsellor handles the termination of clients who do not have a relationship with a community of faith. The pastoral counsellor can never ensure the moral correctness or lasting outcome of counselling.
- Issues concerned with care and service. The final phase of counselling is the turning away from the primary concern for self and its welfare, towards service and concern for others.

Indicators of the ending phase of counselling

Signals of integration and wholeness

- Higher level of energy and the sense of well-being
- Spontaneity of affect (feeling)
- Evidence of shared involvement
- Self-esteem and self-criticism are more realistic.
- Fragmentation is giving way to transformation of the life story.
- Realism is replacing fantasy.

Signals of altered behaviour and altered relationships

- Increased understanding of behaviour and meaning
- Congruency between behaviour in relationships
- Signals of clearer understanding of soul issues
- An awakening to the possibilities of the future
- A growing awareness of one's relationship with other souls.

Signals of openness to travelling beyond, and to, the story

- A style of openness to life experience involving faith
- A growing ability to go beyond the obvious and explicit
- An openness to the flow of events in one's life.

Signals of beginning to accept eschatological (ultimate) identity

- Claiming the Kingdom, not just mental assent to it
- Changed attitude towards self and towards the world
- No longer at war with one's life story
- A realisation that one is a pilgrim among pilgrims
- A greater sensitivity to the suffering of others.

Summary of hermeneutical pastoral counselling

This summary seeks to answer five salient questions.

1. What is the precise relationship between dynamics and narrative patterns of meaning in both intrapsychic and interpersonal life?

- The hermeneutical theory seeks to hold in working harmony the dynamics of force and meaning. Force concentrates on the conflicts and the functions of the self/ego, particularly thinking, analysis and psychological interpretation. Meaning involves a theological interpretation, which stresses the symbolic and imagistic as they influence the life story of the individual.

- Hermeneutical theory emphasises the development of insight through interpretation of the events and experiences of the life story. It uses the language of images, symbols and characterisations. The medium is narrative expression of life conflicts of both force and meaning.
- Hermeneutical theory also deals with soul work, allowing the Spirit to work within the transitional space between the horizons of understanding of counsellor and client.

2. Is pastoral counselling in the hermeneutical mode best seen as a form of spiritual direction or is it best imaged as a theologically oriented form of psychotherapy?

- The hermeneutical model of pastoral counselling lies somewhere between psychotherapy and spiritual direction. Like Janus, it faces both ways, drawing from both, but is distinct from either.
- The hermeneutical model is primarily concerned with the individual's pilgrimage through the problems and crises of everyday life. It is concerned with the person's relationship with God and claiming the Kingdom.
- It is spiritual direction because it is spiritual. It is psychotherapy because it takes account of psychological ways of attending to the client's inner world. At all times pastoral counsellors must be sensitive to the direction of the client's face. To manipulate a client to tread a spiritual path would be as psychologically damaging as pushing a client to perform some behavioural task for which he is unprepared.

3. What are the concerns about short-term versus long-term pastoral counselling?

- Time is probably the major enemy to be overcome.
- Hermeneutical pastoral counselling can only be developed over time.
- Many situations, problems and difficulties are best understood and resolved within the total life story.
- Whenever problem-solving techniques are used, they are best viewed as part of the resolution of the deeper soul issues.

4. Can a hermeneutical approach to a theory of pastoral counselling provide a comparable basis for a theory of pastoral care in the parish?

- Pastoral care involves establishing a pre-counselling relationship with persons and families as they go about their daily business of living and working. Caring provides a connection between the pastor's desire to help and the willingness of people to seek that help.
- The hermeneutical approach provides a structure for listening and responding

to persons in a way that demonstrates deep caring, although such conversations may never reach the depth of long-term counselling.

- The hermeneutical, unified approach offers a ministry theory that is integrated and holistic.

5. Does the hermeneutic approach have broader implications than simply being a theory of pastoral counselling?

- The counsellor using such an integrated model must find ways of moving back and forth between the worlds of theology and personality without collapsing into one or violating the basic integrity of either.
- Hermeneutical pastoral counselling, with its emphasis on object relations and the transformation of self, within a larger context of meaning, has a contribution to offer both theology and psychotherapy.
- Pastoral counselling asserts the standard values of Christian images of what human life, under God, was meant to become and, as such, is an important Christian witness.
- Theology and psychotherapy together offer something more powerful than they could do if kept separated.

Guidelines for working with clients

When working with clients, whether within a pastoral context or not, the following guidelines are helpful. Construct three boxes: Self, Society, Beliefs. Then, together, identify the questions the client could ask that would help both you and the client to achieve greater understanding. Put into each box all the things you have found out.

- **For example, under Self:** What does this person think and feel about himself? What is his level of self-esteem? How does he relate to himself? Is he comfortable with himself and with others? What are his relationships like?
- **Under Society:** How does he relate to society and what does he think of his place in society? What are his relationships with various significant sections of society; parents, siblings, friends? What are his views about society? What are his views about work? Does he fit easily with society or is he uncomfortable in it? Does he feel more at ease with certain groups in society than with others? If so, why?
- **Under Beliefs:** What are his views of God? What is his relationship to God? What are the foundations of his beliefs? How do his beliefs relate to Self and Society?

Tensions: When you have examined the client's statement from all these angles, then you can start to piece them together. From each of the three boxes, take one thing at a time and contrast and compare it with those from the others. In this way you start to get some idea of the tensions that exist between them.

The ending of counselling brings the satisfaction of having been involved with the soul of another. This is often coupled with the humbling acceptance that perhaps not all that was hoped for has been achieved. Added to this is the knowledge that, in the helping, one has been helped; that in sharing the pain of another's wounds, one's own wounds have been touched and transformed. Above all, there is a sense of gratitude that whatever was changed was made possible by the Spiritual Presence.

Further reading

Gerkin, C.V. (1984) *The Living Human Document.* Abingdon Press, Nashville.
Institute of Counselling (1995) *Introduction to Counselling, Lesson 8.* Institute of Counselling, 6 Dixon Street, Glasgow, G1 4AX.

PERSONALITY

Personality is the enduring characteristics of an individual's behaviour, attitude and feelings in everyday social situations. Personality usually refers to what is unique about a person; the characteristics that distinguish that person from other people. Personality implies predictability about how a person will act or react under different circumstances. There are many influences on an individual's personality, including culture, genetic make-up and early family life. Personality psychology encompasses the whole person and the interface of that person with the world.

Psychodynamic approaches

Psychodynamic approaches, based on the work of Sigmund Freud, look at personality not from what could be considered the 'public' side but from the inner world of the person – from the unconscious. Many of Freud's disciples departed from strict psychoanalytic theory to form their own approaches and theories of personality and generally introduced more of a social emphasis in their theories of personality. Underlying development of personality is the belief that it is necessary to understand what motivates the individual. Psychodynamic theories are more concerned with explaining existing neurotic behaviour than with predicting future behaviour.

Freud proposed that early experiences in eating, toilet training and sexual feeling are critical in shaping the developing personality structure. The structure is manifest throughout life in how we view ourselves, in relationships with others and in general ways of relating to the environment.

Psychodynamic theory describes how the structures of the id, ego and superego are in constant conflict and their interaction influences human behaviour. These structures become part of our personality in childhood and become manifest in adult behaviour.

Cognitive-behavioural approaches

Cognition refers to the manner in which we perceive, remember, think and make use of language, and how we organise information about the world. What people think about themselves is an important influence on their behaviour. Other factors that influence personality, according to this model, are how we process information both about the self and the surrounding world; how we attempt to predict and control events; how some people tend to think in a complex, abstract way while others think in a simple, concrete way; how people organise information to make long-range plans and to regulate their behaviour in accordance with these plans.

The behaviourist view of personality is represented by thinkers such as the American psychologist B.F. Skinner, who place primary emphasis on learning. Skinner sees human behaviour as determined largely by its consequences. If rewarded, behaviour recurs; if punished, it is less likely to recur. A common theme running through the cognitive-behavioural approaches is the interplay between the external and the internal or between the person and the situation.

Social-learning approach

Social-learning theory assumes that personality differences result from variation in learning experiences. Responses may be learned through observation, without reinforcement, but reinforcement is important in determining whether the learned responses will be performed. The leading social-learning theorist is Albert Bandura.

Social learning emphasises the importance of environmental or situational factors in determining behaviour. Environmental conditions shape behaviour through learning; a person's behaviour, in turn, shapes the environment. Social-learning theory places much emphasis on cognitive factors such as memory.

The sorts of issue over which social-learning theorists are concerned are:

- **Competence**: What can you do?
- **Interpreting strategies**: How do you see it?
- **Expectancies**: What will happen?
- **Subjective values**: What the person believes.
- **Goals**: How can you achieve them?

Humanistic approaches

The existential-humanistic approach emphasises the growth and self-actualisation of the individual and his conscious subjective experience. Possibly the most influential figures in this field are Carl Rogers – originator of person-centred counselling – and Abraham Maslow.

Rogers' research has explored the conditions that promote positive developments of the self and enhance movement towards self-actualisation. These approaches focus more on the future – what the person can become – than on what the person has been. For Rogers, the most important aspect of personality is the congruence between various aspects of the self and congruence between self and the ideal self.

Personality theory applied to counselling

Personality traits are ill-adjusted if they cause significant impairment in everyday life or if they lead to distress or discomfort. In such cases the personality characteristic is referred to as a personality disorder. These disorders are lifelong patterns of behaving that lead to maladjustment and an inability to cope with ordinary situations.

Personality disorders are not, strictly speaking, illnesses, since they need not involve the disruption of emotional, intellectual or perceptual functioning. In many cases, people with a personality disorder do not seek psychiatric treatment for such unless they are pressured to do so by relatives or by a court. There are many different types of personality disorder; they are classified according to the particular personality traits that are accentuated.

Personality disorders differ from personality change. However, the study of personality disorders is not without its difficulties, for it operates in the grey and ambiguous area between sickness and health, an area that abounds with personal opinion and value judgements. Where do we draw the line between, for example, characterising someone as cautious and determining that person as paranoid? Where is the dividing line between a man who prefers his own company and the schizoid personality? When does a person cross the line from 'normality' to 'personality disorder'?

Personality disorder – also called character disorder – is a mental disorder that is marked by deeply ingrained and lasting patterns of inflexible, faulty or anti-social behaviour. A personality disorder is an accentuation of one or more personality traits to the point that the trait significantly impairs an individual's social or occupational functioning.

For a diagnosis of personality disorder to be made, there must be an evaluation of the person's long-term pattern of functioning. The particular personality features must have been evident from early adulthood. In addition, the disorder must be distinguished from changes that accompany other medical or psychiatric illnesses. Personality disorder tends to appear in late childhood or adolescence and continues to be manifest into adulthood. It is therefore unlikely that the diagnosis of personality disorder will be appropriate before the age of 16 or 17 years.

Personality disorders are treated with various forms of psychotherapy, sometimes by using drugs under the direction of psychiatrists, psychologists, social workers and many other mental-health professionals.

Counsellors who suspect that a client they are dealing with has a personality disorder are advised, in the first instance, to seek psychiatric advice as to the wisdom of continuing.

Further reading

Digman, J.M. (1990) Personality structure: emergence of the five-factor model. *Annual Review of Psychology*, **41**: 417–440.

Mischel, W. (1986) *Introduction to Personality*, 4th edn. Holt, Rinehart & Winston, New York.

PERSON-CENTRED COUNSELLING (SEE ALSO: CORE CONDITIONS, FRAMES OF REFERENCE)

Dr Carl R. Rogers (1902–1987), an American whose study of theology convinced him that he was not suited to the ministry, turned to psychology and psychoanalysis. His study of children led him to question the validity of some of the fundamental tenets of psychoanalysis.

Rogers attached more importance to the counsellor's attitudes than to his technical training or skills. Accurate and sensitive understanding of the client's experiences and feelings is paramount, because it helps the client focus on the experience of the moment. (Rogers used the word 'client' instead of 'patient' to indicate that the treatment is neither manipulative nor medically prescriptive.)

Rogers developed the nondirective approach to counselling, based on his unshakeable belief that clients needed to have much more control over the therapeutic process than they were given in traditional therapy. In nondirective therapy, the aim of the therapist was to engage the client in an equal, participative relationship rather than in organised and structured therapy.

Rogers later replaced the term by 'client-centred' and it is now 'person-centred'. The term is often used to distinguish a process that is different from the directive therapies, particularly behaviour therapy. Rogers' move towards 'person-centred counselling' acknowledged the difficulties of being totally 'nondirective'. It is probably no more possible to be totally nondirective than it is to be totally objective. The very fact that time, venue and length of session are all set removes some of the credibility of being nondirective. What seems to be important is the intention of the counsellor and the underlying philosophy.

To be 'nondirective' means relinquishing some or most of the control to the client. The influence of the counsellor and the wish to help the client to change, some would argue, must in some way be directive, even although it is the client who decides what he wants to change.

The person-centred approach emphasises the capacity and strengths of clients to direct the course and direction of their own therapy. The concept of self-actualisation is at the centre of person-centred counselling, in common with other humanistic therapies, philosophies and approaches.

Fundamental to the method is the relationship established between therapist and client, based on the core conditions of empathy, genuineness or congruence, non-possessive warmth and unconditional positive regard. (See Core conditions for full discussion.)

Person-centred counsellors prefer to talk about attitudes and behaviours and creating growth-promoting climates. Their view of their clients is that they are intrinsically good, capable of directing their own destinies and capable of self-actualisation. Counsellor and client work within a partnership of equals who trust each other.

The focus is on entering the client's frame of reference and understanding and tracking the client's personal meanings. This does not mean that the counsellor is passive. Being able to enter the client's frame of reference means active listening and a continual struggle to lay aside preconceptions that would hinder the process. The person-centred counsellor also believes in the importance of rejecting the pursuit of authority or control over others. Power is there to be shared. Person-centred counselling is not a soft option; neither does it mean that the counsellor does nothing but listen. Not having a set model to work to, yet always remaining in touch with the client's feelings and what those feelings mean to this unique client, means that the counsellor has to be prepared to travel unknown roads, for the experience of every client is totally unique. If the core conditions are present, then growth and change will take place.

The answers to two basic questions are sought in therapy, 'Who am I?' and 'How can I become myself?'

The person-centred approach, in common with many other therapies, is less successful with severely disturbed psychotic clients. Person-centred principles have been applied in the classroom, in colleges, in organisations and in groups. Critics of the approach argue that it is naive and does not help the client face reality.

Table 8: **Stages in person-centred therapy**

Stage 1	Client communicates about externals Feelings are not owned Constructs are rigid The client is reluctant to engage in close relationships
Stage 2	Feelings are sometimes described but not owned Keeps subjective experience at a distance Problems are perceived as external to self
Stage 3	Feelings and personal meanings in the past are described, usually as unacceptable or bad Expressions of self are in objective terms Self tends to be seen as a part of others Personal constructs are rigid Some recognition that problems are personal and not external
Stage 4	Free and full description of feelings and personal meanings Intense feelings are not described in the present The possibility of feelings breaking through causes alarm Unwilling to experience feelings Personal constructs become more free What was absolute now becomes possibility Some recognition of self-responsibility
Stage 5	Easier to express feelings in the present Owning of feelings Immediacy of feelings is less fearful More able to tolerate contradictions and ambiguities Personal constructs and meanings are open to question More acceptance of self-responsibility
Stage 6	Acceptance and immediate expression of previously denied feelings Feelings expressed bring liberation through catharsis Acceptance of the validity of working in the present Self is real, not an object Flexible constructs replace inflexible ones
Stage 7	The client feels comfortable with living in present experience The immediacy of feelings experienced with enhanced richness Able to risk expressing feelings

The counsellor's task is to facilitate clients' awareness of, and trust in, self-actualisation. The therapeutic process is centred on the client and it is the client's inner experiencing that controls the pace and the direction of the relationship.

When clients are accepted and when the core conditions are present, they feel safe enough to explore their problems and gradually come to experience the parts of themselves they normally keep hidden from themselves and from others.

Thus, counselling means helping the client to move away from what is less desirable towards something more desirable or, in Egan's terms, from the present scenario to the desired scenario. Much of the present scenario consists of not living to the fullness of what we are capable of; where we are frequently pulled away from what we want to be by what others want us to be. This is the scenario of the façade, or what Jung calls the Persona, the mask. The desired scenario pulls us towards what we could become, where we know we are being real; where our feelings towards ourselves and others are genuine and positive, yet still being able to express negative feelings appropriately. Being authentic means that we can be real with ourselves and other people.

The person-centred counsellor has no model, structure, strategies or techniques on which to rely, only his own unique self and the intense desire to be at one with the client and to feel with this client within a relationship in which the client feels upheld and able to become himself.

Within the person-centred relationship three stages can be identified:

- **Trust**. This may take many sessions to develop. Trust can never be demanded, it can only be earned, and this will happen as the client feels safe to express whatever feelings need to be expressed without fear of judgement or their being slotted into some preconceived model. Trust is two-way: the counsellor has to trust the client. This does not mean trusting the 'truth' of what the client says, rather it means trusting the client's feelings. More than that, it means having trust in the client's ability to work towards self-healing.
- **Intimacy**. Intimacy can only develop where there is trust. Intimacy does not mean physical closeness or even touch; intimacy means a sharing of feelings, experiences, thoughts, wishes, desires, which we normally do not share readily. When the client allows the counsellor to share in his inner world, to see something from the internal frame of reference, that is intimacy. When client and counsellor sit in silence, just having shared something deeply important, as if sharing in the communion, that is intimacy.
- **Mutuality**. Brian Thorne speaks of this intimacy as the stage of complete trust and transparency, where 'neither is fearful of the other and intimacy comes easily in ways which are appropriate to the counselling setting'. Here the counsellor is likely to become more, but appropriately, self-disclosing. This enhances the counsellor's genuineness as a person, not just a counsellor responding from within a role. This is the stage when the client moves further into, as it were, being his own counsellor; where the client begins to trust himself; where the control is located within, not within the counselling relationship; where the core conditions have been internalised to become

integrated within the personality; where acceptance by the counsellor has been replaced by self-acceptance; where healing, if not complete, is taking place.

Finally, being person-centred not only means having the client at the centre of the counselling relationship, it also means having one's self at the centre. This does not mean being self-centred or egotistical – it means that the core conditions reside deep within and find expression in our relationship with others. If, for example, we are not genuine within, can we be genuine with clients? If we do not accept ourselves as we are, yet never ceasing to change what is unacceptable to our self-image, can we unreservedly accept clients? Can we really listen to the feelings of others and track their meanings, if we do not understand ourselves?

Further reading

Egan, G. (2002) *The Skilled Helper: a problem-management and opportunity-development approach to helping*. Brooks/Cole, Pacific Grove, CA.

Mearns, D. and Thorne, B. (1988) *Person-centred Counselling in Action*. Sage Publications, London.

Rogers, C.R. (1942) *Counselling and Psychotherapy*. Constable, London.

Rogers, C.R. (1951) *Client-centred Therapy: its current practice, implications and theory*. Constable, London.

Rogers, C.R. (1961) *On Becoming a Person: a therapist's view of psychotherapy*. Constable, London.

Rogers, C.R. (1980) *A Way of Being*. Houghton Mifflin, Boston, MA.

Thorne, B. (1985) *The Quality of Tenderness*. Norwich Centre Publications, Norwich.

Thorne, B. (1996) Person-centred therapy. In: *Handbook of Individual Therapy* (ed. W. Dryden). Sage Publications, London.

Thorne, B. (1998) *Person-centred Counselling and Christian Spirituality*. Whurr Publishers, London.

Thorne, B. (2000) *Person-centred Counselling: therapeutic and spiritual dimensions*. Whurr Publishers, London.

PERSON-CENTRED COUNSELLOR ATTITUDES

This entry is adapted from R. Nelson-Jones and C.H. Patterson ((1974) 'Some effects of counsellor training', *British Journal for Guidance and Counselling*, 2(2)) and is used with permission. The original article, and this entry in the second edition of this book, was designed as a questionnaire to be scored; in this edition the questions and answers have been merged.

The interpretations given, resulting from several years in teaching counselling, are purely my views and may not be in agreement with more dedicated person-centred counsellors. Although this is specifically directed at person-centred counsellors, the concepts apply equally to most counselling.

You may disagree with some of the answers. In past experience there have been many students who could not accept the answers as given. The 'Agree' or 'Disagree' verdicts are taken from the original scoring, supplied by Richard Nelson-Jones. The rationale that follows derives from the author's attempt to help students arrive at a greater understanding of what is meant by person-centred counselling. Nelson-Jones and Patterson's paper was based on research and their validation of the questionnaire must be acknowledged. The comments in this entry are not research-based, but this does not make them less valid.

1. The counsellor's goal is to make people better adjusted to society.
Disagree. The counsellor is there for the client, not primarily as an agent of society. To agree with this has implications of conformity and compliance, both of which most counsellors would certainly not agree to.

2. It is the counsellor's job to solve the client's problems.
Disagree. As with 1, most counsellors would agree that the client must solve the problem. The counsellor is there to help clarify and facilitate.

3. A thorough diagnosis is necessary for effective counselling.
Disagree. Unlike medicine, or indeed social work, diagnosing does not play an essential role in counselling. A dictionary definition of diagnosis is: 'determination of the nature of a cause of a disease and the opinion derived from such an examination'. Diagnosis consists of observation, an essential facet of counselling, but it also implies examination by questions and applying preconceived principles and criteria and a process of elimination. Successful treatment is dependent on accurate diagnosis and cannot start until the process of diagnosis is completed. In person-centred counselling, and indeed in most other counselling approaches, the word 'treatment' is not used and the process starts immediately, as counsellor and client begin to interact.

4. The counsellor should plan each session carefully before the client comes.
Disagree. This question is related to the previous one. In person-centred counselling, the counsellor remains as open as possible and it is the client who determines where the session goes. Planning assumes that the planner knows where the session should go.

5. In the session, clients may discuss any area of concern they wish.
Agree. If the client is in charge, then the client will know what to discuss. This may sound a contradiction; this means that the person-centred counsellor has faith in the integrity of the client's psyche. The underlying belief is that the client's psyche is constantly seeking for wholeness and will direct the client accordingly. The counsellor's most difficult task is to make connections among what the client is exploring.

6. The counsellor should be in control of the session at all times.
Disagree. I would imagine that this is self-explanatory, other than for the length of the session. Client and counsellor have an agreed time limit and either may draw it to a close at the appointed time, although normally it is the counsellor who does so.

7. Clients understand themselves best when compared with other people.
Disagree. Comparisons are offensive and are generally either felt to be a put-down or an attempt to offer reassurance.

8. The counsellor should suggest reading material pertinent to the problem, whether it is requested or not.
Disagree. While some approaches recommend and some insist upon homework, this is foreign to the person-centred counsellor. I doubt even if reading material would be suggested, on the premise that, by so doing, the counsellor is giving direction.

9. In order for clients to benefit most from counselling, they must be given unconditional acceptance by the counsellor.
Agree. I would think that this is self-explanatory, although putting it into practice is far from simple.

10. If clients are unable to understand their problem, it is the counsellor's responsibility to explain it to them carefully and clearly.
Disagree. Explanations come from the counsellor's frame of reference and, as such, they could be interpreted as an attempt to convince or gain control.

11. The function of the counsellor is to create and maintain an atmosphere in which clients may explore their feelings and attitudes however they wish.
Agree. When the core conditions are operating, the climate is conducive to exploration.

12. Clients must first establish a dependency relationship upon the counsellor before they can become independent.
Disagree. Unlike some approaches, person-centred counselling works very hard to avoid dependency. The more one takes control and gives direction, the more risk there is of a relationship of dependency being created.

13. The counsellor has the social and professional right not to interfere with the client's choice of an antisocial solution to the problem.
Agree. This often presents difficulty for student counsellors, where their view of themselves as citizens conflicts with their view of themselves as counsellors. The counsellor might hope that counselling would help the client not to be antisocial, but the counsellor cannot interfere. See similar questions 20, 32, 37.

14. The counsellor is always the one to decide when the counselling relationship should end.
Disagree. See question 6. This sometimes causes confusion between the ending of a session and the ending of counselling. Here the meaning is the ending of the counselling relationship. In this instance, it is the client who determines when counselling ends.

15. Clients have within them the capacities to work out a solution to their problems without manipulation by the counsellor.
Agree. I hope that this is self-explanatory, though it does take a great deal of faith in the client to work towards this.

16. If, in the initial session, the counsellor has some negative feelings towards clients, the counsellor should firmly but gently refuse to continue with them.
Agree. I admit to having difficulty with the answer and it could be firmly disputed. The only rationale I can think of is that the counsellor is being truly genuine and open. If the counsellor feels unable to work with a certain client, then it is being genuine to say so. However, there are other points to be considered. If a client engenders negative feelings in me, I would feel it incumbent on me to explore with the client, and with my mentor, the reasons for these feelings. This provides a wonderful opportunity for growth. I find it difficult to believe that any of us can be so sure of our feelings that we could determine after one session if we could work with a client or not. If I have misunderstood the scoring, then I apologise to devoted person-centred counsellors, who may feel outraged at my lack of perception.

17. If counselling is to be successful, the counsellor must depend, for the most part, on the client's own potential for growth.
Agree. The discussion so far should pave the way for an affirmative.

18. A complete case history is necessary before counselling starts.
Disagree. Similar to question 3. For my part, I prefer to build up the picture of the person gradually; otherwise the first session can seem like an interrogation. Very often, clients come for counselling because they are under stress; it would therefore seem inappropriate to deal with the history at the expense of dealing with the crisis.

19. Clients should be permitted to solve their problems in their own way.
Agree. Although the answer is 'Agree', carrying it out may prove difficult for the counsellor. One of the major difficulties is the clash of values. My values are correct for me but I have no right to impose them on others. This question is also tied in with self-determination.

20. The client has the right to choose goals that are antisocial or immoral.
Agree. Similar to question 13. It is necessary to point out that, although the answer is 'Agree', the counsellor is not just a passive bystander. A client who disclosed that an immoral act was contemplated would be helped to explore the various pros and cons of that act so that the client would be making an informed choice.

21. In the session, clients have the right to say anything they wish about the counsellor.
Agree. This would be difficult for most counsellors to accept. I think what underlies this question is that very often clients vent their anger at the counsellor rather than at the person who generated that anger. On the other hand, if I am inept and continually fail to understand the client, then the client has a perfect right to say so. That is my interpretation.

22. The counsellor should offer advice when it is clearly needed.
Disagree. However, it is sometimes very difficult not to offer advice. In my style of counselling I do use advice, simply because I also use other approaches. A client who is stressed, for example, may be advised how to relax and what steps to take to reduce stress levels.

23. The best way to understand clients is to see them as they see themselves.
Agree. This refers to being able to enter the client's frame of reference. Understanding what something means to the other person is what person-centred counsellors call 'tracking the meanings'.

24. People must work out their own solutions to their problems.
Agree. Similar to question 19.

25. If clients talk about a number of problems at the same time, the counsellor should tell them to concentrate on one problem at a time.
Disagree. This is taking control and giving direction, both of which are anathema to person-centred counsellors.

26. The counsellor should praise the client whenever appropriate.
Disagree. This is a difficult one. The strict person-centred counsellor neither praises nor condemns, believing that both are evaluations and judgements. Most other counsellors would give praise appropriate to the situation.

27. One of the counsellor's main functions is to try to convey to clients that their feelings and attitudes are accepted.
Agree. There is generally no problem with this one. If the core conditions are present, then the client feels totally accepted.

28. After clients have decided on their goals, the counsellor should then tell them how they can best be achieved.
Disagree. Person-centred counsellors never tell their clients what to do. They will help them explore what the goals could mean.

29. When clients feel their situation is hopeless, reassurance is in order.
Disagree. Reassurance is often no more than an attempt to diminish the problem. The mere fact that the counsellor is taking time to help the client explore the problem and is creating a climate conducive to foster exploration is adequate.

30. When clients do not understand the meaning of a particular piece of behaviour, the counsellor should explain it to them.
Disagree. The meaning of behaviour would be from the counsellor's frame of reference. Explaining something puts the counsellor in a position of power and control.

31. Clients should be permitted to express attitudes that are contrary to those of the counsellor.
Agree. If the aim of counselling is to encourage self-expression and client control, then this has to be an 'Agree'. Authority does not encourage expression; person-centred counselling is as opposite from authority as Australia is from Britain.

32. Counsellors should try to discourage clients from making mistakes.
Disagree. The counsellor who does try is seeking to gain control.

33. Counsellors should ask questions only when they do not understand what the clients have said.
Agree. The skill of person-centred counselling lies more in creating statements that reflect the client's statement rather than in asking questions. Questions, when asked, are best constructed as open questions.

34. If clients present points of view that are obviously prejudiced or distorted, the counsellor should put them right.
Disagree. What is prejudiced or distorted is very much a question of perception from one's own frame of reference. What the counsellor can do is to present an alternative frame of reference. 'As I see it ... Is that something you would like to explore?'

35. It is essential for client and counsellor to identify and discuss insights.
Disagree. This is another moot point. The strict person-centred counsellor probably feels that insights don't need to be discussed and that to do so would rob the experience of some of the thrill. However, I think that, if the client wishes to, then it's all right to do so, although I would never insist upon it. Insights have to be worked in before they can be worked out.

36. The counsellor should interpret the client's unconscious attitudes and feelings.
Disagree. Interpretation of the unconscious is rarely advisable in counselling unless one is psychologically equipped so to do, by virtue of appropriate training and experience.

37. The counsellor should discourage clients from their intentions to perform criminal acts.
Disagree. Similar to questions 13 and 20. Situations are rarely black or white and quite often counsellors are thrown into conflict. A major consideration must always be: 'Who is at risk if this action is carried through and how will I cope with the knowledge that I did nothing to stop it?' I think another question must also be considered: 'Why is the client telling me?' There may not be a simple answer to that, so my feeling is that the counsellor would be wise to discuss it with the client. Counsellors in the UK must always bear in mind that they can be subpoenaed to disclose information before a court of law.

38. The counsellor's main function is to provide an accepting and permissive atmosphere in which clients are free to work out their problems.
Agree. Similar to question 11.

39. When clients have stated their problems, the counsellor should offer one or more possible solutions to serve as a basis for further discussion.
Disagree. This would remove control from the client to the counsellor. 'What would you like to discuss?' leaves the client in control.

40. Early in the counselling process the counsellor should reassure clients that their problems are not insoluble and thereby reduce their anxiety so that they can start working on their problem.
Disagree. This is false reassurance and puts the client in an inferior position. The anxiety is real and the client must work through it. The anxiety is part of the problem.

41. The counsellor should feel free to ask clients questions in order to obtain pertinent information necessary for the solution of the problem.
Disagree. On the face of it this sounds as if it should be 'Agree'. On closer examination, however, the clue lies in 'solving the problem'. By asking questions that 'investigate' the problem, the counsellor is taking control and showing superior knowledge.

42. Clients should be free to discontinue counselling whenever they wish.
Agree. Although this may not suit the counsellor, can be very frustrating and may break all contracts, the decision must remain with the client. This may be the first decision the client has ever taken to assert his own authority.

43. When counsellors see that clients are solving their problems realistically, they should encourage them.
Disagree. Similar to question 29.

44. If the life situation of clients demands an immediate decision or some course of action and the clients feel unable to make a choice, the counsellor should make suggestions.
Disagree. The counsellor cannot take decisions on behalf of the client; to do so is removing responsibility from the client. However, in a crisis, when the client is immobilised, then the counsellor may have to take action. This course of action would probably be disputed by person-centred counsellors.

45. Clients who wish to spend long periods in silence should be allowed to.
Agree. This may be a frustrating situation to be in, yet it must be the client's choice. Rogers tells a delightful tale of a college counsellor to whom a student was referred. The counsellor explained the process and the number of sessions and so on, ending with something like, 'Now the time is yours to do what you like with'. The student said nothing for the whole session. At the end, the

counsellor said, 'See you next week', and the student left, to reappear next week and to sit in silence again for the whole session. At the end of the contracted number of sessions, the counsellor said something like, 'Do you feel you need to come again?' 'No,' said the student and left. During the sessions, not a word was exchanged. Some time later, the counsellor had a note from the student's teacher: 'I don't know what you did with X, but she's really great now and she's been voted head of the class!'

46. If clients threaten suicide, the counsellor should endeavour to help them explore their feelings.

Agree. This seems logical – in fact it has been suggested that one way to show genuineness is not only to explore feelings, but to explore how the client plans to do it.

47. The counsellor should end every session with some word of reassurance.

Disagree. Similar to question 29. Rather than offer reassurance, here is what I do. Just before the end I usually (I would hesitate to say 'always') say, 'What do you think/feel you are taking away with you from today?' This invites the client to find his own reassurance.

48. When clients ask for advice, they should be given it.

Disagree. Similar to question 22. This time it is if the client asks. The rationale for the 'Disagree' is that once again it puts the counsellor in control and removes responsibility from the client. It increases the power of the counsellor and the helplessness of the client.

49. The counsellor should give an explanation of the counselling relationship in the first session.

Agree. There should be no problem with this. I give all new clients a one-page handout of who I am and my style of working.

50. Resistance to counselling should be accepted, not interpreted.

Agree. What is meant here is that an interpretation could be something like, 'You are resisting the process because you have a problem with authority figures'. Accepting the resistance could be something like, 'It seems that this is difficult to talk about'.

51. In the initial contact, the counsellor should develop a friendly, social relationship with the client as a basis for counselling.

Disagree. The reason for this being 'Disagree' is that counselling is friendly but it is not a social exchange. It is a purposeful relationship, which, when the client so decides, will end.

52. The counsellor should assume the major responsibility for the content of discussion during the session.

Disagree. If we do that, the client is no longer in charge.

53. Most clients are unable to take the responsibility for the solution to their problems; otherwise they would not be in counselling.
Disagree. This is the view of some therapies but certainly not person-centred counselling. The person-centred view would be that the person's inner powers have become temporarily 'frozen' and that within the warmth of the counselling relationship they will become 'unfrozen' and mobilised.

54. The major contribution of the counsellor to the solution of clients' problems is providing an objective, external point of view.
Disagree. Once again, this is linked with the counsellor's frame of reference. Objectivity comes with the way the client's statements are understood and reflected.

55. The client should be allowed to indulge in self-pity.
Agree. It is one thing to recognise that the client is feeling self-pity and another to try to shake him out of it. It is far more constructive to understand what self-pity means from the client's frame of reference.

56. The counsellor should discourage long pauses in counselling, to keep the client from feeling embarrassed or uncomfortable.
Disagree. Similar to question 45. To break silence because we think the client might be embarrassed is putting us in a position of superiority. The truth is that we probably feel embarrassed, not the client. Again, the question could be asked, 'What does this silence mean?'

57. When clients seem unable to talk about themselves, the counsellor should engage in 'small talk' to get them started.
Disagree. Small talk leads to small discussion. Pleasantries such as 'Hello, how have things been with you since we last met?' open the way for exploration. Small talk such as 'Well, what did you think of the football yesterday?' may then make it difficult to get started on the 'real' business.

58. It is rarely helpful for counsellors to tell clients what they would do when faced with the same problem.
Agree. Please notice the qualifying word, 'rarely'. It is tempting, when asked, 'Yes, but what would you do?' to provide an answer.

59. The purpose of the first session is to diagnose the client's problem.
Disagree. Similar to question 3.

60. If counsellors feel that clients persist in wasting interview time, they should be open with the clients and tell them.
Agree. At first glance this may seem contradictory to the philosophy of person-centred counselling. As I interpret it, it is being genuine and open. 'John, there's something that's been bothering me for a few sessions; your time is precious to

you just as mine is to me, yet it seems that you waste our time together by turning up late, then making excuses for wanting to get away before time. What do you think about that?'

61. Counsellors should try to help clients see their problems logically.
Disagree. Similar to question 10. The word 'logically' implies head knowledge, rather than addressing feelings.

62. The counsellor should never take a client's statements at face value, since the client is not fully aware of their hidden significance.
Disagree. Similar to questions 30, 36 and 53. This question implies superior knowledge of the counsellor, based on presupposition and not understanding the client's frame of reference.

63. The counsellor must remain objective and impersonal in the counselling relationship.
Disagree. This question may present difficulties to some counsellors. Part of the counselling process is to bring some objectivity to the relationship, yet too much objectivity creates distance, while too little hampers progress. It means striving for a fine balance between involvement and over-involvement. My own feeling is that one can be objective without being impersonal. At the same time, to become involved demonstrates our humanity. Being involved with another person has its risks. In one training session, Brian Thorne speaks of how at one stage in an interview he was in danger of losing his moorings, as he viewed the enormity of the client's isolation. Experiencing that isolation was temporarily terrifying. Yet it was probably that momentary identification that enabled him to really enter the client's world and make contact other than with words.

64. The more prior information the counsellor has about the client, the easier it will be to understand the client's problem.
Disagree. Information that comes from other people may be biased at best and downright inaccurate at worst. Personally, I prefer not to know anything other than the barest of facts. 'Mr Jones is suffering from stress.' 'Miss Smith has had several abortions and can't come to terms with them.'

65. Clients who deviate from the discussion of a significant problem area should be brought back to it in a gentle, subtle or roundabout way.
Disagree. It is very tempting to want to do this. It can be very frustrating to stay with a client who appears to be going all around the houses – several times. I was facilitating a group for abused women. In the ninth session of 12, the discussion centred on one lady who was obviously angry about her current home situation. My thoughts were, 'What is the relevance to the subject of abuse?' When the penny dropped, I connected the discussion to the main issue by using the phrase 'domestic abuse'. Having made the connection, we explored that issue, which then allowed the group to once more look at other issues of abuse.

66. Successful counsellors are those who are able to suggest solutions to clients' problems in such a way that the clients feel they are their own.
Disagree. This is commonly called 'manipulation', behaviour from which most counsellors would recoil. However, situations are seldom clear cut. There is a fine line between legitimate influence and manipulation. Manipulation always carries with it some benefit to the manipulator. Influence is generally unconscious. In any case, suggesting solutions is not part of effective counselling. There is a difference between exploring alternatives and suggesting solutions.

67. The counsellor should allow the client to make self-derogatory statements.
Agree. This sounds wrong and the natural tendency would be to present a counter-argument. This would not be considered 'good practice'. The person-centred counsellor would probably reflect the feelings. 'I get the feeling that when you say you are a useless no-good that your self-esteem is at rock bottom.'

68. The counsellor should make every effort to get at the true facts of a situation when those facts are in conflict.
Disagree. Counselling is not detective work and counsellors are not investigators. I would draw attention to what appears to be a discrepancy without making a value judgement. When we assert that something is true or untrue we are making a value judgement. If the client is presenting conflicting statements, this could be because of confusion.

69. It is necessary for the counsellor to get a clear picture of the nature and origin of the problem before clients can be helped.
Disagree. Counselling is something like building a jigsaw. The whole picture only emerges as each piece is put into place. The client's problem is made clearer as each bit is put into place and connections are made between different parts of the puzzle.

70. Counsellors should adapt the counselling relationship to the expectations of the client.
Disagree. Counsellors are not professional chameleons. If I were to adapt the counselling relationship with every client, what would happen to my professional judgement? Would I become emotionally fragmented and end up not knowing who I was or what I was supposed to be doing? At the same time, it is in the best interests of clients and for my personal and professional development to remain as open and flexible as I can be, so that I can address this client's needs in the most appropriate way for this client.

Finale

I have tried to give my interpretations of the person-centred approach. As I indicated at the start, I would not call myself a 'person-centred counsellor'; I am person-centred. Therein lies a difference.

If one client finds it difficult to work with reflecting feelings, yet is able to work with images, then I will use images. Another client may prefer a behavioural approach. That, for me, is eclecticism. To be person-centred the client has to be the focus, rather than trying to fit the client into some preconceived therapeutic model. That for me has advantages and disadvantages. To work strictly to a model, I feel, is like trying to fit all people into size 6 shoes. That for me is an impossibility; I take size 12.

Person-centred counselling takes the client where he is and works really hard to stay alongside the client on the particular journey. For some clients, this approach works; others feel it is too woolly and nondirective. The approach does not rely on techniques, yet for some people 'techniques' are helpful.

Clients who are stressed may need help to relax. Marjory liked working with images and, although she was a 'thinker' and found difficulty speaking about feelings, the images she produced were full of feelings. Working with these, as they changed and developed, brought healing.

Every person who engages in counselling is advised to explore many approaches to find one that suits their personality. If there is not a good fit between approach and personality, the approach will sit uneasily and the counsellor will not do the best possible work.

PHENOMENOLOGY (SEE ALSO: EXISTENTIAL THERAPY)

Phenomenology is a school of philosophy that arose in the early years of the 20th century. It is the study of all human experience as free as possible from presupposition or bias. Phenomenology is a way of showing the essential involvement of human existence in the world, starting with everyday perception.

Phenomenologists limit their study to conscious experiences without trying to elicit underlying, hypothetical causes. The data they produce are formulated from the subject's point of view.

Phenomenologists, as a rule, reject the idea of the unconscious. They believe we can learn more about human nature by studying how people view themselves and their world than we can by observing their actions.

In that phenomenologists are more concerned with internal mental processes and the inner life and experiences of individuals – self-concept, feelings of self-esteem and self-awareness – than with behaviour, they have certain similarities to cognitive therapists.

Phenomenologists believe that we are free agents; that we are not acted upon by forces beyond our control, but that we have a great degree of control over our own destiny – the issue of free will versus determinism.

Phenomenological approaches view people as naturally evolving in the direction of psychological growth and maturity. Society may hinder this process by imposing false values and causing the individual to distort his awareness of experience – emotional disorder results from this distortion. The goal of therapy is to restore the patient's natural self-direction by helping him to become aware of distorted or denied feelings and emotions.

The counsellor attempts, as far as possible, to understand the subjective experience of the client and to communicate back – and thus clarify – this experience. The counsellor is an active, empathetic listener who provides an accepting atmosphere and helps the client to regain awareness and thus control of his emotions and behaviour. Emphasis is on present experience as opposed to recollections of early development. Person-centred counselling is a well-developed example of this type of approach. Fritz Perls' Gestalt therapy is a related technique that uses therapy exercises.

The existential approaches of Abraham Maslow and Rollo May can also be grouped here. Phenomenology has made a strong contribution in the field of psychopathology, in which the German Karl Jaspers, a leading contemporary existentialist, stressed the importance of phenomenological exploration of a patient's subjective experience. Jaspers was followed by the Swiss Ludwig Binswanger and several others. The phenomenological strand is also very pronounced in American existential psychiatry, and has affected sociology, history and the study of religion.

Counsellors who use a phenomenological approach concentrate on what is happening now. Most personality theories look at the person from the outside; phenomenology attempts to enter the person's own psychological experience, to try to understand what something means to that person. A phrase often used by Carl Rogers, 'from the internal frame of reference of the individual', sums up the phenomenological experience.

Further reading
Keen, E. (1982) *A Primer in Phenomenological Psychology*. Holt, Rinehart & Winston, New York.

POST-TRAUMATIC STRESS DISORDER (SEE ALSO: CRISIS COUNSELLING)

The term first appeared in the third edition of the Diagnostic and Statistical Manual of Mental Disorders (DSM-III), grouped under anxiety disorders.

Post-traumatic stress disorder (PTSD) is an anxiety disorder brought about by exposure to an exceptional mental or physical event. The symptoms may be felt immediately, although the onset may be three months or more afterwards. The person is beset by persistent reliving of the event and avoidance of anything associated with the trauma. There may be numbing of general responses and manifestations of increased anxiety to other situations.

During the First World War, this disorder was known as 'shell shock'. After the Second World War, the condition became known as 'concentration-camp syndrome'. PTSD is a feature of many catastrophic events and is particularly linked to war conditions.

The essential feature is the development of characteristic symptoms following a psychologically traumatic event that is generally outside the range of human experience, where the symptoms persist for at least one month. The precipitating event would be distressing to almost anyone and would involve, for example:

- Serious threat to life or physical integrity
- Serious threat or harm to one's children, spouse or other close relatives and friends

- Sudden destruction of home or community
- Seeing another person who has recently been, or is being, seriously injured or killed as the result of accident or violence.

The traumatic event is persistently re-experienced in at least one of the following:

- Recurrent and intrusive distressing recollections of the event – children often engage in repetitive play in which themes or parts of the trauma are expressed
- Recurrent, distressing dreams of the event
- Sudden acting or feeling as if the traumatic event was recurring – this may include reliving the experience, illusions, hallucinations and dissociative episodes (flashbacks), which may occur at any time
- Intense psychological distress at exposure to events that symbolise or resemble an aspect of the traumatic event, including anniversaries.

Avoidance of the topic or numbing of responses may show as:

- Strenuous efforts to avoid thoughts or feelings associated with the trauma or to avoid activities or situations that arouse recollections of the event
- Inability to recall an important aspect of the trauma
- Marked lack of interest in significant activities – in young children there may be loss of recently acquired skills
- Feelings of detachment or estrangement
- Restricted range of emotions
- Pessimism about the future.

Symptoms may persist and may show as:

- Difficulty falling or staying asleep
- Irritability or outbursts of anger
- Difficulty in concentrating
- Being ever on the alert
- Being easily startled
- Anxiety when exposed to situations that resemble the traumatic event.

Stressors in PTSD would include:

- Rape or assault
- Military combat
- Natural and manufactured catastrophes
- Physical or sexual abuse.

Planning for crises can reduce anxiety when they do occur. Dealing with a crisis demands fast decision-making and action, clear lines of communication and easy access to all available information. What is not always appreciated is that people who are in the front line of coping with the crisis need support and personal supervision during and following the incident. Suffering can be intensified by official obstruction and insensitivity.

Grief is a natural reaction to most traumatic events, particularly where there is loss of life. Relatives who have an opportunity to see the dead body usually grieve more constructively.

A proactive approach, reaching out to people to offer help, is often more helpful than waiting for people to ask for it. Offering help, however well-meaning the motive, does not guarantee acceptance of the offer. But it does show caring.

Early intervention and opportunity for the survivors to talk through their experiences and their feelings is important, before defences start building up.

Survivor syndrome

The term was introduced in 1926 by R.J. Lifton, an American psychiatrist, for a pattern of reactions frequently observed in those who have survived some terrible ordeal such as an earthquake, a flood or a war. Aspects of the syndrome include chronic anxiety, recurring dreams of the event, a general numbness, withdrawal from and loss of interest in the pleasures of life and, often, survivor guilt.

Survivor guilt was first noticed in those who survived the Holocaust of the Second World War. It has been observed since in people who have survived other severely traumatic events. Part of the sense of guilt seems to be linked to the feeling that those who survived did not do enough to save others who perished.

A crucial point about the survivor syndrome and survivor guilt is the clear link with grief and grieving – grief about the actual event and the event triggering off unresolved grief. It is also worth mentioning the link between guilt and anger – one explanation is that guilt is internalised anger. It would appear, therefore, that counselling should be addressing the feelings of grief.

Critical incident stress debriefing

Many people are affected by a critical incident, and the effects can show for many months or even years.

What is a critical incident?

Davis defines examples of a 'critical incident' 'as a sudden death in the line of duty, serious injury from a shooting, a physical or psychological threat to the safety or well being of an individual or community regardless of the type of incident. Moreover, a critical incident can involve any situation or events faced by emergency or public safety personnel (responders) or individual that causes a distressing, dramatic or profound change or disruption in their physical (physio-logical) or psychological functioning. There are oftentimes, unusually strong emotions attached to the event which have the potential to interfere with that person's ability to function either at the crisis scene or away from it'.

Trauma reactions

Davis describes these as 'cataclysms of emotion' where feelings and thoughts run the gamut and include such diverse symptomatology as shock, denial, anger, rage, sadness, confusion, terror, shame, humiliation, grief, sorrow and even suicidal or homicidal thoughts.

Other responses include restlessness, fatigue, frustration, fear, guilt, blame, grief, moodiness, sleep disturbance, eating disturbance, muscle tremors or 'ticks', reactive depression, nightmares, profuse sweating episodes, heart palpitations, vomiting, diarrhoea, hyper-vigilance, paranoia, phobic reaction and problems with concentration or anxiety. Flashbacks and mental images of traumatic events as well as startle responses may also be observed.

Although some of these symptoms may quickly resolve, others may persist and become long-term crisis reactions, which may lead to aberrant behaviour such as excessive alcohol, tobacco and/or drug use. Interpersonal relations can become strained, work-related absenteeism may increase and, in extreme situations, divorce can be an unfortunate by-product.

Staff who provide support to traumatised and bereaved people need recognition, support, stress relief, adequate supervision and the chance to record their experience and to properly round off their participation when the time is right. Individual counselling may also be required, to help people work through their grief reactions.

What is critical incident stress debriefing (CISD)?

Two components can be identified:

1. **Debriefing.** A specific technique designed to assist others in dealing with the physical or psychological symptoms that are generally associated with trauma exposure.
2. **Defusing.** This allows for the ventilation of emotions and thoughts associated with the crisis event.

The process

Debriefing, ideally, should take place on day two, three or four following the incident. Day one is too soon. After day four, perceptions, feelings and reactions begin to harden and the debriefing begins to have less healing value. As the length of time between exposure to the event and CISD increases, the less effective CISD becomes.

The debriefing should be conducted by an experienced group facilitator who has experience of stress management. Only people with direct experience of the event should be present with the facilitator.

Debriefing is not an evaluation of behaviour but a time for sharing their feelings and experiences, not relating those of other people. It is necessary to warn participants that they may feel worse at first talking about these things, but that it will help to prevent more serious problems developing.

Research shows that people who receive CISD recover more quickly and experience fewer long-term effects than those who do not.

Davis suggests a seven-point debriefing plan:

1. Assess the impact of the critical incident on support personnel and survivors.
2. Identify immediate issues surrounding problems involving 'safety' and 'security'.
3. Use defusing to allow for the ventilation of thoughts, emotions and experiences associated with the event and provide 'validation' of possible reactions.
4. Predict events and reactions to come in the aftermath of the event.
5. Conduct a 'systematic review of the critical incident' and its impact emotionally, cognitively and physically on survivors. Look for maladaptive behaviours or responses to the crisis or trauma.
6. Bring 'closure' to the incident, 'anchor' or 'ground' support personnel and survivors to community resources to initiate or start the rebuilding process (i.e. help identify possible positive experiences from the event).
7. Debriefing assists in the 're-entry' process back into the community or workplace.

Critical incident process and recovery (CIPR)

An alternative model developed by Stephen Galliano (clinical psychologist and clinical director of the Inernational Center for Advanced Studies) has the following phases:

1. Introduction
2. The incident day
3. After the incident
4. Coping mechanisms
5. Closure: individual sessions.

Galliano says:

> I am strongly of the opinion that there should never be any single 'interventions', and that follow-up of people over a period of time is a critical part of a responsible and ethical professional service. This concept of continuity of care also fits much more naturally into the duty of care owed by employers following disasters. Just as important in our view is to identify those people who are not going to make a reasonable recovery from trauma and who run the risk of falling into a state of mental ill health as a result of this. The largest proportion of this vulnerable group (although not all) can be identified in the first eight weeks following an incident.

The process:

- Defusing or psychological first aid to affected people and helpers within 24 hours of an incident
- Trauma debriefing provided no less than three days after an incident and ideally within seven days. Provided on a group basis to people considered emotionally strong enough to handle a group situation and on an individual basis to the others
- Careful and individual assessment of needs after debriefing as well as more prolonged and intense individual debriefing
- Ongoing support or counselling for especially vulnerable people after this first intervention and in the subsequent first few weeks

- Follow-up debriefing interventions at six–eight weeks and where necessary at 12–16 weeks
- Specialist screening for post-traumatic stress disorder (PTSD) at six–eight weeks after the incident
- Ongoing counselling for those clients considered suitable for this
- Specialist treatment for PTSD and other psychological disorders or managing the process of referral to NHS or other agencies for such treatment.

What you can do for family members:

- Listen and empathise. A sympathetic listener is important.
- Spend time with the traumatised person. There is no substitute for personal presence.
- Offer assistance and sympathy. Voiced support is critical.
- Reassure children, the elderly and even adults: they are safe.
- Don't tell traumatised people that they are 'lucky it wasn't worse'. Traumatised people are not consoled by such statements. Tell them instead that you're sorry such an event has occurred, and that you want to understand and assist them.
- Respect a family member's need for privacy and private grief.

What you can do for yourself:

- Physical exercise can help relieve stress. Strenuous exercise alternated with relaxation will help alleviate physical reactions.
- Remember that you're experiencing normal reactions to an abnormal situation.
- Talk to people. Talk is healing medicine.
- Accept support – from loved ones, friends and neighbours. People do care.
- Give yourself permission to feel rotten. You're suffering from loss. And, it's all right to grieve for the loss of material things. You wouldn't have obtained them or kept them around if they didn't have some meaning to you.
- When you're feeling rotten, remember that those around you are also under stress.
- Don't make any big life changes immediately. During periods of extreme stress, we all tend to make misjudgements.
- Eat well-balanced, regular meals and get rest.
- Be kind to yourself.

David Baldwin's Trauma Information Pages at www.trauma-pages.com

Further reading

Cohen, N. (1989) Lockerbie's other victims. *Independent,* 8 February, page 15.

Cunningham, V. (1988) Herald disaster – from the shop floor. *Counselling,* 1–6 August.

Davidson, J.R. (1995) Posttraumatic stress disorder and acute stress disorder. In: *Comprehensive Textbook of Psychiatry,* 6th edn (eds H.J. Kaplan and B.J. Sadock). Williams & Wilkins, Baltimore, MD.

Davis, J.A. (1993). On-site critical incident stress debriefing field interviewing techniques utilised in the aftermath of mass disaster. Training Seminar to Emergency Responders and Police Personnel, San Diego, CA, March.

Figley, C.R. (ed.) (1985) *Trauma and Its Wake: the study and treatment of Post -Traumatic Stress Disorder.* Brunner/Mazel, New York.

Galliano, S. (2002) Critical processing. *Critical Processing Journal.*

Hodgkinson, P.E. (1988) Psychological after-effects of transportation disaster. *Medical Science and Law,* **28(4):** 304–309.

Hodgkinson, P.E. (1989) Technological disaster – survival and bereavement. *Social Science and Medicine,* **29(3):** 351–356.

McCann, I.L., Sakheim, D.K. and Abrahamson, D.J. (1988) Trauma and victimisation: a model of psychological adaptation. *Counselling Psychologist,* **16(4).**

Mitchell, J.T. (1983) When disaster strikes: the critical incident stress debriefing process. *Journal of Emergency Medical Services,* January.

Mitchell, J.T. (1986). Critical incident stress management. *Response,* **24–25,** September/October.

Mitchell, J.T. (1988) Stress: the history and future of critical incident stress debriefings. *Journal of Emergency Medical Services,* 7-52.

Morris, B. (1989) Hillsborough. *Insight,* **9:** 8–9.

Oxfordshire Gulf War Psychosocial Support Group (undated) *Gulf War: advice for staff caring for victims and their relatives.* Oxfordshire Gulf War Psychosocial Support Group, Oxford.

Woodruff, I. (1989) Major incident: impact on staff. *Hospital Chaplain,* 12–17, June.

Wright, M. (1990) Planning a trauma counselling service. *Counselling,* August.

Davis, J.A. *Providing Critical Incident Stress Debriefing (CISD) to Individuals and Communities in Situational Crisis.* The American Academy of Experts in Traumatic Stress Home Page.
www.aaets.org
www.icasgroup.com

PREJUDICE (SEE ALSO: AUTHORITARIANISM)

The *Oxford English Dictionary* defines prejudice as: 'A previous judgement, especially a judgement formed before due examination or consideration; a premature or hasty judgement'. Prejudice, in social behaviour, is a pre-formed and unsubstantiated judgement or opinion about an individual or a group, either favourable or unfavourable in nature. A prejudiced person tends to believe that his own group is superior to others in intelligence, character or behaviour.

From a social psychological perspective, prejudice involves any or all of: derogatory attitudes or beliefs; the expression of negative feelings; the display of hostile or discriminatory behaviour towards members of a group, simply because they belong to that group.

Prejudice has existed for thousands of years and it can manifest itself in many aspects of human behaviour and has led to the most terrible atrocities in all parts of the world. It is often a way of giving expression to personal fears or insecurity. Sometimes prejudice can be extremely subtle and the discrimination may not be evident even to the person who discriminates. When unequal treatment takes the form of systematic abuse, exploitation and injustice, then it becomes social oppression.

Psychologists have sought the origins of prejudice in personality disorders, in the social environment and in attributes of normal thought processes. Prejudice often exists together with social institutions such as segregation, apartheid and other forms of discrimination. But segregation can also apply to the exclusion of a member of a minority group from social clubs or from access to particular jobs or educational opportunities. It is said not to be found among children under three or four years of age. Prejudiced attitudes have often proved extremely difficult to eradicate, even when integration is enforced by law. However, legislation does not readily change attitudes.

A prejudice may be either positive or negative and may be about a particular thing, event, person or idea. Prejudice is characterised by irrational, stereotyped beliefs and views and their accompanying emotions and values. Prejudice tells more about the bearer of the attitude than about the persons who are the objects of the prejudice. Prejudiced behaviour is discrimination.

An essential characteristic of prejudice is the need to separate people into acceptable and unacceptable groups. Our self-image is closely tied to the image of the group as a whole. Prejudice is failure to relate to people as unique individuals with distinct qualities and differences. Rather, people are lumped together as if they all possessed the same stereotyped qualities as one another. Generally, prejudice is an attitude of the majority towards a minority. Prejudice refers to attitudes; discrimination generally refers to behaviours.

Sexism

Sexism is prejudice under a different name; it is belief in (or a set of implicit assumptions about) the superiority of one's own sex, often accompanied by a stereotype or preconceived idea about the opposite sex. Sexism most commonly takes the form of an assumption of male superiority, regarding women as inherently inferior intellectually, psychologically and physically to men. This view, shared by both men and women, has historically shaped institutions of world society. It has been perpetuated through the acculturation of generations of children, with resultant differences between the sexes.

Sexism was not effectively challenged until the 20th century, with the growth of the militant women's rights movements. The term, coined by analogy with racism, was first used in the 1960s by feminist writers to describe language or behaviour that implied women's inferiority. Examples include the contentious use of male pronouns to describe both men and women and the assumption that some jobs are typically or appropriately performed only by one sex.

Institutionalised sexism operates as social oppression. For example, minimum requirements for certain jobs might automatically screen women out, giving the advantage to male applicants. At first glance this might not be obvious discrimination but it becomes clearer when the requirements bear no relation to the ability to do the job.

Racial prejudice

Racial prejudice, or racism, consists of negative attitudes directed in blanket fashion against socially defined groups. It is important to distinguish between the psychological aspects of racism (prejudice) and the social aspects (discrimination), although the one is to the other as ink is to a pen. Societies set groups apart and subject them to discrimination; this is racial prejudice. Conversely, people would not have become segregated unless there had already been widespread prejudice. Prejudice and discrimination feed upon each other. Attitudes can be moderated by experience, for example, when we move from one society to another. Many people keep their prejudices well hidden but in times of stress and threat these prejudices surface.

Racial prejudice is often part of society's way of blaming minorities for its economic and social problems. Racism is the theory or idea that there is a causal link between inherited physical traits and certain traits of personality, intellect or culture and, combined with it, the notion that some races are inherently superior to others. This is prejudice on a grand scale. Technically, any prejudice with a racial basis constitutes racism, just as any based on sex is sexism and any based on ethnicity is ethnicism. This means that prejudice directed against men is sexist, just as prejudice directed by blacks against whites is racist. Some sociologists argue that, while minorities can be just as prejudiced as those who dominate them, concepts such as racism and sexism should be reserved for prejudice whose ideological function is to justify social oppression.

Racial prejudice takes three main forms: xenophobia, the fear of foreigners; ethnic prejudice, the dislike of a person or race because of their different customs, beliefs and attitudes; and colour prejudice, which focuses upon skin colour and outward appearance.

Positive discrimination

Not all discrimination is based on prejudice. Positive discrimination is bias in favour of a particular individual or group of people precisely because they are often the object of prejudice and discrimination, where employment is actively sought out as applicants for jobs, government contracts and university admissions. Although this kind of positive discrimination has been quite controversial, it generally has had little effect on the overall distribution of men, women and members of different ethnic groups among occupations.

Values and beliefs in prejudice

Prejudice and discrimination are very powerful and are bound up with values and beliefs. It is worth repeating: prejudice is an attitude; discrimination is acting out our prejudices. A prejudiced attitude influences relationships with the target group but a society in which prejudice exists must experience difficulty with other relationships and with other societies. Prejudice and discrimination show themselves in many ways.

Probably the most obvious manifestation of racial prejudice was in the millions of Jews who were slaughtered under the Nazi regime. Apartheid in South Africa and the colour-bar in America are other examples of prejudice in action. Those three examples are safe for most of us to talk about without feeling the finger pointing at us. But we don't need to go to those extremes. Taking umbrage against an immigrant family coming to live next door or refusing to patronise a certain shop because the owner is from another country or giving preference to one person over another because of nationality are examples of discrimination.

Prejudice and discrimination have their roots in fear and in inferiority. Inferiority turned on its head becomes superiority. Superiority often accompanies a desire to ensure that the target person or group is kept at an inferior level in hierarchical relationships. For prejudiced people, equality of sorts exists only within their own 'in-group', yet even that semblance of equality is precariously balanced on the strictest conformity to the rules.

A possible reason for racial discrimination is based on the rarely articulated fear of losing one's cultural identity. That is one reason why immigrants, for several generations, tend to group together in communities, to keep alive their culture. Such communities help to cushion culture shock and the feeling of disintegration engendered in the transition from one culture to another.

People who are strongly prejudiced often see things in absolute terms, are closed-minded, do not tolerate ambiguity well and are generally intolerant and judgemental. Prejudices may be defences against feelings of inadequacy. Prejudice is closely linked to the idea of the scapegoat (see Scapegoating). Prejudiced people tend to see the world as being made up of in-groups, which must be supported, and out-groups, which must be avoided or rejected and attacked when they become threatening.

Counselling strongly prejudiced people can be very wearing, for there is often an accompanying lack of insight. If the premise is correct, that such people may be using prejudice as a defence against feelings of inferiority and inadequacy, then working to build up their self-esteem may be an effective way of lessening the prejudice, rather than tackling it head-on.

Further reading

Allport, G.W. (1954) *The Nature of Prejudice.* Addison-Wesley, Reading, MA.

Dovidio, J.F. and Fazio, R.H. (1986) *Prejudice, discrimination, and racism.* Academic Press, Orlando, FL.

Katz, J.H. (1978) *White Awareness: handbook for anti-racism training.* University of Oklahoma Press, Norman, OK.

Lago, C. and Thompson, J. (1989) Counselling and race. In: *Handbook of Counselling in Britain* (eds W. Dryden, D. Charles-Edwards and R. Woolfe). Tavistock/ Routledge, London.

Presenting problem

The presenting problem is what clients complain of – the client's 'admission ticket' to counselling. The presenting problem may be in the nature of a 'trial balloon': not of primary importance, but of sufficient import to generate some anxiety. The presenting problem can be thought of, in musical terms, as an 'overture'. An audience does not judge the performance by the overture; they wait to hear the full work.

In psychoanalytic and humanistic therapies, the presenting problem is regarded as symbolic of the client's underlying difficulties.

In therapies that concentrate on behaviour, the presenting problem is regarded as significant and treated accordingly. The professional discipline and theoretical orientation of the therapist will influence how the presenting problem is handled.

Presenting problems should not be dismissed as unimportant, for they give a clue to whether or not the client is suitable for counselling or whether other specialist help would be more appropriate.

Problem Management

These are goal-directed techniques aimed at improving the abilities of an individual or a family. Symptoms such as anxiety and depression may be due to the client's inadequate attempts at resolving certain situations. When new problem-solving skills are learned, the symptoms may fade.

Effective problem-solving can only take place when well-defined phases are pursued:

- Denying the problem exists
- Ignoring it, hoping it will go away
- Blaming something or someone for it
- Blaming oneself.

Before we can start on the problem-solving process it is necessary to acknowledge that a problem exists and that we intend to do something about it.

Table 9: *Nine-step problem solving*

Step 1 Define the problem This diagnostic stage helps to identify if there is conflict and, if so, where	Whose problem is it? Who is doing what, to whom? Are the perceptions accurate? Is communication distorted? What is at stake? What decisions have to be made? Defining the problem provides clarity, understanding and purpose.
Step 2 Decide a method of attack	Is there anyone else who can help? Do you need any more information? Do you know anyone else who has successfully solved this problem? What sources can you tap?
Step 3 Generate alternatives	Brainstorm, if possible with someone else Think through each alternative, looking at positive and negative aspects.
Step 4 Test alternatives for reality	Don't eliminate possibilities too quickly Try operating the 'detailed response' before rejecting something – this means that, before a suggestion is rejected, you must have generated at least three positive state- ments about it Work out a 'for' and 'against' for each possibility When all possibilities have been filtered through the detailed response, arrange them in a hierarchy of feasibility.

Step 5 Choose an alternative	Use force field analysis (see Goals and goal-setting) The chosen alternative must be within one's capability and within available resources.
Step 6 Plan for action	It is necessary to choose a planning process that is appropriate to the potential solution. There is a danger of becoming so engrossed in the planning that the original problem or the alternatives are lost sight of.
Step 7 Implement the plan	Use Rudyard Kipling's 'six honest serving men', (5WH): Who? What? Why? When? Where? How?
Step 8 Evaluation is at two levels	An evaluation of the action plan itself – how far did the plan meet the set goals and objectives? It may be necessary to go back to step 6. The second level evaluates how effective the overall problem-solving was. Just how far did the plan contribute to the outcome?
Step 9 Next steps	Follow-up is essential. If the original problem still exists, use 5WH. It may be necessary to go back to stage I and work through the process once more. Follow-up may also be helpful to consolidate the learning experience.

Problem solving is aided by:

- Having a healthy self-respect, which also means accepting the consequences of one's own personal worth and contributions
- A healthy other-respect. This may mean giving credit to those who think differently. It also means being able to listen to what others say.
- A healthy optimism that problems can be solved if everyone is willing to work at them to find an acceptable solution
- A respect for, but not fear of, conflict as being potentially creative
- A willingness to invest energy and to take risks.

Skills essential in problem solving:

- Active listening, clarifying, paraphrasing, self-disclosure
- Diagnostic skills (steps 1–2); Decision-making skills (steps 2–5); Data-collecting skills (steps 5–6); Design and planning skills (steps 5–8); Organising/administrative skills (step 7); Analysis skills (step 8)
- Counsellors can help clients to develop their problem-solving skills and so reduce the helplessness they feel at being confronted with a problem that seems insurmountable.

In Chapter 2 of *The Skilled Helper*, Gerard Egan presents a seven-step problem-management process:

1. **Initial awareness.** Identifying issues
2. **Urgency.** As main problem develops
3. **Initial search for remedies.** Trying to get relief; the person in an unhappy marriage starts to complain
4. **Estimation of cost.** Financial, emotional, mental, physical

5. **Deliberation.** Weighing of choices
6. **Rational decision.** Making an intellectual choice
7. **Rational-emotional decision.** Head and heart joined. Decisions based on head and heart are more likely to be fruitful.

Cautions:

- No decision-making process is every strictly sequential
- Uncontrolled emotions can derail the process. The cost may prove too high
- Difficult decisions often result in no decision
- Not enough attention to solution-focused action.

Creative problem management (see also: Left/right brain)

Profoundly creative people are reported to be comfortable using both left and right hemispheres of the brain. Einstein, it is said, relied on geometric mental images rather than language for his analyses.

Creative people are exceptional only in that they have learned to pay attention to, rather than ignore, their insights, visions and altered states of consciousness. At the same time, they subject their visions, insights and intuitions to the most rigorous testing and evaluation. The key to true creativity lies in a balance between the two hemispheres, rather than dominance by one over the other.

The traditional mode of learning and problem-solving is rational, which involves reasoning – a left-brain function. It should be emphasised, however, that many brilliant plans fail because they do not take account of the non-rational, emotional components of the plan.

While it is comparatively easy to teach a rational, logical approach (provided the student is temperamentally suited) it is only possible to *develop* and *train* the right-brain functions.

Most of us face decisions and actions. Many of us have been conditioned to believe in the superiority of the logical and analytical process, and do not trust emotional, intuitive or value-based processing of information.

The creative problem-solving techniques presented in this entry reconcile logic with intuition, facts with emotions.

Table 10: *Left/right brain problem-solving*

The left-brain problem solver:	The right-brain problem solver:
Defines the objectives of the decision to be made	Moderates rational thought with emotional-intuitive preferences
Classifies the objectives according to their importance	Uses various techniques to bring 'out-of-conscious' material into awareness
Identifies alternative courses of action Evaluates alternative courses of actions by the objectives	Avoids censorship of ideas during their 'incubation' Views divergent, even contradictory, ideas with respect rather than with scepticism or defensiveness

Selects the alternative with the best score	Tries not to ignore internal warnings that something is wrong
Identifies and assesses possible consequences of alternatives	Checks any rational problem-solving method to see whether it feels intuitively good in process and in the final decision
Implements the decision with careful monitoring and follow-up of possible negative consequences	Tries to remain constantly self-aware

In counselling, it often becomes necessary to move away from the safety of our preferred way of working in order to help move the client forward. Learning to be creative keeps the counselling mind open and alert.

Further reading

Earley, L.C. and Rutledge, P.B. (1980) A nine-step problem-solving model. In: *1980 Annual Handbook for Group Facilitators*. University Associates, San Diego, CA.

Egan, G. (2002) *The Skilled Helper: a problem-management and opportunity-development approach to helping*, 7th edn. Brooks/Cole, Pacific Grove, CA.

Haley, J. (1976) *Problem-Solving Therapy*. Jossey-Bass, San Francisco, CA.

PSYCHE

The oldest and most general meaning of 'psyche' is that of the early Greeks, who regarded it as 'soul' or the very essence of life. In classical mythology, Psyche was the heroine of the story of Cupid and Psyche.

A certain Greek king had three daughters, of whom Psyche, the youngest, was so beautiful that people worshipped her and neglected Venus. Venus (Aphrodite) was so jealous she sent her son, Cupid (Eros), with instructions to make her fall in love with some ugly, old man.

Cupid, instead, fell in love with Psyche himself. He told her that she must never see him but one night she disobeyed and, while she was looking at him by the light of a lamp, he awoke and he fled.

Psyche was desolate and searched far and wide for him. She finally submitted herself to Venus who set her four impossible tasks: to sort a huge pile of different seeds into their respective piles; to acquire some golden fleece from the terrible rams of the sun; to fill a crystal container from an inaccessible stream; to descend into the underworld and fill a small box with beauty ointment. This last task was made all the more difficult because Psyche would have to harden her heart to compassion.

Psyche completed all her tasks, the first three with assistance from ants, an eagle and a green reed. The final task she accomplished by saying 'No'. Cupid persuaded Jupiter (Zeus), the Father of the Gods, to let him marry Psyche; he agreed and Psyche was made immortal.

In Greek folklore the soul was pictured as a butterfly – another meaning of both 'psyche' and 'soul' – the soul or spirit distinguished from the body.

The mind functions as the centre of thought, feeling and behaviour and consciously or unconsciously adjusting and relating the body to its social and physical environment.

In analytical psychology the psyche is the sum total of all the conscious and unconscious psychic processes. The soul is regarded as the sum total of personality, comprising the persona; the outward face or attitude, the mask; the Anima (in men) and the Animus (in women), the inward attitude or face.

The four main functions of the psyche are intuition, sensing, thinking and feeling. Each approaches reality from a different point of view and with a different question. Each grasps a different part of reality.

Further reading

Jung, C.G. (1958) *The Collected Works – Psychological Types* (vol. 6). Routledge & Kegan Paul, London.

PSYCHIC PAIN

Psychic pain is pain of the heart, mind and spirit. It is as real and powerful as any physical pain. Suppression of psychic pain very often leads to physical disorders.

Psychic pain is often the pain of the deepest sadness, where the person feels 'like a dried-out husk' and where tears – normally therapeutic – dry up in the eyes before they can be shed.

Many people are taught that it is a worthy thing to endure physical pain. In the same way, there is the myth that to admit to psychic pain is a sign of weakness. Suppression of psychic pain drives it deeper into the mind and into the body and healing is therefore made much more difficult. Locked-in pain wastes valuable creative energy and leads to exhaustion.

Many people are now experimenting with new therapies to relieve physical pain. People who can be encouraged to express their psychic pain through counselling are likely to discover a generally improved state of physical health. Pain and anger are close companions. The ability to express anger is one way of expressing the underlying pain.

Psychic pain begins to be experienced at the moment of birth; it is the price we pay for separation. It is also the price we have to pay for forming relationships, for within every relationship lie the seeds of separation.

Speaking of the connection between depression and pain, Professor Lader said:

> If the depressive (person) already suffers from chronic pain, symptoms become much worse. This is particularly important in the management of the terminal patients where the very understandable reactive depression renders the patient miserable and increasingly symptomatic. The close relationship between depression and pain has led some observers to refer to depression as 'psychic pain'.

Psychic pain may be caused by such experiences as:

- Bereavement
- Divorce

- Enforced isolation
- Helplessness
- Loneliness
- Poverty
- Loss of purpose
- Loss of self-esteem.

C.S. Lewis (1961) said:

> Did you ever know, dear, how much you took away with you when you left? You have stripped me even of my past, even of the things we never shared. I was wrong to say the stump was recovering from the pain of the amputation. I was deceived because it has so many ways to hurt me that I discover them only one by one.

Further reading

Lader, M.H. (1981) *Focus on Depression*. Bencard, Great West Road, Middlesex.
Lewis, C.S. (1957) *The Problem of Pain*. Fontana, London.
Lewis, C.S. (1961) A *Grief Observed*. Faber & Faber, London.

PSYCHOANALYSIS (SIGMUND FREUD, 1856–1939) (SEE ALSO: HYPNOTHERAPY, PSYCHODYNAMIC COUNSELLING, TRANSFERENCE AND COUNTER-TRANSFERENCE)

Sigmund Freud, Moravian-born founder of psychoanalysis, studied medicine in Vienna, which became his home until 1938 when, with his daughter Anna, he fled the Nazis and settled in London.

While working with patients under hypnosis (with Joseph Breur), Freud observed that often there was improvement in the condition when the sources of the patients' ideas and impulses were brought into the conscious.

Also, observing that patients talked freely while under hypnosis, he evolved his technique of free association. Noting that sometimes patients had difficulty in making free associations, he concluded that painful experiences were being repressed and held back from conscious awareness. Freud deduced that what was being repressed were disturbing sexual experiences – real or in fantasy.

Repressed sexual energy and its consequent anxiety find an outlet in various symptoms that serve as ego defences. The concept of anxiety now includes feelings of guilt, fear, shame, aggression, hostility and fear of loneliness at the separation from someone on whom the sufferer is dependent.

Freud developed his psychoanalytic method and the technique of free association during the years 1892 to 1895. His basic theory was that neuroses are rooted in suppressed sexual desires and sexual experiences in childhood. He analysed dreams in terms of unconscious desires.

He maintained that many of the impulses forbidden or punished by parents are derived from innate instincts. Forbidding expression to these instincts merely drives them out of awareness into the unconscious. There they reside to affect dreams, slips of speech or mannerisms and may also manifest themselves in symptoms of mental illness.

Freud's view – that the conscious and the unconscious are sharply divided and that access to the unconscious is denied except by psychoanalysis – does not meet with universal acceptance. Rather, many believe that there are various layers of awareness.

In summary, Freud's view was that humans are driven by sex and aggression, the same basic instincts as animals. Society is in constant struggle against any expression of these.

Freud's Psychological Wednesday Circle – the 'inner circle' – was formed by invitation from him to several like-minded people to discuss psychoanalytic matters and later became the Vienna Psycho-Analytic Society.

Psychoanalysis, behaviourism and humanistic psychology are the trilogy of the main orientations of psychotherapy.

Psychoanalysis includes investigating mental processes not easily accessed by other means. It is a method of investigating and treating neurotic disorders and the scientific collection of psychological information. The main purpose of psychoanalysis is to make unconscious material conscious.

Stages of Freudian psychosexual development

1. Oral stage

The oral stage is the earliest phase of both libidinal and ego development, extending from birth to approximately 18 months. The mouth is the main source of pleasure and centre of experience and the libido is satisfied through oral contact with a variety of objects, biting and sucking.

Oral needs are also satisfied by thumb-sucking or inserting environmental objects, such as dolls, other toys or blankets, into the mouth.

The infant's needs and means of expression are centred in all the organs related to the oral zone. Oral sensations include thirst, hunger and pleasurable tactile stimulation, which come by way of the nipple (or substitute). Although the oral stage clearly begins at birth, it is not clear if it ends with weaning.

According to psychoanalytic theory, people who have an oral fixation retain the mouth as the primary erotogenic zone, have a mother-fixation, are prone to mood swings and tend to identify with others rather than relating to them. Fixation is the process by which a person becomes or remains ambivalently attached to an object. Fixation, then, is failure to progress through the appropriate stages of development and is characterised by:

• Infantile and outmoded behaviour patterns, particularly when under stress
• A compulsive tendency to choose objects that resemble the one on which the person is fixated
• Feeling drained of energy, because the energy is being invested in a past object.

Traits said to be associated with incomplete resolution of the oral phase are:

• Excessive optimism or, conversely, pessimism
• Narcissism

- Being demanding of other people
- Dependency, characterised by needing to be looked after
- Weakened self-reliance and self-esteem
- Envy and jealousy.

Freud believed that the oral phase begins to shift to the anal region towards the end of an infant's first year.

2. Anal stage

This describes the second stage of psychosexual (libidinal) development. In the anal phase the anus and defecation are the major sources of sensuous pleasure. The anal stage, generally the second and third years of life, is held to be significant for the child's later development because the way the infant responses to parental demands for bowel control may have far-reaching effects on personality.

The desire of the parent means control over the infant and this develops into a struggle over retaining or expelling the faeces. This results in ambivalence, together with a struggle over separation and independence. Loss of control often brings with it feelings of shame and fear of displeasure or punishment.

This phase is also important in the development of ego, as the infant begins to exercise sphincter control, something so obviously important to the parents and which brings mutual pleasure. Should a person become fixated or locked in the anal stage, that person may develop what has been termed an anal character.

The anal expulsive character typically is said to be excessively pliant, untidy and generous; the anal retentive to be obstinate, orderly and miserly.

The theory proposes that the anal character may be either of these two extreme forms; more commonly, the traits are combined. The theory also says that the anal character is an unconscious reaction formation against finding erotic pleasure in excretion. Although the term was first used by Freud, it still offers a valuable insight into the obsessive-compulsive personality.

People who have resolved the conflicts of this stage are:

- Certain of their own autonomy
- Independent
- Self-determined
- Not overwhelmed by guilt, shame or self-doubt
- Able to cooperate without the need to comply.

3. Phallic stage

This describes the third stage of psychosexual development, in which there is interest in the sexual organs. The phallic stage occurs between the ages of three and five years. Sexual gratification occurs through direct experience with the genitals – the penis or the clitoris.

The penis becomes the primary focus for both sexes; lack of a penis in the female, giving rise to penis envy, is evidence of castration. It is at this stage that we unconsciously desire sexual involvement with the parent of the opposite sex, the Oedipus complex. The guilt over masturbation and Oedipal wishes, coupled with the threat of castration, results in castration anxiety. Successful resolution of the phallic stage provides the foundation for a sexual identity. Resolution of the Oedipal conflict releases energy to be channelled into constructive purposes. It is at this stage that the superego – or conscience – starts to regulate the child's conduct and behaviour.

4. Latency period

This is the period of sexual development between the age of four or five years and the beginning of adolescence, separating infantile from normal sexuality. During this – relatively quiescent – waiting time, memories and wishes remaining from the earlier infantile period are repressed. The latency period is marked by an absence of any great sexual development. Ego and superego development allow the person greater control over potentially destructive impulses.

This is the period of affiliation with others of the same sex and sublimation of energies into learning, play and exploration of the world around, as well as the development of important relationship skills.

Some psychoanalysts, e.g. Erikson, who focus less on sexual development, point to the great social and cognitive developments of this period. The development of social skills, within the education system, may provoke the development of new feelings of inferiority.

This is a period of consolidation and integration, when the child looks forward to adulthood; where industry means growing independence.

Where there is insufficient sublimation into learning and activities, the child might lack internal control, resulting in precocious sexual behaviour or aggression.

5. Genital stage

This describes the final stage of psychosexual (libidinal) development, usually from the onset of puberty until the person reaches young adulthood. In some models this stage is divided into pre-adolescence, early adolescence and late adolescence.

Physiological maturation, with its hormonal changes, increases libidinal drive. While on the one hand this reawakens conflicts of previous stages of development, on the other it also provides opportunity for these conflicts to be resolved and the achieving of a mature sexual identity.

The aims of this stage are:

- Successful integration of the previous stages
- Independence from parents
- To establish successful sexual relationships, free from the Oedipal complex
- To establish a mature personal identity
- To accept a set of adult roles with their accompanying responsibilities
- To accept social expectations and cultural values
- To work toward self-set goals.

The main techniques of psychoanalysis

- Free association (see Free association)
- Interpretation of dreams, resistance and parapraxes (see Humour)
- Analysing and working through the transference (see Transference and counter-transference).

Psychoanalytic assumptions

- The concepts are applicable to normal and abnormal behaviour.
- There is a tripartite mental apparatus – id, ego and superego.
- The idea of psychological adaptation – where the mental apparatus attempts to reduce conflict as much as possible
- The idea of psychic determinism – that all aspects of the mental life are determined, that nothing in the mental life is due to chance, any more than in the physical world
- There is both a conscious and an unconscious world.

Basic concepts

1. The pleasure and reality principles
2. Instincts
3. The conscious and the unconscious
4. The mental apparatus
5. Anxiety
6. Psychical energy, cathexis and anticathexis
7. Bisexuality
8. Normal development.

1. The pleasure and reality principles

Mental activity is governed by the pleasure and the reality principles. The term 'pleasure principle' describes the basic human tendency of the person to maintain a pleasant, tolerable energy level through the relief of inner tension and in so doing to avoid pain and to seek pleasure. The terms 'pleasure' and 'pain' may be misleading – 'gratification' and 'unpleasure' may be more accurate. The pleasure principle is conspicuous in the first years of life and is moderated by the development of the reality principle.

The gratification of pleasure (or the avoidance of discomfort – the reduction of tension) is balanced by the ability of the reality principle (the leading principle in the ego) to accommodate to the facts of, and the objects existing in, the outside world.

The reality principle allows postponement of gratification to accommodate other immediate needs or to secure greater pleasure at a later time.

Normal development is seen as acquiring and strengthening the reality principle so that it acts as a brake on the more primitive pleasure principle.

It is not so much that pleasure is actively sought but that discomfort is actively avoided in order to keep instinctual tension in the best possible balance. Rather than regard the pleasure and reality principles as being in opposition to each other, it might be advantageous to think of them as two integral parts that operate in different ways to keep the organism balanced, in much the say way as do the parts in a thermostat.

2. Instincts

Instincts are innate, inherited, unlearned and biologically useful behaviours. The presence of instincts does not indicate the absence of intelligence or learning. For Freud, instincts bridged the mental and organic spheres. Instinct theory plays a prominent role in psychoanalysis, although it has been modified and now the emphasis is on instinctual behaviour, rather than on the instincts themselves as fixed motivators of behaviour. Human instinct is a fiercely contested topic.

The psychoanalytic classification of instincts is as follows:

- **Ego instincts** are non-sexual, self-preserving and associated with repression.
- **Libido** is the sexual instinct, which has both mental and physiological manifestations. Libido shows itself in ways other than sexual union. Freud considered psychiatric symptoms to be the result of misdirection or inadequate discharge of libido. Jung used the term to encompass all life processes in all species.
- **Aggression**: Freud, unable to reconcile some of the self-destructive elements he observed in his patients, formulated the aggression instinct.
- **Life and death instincts**: With the modification of the instinct theory, Freud concentrated in later writings on the life and death instincts only.
  - Life instinct (Eros): Eros refers to the tendency of particles to reunite or for parts to bind to one another, to form greater unities. Sexual reproduction is an example.
  - Death instinct (thanatos): Thanatos is defined as the tendency to return to an inanimate state. Because all organisms return to the inanimate state Freud considered thanatos to be the dominant force.

3. The conscious and the unconscious

The conscious is the region of the mind that, with the preconscious and the unconscious, makes up the psyche. Freud described the conscious as the 'sense organ of the ego'. The conscious is open to immediate awareness, unlike the preconscious and the unconscious, which are not.

The functions of the ego – reality testing, perception, observation and evaluation – are all at a conscious level. Some of the superego functions – criticism and conscience – are also mainly conscious. The defence mechanism and censorship are not within the conscious.

Some therapies emphasise working directly with what is conscious, as only what is observable or can be described can be accurately interpreted.

The preconscious, a region somewhere between the unconscious and the conscious known as 'the antechamber to consciousness', is also referred to as the descriptive unconscious or the foreconscious. The contents of the preconscious – knowledge, emotions, images – though not immediately in the conscious are accessible to it because censorship is absent. Material can be described as temporarily forgotten – suppressed and not repressed. The preconscious is important in the process of working through, a process necessary to consolidate the insight gained through interpretation.

The unconscious refers to mental processes of which the person is unaware. It is the storehouse of repressed material. Unconscious material is brought into the conscious only through dreams, word associations, free associations, parapraxes and symptoms. The unconscious has two levels: the unconscious proper, which contains repressed material admissible to the conscious only through analysis; and the preconscious, which refers to material that, though unconscious, is available and accessible.

The unconscious exists at the deepest level of the psyche, beneath the conscious and the preconscious. Only the id is entirely within the unconscious. Unconscious material comprises fantasies and images or representations that make their way into the conscious symbolically.

The discovery of the clinical importance of the unconscious became the cornerstone of psychoanalysis.

4. The mental apparatus

The id is one of the three parts of the psyche, a completely chaotic, primitive reservoir of energy derived from the instincts, which demands immediate satisfaction. The id is not synonymous with the unconscious, although it represents a major portion of it. Freud proposed that at birth the neonate is endowed with an id with instinctual drives seeking gratification. It is entirely self-contained and isolated from the world about it and is bent on achieving its own aims.

Characteristics of the id:

- It contains the psychic content related to the primitive instincts of the body, notably sex and aggression, as well as all material inherited and present at birth
- It is oblivious of the external world and unaware of the passage of time
- It functions entirely on the pleasure–pain principle
- It supplies the energy for the development and continued functioning of mental life.

The task of psychoanalysis is to make the ego function more effectively at the expense of the id. Totally effective functioning is never totally achieved or even desirable, for the id provides the creative energy to sustain the ego and superego. The aim should be to integrate the id, not to overpower it.

The id is the oldest of these systems. It contains everything that is inherited and fixed in the constitution. It is filled with energy from the instincts and strives to operate the pleasure principle. It is a chaos, a cauldron of seething emotions. It knows no judgement, values, good or evil and knows no morality. It is not governed by logic.

The ego, literally meaning 'I', is the system of rational and realistic functioning of the personality. The ego is one's perception of self. It is the part that is in touch with reality, influenced by the external world and dealing with stimulation arising from without and within. Ego-psychologists are those who give greater weight to ego processes, such as reality-perception, conscious learning and voluntary control.

The characteristics of the ego:

- It has the task of self-preservation, which it achieves by developing defence mechanisms.
- It gains control over the primitive demands of the id.
- The ego remembers, evaluates, plans and interacts with the physical and social world around.
- It gives continuity and consistency of behaviour.
- It is separate from both personality and body.
- It is capable of change throughout life.

The newborn infant has only the most rudimentary ego. The ego influences the id by what happens in the external world and replaces the pleasure principle with the reality principle. The ego is derived from bodily sensations and mediates between the id and the outside world. It represents reason and common sense and operates the reality principle to control the destructive potential of the id's pleasure principle. It solves problems and perceives. Freud described the id as a horse and the ego as its rider.

An important dimension of the ego has been characterised as ego-strength. As we progress from immediate to directed behaviour, from pre-logical to rational thinking, we move slowly through a number of intermediate stages during childhood. Even in physical maturity, people differ considerably in the forms and effectiveness of ego functioning.

Some behavioural psychologists have adopted the psychoanalytic concept of ego strength – the degree of the ability to adapt oneself to reality. By measuring variables such as self-control, the ability to anticipate the future and the capacity to focus attention, they have found that a stable family life tends to produce greater ego strength in children.

Ego-strength is characterised by:

- Objective appraisal of the world and one's place in it
- Self-knowledge (insight)
- Ability to plan and organise
- Ability to choose between alternatives
- Not being overwhelmed by needs and desires
- Ability to pursue a chosen course
- Theoretically, the 'stronger' the ego, the more able the individual will be to withstand the trials of life, although this would be difficult to ascertain.

On the other hand, people with weak egos are more like the child:

- Their behaviour is impulsive and immediate.
- Their perception of reality and self is distorted.

- They are less capable of productive work because energy is drained into the protection of warped and unrealistic self-concepts.
- They may be burdened by neurotic symptoms.

The superego is the last of the components of the psychic apparatus to develop. It has been called 'the heir to the Oedipus complex'. It is that part of the ego in which self-observation, self-criticism and other reflective activities develop. It is formed gradually within the ego as a mechanism for maintaining the ego-ideal.

The ego-ideal is the standard of perfection we create for ourselves and is derived from loved or admired (rather than judging and threatening) figures and images. It is responsible for the sense of guilt and self-reproaches so typical in neuroses. The ego-ideal consists of precepts ('You ought to be like this') and prohibitions ('You ought not to be like that'). Both precepts and prohibitions result from the struggle to resolve the Oedipus complex, and also represent conscience.

The superego behaves as a moral judge, criticising the thoughts and acts of the ego, causing feelings of guilt and anxiety when the ego gratifies or tends to gratify the primitive impulses of the id.

The superego evolves, to a large extent, as a result of repression of the instincts; it is thus more closely related to the id than to the ego.

In the developing process, standards, restrictions and punishments imposed by authority figures are internalised into the superego, which then becomes self-governing.

The immature superego tends to be rigid and punitive. Modification over time and with experience permits adult sexual behaviour.

The upheaval and aggressive acting-out behaviour of adolescence can be understood in terms of the instinctual release previously curbed by the superego. One of the major tasks of adolescence is to modify the development of the superego. Freud's first use of 'superego' related to his belief that obsessional ideas were self-reproaches for some sexual act performed with pleasure in childhood.

Some people suffer from excessive conscience, characterised by excessive work, earnestness and rituals, rarely allowing themselves pleasure. Only when we can achieve some separateness from superego can we live satisfactorily, even though sometimes the price of disobedience is guilt.

5. Anxiety
Anxiety is a reaction to actual danger or a signal involving the perception of impending danger, which may be realistic (from the environment); moral (from conflict with the superego); or neurotic (from conflict with the id's impulses).

6. Psychical energy, cathexis and anticathexis
The id, ego and superego are charged with psychical energy, similar to an electric charge. Cathexis is a neologism invented by Freud, analogous to the flow of an electrical charge. Anticathexis is a blocking of the discharge of energy.

7. Bisexuality

Freud believed that all human beings are constitutionally psychosexually bisexual. As evidence of this he points to the biological fact that male and female have vestiges of the organs of the other sex and that libido is asexual. Both the woman and the man develop out of the child with a bisexual disposition.

8. Normal development

This may be viewed as:

- Passing through successive stages of sexual maturation without major fixations and regressions
- Developing an ego that copes reasonably effectively with the external world
- Developing a superego based on constructive identifications
- Not developing defence mechanisms that are punitive and moralistic.

Psychoanalytical belief is that neuroses are acquired only during early childhood. The neurotic person is unable to heal the disordered ego and the misery is perpetuated.

The ego pays the price of its defences by being denied access to repressed material by which neurotic conflict would be resolved and is weakened by its repression.

Personality functioning is impaired when psychical energy is used in harmful, defensive anticathexes. Neurotic symptoms will continue so long as the repressions continue.

Psychoanalytic therapy

- A neurotic person is someone who is incapable of enjoyment and efficiency.
- To be capable of enjoyment and to live efficiently, the neurotic person needs to place the libido in real objects instead of transforming it into symptoms.
- To live efficiently, the ego needs to have the energy of the libido at its disposal rather than wasting it in repressions; the superego needs to be allowed libidinal expression and the efficient use of the ego.
- The objectives of psychoanalysis are to free impulses, strengthen reality-based ego-functioning and so to alter the contents of the superego so that it operates less punitively.
- The aim of therapy is to help a person become more self-aware and to achieve insight.

The stages of psychotherapy

- The opening phase
- The development of transference
- Working through
- Resolution of the transference.

The process of psychotherapy

- Free association
- Working with resistance
- Interpretation – the means whereby repressed, unconscious material is made conscious
- Interpretation of dreams.

Schools of psychotherapy using variations of psychoanalysis:

- Freudian psychoanalysis – followers of Sigmund and Anna Freud
- Analytical psychology – followers of Jung
- Individual psychology – followers of Adler
- Interpersonal psychology – followers of Sullivan and Horney
- Object relations or 'British School' – followers of Balint, Fairbairn, Guntrip, Winnicott.

Each of the main schools has developed its own methods of training and accreditation. Knowledge derived from psychoanalysis has led to insights into:

- Art
- Religion
- Social organisation
- Child development
- Education.

Major criticisms of psychoanalysis

- Self-fulfilling
- Overemphasises sexuality
- Untestable and unscientific
- Deterministic and pessimistic
- Politically repressive
- Anti-feminist
- Ignores social and interpersonal dynamics
- Elitist, costly and time-consuming.

Further reading

Erikson, E.H. (1963) *Childhood and Society*. Penguin, Harmondsworth.

Gabbard, G.O. (1995) Theories of personality and psychopathology: psychoanalysis. In: *Comprehensive Textbook of Psychiatry*, 6th edn (eds H.J. Kaplan and B.J. Sadock). Williams & Wilkins, Baltimore, MD.

Karasu, T.B. (1995) Psychoanalysis and psychoanalytic psychotherapy. In: *Comprehensive Textbook of Psychiatry*, 6th edn (eds H.J. Kaplan and B.J. Sadock). Williams & Wilkins, Baltimore, MD.

Kernberg, G.S. (1976) *Internal World and External Reality*. Jason Aronson, New York.

Rycroft, C. (ed.) (1968) *Psychoanalysis Observed*. Penguin, Harmondsworth.

Smith, D.L. (1996) Psychodynamic therapy: the Freudian approach. In: *Handbook of Individual Therapy* (ed. W. Dryden). Sage Publications, London.

PSYCHODRAMA

Psychodrama employs guided dramatic action to examine problems or issues raised by an individual (psychodrama) or a group (sociodrama), in which people dramatise their personal problems within a group setting. The technique was introduced in the 1920s by the Viennese psychiatrist Jacob. L. Moreno.

Although the situations in psychodrama are simulated, they can generate insight and release emotions through catharsis. It is a powerful method of working, which, in the hands of an experienced therapist, can be liberating. A stage setting is generally used, the therapist acting as the 'director', with group members playing various roles.

Using experiential methods, role theory and group dynamics, psychodrama facilitates insight, personal growth and integration on cognitive, affective and behavioural levels. It clarifies issues, increases physical and emotional wellbeing, enhances learning and develops new skills.

The roles

- **The stage**: The physical space in which the drama is conducted.
- **Director**: The group therapist or leader is both director and active participant in the drama, whose role is a catalyst.
- **Protagonist**: This is the person selected from the group and on whom the group focuses its attention. The situation may be chosen by the protagonist or by the director. The protagonist provides all the material, thoughts, feelings and historical details. The director helps the protagonist to work through towards a resolution.
- **Auxiliary ego or egos**: A member or members of the group act(s) out the roles of, for example, significant absent people, e.g. someone who has died.
- **Audience**: Although only a few members of the group may be actively involved, all are involved to the degree that they are observers and are encouraged to identify with parts of what is taking place.

In a classically structured psychodrama session, there are three distinct phases (structural components) of group interaction:

- **The warm-up:** The group theme is identified and a protagonist is selected.
- **The action:** The problem is dramatised and the protagonist explores new methods of resolving it.
- **The sharing:** Group members are invited to express their connection with the protagonist's work.

Some of the techniques are as follows:

- **Soliloquy:** The person verbalises his psychological reactions to various remembered or imagined situations.
- **Self-presentation:** The person plays the part of various significant others.
- **Self-realisation:** the person enacts his past and future life plan.
- **Role playing:** This may be the impromptu enacting of some part of the prota-

gonist's life – past, present or future. It might include acting out a stress-provoking situation.

- **Role reversal**: The person takes the part of someone else with whom inter-action is difficult. Each is encouraged to act, speak and think like the other.
- **Mirroring**: A member of the audience attempts to copy the behaviour of the person, to enable that person to see himself through someone else's eyes.
- **Sculpting**: This is where one person is asked to describe, for example, his place within a group (often a family) by using space/position, not words.

A personal account of psychodrama

www.jkp.com

I never fancied myself as an actor, although I could have followed in my grand-mother's London's West End footsteps. So why did I volunteer? It was certainly not for glory or face, but more of a challenge.

The Institute of Counselling was producing a series of training videos and I appeared on several, counselling clients. When the boss asked for a volunteer to be a Protagonist (client) in a demonstration of psychodrama, that was the challenge. Over the years as a teacher of counselling skills I had put myself on the line many times. Would I have volunteered had I known the outcome of this challenge?

The Director, as he is called in psychodrama, Derek Gale, led the whole group gently into what psychodrama is and the various roles. Then it was crunch time for me. Although I knew what I wanted to portray, that was all. I had rehearsed nothing, not even in my mind.

It was ten years since my dad died, and I knew there was unfinished business to clear up. Was I nervous? No, not nervous, but apprehensive; would I be able to enter in? Would I be able to let go and get in touch with my feelings in front of an audience, all members of the training group?

Over the ten years I had done a lot of thinking and exploration of my relation-ship with my father, so what was the unfinished business I just didn't know, but my gut was telling me that this was my time.

Unfortunately, we were running for some time before the camera crew realised that the cameras weren't switched on! That was a turn-off straightaway. So we started again.

Part of the premise of psychodrama is that you can re-enact so that you change events, and by so doing you change the feelings surrounding the event.

The circumstances were that although dad had been ill, he was only in hospital less than a day when he died, just before my wife and I arrived. So we didn't get the chance to say goodbye. I had seen him the day before he was taken to hospital. It was then he asked me to shave him and trim his finger-nails. We talked about dying and that he would soon be with Mum, to whom he was married for nearly 57 years when she died four years earlier.

He was not a very open man, and didn't find it easy to express his feelings; quite the opposite. He was a stoic of the first order. We had a good father/son relationship and shared a sound Christian faith, and I was immensely proud of him. There were many things I could have wanted to say to him, to tell him that I loved him and how much I appreciated his support of me all through my life. The psychodrama gave me that opportunity.

I remember at one stage asking one of the camera crew to be my father, and it was then, with him lying on the floor, dying, that I was able to pour out my grief and kiss him goodbye.

It is said that actors become so wrapped up in the part they are playing that they are not aware of the audience. That's how it was for me. Part of me was aware that the other members of the group were crying, sharing my grief, yet another part seemed unaware. Yet in a strange way what I was experiencing seemed to act as a catalyst for them, tapping into their own unresolved grief.

I had no idea of the length of time, but the session went on for much longer than normal. Just as in writing a book there is a time to write 'THE END', so it was in my session. I felt drained yet cleansed; tired yet exhilarated.

I had shared something of the deepest part of my whole being, not facts, but deep feelings. I had shared my grief when I realised that I was now an orphan. No longer would I have my dad to talk to and share the joys and sorrows of life with. Yet by sharing my grief and pain I had made new connections and established new links with people who would help to fill the gap. That for me made it all worthwhile.

A bonus is that the video has helped so many people. It is like taking part in a psychodrama master class, which has helped many people to release their own unresolved grief.

For further details contact Video 6, *Counselling in Role Play*, The Institute of Counselling, 6 Dixon Street, Glasgow, G1 4AX.
Tel: 0141 204 2230
Fax: 0141 221 2841
www.CollegeofCounselling.com
E-mail: IofCounsel@aol.com

Further reading

Greenberg, I.A. (ed.) (1974) *Psychodrama Theory and Therapy*. Behavioural Publications, New York.

Moreno, J.L. and Ennis, J.M. (1950) *Hypnodrama and Psychodrama*. Beacon House, Boston, MA.

Wong, N. (1995) Group psychotherapy, combined individual and group psychotherapy, and psychodrama. In: *Comprehensive Textbook of Psychiatry*, 6th edn (eds H.J. Kaplan and B.J. Sadock).Williams & Wilkins, Baltimore, MD.

PSYCHODYNAMIC COUNSELLING (SEE ALSO: KLEIN, MELANIE (1881–1960), PSYCHOANALYSIS)

Before looking at this topic, it might be helpful to recap on the some of the different counselling approaches:

- Psychodynamic and person-centred approaches concentrate on feelings.
- Behaviourists believe that if the behaviour (including thinking) is adjusted, all other aspects will be put to rights.
- Cognitive theories (mainly concerned with thinking) put forward the view that all behaviour is primarily determined by what a person thinks.
- An eclectic or integrated counsellor may use all or any of these theories and approaches.

In this highly simplified introduction to the three main focuses, it may seem that a counsellor who uses one approach only may ignore vital parts of the client – such as thinking or behaviour, if the focus is on feelings – but that is not so. What distinguishes one type of counselling from another is where the attention is focused, and the techniques and skills used.

Understanding the psychodynamic approach

Freud's psychoanalysis gave rise to the word 'psychodynamic', which means every psychological theory that uses the concept of inner drives and the interaction of mental forces within the psyche. Thoughts, feelings and behaviours are viewed as manifestations of inner drives.

Psychodynamic counselling derives from psychoanalysis, but is not psychoanalysis.

A psychodynamic approach is the systematised knowledge and theory of human behaviour and its motivation. Inherent in this is the study of the functions of emotions. Psychodynamic counselling recognises the role of the unconscious, and how it influences behaviour. Further, behaviour is determined by past experience, genetic endowment and what is happening in the present.

Exploring insight

While feelings are not ignored (for to ignore them would be to deny an essential part of the person) feelings are not the emphasis – insight is, and that insight relates to the functioning of the unconscious. For the underlying belief is that it is the unconscious that produces dysfunction. Thus insight, in the psychodynamic model, is:

- Getting in touch with the unconscious; and
- Bringing what is unconscious into the conscious.

Although insight is usually worked towards in those approaches which focus on feelings, in the psychodynamic approach it is considered essential. Clients achieve insight when they understand what is causing a conflict. The premise is that if insight is gained, conflicts will cease. Insight is often accompanied by catharsis, which is the release of emotion, often quite dramatic.

Insight refers to the extent to which you become aware of your problems, origins and influences. It may be sudden – like the flash of inspiration, the 'eureka experience'. More usually it develops stage-by-stage as you develop psychological strength to deal with what is revealed. The counsellor cannot give the client insight. Clients must arrive at it by themselves.

Nothing is more thrilling than when an insight dawns. It may have lingered for days or weeks, gradually working away in the subconscious, even figuring in dreams or with little flashes of sub-insights – something like looking through frosted glass. There the vision is dimmed; the form can be distinguished, but lacks detail. It is thus with some insights. Not all come like bolts from the blue.

Psychodynamic counsellors

Psychodynamic counsellors are trained to interpret what clients say through the psychoanalytic model, and while the counsellor will not analyse, neither will he become as involved as in some other approaches. The psychodynamic counsellor can appear distant and detached, possibly even lacking in warmth, but this is because of the belief that the personal qualities of the counsellor should not intrude into the counselling relationship.

The task of the counsellor is to facilitate the client's insight and understanding by linking the past and present, interpreting some of the client's communication and interpreting transference of past and present relationships.

The psychodynamic approach engages the therapist in three key areas:

- The therapeutic relationship
- Human development, in particular the first five or six years of childhood
- Personality structure and the work of defence mechanisms, and the use of dreams.

The influence of psychoanalysis

Almost every other approach derives from Freud's psychoanalysis, which gives rise to the word 'psychodynamic', meaning every psychological theory that uses the concept of inner drives and the interaction of mental forces within the psyche. Thoughts, feelings and behaviours are viewed as manifestations of inner drives. Psychodynamic counselling derives from psychoanalysis, but it is *not* psychoanalysis.

Thus a psychodynamic approach is the systematised knowledge and theory of human behaviour and its motivation. Inherent in this is the study of the functions of emotions. Psychodynamic counselling recognises the role of the unconscious and how it influences behaviour. Further, behaviour is determined by past experience, genetic endowment and what is happening in the present.

In psychodynamic counselling the counsellor is far less active than in many other approaches and relies more on the client bringing forth material rather than reflecting feelings and inviting exploration, and what the client discloses will be interpreted according to the psychoanalytic model. Just as in psychoanalysis the patient is expected to report anything that comes to mind, so it is in psychodynamic counselling. Hesitation to reveal is interpreted as resistance, which must be worked through before progress is achieved.

Further reading

Jacobs, M. (1992) *Psychodynamic Counselling in Action.* Sage Publications, London.

Smith, D.L. (1996) Psychodynamic therapy: the Freudian approach. In: *Handbook of Individual Therapy* (ed. W. Dryden). Sage Publications, London.
Stewart, W. and Marin, A. (1999) *Going for Counselling.* How to Books, Oxford.
www.valmillscounselling.co.uk/psychodynamic_therapy

PSYCHOSYNTHESIS (ROBERTO ASSAGIOLI, 1888–1974)

Psychosynthesis was developed by Roberto Assagioli, an Italian psychiatrist who broke away from Freudian orthodoxy early in the 20th century and developed an integrated approach to psychiatry.

Psychosynthesis – beginning around 1910 and continuing to the present day – is a synonym for human growth, the ongoing process of integrating all the parts, aspects and energies of the individual into a harmonious, powerful whole. Assagioli drew upon psychoanalysis, Jungian and existential psychology, Buddhism and yoga and Christian traditions and philosophies, and affirmed the spiritual dimension of the person, i.e. the 'higher' or 'transpersonal' self. The higher self is seen as a source of wisdom, inspiration, unconditional love and the will to meaning in our lives. It is said that each person's life has purpose and meaning within this broader context and that it is possible for the individual to discover this. Psychosynthesis has had a profound impact on the human potential movement. For example, the use of guided imagery and the concept of sub-personalities originate in psychosynthesis.

The fundamentals of psychosynthesis

- Psychological pain, imbalance and meaninglessness are caused where the various elements of the psyche are unconnected or clash with one another.
- When these elements merge, we experience a release of energy, a sense of well-being and a deeper meaning of life.
- Assagioli's map of the psyche:
  - The lower unconscious, which contains one's personal psychological past in the form of repressed complexes, long-forgotten memories and dreams and imaginations
  - The middle unconscious, wherein reside the skills and states of mind
  - The higher unconscious or super conscious is an autonomous realm, from where we receive our higher intuitions and inspirations – altruistic love and will, humanitarian action, artistic and scientific inspiration, philosophic and spiritual insight, and the drive towards purpose and meaning in life.
- The field of consciousness lies within the middle unconscious. It is the part of which we are directly aware and contains sensations, images, thoughts, feelings, desires and impulses. It also includes power to observe, analyse and make judgements.
- The conscious self or 'I' lies in the centre of the field of consciousness. One's task is to gain experience of the essence of self or 'I'. Awareness of the conscious self is essential for psychological health. The personal self is a reflection of the transpersonal self; in much the same way as the moon is lit up

by the sun's rays. Since this 'self' has two aspects – the personal and the transpersonal – synthesis happens in two stages; first the personal, followed by the transpersonal.

- The higher or transpersonal self is the true Self, the permanent centre, situated beyond or above the conscious self. Identification with the transpersonal self is a rare occurrence.
- The psyche is bathed in the sea of the collective unconscious of dreams, myths, legends and archetypes.

The lines that delimit the various parts of the diagram are analogous to permeable membranes, permitting a constant process of 'psychological osmosis'. Assagioli's map of the psychological functions (in diagrammatic form, star-shaped) is made up of three dimensions:

- Sensation – Intuition
- Thought – Emotion-feeling
- Impulse-desire – Imagination.

At the centre is the personal self or 'I', surrounded by will. Of will, Brown says:

> The experience and development of the will is basic to Psychosynthesis. Our will is what separates us from being the conditioned automatons envisioned in Huxley's Brave New World. True, we are subject to conditioning, but we can transcend it through the skilful and harmonious use of the will. That is why the will is identified closely with the self in Psychosynthesis models; conditioning is what our environment imposes on us, but the self can still express itself and its inner direction through acts of will.

Key values that psychosynthesis holds in the process of psychotherapy:

- Creating a bridge between the psychological and spiritual realities that many new psychologies now follow
- A deep spiritual understanding of the relationship between parts and wholes and how a spiritual perspective can deepen the experience of Self
- An openness, lack of dogma and inclusiveness to whatever approaches, from raja yoga and esoteric spirituality to humanistic psychology, which fit a holistic perspective
- An optimistic emphasis on the unfolding potential of humans
- Practices such as 'disidentification' to loosen the bonds of outdated personal beliefs and open to being part of a greater sense of self
- A utilisation of imaginative guiding to bring clients to points of higher awareness
- The use of evocative imagery to awaken clients to their own inner wisdom
- An understanding of the importance of meaning and purpose in any individual's life
- An appreciation of the importance of Will in terms of self-responsibility and choice
- A dramatic and easily engaged method of working with personality dynamics called subpersonalities.

Assagioli's personality typology

The will type

The characteristics of the will type are prompt and decisive action, courage and the power to conquer, rule and dominate both physical surroundings and other people.

There is a strong tendency to suppress all emotions and, as a consequence, will types care little for their own or other people's feelings. This suppression of feelings often leads this person into committing heroic acts of courage.

Mentally this person is alert, with clear vision, unencumbered by emotions. Although not trusting of intuition, in the realm of abstract thinking this person excels, having a quick and sure grasp of principles, general laws and universal connections.

The love type

Love types are often attached to material possessions, money or property and the good things of life. The love may be expressed through the mind and emotions. Many love people are underdeveloped sexually, with a distinct possibility of egotistical love. The love type can be self-indulgent and a lover of comfort, with a tendency to laziness and to follow the crowd.

Intuition is highly developed in love types, who have an interest in psychology and a communion with the inner worlds of others.

Generally, love types are kind and receptive, sociable and often afraid of solitude. They are sometimes too readily influenced by others.

The active-practical type

The characteristics of this type are based on intelligent activity and the practical use of tools, coupled with highly developed manual dexterity. Active-practical types are comfortable in the 'real' world of things. Material objects, particularly money, interest them, so they often pursue activities for gain. Money is power.

This type wants immediate and lively reactions; to go slowly is a punishment. Feelings and all that requires psychic sensitivity are foreign to this type, as is the feminine principle of the psyche; the practical mind sees no relevance or meaning in it. Men of this type struggle to understand the psychology of women.

Mentally this type deals well with concrete and practical problems but the more abstract ones leave them cold.

The creative-artistic type

This type is characterised by the search for harmony, peace, union and beauty. Creative-artistic types have an excellent sense of colour and exhibit good taste. They are often beset by unsatisfied ambitions, internal and external conflict.

They are prone to mood swings – between optimism and pessimism; between uncontrolled happiness and despair. They are easily disturbed by violence, vulgarity and ugliness.

They are sensitive to psychic phenomena and rely on their intuition, which is well developed. They are always searching for the meaning hidden behind everything they perceive. They are imaginative, dreamy and impracticable and may live in a fantasy world. Men of this type feel at home with feminine psychological characteristics.

The scientific type

This type is characterised by an interest in the appearance of things, as perceived through the five senses. There is no real interest in moral, aesthetic or any other type of value.

The emotions of this type are totally directed towards impersonal objects. They are passionately attached to ideas and theories and their energies are directed towards intellectual ends.

Their minds are constantly on the alert, investigating, posing questions, solving problems, searching, probing, experimenting, proving and discovering.

The devotional-idealistic type

This type is attracted to an ideal, which is often an ideal personality. The ideal may be religious, political, social or philosophical. Sometimes their severely ascetic attitude turns to hatred of the body as a hindrance towards their spiritual ambition.

Devotional-idealistic types often love or hate with a passion that makes them narrow-minded, intolerant, critical and uncompromising. They generally lack a sense of proportion and humour and have a tendency to impose their views on others. At the same time they are sincere and not egotistical. The Inquisitors are quoted as examples of such a type, torturing and killing in an effort to save the souls of their victims.

The high level of intuition that some develop is identified with the feminine principle. The active subtype does not develop the same degree of intuition and identifies more with the masculine principle, with combativeness and aggression – the person who is always prepared to do battle for a just cause.

The organisational type

Organisational types express themselves in action and are thoroughly objective. They demonstrate will and purpose, a clear mind, constructive activity and practical ability and are methodical and persistent 'doers'. They organise the co-operation and work of other people to achieve the desired end.

This type likes to formalise laws with meticulous care and they tend towards rigidity, which often manifests itself as bigotry. They are strong disciplinarians, both external and internal, and use discipline in order to eliminate loss and waste of time, energy and materials, to avoid friction and to establish, in the end, more productive cooperation.

The organisational type relies heavily on tradition, habit and custom and when these fail or break down organisational types are thrown into confusion; as if their anchor has gone.

The task of psychosynthesis

No person is exclusively one type; we are mixtures. Most of us could identify one or two types that are more of us than the others. When we have identified the type(s), our task is how to use the knowledge we have acquired to effect self-potential.

Expression, control and harmonisation

Each person faces the three-point task.

Expression

- Accepting the characteristics
- Recognising the potentialities
- What our type can teach us
- The opportunities and dangers
- The kind of service to the world.

Control

- Controlling and correcting excesses
- Working on the opposites.

Harmonisation

- Cultivating undeveloped faculties
- Develop the will-to-change
- Seek the company of people who demonstrate the desired attributes.

Psychosynthetic tasks

The will type

- To develop love, understanding, empathy and compassion in such a way that they become capable of expressing goodwill
- To develop sensitivity, intuition and the ability to cooperate with, rather than to solely dominate, compete with and direct others
- To feel comfortable without solitude and to learn to live with others
- To transform egotistical will into service to others.

The love type

- To attain non-attachment and to eliminate from real love the elements of greed and possessiveness and allow for liberty of the other person
- To separate love from the egocentric elements
- To develop a stronger will to help them control their love.

- To cultivate the qualities of the love and creative types
- To recognise the intangible world, intuition, psychological qualities, beauty
- To learn how to relax and be silent.

The creative-artistic type

- To learn to seek a mid path between polarities and extremes
- To work with reality and the practical
- To respect the limitations of others
- To develop more self-discipline, although not at the expense of inspiration
- To develop a more responsible attitude towards money.

The scientific type

- To control the thirst for knowledge and apply it to specific areas
- To approach relationships with warmth, compassion and goodwill
- To cultivate the appreciation of subjective qualities, of internal experiences and intuition, love and beauty.

The devotional-idealistic type

- To distinguish true from idealistic love and to transform devotion to an ideal into true love
- To learn to suspend judgement and to accept that there are other 'ways'
- To learn to be more impersonal and objective
- To develop tolerance and intellectual humility.

The organisational type

- To avoid becoming too identified with the formal and the predictable and to beware of the organisation becoming an end in itself
- To work towards modifying the tendency to rely on the practical and the objective, the concrete and the visible, by developing loving service and the true good of all, free from officiousness and rigidity
- To apply the developed principles of coordination and synthesis to personal or transpersonal development.

Assagioli's concept of subpersonalities

Subpersonalities are distinct, miniature personalities, living together within the personality, each with its own cluster of feelings, words, habits, beliefs and behaviours. They are often in conflict with one another and engaged in a constant jockeying for position.

They are remnants of helpful and unhelpful influences left over from a time when they were needed for survival to meet lower-level needs. For example, a policeman subpersonality is helpful in keeping one on the right side of the law, but becomes tyrannical when it always pushes one into punishing other people for minor breaches of one's self-imposed standards.

Table 11: *Subpersonalities*

boffin	executioner	gaoler
granite	monk/nun	nurse
playboy	policeman	professor
rebel	saboteur	seducer
spider	tiger	donkey

The goals of psychosynthesis

- To free ourselves from the infirmity of illusions and fantasies, unrecognised complexes, of being tossed hither and thither by external influences and deceiving appearances
- To achieve a harmonious inner integration, true self-realisation and a right relationship with others
- To recognise when we have identified with one or another subpersonality and dis-identify from its control.

These goals are achieved through knowledge of one's personality, control of the various elements of the personality and working with the subpersonalities to free oneself from their tyranny. Psychosynthesis speaks of 'guiding', not therapy.

Table 12: *Psychosynthesis methods and techniques*

catharsis	creativity	critical analysis
dialogue	dreamwork	evocative words and affirmation
free drawing	gestalten	guided imagery
homework	journal keeping	meditation
movement	subpersonality work.	

Broad classification of techniques

- **Analytical:** To help identify blocks and enable the exploration of the unconscious
- **Mastery** (see Assagioli's psychological functions, above): The eight psychological functions need to be gradually retrained to produce permanent positive change
- **Transformation:** Creating a soil in which the seeds of change can blossom. The goal is the refashioning of the personality around a new centre
- **Meditative:** To awaken and integrate intuition, imagination, creativity and higher feelings
- **Grounding:** The learning and growth of a session is brought into the concrete terms of daily life – grounding makes use of:

- Carrying out the choices made in the session, actively using imagination
- Standing or moving in ways that express new qualities or attitudes
- Mental images to evoke positive emotional states
- Repeating key phrases or affirmations throughout the day
- Practising chosen behaviours
- **Relational**: To deal with the common obstacles within relationships and communication and to cultivate qualities such as love, openness and empathy.

Psychosynthesis is an evolutionary psychology, to help us to become increasingly aware of our vast potentials and to bring them into service in the world. It can help us to balance all aspects of the human personality: intellect, emotion, body, intuition and imagination.

Psychosynthesis can facilitate courage and patience, wisdom and compassion. It refers to the ongoing synthesis of the psyche, a process that transcends specific models and methods.

People seek counselling and psychotherapy for many reasons:

Table 13: *Reasons people seek counselling*

loss of direction	self-exploration	coping with change
depression	feeling unfulfilled	hopelessness
isolation	relationship difficulties	anxiety
bereavement	addictions	sexuality
identity	self-esteem	. . .and many more

Further reading

Assagioli, R. (1965) *Psychosynthesis: A manual of principles and techniques*. Turnstone Press, Wellingborough.
Assagioli, R. (1969) *Symbols of Transpersonal Experiences*. Institute of Psychosynthesis, London.
Assagioli, R. (1974) *The Act of Will*. Wildwood House, London.
Assagioli, R. (1976) *Transpersonal Inspiration and Psychological Mountain Climbing*. Institute of Psychosynthesis, London.
Assagioli, R. (1983) *Psychosynthesis Typology*. Institute of Psychosynthesis, London.
Brown, M. (1997) *Growing Whole: exploring the wilderness within*. Psychosynthesis Press, Los Angeles, CA. An audiotape and guided journal workshop.
Brown, M. (2004) *The Unfolding Self: psychosynthesis and counselling*, 2nd edn. Psychosynthesis Press, Los Angeles, CA.
Ferrucci, P. (1982) *What We May Be*. Turnstone Press, Wellingborough.
Whitmore, D. (1991) *Psychosynthesis Counselling in Action*. Sage, London.
The Psychosynthesis and Education Trust 92–94 Tooley Street, London Bridge, London SE1 2TH. Tel: 020 7403 2100/fax: 020 7403 5562, enquiries@petrust.org.uk. www.mailmrp.btinternet.co.uk

PUBLIC AND PRIVATE SELF

This is a social psychology concept, in which the self has both a private and public face. The private self consists of what we are inside. The public self is the face we present to others. The one is secret; the other is what we want other people to think of us. Both public and private selves influence our behaviour: the one in how we are when by ourselves; the other in how we react to others and how they will react to what we do.

Confronting ourselves makes us aware of who we are: if faced with a TV camera or an audience, we become more aware of the public self – as indicated by an increased tendency to change our attitudes to conform to the opinions of others.

Some people are prone to introspect, to examine their feelings and motives frequently. Some are habitually concerned with how they appear to others.

Table 14: *Public and private self*

Characteristics of those high on private self (inner-directed):	Characteristics of those high on public self (other-directed):
Tend to be prone to mood changes Prone to anger when provoked Suggestible Reasonably resistant to political propaganda Reasonably accurate in describing their own behaviour Seem to have more self-awareness Able to disclose private aspects of selves to their spouses or intimate partners Tend to behave in accordance with own attitudes and beliefs.	Tend to be sensitive to group rejection Usually good at predicting the kind of impression they make on others Place importance on their 'social' identity A tendency to conform to the values of society A tendency to comply with the expectations and preferences of other people Tend to tailor their actions to fit the social demands of changing situations.
Examples of private self-consciousness statements:	Examples of public self-consciousness statements:
My reflections are often about myself I listen to my inner feelings I'm always trying to work myself out Examining my motives is important to me I'm aware of changes in my mood I like to think I am aware of myself I know how my mind works when I'm thinking through a problem I feature a lot in my own fantasies I am aware that I often watch myself.	My behaviour is influenced by what other people think of me Making a good impression is important to me It is important to me to present myself favourably to other people I'm self-conscious about the way I look My appearance is an important part of me I always check how I look in the mirror before leaving the house.

It needs to be stressed that however 'accurate' personality tests are, they are not absolute. These are not precise instruments but rather indicators of what might be. With reference to this specific indicator, a person's behaviour is likely to be modified by the situation and circumstances – in the real-life world, not in the laboratory. For example, a person who tips the 'private person' scale might be totally different in a group where he is accepted and feels at ease, or when in position of being in control.

Clients may be caught in a trap between these two opposing parts of themselves and not really be sure which of them is the 'real me'. In reality, of course, the majority of people have both a private and a public self. Where it might prove a problem is in having to 'put on a brave face' when caught up in grief, for example, or where one's profession 'demands' a certain attitude, such as happens with doctors and nurses.

The question to be asked is: 'For whose benefit is the public self?' It is possible that putting on a brave face is a defence mechanism; something that maintains our self-esteem (in our own eyes). Being seen to be 'strong' is more important than showing one's feelings. Like all defences, counsellors should recognise them for what they are but not try to break them down. Teasing out the various strands of the two selves might allow the client to develop insight and resolve any conflict there might be.

Further reading

Fenigstein, A., Scheir, M.F. and Buss, A.H. (1975) Public and private self-consciousness: assessment and theory. *Journal of Consulting and Clinical Psychology,* **43**: 522–524.

Q

QUESTIONS

People new to counselling often imagine that they have to ask questions, the more the better. However, in reality, and certainly in person-centred counselling, the counsellor will make statements rather than ask questions. It is not that questions are *wrong*, but it is much easier to frame a question than it is to create a statement that encourages the client to continue. So often, questions are linked to gaining information, rather than getting at the underlying feelings. Counsellors are not psychological detectives, who have to extract all the facts.

Bayne *et al.* make this point:

> *Questions can be the most ensnaring of all skills. In searching for an answer or way to help the client, it can be tempting to take the role of a traditional doctor and ask a series of diagnostic questions. This can easily set up a pattern of question and answer leading to other questions and more answers, with the questioner controlling the direction of the exploration and holding on to the power in the relationship. This type of interaction does little to establish a warm and positive climate in which clients are encouraged to take responsibility... The appropriate use of questions is essential, both in communication and in counselling. Once understood and mastered, your counselling style will be enriched and enhanced.*

Questions should never intrude into the counselling process. They should always be a natural part of what is going on, and the client should always be able to understand the relevance of the question at the time it is asked. There is a time to ask a question and a time not to. A question may occur to the counsellor, but a convenient place to ask it may not present itself. If it is introduced later it may have the effect of stopping the flow; almost like trying to turn the clock back. Introducing it may cause the client to stop, especially if he cannot see its relevance.

Sometimes it is necessary to go back to a previous stage in the session. 'Earlier on you were telling me about ... I wonder if it would be helpful to pick up that thread again', gives a clear indication that the counsellor is still interested and still helping to explore the problem. This theme will be picked up again later, but it is by the counsellor's use of the skills outlined here and the way he communicates, that the counsellor is able to lead the client gently, but with assurance, into identifying the problem.

Asking the right questions

Basically, there are two types of questions: open questions, which help the flow of communication and encourage the speaker to elaborate or be more specific, and closed questions, which tend to shut communication down. Closed questions are those that can be answered with a 'Yes' or 'No'. For example: Did you? Do you think that? Are you going to? Closed questions are useful for getting information.

Some common pitfalls in asking questions

- Asking two or more questions at the same time, which creates confusion in the client's mind
- Usually the client will answer the last question asked
- Wrongly timed questions interrupt and hinder the helping process
- Asking too many questions, which may give the impression that we can provide solutions to other people's problems
- Asking too many questions, which may give the impression of an interrogation
- The emphasis in counselling is on using questions to help people solve their own problems.

A guide to using questions

Examples of *experiencing* questions

- What is going on?
- How do you feel about that?
- What do you need to know to...?
- Would you be willing to try...?
- Could you be more specific?
- Could you offer a suggestion?
- What would you prefer?
- What are your suspicions?
- What is your objection?
- If you could guess at the answer, what would it be?
- Can you say that another way?
- What is the worst/best that could happen?
- Would you say more about that?
- What else?
- And?

Examples of *sharing* questions

- Would you like to share?
- What went on/happened?
- How did you feel about that?
- Who else had the same experience?
- Who reacted differently?
- Were there any surprises/puzzlements?
- How many felt the same?
- How many felt differently?

- What did you observe?
- What were you aware of?

Examples of *interpreting* questions

- How did you account for that?
- What does that mean to you?
- How was that significant?
- How was that good/bad?
- What struck you about that?
- How do those things fit together?
- How might it have been different?
- Do you see something operating there?
- What does that suggest to you about yourself/other people?
- What do you understand better about yourself/other people?

Examples of *generalising* questions

- What might we draw from that?
- What might that be connected to?
- What did you learn/relearn?
- What does that suggest to you about ... in general?
- Does that remind you of anything?
- What principle is being applied there?
- What does that help to explain?
- How does that relate to other experiences you've had?
- What do you associate with that?
- So what?

Examples of *application* questions

- How could you apply that?
- What would you like to do with that?
- How could you repeat this again?
- What could you do to hold on to that?
- What are the options?
- What might you do to help/hinder yourself?
- How could you make it better?
- What would be the consequences of doing/not doing that?
- What modifications can you make to get it to work for you?
- What could you imagine/fantasise about that?

Examples of *processing* questions

- How was this for you?
- What were the pluses/minuses?
- How might it have been more meaningful?

- What's the good/bad news?
- What changes would you make?
- What would you continue?
- What are the gains/losses?
- If you had to do it over again, what would you do?
- What would you add/take away?
- Any suggestions?

Summary of helpful types of question

Elaboration questions give the person the opportunity to expand:

- Would you care to elaborate?
- What else is there?
- Could you expand what you've just said?

Specification questions aim to elicit detail:

- When you say he upsets you, what precisely happens?
- When?
- How many times?

Questions that focus on feelings aim to elicit how the other person feels about something:

- How do you feel about that?
- What would you say your feelings are right now?
- Is it possible that you're feeling. . .?

Personal responsibility questions imply that the other has a responsibility not only for owning the problem but also for making the choices that contribute to solving it:

- How do you see your part in the break-up?
- What skills do you need to develop to help solve the problem?
- What other ways are there to improve the situation?

Wrongly used, questions can create an expectation that we will provide solutions to other people's problems. The emphasis in counselling is on using questions as aids to problem-solving. We may find it expedient to ask questions to fill certain 'gaps' in our understanding. Should we find ourselves asking two consecutive questions without getting a response, then, in all probability, we have asked inappropriately and should return to responding accurately.

Using open questions

Open questions are an open invitation to continue talking, particularly about feelings:

- What would you like to talk about today?
- What happened then? ('What' questions tend to bring out the specific facts of a problem.)

- How did you feel about the situation? ('How' questions often lead towards discussion. When the word 'feel' is included, the client is usually more ready to talk about feelings.) This does not mean that every minute or so the counsellor should say, 'How do you feel about that?' That can become nothing more than a stereotyped response, almost guaranteed to irritate the client.
- Why do you think it happened? ('Why' questions tend to lead clients to talk about their past or present reasoning around an event or situation.) 'Why' questions often take the client away from feeling into thinking and away from the present into either the past or the future and discourage exploration of feelings in the here and now. Sometimes this is helpful – not, however, in this context. If it's information you want, a 'why' question is fine. Another point about 'why' questions is that they are more to do with the counsellor's knowledge than with the client's feelings. 'Why' is not as important as 'how'. 'Why' is investigative; 'how' is facilitative.

Open questions should:

- Seek clarification
- Encourage exploration
- Establish client understanding
- Gauge feelings
- Establish counsellor understanding.

Make effective use of 5WH: Who? What? Why? When? Where? How?

I keep six honest serving-men
(They taught me all I knew);
Their names are What and Why and When
And How and Where and Who.

Rudyard Kipling, 'The Elephant's Child', *Just So Stories* (1902)

Guidelines on questions

- Avoid closed questions unless you want to elicit information or establish facts. Closed questions can usually be answered with a few words and usually begin with 'Is', 'Are', 'Do' or 'Did'. When we preface a statement with 'Could it be?', 'Do you think/feel?', 'Does this mean?', 'Have you considered?', 'Is that...?', 'Am I (would I be) right?' or 'Don't you think?' it usually means a closed question.
- Avoid leading questions, where the desired answer is implied in the question.
- Avoid curiosity questions about areas not yet touched on.
- Avoid too many questions, which give the impression of an interrogation.
- Avoid probing questions that the client is not yet ready to answer.
- Avoid poorly timed questions that interrupt and hinder the helping process.
- Think of responding to what the client has said rather than asking questions.
- Responding is like building a wall, brick by brick. In this way, the counsellor does not rush ahead of the client and cause anxiety by pushing indelicately into sensitive areas that are not yet ready to be explored.

Closed questions derive from a desire to know, to seek information, rather than from an ability to help the client explore or clarify. Closed questions often move the client from the present into the past or from the present into some direction chosen by the counsellor.

However, although it is generally agreed that closed questions stop exploration and the more so if two such questions are asked in succession, creating open questions is sometimes not easy.

Let Gerard Egan have the final say in this discussion on the effective use of questions:

> *Whatever form probes take, they are often, directly or indirectly, questions of some sort. Inexpert helpers often resort to asking questions, in the mistaken belief that the more information they gather the easier it will be to understand the client.*

- Ask a limited number of questions. Don't turn helping into an interrogation: 'When did you first feel like this?' 'Have you discussed this with anyone?' 'What do you do to improve your looks?' 'What is it about your looks that you think others don't like?' These questions are intrusive and insulting. 'Helping sessions were never meant to be question-and-answer sessions that go nowhere.'
- Ask open-ended questions – questions that require more than a simple yes or no or similar one-word answer. One closed question invariably leads to a closed answer and another closed question.
  - Closed: 'Now that you've decided to take early retirement, do you have any plans?' The 'do you' closes it down.
  - Open: 'Now that you've decided to take early retirement, what are your plans?' The 'what' opens it up.
  - If information is essential, a closed question is appropriate.
  - 'In moderation, open-ended questions at every stage and step of the helping process help clients fill in what is missing.'

Further reading

Bayne, R., Horton, I., Merry, T. and Noyes, E. (1994) *The Counsellor's Handbook: a practical A-Z guide to professional and clinical practice.* Chapman & Hall, London.

Drever, J. (1969) *A Dictionary of Psychology*, Penguin, Harmondsworth.

Egan, G. (2002) *The Skilled Helper: a problem-management and opportunity-development approach to helping*, 7th edn. Brooks/Cole, Pacific Grove, CA.

Stewart, W. (1977) *Health Service Counselling.* Pitman Medical, London, page 41.

Sutton, J. and Stewart, W. (1997) *Learning to Counsel: how to develop the skills to work effectively with others.* How to Books, Oxford.

R

RAPE COUNSELLING

Definition (from the Sexual Offences (Amendment) Act 1976):

A man commits rape if:
He has unlawful sexual intercourse with a woman who at the time of intercourse does not consent to it; and
At that time he knows that she does not consent to the intercourse or he is reckless as to whether or not she consents to it.

Rape was traditionally considered an act that occurred only against females and only outside marriage. Traditionally, a man was incapable by law of raping his wife; the argument was that a married woman had given her consent to intercourse by marrying her husband and could not retract it. This interpretation was challenged in the House of Lords in 1992 and no longer applies in most jurisdictions. Until 1994 the rape of a man came under the offence of non-consensual buggery, rather than rape. The law was changed to reflect the general perception that non-consensual buggery is a form of rape.

Sexual intercourse is taken to mean the penetration of the labia by the penis to any degree – full penetration and ejaculation need not take place in order to prove rape. A man can be guilty of rape if he takes advantage of a woman by false pretences, e.g. by impersonating her sexual partner and approaching her just as she wakes from sleep.

Rape can involve the following:

- Intimidation with threats or weapons
- Beating, choking, knifing
- Sexual and mental humiliation
- Urination or spitting on the victim
- Forced oral sex
- Multiple rape by one or more assailants
- Injury to genitals, e.g. bottles, sticks pushed up vagina.

If a woman or child is raped or sexually assaulted, there are very few people to whom she feels she can turn. Some women find it impossible to tell anyone what has happened; those who do sometimes meet with anger, suspicion, recriminations and hostility from those closest to them. And a large number of raped women suffer in silence. Not all women report the crime to the police. It doesn't matter how long ago the attack took place. A raped woman will still need to talk.

Rape is a violation of the person and of human and legal codes of behaviour. It is an anger and a pathological assertion of power. Although rape is a sexual assault, it has more to do with aggression than with sexuality. In fact, one-third of rapists experience either erectile or ejaculatory dysfunction during the assault.

Studies of convicted rapists suggest that the crime is committed to relieve pent-up anger against persons of whom the rapist is in some awe. The feminist theory proposes that the woman serves as an object for displacement of aggression that the rapist cannot express directly towards other men. This theory could be borne out by the incidence of rape during times of war – frequently gang rape – which serves to demoralise the male enemy, relieve pent-up aggression and fear, enhance male bonding and increase feelings of power.

Convicted rapists seem to be part of a general subculture of violence and a great many of them have previous convictions for other offences such as burglary and robbery.

Victims of rape can be any age. The greatest danger exists for females aged 10–29. Rape most commonly occurs in a woman's own neighbourhood, frequently inside her own home. The woman being raped is frequently in a life-threatening situation. During the rape she experiences shock and fear approaching panic. Her prime motive is to stay alive. There is a high incidence of submission, as can be expected, when the rapist uses a knife or a gun. In most cases, rapists choose victims slightly smaller than themselves.

Many women experience the symptoms of a post-traumatic stress reaction. The rape overwhelms them with a sense of vulnerability, fear of living in a dangerous world and loss of control over their own lives. They become pre-occupied with the trauma and it colours their future actions and day-to-day behaviour.

Some typical reactions are:

- A feeling of being unable to wash themselves clean
- Fear of walking out
- Fear of remaining alone in the house
- Fear of being followed
- Fear of being alone – ever
- Nightmares
- Insomnia
- Work problems
- Changes in eating patterns
- Somatic symptoms – headache, nausea, exhaustion, all-over tension
- Sexual difficulties – lack of desire, inhibited orgasm, inhibited excitement, vaginismus.

Few women emerge from the assault completely unscathed. The manifestations and the degree of damage depend on the violence of the attack itself, the vulnerability of the woman and the support systems available to her immediately after the attack. Rape treatment centres that coordinate psychiatric, gynaecological and physical trauma services in one location and with close police cooperation are most helpful to the victim.

The rape victim experiences a physical and psychological trauma when she is assaulted. She is not always believed, in much the same way as the child who discloses incest is not believed. Statements such as 'She was asking for it' or 'She wanted it to happen' are common and they haunt and intimidate the rape victim. If a fruit and vegetable stall-holder displays his wares openly and a thief steals them, would the defence dare to say of the stall-holder 'He provoked my client' and expect the thief to be acquitted on that defence?

Rape is such a terrible experience that the shock itself can distort a person's memory in the immediate period after the attack. The help of experienced counsellors is valuable at this stage, especially if the listener is not connected with anyone who might be concerned with asking necessary questions and making examinations for legal reasons. Long-term counselling is often wise because of the frequency of delayed psychological effects, which can cripple a woman years after the original event.

The rapist, a profile

(Paraphrased from E. Trimmer (1978) *Basic Sexual Medicine,* Heinemann, London.)

Three types of rapist can be identified:

1. The well-adjusted heterosexual who has enjoyed an unusual amount of hetero-sexual activity, including mouth to genital contact, at an early age. Such men are unusually prone to fantasy, particularly sado-masochistic fantasies, and have a marked tendency to behave aggressively towards and feel a pronounced hostility to women. They are also subject to erectile failure.
2. The amoral delinquent or sociopathic personality – in other words, a criminally inclined man who takes what he wants.
3. The incestuous rapist who uses his daughter as a convenient sex object.

Sometimes custodial sentences are necessary for the protection of society and for the safety of the perpetrator. But rapists need skilled help as well as their victims.

This article concentrates on women who have been raped by men. It should be remembered that men and boys who are sexually assaulted by men and women who are forcibly attacked by other women can suffer very similar trauma. Several incidents of male rape have hit the headlines, as have rape by husbands and the more newly reported occurrence of 'date-rape'.

Rape prevention

- Help men to learn to find strength through expressing what are called the 'softer' emotions such as fear, sadness, vulnerability and tenderness. When we hear men talking about women in an abusive, derogatory or dismissive way, we could take it upon ourselves to make them aware of what they are doing.
- Do not condition children by filling them with our own fears and depriving them of their own self-reliance. Let us not lay down blanket rules of do's and don'ts but rather try to instil within them a foundation of resourcefulness by our own openness and willingness to explore the topic of sexuality as one facet of self-awareness.

- For those of us who are older, let us value our age, for it is a tremendous treasure-chest of wisdom and experience. Let us make it available to those with a need to draw from such wisdom and experience.
- Let us help others to learn to say 'no' when that is what they mean; and to say 'yes' only when they are convinced that they do not want to say 'no'.
- Let us not be silent partners to violence and violation. Let us not accept things as 'the way they are' without making our protests heard.
- Let us value ourselves, then we will value others too.

Women's helpline (for victims of rape) 01962 848024
Monday: 11.30 a.m. to 1.30 p.m.
Tuesday and Thursday Evening: 7 p.m. to 9:30 p.m.
Calls answered by women only

Men's helpline 01962 848027
Monday: 11:30 a.m. to 1.30 p.m.
Thursday Evening: 7 p.m. to 9:30 p.m.
Calls answered by men and women

Further reading

Allison, J.A. and Wrightsman, L.S. (1993) *The Misunderstood Crime*. Sage Publications, London.
Sadock, V.A. (1995) Physical and sexual abuse of the adult. In: *Comprehensive Textbook of Psychiatry*, 6th edn (eds H.J. Kaplan and B.J. Sadock). Williams & Wilkins, Baltimore, MD.

RATIONAL EMOTIVE THERAPY (RET)

Rational emotive therapy (RET) is a comprehensive, cognitive-behavioural method of psychotherapy developed by Albert Ellis. RET (also called rational emotive behaviour therapy, REBT) considers dysfunctional behaviour to be the result of faulty beliefs and irrational and illogical thinking.

Ellis considers that emotionally disturbed individuals act in irrational and illogical ways. Greek and Roman philosophers stressed that people are disturbed not by things but by their view of things.

Basic concepts – rationality

All humans have two goals:

- To stay alive
- To feel relatively happy and free from pain.

These goals are choices or preferences, rather than needs or necessities. Rationality enhances goal attainment; irrationality hinders goal attainment. Rationality may be defined as the use of reason in pursuit of chosen short-range and long-range pleasure.

Reason (thinking) and emotion

Thinking and emoting are so closely related that they are essentially the same thing. They take the form of sentences of self-talk. Our internal self-statements are capable of both generating and modifying our emotions.

Appropriate and inappropriate emotions

- RET emphasises appropriate emotions.
- Inappropriate emotions interfere with goal attainment.
- Caution and fear may be appropriate – anxiety is irrational.
- All emotions, not just negative ones, therefore, have both sane and insane sides to them.

Emotions are appropriate when they are accompanied by rational or sane beliefs, which are functional in that they do not block the possibility of effective action and attainment of goals.

How we become irrational

- People have innate and acquired tendencies to be both rational and irrational. People's failure to accept reality almost always causes them to manifest the characteristics of emotional disturbance.
- The emphasis is on how we sustain irrationality, not how we acquired it. Children are indoctrinated with irrationality. People create emotional disturbance because they indoctrinate themselves with prejudices and superstitions acquired during childhood.

RET has elements in common with both cognitive and behavioural counselling. The method uses an A-B-C-D sequence:

- A = activating event; fact, event, behaviour, attitude of another person
- B = beliefs or self-verbalisations of the individual about A
- C = consequence or reaction – happiness or emotional disturbance, which erroneously may be presumed to follow directly from A. That which we believe controls our emotions and behaviours
- Highly charged emotional consequences are invariably created by our belief systems. Undesirable emotional consequences can usually be traced to irrational beliefs. When irrational beliefs are disputed (D), disturbed consequences disappear.

An example of the A-B-C model

A = ACTIVATING EVENT
I went for a job interview and failed to get the job

B = BELIEFS ABOUT A

Table 15: *Outline of RET*

Person A	Person B
rational beliefs (rB) (wants or desires)	irrational beliefs (iB) (demands or commands)
I don't like getting rejected. How annoying! Looks like I'll have difficulty getting the job I want.	How awful to get rejected! I can't stand this rejection. This rejection makes me a rotten person.

C = CONSEQUENCES OF Bs ABOUT A

Table 16: *More about RET*

Person A	Person B
desirable consequences (dC)	undesirable consequences (uC)
desirable emotional consequences	undesirable emotional consequences
(appropriate bad feelings) I felt sorrow and regret; frustrated and irritated; determined to keep trying	(inappropriate feelings) I felt depressed: I felt anxious, worthless and angry
desirable behavioural consequences (desirable behaviours)	undesirable behavioural consequences (undesirable behaviours)
I continued the search for a job. I attempted to upgrade my skills.	I refused to go for other interviews. I felt so anxious that I functioned badly at other interviews.

(Adapted from page 51 of R. Nelson-Jones (1982) *The Theory and Practice of Counselling Psychology*, Holt, Rinehart & Winston, New York, and taken originally from A. Ellis (1976) *Rational Self Help*, Institute for Rational Living, Inc. New York.)

Basic RET propositions

- We are born with the potential to be rational as well as irrational.
- Our tendency to irrational thinking, self-damaging habits, wishful thinking and intolerance is influenced by culture, community and family group.
- We tend to think, feel and behave at the same time.
- RET therapists believe that a highly cognitive, active-directive, homework-assigning, hard-headed and discipline-oriented system is likely to be more effective than other systems.
- A warm relationship is neither necessary nor a sufficient condition for effective personality change.
- RET makes use of a variety of techniques to achieve a deep-seated cognitive change rather than a removal of symptoms.
- All serious, emotional problems can be attributed to magical and faulty thinking; logical, observable and experimental thinking will eliminate these problems.
- Insight is cold comfort if all it does is to let us see we have problems; we must accept that the real difficulty is in ourselves, not in other people nor in what happens to us.

Three basic principles

- While present behaviour is related to the past, it is beliefs about the events and not the events themselves that cause problems in the present.

- Although we may have been emotionally disturbed in the past, our faulty beliefs continue the process; we actively reinforce them by the way we think and act.
- Only repeated rethinking of our irrational beliefs and repeated actions designed to undo those beliefs and the crooked thinking that goes with them are enough to create lasting change.

Table 17: *Aspects of personality*

Physiological	Social	Psychological
We are born with a strong tendency to want, and to insist, that everything should happen for the best in our lives. We condemn ourselves and others when we do not get what we want. We tend to think childishly all our lives and only with great difficulty achieve and maintain realistic and mature behaviour. Self-actualising capacities are frequently defeated by our inborn and acquired self-sabotaging strategies.	When others approve of us and accept us, when we love and are loved, we tend to approve of ourselves as 'good' and 'worthwhile'. Emotional disturbances are often caused when we care too much about what others think – this leads us to believe that we can only accept ourselves when others accept us. A corollary of this is that we have an exaggerated compulsion to do anything to be liked.	We become psychologically disturbed when we feel upset at C, after experiencing a disturbing event at A.

Beliefs at B could run something like:

- 'I can't stand this'
- 'It's awful'
- 'I'd just as soon be dead'
- 'I'm worthless'
- 'It's all your fault'.

The illogicality of this is that:

- We may not like what has happened, but we can stand it.
- Why can't we?
- What is awful?

It would be more precise to say:

- 'It may be very inconvenient'; or
- 'It may be unhelpful'.

Being precise aids logical thinking. To think we can control the world is magical, irrational thinking. When we upset ourselves we then start to condemn ourselves for being upset.

To help people change, concentrate on B. A is past. The feelings of C, although real, are strongly influenced by B. Concentrating attention on B diverts attention from both A and C.

Counselling tasks

Dryden identifies the following counsellor tasks:

- To help clients see that their emotional and behavioural problems are rooted in faulty thinking
- To train clients to identify and change what is irrational to rational
- To teach clients that thoughts, behaviour and feelings can be changed by cognitive, behavioural and emotive methods, including imagery.

The client tasks are:

- To identify the feelings and behaviours that disturb them
- To relate these disturbances to their faulty thinking
- To use behavioural and emotive methods, including imagery, to work at changing their irrational beliefs.

The therapeutic process

- No matter what feelings the client brings out, the counsellor tries to get back to the irrational ideas that lie beneath the feelings.
- The counsellor does not hesitate to contradict and may use personal experience or experience from other people.
- The counsellor never misses a chance to draw attention to and attack 'shoulds', 'oughts' and 'musts'.
- The counsellor will use the strongest philosophic approach possible, saying something like, 'If the worst think possible happened, would you still be worthless?'.
- The counsellor does not dwell on feelings but uses them to point to irrational beliefs and ideas.
- While showing acceptance, unconditional regard and confidence in the client's abilities, the counsellor, when necessary, is stern and insists that the client is capable of doing better.
- The counsellor at all times tries to get the client to see the irrational ideas, without telling or explaining.
- The counsellor may use strong, confrontational language to give the client an emotional shock.
- The counsellor is empathetic but not sympathetic.
- The counsellor constantly checks the client's understanding of what is being taught and does this by getting the client to repeat and clarify what has just been said.
- Unlike some therapies, the RET counsellor does a lot of the talking and taking the lead.

In all of this, the client is understood and, although deep feelings are there, the client is given little chance to become immersed in them or to abreact strongly to them.

The client experiences:

- Full acceptance
- Renewed confidence
- Self-responsibility
- Hope of recovery
- Reduction in defences.

RET is used in numerous settings with individuals and groups.

Behavioural methods used

- Cognitive homework assignments, e.g.:
  - Making lists of current problems
  - Recording irrational beliefs and how to dispute them
  - Filling out RET self-help reports, showing how the client will combat these dysfunctional ideas.
- Activity homework assignments, e.g.:
  - Client and counsellor devise desensitising assignments that are specific to the unique situation of the client
  - Working out a step-by-step plan for overcoming faulty thinking, feeling or behaviour
  - Performing tasks that they dread doing, thereby facing the fear.
- Skills training, e.g.:
  - Communication, intimate relationships, satisfying sex, job-seeking, business relations and time-management
  - Clients are shown how to reinforce what they do and penalise themselves for what they do not do or when they regress to what they know to be dysfunctional.
- Physical methods of therapy, e.g.:
  - Encouraging clients to engage in health-developing activities, which includes diet, exercise, relaxation, biofeedback.

Techniques commonly used

- Repeating forceful, rational, coping statements, e.g.: 'I do not need people's approval. That is a desire'; 'I am not annihilated when people don't approve of me'
- Rational emotive imagery to change inappropriate feelings to appropriate ones
- Unconditional acceptance, even when the client's behaviour is stupid or blame-worthy
- Role-play of difficult situations, during which the counsellor will interrupt to draw attention to faulty thinking
- Clients learn to conduct forceful dialogue with themselves; to express irrational beliefs and then to dispute them.

- These dialogues may be tape-recorded and played back for the counsellor to hear.
- When clients feel strongly ashamed for doing what they want to do, for fear of disapproval, they are encouraged to accept a 'shame-attacking exercise', like doing something ridiculous in public; they work on themselves until they no longer feel ashamed or embarrassed.
- RET uses humour to attack people's over-sensitiveness and dogmatic 'musts'.
- RET discourages dependence by teaching clients to help themselves; to monitor their thoughts, feelings and behaviours; not to blame events or people; to restructure their perceptions and evaluations; and to stand on their own feet.

Major irrational beliefs

- I must do well and must win approval for all my performances or else I rate as a rotten person.
- You must act kindly and considerately towards me or else you are a thoroughly bad person.
- I must live under good and easy conditions, so that I get practically everything I want without too much effort and discomfort – if I don't, the world is doomed and life hardly seems worth living.

Major irrational ideas

- You must have sincere love and approval almost all the time from all people you find significant.
- You must prove yourself thoroughly competent, adequate and achieving; or that you must at least have real competence or talent at something important. The seven great illogical 'Cs':
  - Cheerful
  - Comfortable
  - Compassionate
  - Competent
  - Confident
  - Consistent
  - Controlled
- Life proves awful, terrible, horrible, or catastrophic when things do not go the way you would like them to.
- Emotional misery comes from external pressures and that you have little ability to control your feelings or rid yourself of depression and hostility.
- If something seems dangerous or fearsome, you must become terribly occupied with and upset about it.
- You will find it easier to avoid facing many of life's difficulties and self-responsibilities than to undertake some rewarding forms of self-discipline.
- Your past remains all-important and that, because something once strongly influenced your life, it has to keep determining your feelings and behaviour today.

- People and things should turn out better than they do; you have to view it as awful and horrible if you don't quickly find good solutions to life's hassles.
- You can achieve happiness by inertia and inaction or by passively and uncommittedly 'enjoying' yourself.
- You must always have a high degree of order or certainty to feel comfortable; or that you need some supernatural power on which to rely.
- You can give yourself a global rating as a human and that your general worth and self-acceptance depend on the goodness of your performances and the degree to which people approve of you.
- People who harm you or commit misdeeds rate as generally bad, wicked or villainous individuals and you should severely blame, damn and punish them for their sins.

Characteristics of irrational beliefs

- **Demandingness**: Words such as 'should', 'ought', 'must', which indicate absolutistic or magical thinking, create disturbances. 'Perfectionism', 'grandiosity' and 'intolerance' also indicate this characteristic.
- **Overgeneralisation**: Strive after greater precision in thought and speech. 'I failed at that test' becomes 'I always fail; I have no ability to succeed at it.'
- **Self-rating**: We must accept ourselves unconditionally. We must not attempt to rate personal worth. Some negative effects of self-rating are:
  - it wastes time and energy
  - it tends to be inconsistent
  - it tends to be perfectionistic.
- The favoured philosophic solution to the problem of personal worth is to be truly self-accepting rather than self-evaluating.
- **Awfulising**: Allied to demandingness. If I, someone, or something is not the way I demand that they should be or must be, then this is awful, terrible, horrible or catastrophic. Heightened emotions result and get in the way of perceiving accurately the activating event and hence changing or solving the noxious happenings at point A – the Activating Event.
- **Attribution errors**: Here we attribute causes and motives to our own and others' behaviour and to external physical states. Many irrational beliefs involve misattributions.
- **Anti-empiricism**: An irrational belief cannot be empirically validated or disproven.
- **Repetition**: Irrational beliefs tend, once acquired, to occur again and again. We reindoctrinate ourselves with our self-defeating ideas.

Changing irrational to rational beliefs

1. Focus on changing irrational beliefs (iBs) in the ABC framework. Substitute rational and functional beliefs for irrational and dysfunctional beliefs.
2. Add 'D' for disputing or debating irrational beliefs – 'Why is it awful to get rejected for a job?' 'Why can't I stand this rejection?' 'How does this rejection make me a rotten person?'

3. Add 'E' for the effects of successfully disputing or debating irrational beliefs. The effects are:
   - Cognitive – similar to rational beliefs – 'I can stand rejection, though I'll never like it'
   - Emotional – appropriate feelings – 'I feel concerned but not anxious'
   - Behavioural – desirable behaviour – 'I am sending out more letters for jobs.'
4. Key to detect irrational beliefs:
   - Look for the shoulds and look for the musts
   - Emotional-evocative therapy may include role-playing situations involving irrational beliefs, modelling to show the client how to think and behave differently, and exhortation
   - Behavioural methods include homework sheets, directed readings and cassette recordings of interviews, the use of imaginative techniques and self-reinforcement.

Five steps to help clients towards RETional thinking

Start by selecting a situation that consistently generates stressful emotions.

1. Write down the objective facts of the event as they occurred at the time. Do not include subjective impressions or value judgements.
2. Write down self-talk about the event: 'My subjective impressions, value judgements, assumptions, beliefs, predictions and worries are. . .' My irrational ideas are. . .'
3. Focus on the client's emotional response. Make a clear one- or two-word label to describe it, e.g. 'Angry', 'Depressed', 'Felt worthless', 'Afraid'.
4. Dispute and change the irrational self-talk identified at step 2: 'The irrational idea I am going to dispute is. . .'; 'The rational support for this idea is. . .'; 'The evidence that this is a false idea is. . .'; 'The evidence for the truth of this idea is. . .'; 'If what I want to happen, doesn't, the worst consequence could be. . .'; 'If what I don't want to happen, does, the worst consequence could be. . .'; 'If what I want to happen, doesn't, the benefit could be. . .'; 'If what I don't want to happen, does, the benefit could be. . .'
5. Substitute RETional self-talk.

Making use of RETional imagery

- Get the client to imagine a stressful event in detail; emotions, sight, smell, sound, dress, conversation.
- Encourage the client to feel the main emotion, then transform it.
- Transform anxiety into concern; depression into disappointment; rage into annoyance; guilt into regret; helplessness into discomfort.
- Get the client to examine how to achieve this transformation. Instead of saying, 'I can't handle this. . . This will drive me crazy', the client may now say, 'I've dealt successfully with situations like this before'.

Insight

Three levels of insight are necessary to change:

- Knowledge that we have a problem and awareness of some of the events that may have caused the problem
- Seeing clearly that the irrational ideas we acquired early in life are creating the emotional climate we live in now and that consciously or unconsciously we work fairly hard to perpetuate them
- We will find no other way of eliminating the problem other than steadily, persistently and vigorously working to change our irrational ideas.

Without commitment, altering habitual, irrational responses will prove difficult.

Questions to ask clients

- Identify areas in which you are demanding and perfectionist in relation to yourself.
- Identify areas in which you are demanding and perfectionist in relation to others.
- Place at least one of your areas of irrational beliefs into an ABC framework.
- Assess the extent to which your thinking contains the following characteristics:
  - Over-generalising
  - Self-rating
  - Awfulising
  - Attribution errors.

Further reading

Curwen, B., Palmer, S. and Ruddell, P. (2000) *Brief Cognitive Behaviour Therapy*. Sage Publications, London.

Dryden, W. (1984) *Individual Therapy in Britain*. Harper & Row, London.

Dryden, W. (1996) Rational emotive behaviour therapy. In: *Handbook of Individual Therapy* (ed. W. Dryden). Sage Publications, London.

Ellis, A. (1977) *Reason and Emotion in Psychotherapy*. Secauces, Citadel, NJ.

Ellis, A. (1989) *Why Some Therapies Don't Work*. Prometheus Books, New York.

Ellis, A. and Harper, R.A. (1975) *A New Guide to Rational Living*. Prentice-Hall, Englewood Cliffs, NJ.

Eschenroeder, C. (1982) How rational is rational emotive counsellor? A critical appraisal. *Cognitive Counsellor and Research*, 6: 381–391.

Hargie, O. (ed) (1986) *A Handbook of Communication Skills*. Croom Helm, London.

Nelson-Jones, R. (1982) *The Theory and Practice of Counselling Psychology*. Holt, Rinehart & Winston, New York.

Patterson, C.H. (1980) *Theories of Counselling and Psychotherapy*. Harper & Row, London.

Trower, P., Casey, A. and Dryden, W. (1988) *Cognitive Behavioural Counselling in Action*. Sage Publications, London.

REALITY THERAPY

This therapy proposes that the underlying problem for all clients is that they are either in a relationship that does not satisfy, or what they have could not be called a relationship. Thus, for clients to move on, they must develop a satisfying relationship. Reality therapists teach clients to behave more effectively.

Reality therapy was developed by William Glasser, based on the idea that individuals are responsible for what they do. Responsible behaviour is defined as that which satisfies one's needs while, at the same time, not denying others from satisfying theirs.

Glasser emphasises reality as the basis for responsible behaviour:

- Clients have failed to learn the behaviours necessary for them to meet their psychological needs.
- The task of the reality therapist is to educate them to become more responsible and realistic and hence more successful at attaining their goals.
- Reality therapy focuses on the present and upon getting people to understand that all choices are made in order to meet needs. When needs are not met, we suffer, and often we cause others to suffer also. Reality is based on the concept that our brain works as a control system, like a thermostat.

Survival societies versus identity societies

Western societies were once survival societies concerned with economic goals. They are now identity societies, which emphasise role and personal fulfilment.

People are like a building supported by the five pillars, or needs:

- Survival
  To belong
  To exercise power
  To have fun and
  Experience freedom.

(Compare with Maslow's hierarchy of needs.)

When any one pillar weakens, the whole structure becomes unstable.

People with failed identities are those who have not learned the behaviours necessary for them to meet their psychological needs. They may, therefore, need to learn the behaviours and skills that will help them out of their self-involvement, out of their fantasy world in which they feel more comfortable.

The task of the reality therapist is to educate clients to become more responsible and realistic, and more successful at attaining their goals.

Glasser identifies two basic needs:

1. To love and be loved. This means involvement.
2. To feel self-worth and to feel the worth of others. This means performing tasks of worth.

Reality therapy beliefs

- The concept of mental illness to be a scientific fantasy
- That symptoms are chosen because the individual is lonely and failing now
- That no symptom is chosen without reason
- A symptom serves to reduce the pain of loneliness
- That successful involvement means facing loneliness, pain, and failure
- We choose symptoms

- Symptoms disappear when needs are successfully fulfilled by means of responsible behaviour.

Reality therapy differs from orthodox psychotherapy in that it:

- Rejects the concept of mental illness and all the conventional diagnostic labels
- Concentrates on the present as the razor's edge upon which we live our lives. Our memory of the past is capricious; to remember accurately would be too painful
- Rejects the phenomenon of transference as a misleading and false idea
- Pays little attention to the unconscious and the dreams that go with it. Reality therapy deals only with what the client is presently aware of
- Concentrates on clients' perceptions of their behaviour, and to judge if that behaviour is conducive to meeting their declared goals
- Attempts to teach clients better ways to deal with the world, thus helping them to choose more effective behaviours.

The client has two choices:

1. To deny reality, with its irresponsible behaviour, loneliness, pain and lack of involvement; the failed identity. Responsibility is defined as the ability to fulfil one's needs, in a way that does not deprive others of the ability to fulfil their needs
2. To face reality, with its responsible behaviour, love, worth and involvement; the success identity.

facing reality ↓	denying reality
responsible behaviour	irresponsible behaviour
love and worth (involvement)	loneliness and pain (lack of involvement)
success identity ↓	failure identity

Figure 3: *Facing and denying reality*

The unpleasant truth is that most of us fail at times!

Sources of a success identity

- People we love and admire and who love and admire us
- The causes and concerns on which we spend our time

- Our behaviour in crises
- Feedback from others
- Beliefs, values and philosophy of life
- Status and position in life
- Physical appearance and structure.

A success identity or a failure identity starts to form around the age of four years, as we develop, or fail to develop, social and verbal skills, intellect and thinking ability. Children who identify themselves as 'successful' or 'unsuccessful' quickly associate themselves with similar people. This leads to polarisation.

Parents best teach their children responsibility by behaving responsibly towards them by:

- Being models of responsibility towards each other
- Through appropriate discipline, not punishment
- Through the setting of boundaries.

Reality therapy and education

Many educational systems confirm an embryonic failure identity in children. Many children fail at school because teachers deny children their primary needs for humanity and love. Schools could help to develop a success identity by:

- Focusing on thinking and problem-solving skills, not on rote learning
- Make learning relevant to the child's world
- Giving prime importance to reading, writing and speaking skills
- Having mixed-sex classes and all ages
- Doing away with grading systems
- Having classroom meetings and non-judgemental discussions.

Perpetuating a failure identity

There are two identities:

1. **Success**: Involvement and self-worth
2. **Failure**: Pain and lack of involvement.

Many behaviours only increase the pain and isolation from true involvement. Glasser considers that all symptoms, psychological or psychosomatic, and all hostile, aggressive, irrational behaviour are products of loneliness and personal failure. Such persons may not believe that loving and worthwhile involvements are open to them. This in itself is a denial of reality and one that has profound implications for motivation to change. People with failed identities may need to learn the behaviours and skills, which will help them out of their self-involvement, out of their fantasy world in which they feel more comfortable.

Changing a failure identity

The goal of reality therapy is a successful identity based on being able to meet the needs of love and worth through realism and responsible behaviour.

Essential therapist qualities

- Responsible and able to meet needs within reality
- Strength and integrity to withstand client collusion in irresponsibility
- Accept and understand people who are isolated and in pain through failure to meet their needs
- The capacity to become emotionally involved with irresponsible clients and to be affected by their suffering.

The seven principles of reality therapy

1. **Involvement**: Warmth and friendliness are necessary to break through the sense of failure and self-involvement of the client. This involvement, acceptance and caring means a willingness to discuss personal experiences that are the bridge by which clients develop the confidence to make lasting involvements of their own. Reality therapy discourages long discussions about the client's problems, since this is seen as increasing irresponsible self-involvement.
2. **Focus on current behaviour**: Reality therapy focuses on changing behaviour rather than thinking or feeling; what they are doing, rather than on why they are doing it.
3. **Evaluating behaviour**: The question that is continuously explicit is 'How is this behaviour helping you to meet your needs?'
4. **Planning responsible behaviour**: The client is helped to understand, clarify and define his immediate and long-term life goals.
5. **Commitment**: The client is helped to make a commitment, verbal or written, to carry out a reasonable plan. This commitment is viewed as very important, since the key to feelings of self-worth is the ability to make and follow through plans.
6. **No excuses**: A commitment to a reasonable plan can always be fulfilled.
7. **No punishment**: When a client succeeds, praise is given. Punishment reinforces a failure identity. Any kind of negative statement by the therapist is punishment.

People with successful identities are succeeding in their search for personal fulfilment in the evolving identity society.

Steps in reality therapy

- Establish rapport and empathy and ask the clients what they most want.
- Asking 'What are you doing now?' focuses on goals and behaviours most open to changes to achieve the goals.
- Would their choice get what they want?
- Creating an effective plan hinges on the previous three steps.
- Strong commitment to the plan means strong follow-through.
- Reality therapists are not interested in excuses when plans are not followed through, particularly when clients rake up the past as their excuse.
- The therapist does not resort to punishment, but will use (where appropriate) temporary restriction of freedom or temporary removal of privileges.

- It may take a long time for some people to realise that they can take some control of their world.

Rejecting the idea of transference

Glasser maintains that transference is a way that both therapist and client avoid taking responsibility for who they are now. Thus to the client who says that the counsellor is his father, Glasser would respond that he is not his father, he is himself. The reason this is called reality therapy is that most clients are all too willing to avoid taking responsibility for what they are doing and tend to leap at anything the therapist offers that will help them, and this would include trying to interpret transference. By being themselves, therapists can use the relationship to teach clients how to relate to others in their lives.

The determined therapist will gradually become part of the client's inner world.

The overall goal for therapy, and for living, is a success identity. Attaining a success identity has the following ingredients:

- Neither denying nor ignoring the reality of the world in which we live
- Accepting personal responsibility for our behaviour
- Behaving responsibly, including formulating and carrying out plans
- Loving and being involved with and committed to others as well as being loved in return
- Engaging in activities that are worthwhile to ourselves and possibly to others living up to a reasonable standard of ethical behaviour.

Further reading

Corey, G. (2001) *Theory and Practice of Counseling and Psychotherapy*, 6th edn. Wadsworth. Brooks/Cole, Pacific Grove. CA.

Glasser, W. (1980) *What Are You Doing? How people are helped through reality therapy*. Harper & Row, New York.

Glasser, W. (2000) *Reality Therapy in Action*. HarperCollins, New York.

RECORDS

Counselling records serve four main purposes:

- To aid good counselling practice
- Help administration
- Training
- Research.

The record should show how you set out to help this particular client. It is the first step in evaluation. It is through the record that hypotheses can be tested, characteristic patterns of behaviour perceived and progress assessed. A good record should be readable. A good recording style is plain, clear and as brief as treatment will permit. We cannot record accurately if we have not heard and observed accurately. Clarity and brevity indicate analytical thinking. The record will be a thoughtful reflection of what took place in the interview.

In certain situations, some notes are essential, if only to keep the key issues before your eyes. Before starting a session, if you say something like, 'What do you feel about me taking some notes?' you will rarely meet with a refusal. Such notes need only be single words, enough to act as refreshers later in the session. Single words or short sentences can usually be written without taking your eyes off the client for too long.

Process recording is a term borrowed from social work, in which an interview is recorded as nearly verbatim as possible. It includes not only what both you and the client said, but also significant reactions of the client and changes in mood and response. It preserves the sequence in which the various issues were explored. This is a tremendous discipline, yet an exercise that brings with it great rewards.

Sureness of what material to select grows with experience, if the process is seen as a necessary discipline requiring time and thought. Accurate recording is also an analytical look at the meanings behind the facts and words used.

The early stages of counselling generally require longer records than later sessions. At all times you should be both forward-looking and backward-looking, trying to tie up what took place in past sessions with the present session.

Good observation and perception in the interview will be reflected in the record and, from time to time, particularly with long-term counselling, summaries are recommended.

Suggested items to include:

- How and why the client came to you: was it a referral or self-referred?
- The presenting problem (see Presenting problem)
- The facts
- The relationship between the client and any significant others
- Personal history
- Any significant quotes made either by you or the client that bring out important feelings, attitudes, opinions or refer to the 'larger problem'
- Your own activity within the session: thoughts, feelings, behaviours, interactions
- As counselling continues, the record should reflect development and include your periodic evaluations and statements of aims
- Future dates for sessions
- Referrals if any.

However, it is not essential that all these data be gathered in the first session, although some counsellors do work with a 'history' sheet completed in the first session.

To be serviceable, a record must be orderly in its arrangements; this hinges on thinking through what has to be included, even although how it was presented may not be logical. A page with margins for headings can be a useful way of making quick reference to material. Counselling records are not an end in themselves; they are tools, not works of art, yet they should be legible, readable and logical. You may wish to refer to your notes for research purposes. Records often provide evidence that changes need to take place within an organisation or a community.

You may wish to consider using a tape recorder. Although some clients may refuse your request to do so, I have never had a client refuse. Taped sessions are useful because they are an accurate record of what took place and although the listening and transcribing time is considerable, the benefits are a tremendous compensation.

When I first started using a tape recorder, in the early 1970s, John, the client I was then working with, asked if he could listen to the tapes when I had finished with them. So, before the next session, I would have listened, transcribed and analysed the session; he then had the tape, listened to it in the intervening week and we would discuss any particular points raised by listening to the tape. There were many times when he said something like 'I hadn't remembered saying that' or 'I've had some new thoughts on that' or 'Listening again to that made me quite upset'. Our relationship lasted nine months and, in the evaluation, he said how much he had gained from listening to the tapes. In effect, he was having two counselling sessions a week – one he paid for, one for free!

For one's own professional development, some time should be devoted to making a summary of what has taken place throughout counselling. It is possible that what is included in the summary may never be read by anyone else. But the fact that you have taken time and effort to commit it to paper may at some time be a useful resource for you when pondering on a particular point in counselling.

Experience can never be wiped out but, when experience is reinforced by evaluation, many of the interactions, the words, the nuances that so quickly fade from the memory are captured in a way that experience by itself cannot do. If you feel that the final evaluation is proving too difficult, that may be because evaluating your own part in the process is eluding you. It is possible, for example, that some aspect of the relationship between yourself and the client is proving a stumbling block. If the stumbling block is not removed it will remain an obstacle in the way of effective counselling. Stumbling blocks can be turned into stepping stones by an honest and in-depth evaluation assisted by honest recording.

A final point should be made about computer-kept records. The whole issue of record-keeping presents difficulties of confidentiality; counsellors certainly must consider the implications of keeping client records on computer. Such questions as: storing (on hard disk or on floppy); security of material (where is it kept?); access (password; who has access?); how long the records are kept and for what purposes; and, if you are part of a computer network, how you protect the material, all have to be considered. Computer-kept records can save an enormous amount of time and space but client confidentiality must always be uppermost in our minds.

Further reading

Sutton, J. and Stewart, W. (1997) *Learning to Counsel: how to develop the skills to work effectively with others.* How to Books, Oxford.

REDUNDANCY COUNSELLING (SEE ALSO: DYING – STAGES AND TASKS OF, RETIREMENT)

The effects of redundancy can be devastating to the person, to the immediate family and also to society. It may be the most psychologically mutilating event the individual has ever experienced.

Redundancy affects the person concerned and the one having to give the news. The whole organisation is subjected to the trauma. Whatever the reasons, when the axe falls the innocent often feel they have a hand in the execution.

A disturbing fact is that people, particularly managers, who have once been made redundant are more at risk of a second or third redundancy.

The stages of redundancy

1. Planning in secret; often accompanied by rumours and suspicion
2. Announcement of redundancy and selection of personnel to go
3. Individuals leave the organisation and enter a period of unemployment
4. Search for new jobs.

The psychological phases of redundancy

1. **Shock**: 'I can't believe it', 'I won't survive'
2. **Optimism**: 'Something is bound to turn up'
3. **Pessimism (or depression)**: 'Nobody wants me'
4. **Fatalism**: 'I might as well give up.'

Redundancy can also be regarded as a bereavement – the loss of something precious, suggestive of the Kubler-Ross model. All models have their limitations and it does not mean that every person will follow the model through as presented. Neither does it mean that there is a logical progression through the stages. It is more likely that the person will fluctuate between the various stages and perhaps experience all of them within a short space of time and return to a previous stage many times before 'acceptance'. In many cases of redundancy, acceptance only comes with being re-employed.

Stress following redundancy is to be expected for the following reasons:

- Expectations have been cut short
- Being unemployed is not the norm.

People may not find the answer to the question 'Why me?' It is possible that the individual does have a part to play in what has happened, e.g. he may not have kept abreast of personal development, something expected by many organisations. This expectation may be justified, particularly where the organisation provides opportunity for self-development. At the same time, effective management might have detected the lack before and been able to take constructive action, not redundancy.

Redundancy counselling, which covers dismissal or other severance, is concerned mainly with helping people change in order to improve their chances of new employment. New employment may have to be different from the previous one but it should feel psychologically good, according to the following criteria:

- Provides an opportunity to use one's special abilities
- Permits one to be creative and original
- Enables one to look forward to a stable and secure future
- Provides one with a chance to earn a reasonable income
- Gives one an opportunity to be of service to others.

Some people want only practical advice; others need an opportunity to explore their feelings before they can make a decision, having explored various options.

The stages of redundancy counselling

1. Dealing with the crisis
2. Careers advice
3. Coaching (interviewing skills, preparing CVs and presentation)
4. Where to look, whom to approach, coping with rejections and follow-up after re-employment.

Counselling should be an integral part of the organisation's redundancy package. Some people have the necessary coping skills and have an already established network of support and contacts, but may need some help with the practicalities. Some, because of their stress levels (which may, of course, involve the family), may need more personal counselling before they are able to think clearly enough to take action. Some are so devastated that they experience a full-blown grief reaction and will need a lot of personal counselling.

Redundancy counselling benefits the organisation by:

- Taking the problem off the organisation's shoulders
- Showing concern, thereby keeping up morale
- Enabling difficult decisions to be made
- Helping to keep confidence in the organisation.

Services usually offered by companies specialising in redundancy counselling:

- Negotiating the 'golden handshake'
- Financial, pensions and investments advice
- Legal advice
- Health check-up
- Crisis/personal counselling
- Vocational/career guidance
- Analysis of interests and skills, strengths and weaknesses, aptitude and psycho-metric tests and advice from clinical psychologists
- Self-marketing skills: interviewing, presentation, preparing CVs and letters
- Exploring new opportunities: working abroad, self-employment, retraining

- Getting lists of vacancies and contacting recruiting agencies
- Providing office facilities, including secretarial assistance
- Advice on handling offers of work.

An important step forward is when the person can say, 'My job is redundant, I am not'.

Further reading

British Association for Counselling and Psychotherapy (1983) *Redundancy and Unemployment.* BAC, Rugby.

Burrows, G. (1985) *Redundancy Counselling for Managers.* Institute of Personnel Management, London.

De Board, R. (1983) *Counselling People at Work.* Gower, Aldershot.

Weatherley, M.J. (1982) Counselling in career self-management courses for the mature executive. *British Journal of Guidance and Counselling,* **10(1):** 88–96.

Webb, S. (1984) *Guidelines for the Redundant Manager.* British Institute of Management, London.

REFERRING A CLIENT

Not every counsellor is the best person for all clients, so from time to time it may become necessary for the client's development that he is referred to another counsellor or counselling agency.

It may become necessary, therefore, to refer a client for one or a combination of the following reasons:

- Medical
- Social
- Pastoral
- Psychiatric
- Psychological
- Emotional
- Spiritual
- Legal.

It is helpful, therefore, to know the resources available in your own locality – agencies as well as people. In addition, it might become necessary to refer clients because:

- You are moving to a different area
- The client requests it
- The client requires more in-depth work than you feel comfortable with
- The agency you work for does not take on clients with this type of difficulty
- The problem is outside your competence
- Your style of counselling does not suit the client
- You discover that you and the client share a relationship with a third party and there is a conflict of loyalty or confidentiality
- It becomes apparent that the client might do better in couple counselling or group counselling

- The client wants to explore sensitive areas such as sexuality and needs a counsellor of the same sex
- The client is of a different culture and this is creating difficulty in the relationship – this might also apply to people whose first language is not the same as yours.

Referral is likely to be delayed because of:

- The counsellor's hurt pride at not being able to continue with the client until completion
- Not creating an awareness in the mind of the client from the start that referral is a possibility
- Not admitting limitations
- Not working through and helping the client understand why referral is indicated
- Not being able to separate from the client.

The client might see referral as rejection rather than development. Sometimes there is the tendency to refer too quickly. Perhaps the counsellor may see a need for referral but this is totally rejected by the client. The limitations should then be brought into the open and discussed. The counsellor then may need to seek expert help if work with the client is to be productive. Working with a client who refuses to be referred is both demanding and exciting but the counsellor will need a great deal of support.

Referral is particularly difficult for clients who feel they have already been pushed from one counsellor to another; this could lead to a feeling that they are beyond help. It is certainly true that the longer the relationship the more difficult referral might be, even though the need is recognised by the counsellor and accepted by the client. But just as it is possible to work towards separation at the end of counselling, so it is equally possible to achieve this in referral.

You should do all you can to make the transition easy – talk about the other counsellor or agency, arrange a visit, let the client make contact, work with the client to prepare a summary of what has been achieved so far. Clients who feel totally involved in the referral are likely to get the most out of the new relationship.

Further reading

Bayne, R., Horto, I., Merry, T. and Noyes, E. (1994) *The Counsellor's Handbook: a practical A-Z guide to professional and clinical practice.* Chapman & Hall, London.
Jacobs, M. (1982) *Still Small Voice.* SPCK, London.

RELATIONSHIP PRINCIPLES

To work effectively with people we need to be able to:

- Build on other people's ideas
- Express warmth and affection
- Handle personal anger constructively
- Be aware that we influence others

- Listen with understanding
- Receive warmth and affection
- Tolerate conflict and antagonism
- Tolerate conflicting views of others
- Tolerate other people's behaviour
- Have aspirations for self
- Be aware of our own feelings
- Have an awareness of other people's feelings
- Be willing to continue developing self-awareness
- Have close personal relationships
- Value independence
- Value innovativeness
- Strive to be open-minded
- Show peace of mind
- Maintain physical energy
- Work towards maintaining high self-esteem/self-worth
- Be self-expressive
- Tolerate differences in others
- Trust people
- Be versatile
- Be willing to discuss our own feelings.

Seven relationship principles can be identified:

1. Individualisation
2. Expressing feelings
3. Involvement
4. Self-determination (self-direction)
5. Confidentiality
6. Acceptance
7. Non-judgement.

1. Individualisation (uniqueness)

- Individualisation means recognising and respecting the other person's uniqueness.
- It recognises not just a human being but *this* human being – just as he or she is.
- Every person has the need and the right to be related to as unique.
- Clients need our undivided attention and privacy, to be able to discuss their unique problem.
- People whose uniqueness is not respected react by only giving information and not disclosing feelings.
- When people are related to with uniqueness, when they feel understood, they will enter more willingly into the helping relationship.
- Relating to others in this way may not come easily.
- Training is essential to:
  - Recognise and deal with our biases and prejudices

- Acquire knowledge of human behaviour
- Develop listening and responding skills
- Learn to move at the client's pace
- Learn to respond with empathy
- Develop perspective
- Develop a flexible approach.
- We can enhance individualisation by:
  - Thoughtfulness and care
  - Privacy
  - Preparation
  - Engaging the client
  - Flexibility.

2. Expressing feelings

- Every client has the right to be permitted, and indeed encouraged, to express both positive and negative feelings within an atmosphere of understanding and acceptance and without feeling judged.
- We should neither discourage nor condemn feelings – it is often therapeutic to encourage the expression of feelings.
- Any problem, however practical its focus, has an emotional component.
- The expression of feelings is encouraged:
  - To relieve pressures and tensions and free the client for positive, constructive action
  - To understand more clearly the client and the problem
  - To help us assess the client's strengths and weaknesses
  - To provide psychological support – feelings shared brings closeness
  - Because when feelings are brought into the open there is more chance that something constructive can be done with them
  - Because feelings shared help to deepen the counselling relationship
  - To create a safe environment.
- Feelings are facts.
- Feelings have a voice; they will speak for themselves – we must ensure that we listen to them.
- We can enhance the expression of feelings by:
  - Being relaxed
  - Adequate personal preparation
  - Active and purposeful listening
  - Not trying to rush the process.

Some cautions:

- Psychological awareness is essential to deal constructively with other people's feelings and the feelings generated within us.
- The relationship must encourage true expression of feelings.
- Give free time and space to the client.

- Keep your foot on the emotional brake – feelings expressed too soon, too much, may be destructive.
- Clients' feelings should not become our burden.
- Do not fall into the trap of offering premature or empty verbal reassurances.

Thinking and feeling

Trainee counsellors learn quickly that beginning sentences with 'I think' is bad form, so they preface their remarks with 'I feel' and go on to report thoughts. This use of 'I feel' often results in muddled communication. Thinking (head talk) seeks to explain interaction – the prose of communication. Feeling (heart talk) seeks to understand interaction – the poetry of communication.

Thinking:

- 'Think' statements refer to what the environment means to us.
- They attempt to define, assert, offer an opinion, rationalise or make cause and effect connections between different events.
- 'Think' statements are bound by the rules of logic and scientific inquiry; they may be true or untrue.
- A 'think' statement can generally be proved or disproved.
- 'Think' statements require words to be communicated.
- Most of us have been trained to make 'I think' statements exclusively.
- We are constantly engaged in cognitive work: observing, inferring, categorising, generalising and summarising.
- Occasionally we report to others what goes on in our head.
- Frequently we are asked for:
  - Facts: 'Where did you put the car keys?'
  - Opinions: 'Which tastes better, French or Spanish wine?'
  - Speculation: 'What happens when we achieve population saturation?', 'What are you thinking about?'

Human beings like to think and our ability to do it is usually on the shortlist of characteristics that distinguish us from other species.

Feeling:

- 'Feel' statements refer to what is implied, internal, affective, immediate, non-rational, emotional – a 'gut' response to something personal and distinctive happening within.
- Like dreams, feel statements are neither true nor false, good nor bad; they can only be honestly or dishonestly communicated.
- Many of us have conditioned ourselves to screen out our internal reactions: we allow ourselves to say we feel 'interested', 'uncomfortable' but are scared to disclose our more intense feelings.
- By getting in touch with what is happening within us, we enrich our own lives and those with whom we communicate.
- Internal changes provide direct cues to the feelings we are experiencing: a change in bodily functioning – muscle tightness, restlessness, frowning,

smiling, inability to stay with a conversation – tell us how we are reacting to what is happening.

Watch yourself when you say 'I feel that...'. The 'that' is a tip-off that you are making a think statement with a feel prefix.

Examples of thinking and feeling statements:

- Example: 'I feel like having a drink'. Rephrased: 'I'm thirsty, so I think I'll have a drink'.
- Example: 'I feel your brashness is a cover for your insecurity'. Rephrased: 'It's my opinion that you cover up your insecurity with brashness'.
- Example: 'I feel that all men are created equal'. Rephrased: 'I believe that all men are created equal'.

3. Involvement

Involvement must be controlled:

- No emotional involvement means separation.
- Controlled emotional involvement means effective contact.
- Over-involvement leads to feelings of being engulfed.
- Over-involvement/over-identification is caused by a deficiency of self-awareness. The components of controlled involvement are:
  - Sensitivity: Listening to feelings, verbal cues, non-verbal cues, paralinguistic cues
  - Understanding what these feelings mean to this person: Getting inside the client's frame of reference, seeing through the client's eyes, hearing through the client's ears, feeling through the client's experience
  - Responding: Responses convey understanding – a response may be internal, founded on attitudes, feelings and understanding, or external; verbal or non-verbal
  - Avoid empty phrases such as: 'I know how you feel', 'This must be hard on you'. We can never know how another person feels. We only know how we feel, how we felt. We trust that our level of understanding is helping us get somewhere near the client's feelings.

4. Self-determination (self-direction)

- Self-determination is our basic right of freedom to choose our own direction, even though that decision may clash with the values, beliefs and desires of other people.
- We all have the responsibility to live our own life and achieve life's goals as we perceive them.
- One of the functions of counselling is to help clients mobilise their inner resources so that they are more able to make balanced decisions.
- Many people feel helpless to make decisions because the alternatives are

unclear; helping them tease out what is involved often enables them to make a decision and to take responsibility for what they decide to do.

- We may face a dilemma: if, in our view, a proposed course of action is destructive, could we still be objective and positive towards the client? If our values clashed, could we continue counselling without trying to persuade, manipulate, taking responsibility or trying to control the client?
- Clients need help to:
  - See their problem in a new perspective
  - Explore alternatives and the possible consequences
  - Express their thoughts and feelings about choices
  - Explore their thoughts, feelings and behaviours within a relationship in which they feel safe.

The counsellor, as it were, helps clients clear some of the mist away from the window, thus allowing them to look out and see a little more clearly.

Self-determination is not licence. It is influenced by:

- The rights of others
- The client's capacity to make informed decisions
- Civil and criminal law and the client's own moral law
- In work, the contract of employment
- Clients who violate their own moral law do spiritual harm to themselves. If a decision would be so contrary to the client's own moral law as to be destructive, it is questionable if we are really helping to solve a problem if we do not challenge that decision.

For every individual right of choice there are accompanying duties and responsibilities in our relationship with others. When we practise self-determination it does not mean that we are indifferent to what clients do; neither does it mean that we have to approve. We accept their basic right.

However, being able to work with a client who challenges our willingness not to interfere might also challenge how willing we are not to control or to possess the client. Possessiveness refers to any tendency to attempt to gain and hold ownership over things; however, it is generally applied to possessiveness of people. It is the tendency to maintain power and control over others, to treat them as though they were one's owned possessions. It is most commonly observed in parents' attitudes towards their children and husbands and wives towards each other. Possessiveness – the opposite of self-determination – is anathema in counselling.

5. Confidentiality (see Counselling ethics)

Counselling touches human lives intimately, possibly more so than any other helping relationship. The counsellor is frequently the observer, and often the recipient, of confidential material about people, their life situations and intimate details of their families. Confidentiality is both an ethical consideration and an element in the counselling relationship. At first glance, it is deceptively simple.

- Confidentiality means not passing on secret details about another person disclosed during counselling.
- Everything said in a counselling interview is confidential; not everything is secret – what are secrets?
- The private secret is that which, if we reveal it, would libel, injure or cause great sadness to the person concerned.
- The pledged secret is when one person shares something with another and is assured that it will remain in confidence.
- The entrusted secret is the explicit or implicit understanding that the confidant will not divulge the information.
- A belief that absolutely everything the client says must never be shared with anyone else can lead to problems.
- If it becomes imperative that some information must be passed on, full discussion with the client is essential.
- The professional counsellor is bound by certain ethics, which are not applicable in their totality to people using counselling skills as part of their repertoire of work skills. People who use counselling at work, as distinct from independent counsellors, must consider the rules of professional conduct of their organisation. It is helpful to ask: Is this information concerned mainly with the client as a person with the organisation? Purely personal material, unless it impinges on the client's working life and influences performance, is of no concern to anyone else. The dividing line between 'personal' and 'organisa-tional' is finely drawn. Only after a weighing up of all the pros and cons will we realise why the balance is tipped the way it is and so make our decision to keep something or pass it on.
- Wherever possible agreement to disclose should be received, to avoid feelings of betrayal.
- Feelings as well as facts should not be shared indiscriminately.
- Confidentiality is limited by:
  - Whose needs predominate
  - Who would be harmed
  - The organisational needs
  - The needs of the wider society.

Counsellors need to be quite clear what information gleaned during counselling they may pass on and to whom. Some clients need to be reassured of confidenti-ality and counsellors should take time to clarify precisely what the client under-stands by 'confidentiality'.

The person's right to secrecy is never absolute. Counsellors may be required by a court to disclose secret information. Failure to do so may lead to impri-sonment for contempt of court.

6. Acceptance

Acceptance is:

- A warm regard for people as persons of unconditional self-worth

- Valuing people no matter what their condition, thoughts, behaviours or feelings
- Respect and liking for people as separate, unique persons
- Willingness to allow people to possess their own feelings
- Regard for the attitudes of the moment, no matter how negative or positive; no matter how much such attitudes may contradict other attitudes the person held in the past
- Inherent in the idea of acceptance is that the counsellor does not judge the client by some set of rules or standards.
- Counsellors who are unable to suspend their own judgement will find that they intrude on the interaction and influence their impartiality.
- Acceptance is a special kind of loving that moves out towards people as they are – warts and all; maintaining their dignity and personal worth, with their strengths and weaknesses, with their likeable, unlikeable qualities; with their positive and negative attitudes, constructive and destructive wishes, thoughts, feelings and behaviours. There is no wish to apply pressure to make the person to be someone else, no wish to control, criticise or condemn and attaching of 'if' clauses; e.g. 'I will love you if...'. Clients will test our unconditional acceptance.
- When we accept clients just as they are, they accept us just as we are and this helps them to accept other people as they are.
- Acceptance is dependent on self-awareness: the more psychologically aware we are, the more able we shall be to help others mobilise their feelings and energies and to direct them towards change, growth and fulfilment.
- Obstacles to acceptance are:
  - Lack of knowledge of human behaviour
  - Blockages within self
  - Attributing one's own feelings to the client
  - Biases and prejudices
  - Unfounded reassurances
  - Confusion between acceptance and approval
  - Loss of respect for the client
  - Over-identification with the client.

Acceptance is the feeling of being accepted as we really are, including our strengths and weaknesses, differences of opinion, no matter how unpleasant or uncongenial, without censure. We do not feel accepted unless the very worst in us is accepted too. We never feel accepted when judgement is passed on us.

If we want to guide someone, even one step of the way, we must feel with that person's psyche. We may not put our judgements of other people into words; we may keep them to ourselves; this makes not the slightest difference. Judgement in the heart will be revealed.

We cannot change anything unless we accept it. Condemnation (which lies at the heart of rejection) does not liberate, it oppresses. We can only truly accept when we have already seen and accepted ourselves as we are.

Acceptance enables the counsellor to distinguish between the client's 'self' and 'behaviour'. It means maintaining all the while a sense of the client's innate dignity and personal worth. Unconditional acceptance demonstrates to clients that no matter how badly they act – towards us or towards others – we can still accept them and teach them to unconditionally accept themselves.

Acceptance does not mean approval of deviant attitudes or behaviour. The object of acceptance is not the 'good' but the 'real'.

Acceptance is not an all-or-nothing phenomenon, like perfect sight or total blindness. Rather, every counsellor has a certain degree of acceptance, which may vary from day to day or from client to client. No counsellor has or is expected to have perfect acceptance, for that would require godlike wisdom and an immunity from human frailties.

Acceptance is based upon the conviction that we have an innate dignity and worth and that acceptance cannot be lost by any weakness or failure on our part. It is possible that, in counselling, the client can lose this consciousness and feeling of personal dignity and value if the counsellor loses respect for the client.

Acceptance requires the quality of love. In real love, of whatever variety, the two persons know each other; they know their weaknesses and strengths, their successes and failures, and in spite of them, possibly even because of them, mutual respect continues and even increases. Love and acceptance cease with a loss of respect. Respect for other people necessarily implies a recognition of their innate dignity and value. This internal attitude is expected of a professional helping person and is the result of self-awareness and philosophy of life.

7. Non-judgement

- People who are troubled need help, not judgement.
- An attitude of non-judgement is based on the firmly held belief that assigning guilt or innocence, or the degree to which the client is responsible or not for causing the problem, has no place in the therapeutic relationship.
- Judgement without the appropriate authority is a violation of basic human rights.
- Clients who are nurtured within a relationship of non-judgement learn not to pass judgement upon themselves.
- When in such a relationship, people find the courage and the strength to change.
- When we pass judgement upon others, if we examine ourselves, we will find the very thing on which we pass judgement also present within us.
- 'Non-judgement' does not mean being valueless or without standards. It does mean not trying to mould others to fit into our value systems. Our values may be right for us, but totally wrong for other people. Counsellors, however, are not human chameleons. They must remain true to their own values and standards.
- Guilt or innocence, blame, condemnation and punishment are all part of judgement.

- People feel attacked when judgement is passed on them and less attacked when their observed behaviour is questioned.
- We communicate the unspoken judgement lurking within; when we feel non-judgement, that feeling is communicated.
- We may not like all clients, but it is our duty to strive towards freedom from prejudices that will lead us into passing judgement.
- We can work towards non-judgement by:
  - Recognising and carefully scrutinising our own values and standards, some of which we may need to jettison
  - Trying to see the world from the client's frame of reference
  - Not jumping to conclusions
  - Not saying, 'I know how you feel'
  - Not comparing the client to someone else
  - Not becoming over-involved
  - Not responding to the client's inappropriate feelings towards us, which may indicate transference.

Judgement is to do with law, blame, guilt or innocence and punishment. If relationships are to work, we must learn to suspend judgements and standards and not to impose them on others. Judgementalism takes no account of feelings. It is critical and condemns others because of their conduct or supposed false beliefs, wrong motives or character. Judgementalism is arbitrary, without room for negotiation or understanding. It is an evaluation and rejection of another person's worth.

The result of judgementalism is that it dims, divides and fragments relationships. Judgementalism seeks to elevate one person above another. Within it are the characteristics of self-exaltation, self-promotion and the determination to be first on every occasion. Judgement invariably attacks the person rather than the behaviour. It creates massive blind spots in our relationships. We cannot relate to people effectively while we are judging and condemning them.

Judgementalism can often be detected by such words as 'should', 'ought', 'must' and 'don't' and by such phrases as 'In my opinion', 'I think…' and 'This is what you should do'. It is moralistic, based on norms and values, warnings, approval/disapproval and instruction. Judgementalism induces inferiority and evokes inhibition, guilt and distress. Judgementalism is often associated with authority, control, hierarchy, rules and regulations that impose standards of behaviour.

Judgementalism and acceptance are opposites – judgementalism paralyses; acceptance affirms and encourages action. People with a strong attitude of judgementalism are very often highly critical of themselves and find it almost impossible to forgive others or themselves.

Judgement does not fit with being judgemental. If judgement is the opposite of acceptance, then to judge is to reject and that negates the whole idea of counselling. Counsellors might not like what a person is or does, but acceptance goes far beyond liking; it goes beyond the surface and makes contact with the real person.

Further reading

Biestek, F.P. (1957) *The Casework Relationship.* George Allen & Unwin, London.
Billheimer, P.E. (1981) *Love Covers: a viable platform for Christian Unity.* Christian Literature Crusade, Arlesford, Hampshire.
Dryden, W. (1988) *Therapists' Dilemmas.* Harper & Row, London.
Friedman, M. (1972) *Touchstones of Reality.* E.P. Dutton, New York.
Rogers, C.R. (1961) *On Becoming a Person.* Houghton Mifflin, Boston, MA.
Rogers, C.R. (1980) *A Way of Being.* Houghton Mifflin, Boston, MA.

RELAXATION THERAPY (SEE ALSO: STRESS MANAGEMENT)

The purpose of relaxation is to do away with certain activities that place undue stress upon the body. Most of the techniques of relaxation therapy involve retraining the muscles of the body to get rid of hidden underlying tension.

When an individual is stressed, then the so-called 'fight or flight response' is activated, with the person experiencing increased heart rate, blood pressure and respiratory rate. One of the major tools employed by relaxation therapists is deep breathing, as tension per se causes breathing changes.

Relaxation is a state of low tension in which emotional level is diminished, especially the level of emotions such as anxiety, fear, anger and the like. Relaxation therapy, generally, is any psychotherapy that emphasises techniques for teaching the client how to relax, to control tensions. The procedure used is based upon Jacobsen's progressive relaxation techniques in which the client learns how to relax muscle groups one at a time, the assumption being that muscular relaxation is effective in bringing about emotional relaxation. Jacobsen's techniques are often used in various forms of behaviour therapy, for example, desensitisation procedure.

Relaxation quietens our physical and psychological internal worlds and, therefore, aids in reducing arousal level. One can relax immediately and quickly by starting to breathe slowly and deeply.

There are many excellent tapes on the market that teach progressive relaxation techniques. A regular programme of relaxation is preventive as well as curative if you practise the following routine.

1. Choose a comfortable position.
2. Close your eyes.
3. Relax your muscles.
4. Become aware of your breathing.
5. Maintain a passive attitude when thoughts surface.
6. Continue for a set period of time (20 minutes is recommended).
7. Practise the technique twice daily.

If the above technique is practised with a phrase or word that reflects your basic belief system, then relaxation and its curative powers will be enhanced.

Some examples of phrases used in teaching the expanded relaxation response are: 'My peace I give unto you' or 'Shalom' (the Hebrew word for peace).

Relaxation for better health and well-being

Rewards

- A person who uses regular relaxation needs less sleep.
- Body and mind have more energy, and consciousness has more clarity.
- Concentration improves.
- Living is more joyful and fulfilling.
- The journey towards self-actualisation is made easier.

Medical findings about regular relaxation

- Heart rate decreases by about three beats a minute.
- The body's consumption of oxygen decreases.
- The metabolism reduces by around 20 per cent.
- Anxiety is reduced.
- Blood pressure is reduced.
- The brain produces Alpha and perhaps Theta waves. Beta waves denote activity whereas others produce a relaxed condition.

People under stress tend to breathe with relatively short, shallow breaths. Yoga is a form of relaxation that employs breathing and positioning of the body to improve agility, both mental and physical, and reduces tension by allowing the body to relax. Yoga promotes happiness in a state of inner tranquillity and balance, with inner peace and harmony at the root of the therapy.

Clients who are stressed and anxious can be taught to control their anxiety by teaching them how to relax. This is more than a technique, for it gives the client a strong element of control over what they feel is something out of control. Another bonus for relaxation is that if behavioural counselling is indicated, to help with panic attacks or phobias, relaxation is vital. As counsellors we cannot justifiably proclaim the virtues of relaxation if we do not practise it, and have ourselves proved the benefits of it.

Relaxation therapy is helpful for people with learning disabilities who have an increased likelihood of demonstrating maladaptive behaviours such as stereotyped rocking or aggression towards others.

Main relaxation therapies:

- Aromatherapy
- Art therapy
- Biofeedback
- Dream therapy
- Guided imagery
- Hypnotherapy
- Massage
- Meditation and prayer
- Music therapy

- Reflexology
- T'ai chi
- Yoga.

Further reading

Cooper, C.L., Sloan, S.J. and Williams, S. (1988) *Occupational Stress Indicator.* NFER Nelson, Windsor.

Davis, M., Robbins, E. and McKay, M. (1982) *The Relaxation and Stress Reduction Workbook.* New Harbinger Publications, Oakland, CA.

Holmes, T.H. and Rahe, R.H. (1967) The social readjustment rating scale. *Journal of Psychosomatic Research,* **11:** 213–218.

Jacobsen, E. *Progressive Relaxation.* University of Chicago Press, Chicago.

Livingstone-Booth, A. (1985) *Stressmanship.* Severn House Publishers, London.

Lovelace, R.T. (1990) *Stressmaster.* John Wiley, Chichester.

Spencer, J. (2004) Relaxation can't wait. *Reader's Digest,* June, pages 119–122.

Sutton, J. (1998) *Thriving on Stress: how to manage pressures and transform your life.* How to Books, Oxford.

www.lut.ac.uk

www.nassdb.org.uk

RESISTANCE (SEE ALSO: TRANSFERENCE AND COUNTER-TRANSFERENCE)

In psychoanalysis, resistance describes the client's unconscious efforts to thwart the aims and process of therapy, sometimes referred to as 'sticking points'. The client does this by blocking unconscious, repressed material from breaking through into the conscious. This may take the form of being unwilling to continue exploring a particular theme, with its thoughts and feelings. This might be due to anxiety about the disclosure or fear of how the counsellor will react. If the client deliberately blocks something, then this is more avoidance than resistance, which, in its original sense, is an unconscious mechanism.

Because of the client's resistance, access to the unconscious can be gained only by indirect means, the chief of which is free association. Resistance must be overcome if the client is to integrate unconscious material into the conscious and move forward towards the loss of symptoms. However, this 'overcoming' is not an aggressive breaking down of the defence; rather it is achieved as client and counsellor work through the need for resistance. Neither does resistance mean that the client does not comply with what the counsellor wants or desires.

Resistance is not a 'once-and-for-all' phenomenon; it is continually being experienced. By analysing the resistances, the client gains freedom from them. The analyst uses positive transference to overcome resistance.

The paradox is that many people who engage in counselling experience resistance to it. Most people would experience resistance if they felt, for example, censured and judged.

Anticipated change may also create resistance. Clients are more likely to undertake change with less resistance when in a supportive relationship than when they feel undesired change is being forced upon them.

Resistance occurs as the client's unconscious senses that something is waiting in the wings to be disclosed and this something is likely to increase the client's distress or anxiety. It may be concerned with guilt over some 'forgotten' experience or some feeling of shame or disgrace, or just some vague feeling of something not quite right.

Overcoming resistance cannot be hurried; it can be helped by:

- The client's need for recovery
- The client's intellectual interest
- Positive transference
- Making the expression of resistance as safe as possible
- Honouring the resistance by careful listening, without discounting what is revealed
- Acknowledging the resistance, not by agreeing with it but by recognising the difficulty the client is experiencing
- Reinforcing that there must be valid reasons for resisting at this time.

Exploring the resistance

- Distinguish between valid and invalid resistance. Valid resistance is directed at the specific topic; invalid resistance is a smokescreen of feelings to divert the counsellor's attention. Invalid resistance is often linked to generalities and bringing up the past.
- Any probing of the resistance must be carried out with extreme caution. The probing is carried out with the express consent of the client.
- The aim is to reduce needless resistance that interferes with the client's healthy functioning.

Indicators of resistance include:

- A tendency to argue
- Avoidance of new learning
- Refusal to cooperate in suggested programmes
- Refusal to look at new possibilities
- Always wanting to generalise and not deal with specifics
- Intellectualising and refusing to work with feelings
- Rudeness, antagonism, anger or any other strongly negative feeling
- Silences and passivity
- Verbal aggression
- Projecting feelings on to the counsellor
- Denial, without desire to explore
- Insistence that there is no improvement
- Talking about trivia
- Talking about external events and other people
- Premature ending of counselling
- Refusal to terminate counselling.

Resistance may be created by the counsellor, either from what is said or done or from what is not said or done. The counsellor whose empathy has lapsed and who is no longer relating to the client from the internal frame of reference is in danger of creating the conditions in which resistance will flourish.

Further reading

Jacobs, M. (1988) *Psychodynamic Counselling in Action.* Sage Publications, London.
Jacobs, M. (1993) Client resistance. In: *Questions and Answers on Counselling in Action* (ed. W. Dryden). Sage Publications, London.
Karp, H.B. (1988) A positive approach to resistance. In: *1988 Annual: Developing Human Resources.* University Associates, San Diego, CA.
Rosenthall, L. (1980) Resistance in group psychotherapy. In: *Group and Family Therapy* (eds L. Volberg and M. Arunsen). Brunner/Mazel, New York.
Wachtel, P.L. (ed.) (1982) *Resistance: psychodynamic and behavioural approaches.* Plenum Press, New York.

RETIREMENT

Retirement is more than a date on the calendar when we become entitled to the state pension. An estimate of the likely total stress of retirement, using the life change units (see Stress management) is made up of:

- Retirement from work   45
- A significant change in financial state   38
- Significant change in living conditions   25
- A revision of personal habits   24
- Change in residence (perhaps)   20
- A significant change in the person's usual type and/or amount of recreation 19
- A significant change in social activities   18

This does not take into account many other items, not included above, such as:

- Loss of friends and colleagues
- Disrupted routine
- More contact with spouse – this may produce friction, as neither is used to having the other around for such long periods
- Time hangs heavily
- Loss of status – joins the ranks of the 'retired'
- A new status, which has overtones of ageing
- Loss of purpose and meaning
- Reduced income.

All is not negative. The retired person does have more time to 'do all those things that, over the years, have been left'. Yet this can produce strain. Over the years at work, the body has become accustomed to a certain routine of sleep, work, rest, diet and recreation.

Many people go hell-for-leather at redecorating the house, carrying out major structural alterations to the garden, etc. These new activities use different groups of muscles and very often the result is strain and frustration.

There are definitely many positives: being able to please oneself as to where to go and when; being able to resume activities such as walking and swimming, which are thoroughly recommended.

Many people, with more time on their hands, turn to developing hobbies that have lain dormant and discover another 'career'. Sadly, however, many feel that when the work gate closes (symbolically, if not actually) life stops and all they can see is the scrapheap.

When retired people complain of feeling stressed, what they complain of is associated with the ageing process. They show a higher tendency to leave things until the last minute and may also exhibit anxiety, heart trouble, fear of health breakdown, loss of temper, irritability, sleeplessness and periods of depression.

Counselling might mean helping such a person find a new direction in life, for with retirement often come feelings similar to grief, grieving over what has been lost and can never more be. Recognising that the client is grieving, although this might not be acknowledged, might be the first step towards something new.

Retirement, like old age, comes to us all. People who resist getting old may not tolerate enforced retirement very well, for it is accompanied by many dramatic changes of lifestyle. Whether we accept these changes, and get them to work for us instead of against us, is entirely our choice. However, choice often seems to be predetermined by the life philosophy we have developed. Retirement means letting go, in much the same way as getting older means letting go of what once was, and what never again can be.

Retirement and redundancy are closely bound up with self-esteem. Many of us are likely to become involved in listening to someone whose job either is to be made redundant, or has been. This experience is shattering to one's self-esteem, and is often handled very badly by whoever breaks the news. Telling people that their job is finished is like breaking the news that someone has died; only it's not someone else, it's you.

S

SCAPEGOATING

Although the idea of the scapegoat is commonly associated with early Jewish history, the use of scapegoats has a long and varied past involving many kinds of animals, as well as human beings.

In ancient Greek religion, the ritual of the scapegoat was associated with the festivals of Apollo at Athens, celebrated on the sixth and seventh days of Thargelion (May–June). This festival was a vegetation ritual named after the first fruits or the first bread from the new wheat. On the first day of the festival, one or two men (or a man and a woman), representing the deity but also acting as scapegoats for community guilt, were chosen. After being feted, the couple were led around the town, beaten with green twigs, driven out of the city and possibly even stoned. In this way the city was supposedly protected from ill fortune for another year. Occasionally, as in times of heavy calamity, they were sacrificed, being either thrown into the sea or burned on a funeral pyre. On the second day of the festival, there was a thanks-offering, a procession and the official registration of adopted persons.

During the Roman feast of Lupercalia, priests *(luperci)* cut thongs from the sacrificial animals (goats and a dog), then raced around the walls of the old Palatine city, striking women (especially) as they passed with the thongs. A blow from the hide of the scapegoat was said to cure sterility. In early Roman law an innocent person was allowed to take upon himself the penalty of another who had confessed his own guilt.

In the Old Testament it is stated that, on the Day of Atonement, Aaron would sacrifice two goats, a ram and one bullock. One goat and the bullock would be sacrificed immediately as a sin offering. The second goat was allotted to the demon Azazel, symbolically burdened with the sins of the Jewish people and driven off into the wilderness and abandoned (Leviticus 16:7–10 and 20–22).

The same ritual was carried out in the purification of lepers but using two birds (the variety is not named but in Leviticus 14:22 two pigeons are mentioned as sin offerings, so the 'birds' might have been pigeons). One of the birds was killed and the leprous person was sprinkled with its blood. The second bird was sprinkled with the blood and was allowed to fly free, carrying with it, symbolically, the remnants of the disease.

In *The Golden Bough*, Sir James Frazer, drawing attention to variations on a theme, quotes cases of certain African Moors who, when experiencing a headache, would beat a lamb or a goat until it fell down, believing that the headache will be transferred to the animal. Similarly, in Morocco, wealthy Moors were known to keep a wild boar in their stables in order that the jinn and evil spirits would be diverted from the horses and enter the boar.

In certain South African tribes, when all known remedies have failed to cure a sickness, a goat will be brought in and the sick person will confess his sins over it. Then the animal is turned out to fend for itself. When plague hits Arabia, the people have been known to lead a camel through all the quarters of the town in order that the animal may take the pestilence on itself; then the animal is strangled in a sacred place. Similarly, in Taiwan, to get rid of smallpox, the people used to drive the demon of disease into a sow, then cut off the animal's ears and burn them or it.

In all these rituals, the belief is that the 'curse' will be averted, the illness cured or sins will be forgiven.

By extension, a scapegoat has come to mean any individual or group that innocently bears the blame of others. Christianity reflects this notion in its doctrine of justification and in its belief that Jesus Christ was the God-man who died to atone for the sins of all mankind. Christ's death and atonement reflects the notion of the innocent suffering for the guilty.

The concept of scapegoating applied to counselling

In groups, scapegoating describes the way in which one person can be isolated and excluded in order to relieve group tension and stress. The scapegoated person usually possesses one or more characteristics that influence the process, such as:

- Mental or physical disability or illness
- Racial, sexual, colour or language difference
- Vulnerability – difference in rank or status or, in families, low rank order.

Scapegoating can be seen within societies, where minority groups are blamed for everything that goes wrong in the community, which relieves the others from having to take any responsibility. Scapegoating uses the defence mechanisms of displacement (where emotions, ideas or wishes are transferred from their original object to a more acceptable substitute), projection (where what is emotionally unacceptable in the self is unconsciously rejected and attributed – projected – to others) and projective identification (attributing unacceptable parts of self – feelings, thoughts and impulses – on to another).

Scapegoating is also seen in family therapy, where one member is designated as 'the sick one', the one in need of being 'cured'. Then the family would be 'normal'. It is also seen in therapy groups or, indeed, in any growth group, where one member will be ganged up against and blamed for the non-progress of the group task. If the group leader does not draw attention to what is happening, the 'scapegoat' can be demoralised and psychologically destroyed. In individual counselling, clients may engage in this as they lay blame at the door of someone else. Scapegoating is thus an effective way of avoiding dealing with something relevant in counselling; if it goes unrecognised, counselling will cease to be effective.

Further reading

Frazer, J. (1993) *The Golden Bough*. Wordsworth Reference, London.

Gaskell, G.A. (1981) *Dictionary of All Scriptures and Myths*. Random House, New York.

SELF

Self refers to the organised, consistent perceptions of the 'I' and the relationship of 'I' to others. In modern psychology, the notion of the self has replaced earlier conceptions of the soul. The concept of the self has been a central feature of many personality theories, including those of Sigmund Freud, Alfred Adler, Carl Jung, Gordon W. Allport, Karen Horney, Carl Rogers, Rollo May and Abraham H. Maslow.

The self is a relatively stable set of perceptions of who we are in relation to ourselves, to others and to social systems. Personality and ego are commonly used synonyms, although they do not have exactly the same meaning. The personality is more outwardly observable (by others, that is) and the ego, as a psychoanalytical term at least, contains unconscious elements that the self does not recognise.

The development of self is shaped through interaction with other people and draws upon social materials in the form of cultural imagery and ideas. We are not passive participants in this process of socialisation; we exert a powerful influence over how this process and its consequences develop.

Self-concept

The self is organised around a self-concept, the ideas and feelings that we have about ourselves. Charles H. Cooley referred to the looking-glass self, based on how we think other people see and evaluate us (which, of course, is not necessarily how they actually see us).

The self is also based on cultural ideas about the social statuses and roles that we occupy. In this way, for example, a man who is a father will draw upon cultural ideas about fathering in constructing his idea of who he is. This component of a self-concept, which is based on the social positions that a person occupies, is known as a social identity. Self experiences are the basic material from which the self-concept is formed.

Confusion and tension result in a state of vulnerability when there is incongruity between the self-concept and actual experience. Lack of awareness of incongruity between self and experience makes us vulnerable to anxiety and disorganisation. Many people resist feedback that would alter their views of themselves, even rejecting feedback of a flattering nature that tells them they are better than they thought. On the other hand, some people seek positive flattering feedback in order to make a good impression on others.

Ideal self

We all possess an actual self and an ideal self. The ideal self is what we know we could be, should be or would like to be. Low self-esteem operates in the gap between the actual self and the ideal self. The ideal self is influenced by three major factors:

• Parental expectations and instructions received on how to behave

- The values of parents
- The values of heroic figures from real life, biography and fiction.

A related concept is that of undesired self, that which we would not like to become, similar to Jung's concept of the Shadow. This motivates us to do all we can to avoid becoming that person.

Self-esteem

Self-esteem is the positive and negative evaluation we make of and apply to ourselves. Self-esteem indicates the extent to which we believe ourselves to be significant, capable and worthy. Self-esteem is generally applied to feelings of worthiness. We may have a good, average or bad opinion of ourselves; the views we hold about ourselves are not always held by other people.

Self-esteem is also affected by evaluations that are part of the looking-glass self. Generally we see our value mirrored in the eyes of society, a process that starts in childhood. To some extent, our self-esteem is derived from a comparison between ourselves and other people. On the other hand, we may think well of ourselves if we occupy positions of high status, because other people look up to us. Comparison with the peer group, for example, is important and is based on popularity, power over others, task competence and honour or virtue.

A surprising point about self-esteem is the enormous variation that exists between individuals. Some people think the whole world is theirs for the taking; others almost feel they have no right to exist. Some people attempt to bolster their self-esteem at the expense of that of others but this, in the long term, is not fruitful.

There is a general need to regard one's self favourably and one way we do this is to exaggerate our good points. Another way is to alter our behaviour so that we conform to the expectations and standards of our ideal self. Self-esteem includes self-significance, self-competence and self-like.

Freud believed that the male child who has been the mother's favourite will forever keep the feeling that he is a conqueror. Yet other children, even within the same family, grow up with the feeling that their very existence is a terrible mistake. There is no 'self-esteem blueprint' for parents to work on.

At the highest level, self-esteem depends on making sense of our relationship to the rest of the universe. Low self-esteem operates in the gap between the actual self and the ideal self. Low self-esteem is often associated with:

- Abuse
- Anxiety states
- Delinquency
- Depressive illness
- Disability, disfigurement
- Prejudice
- Psychosomatic disorders.

Self-esteem rating scales correlate strongly with scales measuring anxiety, depression and neuroticism and in many cases there is overlap of items. Low self-esteem is an enormous public health problem. People who report low self-esteem usually say that it has been present since early childhood or at least since adolescence.

- **Self-significance** refers to feelings of being significant, important, worthwhile and meaningful as opposed to feeling unimportant, meaningless and of no value.
- **Self-competence** refers to feelings of competence, intelligence, ability and strength as opposed to weakness, incompetence and the inability to cope.
- **Self-like** refers to feeling good in the presence of the self, i.e. when alone, as opposed to not enjoying one's own company.
- **Self-attentiveness** (also called self-consciousness): People differ in the degree to which they habitually attend to themselves as well as in the focus of their self-preoccupations. For example, some people are prone to introspect, to examine frequently their feelings and motives. Some are habitually concerned with how they appear to others.

Public and private self

The self has both a private and public face. The private self consists of our personal thoughts, feelings, values and beliefs. The public self is what we present to others – the behaviour, mannerisms and ways of expressing ourselves that create people's impressions of us. Both aspects of the self influence behaviour: our actions are guided by our personal feelings and beliefs as well as by the social context in which we find ourselves, i.e. by considering how others will react to what we do (see also Public and private self).

Private and public self-consciousness

Persons who score high in private self-consciousness (i.e. the disposition to introspect) tend to be more responsive to transient affective states than do persons who score low in that category. They show more behavioural signs of anger when provoked and are more affected by viewing pleasant and unpleasant slides. They are also less suggestible, more resistant to political propaganda and more accurate in describing their own behaviour. It seems they know themselves better than do those low in private self-consciousness. They are also more likely to disclose private aspects of selves to their spouses or intimate partners.

People who score high on the scale of public self-consciousness seem more sensitive to group rejection than those who score low on this dimension. Individuals high in public self-consciousness are also better at predicting the kind of impression they make on others and place more importance on their 'social' identity in describing themselves – e.g. their physical characteristics, gestures and mannerisms and group memberships. If they are female, they are apt to wear more make-up than are those who score low on public self-consciousness.

The dimensions of private and public self-consciousness have implications for the question of personality consistency. Individuals who score high on private and low on public self-consciousness have greater consistency in behaviour over different situations than do people who score low on private and high on public self-consciousness. People high in private self-consciousness tend to behave in accordance with their own attitudes and beliefs rather than tailoring their actions to fit the social demands of changing situations.

It needs to be stressed that however 'accurate' personality tests are, they are not absolute. They are not precise instruments, but rather indicators of what might be. For example, a person who tops the 'private person' scale might be totally different in a group or in a one-to-one relationship, where the person is accepted and feels at ease or when in the position of being in control.

The self in counselling

Self-esteem is part of the ego and, when the ego suffers, self-esteem suffers with it. Difficulties with self-esteem are present in many clients. Self-esteem is at the very core of our personality and low self-esteem is characteristic of depressive personality. Loss of self-esteem often accompanies depression and may result from the symbolic (and symbolic does not mean worthless) losses of, for example, power, status, roles and values, all of which influence, to one degree or another, the way we live our lives. When we feel good about ourselves, it is almost certain that most of our activities will be successful. We derive great joy from them. People who feel good about themselves:

- Take risks with confidence – they do not have to be either foolhardy or over-cautious
- Can keep on being what they are, confident and likeable – the thought of not being liked or supported does not shatter them
- Can take orders without resentment and give orders without guilt or without fearing punishment
- Can take criticism and make constructive use of it
- Can take a compliment graciously without suspecting the sincerity of the giver
- Can give compliments without being afraid that they will gain an advantage; they do not think that others need to feel the same way about them
- Can speak directly and honestly to people with whom they have a problem instead of talking behind their backs.

The basic components of self-awareness are:

- **The reality and integrity of self**: I am one person.
- **The continuity of self**: I am the same person now that I was yesterday and that I will be tomorrow.
- **The boundaries of self**: I can distinguish between myself and the rest of the world as being non-self.
- **The activities of self**: I know that I am thinking, feeling and doing.
- **Body-image**: my mental representation of my body.
- **Ego ideal**: the positive standards, ideals and ambitions that according to psychoanalytic theory form a person's conscious goals.

Disturbances of these basic components are seen in certain mental illnesses and indicate the urgent need for psychiatric help.

Further reading

Becker, J. (1979) Vulnerable self-esteem as a predisposing factor in depressive disorders. In: *The Antecedents of Self-esteem* (ed. S. Coopersmith). W.H. Freeman, San Francisco, CA.

Lowry, R.J. (ed.) (1973) *Dominance, Self-esteem, Self-Actualisation: germinal papers of A. H. Maslow.* Brooks/Cole, Pacific Grove, CA.

Stewart, W. (1998) *Building Self-esteem: how to replace self-doubt with confidence and well-being.* How to Books, Oxford.

SELF-COUNSELLING

Self-counselling is the systematic investigation of one's own psychic processes using psychoanalytic techniques such as free association, the recording and analysis of one's own dreams and the investigation of minor symptoms such as lapses of memory, headaches and slips of the tongue.

Originally Freud recommended the technique and engaged in self-analysis himself. Later, however, he concluded that such a procedure was a poor substitute for being analysed by someone else. Karl Abraham believed that self-analysis was in fact resistance to psychoanalysis, but Karen Horney suggested that it was both feasible and useful, though limited in its results as compared with analysis by someone else. It is now regarded as a highly desirable procedure in its own right, but not as a substitute for one's own therapeutic or training analysis.

In her introduction to *Self-Analysis* (1942 and reissued in 1994), Horney says: 'To an increasing degree people turn to analysis not because they suffer from depressions, phobias or comparable disorders but because they feel they cannot cope with life or feel that factors within themselves are holding them back or injuring their relationships with others.' Written over 60 years ago, this applies with even more force to the rapid development of counselling, and the awareness that counselling can help people to live life more effectively.

Journeying towards self-discovery

Being your own counsellor will take you out of your accepted way of thinking about things. Some people might criticise this as being 'pie in the sky' or just fantasy. It might be fantasy, it might be fantastic, but so is the journey towards self-discovery, for it is a journey that has no map, no signposts, no known way, yet countless thousands have travelled this way; and every journey is different. Every pilgrim creates his own map and signposts, and every pilgrim finds his own solutions to problems. Like Christian in Bunyan's *Pilgrim's Progress,* they are all making their way to some Celestial City, yet for each it is different. Life is a paradox; so is the journey towards self-awareness.

Self-counselling is a bit like learning by correspondence – you go at your own pace. Some students are really focused on the course, and apply themselves to every lesson and the accompanying assignments. Others look upon the lessons as a chore, and the assignments as drudgery. But what they have in common is that they are doing things at their own pace, not being pushed by a zealous (or over-zealous) teacher. So it is in self-counselling.

Identifying the limitations of self-counselling

It would be irresponsible to assert that there are no limitations. However, it is equally possible that the limitations that apply to any counselling also apply to self-counselling. Counselling is often inappropriate for the more florid mental illnesses, but even here, a degree of self-counselling might help; it would certainly be unlikely to make the condition worse.

A second possible reason why self-counselling might not be feasible is the degree to which the person is enmeshed in the problem – in other words, how deeply embedded in the unconscious it is. It could be argued that such cases are not suitable for counselling, but rather for psychoanalysis.

The main approaches are:

- Free association
- Dream analysis
- Meditation
- Relaxation
- Religious approaches
- Autogenic training.

Self-analysis is not an easy option, although it is certainly not as expensive as psychoanalysis. However, it is not to be undertaken lightly or by the faint of heart. It is time-consuming, emotionally demanding, frustrating and rewarding. As with most other activities – what you put in, you get out. Motivation is the first hurdle to be jumped. Why are you doing it? What is your goal? Your motivation may be severely tested when insights seem slow in coming, and frustration tugs at your heels. But that may be the very sticking-point you must overcome before insights come.

Have you ever sat down with all good intentions to write an essay, and then discovered that there are several other tasks that seem more important? Distractions! Habit is a wonderful ally, provided it does not become a tyrannical gaoler, so setting aside a regular time and quiet place for self-analysis will pay dividends.

Privacy is essential. You will not be able to get in touch with your inner self with the children flying around, making demands on you. You may have to shut your bedroom door, and let everyone know that this is your special time.

Progress for you may be discovering the link between why you do things the way you do them and remembering that that was the way you saw your grandmother do them, and she died before you went to school. Progress may be you being able to cry about the death of a pet. It may be that you can complete some unfinished business with someone who has died. You cannot predict progress; you can only recognise it when it happens – when your psyche lets you know.

Further reading

Horney, K. (1942, reprint 1994), *Self-Analysis*. W.W. Norton, New York.
Shepard, M. (1973, reprint 1994) *Do-it-yourself psychotherapy*. Optima, Little, Brown and Co., London.
Stewart. W. (1998) *Self-counselling: how to develop the skills to positively manage your life*. How to Books, Oxford.

SELF-DISCLOSURE

Self-disclosure is the process by which we let ourselves be known to others. In the process, we enhance our self-awareness.

Disclosures may be:

- Intentional (mainly conscious)
- Unintentional (mainly unconscious)
- Verbal (mainly conscious)
- Non-verbal (mainly unconscious)
- Thoughts, feelings and behaviours.

Clear verbal and non-verbal disclosures increase the chance of accurate reception without the need for complicated decoding.

Appropriate disclosure is critical in relationships, for it enhances them, keeps them alive and helps to avoid alienation. One person's low disclosure is likely to block another person's willingness to disclose.

People who are genuine, in touch with their own inner empathy, are also in touch with what they are experiencing and send authentic messages to others.

Disclosure involves both negative and positive aspects of self. Not everyone finds it easy to disclose positive aspects of themselves, possibly because of low self-esteem.

Disclosing means that we have to anticipate:

- Our own feelings
- The other person's reactions
- The possible effect on the relationship.

We may interfere with people's genuine self-disclosure by:

- Being secretive; this leads to a high degree of information control
- Colluding with them, in which case fantasy and reality become confused
- Faking disclosures, which prevents the other person from making genuine disclosures.

Questions of appropriateness of self-disclosure:

- How much can I disclose?
- What area can I disclose?
- How many areas should I disclose?
- How intimate should the disclosures be?

- To whom could I disclose?
- In what context could I disclose?
- Why am I disclosing?

Encouraging self-disclosure

- **Assertion**: Learning to express, where appropriate, positive and negative feelings
- **Challenging**: To give feedback non-aggressively
- **Development of relationships**: Breadth and depth of disclosures tend to increase naturally as relationships develop
- **Expressiveness**: To be able to express feelings appropriately (or not express them, but recognise and acknowledge them), not just talk about them
- **Feedback options**:
  - To agree
  - To restate the initial disclosure
  - To reflect the other person's message
  - To send an I message
  - To remain silent
- **Immediacy**: To be able to respond immediately and say what otherwise would remain unsaid
- **Positive/negative disclosure**: Genuine intimacy is characterised by a willingness to let ourselves be known genuinely
- **Questions**: Questions often avoid having to disclose; they should be used with discrimination
- **Reciprocity**: Relationships can be prevented from becoming shallow by matching levels of disclosure
- **'I' messages**: Recognising, owning and expressing one's own feelings, not someone else's
- **Specificity**: Generalisations are too vague for people to relate to
- **Verbal and non-verbal disclosures**: People can be taught to disclose by such means as:
  - Modelling/teaching
  - Rehearsal/practising
  - Homework
  - Audio-visual aids.

Self-disclosure (client)

This is where the client makes a conscious decision to disclose feelings, thoughts, attitudes, behaviours – past or present – to the therapist. Client disclosure is an essential element of most types of psychotherapy.

Where this is not happening, counselling is seriously impeded. The degree of disclosure is related to the degree of trust within the relationship. Counsellor trustworthiness, a non-judgemental attitude and acceptance all facilitate disclosure.

Exploring how disclosure could facilitate or hinder counselling may help those clients who have difficulty disclosing. Clients may be helped towards disclosure by considering the potential gains and risks.

Table 18: *Gains and risks of self-disclosure*

Possible gains:	Possible risks:
Lessened loneliness and alienation	Rejection
Greater intimacy	Not liking self
More friendships	Feelings of shame
Self-responsibility	Being misunderstood
More assertive	Wary of confidentiality
Makes it easier for others to disclose	Feeling tense/vulnerable
Discovering others	Too much intimacy, too soon
Self-acceptance	Too many close relationships
More control of own life.	Too much self-knowledge
	Equilibrium of relationship disturbed
	Breaking taboos about disclosures.

Reluctance to disclose may also be related to ethnic or religious influences. It may also be an indication of resistance.

Self-disclosure (counsellor)

Where counsellors are open and use disclosure appropriately, clients are more likely to be equally disclosing. Counsellor disclosure involves appropriate sharing of:

- Attitudes
- Experiences
- Feelings
- Reactions to the client
- Views.

Appropriate self-disclosure is critical in relationships; it helps to keep us real. One of the dangers of self-disclosure is that it can remove the focus from the client, particularly if the disclosure goes into too much detail. This can be an effective way of the client engaging the counsellor as a defence against exploration and of the counsellor avoiding challenging the client. Being clear about the motive for disclosing is essential.

Counsellor disclosure may be more appropriate in well-established relationships. Disclosures should reflect the needs of the client, not of the counsellor.

It is also useful to distinguish between supplying information requested by the client and choosing to disclose something that is designed for the client's benefit. Asking for information may indicate that the client wants to reduce the client-counsellor distance, effecting a change in the relationship.

Self-disclosure is embraced in humanistic therapies but seldom in psychoanalytic therapies, where to self-disclose would get in the way of working through the transference.

Inappropriate or mistimed disclosures may increase rather than decrease the client's anxiety. The focus may be removed from the client if the disclosure is lengthy or inappropriate.

The counsellor must always remember who is the client; any discussion of personal problems is inappropriate and will lead to confusion of roles, because the boundaries have been blurred.

While the counsellor might feel that disclosing something could deepen empathy, and there is no doubt that it could, unless the disclosure is brief and to the point and the focus is returned to the client, any empathy could be destroyed.

Disclosure is appropriate if:

- It keeps the client on target and does not distract
- It does not add to the client's burden
- It does not occur too often.

The greatest block to self-disclosure is fear of not being accepted; of thinking oneself to be different, odd, unworthy, fit only to be judged. Cautious, ritualised communication inhibits self-disclosure.

To build self-disclosure skills:

- Be direct
- Be sensitive
- Be relevant
- Be non-possessive
- Be brief
- Be selective.

Example

Peter was talking to his counsellor, Roy, about his father's recent death. He was having difficulty expressing himself until Roy said, 'My father died four years after my mother. When he died I felt I'd been orphaned. Maybe that is something like how you feel.'

Peter sat for several minutes in deep silence before saying, 'You've put into words exactly how I feel. May I talk about my childhood and how Dad and I got on?'

Gerard Egan makes the following points about helper self-disclosure:

- Indirect self-disclosure goes on all the time, through what we say, the tone of voice and our body language, as well as our emotional responses, and the way we relate to clients.
- Direct self-disclosure is problematic and contradictory. It can frighten clients. They may see helpers as not as well adjusted as they thought.
- Helper self-disclosure might place another burden on clients.
- On the other hand, helper self-disclosure is appreciated by some clients; some clients see self-disclosing helpers as down-to-earth and honest.

- Direct self-disclosure can serve as a form of modelling for clients. Self-help groups such as Alcoholics Anonymous use such modelling extensively.
- Helper self-disclosure is challenging:
  - It is a form of intimacy and some clients do not find intimacy easy to handle.
  - Helpers need to know precisely why they are divulging information about themselves.
  - The indirect message to the client indirectly is a challenging 'You can do it, too'. Helper revelations, even when they deal with past failures, often centre on problem situations they have overcome or opportunities they have seized.
  - When done well, such disclosures can be very encouraging for clients.
  - Helper self-disclosure is not a science but an art.

Guidelines for using self-disclosure

- Include helper self-disclosure in the contract. At some time towards the beginning of the counselling process, you might say something like this: 'From time to time, I might share with you some of my own life experiences if I think they might help.'
- Make sure that your disclosures are appropriate. Sharing yourself is appropriate if it helps clients achieve treatment goals, and is not you showing off.
- Be careful of your timing. Premature helper self-disclosure can turn clients off.
- Keep your disclosures selective and focused. Don't distract clients with rambling stories about yourself.
- Don't disclose too frequently. Too frequent disclosure may give the client the impression of 'Who is the client?'
- Do not burden already overburdened clients. Don't cause clients to say, 'Don't tell me your problems, I've got enough of my own.'
- Remain flexible. Adapt your disclosures to differences in clients and situations. Every client is unique. Not every client in every situation needs or would benefit from helper self-disclosure.

Further reading

Egan, G. (2002) *The Skilled Helper: a problem-management and opportunity-development approach to helping*, 7th edn. Brooks/Cole, Pacific Grove, CA.

Johnson, D.W. and Noonan, M.P. (1972) The effects of acceptance and reciprocation of self-disclosures on the development of trust. *Journal of Counselling Psychology*, **19**: 411–416.

Jourard, S.M. and Friedman, R. (1970) Experimenter-subject 'distance' and self-disclosure. *Journal of Personality and Social Psychology*, **15**: 278–282.

Jourard, S.M. and Friedman, R. (1971) *The Transparent Self*. Van Nostrand Reinhold, Toronto.

Segal, J. (1993) Against self-disclosure. In: *Questions and Answers on Counselling in Action* (ed. W. Dryden). Sage Publications, London.

SEX THERAPY

Sex therapy involves the treatment of sexual disorders, variances and dysfunctions. In particular, sex-therapy programmes are directed toward the solution of such sexual problems as impotence, premature ejaculation, retarded ejaculation, painful coitus, sexual unresponsiveness and orgasmic dysfunction.

A common assumption underlying many modern sex-therapy programmes is that sexual problems are often learned and hence can be alleviated or corrected through relatively brief intervention measures. Intensive psychotherapy and medical treatment may be given when emotional disturbances and/or physical disorders compound sexual difficulties.

Sex-therapy programmes generally attempt to help people by providing appropriate sex information, alleviating anxieties and fears about sexual performance and facilitating verbal, emotional and sexual communication between sex partners. Sex instruction, followed by private home assignments in which a couple practises newly learned, healthier ways of interacting, is an integral part of many sex-therapy programmes.

Both partners in the couple are often included in sex-therapy programmes. Sometimes, however, it is reasonable for a single person or only one member of a couple to be counselled alone, depending upon the nature of the sexual problem. Group-therapy techniques, including groups of individuals and/or groups of couples, are often used in sex-therapy programmes.

Some sex therapists believe that sex problems can be treated best if one therapist counsels both partners. Other therapists believe that a therapy team composed of a male and a female therapist is the best way to help couples overcome their difficulties. Still other therapists believe that couples with sexual difficulties can engage in self-treatment if given instructions through books, videos and DVDs, along with brief intensive counselling.

Physicians, psychiatrists, psychologists, social workers and marriage and family counsellors can usually either provide effective sex therapy or make referrals to other sources that can provide such therapy.

The couple approach recognises that sexual dysfunction results from the interaction between two people and is not the exclusive problem of one member of the pair. Individual counselling is employed for those without cooperating partners and may involve the use of a surrogate partner or may focus on exercises that can be practised by an individual to improve his or her sexual interactions. Group therapy, in which individuals discuss feelings about sex, is also employed for both single-sex and male–female groups.

Sexual dysfunction

One of the most potent sources of anxiety is that surrounding sexuality and sexual difficulties. A satisfactory sex life increases energy and creates a sense of well-being. What produces anxiety is internal conflict and a sense of frustration.

Sexual problems may be classified as physiological, psychological and social in origin. Any given problem may involve all three categories; a physiological problem, for example, will produce psychological effects and these may result in some social maladjustment.

Understanding human sexuality

Human sexuality is concerned with the organs of sex and their functions; the sex impulses, instincts and drives; the thoughts, feelings and behaviours associated with sexual gratification, the attraction of one person to another, and the possibility of reproduction.

Sexuality is an essential part of one's personality, and cannot be separated from it. It is part of one's biological make-up, and includes one's perception of being male or female. Abnormal sexual behaviour is that which is destructive and harmful to one's self or others.

Identifying the characteristics of normal sexual response

Desire
Sexual fantasies and the urge to engage in sexual activity.

Excitement
Physiological stimulation through kissing and touch; a felt sense of pleasure; erection or vaginal lubrication; nipples of both sexes become erect, though this is more common in women; firming up of the clitoris, with venous engorgement of the lips of the vulva; rate of heartbeat and respiration increase and blood pressure rises.

Orgasm
Peaking of sexual pleasure, with release of sexual tension. Ejaculation occurs in the man, with emission of semen. The female experiences orgasm by strong, sustained contractions of the uterus. Both men and women experience rise in blood pressure, and the heart rate increases, maybe up to 160 beats a minute. Orgasm lasts from 3 to 25 seconds and is associated with a slight clouding of consciousness.

Resolution (detumescence)
The blood leaves the sexual organs, bringing the body back to its resting state. Orgasm is followed by a sense of well-being, general and muscular relaxation. It may take a man several hours (a refractory period) before he can be sexually aroused to orgasm again. This does not always apply to women.

Understanding the male sexual function

- Concern (often amounting to severe anxiety) over the size of the penis is practically universal among men, but size has nothing to do with function.
- Ejaculation is the forceful propulsion of semen and seminal fluid into the urethra (the tube through which urine is voided from the bladder).
- The passing of seminal fluid as it passes through the prostate provides the man with a sensation of impending climax.
- The ejaculation is aided by the action of muscles of the pelvis and at the root of the penis.

- Erection depends on a complex interaction of the autonomic nervous system. Blood flows into the spongy tissues on the underside of the penis. Muscles at the base of the penis contract, so preventing the blood flowing back until ejaculation takes place.
- Impotence, or failure of the man to get or maintain an erection, can thus result from a number of causes, which may be psychological or physiological. If not enough hormones are pumped into the body, or if there is muscle weakness, or if there are problems with the blood supply, impotence may result.

Understanding the female sexual function

- The sexual organs of the female consist of the external sexual organs and the internal organs of reproduction.
- To accommodate the erect penis, the vaginal canal expands both in length and width.
- After the menopause the vagina loses much of its elasticity.
- The clitoris is the primary sexual organ, because orgasm depends on adequate clitoral stimulation.
- The clitoris has a nerve net that is proportionally three times as large as that of the penis.
- Many women describe the so-called 'G' spot, an area near the urethra, as giving great pleasure, enough to induce orgasm.

Exploring physiological problems of sexual function

Physiological problems of a specifically sexual nature are rather few. Only a small minority of people suffer from diseases of or deficient development of the genitalia. Many people, however, at some time experience sexual problems that are by-products of other pathologies or injuries.

Anything that seriously interferes with normal bodily functioning generally causes some degree of sexual trouble. Fortunately, the great majority of physiological sexual problems are solved through medication or surgery. Generally, only those problems involving damage to the nervous system defy therapy.

Looking at particular disorders

Understanding disorders of sexual desire

The need for sexual contact and satisfaction varies greatly from person to person. Lack of desire may be an unconscious defence against fear of sex. Lack of desire can also be related to periods of stress or depression. Lack of sexual activity for a prolonged period can lead to suppression of sexual desire.

Sexual desire is a complex mix of biological drive, adequate self-esteem, previous experiences of good and bad sex, and the availability of a suitable partner.

Some people are brought up to believe that sex is all right for men, but for women it is disgusting and degrading, and only for the purpose of producing children. It might be thought that this is an attitude of an older generation and would not apply to the liberated young people of the 21st century, but attitudes like that have a pernicious habit of hanging on from generation to generation.

Sexual aversion

When the prospect of sexual interaction with a sexual partner is associated with strong negative feelings, it can produce sufficient fear or anxiety that sexual activity is avoided. The dysfunction, when persistent, usually causes difficulties within the person and between couples. The aversion may be to a specific part of sex; genital contact (secretions, smell) may arouse feelings of disgust; kissing and touching on certain parts of the body may generate enough negative feelings to stop the process. The dividing line between a lack or loss of desire and aversion to sex is finely drawn, but sexual aversion has certain elements of phobia in it.

Freud postulated that sexual aversion was unresolved oedipal conflict, and fixation at the phallic stage. According to Freudian theory, some men who are fixated at the phallic stage believe that the vagina is something to be feared; that they will be castrated; that the vagina has teeth. Hence they avoid all contact with the female genitalia. Aversion may be attributed to traumatic sexual experiences when young, that have left the person carrying a load of guilt and shame.

Understanding disorders of sexual arousal

Male erectile disorder or dysfunction, also called impotence, is divided into:

- **Lifelong**: Never having had an erection that has culminated in vaginal penetration
- **Acquired**: Has successfully achieved vaginal penetration at some stage, but is later unable to do so
- **Situational**: Able to achieve penetration in one situation but not in another; for example, with a prostitute or with another man, but be impotent with his female sexual partner.

Potential causes

The man who has never been able to achieve orgasm (primary inhibited male orgasm) may have had a puritanical upbringing where sex equates with sin, where genitals are dirty and the whole process is laden with guilt. The same person may experience difficulty with intimacy in any shape or form.

Secondary ejaculatory inhibition may be a reflection of interpersonal difficulties, the sexual difficulty being the man's (unconscious) way of coping. For example, the female partner wishes to become pregnant, the man is ambivalent, so (again unconsciously) he becomes disabled and cannot achieve orgasm, although he may be perfectly able to do so through masturbation. At a deeper and more dynamic level, not achieving orgasm may be veiled hostility towards the woman, or towards all women.

Premature ejaculation is a common problem, especially for young males. Sometimes this is not the consequence of any psychological problem but the natural result of excessive tension in a male who has been sexually deprived. In such cases, more frequent intercourse (or masturbation) solves the problem.

Premature ejaculation is difficult to define. Masters and Johnson say that a male suffers from premature ejaculation if he cannot delay ejaculation long enough to induce orgasm in a sexually normal female at least half the time.

Impotence is more common than most people believe. The cause is often something physical. It should not be dismissed as 'all in the mind'. Almost every single case can be treated medically, reliably and inexpensively.

Physical factors

Hormone deficiency
A deficiency of testosterone and other hormones occurs in a small percentage of men with impotence.

Diabetes
Between 30 and 50 per cent of diabetic men suffer from impotence. Among the effects of diabetes are high blood sugar levels, poor circulation, damaged nerve endings, narrowed arteries and high blood pressure.

Blocked arteries
The extra blood needed for an erection may not be reaching the penis.

Leaking veins
To achieve and maintain an erection, veins must trap blood in the penis. Venous leaks are found to be the cause for a small number of men with impotence.

Psychological factors

Stress/anxiety
A man may experience normal erections in the early mornings but fail during sex with a partner.

'Male menopause'
The female menopause is well known. But some doctors say that a man can also suffer from a mid-life crisis, causing depression, hot flushes, lack of energy and low sex drive, night sweats and circulatory problems, leading to impotence.

False expectations
Expectations about performance found in the media – magazines, newspapers and television – lead to disappointment and despair if the reality seems quite different to the stereotypical image.

Damaged nerves
Damage caused by spinal cord injuries, multiple sclerosis and alcoholism, bladder and bowel surgery can also affect the nervous system.

Drugs
Impotence may be a side-effect of anti-depressants and anti-ulcer drugs. Drugs

for the treatment of high blood pressure and even simple over-the-counter decongestant cold remedies have also been found to lead to impotence.

Alcohol
Small quantities often enhance a man's sexual response, but heavy or prolonged drinking can cause impotence.

- Many men fear impotency, particularly as they reach middle age.
- Many medical conditions produce physiological impotence, but these do not account for all cases of men for whom impotence is the dysfunction for which they seek help.

Impotence can be caused by a combination of factors, partly physical, partly psychological. Usually the physical problem will start first and gradually worsen. Secondary psychological fears and anxieties then begin to set in and sex becomes a very anxiety-provoking experience, sometimes coupled with depression.

Understanding disorders of orgasm

In males, orgasmic disorders or retarded ejaculation mean that the man only achieves climax with great difficulty. Some practitioners make a distinction between orgasm and ejaculation, though the two are so bound together that it is difficult to make a clear distinction. Although not strictly an orgasmic disorder, premature ejaculation is closely connected in that both conditions are to do with climax. Retarded ejaculation may be due to the effects of drugs – certain antihypertensive drugs and tranquillisers, for example. Recent excessive alcohol intake may also influence retarded orgasm.

Understanding sexual disorders that involve pain

Dyspareunia
This is persistent pain during intercourse. In women it is often associated with vaginismus (see below); the one may lead to the other. It is often found to be linked to pelvic disease, and is a common complaint in women who have been raped or sexually abused.

Pain after intercourse is thought to be due to violent uterine contractions during orgasm, in women who suffer from endometriosis. Post-menopausal women may experience pain through the thinning of the lining of the vagina and lack of lubrication. Some inexperienced females fear they cannot accommodate a penis without being painfully stretched. This is a needless fear since the vagina is not only highly elastic but enlarges with sexual arousal, so that even a small female can, if aroused, easily receive an exceptionally large penis. If the man proceeds with intercourse, irrespective of his partner's vaginal readiness, then pain is almost inevitable.

Dyspareunia can also occur in men, but is uncommon and usually associated with some medical condition, such as inflammation of the prostate. Persistent erection without ejaculation may also produce pain. Pain may sometimes be experienced at the moment of ejaculation.

Vaginismus

This is a recurrent or persistent powerful and involuntary spasm of the pelvic muscles constricting the vagina so that penetration is painful or impossible. It may be due to anti-sexual conditioning or psychological trauma and serves as an unconscious defence against intercourse. While the woman may consciously wish to have intercourse, unconsciously there may be something preventing penile penetration. Rape or previous experiences of sexual abuse may set the scene for vaginismus. Painful physical examinations in the past can act in the same way. A final point is that where women feel unappreciated, and where sex is merely an act and not the sharing of love, then resentment may find an expression in vaginismus.

Understanding treatment for sexual dysfunction

Treating men

Because there are a number of factors involved, the combination of treatments is varied for each man, but usually includes counselling. Where a physical cause is detected, explanation helps the man realise that the physical problem that caused the difficulty in the first place can be treated.

It is important not to presume that all cases have a common cause. For this reason it is best to view impotence as a medical problem. The doctor will treat this just like any other, and perform a full and proper diagnosis of the physical cause(s). Once this is done, treatment is usually very simple and offers a complete restoration of normal function.

Treating women

For females, sexual arousal dysfunction takes the form of persistent inability to attain or maintain adequate sexual excitement to completion. Women who experience difficulty in the excitement stage often experience problems with orgasm too. Less research has been done on sexual dysfunction in females than in males, though it has been suggested that women who experience sexual dysfunction are less aware of the physiological responses of their bodies during arousal.

Certain drugs – antihistamines for example – are known to lessen vaginal lubrication and interfere with arousal. An artificial lubricant is frequently useful for women who experience dryness.

Sex therapy, after the style of Masters and Johnson, deals with the couple; there is no credence given to the idea that only one of the couple is 'sick', needing to be 'cured'. The relationship is treated as a whole. The sexual dysfunction may be symptomatic of other relationship difficulties, and these may need to be brought into the open before the sexual difficulty can be resolved.

Further reading

Masters, W.H. and Johnson, V.E. (1970) *Human Sexual Response*. Little, Brown, Boston.

Sadock, V.A. (1995) Normal human sexuality and gender identity disorders. In: *Comprehensive Textbook of Psychiatry*, 6th edn (eds H.J. Kaplan and B.J. Sadock). Williams & Wilkins, Baltimore, MD.

Stewart, W. (2000) *Controlling Anxiety*, 2nd edn. How to Books, Oxford.

Sexual harassment

Sexual harassment is a subject which, like child abuse, has hit the headlines as if it was something new, yet it has been around for centuries. Sexual harassment is abuse, perpetrated often, although not exclusively, by men. The discussion centres on harassment by men, because this is what is most reported. Perhaps the next decade will reveal the prevalence of sexual harassment of men by women. What has come to light in recent years is that boys are abused by women more than was imagined. So if men are being harassed, they can take heart from women and disclose it. Then perhaps that might alter the balance of power somewhat.

It could be conjectured that, just as men who have themselves been abused as children are said to turn into abusers of children, so boys who have been abused by women may turn into adults who harass women sexually.

Whatever the dynamics of sexual harassment, we still have to struggle with the stereotypes of the macho man and the compliant, weaker woman who has no rights except to satisfy the sexual desires of men. These are powerful stereotypes to break. It can be done, but it will only come about as we all relate to one another as people, with respect and regard, and not through the sexual male and female stereotypes.

Sexual harassment in the workplace has received increased attention lately in the general press and in professional journals. Sexual discrimination is sexual harassment. Discrimination is any action that does not extend to people of one gender the same job conditions, courtesy, benefits, salary, training and development and advancement opportunities that are extended to the other.

Who is vulnerable?

Sexual harassment is often based on men not being willing to share power or control with women. It is more to do with 'keeping women in their place' than with 'sex'. Women are most vulnerable to being sexually harassed:

- When they are the first of their sex to break into an area of employment
- When they make up less than 25 per cent of the workforce
- When they enter hitherto male-dominated positions, e.g. female police officers, fire fighters, factory workers, maintenance and repair workers.

Many of the harassing behaviours are intended to actually cause the woman to be fired or to resign from the job.

Men who are pioneers in occupations typically held by women are also more vulnerable to harassment:

- Male nurses may still experience discrimination and harassment
- Those who want to work as baby-minders or au pairs.

Sexual harassment may be motivated by feelings of power, anger or cruelty, while other harassment is motivated by sexual desires.

Harassment can include:

- Insulting, degrading, hurtful or rude comments
- Offensive talk, language, pictures or physical actions
- Bad reviews and appraisals
- Attempts to force the person out of the job.

Costs of harassment at work
Effects on the victim:

- Psychological damage
- Loss of productivity
- Loss of wages and benefits
- Loss of employment and future benefits
- Claims to a court or tribunal may result in further victimisation.

The effects on others in the workforce:

- Psychological damage (such as anger, resentment, fear)
- Loss of productivity
- Loss of esteem for the persecutor and/or supervisors involved
- Divisions, as people 'take sides'
- Demoralisation of the workforce.

Investigating or dealing with a complaint:

- Inquiries or in-depth investigations create tension
- If in-house personnel carry out the investigation, they may be accused of bias and 'cover-up'; if outside people are brought in, they may meet a stone wall of silence and passive aggression.

Other costs:

- Loss of morale and absenteeism
- Administrative
- Counselling
- Impact on other workers, supervisors
- Rescheduling of tasks
- Redeployment
- Training of new employees.

Sexual harassment may amount to indecent assault (a hostile act accompanied by circumstances of indecency). In this instance, 'hostile' means that the person receiving the act is an unwilling victim and the act is a criminal offence. In the USA, sexual harassment (which applies to men and women) means:

- Unwelcome sexual advances
- Requests for sexual favours
- Other verbal or physical conduct of a sexual nature.

Sexual harassment exists when:

- Submission to such conduct is made – either explicitly or implicitly – a term or condition of an individual's employment
- Submission to or rejection of such conduct is used as the basis for employment decisions affecting the individual
- Such conduct has the purpose or effect of unreasonably interfering with an individual's work performance or creating an intimidating, hostile or offensive working environment.

A third party also may file a complaint if behaviour offends her or him, even if the victim has not complained. For example, if two men are telling sexual jokes in the work setting in the presence of a female employee and a third person who overhears them is offended, that person may complain.

What we can do about harassment

- Help people distinguish between what is acceptable and what is offensive behaviour.
- Help people to deal with offensive behaviour, when it happens, in an assertive manner that gives a clear, unambiguous message.
- Help people to recognise when they are sending mixed messages.
- Undertake experiential training in how to handle harassment.

Experiential learning helps people to:

- Develop their listening skills
- Become aware of their own values and assumptions
- Learn about the values and assumptions of others
- Practise constructive confrontation techniques
- Learn to use third-party intervention
- Learn to use direct statements and I statements
- Distinguish between 'thinking' and 'feeling' statements
- Explore and understand different social styles
- Understand other people's motivations to work.

In mixed-gender, experiential-learning groups, people can explore underlying issues at first hand and develop interpersonal skills. Within the safety of an experiential group, people can sort through their feelings, assumptions and values as they hear about and relate to the values of others. Participants learn from their own experiences, including their emotional responses, reflections, insights and discussions with others.

Summary of sexual harassment

- We must all do everything possible to reduce and eliminate sexual discrimination and sexual harassment. Managers must effectively resolve each instance of sexual harassment in the workplace.
- Legislation cannot remove personal prejudices but it requires that we do not act out those prejudices and persecute other people.

- We all have a responsibility to ensure that others do not use discriminatory behaviour.
- We all have a responsibility to behave in ways that do not intentionally cause offence.
- We must demonstrate, not only by policy but also by example, that sexual harassment is not appropriate nor is it to be tolerated in our society.
- At a personal level, when people believe in equality and work hard to put their belief into practice, when they work hard not to exert undue power over other people, then sexual harassment will cease to exist.
- On a counselling level, helping a client deal with sexual harassment is akin to helping a client deal with sexual abuse. It is embarrassing to disclose, frightening in its consequences and likely to arouse feelings of helplessness, similar to feelings experienced in childhood over bullying. Above all, the complainant has to be believed and, as with the rape victim who is often not believed, the counsellor must believe. The counsellor is not in the position of proving or disproving a client's statement. That is for the court to decide. Counselling may provide the psychological strength for the client to confront the harasser.

Stalking

More recently, stalking, which is harassment by another name, has, in the UK, become a criminal offence. It would appear that stalking is causing concern worldwide:

1. 'Two sisters will appear in Orange Local Court next month to face charges of stalking and harassing rugby league star Andrew Johns and his girl-friend Catherine Mahoney.' *Melbourne Herald Sun Australia*, Tuesday, 8 June 2004.
2. 'There are about 20 cases of stalking reported in the state of Tasmania, Australia, each year, with victims harassed or terrorised in person or by phone, mail or e-mail.' *Australian Broadcasting Corporation*, 2004.
3. 'Trooper Robert J. Gebhart, state police at Gettysburg, was accused of sending 113 unwanted e-mails, making hundreds of unwanted telephone calls, and making unwelcomed visits to the home of his ex-girlfriend, from December 2002 to August 2003.' Taci George – *Times Staff Writer*.
4. 'In Finland, harassment and stalking – usually by a former partner or spouse – has risen by a fifth. This is despite the introduction of a system of restraining orders five years ago. Repeated phone calls, a flood of text messages, and stalking are some of the most typical types of harassment.' *Finnish News Agency*, 7 June 2004.

Types of stalkers

A study of 50 stalkers by the Royal Free Hospital and University College Medical School, London, found that women are much more likely to be stalked and attacked by a former sexual partner than by a stranger. Stalking has become

Britain's fastest growing crime with over 4000 prosecutions under the Protection from Harassment Act each year. The UK's first national anti-stalking police unit was authorised by Home Secretary Jack Straw in January 2000.

Three broad categories of stalkers:

1. **Intimate partner stalkers:** The person who can't (or won't) 'let go'. These are not sympathetic, lonely people who are still hopelessly in love, but what they are doing is carrying on the controlling abusive behaviour of the old relationship. Trying to 'let him down gently', or telling him 'I need some space', is only likely to encourage the stalker.
2. **Delusional stalkers:** The delusional belief is that the victim loves him. He is likely to be an unmarried and socially immature loner, unable to establish or sustain intimate relationships, and have a poor sense of his own identity.
3. **Vengeful stalkers:** Politicians, for example, get many of these types of stalkers who become angry over some piece of legislation. But disgruntled ex-employees can also stalk, whether targeting their former bosses, colleagues or the entire company.

www.antistalking.com

Cyber-stalking

Although there is no universal definition of cyber-stalking, which is simply an extension of the physical form of stalking, the term is generally used to refer to the use of the internet, e-mail or other telecommunication technologies to harass, communicate a threat or stalk another person.

- The internet offers new opportunities for stalking, hence the term cyber-stalking.
- The stalker can, from the safety of his or her home, or the anonymity of an office environment, trace, track and find out personal details of the target, including address, phone number and, more sinisterly, addresses and details of the target's family.
- The internet also offers unlimited opportunity to befriend lonely, vulnerable and nice people who can be persuaded to start a relationship.
- Little do most people know when a stalker targets them.

www.stalkingbehehavior.com
http://www.cyberangels.org/stalking/
http://www.safetyed.org/help/stalking/cyberstalking.html
http://www.sfwa.org/gateway/stalking.htm

Further reading

Becker, G. de (1997) *The Gift of Fear: survival signals that protect us from violence.* Bloomsbury, London.
Carbonnell, J.L., Higginbotham, J. and Sample, J. (1990) Sexual harassment of women in the workplace. In: 1993 *Annual: Developing Human Resources.* University Associates, San Diego, CA.

Lee, C. (1992) Sexual harassment: after the headlines. *Training,* March, 25.
Pattinson, T. (1991) *Sexual Harassment.* Futura, New York.

SILENCE

- Silence is referred to in psychotherapeutic literature as:
  - An indicator of resistance
  - A necessary and productive part of the therapeutic process
  - An intervention by the counsellor
  - An integrating process.
- Silences enable the client to make associations and connections and engage in problem-solving; breaking the silence may interfere with the client's internal processes.
- The positive value of silences is stressed in the person-centred and humanistic approaches, as a means of adding depth to the relationship.
- Silence enables clients to hear what they and the counsellor have said and releases attention to observe non-verbal behaviour.
- Silences give clients the opportunity to explore their own inner world without the pressure of having to respond.
- Counsellors who are never silent deprive themselves and their clients of the opportunity to listen to the deeper meanings that lie beyond words.
- Silence happens between people, rather than within one of them, and is an essential characteristic of the relationship.
- Silences may arise from resentment, through not having been listened to, being argued with, put down or given incorrect, mistimed or unacceptable interpretations.
- In family therapy, 'dysfunctional silence' is used by one member of the family in order to sabotage change.
- Silence, on the other hand, is essential in techniques such as meditation, relaxation and imagery.
- When silence is thought to be resistance or blocking, the counsellor may use a prompt, by repeating something previously said or by drawing attention to the nature of the silence.
- Counsellors may have to work hard on their ability to tolerate silence – what could be a constructive silence is easily ruined by too quick an intervention.
- Some silences are as deep as communing with another spirit.

Further reading

Biestek, F.P. (1961) *The Casework Relationship.* George Allen & Unwin, London.
Buber, M. (1958) *I and Thou.* T. & T. Clark, Edinburgh.

SIX CATEGORY INTERVENTION

Six category intervention is a method developed by John Heron. It is client-directed, with counsellor interventions directed towards catharsis and support.

The six interventions

1. Prescriptive
Prescriptive interventions aim to influence and direct the client's behaviour in such a way that:

- The client is free to accept or reject them
- They do not interfere with the client's freedom of choice.

Prescriptive interventions take the form of:

- Advice, in a specific area of expertise
- Suggestions or commendations
- Requests
- Demands or commands
- Modelling behaviour
- Giving a lead
- Verbally and non-verbally directing the client's behaviour
- Attitudes and beliefs about behaviour
- Particular goals to be achieved.

2. Informative
Informative interventions aim to impart new knowledge:

- That the client sees as relevant
- That does not increase dependence
- In such a way that the client is encouraged to be an active partner in the learning process.

Informative interventions give:

- General knowledge
- Information specific to the client's situation
- Information about the client's behaviour.

3. Confronting
Confronting interventions:

- Challenge attitudes, beliefs and behaviours
- Support the client while highlighting the defences being used
- Enable the client to achieve insight.

Confronting interventions include:

- Direct, descriptive, non-judgemental, personal-view feedback
- Interrupting the pattern of negative thinking or acting by:
  - Distraction
  - Introducing a new topic
  - Contradicting
  - Proposing a total change of activity

- Mirroring, in a supportive way, the client's negative verbal or non-verbal behaviour
- Using direct questions to get at what is being defended
- Challenging restrictions – e.g. the use of 'shoulds' and 'oughts' and generalisations
- Unmasking, which uses information not given by the client
- Interpretation of the client's defences
- Discharge feedback, which is demonstration by the counsellor, in sound and movement, of pent-up anger and frustration.

Confronting interventions that are punishments or attacks cause the client to counter-attack. They only succeed when clients feel that the counsellor is attacking their defences, not them.

4. Cathartic

Cathartic interventions aim to help the client release repressed emotions:

- Anger, through storming
- Grief, through tears and sobbing
- Fear, through trembling
- Tension, through yawning
- Embarrassment, through laughter.

Cathartic interventions include:

- Literal description, where, in the first person and in the present tense, the client describes a traumatic event in detail. Detail would include sounds, sights, smells, and what people said and did.
- Repetition, where the client repeats emotionally charged words or phrases. Non-verbal cues indicate emotionally charged content such as faltering tone, sudden emphasis, puckering of mouth or eyes, twitching of fingers or limbs, sudden change of posture, or a change in breathing pattern.
- Association, when the client is encouraged to verbalise a sudden, unbidden thought or to repeat a slip of the tongue. Unbidden thoughts may be detected mainly by the eyes looking anywhere but at the counsellor and by hand movements, indicating discomfort.
- 'Acting into' means encouraging the client to deliberately act out the sounds and movements of the emotions, to tap into a genuine discharge of emotion.
- Self-role-play is a basic cathartic intervention. Clients become themselves in a past traumatic scene, with its words and wishes and feelings. The counsellor becomes the recipient of the client's emotionally charged message.
- Monodrama (see also Gestalt counselling) is where the client has a different chair for each role in the conflict. The client switches from chair to chair and creates a dialogue between the characters in each chair.
- Primary contact: The counsellor gazes into the client's eyes and, at the same time, holds the client's hands and gives total attention.

- Touch: When the client is on the verge of tears and sobbing, touch is supportive and may allow the floodgates to open.
- Body work, with breathing and exaggerated movements.
- Contradiction encourages the client to use phrases that:
  - Contradict the negative self-image, accompanied by voice tone and body language that agree with the verbal message
  - Express negative views with voice and body language that contradict the feelings
  - Use a double negative to exaggerate tone of voice, facial expression and body language.
- Fantasy may be used in a number of ways to bypass intellect.
- Relaxation and reverie to work on associations.
- Transpersonal work, e.g. meditation.
- Balance of attention: Old, painful emotions cannot be discharged unless the client has sufficient attention outside the traumatic experience. The counsellor may help to generate attention by directing the client's attention to something in the immediate environment or to the counsellor, by getting the client to describe a recent, pleasant experience, to relax or do controlled breathing.

5. Catalytic

Catalytic interventions are those that:

- Enable the client to work towards self-determination and self-discovery
- Convey to the client that the counsellor is paying attention, is supportive and is trying to understand.

Catalytic interventions include:

- Free attention, not being distracted either by the external or by internal thoughts and feelings, using gaze, posture, facial expressions and touch, being totally supportive, waiting and expecting with hope, being non-anxious, being tuned into the client
- Active listening skills, such as:
  - Reflecting the last words after a pause, where attention is focused on significant words or phrases
  - Paraphrasing, putting into one's own words the gist of what the client has said
  - Empathy building, making every effort to work within the client's frame of reference; checking for understanding is a summary that reinforces understanding, aids empathy building and encourages further elaboration
  - Discreet self-disclosure by the counsellor, which encourages trust and acceptance
  - Open questions by the counsellor, which encourage further exploration
  - Problem-solving structured exercises, which work logically from identifying symptoms towards an agreed action plan
  - Self-discovery, through reality games and growth games
  - Theoretical structure, where the counsellor offers relevant theories and conceptual models

  – Analysis of variables as they relate to how the counsellor perceives the possible causes
  – Examination of options: how the counsellor perceives the various alternatives to the client's decision.

6. Supportive

Supportive interventions are those that:

- Affirm the person's worth and value
- Are given unconditionally
- Are caring and authentic
- Do not collude with the client's defences and negative self-opinions.

Supportive interventions include:

- Free attention
- Touch
- Expressing positive feelings
- Expressing care and concern
- Validation, and positive affirmation
- Sharing what is happening in the relationship
- Self-disclosure.

A negative self-image makes it difficult for some clients to accept supportive interventions. Productive interventions fall into one or other of the six categories. No one intervention is superior to another. To be productive, any intervention has to be caringly supportive. All interventions must have a catalytic element.

Counsellors who are not drawn to using the full-blown model may find some of the interventions worth including in their repertoire of skills.

Further reading

Heron, J. (1972) *Experience and Method*. Human Potential Research Project, Guildford.
Heron, J. (1973) *Experiential Training Techniques*. Human Potential Research Project, Guildford.
Heron, J. (1974) *Reciprocal Training Manual*. Human Potential Research Project, Guildford.
Heron, J. (1975, 5th edn 2001) *Six Category Intervention Analysis*. Human Potential Research Project, Guildford.
Heron, J. (1999) *The Complete Facilitator's Handbook*. Kogan Page, London. Revised second edition and compilation of the complete texts of both *The Facilitators' Handbook* (1989) and *Group Facilitation: Theories and Models for* Practice (1993).
Heron, J. (2001) *Helping the Client: a creative, practical guide*, 5th edn. Sage, London.

STRESS MANAGEMENT (SEE ALSO 'A' TYPE PERSONALITY, ANXIETY, POST-TRAUMATIC STRESS DISORDER)

Stress is the result of any change to which a person must adjust. It is an effect and not a cause; the effect is felt only within the individual and is essentially the rate of wear and tear in the body. The subjective sensations of stress are feeling tired, jittery or ill.

Hans Selye says that stress produces 'adaptive reactions' as a defence. He refers to this as the 'general adaptive syndrome'. The general adaptive syndrome has three stages:

1. Alarm reaction
2. Resistance
3. Exhaustion.

When we interpret something as threatening, the body prepares us to fight or run away. This is known as the fight/flight response.

The effect of a stressor is to mobilise the body's fight/flight system to combat a perceived enemy. Stress stimulates chemical, physical and psychological changes to prepare the body to cope with a potentially life-threatening situation. The process is controlled by the autonomic nervous system and the endocrine system. The process is:

- The liver releases extra sugar to fuel the muscles
- Hormones are released that stimulate the conversion of fats and proteins to sugar
- The body's metabolism increases in preparation for increased activity
- Certain unessential activities, such as digestion, are slowed up
- Saliva and mucus dry up, so increasing the rise of the air passages to the lungs and giving rise to the early sign of stress, a dry mouth
- Endorphins, the body's natural painkillers, are secreted
- The surface blood vessels constrict to reduce bleeding in case of injury
- The spleen releases more red blood cells to help carry oxygen, and the bone marrow produces more white cells to help fight infection.

The autonomic nervous system, regulated by the hypothalamus (the stress centre) with the pituitary, is responsible for releasing more than 30 hormones that control these physiological responses to an emergency.

When neither response – to fight or to run away – is appropriate, the bio-chemical changes have already been aroused and the body takes time to return to normal. It is the continued presence of the stress hormones that give rise to the prolongation of bodily symptoms described above. When appropriate action is taken, the chemicals are used up and the body returns to normal functioning. People who experience stress live in a state of constant readiness to respond to fight or flight:

- Blood flow to the brain increases
- Blood is redirected from the extremities to the trunk and head
- Hands and feet become sweaty
- Hearing becomes more acute
- Heart and respiratory rates increase
- Muscles tense
- Thought processes speed up
- Vision becomes clearer.

Chronic stress is the result of the body not being given relief from the biochemical changes that occur during the 'fight or flight' response.

What produces stress in one person may have no effect whatsoever in someone else. One person cannot make assumptions about what is not 'distressing' for another person.

Only when something is perceived as hostile does it have the power to act as a stressor, although stress events are not necessarily negative or unpleasant.

Stress has been found to be related to many physical ailments and every organ of the body may become the focus for felt stress.

Sources of stress

- **Environmental**: Crowds, time pressures, noise, work demands, finance, weather
- **Physiological**: Ageing, illness, diet, endocrine, poor sleep, pregnancy
- **Emotional**: Ambitions, relationships, desires, drives
- **Mental**: Thoughts, judgement, reason, intelligence, memory
- **Behavioural**: Outgoing/withdrawn, quiet/excitable, aggressive/placid
- **Transpersonal**: Values, attitudes, ideals, beliefs, spirituality.

The 'social readjustment rating scale' of Holmes and Rahe identifies ten significant areas related to life events and stress:

1. Economics
2. Education
3. Family
4. Group and peer relationships
5. Health
6. Marriage
7. Occupation
8. Recreation
9. Religion
10. Residence.

Holmes and Rahe developed a scale of 43 'life change units' (LCUs). People who accrue 200 or more points at any one time, over a period of about a year, are prone to physical disease or psychiatric disorder.

The top ten LCUS

• Death of spouse (partner)	100
• Divorce	73
• Marital/partner separation	65
• Death of close family member	63
• Detention in prison or other institution	63
• Significant personal injury or illness	53
• Marriage	50

- Being dismissed from work   47
- Reconciliation with partner   45
- Retirement from work   45

Measures to reduce life events stress

- Become familiar with life events and their degree of change
- Display your life change chart in a prominent place and review it frequently
- Practise recognising significant life events
- Identify feelings about significant events
- Learn to control events, not vice versa
- Do not make decisions in a hurry
- Plan significant events well in advance
- Practise keeping calm.

Helping people recognise and deal with stress
How many of the following phrases do you regularly use?

- I'm just as tired when I wake up
- I can't face another day
- I'll take another day off sick
- Oh God! Another dreary day
- I couldn't care less
- If I sit down, I'll never get started again
- I'm bad tempered lately; it's not like me
- Life's one long, boring slog
- Life's maddening, nothing's ever right
- I need a drink.

Mind indicators of stress

- Frequent headaches
- Lapses in memory
- Ringing/buzzing in the ears
- A particular thought that won't go away
- Inability to settle down to get on with things
- Constantly putting tasks off
- Great difficulty in concentrating
- Head feels full of cotton wool
- A feeling as if thinking through a fog.

Social indicators of stress

- People are more difficult than usual
- People make too many demands
- Too much change is happening
- No one to confide in

- Life is nothing but work and sleep
- Family problems
- Don't really know anyone really well.

Body indicators of stress

- Legs twitch in bed
- Frequently have cramp in bed
- Aches and pains in the back of the neck
- Shoulders, neck and back ache a lot
- Hands often tremble
- Sigh often
- Can't get enough breath in the lungs
- Suffer from diarrhoea
- Rings on fingers get very tight
- Tummy feels knotted
- Tummy gets very gassy
- Bladder needs to be emptied a lot
- Sleep is difficult
- Wake in the early hours
- Difficulty getting back to sleep
- Get very hot at night
- Heartbeat seems loud and fast at night
- Heart seems to skip a beat.

Emotional indicators of stress

- Often very near to tears
- Rarely laugh these days
- Can't react with the same feeling
- Life is flat
- Upset by the least little thing
- Feel as taut as a violin string
- Don't feel or care about anything/anybody.

Type 'A' personality and stress (see also 'A' type personality)

- Undertakes more than one job at any one time, which results in poorly done work
- Tries to cram too much work into a given time, which results in a race against the clock
- Competitive about almost everything, sometimes with hostility and aggression
- An intense, sustained drive to achieve self-selected but usually poorly defined goals, coupled with extraordinary mental alertness.

Categories of occupational stress

- Workload

- Occupational frustration
- Occupational change.

The stress levels of people caught on the occupational treadmill of long hours, intensive study, promotion and relocation (usually with increased financial commitments) will inevitably increase. The spirit of work of the 21st century is geared towards the 'A' type personality.

Assertiveness and stress (see also Assertiveness)
Assertive behaviour is a middle way between passive and aggressive behaviour. People who behave passively feel humiliated, put down, worthless, not appreciated and stressed because they have allowed someone to walk all over them. People who behave aggressively feel stressed because of the angry feelings generated within themselves and in other people.

When people feel good after communicating with others, it is usually because:

- They have said what they want to say
- They have listened and been listened to
- They have maintained their self-esteem.

Making decisions often causes stress and conflict because of the way difficult events are perceived and interpreted. Fears about making a faulty decision add to the stress.

Symptoms of decisional stress

- Feelings of imminent loss if a wrong decision is made – losses may be material, social or affecting reputation or self-esteem.

Effects of stress on decision-making

- One's ability to handle information is undermined.
- Crisis management becomes the norm.
- There is a tendency to make irrational/hasty decisions.
- Sometimes the inability to make a decision is total.

Helping people reduce decisional stress

- Explore and evaluate alternative choices.
- Explore and evaluate risks.
- Encourage action, however small.
- Don't overload with information.
- Don't encourage making 'any old decision'.
- Teach relaxation and positive imagery.
- Use a 'for and against' approach.

Helping people manage time
Time is a conveyor belt of small and large decisions, all of which shape our lives. Some decisions produce frustration, lowered self-esteem and stress.

Inappropriate decisions give rise to the symptoms of ineffective time management:

- Rush and hurry
- Chronic hesitation between alternatives
- Fatigue or apathy alternate with non-productivity
- Deadlines are often missed
- Few periods of rest or companionship
- Sense of being overwhelmed by demands and details
- For most of the time having to do what they don't want to do
- Often no clear idea what they would prefer to be doing.

People can be helped towards effective time management by:

- Establishing goals
- Establishing goal priorities
- Creating time by constructing a realistic and practical programme to take care of essential tasks
- Taking time to learn how to make decisions.

Encourage them to take time to reflect on:

- How their day has gone
- Were intervals between work genuine times of recreation? Was their eating healthy?
- Did they eat/drink more than they could handle? What mood are they in at bedtime?
- Are they on the emotional treadmill of anxiety about some aspect of work? Are they having a relationship problem?

Helping people set goals (see also Goals and goal-setting)
One step towards a goal is progress. Focus on the goal, not on the route.

Help them to think how not to spend 80 per cent effort to get 20 per cent reward.

Some golden do's to help people avoid stress

- Learn to say 'No' assertively – the consequences of saying 'No' have to be weighed against the consequences of saying 'Yes' when it's really 'No' you want to say.
- Tackle high-priority tasks first – low-priority tasks may go away.
- Don't become so schedule-conscious that interruptions create more stress.
- Create personal time and space every day – everyone around benefits.
- Make one decision every day – start with something small but significant.
- Practise deep relaxation daily.

Stressful thinking (see also Cognitive therapy)
Many people are caught in the trap of negative thinking. A sense of inferiority or inadequacy puts a stumbling block in the pathway of achievement. Negative

thinking is destructive and wasteful of precious energy. Negative thoughts interfere with relaxation and increase stress. Self-confidence leads to self-realisation and successful achievement.

Aids to thought control:

- Explore and list negative thoughts.
- Use imagination positively.
- Use 'thought stop': every time a thought comes, say – aloud if you can – 'Stop!'
- Substitute a positive thought to replace the invasive negative thought.
- Make positive thinking an ally.

Irrational ideas and stress (see also Rational emotive therapy)

- Negative thinking uses irrational ideas.
- Negative thinking creates stress.
- Negative self-talk leads to negative feelings.
- Many irrational ideas are based on impossible standards, generally imposed on us by other people and taken on board, lock, stock and barrel.
- Rationality enhances goal attainment.
- Irrationality hinders goal attainment.

Main stress-management techniques

- Assertiveness training (see Assertiveness)
- Autogenic training (a series of mental exercises designed to reduce the 'fight/flight' response and switch on to rest and relaxation)
- Body awareness
- Biofeedback (a technique of body awareness designed to reduce stress)
- Breathing (as practised in yoga)
- Coping skills training
- Exercise
- Imagination (see Imagery)
- Meditation
- Nutrition
- Relaxation – can be learned in one week, practising two 15-minute sessions a day
- Rational emotive counselling (see Rational emotive therapy)
- Self-hypnosis
- Thought stopping (see Cognitive therapy)
- Time management.

In a *Reader's Digest* article, Jane Spencer draws attention to the myth that going on a pampering holiday is an effective stress-reducer. What is important is that we build stress-relieving moments into every day of our lives, and particularly, '…women may naturally cope with stress not just by fighting or fleeing, but by finding comfort in friends, too'. This could be called the 'cuddling response'. People who find what works for them will help to beat the build-up of stress.

Fight/flight defences in counselling

In addition to the listed defence mechanisms, various manoeuvres by the client (and sometimes by the counsellor) may be included in this section on the fight/flight response.

Fight manoeuvres

These are based on the premise that a good attack is the best defence.

- **Competing with the counsellor**: The client who struggles to control the counsellor is very probably doing so to avoid dealing with some hidden agenda.
- **Cynicism**: This is characterised by frequent challenging of the counsellor's role and method of working, questioning genuine behaviour in a sceptical way.
- **Interrogation**: Here the client cross-examines the counsellor 'to gain helpful information and understanding'.

Flight manoeuvres

- **Intellectualisation**: This is a deliberate avoidance of dealing with feelings by filtering and analysing everything through head logic.
- **Generalisation**: This is a refusal to get to grips with specifics, applying to someone else what we ourselves are experiencing.
- **Rationalisation**: This is an attempt to justify certain behaviour by substituting 'good' behaviour for the real one; an example would be: 'I would be able to look at my feelings if I had a different counsellor'.
- **Projection**: Here the client attributes to other people the traits of his own personality.
- **Withdrawal**: This may vary from boredom to actual physical removal from the session – the tendency to avoid dealing with the 'here-and-now' is also a flight response.

Further reading

Cooper, C.L., Sloan, S.J. and Williams, S. (1988) *Occupational Stress Indicator*. NFER Nelson, Windsor.

Davis, M., Robbins, E. and McKay, M. (1982) *The Relaxation and Stress Reduction Workbook*. New Harbinger Publications, Oakland, CA.

Holmes, T.H. and Rahe, R.H. (1967) The social readjustment rating scale. *Journal of Psychosomatic Research,* **11**: 213–218.

Livingstone-Booth, A. (1985) *Stressmanship*. Severn House Publishers, London.

Lovelace, R.T. (1990) *Stressmaster*. John Wiley, Chichester.

Selye, H. (1957) *The Stress of Life*. Longman Green, London.

Spencer, J. (2004) Relaxation can't wait. *Reader's Digest,* June, pages 119–122.

Sutton, J. (1998) *Thriving on Stress: how to manage pressures and transform your life*. How to Books, Oxford.

SUICIDE (SEE ALSO: EUTHANASIA)

- Suicide is the intentional of killing oneself.
- Attempted suicide is where such an act has failed or has been prevented. Parasuicide is where there is little or no intention that death should result.

Historical perspective

In Ancient Greece, convicted criminals were permitted to take their own lives but the Roman attitude towards suicide hardened toward the end of the empire as a result of the high incidence among slaves, who thus deprived their owners of valuable property.

To St Augustine, however, suicide was essentially a sin. Several early church councils decreed that those who committed suicide should be deprived of the ordinary rites of the church and by the Middle Ages the Catholic church condemned all suicides. Until the Reformation, suicides were condemned by both church and state and burial in consecrated ground was prohibited. The state confiscated the suicide's possessions. Traditionally, suicides were buried at a crossroads with a stake through their bodies. Even until 1823 burial was carried out at night, without a burial service and with a stake through the heart.

Following the French Revolution of 1789, criminal penalties for attempting to commit suicide were abolished in European countries, the United Kingdom being the last to follow suit in 1961. The change in the legal status of suicide, however, had no effect on the suicide rate.

Many countries and numerous American states also adopted laws against helping someone to commit suicide. Under English law, to aid and abet another's suicide is an offence and euthanasia or mercy killing may amount to aiding in this context. Where there is a suicide pact and one partner survives, the partner may be charged with manslaughter.

Sociological perspective

Suicide is an important subject in sociology, because of the systematic study of suicide by Emile Durkheim (1858–1917), published in 1897. He argued that suicide was not simply a result of individual pathology and psychology but that weak social ties resulted in higher rates of suicide. He predicted that Protestants would have higher rates of suicide than Catholics, since Protestantism emphasised personal autonomy and achievement more than did Roman Catholicism.

Durkheim's classification of suicide is:

- **Egoistic suicide** results from a deep sense of personal failure coupled with lack of concern for the community, with which the person was inadequately involved. Persons not involved in society and its institutions are not constricted by its rules, including those that regulate – and often prohibit – suicide. Instead they are regulated only by their own rules of conduct and in terms of their own private interests.

- **Altruistic suicide** results from excessive integration into society and insufficient individuation. The behaviour of the individual is almost completely determined by the social group. Such an individual may commit suicide as a sacrifice to benefit the collective good.
- **Anomic suicide** is based on the belief that life no longer has meaning, resulting from a sense of anomie, loneliness, isolation and loss of contact with the norms of society. When changes – usually of an abrupt nature – occur in the situation of an individual or culture, equilibrium is disrupted and a state of deregulation exists. Under such circumstances the anomic individual is left without clear norms to guide behaviour. Suicide is one possible result.

Social influences

Social conditions frequently result in a marked increase in the suicide rate. This happened, for instance, among young people in Germany after the First World War (1914–1918). Many social scientists believe that the various pressures on young people to succeed at school and the inevitable failure of some of them are leading to significant increases in suicides among students. Some psychologists think that growing feelings of loneliness, rootlessness and the meaninglessness of life are contributing to more suicides in industrialised nations.

Psychological perspective

Freud viewed suicide as an instinctual human tendency towards aggression and destruction. In suicide the death instinct (thanatos) somehow manages to overcome the life instinct (Eros). Freud's second explanation was based on the notion that an individual who commits suicide feels aggression and anger over the loss of love objects but turns these feelings inwards on himself.

Psychic pain: One of the characteristics of people who feel they want to commit suicide is the amount of psychic pain they experience, an unbearable psychological pain from which the person desires to escape (see Psychic pain).

Who is at risk?

Married couples and those in stable relationships have the lowest rates of suicide, while single people have twice the rate and the rates for divorced, separated and widowed people are considerably higher. Family and religious affiliations influence the suicide rates: Catholics and Jews have lower rates than Protestants. People of higher social class have a higher incidence of suicide than those from lower classes, although the risk does increase at the lower end of the scale, possibly because of socioeconomic conditions and stressful life circumstances.

Many people experience feelings of loneliness, depression, helplessness and hopelessness from time to time. The death of a family member, the break-up of a relationship, blows to our self-esteem, feelings of worthlessness and/or major financial setbacks are serious blows that all of us may have to face at some point in our lives. Because each person's emotional make-up is unique, each of us responds to situations differently.

In considering whether a person may be suicidal, it is imperative that the crisis be evaluated from that person's perspective. What may seem of minor importance to one person can be extremely distressful to another. Regardless of the nature of the crisis, if a person feels overwhelmed there is a danger that suicide may seem an attractive solution.

Depression is the chief cause of suicide. Some depressive conditions do respond to counselling, for example where there is a definite known cause, such as depression following bereavement. Major depressive illness is difficult to handle with psychotherapy but usually responds to medical intervention. Loneliness often leads to what is known as situational depression. Relationship difficulties may also lead to depression and are a common cause of suicide and parasuicide. Chad Varah of the Samaritans says that befriending often swings the ambivalent person in favour of living and towards finding an alternative to death.

The effects of suicide

Recognition of suicide today exists within the context of wider awareness of mental health problems, so that there is a decreased tendency to moralise and condemn suicide. Frequently, however, stigma and shame are still associated with such deaths. Surviving family members and friends of the suicide are particularly affected and may experience altered grieving and bereavement associated with the mode of death of their loved one.

The common link among people who kill themselves is the belief that suicide is the only solution to a set of overwhelming feelings. The attraction of suicide is that it will finally end these unbearable feelings. The tragedy of suicide is that intense emotional distress often blinds people to alternative solutions, yet other solutions are almost always available. Suicide is often used as an escape from painful circumstances or as an act of revenge on another person who is blamed for the suffering that led to the suicide. These feelings are sometimes revealed in suicide notes and in the place where the suicide takes place.

The ambivalence of suicide

Almost all people in the 'pre-suicidal' state experience ambivalent feelings. They want to die and also to be saved. They want to escape from an intolerable situation and they also wish that the intolerable situation could be so transformed that they could continue living. Prevention may be possible in the presuicidal state because of the ambivalence, but people of immature personality may not experience ambivalence.

Many people are now experimenting with new therapies to relieve physical pain. People who can be encouraged to express their psychic pain through counselling are likely to discover a generally improved state of physical health. Pain and anger are close companions. The ability to express anger is one way of expressing the underlying pain.

Myths about suicide

● **Myth**: 'You have to be crazy even to think about suicide.'

- **Fact**: Many people have thought of suicide from time to time. Most suicides and suicide attempts are made by intelligent, temporarily confused individuals who are expecting too much of themselves, especially in the midst of a crisis.
- **Myth**: 'Once a person has made a serious suicide attempt, that person is unlikely to make another.'
- **Fact**: The opposite is often true. Persons who have made prior suicide attempts may be at greater risk of actually committing suicide; for some, suicide attempts may seem easier a second or third time.
- **Myth**: 'If a person is seriously considering suicide, there is nothing you can do.'
- **Fact**: Most suicide crises are time-limited and based on unclear thinking. Persons attempting suicide want to escape from their problems. Instead, they need to confront their problems directly in order to find other solutions – solutions that can be found with the help of concerned individuals who support them through the crisis period until they are able to think more clearly.
- **Myth**: 'Talking about suicide may give a person the idea.'
- **Fact**: The crisis and resulting emotional distress will already have triggered the thought in a vulnerable person. Your openness and concern in asking about suicide will allow the person experiencing pain to talk about the problem, which may help reduce his anxiety. This may also allow the person with suicidal thoughts to feel less lonely or isolated and perhaps a bit relieved.
- **Myth**: 'People who commit suicide are people who were unwilling to seek help.'
- **Fact**: Studies of suicide victims have shown that more than half had sought medical help less than six months before their death.

Recognising potential danger

- At least 70 per cent of all people committing suicide give some clue as to their intentions before they make an attempt – becoming aware of these clues and the severity of the person's problems can help prevent such a tragedy.
- If a person is going through a particularly stressful situation – perhaps having difficulty maintaining a meaningful relationship, having consistent failure in meeting goals or even experiencing stress at having failed an important test – watch for other signs of crisis.
- Many persons convey their intentions directly with statements such as 'I feel like killing myself or 'I don't know how much longer I can take this'.
- Others in crisis may hint at a detailed suicide plan, with statements such as 'I've been saving up my pills in case things get really bad' or 'Lately I've been driving my car like I really don't care what happens'.
- In general, statements describing feelings of depression, helplessness, extreme loneliness and/or hopelessness may suggest suicidal thoughts; it is important to listen to these 'cries for help' because they are usually desperate attempts to communicate to others the need to be understood and helped.

- Often persons thinking about suicide show outward changes in their behaviour – they may prepare for death by giving away prized possessions, making a will or putting other affairs in order; they may withdraw from those around them, change eating or sleeping patterns or lose interest in prior activities or relationships.
- A sudden, intense lift in spirits may also be a danger signal, as it may indicate that the person already feels a sense of relief at knowing the problems will 'soon be ended'.

How you, the counsellor, can help

Most suicides can be prevented by sensitive responses to the person in crisis. If you think someone you know may be suicidal, try to:

- Remain calm. In most instances, there is no rush. Sit and listen to what the person is saying. Give understanding and active emotional support for the person's feelings.
- Deal directly with the topic of suicide. Most individuals have mixed feelings about death and dying and are open to help. Don't be afraid to ask or talk directly about suicide.
- Encourage problem solving and positive actions. Remember that the person involved in an emotional crisis is not thinking clearly; encourage him to refrain from making any serious, irreversible decisions while in a crisis. Talk about the positive alternatives that may establish hope for the future.
- Get assistance. Although you want to help, do not take full responsibility by trying to be the sole counsellor.
- Seek out resources that can lend qualified help, even if it means breaking a confidence.
- Let the troubled person know you are concerned – so concerned that you are willing to arrange help beyond that which you can offer.
- Tell the person, 'The suicidal crisis is temporary. Unbearable pain can be survived. Help is available. You are not alone.'

Further reading

Durkheim, E. Suicide. In: J.P. Gibbs and W.T. Martin (1964) *Status integration and suicide.* University of Oregon Books, Oregon.
Roy, A. (1995) Suicide. In: *Comprehensive Textbook of Psychiatry*, 6th edn (eds H.J. Kaplan and B.J. Sadock). Williams & Wilkins, Baltimore, MD.

Summarising

Summarising is used to:

- Focus scattered facts, thoughts, feelings and meanings
- Prompt the client to further explore a particular theme
- Close a particular theme
- Help the client to find direction

- Help to free a client who is stuck
- Provide a 'platform' to view the way ahead
- Help the counsellor when feeling stuck
- Help clients to view their frame of reference from another perspective.

A summary:

- Outlines the relevant facts, thoughts, feelings and meanings
- May include a mixture of what was said and what was implied
- Gives a sense of movement
- Requires checking with the client for accuracy
- Should be simple, clear and jargon-free.

Further reading

Sutton, J. and Stewart, W. (1997) *Learning to Counsel: how to develop the skills to work effectively with others.* How to Books, Oxford.

SUPERVISION (SEE ALSO: EVALUATION)

Why counsellors need supervision

For counselling to be productive, counsellors must be continually moving forward towards increased understanding of themselves in relation to other people. Time and again they will be brought into contact with clients whose problems will awaken within them something that will create resistance or conflict within that relationship and specific to it. The client's difficulty will not be adequately resolved until the counsellor's own resistance or conflict is resolved.

The client may seek help from other sources, but if he does the counsellor's personal development may be retarded. When faced with a situation where their own emotions are thrown into turmoil or where counselling appears to have reached stalemate, there are three courses of action that counsellors may take. They can pull the blanket over their heads and hope that the problem will go away, they can work at it on their own or they can seek help.

In counselling we hope that clients will achieve a degree of insight in order to see their problem more realistically. If insight is essential for the client, how much more is it essential for the counsellor? If it is necessary for clients to seek help from someone to work through their problems, it is equally important for the counsellor.

Supervision helps counsellors to increase their skills and develop understanding and sensitivity of their own and the clients' feelings. The supervisory relationship is not primarily a therapeutic one. The task of the supervisor falls somewhere between counselling and tutoring. Supervision is developmental, helping the counsellor examine his/her relationship with particular clients and the counselling process.

The supervisory relationship forms a three-way relationship of client, counsellor and supervisor. Supervision is often resisted, because people don't use it fully. Counsellors who disregard the supervision relationship will lose out and run the risk of their counselling becoming stale.

Supervision is a requirement of membership of the British Association for Counselling and Psychotherapy.

The components of supervision:

- Support and encouragement
- Teaching and integrating theoretical knowledge and practice
- Assessment in the maintenance of standards
- Transmission of professional values and ethics.

Table 19: **Approaches to supervision**

Characteristics of case-centred supervision	Characteristics of counsellor-centred supervision	Characteristics of interactive supervision
Exploration of case material Concentrated mainly on what took place Little exploration of the counselling relationship A teacher/pupil relationship Discussion is more in the 'then-and-there', than in the 'here-and-now'.	The counselling relationship and what is happening within the counsellor Feelings are more readily acknowledged Carried out in an uncritical atmosphere Transference and counter-transference are more openly explored.	Takes into account both the case and the counselling relationship The interaction between client and counsellor may, in some way, be reflected in the supervisory relationship. Recognising the interaction and working with it, is likely to provide the counsellor with invaluable first-hand experience.

Supervision can be achieved in a number of ways:

- One-to-one, supervisor and counsellor
- Co-supervision between peers – usually recommended for experienced counsellors
- Group supervision, where a supervisor works with a number of counsellors
- Peer supervision, where a group of experienced counsellors meet on a regular basis.

Further reading

British Association for Counselling and Psychotherapy (1987) Supervision. *News-Letter of the Counselling at Work Division*, Spring.

Marteau, L. (1976) *Ethical Standards in Counselling*. British Association for Counselling and Psychotherapy, Rugby.

T

TAVISTOCK METHOD (SEE ALSO: GROUPS)

The Tavistock method originated with Wilfred R. Bion, working with small study groups at the Centre for Applied Social Research in the Tavistock Institute of Human Relations, London. Bion's experience in military psychiatry convinced him that the individual could not be considered except as part of a group. The emphasis later gradually shifted from the roles adopted by people in groups to the dynamics of leadership.

Basic assumptions of groups

- A group is formed from a collection of people when there is interaction between members who are aware of their shared relationship, from which a common group task emerges.
- Various forces bring groups into being, such as external threat, collective regressive behaviour and attempts to satisfy needs for affection, dependency, safety and security.
- When a collection becomes a group it behaves as a system and is greater than the sum of its parts, though the primary task may be masked.
- The primary task of any group is to survive.
- The fantasies and projections of its members give the group a life of its own.
- Group members are used in the service of the primary task.
- A person's present behaviour is an expression of that person's individual needs and also the needs of the group.
- Whatever the group says or does, the group is always talking about itself.
- Knowledge of the group process increases people's insights into their own and other people's behaviour in the group.
- Groups have manifest (overt) and latent (covert) aspects.
- People always have hidden agendas – parts of themselves that they consciously or unconsciously do not intend to reveal.
- The basic assumption group is composed of the combined hidden agendas of:
  - Unconscious wishes
  - Fears
  - Defences
  - Fantasies
  - Impulses
  - Projections.
- The basic assumption group is in conflict with the task.
- The tension between the task and the basic assumption group is usually balanced by:
  - Individual defence systems

- Ground rules
- Expectations
- Group norms
- Survival assumptions:
  - Dependency
    - The aim is to gain security and protection from either the designated leader or the assumed leader.
    - The group behaves in such a way that it hopes it will be rescued, controlled and directed by the leader.
    - The group expresses disappointment and hostility when the leader does not rescue.
    - Authoritative leaders often fall foul of the dependency assumption.
  - Fight/flight
    - Fight is characterised by active aggression, scapegoating and physical attack.
    - Flight is characterised by withdrawal, passivity, avoidance and ruminating on past history.
    - Fight leadership is bestowed on the person who mobilises the group's aggressive forces but this leadership is generally short-lived.
    - Flight leadership is bestowed on the person who successfully moves the group away from the 'here and now' to the 'then and there' and so reduces the importance of the task.
  - Pairing, characterised by warmth and affection, creates intimacy and closeness and by mutual support that excludes others in the group.
  - Oneness exists when the group surrenders self to some outside cause or all-powerful force, in order to feel a sense of well-being and wholeness.

Organisations seek to satisfy one or other of the survival assumptions. Examples are:

- Dependency, e.g. the Church
- Fight/flight, e.g. the military and industry
- Pairing, e.g. the political systems
- Oneness, e.g. mysticism and cosmic consciousness.

The function of the facilitator:

- To confront the group without intentionally offending group members
- To draw attention to group behaviour but not to individual behaviour
- To point out how the group uses individuals to express its own emotions
- To show how it exploits some members so that others can excuse themselves
- To focus on what is happening in the group
- To present observations in such a way as to increase the group's awareness.

Facilitator interventions may be:

- Description of what is observed
- Process observation – how the group pursues its task

- Thematic development – interactions that threaten the performance of the task, often drawing analogies from myth, legend and fairy tale
- Enlightenment – remarks aimed at instant enlightenment
- Shock – remarks that point to absurdities, aimed at producing shock and immediate awareness.

Issues confronting group members

- **Authority**
- **Responsibility**
- **Boundaries:** A fundamental precept of group relations is that work is not possible unless some boundaries – known to all members – are established and maintained. Boundaries must be strong yet permeable.
- **Projection** occurs in all human relationships and is particularly observable in groups in the form of:
  - Scapegoating
  - Hostility, often directed at the facilitator
  - Struggles for power
  - People who project their weaknesses on to others are also in danger of giving away their strengths.
- **Group structure**
  - Control: the group objectives and contract
  - Restraints: ground rules
  - Selected emphasis: expectations and assumptions of both facilitator and members
  - Elaborate structures hinder the group process.
  - Minimal structures enhance the group process.
  - Visible structures build trust.
  - Invisible structures open the door to manipulation.

Further reading

Bales, R.F. and Cohen S.P. (1979) *SYMLOG: a system for the multiple-level observation of groups*. Free Press, New York.
Bion, W.R. (1961) *Experiences in Groups*. Tavistock, London.
Brown, R. (1988) *Group Processes: dynamics within and between groups*. Basil Blackwell, Oxford.

TELEPHONE COUNSELLING

Telephone counselling can be a practical solution if a client lives at a distance or is unable to travel for any reason. Telephone counselling works on the same principles as other forms of therapy.

The telephone, a central feature of many crisis intervention agencies, is now being used for counselling over longer periods. Potential clients, those who have not yet plucked up courage to engage in a more formal counselling relationship, can use the telephone.

The telephone allows for anonymity, gives control to the client and reduces intimacy, something that many clients find frightening.

Difficulties of telephone counselling mainly arise from the lack of visual contact and total reliance on verbal language. However, for many people this service is proving useful.

Listening, essential in any counselling, is crucial in telephone counselling. Effective listening is listening to what is said, the way it is said (paralinguistics) and what is not said, and being aware of silences.

The way the person responds helps to build rapport and is aided by the frequent (but not habitual, nor unrelated) use of minimal responses such as 'Hmm', 'Yes', 'Right', 'OK', 'Carry on'.

Non-verbal language is always being transmitted, so we should avoid doing anything we would not normally do in face-to-face counselling. Taking notes or doodling may create an intuitive distraction.

Telephoning advice:

- Look welcoming.
- Imagine you are looking the speaker in the eye.
- Try to convey warmth by avoiding a clipped, crisp, business-like, hurried approach.
- Avoid looking at the clock, aware of a pressing engagement – be honest, tell the caller and arrange a return call.
- If the telephone is held in your left hand, you are more likely to use your right brain function for feelings and to explore.
- If the telephone is held in your right hand, you are more likely to use your left brain to analyse and to be precise.
- Empathy is more right- than left-brain oriented.

Similar to telephone counselling is online counselling. For people using the internet, a search of 'telephone counselling' and 'online counselling' will bring up hundreds of sites. A useful one is http://www.thehumantouch.co.uk which will give you links to dozens of sites.

Further reading

CEPEC, N16 (1.8 7C) (1987) *Notes on the Use of the Telephone in Counselling.* CEPEC, London SW1Y 6NY.

Kennedy, E. (1981) *Crisis Counselling: the essential guide for non-professional counsellors.* Gill & Macmillan, Dublin.

TEN TRAPS FOR THERAPISTS

James Chu, speaking from a psychoanalytical perspective, draws attention to the fact that clients who have experienced trauma are difficult to treat. Although he was referring mainly to victims of childhood abuse, the ten traps, or therapeutic impasses, are applicable to many types of trauma.

When caught in a trap, both client and therapist feel immobilised, and therapy stands still or even regresses. The steps in resolving resistance have been identified as:

- Confrontation
- Clarification
- Interpretation
- Working through.

The nature of traps

Trauma survivors who come from pathological backgrounds are likely to go on to develop psychiatric disorders. Such a background is characterised by:

- Incestuous abuse
- Lack of familial support
- Contradictory messages: loved yet abused; nurtured yet abandoned and betrayed.

An abusive background may lead to dissociation and repression.

Both therapist and client may feel overwhelmed by the depth of the client's pain. Many such clients have poor ego functioning and place heavy demands on the therapist, in order to feel loved and cared for. It is essential that therapists recognise their own feelings and how they might influence the therapeutic relationship.

Traps are created by:

- The client's acute distress
- The emerging traumatic experiences
- Resistance, as the client finds treatment painful
- Difficulty in maintaining the therapeutic alliance.

Trap 1 – trust

- Clients who have suffered trauma, particularly abuse, neglect or abandonment, have difficulty creating and maintaining trusting relationships. Learning to trust the therapist may not happen until nearing the end of a long relationship.
- Clients who have been betrayed are hyper-alert to any indications of what they perceive as untrustworthiness in the therapeutic relationship.

Trap 2 – distance

- In this, the therapist creates distance in response to the client's resistance in learning to trust and neediness. This might be a particular difficulty for therapists trained in psychoanalysis, where distance is encouraged. 'However, it is worth considering,' says Chu, 'whether distance is appropriate for patients who have major problems in maintaining basic relations.' They may perceive withdrawal as further evidence of abandonment.
- This is where person-centred 'core conditions' would help to come closer and lessen distance.
- Therapy is a partnership, where client and therapist both contribute and both gain.

Trap 3 – boundaries

- Inconsistent nurturing and grossly distorted family roles create blurred boundaries for the child. That is why therapeutic boundaries are clearly established.
- The client might want to know more about the therapist's private life, to help feel secure. Some therapist self-disclosure might be therapeutically helpful; however it is the therapist who sets and maintains the boundaries.
- Clients, too, must feel comfortable about the boundaries of what they disclose in therapy.

Trap 4 – limits

- This relates to failing to set time limits. What therapists set out to do is to provide a basic 'good enough' environment. This means providing a containing environment, that includes setting time limits. Flexibility does not equate with an endless gratification of client demands. This concept applies to all relationships, particularly the parent/child relationship, and this child/parent dynamic must not be overlooked in the therapeutic relationship.
- Clients who have been severely deprived may be very demanding of the therapist's time. Therapists who attempt to meet these demands may well end up immobilised and powerless. Some clients come with a bottomless well of need, which no therapist could ever fill.
- Failure to meet demand is likely to result in client anger and therapist guilt.

Trap 5 – responsibility

- Although the aim of therapy is that it will have some benefit for the client, sometimes it seems that the picture becomes less clear.
- The trust the client has in the therapist (and in the therapy) is stretched to breaking point, as the pain of the process in the here-and-now seems more than the long-term gains.
- Clients may attempt to escape through leaving therapy, or by threatening suicide – the ultimate escape.
- Attempts by the therapist to persuade the client to stay in therapy are met with persuasive counter-arguments. This places the therapist in the position of taking responsibility for the client's life and treatment.
- Therapists must have the ability to step back and allow the clients to take responsibility for their treatment and well-being.
- The more that the therapist pursues such a client, the more it emphasises to the client that it is the therapist who has the ultimate responsibility.

Trap 6 – control

- Clients with a traumatic past present intrusive responses similar to people who have suffered from PTSD: hyperactivity, explosive aggressive outbursts, startle response, recollections, nightmares and flashbacks, and re-enactment of the situation. All of these are combined with numbed responses, retreat from family obligations and a feeling of estrangement.

- The client may experience violent swings between feeling totally out of control and exercising rigid control.
- Therapy encourages clients to let go and to start exercising some control over the flashbacks. It also must be accepted that flashbacks do serve the function of relieving internal pressure, albeit temporarily, though without abreaction or integration.

Trap 7 – denial

- Denial – that the experience didn't happen, or that the effects are nothing to worry about – is the core defence for clients who have suffered trauma.
- Denying the horror ensures that these painful feelings will not be addressed.
- Another form of denial is to fabricate stories about a good upbringing within a loving, caring family.
- While clients might admit to events, they deny the significance, or maintain that they have worked through them. However, the therapist must challenge the difference between cognitive and affective understanding.

Trap 8 – projection

- Clients may project intolerable experiences and conflicts on to different parts of themselves, or on to something external.
- It is easier for the client to project than it is to resolve internal conflicts. The therapist often becomes the object of such transferences, and may be perceived as cold/empathic; nurturing/abusive; friendly/hostile.
- The therapist, however competent, may be perceived as incompetent, and be blamed for not knowing enough or not doing enough.
- Therapists must not act out their own feelings, but must interpret them. Not do to do so is collusion.
- Therapist self-disclosure, because of its intimacy, may be too difficult for the client to handle, and may be too intrusive. So self-disclosure must be handled with great care.

Trap 9 – idealisation

- Idealisation can boost one's ego, but it can be unhealthy and destructive.
- Ignoring idealisation, which is a negative transference, can block progress, and may lead to client self-destructive behaviour.
- Clients who have a fragmented self-image view others in the same way.
- Eroticised idealised transference is particularly pernicious and difficult to handle, because of the intensity and the degree of dependency on the therapeutic relationship.

Trap 10 – motivation

- Ego strength, the ability to maintain relationships (however conflicted) and motivation all play an important part in determining the outcome of therapy.
- Ingrained, severe character pathology, marked negativity in coping mechanisms or insufficient motivation all suggest poor prognosis.

However, motivation and all the other factors can only be judged over time. We can only judge by what the client does, not what the client says.

For some, the gains of maintaining the status quo are more than the possible gains of change.

Chu says, 'Not all patients are interested in resolving past events or in personality change and integration, and it is certainly acceptable to help a patient achieve some level of stability and more harmonious functioning and relationships.'

Clients may be caught in the double-bind of 'If I make too much progress I'll lose the only relationship that's worthwhile.'

Chu's summary

Finding a balance in such issues as flexibility versus limits, acceptance versus confrontation, or even the patient's versus the therapist's needs, are all part of the skill, judgement and art of psychotherapy... Knowledge, understanding, patience, and compassion on the part of the therapist will enhance the therapeutic process, and may make it more productive for the patient and the therapist.'

Further reading

Byer, J.B., Nelson, B.A., Miller, J.B. and Krol, P.A. (1987) Childhood sexual and physical abuse as factors in adult psychiatric illness. *American Journal of Psychiatry*, 144(11): 1426–1430.

Chu, J.A. (1988) Ten traps for therapists in the treatment of trauma survivors. *Dissociation*, 1(4): 24–32, December.

Sutton, J. (2004) Understanding dissociation and its relationship to self-injury and childhood trauma. *Counselling and Psychotherapy Journal*, 15: 03, April.

TOUCH

The touch of significant others, especially the mother or principal caregiver, plays an important part in the development of security in the infant. Through its senses the infant learns that it is loved and develops a confident personality.

Deprivation of touch can give rise to neurotic or psychotic behaviour in later life, such as 'touch hunger' or 'touch revulsion'.

Touch can be an important element in transference. Touch can soothe the grieving soul or inflame passion. That is one reason why touch should be carefully used.

The psychoanalytic approach, which is exclusively verbal, operates a 'no touch' rule, which affords no escape for the client and frees the counsellor from possible collusion and self-gratification. On the other hand, full expression of thoughts, feelings and fantasies is encouraged.

Body therapies, however, use a great deal of touch. For them, touch is healing. The cardinal guideline is that the counsellor is not 'touch hungry' or seductive. The touch should be for the benefit of the client, not the counsellor.

Touch can soothe and also inflame great passion. Touch can relax tired and tense muscles; it may also cause a person to shrink away in fear. We can enjoy being touched, embraced, hugged or cuddled or we can detest these touchings.

John Rowan, speaking of humanistic therapies and the part touching plays, says, 'As babies we all had strong needs to be touched and cuddled. If these were not met, we may go through life looking for the touch we missed.' In another part of the same book, *The Reality Game*, he says:

> *Many humanistic practitioners touch the bodies of their clients, whether out of ordinary human sympathy, encouragement to regress, provocative massage designed to bring out feelings, re-enactment of birth, etc. In opening up the whole inner world which has been blocked off, we use a lot of gratification (whole body massage, cuddling and comforting, giving of bottles or breasts, immersion in warm water, group rocking and lullabies, affirmation of good qualities and general loveableness and so on) because we find it to be highly therapeutic and very effective in producing real change, if used in the right way.*

Thus on the one hand there is the psychodynamic counsellor who avoids touch and, on the other, the body-awareness counsellor who will use any or all of the approaches mentioned by Rowan. Touch, like any other response, needs to be carefully used and we need to know why we want to touch the client. It can convey warmth but it may also evoke feelings of the parent–child relationship. Touch can be welcoming but it may also be perceived as threatening, an invasion of personal space. Touch can be encouraging; it may also have the effect of drying up emotions, almost like the patronising 'There, there; everything will be all right'.

We need to ask ourselves: 'Why do I want to touch this person?' Is it to comfort the person or to comfort ourselves? Is it that we cannot cope with the person's distress? As in most aspects of counselling there are no hard and fast rules about touch, however, one guiding principle would be: know your client. Never make assumptions about your client's wish for touch, whether it is holding hands or hugging. More than that: the same client might change from session to session. The client who rejected your touch when he was distressed might ask for a hug on leaving after achieving a major breakthrough.

Further reading

Rowan, J. (1983) *The Reality Game*. Routledge & Kegan Paul, London.

TRANSACTIONAL ANALYSIS (TA) (E. BERNE, 1910–1970)

Transactional analysis (TA) is a system of analysis and therapy developed by Eric Berne, and comprises a theory of personality, a theory of social interaction and an analytical tool for psychotherapy.

Philosophy and concepts

Although an infant starts off from the position of being OK, obstacles and difficulties often prevent him from developing his potentialities to his best advantage and to the advantage of others. These obstacles and difficulties also interfere with his ability to be able to work productively and creatively, and to be free from psychological disturbances.

TA is also a method of group work that emphasises the person's ability to change, the role of the inner parent in the process of change and the person's control of the ego states.

Berne identifies four forms of hunger-need:

1. **Tactile**: Intimacy and physical closeness. This need continues through life.
2. **Recognition**: 'I cannot physically touch you, but I will verbally stroke you.' (The stroke is a basic unit of social interaction.) A transaction is an exchange of strokes.
3. **Structure**: 'I must fill my time to prevent boredom.'
4. **Excitement**: 'I must fill my life in interesting and exciting ways.' Leaders provide structure for others to fill their time. However, many of us are brought up to believe that seeking excitement is bad and should be shunned.

Intimacy

Intimacy is the most satisfying solution to stimulus, recognition and structure hunger. To be able to enter into intimacy, a person must have awareness and enough spontaneity to be liberated from the compulsion to play games.

Facets of intimacy

- **Sexual**: Expression of caring and enjoyment of each other
- **Emotional**: Sharing of significant meanings and feelings, being tuned to one another's wave length. Child–Child communication
- **Intellectual**: Closeness in the world of ideas
- **Aesthetic**: Sharing experiences of beauty
- **Creative**: Sharing the experience of creating
- **Recreational**: Relating in experiences of fun and play
- **Work**: The closeness of sharing common tasks
- **Crisis**: Closeness in coping with problems of pain
- **Conflict**: Facing and struggling with differences
- **Commitment**: Mutuality derived from self-investment
- **Spiritual**: The we-ness in sharing ultimate concerns
- **Communication**: The source of all types of true intimacy.

Personality structure comprises:

- Three various 'selves' or ego states: Parent; Adult; Child (PAC). (Parent, Adult, Child are capitalised to identify them as distinct states.) We all incorporate all three. At any given moment we will exhibit one (and only one) or another of these states. An ego state involves thinking, feeling and behaving.
- Transactions between people and between one's various selves.
- An individual existential position.
- A preconscious life-plan or 'script'.

1. The Parent ego state

A set of feelings, thoughts, attitudes and behaviours, which resemble those of parental figures, characterised by postures, gestures, verbalisations and feelings. The function of the Parent is to conserve energy and to diminish anxiety by making certain decisions 'automatic'. The Parent in you feels and behaves in the same ways you perceived the feelings and behaviour or your mother, father or significant others who raised you. The Parent state consists of:

The critical Parent

- The basic need of the critical Parent is power.
- Critical Parent functions are to set limits, discipline, make rules and regulations about how life should be; the do's and don'ts.
- The critical Parent ego state criticises and finds fault and is contrasted with the nurturing Parent.
- The critical Parent may also be assertive and self-sufficient.
- The critical Parent uses such words as 'always', 'never', 'should', 'should not', 'must', 'ought to', 'have to', 'cannot', 'good' and 'bad'.
- The critical Parent judges and criticises and uses such language as 'Because I said so', 'Brat', 'Childish', 'Naughty', 'Now what?', 'What will the neighbours say?'.
- Some typical gestures and postures – eyes rolling up in disgust, finger-pointing, folded arms, tapping of feet in impatience.
- Some typical voice tones – condescending, punishing, sneering.
- Some typical facial expressions – angry frown, disapproving, furrowed brow, hostile, pursed lips, scowl, set jaw.

The nurturing Parent

- The basic need of the nurturing Parent is caring.
- Nurturing Parent functions are to give advice, guide, protect, teach how to and keep traditions – group work helps people become aware of the influence of Parent, then to sort out what makes sense and what does not.
- The nurturing Parent ego state is characterised by warmth, support and love.
- Some typical words and phrases – 'Don't worry', 'Good', 'Darling', 'Beautiful', 'I'll take care of you', 'Let me help you', 'Smart', 'There, there'
- Some typical gestures and postures – consoling touch, head nodding – 'Yes', pat on the back
- Some typical voice tones – encouraging, supportive, sympathetic
- Some typical facial expressions – encouraging nod, loving, sympathetic eyes.

2. The Adult ego state

The Adult is the part of you that figures out things by looking at the facts. It is the part that computes, stores memories and uses facts to make decisions. The Adult is unemotional and is concerned with 'what fits' or what is most expedient and useful. *Adult* does not mean *mature*.

- The basic need of the Adult is rationality.
- Adult functions are to work on facts, to compute, store memories and feelings, and to use facts to make decisions.
- The Adult decides what fits, where and what is most useful.
- The Adult gathers data on the Parent and the Child, makes decisions based on available data and plans the decision-making process.
- The Adult is an analytical, rational and non-judgemental ego state.
- The Adult problem-solves and obtains information.
- Some typical phrases – 'According to statistics', 'Look for alternatives', 'Check it out', 'Have you tried this?', 'What do the results suggest?', 'How do you arrive at that?'
- Some typical gestures and postures – active listening; checking for understanding; giving feedback; pointing something out
- Some typical voice tones – calm; clear, with appropriate emotion; confident; informative; inquiring; straight
- Some typical facial expressions – attentive; confident; eyes alert; direct eye contact; lively; responsive; thoughtful.

3. The Child ego state

Every adult was once a child. Feelings, thoughts and behaviour patterns exist in later life as relics of the individual's childhood. Berne considers that we all carry within ourselves a little boy or girl who feels, thinks, acts and responds just as we did when we were children of a certain age. The behaviour of the Child is not childish but *childlike.*

It is a basic ego state consisting of feelings, impulses and spontaneous acts. As a result of learning, the Child ego state takes the form of the adapted Child or the natural Child.

The natural (or free) Child

- The basic need of the natural Child is creativity.
- The natural Child is loving, spontaneous, carefree, fun-loving and exciting.
- The natural Child is adventurous, curious, trusting and joyful.
- The natural Child describes the spontaneous, eager and playful part of the personality.
- People whose natural Child is too dominant generally lack self-control.
- Some typical words: 'Eek', 'Gee whiz', 'Gosh', 'I'm scared', 'Let's play', 'Look at me now!', 'Wow!'
- Some typical gestures and postures – joyful, skipping, curling up, pretending
- Some typical voice tones – belly-laughing, excited, giggling, gurgling, whistling, singing.
- Some typical facial expressions – admiration, wide-eyed and curious, excited, flirty.

The adapted Child

- The basic need of the adapted Child is for approval.
- Adapted Child functions are being angry, rebellious, frightened and conforming.
- The adapted Child functions are to conform to, or rebel against, what another person wants.
- Some typical words and phrases – 'Can't', 'Did I do all right?', 'Do it for me', 'I didn't do it', 'It's all your fault', 'It's all my fault', 'Nobody loves me'.
- Some typical gestures and postures – batting eyelashes; dejected; nail-biting; obscene gestures; temper tantrums.
- Some typical voice tones – asking permission; annoying; spiteful; sullen silence; swearing; whining.
- Some typical facial expressions – eyes directed upwards/downwards, helpless, pouting, woebegone.

In other words:

- Parent is our 'Taught' concept of life
- Adult is our 'Thought' concept of life
- Child is our 'Felt' concept of life.

Berne considered the natural Child to be the most valuable part of the personality. The proper function of a 'healthy' Child is to motivate the Adult so as to obtain the greatest amount of gratification for itself. This it does by letting the Adult know what it wants and by consulting the Parent about its appropriateness. The Adult can turn off either or both of the other ego states. Control is not repression; it means changing the ego state. Control is about choice and decisions.

Table 20: *A recent variation of the PAC states*

Parent	Nurturing	Nurturing (positive)
		Spoiling (negative)
	Controlling	Structuring (positive)
		Critical (negative)
Adult	Adult remains as a single entity, representing an 'accounting' function or mode, which can draw on the resources of both Parent and Child.	
Child	Adapted	Cooperative (positive)
		Compliant (negative)
	Free	Spontaneous (positive)
		Immature (negative)

www.businessballs.com/transact.htm

Personality function

The three systems of personality react in the following ways:

- The Parent judgementally attempts to enforce external standards.
- The Adult is concerned with processing and storing information.
- The Child reacts more impulsively on poorly differentiated perceptions.
- Transactional analysis recognises four basic life positions (see table below).

Table 21: *Transactional analysis's four life positions*

I'm OK, You're not OK The basic attitude is: 'I'm going to get what I can, though I'm not much. Your life is not worth much; you are dispensable. Get out of my way.' This is a distrustful position and is taken up by a Child who is suspicious of people.	Words to describe this state: Arrogant, Do-gooder, Distrustful. Bossy
I'm not OK, You're OK The basic attitude is: 'My life is not worth much; I'm nothing compared to you.' The position of the Child who usually feels low or depressed.	Words to describe this state: Depression, Resignation, Suicide
I'm not OK, You're not OK The basic attitude is: 'Life is not worth anything at all; we might as well be dead. So, it doesn't matter what we do or who we hurt.' Such people may yearn for warmth, but cannot accept it and cannot trust the person who gives it. The position of a Child who feels that life just isn't any good and that there is no escape from it.	Words to describe this state: Futility, Alienation, Severe withdrawal
I'm OK, You're OK The basic attitude is: 'Life is for living; let's live it to the full.' Only this state puts people on equal terms. The healthy position.	Words to describe this state: Good, Healthy, Successful, Competent, Confident, Challenging, Creative

Transactions

Transactions are the basic units of human communication; any exchanges between the ego states of any two people. Transactions may be verbal and non-verbal. Transactions operate at an overt social level and at a covert psychological level.

Transactions may be:

- Parallel, e.g. Parent to Parent and Parent to Parent
- Crossed, e.g. Parent to Parent and Parent to Child
- Ulterior, e.g. Adult to Adult and Child to Adult.

Contamination

This is where the Child takes on the values, prejudices, opinions and feelings of significant others without filtering them through the Adult.

Strokes

Strokes describe the recognition we receive from others. Strokes can be verbal, non-verbal or both. A wave of the hand. 'Hello, how are you today?' A slap.

- Positive strokes are warm and enhance self-esteem and evoke the feeling of 'I'm OK, you're OK'. Expressing love, caring, respect and responding to an expressed need are all positive strokes.
- Negative strokes are cold and knock self-esteem and evoke the feeling of 'I'm not OK'. Expressing hating is a negative stroke. 'I can't stand you' is a negative stroke.
- Conditional strokes are given to get something in return. 'I will love you if...'. (See also unconditional positive regard, in Core conditions.)
- Unconditional strokes are given without any strings attached; with no hidden motives.

We need positive strokes to maintain physical and mental well-being. Institutionalised infants have been known to die when deprived of stroking. As we grow, words are often substitutes for the physical stroking we received as children.

So often, strokes are given when we have done something. We also need strokes just for being who we are. We also need to learn to ask for strokes when we need them. 'I'd really appreciate a big hug right now.' 'Give me a kiss, darling.'

A positive self-esteem makes it in order to stroke oneself. 'I did a really good job and I'm pleased with myself.' Recognition from others may be:

- Positive, evoking the feeling of 'I'm OK, You're OK'
- Negative, evoking the feeling of 'I'm not OK, You're OK'
- Conditional strokes are given for something done – 'I will love you if...'
- Unconditional strokes are given just for being
- Positive, unconditional stroking benefits the giver as well as the receiver.

People whose Child feels 'not OK' become more used to negative strokes than to positive ones. They may yearn for compliments, but cannot accept them and cannot trust the person who gives them.

Existential or basic positions (scripts)

A script is our preconscious life plan by which we structure our time, decided by the child before the age of six or seven. It is based on injunctions ('Don't do...') and counter-injunctions (usually in the form of slogans). A counter-script is a preconscious life-plan decided by the child's Parent.

Scripts determine our destinies, including our approach to relationships and to tasks. They are based on childlike illusions, which may persist throughout life. Very often we live in the illusion that we live our lives autonomously. In reality much of what we do as Adults bears parental and other influences. The aim of therapy is to free people from following their scripts and counter-scripts.

Stamps and rackets

'Stamp collecting' is storing bad feelings as an excuse for doing things you might not otherwise do. Stamps are not needed if the basic position is 'I'm OK; You're OK'.

Rackets is a term to describe the habitual ways of feeling bad about oneself, learned from parents and other significant people. They are the feelings of our parents, they do not rightly belong to us, but we act as if they do.

An example would be that, when our parents were under pressure, they may have become anxious, depressed, confused or nervous. If they did not take appropriate Adult action to eliminate the tension or pressure, the likelihood is that we learned a racket by responding in the same way. Rackets originate from the 'not OK' Child of our parents; our Child then repeats these to avoid taking constructive action.

Time structuring

We fill our time depending on which of the four basic positions our Child has taken and what kind of stroking our Child wants.

- **Withdrawal**: No overt communication, e.g. in a railway carriage
- **Rituals**: Socially prescribed forms of behaviour, e.g. the 'Hello–Goodbye' sequence
- **Activities**: These are socially significant because they offer a framework for various recognitions and satisfactions
- **Pastimes**: Semi-ritualistic – topical conversations that last longer than rituals but are still mainly socially programmed, e.g. 'Let's talk about cars/babies/the weather'
- **Games** (over 90 have been described): These are unconscious (a conscious game is manipulation) and involve stamp-collecting
- **Intimacy**: The most satisfying solution to the need for positive stroking. To be able to enter intimacy, a person must have awareness and enough spontaneity to be liberated from the compulsion to play games.

Games

- Games describe unconscious, stereotyped and predictable behaviours. When games are conscious, it is manipulation. The transactions in games are partially ulterior and result in negative payoffs for the players.
- Games are classified as first-, second- or third-degree depending on the seriousness of the consequences. They allow the player to collect 'stamps'. Stamps are stored up feelings, positive or negative. When we have amassed enough stamps we may cash then in for a 'prize': letting fly at someone with whom we have been really tolerant over a long period; allowing oneself a period of relaxation, for example.
- Brown stamps are for negative feelings; gold stamps are for positive feelings.
- Stamp collecting is a way of trying to help the Child to feel OK.

A game consists of:

- An apparent (conscious) transaction (usually Adult–Adult)
- A hidden (unconscious) transaction (usually Parent–Child or Child–Child)
- A sudden and unpleasant reaction (a stamp).

The most common games are:

- 'If it weren't for you'
- 'Kick me'
- 'I'm only trying to help'.

Injunctions, attributions and discounts

Although directives from parents can be nurturing and conducive to the child's emotional development, they can also be restrictive, reflecting the fears and insecurities of the Child in the parent.

Injunctions are irrational negative-feeling messages expressed pre-verbally and non-verbally. They are restrictive, reflecting fears and insecurities.

Examples of injunctions

- Don't be you, be me, or someone else
- Don't grow up
- Don't be well, be sick
- Don't be a child, be grown up
- Don't make it, don't be a success
- Don't be close to people
- Don't be sane, be crazy
- Don't count, be unimportant
- Don't think/feel what you think/feel (angry, sexy, happy, good), think/feel only what I think/feel.

Examples of slogans as injunctions:

- Be a man, my son.
- God helps those who help themselves.
- Raise yourself up by your own bootlaces.

The following injunctions block intimacy:

- Do not give strokes if you have them to give.
- Do not ask for strokes when you need them.
- Do not accept strokes even if you want them.
- Do not reject strokes even if you do not want them.

Attributions

This means being told what we are, what we must do and how we must feel. Family reinforcement schedules tend to reward children who follow attributions and punish children who disobey injunctions.

Where a child (pre-school development) is given unconditional protection he is less likely to develop a restrictive script. When parents make their nurturing conditional on their child's submission to their injunctions and attributions, the child may make a conscious decision to adhere to parental wishes even though this means the sacrifice of autonomy.

Attributions are:

- Being told what we are, what we must do and how we must feel
- Generally approving of obedience and disapproving of disobedience.

Injunctions and attributions lie at the heart of a judgemental attitude. The developing child's autonomy may be sacrificed at the altar of parental control.

Scripts

- A script is a preconscious set of rules by which we structure our life plan.
- Scripts are decided before the age of six or seven years.
- Scripts are based on injunctions and attributions.
- Scripts determine how we approach relationships and work.
- Scripts are based on childlike illusions that automatically influence our lives.

Attempts to move out of script produce discomfort. Comfort is re-established when the script is picked up, when once again there is acquiescence to parental wishes.

Berne proposed that the parent of the opposite sex tells the child what to do and the parent of the same sex demonstrates how to do it.

Considerations for counselling

1. Assumptions
Therapist cannot change clients; they can only:

- Bring clients to an awareness of how they make themselves and others sick, bad, stupid or crazy
- Help them develop permission to change
- Give them protection while they change.

If clients are aware of how they hurt themselves, they are aware of the changes they need to make, if they wish to. The counsellor may need to help the person give himself permission to make the change.

2. Bases for change
Therapeutic change is based on decisions and action. If the person does not do this, no one else will; hence the necessity to emphasise:

- The Adult's ability to turn off inappropriate Child and Parent states
- Permission
- Protection
- Decision

- What the client can do. If the counsellor accepts a 'can't', he agrees with the person that he is helpless and/or hopeless.

3. Contract
The client commits himself to a plan for behaviour change. Important contracting conditions:

- The person makes the contract with himself: the facilitator is only a guide and a witness. With a dishonest contract, the person thus defeats only himself.
- The more explicit the contract the better. The person has the right to refuse a contract, which is another way of clarifying his readiness for change.
- The more operational the contract the better (e.g. 'happiness' is not operational; there are no criteria to measure it by). You might ask the person:
  - What would you be doing better if you were happier?
  - How do you make yourself unhappy?
  - What do you want to stop doing?
- The contract can be renegotiated.
- Contracts are most useful if satisfactory to all of the three ego states of both the facilitator and the person.
- The contract is one way of assuming that what goes on between the facilitator and the person is more likely to be an activity that promotes growth towards personal fulfilment.

Drama triangle (also known as the rescue triangle)
A significant part of transactional analysis is identifying the games people play. One of these games is the rescue triangle of Rescuer, Persecutor and Victim.

- We adopt the role of Rescuer by helping and keeping others dependent on us.
- We adopt the role of Persecutor when we set unnecessarily strict limits on behaviour or are charged with enforcing the rules, but do so with brutality.
- We adopt the role of Victim when (without cause) we feel we are being unjustly treated.
- All three roles are interchangeable and we may play them all in turn.

The Rescuer
There are many situations in life where one person is in need of help and another person is capable of offering it. In a fire, the fire-fighter is in a legitimate role of 'rescuer'. This does not qualify as a 'game'. True helping is based on the life position of 'I'm OK, You're OK'.

We drop into the game when we see the person as helpless and hopeless and not able to manage without our help. In such a situation, we assume the complete burden of caring and helping, thus relieving the other person of any responsibility for helping themselves.

The Persecutor
In the rescue game, the Victim poses a question from a position of powerlessness; the Rescuer attempts to give answers. Every suggestion is rejected; a new one is

suggested, until eventually the Rescuer becomes angry, switches roles and persecutes the Victim.

When we rescue people who don't need it, we put them down, emphasise their helplessness and exalt our own superiority and they will become angry with the Rescuer.

Every Rescuer–Victim transaction will result in a Persecutor–Victim transaction.

The Victim

In a Rescue situation, the person helping is the Rescuer and the person being helped (often without asking for it) is called the Victim.

There are situations in life when a person is truly a victim, e.g. someone who has been burgled. However, the Victim in the rescue game generally contributes to the situation.

When the Victim is being overpowered or oppressed by a person or situation, the Victim colludes with the Persecutor, to the extent that he discounts feelings of being persecuted. In addition, the Victim doesn't use all of his own power to overcome the oppression.

The fire-fighter rescuer would be thanked by his victim; a Rescuer would normally be persecuted by his Victim.

How it begins

The family is the training ground for the three basic roles of the rescue triangle, which is, in effect, training for powerlessness. Children are forced into the Victim role, while the roles of Rescuer and Persecutor are taught by example, as provided by the parents. We train children into the Victim role of powerlessness by attacking all the areas in which they have potential power.

Areas of power attacked by the 'game':

- The power to love; to successfully relate to other human beings
- The power to think; the capacity to understand the world
- The power to enjoy ourselves; the capacity to experience and make full use of our bodies and emotions.

The degree to which children are not allowed to love, to understand the world and themselves, forces them into a Victim position. The parents (and others in authority) are either Persecutors who oppress their children in their abilities or Rescuers who then do what they have actually prevented the children from doing for themselves.

Training children in powerlessness

- In relationships, by not allowing children to make their own social contacts and their own decisions about who they want to be with and when (all such decisions must be appropriate to age)
- In knowledge of the world, by not allowing children to come up against

situations in which they have to understand the world well enough to make decisions and to think in it

- To learn about themselves, what gives them pleasure, how they feel and how to act upon those feelings
- Many parents treat males differently from females, so that male children are trained to be powerless in the capacity to know themselves; female children are trained to be powerless in their capacity to think and to know the world
- Powerlessness is a requirement of an oppressive family, community or society. In the typical authoritarian family, father is the Persecutor, mother is the Rescuer and the children are Victims.

As the children grow up, they often take over the Persecutor role, while the parents become the Victims, which may appear as children's poor school records, refusing to work, drug-taking, violence or lawlessness.

Children raised in the shadow of the Rescue triangle are excellent candidates for accepting the vertical relationships of hierarchies, although they often carry their rebellion over and become misfits.

Caught in the drama triangle trap

Selflessness, doing for others, generosity and cooperation are encouraged, even when people are selfish, stingy and do not cooperate with us. This is exploitation and characteristic of the Rescuer role.

Being one-down in a relationship is the experience of many women, while the reverse is true of many men. Women are more likely to be trained into the playing of the Rescuer role, to always be available.

Don't rescue me! If we don't want to be a Victim, we must demand not to be rescued. We may have to repeat our demand many times, because people who are confirmed Rescuers experience tremendous feelings of guilt if deprived of the Rescuing role.

Counsellors, too, can get caught up in the game. The client who ends a long recital of what is wrong in his life by saying, 'I really don't know what to do. I feel so helpless. It's not my fault, is it?' is casting himself in the Victim role. The unwary counsellor, intent on action rather than on exploring and challenging, who agrees that life is cruel and that the client is entirely innocent, is falling into the role of Rescuer. A simple, 'You feel as if you are an innocent victim in all this. Perhaps it would be productive to look at your part in the break-up of your marriage,' would be enough to convey to the client that he has the resources within him to challenge himself and the counsellor would not become the Rescuer and run the risk of the client becoming the Persecutor.

TA helps clients to become aware of how they hurt themselves, the changes they need to make and the inner forces that hinder change. Therapeutic change is based on decisions and action. If we do not decide or act, no one will or can do it for us. When we accept a 'can't', we agree with clients that they are helpless. Clients make a contract with themselves to work towards specific changes in behaviour. Change is for the purpose of the client assuming responsibility for his life and achieving a degree of self-actualisation.

TA is an ideal model for eclectic counsellors to add to their repertoire, mainly because it does not clash with other models and secondly because clients readily understand the basic principles of the Parent–Adult–Child ego states and are normally adept at identifying which ego state they are speaking from.

Intimacy is the most satisfying solution to the need for positive stroking. To be able to enter intimacy, a person must have awareness and enough spontaneity to be liberated from the compulsion to play games. Intimacy is like a harp. The music it produces comes from all its strings. Within the intimacy of the counselling relationship the client will learn how to ask for and receive positive strokes.

Another point is the triangular relationship. When a couple add a child and become a family, a triangle is formed. In a stable, functional family, the child is at the apex, supported by the firm base of the parents. However, in a child-centred family, the triangle is reversed and the child supports the parents, for all attention is directed at the child. This can only lead to dysfunction, as this configuration prevents integration, where the child feels supported. Children will exploit the family relationship and strive to drive a wedge between the parents, and create alliances. Unless the parents stand united, such alliances will lead to dysfunction.

Further reading

Anderson, J.P. (1973) A transactional primer. In: *1973 Handbook for Group Facilitators*. University Associates, San Diego, CA.

Berne, E. (1961) *Transactional Analysis in Psychotherapy*. Grove Press, New York.

Berne, E. (1964) *Games People Play*. Grove Press, New York.

Berne, E. (1972) *What Do You Say After You Say Hello?*. Grove Press, New York.

Harris, T.A. (1969) *I'm OK– You're OK*. Harper & Row, New York.

Karpman, S.B. (1968) Fairy tales and script drama analysis. *Transactional Analysis Bulletin* 7(26): 39–43.

Nelson-Jones, R. (1983) *The Theory and Practice of Counselling Psychology*. Holt, Rinehart & Winston, New York.

Pareek, U. (1984) Interpersonal styles: the SPIRO instrument. In: *1984 Handbook for Group Facilitators*. University Associates, San Diego, CA.

Patterson, C.H. (1986) *Theories of Counselling and Psychotherapy*, 4th edn. Harper & Row, London.

Pitman, E. (1984) *Transactional Analysis*. Routledge & Kegan Paul, London.

Stewart, I. and Joines, V. (1987) *TA Today*. Lifespace Publishing, Nottingham.

Stewart, W. (1998) *Building Self-esteem*. How to Books, Oxford.

TRANSFERENCE AND COUNTER-TRANSFERENCE (SEE ALSO: BONDING AND CHILD ABUSE)

Freud's first reference to transference came early in *Studies on Hysteria*. He noted that some patients consistently tended to bring their intense personal feelings towards the analyst into treatment, transferring to the physician disturbing ideas that arose from their past and that recapitulated earlier ties with significant persons from their childhood, thereby making a false connection onto the analyst.

The case of Dora, in 1905, was a turning point in psychoanalytic technique by highlighting for Freud the necessity to interpret feelings transferred onto the analyst. Dora's hostile feelings resulted in her breaking with Freud (acting out), something she had not dared to do with her lover. Disturbed by her premature termination, Freud recognised the need to analyse resistance and transference manifestations. This was a therapeutic failure that instigated the change in his approach.

Freud's papers, dealing with the dynamics of transference and resistance, their positive and negative aspects, as well as with warnings to analysts about how to behave in order to manage their inherent difficulties, spanned the years 1912 to 1917.

Introduction

Transference describes the situation in therapy in which the client displaces onto the counsellor feelings, attitudes and attributes that derive from previous figures in the client's life. The client then responds to those feelings as though the counsellor were a significant figure in the client's past. Transference is a form of memory in which repetition in action replaces recollection of events.

What happens is that something is said that hooks into the past, with all the accompanying feelings, and that hook is then thrown onto, in this instance, the counsellor. Of course transference can happen in many situations, but because of the intensity of the counselling relationship, transference is more likely to happen. When it does happen, the person, the client, is unlikely to know why he feels the way he does.

Extreme forms of transference (while rare) can turn into a full-blown obsession if not dealt with, and can result in accidents, dangerous choices, nightmares, fantasies, stalking someone, psychotic reactions and sometimes violence.

Qualities that distinguish transference:

- Inappropriateness
- Intensity
- Ambivalence
- Inconsistency.

Transference may be positive, e.g. feelings of liking or love, or negative, e.g. feelings of dislike, insecurity, nervousness, anger and hostility.

The term is also used to describe the tendency to transfer onto any current relationship feelings and emotions that properly belong to a previous relationship.

Transference allows old conflicts to resurface and to be worked through. The counsellor is careful to avoid responding to the displaced feelings and behaviour.

Negative transference will interfere with therapy. It shows in direct attacks on the counsellor or in acting out negative feelings rather than exploring them and unwillingness to work through resistances.

Intense positive transference may make excessive emotional demands on the counsellor and prevent exploration of feelings.

Freud's position

- Transference is a resistance to true remembering.
- Transference produces a conflict between getting better and getting the better of the counsellor.
- Negative transference feelings are more likely to occur in male clients.
- Narcissistic people are not likely to experience transference.
- Transference means wanting to change the therapeutic relationship into something else.

In positive transference the counsellor is:

- All-important to the client
- A constant topic of conversation
- Idealised
- Constantly praised
- A significant person in dreams and fantasies.

Transference, if not recognised and worked through, may lead to a deterioration in the relationship, little progress and a plateau in therapy.

Jung's position

- Almost all cases requiring lengthy treatment involve transference.
- Transference, of some degree, is present in any intimate relationship.
- Transference is natural, it cannot be demanded.
- Accurate empathy reduces transference.

Carl Rogers' position

- Understanding the client is easier than handling the transference.
- Strong transference (in person-centred counselling) occurs in a relatively small number of cases, although some is present in all.
- When the displaced feelings become realistically placed, transference attitudes disappear because they have become meaningless.
- The more the counsellor interprets, controls, questions, directs, criticises, questions and evaluates, the more dependency is created and the stronger the degree of transference.
- In client-centred therapy, this involved and persistent dependency relationship does not tend to develop.
- Transference is likely to develop where the counsellor is perceived as 'the authority'.

For an argument from a person-centred perspective, see *A Counter-Theory of Transference*, by, John M. Shlien, Harvard University, on www.person-centered-counseling.com.

Signs of transference

- The client frequently asks you personal questions.
- The client calls you at home, knowing that calls should be made to your office.

- After only one or two treatments, the client is overly complimentary of you and your work.
- The client tries to bargain with you for a reduced rate.
- The client regularly requests that you change your schedule to accommodate his schedule.
- The client brings you gifts.
- The client repeatedly invites you to social engagements and feels rejected when you explain your policy of separating your work and social life.
- The client asks you to do 'a little bit more' at the end of most treatment sessions and expresses disapproval if you don't comply.
- The client asks you to help him solve personal problems.
- The client frequently asks you questions in areas that you've previously explained aren't within your scope of practice.
- This client often mentions that you remind him of someone.
- The client has difficulty maintaining a physical boundary and attempts to inappropriately hug or touch you at the end of each session.
- The client has difficulty leaving after the session and tries to engage you in conversation.
- The client gives you intimate details about his personal life.

Transference patterns

Idealising the counsellor
This is characterised by:

- Profuse complimenting
- Agreeing
- Bragging about the counsellor to others
- Imitating the counsellor's behaviour
- Wearing similar clothes
- Hungering for the counsellor's presence
- Dreams that involve the counsellor.

Attributing supernatural powers to the counsellor
This is characterised by regarding the counsellor as:

- All-knowing
- Godlike
- The 'expert'
- Able to grant requests for advice
- Someone to be afraid of.

Regarding the counsellor as provider
This is characterised by the client:

- Displaying out-of-place emotion and weeping
- Displaying helplessness and dependence

- Being indecisive
- Asking for advice
- Asking for touch, to be held
- Professing to have no strength without the counsellor
- Being effusively grateful.

Regarding the counsellor as one who thwarts
This is characterised by being:

- Self-protective
- Watchful
- Reticent
- Resentful
- Annoyed at lack of direction
- Hostile.

Regarding the counsellor as unimportant
This is characterised by:

- Always changing the subject
- Talking and never listening
- Being unwilling to explore
- Being dismissive of ideas.

Working with transference

Working with transference means focusing directly on the expressed feelings and making them explicit. Re-evaluation counselling provides a useful two-part way of working with transference.

- Getting the client to identify and verbalise just how the counsellor is like someone else towards whom feelings are directed. This is repeated until no more likenesses remain.
- Getting the client to identify and verbalise just how the counsellor is not like the other person, so that the counsellor is perceived as the person he really is.

Counter-transference

If we as counsellors react to these projected feelings, this is called 'counter-trans-ference'. For example, if the client is angry with the counsellor, as if the counsellor is the perceived parent, transference is taking place. If the counsellor then reacts by relating to the client in an authoritarian manner, in a parental way, that is counter-transference.

Counsellors, in contrast to psychoanalysts, do not deliberately foster transfer-ence. In psychoanalysis much use is made of transference and of working through it. But we should be aware that clients may be investing feelings in us that would be more appropriately directed towards another person.

These feelings are more likely to develop in psychoanalysis than in counselling, partly because of the depth at which analysts work, but also because of the greater frequency of contact. Psychoanalysts will interpret these feelings to the client: counsellors may be well advised not to. To acknowledge them may be sufficient. By so doing, we are opening the way for clients to discuss their feelings at that moment. This supports the view that counselling deals more with the present than with the past and more with the conscious than with the unconscious.

We are more likely to experience counter-transference when something being related by the client resonates within us, possibly because of some unresolved part of our life. We may detect this transference by wanting to take action on behalf of the client, even though that would be inappropriate.

Counsellors also have a history and unconscious desires. They then experience the same process as the client and sometimes they re-enact their own traumatic experiences through the client history. This process is also called counter-transference.

Counter-transference refers to unconscious needs, wishes or conflicts of the counsellor evoked by the client, which are brought into counselling and influence the counsellor's objective judgement and reason. This might happen because counselling is a two-way street.

It is very important for the therapist and the client to work through these reactions to overcome difficulties in order to optimise the work of professionals, taking into account the self-care of the psychotherapist.

Possible indicators of counter-transference

- Altering the length of sessions or forgetting sessions with certain clients
- Being overly strict with certain clients and lenient with others
- Being preoccupied with certain clients
- Developing fantasies about the client
- Dreaming about certain clients
- Emotional withdrawal from the client
- Experiencing unease during or following sessions
- Feeling drowsy without cause
- Needing the approval of certain clients
- Not being willing to explore certain issues
- Not wanting the client to terminate
- Promising unrealistic rescue
- Reappearance of immature character traits in the counsellor
- Using the client to impress someone
- Having sexual feelings towards the client.

Theoretical perspectives

- **The classical viewpoint**: The counsellor displaces on to the client feelings that would be more appropriately directed at another person, either in the present or, more probably, in the past. Counter-transference feelings thus arise from the counsellor's own needs and are not directed to meet the needs of the client. Counter-transference interferes with counsellor neutrality and therefore has an adverse effect on therapy.

- **An integrated viewpoint:** Counter-transference is not pathological but is inevitable and an integral part of the relationship. How the counsellor uses feelings and thoughts all help to increase understanding of the counsellor and client within the relationship.
- **A 'totalistic' viewpoint:** All the counsellor's thoughts, feelings and behaviours are indicators of counter-transference.
- **A realistic viewpoint:** The counselling relationship possesses both positive (constructive) and negative (destructive) elements. Research supports the point of view that the client influences the counsellor much more than the literature would suggest.

Over-identification or disidentification

Counter-transference may be either over-identification or disidentification and may be one of four forms:

1. **Overprotective** (over-identification): Characterised by Parent–Child interaction, collusion (allowing the client to blame others), cushioning the client from pain.
2. **Benign** (over-identification): Characterised by talk-talk, as friends, where distance is closed.
3. **Rejecting** (disidentification): Characterised by being cool/aloof with minimal involvement and increased distance, failure to intervene, allowing client to struggle and stumble – the counsellor fears demands and responsibility.
4. **Hostile** (disidentification): Arises from fear of contamination and is characterised by the counsellor being verbally abusive, curt or blunt.

Aids to managing the transference:

- Self-analysis
- Personal therapy
- Supervision
- Genuineness and self-disclosure
- Refer the client.

The counsellor and counter-transference

Working with clients who have deeply ingrained personality problems or those who display self-defeating behaviour may provoke similar behaviour in the counsellor.

Counter-transference behaviour may take the form of:

- Anger
- Losing concentration
- Wishing to control

- Feeling defensive
- Denying the truth.

Anticipation, understanding and adequate supervision allow counsellors to avoid becoming engulfed in counter-transference. Concern over counter-transference is especially warranted when dealing with people who are depressed or manic, and those contemplating suicide.

www.crisiscounseling.com/Articles/Transference.htm
www.asetts.org.au/transference.htm

Transference and counter-transference positions in treating the adult survivor of childhood sexual abuse

Davies and Frawley identify the following transference and counter-transference positions when dealing with survivors of childhood sexual abuse. They make an important point: 'It is in the counter-transferential reactions that the clinician [the authors are working from a psychoanalytical perspective] experiences powerful projective identification with aspects of the patient's self and object worlds.' Thus it would seem that in order to get in touch with the client's world, the therapist must be prepared to work through his own feelings towards the client.

1. **The unseeing, uninvolved parent and the unseen, neglected child:** Whenever a child is abused, someone's eyes are closed.
   - The client may try to protect the therapist.
   - The therapist might collude with the client and not recognise the false self the client is presenting; not recognise when the client is 'acting out', when the client engages in self-harm.
   - The client might accuse the therapist of being blind to what the child suffered as a child.
   - The therapist might react by not understanding (symbolically 'not seeing').
2. **The sadistic abuser and the helpless impotently enraged victim:** A child who is 'sexually traumatised' will identify with certain aspects of the abuser, the more so if the abuser is a loved and trusted figure in the child's life.
   - Identification – to be like the parent – is a normal process in the development of all children, so it is logical that this will happen in the abused child. At the same time, this identification is necessary for the child to express unconsciously all the rage and contempt the child feels for the abuser.
   - In therapy, this may take the form of the client expressing negative feelings towards the therapist by 'invading the therapist's personal and psychic boundaries.'
   - In some ways the client seeks to control the therapist as the abuser controlled the client, by extra demands for more and more time, ending up with the therapist feeling used, a good indication of counter-transference.
   - The therapist who starts to dread the upcoming session may very well be experiencing the feelings the client had about the abuser's 'session'.

- Clients who engage in self-destructive behaviour may be testing the therapist's ability to hold in there. The feelings such self-abuse generates in the therapist may be exactly the feelings aroused in the client by the abuser. The therapist who feels impotent may be feeling exactly how the abused child felt, and how the abused adult now feels.
- The Bible says (Prov. 13:12), 'Hope deferred makes the heart sick.' What does the abused child have to hope for? So the abused adult often engages in acts that destroy hope; good things don't last – threatening premature termination, self-mutilation after long periods of abstinence, developing psychosomatic disorders, sabotaging relationships or jobs.
- Again, if the therapist feels deflated and impotent, this is likely to be a reflection of the client's feelings – at the time and in the present.
- Clients may feel shame and guilt if they recognise that they have victimised the therapist, and in a sense this picks up on the feelings of identification of a loved abuser and the conflict of love/hate generated.
- It is crucial for the treatment for the therapist to experience and enact the role of the victim to the patient/abuser. Only in this way can the clinician truly appreciate at a visceral level the terror, paralysis, hopelessness and impotent rage lived by the patient when the patient was a child.
- Sexual encounters between patient and therapist. The most serious enactment of analysis abusiveness/patient victimisation occurs when the parties engage in an explicit sexual relationship, where the transference and counter-transference are actual and no longer symbolic.
- In the survivor's identification with the abuser, the adult survivor of childhood sexual abuse plays out a truly dazzling array of seductive, cajoling, pleading behaviours that, via projective identification, are capable of evoking within the clinician confusion and disorientation comparable to that of the child whose experience of reality was so seriously impinged upon. This desire to repeat the abuse is linked to the child's original love/hate identification with the abuser.
- Evidence may be in the form of intrusive sexual demands, by way of erotic phone calls, stalking or the therapist 'is confronted by the patient undressing'.
- When an actual sexual relationship comes between therapist and client 'any hope of further therapeutic work is destroyed'. While this is self-evident, the counter-transference pull should not be taken lightly.
- Only as client and therapist are able to work through the transference and counter-transference will the client be able to integrate into her self the split-off parts and the loss of childhood innocence, as well as her fantasised good parents.

3. **The idealised omnipotent rescuer and the entitled child:** The adult survivor of child abuse invariably seeks an omnipotent rescuer. (See the drama triangle in Transactional analysis.)
    - The therapist who acts out the rescuer may be re-enacting what the child was doing, in her attempts to rescue the abuser by 'sacrificing her own

needs and growth', albeit at tremendous emotional cost. That cost is likely to be shame, because she was not able to rescue the victimiser who continued the abuse.

- Rescuing seems more likely to occur during the integration stage, when the suffering is intense. Any attempt to rescue would interfere with the client's experiencing the grief and loss in full measure.
- While the client might wish that the therapist reverse all that happened in childhood, that cannot happen.
- The therapist cannot compensate for a lost childhood. However, taking a leaf out of the psychodrama book, allowing the client to engage in a re-enactment of what might have been might well assist in the development of something more healthy.

3. **The seducer and the seduced:** 'Pervading the psychoanalytically orientated treatment of adult survivors of childhood sexual abuse is an ambivalence of seduction. Through the work, therapist and patient seduce and are seduced by each other. If therapy is successful, however, there will be, over time, a shift in the nature and experience of mutual seductions.' (Davies and Frawley)

- From a young age the client was trained to seduce and to be seduced. That was the only way she could maintain the relationship that was important to her.
- The seduction in the therapeutic relationship is, of course, at an unconscious level. For example, she may dress provocatively, and act in a 'come hither' manner, yet at the same time denounce females who try to seduce.
- The therapist who feels sexually aroused may well feel guilty, because she is a client and he is an authority figure. It is important for the therapist to remain engaged and not to withdraw.
- Some clients hide their sexuality in the way they dress.
- Clients may seduce the therapist by only disclosing inducements, thus keeping the therapist dangling.
- The therapist, caught up in counter-transference, may hear his own flirtatious tone, or may tease the client to 'reveal more about herself in a way that is erotically tinged'. On the other hand, guilt and shame may cause the therapist to become over-rigid and controlling.
- It is important that the therapist conveys to the client that sexual feelings and thoughts are part and parcel of human experience. 'It is this combination of acceptance, availability, and boundaries that eventually allows the patient to differentiate between benign seductions, opening a pathway to integration of her own sexuality.' (Davies and Frawley)
- The fact that therapist and client do have sexual feelings towards each other, without acting them out, is positive and healthy, and demonstrates a positive therapeutic relationship.

Nothing is straightforward in this line of work. The therapist treads a thin line between victim and rescuer. The therapist will be tried almost to breaking point as the client dredges the depths of her pain and loss as she struggles to make sense of the abuse and the abuser, and the conflict of love and hate, and often projects this love and hate on to the therapist.

Further reading

Davies, J.M. and Frawley, M.G. (1994) *Treating the Adult Survivor of Childhood Sexual Abuse: a psychoanalytic perspective.* Basic Books, New York.
Jacobs, M. (1988) *Psychodynamic Counselling in Action.* Sage Publications, London.
Jung, C.G. (1946) *The Psychology of the Transference.* Routledge & Kegan Paul, London.
Klein, M. (1952) The origins of transference. In: *Envy and Gratitude and Other Works.* Hogarth Press, London.
Patterson, C.H. (1985) *The Therapeutic Relationship: foundations for an eclectic psychotherapy.* Brooks/Cole, Pacific Grove, CA.
Rogers, C.R. (1951, reprint 1981) *Client Centred Therapy.* Constable, London.
Watkins, C.E. (1989) Transference phenomena in the counselling situation, and Counter-transference: its impact on the counselling situation. In: *Key Issues for Counselling in Action* (ed. W. Dryden). Sage Publications, London. Originally published (1983) in *Personnel and Guidance Journal,* **62**: 206–210 and **63**: 356–359.
Transference, by Ben Benjamin, adapted by the author from *The Ethics of Touch: the hands-on practitioners guide to creating a professional safe and enduring practice*, by Ben Benjamin and Cherie Sohnen-Moe. BB@mtti.com
Conner, M.G. (2001) *Transference: are you a biological time machine?.* The Source, June, www.CrisisCounseling.Com. Conner@CrisisCounseling.Com or www.Education-Options.Com

TRANSPERSONAL PSYCHOLOGY (SEE ALSO EXISTENTIAL THERAPY AND PSYCHOSYNTHESIS)

Sometimes referred to as the 'fourth force', transpersonal psychology is the successor to humanistic psychology. It seeks to expand or extend consciousness beyond the usual boundaries of the ego personality and beyond the limitations of time and/or space. It is concerned with the ultimate questions about human existence.

The term 'transpersonal' means 'beyond the personal' and a common assumption in transpersonal psychology is that transpersonal experiences involve a higher mode of consciousness in which the ego self is transcended.

Transpersonal psychotherapy has traditional concerns but includes personal awareness and growth beyond the reaches of the traditionally accepted limits of health. What matters is the experience of being at one with humanity.

Transpersonal experiences are distinguished from 'religious' or 'spiritual' experiences in that they are not required to fit into some prearranged pattern of dogma.

A transpersonal view of the world goes beyond ego boundaries and sees all parts as being equal in their contribution to the whole and all humans as having the same needs, feelings and potentials.

Transpersonal counsellors have trained themselves to see the light within themselves and others. Transpersonal work is not about learning something new but unlearning distorted knowledge already acquired.

Transpersonal psychology is not without its critics. Transpersonal counselling is at the opposite end of the scale from behavioural counselling. Albert Ellis maintains that transpersonal counselling adds to people's burdens rather than relieving them. This criticism is applied to handling such florid conditions as phobias, obsessions and compulsions. This criticism is probably fair, for there is little doubt that these conditions fare better with a cognitive/behavioural approach.

Possibly one of the major criticisms is that transpersonal counselling does not have one core theory (see Eclectic counselling), but is a hotchpotch of what some consider 'way-out' theories and techniques.

One example must suffice – anger. The transpersonalist will encourage the client to get in touch with the feelings – experience the feelings – but this is often an end in itself. If the person does not end up knowing what to do with the feelings, if there is no change, then the question must be asked: 'What use has it been?' This is the argument of those who work from a cognitive/behavioural perspective.

On the other hand, for people who want to develop their creativity, imagination and intuition, rather than just to control dysfunctional behaviour, transpersonal work has much to offer. Many people are searching to know more of themselves; transpersonal psychology is one of the possible avenues, as are any of the other forms of therapy and counselling. Insight and self-awareness are not exclusive to one method.

A transpersonal counsellor would assist a client, not to come to terms with a dysfunctional society, for example, but to discover inner potential in order to transcend the difficulty. In addition to using techniques from all the traditional approaches, the transpersonal counsellor may use:

- Meditation
- Voluntary disidentification to provide a means of avoiding the effects of stress
- Learning to enter altered states
- Bodywork
- Breathing exercises
- Movement.

What transpersonal psychology is not:

- It is *not* a religion or an ideology, even though there are strong spiritual and religious influences and practices, such as meditation and devotion.
- It is *not* the New Age. It seeks to distance itself from certain elements of the so-called counter-culture. It does not embrace crystals, UFOs, alien abduction, chakras, auras, fairies, psychism, aromatherapy, levitation or fire-walking.
- It is *not* metaphysics, i.e. a belief in a spiritual, divine or transcendent realm. This does not exclude the personal belief in God, but such a belief is not at the core of transpersonal psychology. Such beliefs are purely personal.
- It is *not* anti-rationalist. It does not dismiss or devalue rational and intellectual analysis. However, it acknowledges the reality and importance of non-

rational modes of knowing, such as intuition, integrative awareness and contemplation.

Core concepts in transpersonal psychology

- **Self**: I am not defined by others; neither do I define myself; I am defined by the other.
- **Motivation**: My motivation is not to satisfy need nor to exercise choice; it is to surrender.
- **Personal goal**: My personal goal is not adjustment nor is it self-actualisation; it is union.
- **Social goal**: My social goal is not socialisation nor is it liberation; it is salvation.
- **Process**: The process I go through is not healing, ego-building or ego-enhancement; it is enlightenment and ego-reduction.
- **Role of helper**: The role of my helper is not that of analyst or facilitator; it is guide.
- **Focus**: The focus of my attention is not towards the individual nor towards the group; it is towards a supportive community.

Some transpersonal counselling beliefs

- To do therapy is to receive therapy.
- We cannot help anyone; we can only help ourselves.
- Therapy is a day-by-day process.
- We demonstrate what we believe.
- What a counsellor is saying is only a small part of the therapeutic effort.
- Everyone has the potential to be someone else's counsellor, client or both.
- Therapy focuses on internal rather than on external resources.
- Focus is on self-energy, not allowing others to invalidate us.
- Thoughts determine outcome.
- We have to find our own unique pathway, then tread it.
- We need to learn to trust our internal voices.

Criticisms of transpersonal psychology

Ellis criticises transpersonal counselling methods because they ignore effective, planned behavioural methods, relying instead on what he calls 'temporary distractions'. Ellis maintains that transpersonal counselling is not effective against many of the more florid disturbances of obsessions, phobias and compulsions, working rather with methods such as yoga, which often create their own rituals.

Thus there are many differences between transpersonal and behavioural psychology and between the two approaches to counselling. Yet to ignore one without exploring it might be closing one's mind to something that will help a particular client. While working exclusively with a transpersonal approach might do what Ellis says, perhaps it is appropriate for other cases where behavioural methods are not.

itp.edu/about/tp.html

Further reading

Bolen, J.S. (1984) *Goddesses in Everywoman*. Harper & Row, London.

Bolen, J.S. (1989) *Gods in Everyman*. Harper & Row, London.

Ellis, A. (1989) *Why Some Therapies Don't Work*. Prometheus Books, New York.

Gordon-Brown, I. and Somers, B. (1988) Transpersonal psychotherapy. In: *Innovative Therapy in Britain* (eds J. Rowan and W. Dryden).Open University Press, Milton Keynes.

Grof, S. (1992) *The Holotropic Mind*. Harper, San Francisco.

Hendricks, G. and Weinhold, B. (1982) *Transpersonal Approaches to Counselling and Psychotherapy*. Love Publishing, Denver, CO.

Maslow, A.H. (1964) *Toward a Psychology of Being*. Van Nostrand, Princeton, NJ.

Maslow, A.H. (1971) *The Farther Reaches of Human Nature*. Viking Press, New York.

Rowan, J. (1983) *The Reality Game*. Routledge & Kegan Paul, London.

Tart, C. (1969) *Altered States of Consciousness*. John Wiley, New York.

Tart, C. (1983) *Transpersonal Psychologies*. Psychological Processes, California.

Walsh, R. and Vaughan, F. (1980) *Beyond Ego: transpersonal dimensions in psychology*. J.P. Tarcher, Los Angeles, CA.

Daniels, M. *An Introduction to Transpersonal Psychology*. www.transpersonalpsychology.co.uk

V

VALUES

Over the course of our lives, we develop assumptions and beliefs about ourselves, other people and the world around us. Values are what we consider good or beneficial to our well-being. Values are learned beliefs, largely culturally determined and show in our attitudes. Values are part of our personality, direct how we behave and think, and therefore influence how we feel. Values are acquired through experience; needs, on the other hand, are innate.

Egan says this:

Assumptions and beliefs, interacting with values, generate norms – the 'do's and don'ts' we carry around inside ourselves. These norms drive patterns of behaviour, and these patterns of behaviour constitute, as it were, the bottom line of personal or individual culture – 'the way I live my life'.

Six basic value systems

- **Political**: The pursuit of power, characterised by:
  - Influence
  - Personal prestige
  - Control
  - Authority
  - Strength
  - Money as evidence of success
  - Social status and recognition
- **Aesthetic**: The pursuit of beauty, symmetry and harmony, characterised by:
  - Artistic expression
  - Style and charm rather than practicality
  - The dignity of people
  - Self-sufficiency and individuality
  - Taste, appearance and elegance
  - Money as a means to an end
  - Perhaps regarded as 'snobs', with expensive tastes
- **Social**: The pursuit of humanitarianism, characterised by:
  - Love of fellow beings
  - Being kind, sympathetic, warm, giving
  - Charity, unselfishness
  - Belief in freedom
  - Readiness to offer aid and assistance
  - Consequences of actions carefully considered
  - Frightened off by cold, unsympathetic people
  - Social does not mean 'outgoing'

- **Theoretical**: The pursuit of truth and knowledge, characterised by:
  - Thinking, learning, probing, analysing, explaining
  - Being critical, logical, empirical
  - Science, research, information, theory
  - Organisation of material
  - Detachment, lack of emotion
  - Problem-solving, development of theories, formation of questions
  - Knowledge is power
  - Often a low tolerance of people who do not place the same value on knowledge
- **Economic**: The pursuit of what is practical and useful, characterised by:
  - Belief that knowledge is useful only if it can immediately be applied to produce something useful
  - Efficiency and effectiveness measured by profit and prosperity
  - Extreme frugality, giving the impression of being stingy or selfish
  - A feeling that we must conserve resources and use them wisely
  - May judge the success of others by their wealth
- **Religious**: The pursuit of faith, characterised by:
  - Renunciation of experience and logic
  - Seeking the mystic, unity with nature
  - Life is a divine creation
  - Life is ordained and planned
  - Self-denial, prayer, meditation.

Values clarification

In counselling, the following questions are useful to help clients understand full values:

- How freely was it chosen?
- What alternatives were there?
- What effects would any alternatives have?
- How has the value been acted upon?
- Is the value acted upon repeatedly?
- How does the value help reach potential?
- Has the value been publicly affirmed?
- A full value must satisfy all seven criteria.

Some work values

Work values are the degree of worth a person attributes to particular aspects of work. Dimensions of work include the opportunities offered by the work for a person to satisfy the following needs:

- To be creative
- To earn money
- To be independent
- To enjoy prestige and status

- To serve others
- To do academic work
- To have a stable and secure job
- To enjoy one's colleagues
- To have good working conditions.

The counsellor's values are an important part of his frame of reference, just as the clients' values are to them. Values are closely linked to judgementalism and probably our values are one of the major areas that will bring us into conflict with clients. Just as we have to suspend our judgements if counselling is to be effective, so must we learn that our values are right for us but we have no right to try to impose them on other people, let alone on clients.

Values are incredibly difficult to work with. As counsellors we need to have our own value system firmly established and yet not let our values get in the way. This requires something of a balancing act. If there is one thing that will get in the way of understanding the client, of really being in empathy, it is our values. At the same time, it is part of our professional duty to explore our values. Many of us take on our parents' (and others') values lock, stock and barrel, then in counselling training comes the painful process of re-evaluating our values and perhaps getting rid of some of them. That process of evaluating and getting rid of outworn values should never stop and every new client presents the opportunity to take another look at what we value.

Moira Walker raises an interesting point: If there is value clash, what does the counsellor do? She says, 'My contract with [him] did not have an exclusion clause allowing me to withdraw if I found it I did not like his views'. She goes on to say that it is her professional duty to 'work on and with my own counter-transference'. Thus another factor has been introduced – counter-transference. Every clash of views, values or ideology gives us a wonderful opportunity to get to know more of ourselves.

Walker goes on to say that many people in the caring professions do not have the choice of whom they work with; their clients (or patients) are chosen for them, so they cannot opt out of a relationship simply because their values clash.

Clients can feel trapped between two opposing sets of values. For example, Sandra is experiencing a value-clash with her mother because Sandra is living with her boyfriend and her mother won't let them sleep together when they visit the parental home. A useful way of working with Sandra would be to get her to itemise the various values and their consequences in two columns – hers and her mother's. This might then lead to a discussion of how compromises could be reached. However, compromise can only be arrived at if both sides are willing to seek a middle path.

Further reading

Egan, G. (2002) *The Skilled Helper: a problem-management and opportunity-development approach to helping*, 7th edn. Brooks/Cole, Pacific Grove, CA.

Oliver, J.E. (1985) The personal value statement: an experiential learning instrument. In: *1985 Annual: Developing Human Resources*. University Associates, San Diego, CA.

Rao, T.V. (1991) Managerial work-values scale. In: *1991 Annual: Developing Human Resources*. University Associates, San Diego, CA.

Walker, M. (1993) When values clash. In: *Questions and Answers on Counselling in Action* (ed. W. Dryden). Sage Publications, London.

Working through

Working through is a psychoanalytic term to describe the period that elapses between one part of counselling and another. It may be between interpretation and its acceptance and integration or the transference, in which the client moves from resistance to insight and permanent change.

The concept, although introduced by Freud and central to psychoanalysis, is common to most of the psychodynamic therapies. The term is also used to describe the gradual acceptance of loss in the process of grief and mourning.

Working through, according to psychoanalytic theory, comes as a result of the client confronting the particular mental event that is causing the difficulty, clarifying the various components of the particular event and interpreting the conflict. Constant and repetitive exploration is made until unconscious material is fully integrated into the conscious. For example, interpreting someone once is not enough; the interpretation has to be repeated, albeit focusing on different aspects as the client achieves insight. Working through means giving the client time for the interpretation to take root, then to deal with the resistance invoked by the interpretation.

Working through is, thus, an ongoing process or stage of analysis, rather than a technique. It is the culmination of three distinct techniques: confrontation, clarification and interpretation:

- **Confrontation** points out or highlights the particular mental event that the client must face.
- **Clarification** brings into focus an event that is confusing or unclear. It does this by separating the main issue from its surrounding issues.
- **Interpretation** makes the client aware of the psychic content and conflict, which the client has been warding off.

The process of working through will repeat the three techniques until the material is integrated into the client's ego.

Working through thus helps the patient to gain some measure of control over inner conflicts and to resolve them or minimise their power.

Insight alone does not automatically lead to behavioural change. Sometimes insight comes in a flash, but more often it develops gradually over time.

Wounded healer

This is a Jungian term used to describe the potential healing power of the therapist's own suffering, pain and loss. Therapist and client are both part healer and part sufferer, the one for the other.

It would seem that most healers have experienced great pain and suffering and are here to help others release their pain and create balance. Counsellors draw on their own experience of being wounded in order to know the clients in an emotional sense. Counsellors who do not acknowledge their own woundedness erect barriers between themselves and their clients instead of being channels. When the counsellor's vulnerability is acknowledged, the client becomes an active partner in the process and not just a passive recipient of help. The counsellor is not then perceived as the perfect, healthy expert and the client as sick and unskilled.

The concept of the wounded healer finds an echo in Hephaestus (Vulcan), the mythical lame son of Zeus and Hera, queen of Olympus. Ridiculed in the hostile world of Olympus because of his club foot and rolling gait, he found refuge in his work. As a craftsman at the forge fire, he transformed raw material into beautiful objects.

Hephaestus, the only imperfect major deity, is the archetype of the wounded healer whose creativity cannot be separated from his emotional wounds. The motivation to heal comes from our own sense of being wounded.

Hephaestus could never (in his eyes) be beautiful, so he created beauty. His body didn't work perfectly, but what he created was perfect.

A second view is that the concept originates with the Greek myth of Chiron who was physically wounded, and by way of overcoming the pain of his own wounds Chiron became the compassionate teacher of healing.

People who come for pastoral counselling may have only a hazy awareness of the suffering that comes from being stuck in their history. Counselling aims to liberate the clients' inner resources so they can handle the suffering more positively and help to restore their identity. For the pastoral counsellor, change involves the work of the Spirit.

The Spirit is seen as an energy or power, whose subject is God or Christ. The counsellor cannot force change; change is achieved through the mediating influence of the Spirit. The counselling relationship is undertaken in the hope, and with the expectation, that in the search for new directions the client will be accompanied by the Spirit. Jesus is the perfect example of the wounded healer whose work of healing cannot be separated from his/her own emotional wounds. Our motivation to heal comes from our own sense of being wounded and having travelled some way along the road towards healing.

The 'wounded healer' suggests a cost to the counsellor. Counsellors who are involved in this gradual transformation process of another require a level of personal involvement and interpersonal engagement that taps the deepest sufferings of the soul at four different but related levels:

- **Anxiety**: No counsellor has pre-knowledge of a client's journey and cannot plan the way.
- **Vulnerability**: Certain themes of the client's life story may awaken unfinished business within the counsellor, which require reworking. The experience of the client may be just the catalyst that the counsellor needs, at that moment, to be able to move one step forward towards his own healing.

- **Balance:** As client and counsellor move in the transitional space between their worlds, a balance between objectivity and subjectivity is essential. This is the space where the Spirit works and transformation begins to take place. It is there that one's own vulnerabilities become open to challenge and change, in the light of the Spirit's work with the client.
- **Transference:** This is the unconscious process whereby the counsellor becomes the focus of the client's unresolved feelings towards significant others.

The client who works through his woundedness with the help of the wounded therapist can then become the wounded healer for someone else. Generally the counsellor is aware of significant movement in the client when the client starts to relate to the suffering of other people.

Further reading

Jung, C.G. (1961, reprinted 1989) *Memories, Dreams, Reflections.* Vintage Books, London.
www.jelder.com/quotations/woundedhealer.html
www.healingwaterssacredsprings.com

COUNSELLOR TRAINING

There are too many organisations offering counsellor training to include in this book. The following information might help those who wish to embark on such a course.

Most colleges and universities offer counsellor training from Certificate to Master's degrees. The Universities Handbook will contain information on which courses are available.

In addition, counselling and related courses are offered by:

- The National Extension College, Open Learning Centre International, 24 King Street, Carmarthen SA31 1BS. Tel: **Freephone 0800 393 743**. Email: info@olci.info, or www.olcinternational.com or www.nec.ac.uk.
- The Open University, Walton Hall, Milton Keynes MK7 6AA. Tel: 01908 274066. www.open.ac.uk You can find the Area office in your telephone directory.
- The Institute of Counselling, Clinical and Pastoral Counselling, 6 Dixon Street, Glasgow G1 4AX. Tel: 0141 204 2230. In addition to many distance learning counselling skills courses, the Institute offers Psychology for Counsellors, and an Introduction to Stress Management course, which includes a relaxation instruction tape.
- The British Association for Counselling and Psychotherapy, 1 Regent Place, Rugby, Warwickshire CV2 2PJ. Tel: 01788 5788328, produces a *Training in Counselling and Psychotherapy Directory*. This would probably be the best one-book resource. You may find it in your local library. You can find out more details on the BACP website: www.counselling.co.uk. The following information is taken from the Association's website: 'The Directory has 400 pages of information to help you make a decision about Counselling and Psychotherapy training, with useful tips on funding, open learning and setting samples. Courses listed on a regional basis of Institutions with brief notes on course duration and entry requirements. BACP Code of Ethics & Practice for Trainers in Counselling & Counselling Skills. Another excellent nationally recognised reference book is the *Training World of Counsellors & Psychotherapists*.'
- The Westminster Pastoral Foundation, 23 Kensington Square, London W8 5HN. Tel: 0207 937 6956, is a well-established and respected training organisation.
- RELATE Marriage Guidance National Headquarters, Herbert Gray College, Little Church Street, Rugby, Warwickshire CV21 3AP. Tel: 01788 573241.
- Centre for Stress Management, 156 Westcombe Hill, London SE3 7DH. Tel: 0208 293 4114.
- CRUSE (Bereavement Care) Cruse House, 126 Sheen Road, Richmond, Surrey TW9 1UR. Tel: 0208 332 7227.

USEFUL ORGANISATIONS

The following resources are provided for information purposes and do not necessarily constitute a recommendation. For information on special-rate telephone numbers (08–) or premium-rate numbers (09–), see your BT phone book.

ABUSE, RAPE AND SELF-HARM/SELF-INJURY SERVICES

Association of Child Abuse Lawyers (ACAL), PO Box 466, Chorleywood, Rickmansworth, Hertfordshire WD3 5LG.
Tel: (01923) 286888 (10 a.m.–1 p.m. and 2 p.m.–4 p.m. Tuesdays and Thursdays only).
Email: info@childabuselawyers.com
Website: http://www.childabuselawyers.com
 Description: Practical support for survivors and professionals working in the field of abuse. Can recommend a solicitor with some understanding of childhood abuse cases, and site contains some useful links and information.

Bristol Crisis Service for Women, PO Box 654, Bristol BS99 1XH.
National Helpline (for women): 0117 925 1119. Contact times: Friday and Saturday nights 9 p.m.–12.30 a.m. Sunday evenings 6 p.m.–9 p.m.
Email: bcsw@btconnect.com
Website: www.users.zetnet.co.uk/BCSW
 Description: A national voluntary organisation that supports women in emotional distress. Particularly helps women who harm themselves (often called self-injury). Provides talks and training courses to professionals, runs and supports self-help groups, and produces information and publications about self-injury.

ChildLine UK
Tel: 0800 1111.
Website: www.childline.org.uk
 Description: UK's free, 24-hour helpline for children and young people in trouble or danger. The lines can be busy so please keep trying.

Directory and Book Services (DABS), 4 New Hill, Conisbrough, Doncaster, DN12 3HA.
Tel/fax: 01709 860023.
Email: books@dabsbooks.co.uk
Website: http://www.dabsbooks.co.uk
 Description: Books and information for adults who were abused as children, for counsellors and workers, and for anyone affected by child abuse.

Kidscape, 2 Grosvenor Gardens, London SW1W 0DH.
Tel: 0207 730 3300. Fax: 0207 730 7081. Helpline: 08451 205 204.
Website: http://www.kidscape.org.uk
Description: Registered charity committed to keeping children safe from harm or abuse. Kidscape is the only national children's charity that focuses upon preventative policies – tactics to use before any abuse takes place. Kidscape has practical, easy to use material for children, parents, teachers, social workers, police and community workers.

Mothers of Sexually Abused Children (MOSAC), 141 Greenwich High Road, London SE10 8JA.
Helpline: 0800 980 1958.
Website: http://www.mosac.org.uk
Description: A voluntary organisation supporting all non-abusing parents and carers whose children have been sexually abused, to provide support, advice, information and counselling following the discovery of sexual abuse.

NSPCC (National Society for the Prevention of Cruelty to Children), Weston House, 42 Curtain Road, London EC2A 3NH.
Tel: 0207 825 2500. Fax: 0207 825 2525. Helpline: 0808 800 5000.
Website: www.nspcc.org.uk
Description: The UK's leading charity specialising in child protection and the prevention of cruelty to children.

SAFELINE, King Tom House, 39b High Street, Warwick CV34 4AX.
Tel: 0808 800 5005.
Email: safeline@bigfoot.com
Website: http://www.safelinewarwick.co.uk
Description: A voluntary association based in the UK established by people who were sexually abused as children. Offers counselling, support, a free information pack, newsletter, lending library, volunteer training and workshops. Website includes a comprehensive list of links to related sites.

Survivors UK, PO Box 2470, London SW9 6WQ.
Helpline: 0845 1221201 Tuesday and Thursday 7 p.m.–10 p.m.
Email: info@survivorsuk.org.uk
Website: http://www.survivorsuk.co.uk/
Description: Help and support for men who have been sexually abused or raped. Adult male survivors of sexual abuse and rape. London based. Site contains useful information, links to other sites and a list of accredited counsellors.

The Basement Project, PO Box 5, Abergavenny, South Wales NP7 5XW.
Tel: 01873 856524.
Website: http://freespace.virgin.net/basement.project/default.htm
Description: A community resource providing support groups and helpful literature for individuals. Their work has a particular focus on abuse and self-

harm. They offer an educational programme for workers, which includes training, supervision, consultation, research and publications.

Internet resources

National Association for People Abused in Childhood (NAPAC)
Contains useful information for survivors.
Tel: 0800 085 3330 (Information Line).
http://www.napac.org.uk

Self-injury and related issues (SIARI) (Jan Sutton's site)
Information and support for self-injurers and their supporters. Includes creative works of self-injurers, message board for self-injurers, moderated online support group for helpers, bookstore, articles and extensive list of resources on self-injury and related issues (self-harm, abuse, eating disorders, PTSD, bipolar disorders, dissociative disorders, counselling and therapy).
http://www.siari.co.uk

Survivors of Incest Anonymous (World Service Office)
http://www.siawso.org

Young people and self harm resource
http://www.ncb.org.uk/selfharm

ADDICTION SERVICES

Addiction Recovery Foundation, 122A Wilton Road, London SW1V 1JZ.
Tel: 0207 233 5333.
Email: enquiries@addictiontoday.co.uk
Website: http://www.addictiontoday.co.uk
Description: Publishes *Addiction Today*, the most influential information in the UK on addiction recovery. Articles include therapeutic techniques, lists of self-help groups and treatment centres, details of seminars and workshops for professionals and people in recovery, research, news, complementary medicines, relevant legislation.

Al-Anon Family Groups UK and Eire, 61 Great Dover Street, London SE1 4YF.
Tel: 0207 403 0888. Fax: 0207 378 9910.
Website: http://www.al-anonuk.org.uk/
Description: Provides understanding, strength and hope to anyone whose life is, or has been, affected by someone else's drinking.

Alcohol Concern, Waterbridge House, 32–36 Loman Street, London SE1 0EE.
Tel: 0207 928 7377.
E-mail: contact@alcoholconcern.org.uk
Website: http://www.alcoholconcern.org.uk/
Description: National agency on alcohol misuse. Works to reduce the incidence and costs of alcohol-related harm, and to increase the range and quality of services available to people with alcohol-related problems.

Alcoholics Anonymous, PO Box 1, Stonebow House, Stonebow, York YO1 7NJ. Tel: 01904 644026.
Website: http://www.alcoholics-anonymous.org.uk
Description: Offers advice and support to alcoholics. In the UK and Ireland, look for 'Alcoholics Anonymous' in any telephone directory.

Drinkline (National Alcohol Helpline). Tel: 0345 320202 (11 a.m.–11 p.m.).

European Association for the Treatment of Addiction (EATA), Waterbridge House, 32–36 Loman Street, London SE1 0EE. Tel: 0207 922 8753.
Email: secretariat@eata.org.uk
Website: http: www.eata.org.uk
Description: A charity working to help ensure people with substance dependencies get the treatment they need.

Gamblers Anonymous (UK), PO Box 88, London SW10 0EU. Tel: 0870 050 88 80.
Website: http://www.gamblersanonymous.org.uk/
Description: A fellowship of men and women who have joined together to do something about their own gambling problem and to help other compulsive gamblers do the same. Includes a list of helpline numbers.

Narcotics Anonymous (UK), 202 City Road, London EC1V 2PH. Helpline UK: 0207 730 0009.
Email: helpline@ukna.org
Website: http://www.ukna.org
Description: A fellowship of men and women for whom drugs had become a major problem. They meet regularly to help each other stay clean. The only requirement for membership is the desire to stop. Details of meetings throughout the UK.

National Treatment Agency for Substance Misuse, 5th Floor, Hannibal House, Elephant and Castle, London SE1 6TE. Tel: 0207 972 2214.
Email: nta.enquiries@nta-nhs.org.uk
Website: http://www.nta.nhs.uk/
Description: The NTA is a special health authority established in 2001, to increase the availability, capacity and effectiveness of treatment for drug misuse in England.

Talk to FRANK (National Drugs Helpline) Helpline: 0800 77 66 00
Email frank@talktofrank.com.
Website: www.talktofrank.com
Description: Free confidential drugs information and advice 24 hours a day.

Internet resources

12 Step Cyber Café
http://www.12steps.org

Alcoholism and Addiction Prevention, Treatment and Recovery Resources
http://www.alchemyproject.net/Links/twelve_step.htm

BBC addictions message board
http://www.bbc.co.uk/cgi-perl/h2/h2.cgi?state=view&board=health.10addictions

Drugs.gov.uk (cross-government website to support the National Drugs Strategy
and the work of Drug Action Teams)
http://drugs.gov.uk/

DrugScope
The UK's leading independent centre of expertise on drugs. Its aim is to inform
policy development and reduce drug-related risk.
http://www.drugscope.org.uk/

Sex Addicts Anonymous: details of meetings in the UK. http://www.sexaa.org/
meetings.htm

The Way – Confronting Addiction
Links to organisations offering help with addictions.
http://www.theway.uk.com/links.htm

ADOPTION SERVICES

British Agencies for Adoption and Fostering (BAAF), Skyline House, 200 Union
Street, London SE1 0LX.
Tel: 0207 593 2000
Email: mail@baaf.org.uk
Website: http://www.baaf.org.uk
   Description: BAAF, based in London and with offices in Wales, Scotland and
England, is the leading membership organisation for agencies and individuals
concerned with adoption, fostering and work with children and families. It is also
a major publisher, training provider and family finder.

Office of National Statistics: Adopted Children Register, Adoptions Section,
General Register Office, Smedley Hydro, Trafalgar Road, Southport PR8 2HH.
Tel: 0151 471 4830.
Email: adoptions@ons.gov.uk
Website: http://www.gro.gov.uk/gro/content/adoptions/
   Description: The Adopted Children Register is kept by the Registrar General,
and contains a record of every person who has been adopted through a court in
England or Wales. Website gives information on applying for adoption certifi-
cates, receiving information on original birth details, and making contact with
adopted people and their relatives.

COUNSELLING AND PSYCHOTHERAPY SERVICES

Association for Family Therapy and Systemic Practice in the UK,
7 Executive Suite, St James Court, Wilderspool Causeway, Warrington, Cheshire
WA4 6PS.

Tel: 01925 444414.
Email: s.kennedy@aft.org.uk
Website: http://www.aft.org.uk/
Description: Aims to develop the profession and to establish standards for training and registration through the UK Council for Psychotherapy.

British Association for Behavioural and Cognitive Psychotherapies (BABCP), PO Box 9, Accrington BB5 2GD.
Tel: 01254 875277. Fax: 01254 239114.
Email: babcp@babcp.com
Website: http://www.babcp.org.uk/
Description: A multi-disciplinary interest group for people involved in the practice and theory of behavioural and cognitive psychotherapy. Produces a range of publications including pamphlets on anxiety, depression, schizophrenia, PTSD, general health, OCD, agoraphobia, learning disability, insomnia, chronic fatigue syndrome, eating disorders, understanding CBT (cognitive behavioural therapy), sexual dysfunction, chronic pain, conduct disorder and bipolar disorders.

British Association for Counselling and Psychotherapy, BACP House, 35–37 Albert Street, Rugby, Warwickshire CV21 2SG.
Tel: 0870 443 5252. Fax: 0870 443 5161.
Email: bacp@bacp.co.uk
Website: http://www.bacp.co.uk
Description: The association's aims are to promote understanding and awareness of counselling throughout society, increase the availability of trained and supervised counsellors, and maintain and raise standards of training and practice. Produces a range of publications and a quarterly counselling journal. The United Kingdom Register of Counsellors (UKRC) is part of the British Association for Counselling and Psychotherapy.

British Association of Psychotherapists (BAP), 37 Mapesbury Road, London NW2 4HJ.
Tel: 0208 452 9823. Fax: 0208 452 0310.
Email: mail@bap-psychotherapy.org
Website: http://www.bap-psychotherapy.org
Description: Specialises in individual psychoanalytic psychotherapy for adults, adolescents and children and is one of the foremost psychoanalytic psychotherapy training organisations in the UK.

British Association of Sexual and Relationship Therapists (BASRT), PO Box 13686, London SW20 9ZH.
Tel: 0208 543 2707.
Email: info@basrt.org.uk
Website: http://www.basrt.org.uk/
Description: Promotes the education and training of clinicians and therapists working in the fields of sexual and couple relationships, sexual dysfunction and sexual health, and raises public awareness of sexual and relationship therapy.

British Psychological Society (BPS), St Andrews House, 48 Princess Road East, Leicester LE1 7DR.
Tel: 0116 254 9568. Fax: 0116 247 0787.
Email: enquiry@bps.org.uk
Website: http://www.bps.org.uk
Description: Aims: to encourage the development of psychology as a scientific discipline and an applied profession, to raise standards of training and practice in the application of psychology, and to raise public awareness of psychology and increase the influence of psychological practice in society.

Institute of Family Therapy, 24–32 Stephenson Way, London NW1 2HX.
Tel: 0207 391 9150. Fax: 0207 391 9169.
Email: clinical@instituteoffamilytherapy.org.uk (clinical department)
Email: training@instituteoffamilytherapy.org.uk (training department)
Website: http://www.instituteoffamilytherapy.org.uk
Description: Provides a range of services for families, couples and other relationship groups, family mediation service, training courses, conferences and workshops.

Relate: The relationship people, Central Office, Herbert Gray College, Little Church Street, Rugby, Warwickshire CV21 3AP.
Tel: 01788 563853 Central Office Personnel Department. Helpline: 0845 130 4010 (calls are charged at local rates).
Email: enquiries@relate.org.uk
Website: http://www.relate.org.uk.
Description: UK's largest and most experienced relationship counselling organisation. Whether you are having problems getting on with your partner, your kids, your siblings or even your boss – Relate can help. Local branches can be found by entering a postcode on the website.

The Samaritans, General Office, The Upper Mill, Kingston Road, Ewell, Surrey KT17 2AF.
Tel: 0208 394 8300 (enquiries only). National numbers: UK 0845 790 90 90. Republic of Ireland: 1850 60 90 90.
Email: admin@samaritans.org
Website: www.samaritans.org.uk
Description: Provides confidential and emotional support to any person who is suicidal or despairing (24-hour-a-day service – all year round). For details of your nearest branch consult website or your local telephone directory.

United Kingdom Council for Psychotherapy, 167–169 Great Portland Street, London W1W 5PF.
Tel: 0207 436 3002. Fax: 0207 436 3013.
Email: ukcp@psychotherapy.org.uk
Website: www.psychotherapy.org.uk
Description: Promotes and maintains the profession of psychotherapy and high standards in the practice of psychotherapy for the benefit of the public throughout the UK.

Westminster Pastoral Foundation Counselling and Psychotherapy, 23 Kensington Square, London W8 5HN.
Counselling and Psychotherapy Services
Appointments: 0207 361 4803/04 (9 a.m. – 4.30 p.m.).
Email: counselling@wpf.org.uk
Training Department
Tel: 0207 631 4846. Fax: 0207 631 4819.
Email: training@wpf.org.uk
Website: http://www.wpf.org.uk/
Description: Exists to extend access to high-quality, professional counselling and psychotherapy and to strive for excellence in the training of counsellors and psychotherapists. Provides a list of UK affiliate training centres.

DISTANCE LEARNING COURSES IN COUNSELLING SKILLS AND RELATED SUBJECTS

National Extension College, The Michael Young Centre, Purbeck Road, Cambridge CB2 2HN.
Tel: 01223 400 200. Fax: 01223 400 399.
Email: info@nec.ac.uk
Website: http://www.nec.ac.uk/

The Open University, Customer Contact Centre, PO Box 724, Milton Keynes MK7 6ZS.
Tel: 01908 653231. Fax: 01908 655072.
Email: general-enquiries@open.ac.uk
Website: http://www.open.ac.uk

The Institute of Counselling, Clinical and Pastoral Counselling, 6 Dixon Street, Glasgow G1 4AX.
Tel: 0141 204 2230.
Email: IOfCounsel@aol.com
Website: http://www.collegeofcounselling.com
Description: The College of Counselling is the accredited distance learning college of the Institute of Counselling. The College offers a wide range of tutor supported correspondence courses, videos, audio cassettes and books; specialising in counselling skills training.

DIVORCE, MEDIATION AND LONE PARENT SERVICES

Families Need Fathers, 134 Curtain Road, London EC2A 3AR.
Tel: 0207 613 5060. Helpline: 0870 760 7496 (7 p.m.–10 p.m.).
Email: fnf@fnf.org.uk
Website: http://www.fnf.org.uk
Description: Provides information and support to parents, including unmarried parents, of either sex. FNF is chiefly concerned with the problems of maintaining a child's relationship with both parents during and after family breakdown.

Gingerbread, 7 Sovereign Close, Sovereign Court, London E1W 3HW.
Tel: 0207 488 9300. Fax: 0207 488 9333. Advice Line and Membership: 0800 018 4318.
E-mail: office@gingerbread.org.uk
Website: http://www.gingerbread.org.uk
Description: Provides information about support for lone parent families.

National Council for One Parent Families, 255 Kentish Town Road, London NW5 2LX.
Tel: 0207 428 5400. Fax: 0207 482 4851. Helpline: 0800 018 5026.
Email: info@oneparentfamilies.org.uk
Website: http://www.oneparentfamilies.org.uk
Description: Promotes the welfare of lone parents and their children.

National Family Mediation (NFM), Alexander House, Telephone Avenue, Bristol BS1 4BS.
Tel: 0117 904 2825. Fax: 0117 904 3331.
Email: general@nfm.org.uk
Website: http://www.nfm.u-net.com
Description: NFM is a network of over 60 local not-for-profit Family Mediation Services in England and Wales offering help to couples, married or unmarried, who are in the process of separation and divorce. They are committed to providing mediation to everyone who needs it in all communities.

EATING DISORDER SERVICES

Eating Disorders Association (EDA), 103 Prince of Wales Road, Norwich NR1 1DW.
Tel: Admin 0870 770 3256. Adult Helpline: 0845 634 1414. Over 18 years of age. Open 8:30 a.m.–8:30 p.m. Monday to Friday, and 1 p.m.–4.30 p.m. Saturday.
Helpline e-mail service helpmail@edauk.com
Youthline: 0845 634 7650. Up to and including 18 years of age. Open 4 p.m.–6.30 p.m. Monday to Friday, and 1 p.m.–4.30 p.m. Saturdays.
Youthline e-mail service talkback@edauk.com
Youthline TEXT service 07 977 493 345.
Text-phone service for the hard of hearing only: 01603 753322. Open 8.30 a.m.–8.30 p.m. weekdays.
Recorded Information Service 0906 302 0012 (24 hours, calls cost 50p per minute and the message lasts approximately eight minutes).
Email: info@edauk.com
Website: http://www.edauk.com
Description: Help on all aspects of eating disorders, including anorexia nervosa, bulimia nervosa, binge eating disorder and related eating disorders.

The National Centre for Eating Disorders, 54 New Road, Esher, Surrey KT10 9NU.
Tel: 01372 469493.

Website: http://www.eating-disorders.org.uk
Description: Effective solutions for eating disorders such as compulsive eating, unsuccessful dieting and bulimia. Counselling, training and information.

The Priory Hospital, Eating Disorder Unit, Priory Lane, Roehampton, London SW15 5JJ.
Tel: 0208 876 8261. Fax: 0208 876 4015.
Email: peter.rowan@priory-hospital.co.uk
Website: http://www.priory-hospital.co.uk/htm
Description: The Eating Disorder Unit consists of 14 bedrooms on three floors. Most of the patients are aged from 14 to 25 years old. Although the large majority of patients are female, the unit can also cater for males with eating disorders. In addition to offering treatment for eating disorders, The Priory Hospital offers treatment for other psychiatric conditions, including anxiety, depression and schizophrenia, alcoholism, drug abuse and stress related disorders.

Internet resources

BBC eating disorders message board
http://www.bbc.co.uk/cgi-perl/h2/h2.cgi?state=view&board=health.11eatdisorders

Eating disorder links – extensive list of links to organisations and conference transcripts (SIARI – Jan Sutton's site)
http://www.siari.co.uk/RS7_Eating-Disorder_Links.htm

UK Treatment Facilities (Something Fishy Site)
http://www.something-fishy.org/treatment/uk.php

FERTILITY SERVICES

British Fertility Society, 22 Apex Court, Woodlands, Bradley Stoke, Bristol BS32 4JT.
Tel: 01454 642217. Fax: 01454 642222.
Email: bfs@bioscientifica.com
Website: http://www.britishfertilitysociety.org.uk
Description: A national multidisciplinary organisation representing professionals practising in the field of reproductive medicine. Its members include gynaecologists, research scientists, counsellors, nurses, embryologists, andrologists and urological surgeons.

Infertility Network UK, Charter House, 43 St Leonards Road, Bexhill on Sea, East Sussex TN40 1JA.
Advice line: 0870 118 80 88.
Website: http://www.infertilitynetworkuk.com/
Description: Aims to help all those affected by fertility problems.

LOSS AND BEREAVEMENT SERVICES

Child Death Helpline
Tel: 0800 282 986 (Open 365 days a year. Every evening 7 p.m.–10 p.m.,
Monday to Friday 10 a.m.–1 p.m., and Wednesday afternoon 1 p.m.–4 p.m.).
Website: http://www.childdeathhelpline.org.uk
Description: A helpline for all those affected by the death of a child. Provides
local contacts.

Cruse Bereavement Care, Cruse House, 126 Sheen Road, Richmond, Surrey
TW9 1UR.
Tel: 0208 939 9530. Fax 0208 940 7638. Helpline: 0870 167 1677.
Email: helpline@crusebereavementcare.org.uk
Website: www.crusebereavementcare.org.uk
Description: Offers help and counselling for bereaved people as well as a range
of useful publications.

Foundation for the Study of Infant Deaths, Artillery House, 11–19 Artillery Row,
London SW1P 1RT.
Tel: 0870 787 0885 (general enquiries). Helpline: 0870 787 0554.
Email: fsid@sids.org.uk
Website: http://www.sids.org.uk/fsid
Description: Aims to prevent unexpected infant death and promote baby
health. Offers a range of support leaflets for bereaved families. Also produces a
series of leaflets, books, posters, fact files and videos for parents, students,
carers, health professionals and anyone interested in knowing more about cot
death.

Miscarriage Association, Head Office, c/o Clayton Hospital, Northgate,
Wakefield, West Yorkshire WF1 3JS.
Tel: 01924 200795 (admin). Helpline: 01924 200799. Scottish helpline: 0131
334 8883.
Email: info@miscarriageassociation.org.uk
Website: http://www.miscarriageassociation.org.uk/
Description: Offers support to those who have suffered the loss of a baby in
pregnancy. Has 50 support groups across the UK, where people can meet and
share their experiences and feelings. Produces leaflets, factsheets and audio tapes
and works to raise awareness and sensitivity among health care professionals
through lectures, workshops and articles in professional journals. Site contains a
useful list of links to related sites.

SANDS (Stillbirth and Neonatal Death Society), 28 Portland Place, London W1B
1LY.
Tel: 0207 436 7940. Fax: 0207 436 3715. Helpline: 0207 436 5881 (10 a.m.–3
p.m. Monday to Friday).
Email: support@uk-sands.org
Website: http://www.uk-sands.org/

Description: Provides support for parents and families whose baby is stillborn or dies soon after birth.

The Compassionate Friends for Bereaved Parents, 53 North Street, Bristol BS3 IEN.
Tel: 0845 120 37 85. Helpline: 0845 123 23 04.
Email Information and Support: info@tcf.org.uk
Website: http://www.tcf.org.uk
Description: Offers understanding, support and encouragement to others after the death of a child or children.

MENTAL HEALTH SERVICES

Association for Post-Natal Illness, 145 Dawes Road, Fulham, London SW6 7EB.
Helpline: 0207 386 0868. Fax: 0207 386 8885.
Email: info@apni.org
Website: http://www.apni.org
Description: Provides support to mothers suffering from post-natal illness. Aims to raise public awareness of the illness and to encourage research into its cause.

Depression Alliance, 35 Westminster Bridge Road, London SE1 7JB.
Tel: 0845 123 23 20.
Website: http://www.depressionalliance.org
Description: Leading UK charity for people affected by depression. Works to relieve and to prevent depression by providing information, support and understanding. It also campaigns to raise awareness among the general public about the realities of depression.

Fellowship of Depressives Anonymous, Box FDA, Ormiston House, 32–36 Pellam Street, Nottingham NG1 2EG.
Tel: 0870 774 4320 (Information line). Fax: 0870 774 4319.
Website: www.depressionanon.co.uk
Description: FDA is a UK nationwide self-help organisation made up of individual members and groups that meet locally on a regular basis for mutual support.

Manic Depression Fellowship, Castle Works, 21 St. George's Road, London SE1 6ES.
Tel: 0207 793 2600. Fax: 0207 793 2639.
Email mdf@mdf.org.uk
Website: http://www.mdf.org.uk
Description: The Manic Depression Fellowship works to enable people affected by manic depression to take control of their lives.

Mind, 15–19 Broadway, London E15 4BQ.
Tel: 0208 519 2122. Fax: 0208 522 1725. MindinfoLine: 0845 766 0163.
Email: contact@mind.org.uk
Website: http://www.mind.org.uk

Description: Mind is the leading mental health charity in England and Wales. It works to create a better life for everyone with experience of mental distress. Also publishes a wide range of books, factsheets, booklets and reports.

The ME Association, 4 Top Angel, Buckingham Industrial Park, Buckingham MK18 1TH.
Tel: 0871 222 7824 (Information line). Fax: 01280 821602.
E-mail: meconnect@meassociation.org.uk
Website: http://www.meassociation.org.uk
Description: Informing and supporting those affected by myalgic encephalopathy (ME), chronic fatigue syndrome and post-viral fatigue syndrome.

The Mental Health Foundation, 83 Victoria Street, London SW1H 0HW.
Tel: 0207 802 0300. Fax: 0207 802 0301.
Email: mhf@mhf.org.uk
Website: http://www.mentalhealth.org.uk/
Description: Comprehensive website on mental health (and mental illness). Carries out vital work in supporting people with mental health problems. Information on a wide range of specific mental health issues from attention deficit disorder to obsessive compulsive disorders to eating disorders to stress to self-harm, etc.

SENIOR CITIZENS

Age Concern England, Astral House, 1268 London Road, London SW16 4ER.
Tel: 0208 765 7200. Information Line: 0800 00 99 66.
Email: ace@ace.org.uk
Website: http://www.ageconcern.org.uk
Description: Provides a wide range of information on issues such as money, legal topics, health, community care, housing, transport, heating, and leisure and education. Also campaigns and researches age-related issues. Local groups throughout UK.

Help the Aged, Head Office, 207–221 Pentonville Road, London N1 9UZ.
Tel: 0207 278 1114.
Email: info@helptheaged.org.uk
Website: http://www.helptheaged.org.uk
Description: Provides a range of services to help older people live independent lives, particularly those who are frail, isolated or poor.

Internet resources

Action on Elder Abuse
Helpline: 0808 808 8141.
http://www.elderabuse.org.uk

Seniors' Health (List of links from Patient UK)
http://www.patient.co.uk/seniors_health.htm

VICTIMS OF CRIME

Victim Support, National Office, Cranmer House, 39 Brixton Road, London SW9 6DZ.
Tel: 0207 735 9166. Victim Supportline: 0845 30 30 900.
Email: contact@victimsupport.org.uk
Website: http://www.victimsupport.org/

Description: Victim Support is committed to providing people affected by crime with support and information to help them cope with their experience.

INDEX